THE NIV STANDARD LESSON COMMENTARY

International Sunday School Lessons

2000-2001

edited by

DOUGLAS REDFORD AND JONATHAN UNDERWOOD

published by
Standard Publishing
Eugene H. Wigginton, President
Mark A. Taylor, Publisher
Richard C. McKinley, Director of Curriculum Development
Carla Crane, Assistant Director of Curriculum Development
Jonathan Underwood, Senior Editor
Cheryl Frey, Office Editor

Seventh Annual Volume

FREE CD-ROM INCLUDED

The electronic version of *The NIV® Standard Lesson Commentary* and the *QuickVerse®* STEP Book Reader are contained on the CD-ROM so you can:

- Instantly search the complete text of the Commentary for any word, phrase, or Bible reference. Search options include full-text, title-only, case-sensitive, and support of Boolean operators (AND, OR, NOT, etc.).
- Access related articles or information via hyperlinks within the text of each book. (Double-clicking on a highlighted word will access related articles.)
- Print lessons directly from the *QuickVerse®* or customize in any Windows® word processor.
- Access Bible maps from *PC-Atlas®!*

PLUS, you'll find additional reference titles locked on the CD. NOTE: These additional resources are made available for your convenience. Standard Publishing does not necessarily endorse the complete contents of any of them.

The electronic version of this book is fully compatible with the new Bible Software Industry standard for reference titles, STEP (Standard Template for Electronic Publishing).

System Requirements:
An IBM or compatible PC running Windows 95/98 or Windows NT 4.0 or later; 8MB RAM, and 45 MB hard drive space.

For technical support call Parsons Technology at (319) 395-7314.

© 2000
STANDARD PUBLISHING
a division of STANDEX INTERNATIONAL Corporation
8121 Hamilton Avenue, Cincinnati, Ohio 45231
Printed in U.S.A.

In This Volume

Special Features

Fall Quarter, 2000
Rulers of Israel

Writers

Lesson Development ....*Orrin Root*   Discovery Learning.............*Ronald L. Oakes (1-9),*
Verbal Illustrations ....*Charles R. Boatman*   *Robert L. Kitchen (10-13)*
What Do You Think? ....*Kenton K. Smith*   Reproducible Activities........*Ronald L. Oakes (1-9),*
                                                      Robert L. Kitchen (10-13)

Winter Quarter, 2000-2001
Good News of Jesus

Writers

Lesson Development ......*J. Michael Shannon (1-5),*   Discovery Learning and Reproducible Activities....
   Johnny Pressley (6-9), Terry A. Clark (10-13)   *Virginia Beddow and Greg Delort (1-5),*
Verbal Illustrations....................*Robert C. Shannon*   *Rick Shonkwiler (6-9),*
What Do You Think? ....*David Baynes*   *Richard A. Koffarnus (10-13)*

Spring Quarter, 2001
Continuing Jesus' Work

Writers

Lesson Development ....*Mitch Simpson (1-4),*   Verbal Illustrations ....*Charles R. Boatman*
   Edwin V. Hayden (5-8), Marshall Hayden (9-13)   Discovery Learning..........................*Everett Brewer*
What Do You Think?.............*Richard A. Lint (1-4),*   Reproducible Activities....................*Everett Brewer*
   Charles E. Cook (5-8), Kenton K. Smith (9-13)

Summer Quarter, 2001
Division and Decline

Writers

Lesson Development ....*John W. Wade*   Discovery Learning..............................*Alan Weber*
What Do You Think? ....*Matt Carswell (1-4),*   Verbal Illustrations ....*Richard W. Baynes*
   Kenneth L. Beck (5-9), Ken Goble (10-13)   Reproducible Activities ....*Alan Weber*

Index of Printed Texts, 2000-2001

The printed texts for 2000-2001 are arranged here in the order in which they appear in the Bible. Opposite each reference is the page number on which the lesson that treats the passage begins in this volume.

Cumulative Index of Printed Texts

A cumulative index for the Scripture passages used in *The NIV Standard Lesson Commentary* for September, 1998—August, 2001 is presented here for your convenience.

Introducing *The NIV®*
Standard Lesson Commentary

This is the seventh year teachers following the Uniform Lesson Plan have had available this popular commentary based on the *New International Version* of the Scriptures. Teachers familiar with *The NIV® Standard Lesson Commentary* will find in this volume all the features they have come to expect; new users of the *Commentary* will find a wealth of resources never before so close to their fingertips! For the fourth year a free CD-ROM is included for the convenience of computer users. Continuing a practice begun with the 1998-99 volume, we have included maps and chronological charts with each quarter. By the end of the current six-year series (see page 12), you can compile quite a handy Bible atlas!

Whether you have used *The NIV® Standard Lesson Commentary* before or not, however, you will quickly find this volume a helpful companion in preparing your Sunday school lessons.

LESSON DEVELOPMENT

The first page of each lesson clearly identifies the title, Scripture, current unit, and lesson aims for the session. A thumb tab identifies the date the lesson will be taught so that it can be found quickly. The date is repeated on each page at the top outside corner.

Application from the start!

The first item in the lesson development is a brief rationale for the lesson: **"Why Teach This Lesson?"** Tying the lesson theme to contemporary life, this section puts application at the forefront of your preparation. Then comes the lesson treatment itself, following a three-point structure: introduction, exposition, and conclusion. The **introduction** provides background and other useful information to set the stage, tie the current lessons with earlier ones, and generally give you a handle on the context for the current lesson.

Verse-by-verse exposition.

What follows is a **verse-by-verse Scripture exposition**. The text is printed in the *New International Version*, usually one verse at a time. Bold type sets the text off from commentary so you can read it easily, even if you just want to read through the passage without comment at first. The commentary is interspersed so you can relate the comments to the specific Scripture passage they illuminate.

The **conclusion** leans heavily toward **application**, giving specific examples of how the principles of the lesson Scripture can be put to practice in real life.

Verbal illustrations.

Verbal illustrations, usually two to a lesson, help to illuminate the concepts of the lesson. These are found in the exposition section, providing yet another tool for you to illustrate the Scripture. These are set off in block quotes so they can be easily found or easily jumped over if you choose not to use them.

MARGINAL NOTES

Many of the most helpful features of this lesson commentary are found in the margins. Occasionally the text suggests some interesting point for discussion.

Discussion starters.

These issues are raised under the heading of **"What Do You Think?"** The question is raised, sometimes from more than one perspective. The Scripture in the main section is relevant, and other Scriptures may also be suggested. No answers are given, however, because these are questions without pat answers. These will encourage your students to wrestle with the big issues without being trite.

Visual illustrations.

"Visuals" are pictured in the margins, also. These are reproductions of the classroom visuals available from Standard Publishing each quarter to help your students visualize the points being made. Again, these appear in the margin along-side the Scripture or other part of the lesson where they are most appropriate. NOTE: These are mere **reproductions** of large, colorful classroom visuals available to enhance your lesson presentation. Contact your curriculum supplier to order yours each quarter.

Daily Bible readings, points to remember, and even prayer ideas are included in the margin near the end of each lesson.

Daily Bible readings.

DISCOVERY LEARNING

For teachers who like to involve their students in the learning process, a page of **Discovery Learning** is included in each lesson. These alternate lesson plans are designed to get the students busy in Bible study and application to discover for themselves the timeless truths of the Scriptures. Each discovery learning plan includes an activity to begin the lesson, a Bible study activity, and an application activity.

Student involvement!

The last page of each lesson is a **reproducible page**. These, too, are designed to involve the students in discovery learning. Sometimes they are an integral part of the discovery learning plan. At other times, they provide optional activities that may be introduced at various points in the lesson. Marginal "Option" notes fre-quently call your attention to an activity on this page. Or you can start with the whole page and build your lesson plan around it, using the other resources in this book.

Reproducible pages!

OPTIONS

This is a lesson planner with lots of options! No matter what style you pre-fer—lecture, discussion, activities—you'll find resources to plan a great lesson. If you like variety, this will help you design an easy-to-teach lesson unique to your personality and that of your class. Or, if you like a ready-made plan you can teach with minimal preparation time, you'll find that, too. It's all here.

Make it personal.

PLANNING SHEET

Use the lesson planning sheet on page 10 to plan each of your lessons. The page is reproducible, so you can use it to fill in the blanks and plan out your complete lesson each week. List the options and features you have chosen for each lesson, and use it to guide you quickly and easily from one activity to the next.

Map out your game plan.

EASY-TO-READ QUARTERLY FORMAT

Some users of *The NIV® Standard Lesson Commentary* have wished for a quar-terly format to use in teaching. Others have wished the type were a little larger and easier to read. Both those desires have been answered with the *NIV® Bible Teacher*, available from your Christian bookstore or from Standard Publishing. It contains the same content as this volume but is published in four quarterly is-sues and in a larger typeface. Order number 184 for fall, 284 for winter, 384 for spring, and 484 for summer.

NIV® BIBLE TEACHER

Lesson Planning Page

List the aims here, either directly from the lesson or revised to suit your individual needs.

LESSON AIMS

Begin with an opening activity like the illustration from the beginning of the lesson, "Into the Lesson" from the Discovery Learning page, a discussion question, or some other appropriate opener.

GETTING STARTED

List in order the activities you will use. These include discussion questions, activities from the discovery learning page and the reproducible page—as well as key points from the commentary section.

LESSON DEVELOPMENT

I.

II.

III.

How will you bring the lesson to a climax, stressing the key point and desired action steps?

CONCLUSION & APPLICATION

Dismiss the class with an activity that reinforces the Bible lesson.

CLOSING ACTIVITY

Fall Quarter, 2000

Rulers of Israel

(Judges, 1 and 2 Samuel, 1 Kings)

Special Features

Lessons

Unit 1: Judges of Israel

Unit 2: Saul and David

Unit 3: David and Solomon

About These Lessons

The lessons in this quarter survey the history of Israel from the period of the judges to the end of the united kingdom. They do so with a look at each of several great leaders of the nation during that time. From their successes and from their failures we can learn valuable lessons of faith.

Sep 3
Sep 10
Sep 17
Sep 24
Oct 1
Oct 8
Oct 15
Oct 22
Oct 29
Nov 5
Nov 12
Nov 19
Nov 26

Triumph and Trouble

by Orrin Root

Do you remember what we were doing in Sunday school a year ago? We were leaving Egypt with the children of Israel to travel to their promised land. For three months we followed them over the journey that took them forty years. At the end of November last year we saw them cross the Jordan into the promised land. There they followed God's leading, and he led them in triumphant conquest.

Now we are to take up the story of Israel at that point. During the upcoming thirteen lessons we shall consider what those people did for approximately the next four and a half centuries. It is a tale of both triumph and trouble.

SEPTEMBER | **UNIT 1: JUDGES OF ISRAEL**

Living in peace and prosperity year after year, the people of Israel began to think more about pleasure and comfort and less about God and his law. Carelessly they drifted into wrongdoing, and even joined in pagan religious rites.

International Sunday School Lesson Cycle
September, 1998—August, 2004

YEAR	FALL QUARTER (Sept., Oct., Nov.)	WINTER QUARTER (Dec., Jan., Feb.)	SPRING QUARTER (Mar., Apr., May)	SUMMER QUARTER (June, July, Aug.)
1998-1999	God Calls a People to Faithful Living (Old Testament Survey)	God Calls Anew in Jesus Christ (New Testament Survey)	That You May Believe (John)	Genesis: Beginnings (Genesis)
1999-2000	From Slavery to Conquest (Exodus, Leviticus, Numbers, Deuteronomy, Joshua)	Immanuel: God With Us (Matthew)	Helping a Church Confront Crisis (1 and 2 Corinthians)	New Life in Christ (Ephesians, Philippians, Colossians, Philemon)
2000-2001	Rulers of Israel (Judges, 1 and 2 Samuel, 1 Kings 1-11)	Good News of Jesus (Luke)	Continuing Jesus' Work (Acts)	Division and Decline (1 Kings 12-22, 2 Kings 1-17, Isaiah 1-39, Hosea, Amos, Micah)
2001-2002	Jesus' Ministry (Parables, Miracles, Sermon on the Mount)	Light for All People (Isaiah 9:1-7; 11:1-9; 40-66; Ruth, Jonah, Nahum)	The Power of the Gospel (Romans, Galatians)	Worship and Wisdom for Living (Psalms, Proverbs)
2002-2003	Judgment and Exile (2 Kings 18-25, Jeremiah, Lamentations, Ezekiel, Habakkuk, Zephaniah)	Portraits of Faith (Personalities in the New Testament)	Jesus: God's Power in Action (Mark)	God Restores a Remnant (Ezra, Nehemiah, Daniel, Joel, Obadiah, Haggai, Zechariah, Malachi)
2003-2004	Faith Faces the World (James, 1 and 2 Peter, 1, 2, 3 John, Jude)	A Child Is Given (Samuel, John the Baptist, Jesus) Lessons From Life (Esther, Job, Ecclesiastes, Song of Solomon)	Jesus Fulfills His Mission (Death, Burial, and Resurrection Texts) Living Expectantly (1, 2 Thessalonians, Revelation)	Hold Fast to the Faith (Hebrews) Guidelines for the Church's Ministry (1, 2 Timothy, Titus)

Then came trouble. The Lord withdrew his protection. Armed raiders swept in from a neighboring country to drive away or destroy livestock and steal new harvests, killing anyone who got in their way.

In their misery the people remembered how God had helped them before. When they appealed to him and went back to obeying his law, God provided a leader who rallied the people to resist and defeat the invaders. Peace and prosperity returned. But when all was well, the people again drifted away from God and his law.

That same pattern was repeated over and over through approximately three hundred years. (See the summary in Judges 2:11-19.) The leaders who rallied God's people are called *judges*. Twelve of them are named in the biblical record, and four will be considered during our September lessons.

Lesson 1: Deborah. God chose this lady to be his prophetess, and men of Israel went to her to have their disputes settled according to God's law. Deborah instructed Barak to gather an army to defeat the Canaanites. So he and ten thousand men prepared to meet the fearsome Canaanite army, which was equipped with nine hundred iron chariots and countless horsemen and foot soldiers. Then the Lord took a hand in the battle. A terrific rainstorm and flood made the chariots and horses useless, and the Canaanites were soundly defeated.

Lesson 2: Gideon. God called Gideon to raise an army and drive out the Midianites and the Amalekites. Gideon recruited thirty-two thousand men to help him, but the Lord said they were too many. The number was reduced to ten thousand, but that was still too many! When the number was reduced to three hundred, God used the tiny force to defeat countless thousands of the enemy.

Lesson 3: Samson. This hero raised no army—and needed none! Single-handedly he engaged the Philistines in conflict and won. On one occasion he was able to kill a thousand of them in a day; but he was not able to resist the charms of their women, especially the infamous Delilah.

Lesson 4: Samuel. Born to a godly mother who dedicated him to the Lord's service, Samuel was brought up by Eli the priest. In his youth he became recognized as God's prophet. That helped him to turn God's people back to the Lord and to end the long oppression of the Philistines. Prophetic insight also helped Samuel administer justice, and he became a loved and trusted judge of Israel.

UNIT 2: SAUL AND DAVID

OCTOBER

Samuel's one notable failure was neglecting to bring up his sons to be like him. When he appointed them to be judges, they turned out to be mercenary scoundrels. Facing the prospect of being judged by such crooks, the elders of Israel asked Samuel to appoint a king for the nation.

That was not the best way to solve Israel's problem. Israel was designed to acknowledge God as their primary King, and he saw their request to Samuel as a rejection of him (1 Samuel 8:7). The Lord warned that a monarchy would become expensive and oppressive. Still, the elders persisted in their request. The Lord consented without approving, and Israel became a monarchy. The lessons for October and November will tell of the first three kings.

Lesson 5: Saul Becomes King. God chose Saul to be Israel's first king. He was tall and handsome. Well pleased with the choice, the people voiced their approval with excitement.

Lesson 6: Saul Rejected and David Anointed. Saul began his reign with a glorious victory, but success seemed to go to his head. Soon he began to ignore God's leading and go his own way. His reign was then doomed to end in failure. The Lord sent Samuel to anoint David to be the next king; but that was not made known to the public, for it was not yet time for Saul's rule to end.

Lesson 7: David Mourns Saul and Jonathan. By exhibiting valor in battle, David became a national hero. Saul became insanely jealous and ordered David killed. David fled to the desert and remained an exile until the Philistines defeated Israel and killed Saul and his son Jonathan. That opened the way for David to become king; but instead of rejoicing, David mourned sincerely for Saul and his son.

Lesson 8: David Becomes King of All Israel. When Saul was dead, the tribe of Judah promptly chose David to be its king. But Abner, general of Saul's army, named Saul's son Ish-Bosheth as king. For seven years Israel was divided. Then both Abner and Ish-Bosheth died, and David became king of the entire nation.

Lesson 9: God's Covenant With David. When David made Jerusalem his capital city, he soon brought the ark of the covenant there. He kept it in a tent, but proposed to build a house for it—a temple of stone and wood. That was a good thought, but it came before its time. The house for the Lord was to be built by David's son Solomon, who would be the next king. However, God promised to build an enduring house for David: a dynasty that would rule forever. Kings of David's family did rule in Jerusalem for centuries; but here we see a clear prophecy of Jesus, the King eternal. On the human side he is a son of David, and on the divine side he is the Son of God. He is ruling now, and his kingdom is forever.

UNIT 3: DAVID AND SOLOMON

NOVEMBER

Young King David did the Lord's will, and the Lord blessed him with success and made little Israel into a mighty empire. But during what should have been David's mature years, he committed the sins of adultery and murder; and the latter years of his reign were plagued with trouble and sorrow. With difficulty he held the empire together and passed it on to his son Solomon.

Young King Solomon began his reign by serving God with a devotion like that of young King David. But at the end of November we shall see that old King Solomon drifted into sins more shameful than the sins of old King David.

What a warning is here for all of us! A good beginning is not enough. God's people must serve him faithfully to the end.

Lesson 10: David and Bathsheba. Walking on the roof of his palace, David caught sight of a woman bathing on a neighboring roof or in a courtyard. Struck by her beauty, he brought her to his palace and to his bed. Then he plotted the death of her husband. Nathan the prophet pronounced God's sentence: "Now, therefore, the sword will never depart from your house" (2 Samuel 12:10). David's latter days were plagued by rebellions—led chiefly by his own sons.

Lesson 11: Solomon Succeeds David. In spite of these rebellions, David held his empire intact and handed it over to Solomon. He advised his son to obey God's law continually. Given a unique opportunity by God, Solomon requested and received a special gift of wisdom. His reign seemed to be bright with promise.

Lesson 12: Solomon Builds the Temple. Solomon amassed a fabulous income from taxes, from the tribute of pagan nations, and from his own business ventures. He built palaces and forts on a grand scale. Most significant of all his buildings was the exquisite temple of the Lord.

Lesson 13: Solomon's Mistakes. To maintain the stability of his empire, Solomon made treaties with foreign kings, taking daughters of those kings as his wives. But he allowed his pagan wives to bring their gods with them to Jerusalem. If that were not bad enough, Solomon then built shrines for those false gods. Finally, he actually joined in the pagan worship. So Solomon's efforts to strengthen his empire actually brought it to the brink of ruin.

Can you believe that the wisest ruler in the world blundered so foolishly? The warning to us should be clear: no good purpose is well served by disobeying God.

Rulers of Israel
Judges and Kings

• Sidon

• Dan

• Kadesh-Naphtali

Hazor
•

The Great Sea

Harosheth
Kishon River

Mount Carmel

Sea of Chinnereth

Mount Tabor

Jezreel Valley

• En-dor

Well of Harod

Mount Gilboa

• Ophrah

• Jabesh-gilead

Beth-shan
•

• Penuel

Jordan River

• Succoth

Jabbok River

Shiloh
•

AMMON

• Bethel

• Rabbah

• Mizpeh

• Ekron   Gibeon

• Gilgal

Michmash

Ashdod
•

Zorah Gibeah

Ramah
•

Valley of Sorek

Timnath
•

• Jerusalem

Beth-shemesh

Ashkelon
•

PHILISTIA

Bethlehem
•

Salt

Gaza •

• Gath

Hebron •

Sea

En-gedi •

Beersheba •

MOAB

Important Sites in the Life of
Deborah
Gideon
Samson
Samuel
Saul
David
Solomon

From Slavery to Slavery

Era	Leaders	Dates (B.C.)
Exodus and Wandering	Moses	1446-1406
Conquest and Settlement	Joshua	1406-1380
Judges	Deborah Gideon Samson Samuel	c. 1380-1050 c. 1250-1210 c. 1212-1172 c. 1110-1082 c. 1075-1020
United Kingdom	Saul David Solomon	1050-931 1050-1010 1010-970 970-931
Divided Kingdom	19 Kings of Israel 12 Kings of Judah 1 Queen of Judah	931-722
Judah Alone	7 Kings	722-587
Captivity		604-538

DEBORAH

LESSON 1

WHY TEACH THIS LESSON?

Some of your students are outgoing and effervescent. Others are more reserved and quiet. Some are comfortable "up front" and at the center of attention—in fact, they may relish such a position. Others work more comfortably behind the scenes. And some would like to be up front but never seem quite able to get there. Yet all of them can be instrumental in the work of the church.

This lesson will give you an opportunity to assure the folks who work behind the scenes that their contribution is as vital as that of those who stand up front. And it will enable you to remind the folks up front that it is really the Lord, not they themselves, who gets the glory.

INTRODUCTION

"Johnny!" Mom's voice was sharp as the family gathered around the table. "Why do you keep coming to supper without washing your hands? You know I always send you back to do it."

Said Johnny, "Once you forgot."

One lapse in Mom's vigilance gave Johnny the hope that there would be another, thus allowing him to escape the onerous task of washing his hands.

A. No Lapse in God's Vigilance

As we read through the book of Judges, it seems that the people of Israel always began to do wrong when they were prosperous and happy, and that God always punished them by allowing other peoples to ravage their land and put an end to their prosperity. Not once did God forget. There was no lapse in his vigilance that would give the Israelites reason to hope there would be another. They often stopped thinking about God and his law, but God never stopped disciplining them and reminding them of the high cost of their disobedience.

B. Lesson Background

One year ago we began a series of thirteen lessons that traced the progress of Israel from slaves in Egypt, to wanderers in the wilderness, and finally to conquerors of the land that God had promised to give them. With rare exceptions the people were faithful to God through those years of conquest, and he gave them victory over the pagan peoples who had lived there.

With undisputed possession of all the land they needed, God's people settled down to peaceful and prosperous living. This happy state continued as long as Joshua lived to lead them, and then for a few years more. As the faithful old leaders died, a new generation arose—a generation that did not remember the mighty miracles God had done to give them their good land. In their pursuit of profit and pleasure they forgot God and his law. So God allowed pagan tribes to invade Israel, stealing livestock and harvests and leaving the people in poverty and misery.

In their poverty and misery God's people remembered him. They turned to him and pleaded for his help. In response, God provided a leader who rallied the

DEVOTIONAL READING:
PSALM 68:1-6

BACKGROUND SCRIPTURE:
JUDGES 4, 5

PRINTED TEXT:
JUDGES 4:1-9, 14, 15, 17a, 21, 22

LESSON AIMS

After participating in this lesson, each student will be able to:

1. Tell how God used Deborah to deliver his people from Canaanite oppression.

2. Explain how Deborah's example shows that supportive, behind-the-scenes leadership can be effective.

3. Seek a specific opportunity to serve the Lord and to give him all the praise rather than to seek praise for oneself.

KEY VERSE

Then Deborah said to Barak, "Go! This is the day the LORD has given Sisera into your hands. Has not the LORD gone ahead of you?"   —Judges 4:14

The visual for today's lesson will help your students place the events of the quarter's lessons in chronological order.

WHAT DO YOU THINK?

Even though the Israelites cried out to the Lord for relief from the Canaanite oppression, he did not answer for twenty years. Actually, the text says that Jabin oppressed the Israelites for twenty years and that they cried to the Lord. We do not know how many of those twenty years the Israelites spent in denial, refusing to address the Lord with their complaint, and then how many more they spent in unrepentant complaining. Why do you suppose it took so long either for Israel to acknowledge their sin or

people to drive out the invaders and repossess their country. Peace and prosperity returned. Sadly, this same cycle of events was repeated over and over for approximately three hundred years.

Judges is the name given to those leaders whom God raised up to lead his people back to him. This week our lesson concerns one of them. This judge was a lady. With the direction of God and the help of a man, she brought Israel from sin and misery to faithfulness and prosperity.

I. ISRAEL IN TROUBLE (JUDGES 4:1-3)

A. SIN (v. 1)

1. After Ehud died, the Israelites once again did evil in the eyes of the LORD.

Ehud was a judge of Israel prior to the time described in our lesson text. His efforts on behalf of God's people are told in Judges 3:12-30. As indicated in Judges 2:18, 19, Ehud's strong influence kept the nation faithful to God as long as he lived. But *after Ehud died*, there was no one of like faithfulness and influence to take his place. In time *the Israelites . . . did evil in the eyes of the Lord.*

B. PUNISHMENT (v. 2)

2. So the LORD sold them into the hands of Jabin, a king of Canaan, who reigned in Hazor. The commander of his army was Sisera, who lived in Harosheth Haggoyim.

So the Lord sold them into the hands of Jabin. This does not mean that Jabin paid anything to the Lord in return for his control of Israel; it means merely that God delivered Israel, or handed the people over, as if they had been sold. Back in the days when Joshua was leading and God was helping Israel, Joshua had promised two of the tribes a victory over the Canaanites in spite of their intimidating iron chariots (Joshua 17:17, 18). But now there was no godly leader like Joshua, and God was giving victory to Israel's enemies rather than to Israel.

King Jabin's capital was located at *Hazor*, far north in Israel's land (approximately nine miles north of the Sea of Galilee) in the territory belonging to the tribe of Naphtali. This means that we should understand *Canaan* in this verse to include, not the entire promised land (sometimes referred to as the land of Canaan), but the northern region of Canaan where the Canaanites were particularly strong. Apparently a large part of Jabin's army was stationed in *Harosheth*, located farther south in the plain of Jezreel. The troops there were commanded by *Sisera*. The word *Haggoyim*, which is attached to Harosheth, means "of the Gentiles" and may indicate that peoples of different nationalities lived there.

C. DISTRESS (v. 3)

3. Because he had nine hundred iron chariots and had cruelly oppressed the Israelites for twenty years, they cried to the LORD for help.

With his impressive array of *iron chariots*, Sisera easily terrorized the farmers of the valley and took whatever share of their harvests and livestock he chose to demand. The people of Israel did not have the capability to oppose those chariots. *They cried to the Lord for help*, but he left them in their distress *for twenty years.*

LOSING STREAKS

Prairie View A & M (a small Texas college fifty miles northwest of Houston) once had a nearly invincible football team. They won five NCAA divisional titles in the 1950s and 1960s. But in 1989 the team began an eighty-game losing streak that broke the previous NCAA consecutive loss record by thirty games! The worst loss in the streak was by a score of 92-0! The nightmare finally came to an end on September 26, 1998, with a 14-12 victory over Langston University, nearly nine years after their last win.

Many factors contributed to the losing streak: unethical coaches, powerful opponents, lack of scholarships to attract good players, and perhaps even a losing mentality that developed as the streak went on.

In our text today, we see Israel in the throes of a twenty-year period of decline. After the death of the God-fearing judge Ehud, Israel had no strong leader. Her enemies—the Canaanites—were superior militarily. However, the most important factor in Israel's twenty-year "losing streak" was the attitude of the people: they had forgotten God. Only when they returned to him in repentance and obedience did their dismal "streak" end. —C. R. B.

II. LADY TO THE RESCUE (JUDGES 4:4-9)

During the long tyranny of the Canaanites, everyone felt helpless—well, nearly everyone. With calm assurance, one lady took charge: Deborah the prophetess.

A. THE PROPHETESS (vv. 4, 5)

4. *Deborah, a prophetess, the wife of Lappidoth, was leading Israel at that time.*

Like the other judges, *Deborah* was not elected by the people or appointed by anyone. God raised her up to help his people, and this is why she *was leading Israel at that time*. Here she is also described as a *prophetess*. Thus Deborah was not only the only judge who was a woman, but also the only one who is described as having the gift of prophecy. She needed no written law before her; her judgments came by direct inspiration from the Almighty Author of the law himself.

5. *She held court under the Palm of Deborah between Ramah and Bethel in the hill country of Ephraim, and the Israelites came to her to have their disputes decided.*

No map can pinpoint the exact location of this palm tree, but it would have been somewhere in the hilly country near the middle of Israel's territory and within the land belonging to the tribe of Benjamin. Here Deborah *held court* and regularly dispensed justice to those who *came to her to have their disputes decided*. Apparently this location became so familiar that it was known as *the Palm of Deborah*.

B. THE ARMY (vv. 6, 7)

6. *She sent for Barak son of Abinoam from Kedesh in Naphtali and said to him, "The LORD, the God of Israel, commands you: 'Go, take with you ten thousand men of Naphtali and Zebulun and lead the way to Mount Tabor.*

Barak lived approximately eighty miles to the north of where Deborah held court, but it appears that he came promptly when Deborah *sent for* him. When he came, Deborah first made it clear that she was giving him the message of *the Lord, the God of Israel*, not her own. God wanted Barak to assemble an army of *ten thousand men* from the tribe of *Naphtali* (Barak's own tribe) and the neighboring tribe of *Zebulun*. He was to lead that army to *Mount Tabor*, a mountain (1,843 feet high) overlooking the valley of Jezreel. The Kishon River, mentioned in the next verse, flowed through that valley.

7. *I will lure Sisera, the commander of Jabin's army, with his chariots and his troops to the Kishon River and give him into your hands.'"*

---

for God to respond? What does this twenty-year wait suggest to you about problems our own country faces and about which Christians have been praying?

HOW TO SAY IT

Abinoam. Uh-BIN-o-am.
Barak. BAIR-uk.
Bethel. BETH-el.
Canaan. KAY-nun.
Ehud. EE-hud.
Ephraim. EE-fray-im.
Haggoyim. Hah-goy-EEM.
Harosheth. Huh-ROE-sheth.
Hazor. HAY-zor.
Heber. HEE-ber.
Hobab. HO-bab.
Jabin. JAY-bin.
Jael. JAY-ul.
Jezreel. JEZ-ree-el or JEZ-reel.
Kedesh. KEE-desh.
Kenite. KEN-ite.
Kishon. KYE-shon.
Lappidoth. LAP-ih-doth.
Naphtali. NAF-tuh-lye.
Ramah. RAY-muh.
Sisera. SIS-er-uh.
Zebulun. ZEB-you-lun.

WHAT DO YOU THINK?

The narrative in Judges 4 places a great deal of emphasis on Sisera's nine hundred iron chariots. The Israelites apparently had none, but still they were willing to do battle. How do we today face seemingly unbeatable forces with confidence? What are some of the "iron chariots" that we face? (Be sure to consider Psalm 20:7 in your discussion.)

VISUALS FOR THESE LESSONS

The visual pictured in each lesson (e.g., page 18) is a small reproduction of a large, full-color poster included in the Adult Visuals packet for the Fall Quarter. The packet is available from your supplier. Order No. 192.

WHAT DO YOU THINK?

Knowing that he would not receive the major credit for the triumph, Barak led his army into battle. How many Christians today do you think would undertake a significant ministry or project if they knew someone else would get the credit for any success achieved? How much should getting credit matter? Why? (See Matthew 6:1.)

As mentioned in verse 2, *Jabin's army* was stationed at Harosheth, several miles to the west of Mount Tabor where the valley of Jezreel widened into a plain. The Lord promised to *lure* his army from that location and down the river to a point near Barak's position on Mount Tabor. *Sisera*, commander of that army, would bring his aforementioned nine hundred iron *chariots* (v. 3). Probably *his troops* included a large force of infantry that would accompany the chariots. The Lord planned to *give* those men *into* Barak's *hands*: that is, he promised victory to Barak and his army.

C. THE LEADERSHIP TEAM (vv. 8, 9)

8. Barak said to her, "If you go with me, I will go; but if you don't go with me, I won't go."

It is to Barak's credit that he trusted the Lord and recognized that Deborah was his "link with headquarters." He did not intend to be caught on Mount Tabor with ten thousand men and without God's guidance as to what to do next. If God's prophetess would not *go with* him on this mission, then he also would not *go.*

Still, it seems to indicate some limitation in Barak's faith that he would set conditions on which he would obey what the Lord had commanded him to do (v. 6). As in the case of Gideon and his fleece (Judges 6:36-40), it seems the Lord responded on the basis of the faith that was expressed in spite of the clear need to grow in that faith.

9. "Very well," Deborah said, "I will go with you. But because of the way you are going about this, the honor will not be yours, for the LORD will hand Sisera over to a woman." So Deborah went with Barak to Kedesh.

Thus the leadership team was formed. God would be the commander; Deborah would convey his orders to Barak; Barak would command the army. However, Deborah warned Barak that he would not receive the primary credit for Israel's victory. That would be given to *a woman*. At this point in the story, we might expect Deborah to be that woman, but she would not be.

Quickly Barak enlisted ten thousand men and led them to Mount Tabor, and so "Deborah also went with him" (v. 10). Such a mobilization could not be kept secret, and Sisera soon learned about it (v. 12). To him it must have had all the appearances of an armed revolt among the Israelites. Sisera readied his chariots and infantry and set out from Harosheth to put the impudent rebels in their place. From his position on Mount Tabor, Barak and his men could see them coming.

III. WAR AND VICTORY (JUDGES 4:14, 15, 17a, 21, 22)

A. ISRAEL'S ATTACK (v. 14)

14. Then Deborah said to Barak, "Go! This is the day the LORD has given Sisera into your hands. Has not the LORD gone ahead of you?" So Barak went down Mount Tabor, followed by ten thousand men.

The prophetess gave the command, and with it the promise of victory and the assurance that *the Lord* himself was advancing to battle ahead of the *ten thousand men*. Encouraged by that promise, Barak led his troops down the slope of *Mount Tabor* and across the valley floor to meet the chariots and infantry by the river.

It should be noted that this strategy seemed to favor Sisera, for it allowed him to fight where his iron chariots could be used to their greatest advantage—in the level valley rather than on the slopes of the mountain. Perhaps Sisera anticipated an easy victory at little cost to himself or his men. The Lord, of course, had other plans.

B. ENEMY'S DEFEAT (v. 15)

15. At Barak's advance, the LORD routed Sisera and all his chariots and army by the sword, and Sisera abandoned his chariot and fled on foot.

The Lord routed Sisera. For more about the Lord's action in this conflict, we turn to the song of victory in the next chapter of Judges. There we read that the Lord caused a spectacular cloudburst to come from the south (Judges 5:4, 5). Without being told all the details, we know that such a rain would have produced a flash flood on the Kishon. Quickly the river came forth from its banks. The soft ground turned to mud; the chariots bogged down to their axles. The rising flood overwhelmed both horses and men, drowned them, and swept their dead bodies away (5:21).

Those men who managed to make their way to dry ground above the flood were met with the edge of *the sword*—ten thousand vengeful swords in the hands of men smarting from twenty years of severe oppression. The Canaanites who did not die immediately raced back by the way they had come, but the men of Israel chased them all the way to Harosheth and killed every one of them (Judges 4:16).

C. A GENERAL'S DEATH (vv. 17a, 21, 22)

17a. Sisera, however, fled on foot to the tent of Jael, the wife of Heber the Kenite.

Heber is described as a *Kenite*, meaning that he belonged to the tribe of Hobab, who was a relative of Moses (Judges 4:11). Originally the Kenites had become affiliated with the tribe of Judah to the south (Judges 1:16), but Heber and his wife *Jael* had chosen a more solitary life in the north. Apparently they were nomadic shepherds. On this occasion Jael was alone in the tent; perhaps Heber was away with the sheep.

The Kenites were not included among the oppressed Israelites; they were at peace with the Canaanites, as the latter part of this verse notes. Still, it seems that Jael's heart was with Israel. She recognized Sisera when he appeared, wearied by his long flight from the battlefield. Cordially she welcomed him into the tent and agreed to hide him there. After a drink of milk, he fell soundly asleep (vv. 18-20).

21. But Jael, Heber's wife, picked up a tent peg and a hammer and went quietly to him while he lay fast asleep, exhausted. She drove the peg through his temple into the ground, and he died.

Quickly Jael *picked up a tent peg*, along with a heavy *hammer* used to drive such pegs. Apparently Sisera was sleeping with his head flat on the ground. Jael came to him stealthily. With a few sharp blows, she drove the stake through his head and *into the ground*. It was hardly necessary to add: *and he died.*

22. Barak came by in pursuit of Sisera, and Jael went out to meet him. "Come," **she said, "I will show you the man you're looking for." So he went in with her, and** **there lay Sisera with the tent peg through his temple—dead.**

The record seems to indicate that some men of Israel saw Sisera leave his panic-stricken troops and race away alone to the north. But they proceeded to exterminate the army, and then returned to pursue the general. It was not hard to guess that he would hurry to his king at Hazor (v. 2), so they traveled in that direction. Perhaps they reached Jael's tent a day or two behind Sisera, but she had left Sisera's body undisturbed. Now, perhaps with some pride, she showed Barak what she had done. Thus, as Deborah had foretold (v. 9), the outstanding champion of the campaign was not Barak, but a woman—Jael.

At this point the war was not over, but a major blow had been struck against Israel's oppressors. Barak and his men pressed on until the Canaanites were subdued and their king was destroyed (Judges 4:23, 24). The oppression was ended, and "the land had peace forty years" (Judges 5:31).

DAILY BIBLE READINGS

Monday, Aug. 28— *Canaanites Oppress the Israelites* *(Judges 4:1-3)*

Tuesday, Aug. 29—The *Leadership of Deborah (Judges* *4:4-10)*

Wednesday, Aug. 30— *Defeat of the Canaanites (Judges* *4:11-16)*

Thursday, Aug. 31—Death *of Sisera (Judges 4:17-24)*

Friday, Sept. 1—The Song of *Deborah (Judges 5:1-9)*

Saturday, Sept. 2—Praise *for the Tribes (Judges 5:10-23)*

Sunday, Sept. 3—God's *Enemies Will Perish (Judges* *5:24-31)*

WHAT DO YOU THINK?

We can compare Jael's act with that of David in slaying Goliath (1 Samuel 17). In each case the victim was an enemy of God and his people. In one instance God used a woman with a tent peg and hammer to defeat that enemy, and in the other he used a boy with a sling and a stone. On both occasions God was given praise for the enemy's destruction (Judges 5:2-5; 1 Samuel 17:45-47). We are in the habit of viewing young David as a hero, but some have regarded Jael as a murderer. Why do you think that is so, and why should we regard Jael as heroic?

PRAYER

Thank you, Father, for setting our tasks before us. Give us true hearts and willing minds and energetic bodies, we pray, that we may "do with our might what our hands find to do."

THOUGHT TO REMEMBER

"There's a place for every worker In the vineyard of the Lord."
        —Noel A. McAulay

WHAT DO YOU THINK?

The lesson writer says winning people to Christ is the best solution to resolving our society's serious moral problems. Some critics may scoff that such a statement is too simplistic. After all, many professing Christians have made the news because of their involvement in adultery, pornography, political corruption, and other moral evils. How would you answer?

MISPLACED TRUST

Ferdinand Marcos, who ruled as president of the Philippines from 1966 to 1986, once wrote in his diary: "I am president. I am the most powerful man in the Philippines. All that I have dreamt of I have. . . . . But I feel a discontent."

Marcos's discontent was appropriate. His delight and trust in the things that represented his worldly power became his undoing. Eventually, he was toppled from power, disgraced by charges that he had embezzled several billion dollars from the national treasury. The Swiss government returned to the Philippines more than $500 million that Marcos had hidden in private Swiss bank accounts. He died in exile—a broken, lonely man.

Sisera was a powerful general whose troops greatly outnumbered the ragtag army of Israelites and whose weaponry was vastly superior to theirs. His first mistake was to place his trust in military might, since the forces of nature's God made his armaments of no value. His second mistake was to place his trust in Jael, a woman unknown to him, whose hospitality would prove fatal.

Where do we place our trust? In the possessions that delight us, in the power we have at our disposal, or in the God whose wisdom can give us the proper perspective on life?   —C. R. B.

CONCLUSION

A. OUR OWN COUNTRY

These lessons are used most in English-speaking countries. Not for centuries has one of these countries been overthrown and oppressed by a foreign power. Does that mean we are as godly as we ought to be?

We doubt it. This dying century has seen such a surge of paganism in Europe and America that students of our time are calling it "the post-Christian era." Hardly any thoughtful observer will deny that our country is moving away from obedience to God rather than toward it.

B. WHAT CAN WE DO?

We cannot recruit an army of ten thousand and "rout" all the sinners with the edge of the sword. What can we do for the salvation of our friends, our neighbors, our enemies, our country, our era?

We can bring people to Christ one by one. That was what Christians did when the church was beginning. They "preached the word wherever they went" (Acts 8:4). Whom do you know who is not a Christian? Are you really trying to reach him?

You don't know how? Then whom do you know who does know how? Perhaps you can go with him a few times, or many times, and see how he does it. Perhaps some more people in your church would like to know how. You can gather a class of six or ten or twenty and ask your minister to teach you how to approach people and win them. Then you can form teams of two, divide the nearby homes among the teams, and cover your town with the gospel.

Of course, when someone is won to Christ, that is only the beginning of what we can do. The next step is to make that person truly one of us. We can help him find his place in the work of the Lord. It may be mowing the lawn or singing in the choir. It may be trimming the shrubbery or teaching a Sunday school class. It may be repairing the roof or going out with another Christian to win his non-Christian friends.

Our problem is not that there is nothing we can do. Our problem is that we are not doing what we can. And that is a problem we can solve.

Discovery Learning

*This page contains an alternate lesson plan emphasizing learning activities. Classes
desiring such student involvement will find these suggestions helpful. The next page
is a reproducible activity page to further enhance discovery learning.*

LEARNING GOALS

After this lesson each student will be able to:

1. Tell how God used Deborah to deliver his people
from Canaanite oppression.

2. Explain how Deborah's example shows that supportive, behind-the-scenes leadership can be effective.

3. Seek a specific opportunity to serve the Lord and to
give him all the praise rather than to seek praise for oneself.

INTO THE LESSON

Prior to class prepare a poster with the phrase, "An encourager is one who. . . ." Place this poster near the door
to the classroom and attach a couple of markers. Ask
each person coming into the room to complete the sentence by writing potential endings. (*Possible answers include: supports what you are doing; stands beside you in
times of crisis; provides words of encouragement; believes in
you; trusts in your ability to lead; stands behind you.*) When
everyone has arrived, bring the poster to the front of the
room and read the endings. State: "Now that we've listed
some ways people encourage others, let's examine our
text. Turn to the book of Judges, and let's learn from
Deborah's example how we can be encouragers."

Option. Make a transparency of the reproducible activity, "Cycle of Redundancy." Use this chart to guide you in
giving a brief lecture to set the stage for today's lesson.

INTO THE WORD

Divide the class into three groups and give each
group one of these assignments. After ten minutes have
each group report to the class.

Group 1: Read Judges 2:6-19 for the lesson background. Answer the following questions:

1. What happened after Joshua died? (*The Israelites
did evil, forsaking the Lord, vv. 11, 13.*)

2. Why did they forsake the Lord? (*They did not know
him or what he had done for Israel, v. 10.*)

3. How did the Lord respond to their sin? (*He handed
them over to their enemies, v. 14.*)

4. How did God deliver the Israelites from their enemies? (*He raised up judges, vv. 16, 18.*)

5. What happened when the judge died? (*They returned to their evil ways and forsook the Lord again, v. 19.*)

Group 2: Read Judges 4:1-9 and prepare to give a
brief, one-minute summary of Ehud (from Judges 3:12-
30). Then answer these questions:

1. Why did Israel cry out to the Lord? (*Sisera had nine
hundred iron chariots and cruelly oppressed Israel for twenty
years, v. 3*)

2. What evidence from the text suggests how the Israelites regarded Deborah? (*Prophetess, v. 4; Israelites
came to her for judgment, v. 5; Barak came eighty miles in
response to her request, v. 6; Barak accepted God's message
through her, v. 8.*)

3. Why did Barak want Deborah to go with him to
the battle? (*He believed she spoke God's message and
wanted assurance that God was behind this operation.*)

Group 3: Read Judges 4:14, 15, 17a, 21, 22; and 5:4,
5, 21. Answer the following questions:

1. How was Israel able to overcome the nine hundred
chariots? (*Soldiers fought; the Lord routed Sisera and all his
chariots, 4:15; severe rainstorm and flood, 5:4, 5, 21.*)

2. Explain the meaning of v. 9, "for the Lord will hand
Sisera over to a woman." (*Reference to Jael, who drove a
tent peg through Sisera's head so that he died, 4:21.*)

INTO LIFE

Photocopy the reproducible activity called "Principles
to Apply" from the next page and pass out one copy to
each person. Make an overhead transparency of this
chart, too. Divide the class into three small groups and
ask them to draw from this account at least one principle from each biblical character. After two minutes, ask
each group to state the principles it discovered. Write
those principles on the projected chart. Several principles could be suggested for each column, but make certain that the following principles are suggested and
written on the chart. (*Deborah: gave supportive, behind-the-scenes leadership; Barak: did not seek his own glory, v. 9;
Jael: took advantage of an unexpected opportunity.*)

Circle the Deborah principle stated above and compare
it with the encourager list from "Into the Lesson." State:
"Deborah was an encourager: she supported Barak in a
dangerous situation; she got involved in community concerns; she shared God's word and stood beside Barak."

State: "I want each of you to select one person whom
you can encourage. Tell the person sitting next to you
how you will do that." Ask the class to pray in twos or
threes for each other's commitment to encourage someone. Then lead the class in a prayer that God will help
them take advantage of every opportunity to encourage
someone and to give all the glory to God.

Principles to Apply

Read Judges 4:1-9, 14, 15, 17a, 21, 22. In this account each character cited below demonstrates some good principles by which to live our lives. Write at least one principle that you see demonstrated in the life of each character. (One example has been given for each to get you started.)

DEBORAH

Gave supportive, behind-the-scenes leadership

BARAK

Willing to serve but did not seek his own glory

JAEL

Took advantage of the unexpected opportunity

Israel's Cycle of Redundancy

Israel Serves the Lord

Judge Dies

Israel Sins

The Lord Delivers Israel to Enemy

Israel Cries to the Lord

Judge Raised Up

Israel Delivered

GIDEON

LESSON 2

Sep
10

WHY TEACH THIS LESSON?

Why do you teach an adult class? Did you volunteer, or did someone "recruit" you? Did you agree eagerly, or were you hesitant? Do you face your class each time with confidence, or are there times when you wonder why you ever agreed to this ministry in the first place?

Most of us have occasional doubts and misgivings. The key is not letting those doubts control us. People who do not serve are letting their doubts control them. Like Gideon in our lesson today, they need someone to reassure them that they, with the help of God, can make a difference for the Lord. Some of these people are in your class. They need this reassurance. That's why you'll teach *this* lesson!

INTRODUCTION

A. RELUCTANT LEADERS

Have you ever had difficulty getting someone to accept some task in the church? Reluctant leaders are not a new phenomenon in the work of the Lord. Isaiah volunteered, "Here am I. Send me!" (Isaiah 6:8); but some other outstanding leaders had to be "drafted." Do you remember how Moses protested when God appointed him to lead his people out of slavery (Exodus 3:11, 13; 4:1, 10, 13)? In this lesson we meet another reluctant leader.

B. LESSON BACKGROUND

Last week we read that God used Deborah, Barak, and a powerful rainstorm to defeat the Canaanites and end their twenty-year oppression of Israel. "Then the land had peace forty years" (Judges 5:31). By that time most of the Israelites under sixty years old had no memory of the terrible oppression that had come because Israel had disobeyed God. They had not been involved in the momentous battle against the Canaanites. So this new generation began their own path of disobedience. For that reason, for seven years the Lord "gave them into the hands of the Midianites" (Judges 6:1).

The Midianites were nomads from the deserts east and south of Israel. They crossed the Jordan in great numbers, bringing countless thousands of sheep and cattle to pasture on the young barley and wheat in Israel. Thus deprived of their harvests, the Israelites found it hard to survive. Desperately they "cried out to the Lord for help" (Judges 6:6).

I. FINDING A LEADER (JUDGES 6:11-14)

Naturally the invaders from Midian were most interested in securing control of the plains with their wide stretches of fertile farmland. As a result, many Israelites fled to the hill country, where they found hiding places (Judges 6:2).

A. AN ANGEL VISITS (vv. 11, 12)

11. *The angel of the LORD came and sat down under the oak in Ophrah that belonged to Joash the Abiezrite, where his son Gideon was threshing wheat in a winepress to keep it from the Midianites.*

DEVOTIONAL READING:
JOSHUA 1:1-9

BACKGROUND SCRIPTURE:
JUDGES 6–8

PRINTED TEXT:
JUDGES 6:11-14; 7:1-7, 20, 21

LESSON AIMS

After studying this lesson, each student will be able to:

1. Recount the story of the unusual way in which God used Gideon to rescue Israel from the Midianites.

2. Explain why one's reluctance to serve the Lord should not be allowed to keep him or her from such service.

3. Seek an opportunity to encourage an individual who has been rather timid in serving the Lord to use his or her talents in his service.

KEY VERSE

The LORD turned to him and said, "Go in the strength you have and save Israel out of Midian's hand. Am I not sending you?" —Judges 6:14

LESSON 2 NOTES

An *Abiezrite* was a member of one of the families of the tribe of Manasseh. *Ophrah* probably was located in the hills southeast of the plain of Jezreel, where Barak and the Israelites had routed the Canaanites. It seems that *Joash* and *his son Gideon* somehow had been able to grow and harvest a little *wheat*. Gideon was secretly *threshing* some of it in order to provide food.

A *winepress* usually consisted of a pit cut into the limestone rock that was common throughout Israel. There grapes were trampled to crush the juice out of them for wine—only now the pit also served as a hiding place. No doubt Gideon was actually *in* the winepress—down in the pit and out of sight as much as possible, since the Midianites would steal his wheat if they saw it. As Gideon worked, *the angel of the Lord came and sat down under the oak* nearby.

12. When the angel of the LORD appeared to Gideon, he said, "The LORD is with you, mighty warrior."

For Gideon to hear himself described as a *mighty warrior* must have sounded like cruel sarcasm. Some warrior—hiding in a winepress to thresh a bit of wheat! *The Lord is with you* must have sounded unbelievable, too. Gideon had an immediate response to that claim.

WHAT DO YOU THINK?

The angel of the Lord greeted Gideon as a "mighty warrior." At the time Gideon seemed a man of cowardice more than courage. What is the value of speaking of others' potential more than what they have actually demonstrated?

B. GIDEON OBJECTS (v. 13)

13. "But sir," Gideon replied, "if the LORD is with us, why has all this happened to us? Where are all his wonders that our fathers told us about when they said, 'Did not the LORD bring us up out of Egypt?' But now the LORD has abandoned us and put us into the hand of Midian."

The Lord had indeed brought the people of Israel *out of Egypt* by means of *his wonders*. Gideon, however, had seen no wonders in his own time. He was quite right in saying, *The Lord has . . . put us into the hand of Midian.* Judges 6:1 tells us exactly the same thing. But Gideon was wrong in saying, *The Lord has abandoned us.* The Lord had delivered his people to the Midianites to turn them away from idolatry and other sins and to bring them back to worshiping and obeying him alone.

C. THE LORD SENDS (v. 14)

14. The LORD turned to him and said, "Go in the strength you have and save Israel out of Midian's hand. Am I not sending you?"

Here, as in several places in the Old Testament, there appears to be no clear distinction between the angel of the Lord and the Lord himself. Someone has suggested that the angel was God "in one particular phase of his self-revelation." That seems to explain a concept that is difficult to understand fully.

Hiding in the winepress, Gideon must have wondered how he could have possessed any *strength* of his own. How could someone like him *save Israel*? His family was a poor one in its tribe, and he was the least in his family (v. 15). But the Lord had a ready answer for him: "I will be with you" (v. 16).

After some further convincing, and at God's command, Gideon began to display his might. He destroyed an altar used in the worship of the imaginary god Baal (vv. 25-27). Men of the city wanted to kill Gideon for destroying Baal's altar, but his father dissuaded them (vv. 28-32).

Events moved swiftly after that. The Midianites assembled in a huge camp in the valley of Jezreel (v. 33). Gideon called for volunteers, and men from his tribe and three others responded (vv. 34, 35).

HOW TO SAY IT

Abiezrite. AY-by-EZ-rite.
Baal. BAY-ul.
Barak. BAIR-uk.
Canaanites. KAY-nun-ites.
Deborah. DEB-uh-ruh.
Ephraim. EE-fray-im.
Gideon. GID-ee-un.
Gilboa. Gil-BO-uh.
Gilead. GIL-ee-ud.
Harod. HAY-rod.
Isaiah. Eye-ZAY-uh.
Jerub-Baal. JAIR-ub-BAY-ul.
Jezreel. JEZ-ree-el or JEZ-reel.
Joash. JO-ash.
Manasseh. Muh-NASS-uh.
Midian. MID-ee-un.
Midianites. MID-ee-un-ites.
Moreh. MO-reh.
Ophrah. AHF-ruh.

"LOOK WHAT I'VE DONE!"

For many years, the tallest building in the world was New York City's Empire State Building. In 1966 New York's World Trade Center claimed the title at 1,377 feet. Chicago's Sears Tower took the honor in 1973 (1,454 feet). In 1996 the crown passed to Kuala Lampur, Malaysia, where the Petronas Towers reached 1,483 feet.

A few years ago, top architects around the world claimed in a survey that the reason for such buildings is primarily "self-advertising" and "ego." We could have guessed that, couldn't we? How interesting, then, that God often looks elsewhere when he has a significant task to be done. When he looked for someone to lead his people against the Midianites, Gideon was working in a winepress, desperately hoping *not* to be noticed! Such people are more likely to credit God for their successes, but God often has to prod them into action.

Where do we fit in this picture? Are we willing to serve but wanting the credit, or humble but reluctant to serve? The story of Gideon teaches us a lesson about the kind of people whom God can use.   —C. R. B.

II. REDUCING AN ARMY (JUDGES 7:1-7)

An army of thirty-two thousand assembled in answer to Gideon's call. Gideon may have thought that this number was much too small to fight the multitude of Midianites that filled a wide camp in the valley. But the Lord told Gideon that the army was too big!

A. FROM 32,000 TO 10,000 (vv. 1-3)

1. Early in the morning, Jerub-Baal (that is, Gideon) and all his men camped at the spring of Harod. The camp of Midian was north of them in the valley near the hill of Moreh.

Jerub-Baal means "let Baal plead," a nickname Gideon picked up when he destroyed Baal's altar. When the people of the city came for Gideon, his father said, "Are you going to plead Baal's cause? Are you trying to save him? . . . If Baal really is a god, he can defend himself" (Judges 6:31). So from that day Gideon was known as Jerub-Baal, "let Baal plead" (v. 32). The name appears fourteen times in Judges and 1 Samuel.

Gideon and his men made their camp on an elevated area where *the spring of Harod* provided an ample water supply. Since this spring was located at the northern foot of Mount Gilboa, this is most likely where Gideon and his men were camped. From this position they could look down on the enemy camp *in the valley* that was *north* of them.

2. The LORD said to Gideon, "You have too many men for me to deliver Midian into their hands. In order that Israel may not boast against me that her own strength has saved her,

The Lord explained why the army must be reduced in size. The battle must be won by a force so small that everyone would know without question that God had given the victory.

3. . . . announce now to the people, 'Anyone who trembles with fear may turn back and leave Mount Gilead.'" So twenty-two thousand men left, while ten thousand remained.

The proclamation went out through the camp of Israel: *anyone who trembles with fear* may be excused. More than two-thirds of the men happily left *Mount Gilead* (most likely another name for Mount Gilboa).

B. FROM 10,000 TO 300 (vv. 4-7)

4. But the LORD said to Gideon, "There are still too many men. Take them down to the water, and I will sift them for you there. If I say, 'This one shall go with you,' he shall go; but if I say, 'This one shall not go with you,' he shall not go."

WHAT DO YOU THINK?

The account of God's reducing Gideon's army is just one example of God's working with small numbers to accomplish tremendous results. The Lord is not dependent on the bigness of human organizations to accomplish his work. What is the significance of that fact for the church today? How should we apply that truth to our ministries?

There were *still too many men* in Gideon's army to serve the Lord's purpose. The number had to be reduced again. A small stream flowed from the bigger spring near the camp. The men were to go down there for a drink, and God would make known to Gideon which ones should be selected for the coming battle.

5. So Gideon took the men down to the water. There the LORD told him, "Separate those who lap the water with their tongues like a dog from those who kneel down to drink."

There are different ways of drinking from a running stream. Some men would *lap the water with their tongues like a dog*. This action is further explained in verse 6. One man would cup the palm of his hand to dip a little water from the stream; then he would lap it from his hand with his tongue. Another man, however, would *kneel* on both knees and bend forward, bringing his lips to the surface of the stream.

These ways of drinking seemed to show something about the attitudes of the men. They were camped in sight of the enemy, an enemy that greatly outnumbered them. At any time that enemy might decide to attack rather than wait to be attacked. A man who lifted a little water with his hand showed himself to be more alert and watchful, and more concerned about the possibility of sudden attack.

In contrast, one who put his face down to the water showed himself to be overconfident or careless, unaware of the potential danger. While he drank, the enemy could approach without his being aware of it. And he would drink more than the one who cupped a little in his hand. If he rose from his knees and discovered the enemy charging up the hill, his full stomach might keep him from doing his best in battle.

6. Three hundred men lapped with their hands to their mouths. All the rest got down on their knees to drink.

By far the greater number of men relaxed and drank freely. It was obvious that they were more interested in satisfying their thirst than in staying ready for the possibility of conflict.

7. The LORD said to Gideon, "With the three hundred men that lapped I will save you and give the Midianites into your hands. Let all the other men go, each to his own place."

At this point, let's try to imagine what the *Midianites* were thinking in their camp in the valley. They had seen thirty-two thousand men of Israel gather on the hill above them. Then they had seen most of those Israelites go away. They must have wondered where all those men were going, and why. Were they planning to meet with other Israelites—thousands of them? Were they preparing to surround the camp of Midian with an overpowering army? When the number of men on the hillside shrank to *three hundred*, the thousands of Midianites likely felt more uneasy rather than more secure.

That was confirmed when later, under cover of darkness, Gideon and an aide sneaked near the enemy camp and heard the men of Midian talking. They learned that the Midianites indeed were apprehensive, fearing a devastating attack by Gideon and his men (Judges 7:9-14).

Encouraged by this information, Gideon went back to his own camp to prepare to carry out God's plan. The Midianites were to be routed by clever strategy rather than by force of arms. Gideon divided his three hundred men into three groups. Each man lighted a torch but hid its flame in a clay jar. Each man also took a trumpet. The three groups crept away silently in the darkness to their assigned places.

WHAT DO YOU THINK?

The three hundred men who comprised Gideon's army were the ones who demonstrated their readiness for battle. Why is it important that we be alert and ready for battle today? What is the most intense "battle" being fought in our community? How can we better equip ourselves with God's might for this battle?

WHAT DO YOU THINK?

God's strategy for defeating the Midianites called for the use of empty jars, torches, and trumpets. God still uses ordinary things to accomplish his purposes today. What are some common human attributes that Christians can employ in God's service?

III. DEFEATING AN ENEMY (JUDGES 7:20, 21)

The twelve hours of "night" (from 6:00 P.M. to 6:00 A.M.) were divided into three "watches" of four hours each. Near the end of the first watch Gideon and his men moved into position. At the beginning of the "middle watch," about 10:00 P.M. (v. 19), while sentries just roused from sleep were nervous amid the darkness around Midian's camp, Gideon blew his trumpet. The response was spectacular.

A. LIGHTS AND NOISE (v. 20)

20. The three companies blew the trumpets and smashed the jars. Grasping the torches in their left hands and holding in their right hands the trumpets they were to blow, they shouted, "A sword for the LORD and for Gideon!"

Three hundred *torches* gleamed in the darkness. Three hundred breaking *jars* shattered the silence. Three hundred *trumpets* blared, and three hundred voices shouted the battle cry to let the Midianites know what was upon them: *"A sword for the Lord and for Gideon!"*

B. PANIC (v. 21)

21. While each man held his position around the camp, all the Midianites ran, crying out as they fled.

The men of Israel did not need to draw their swords and charge. *Each man held his position.* They waved their torches; they blew their trumpets; they shouted their battle cry—as they had been instructed to do.

In the dark camp of Midian, uneasy sleepers woke to the sound of three hundred trumpets and looked out at three hundred torches like a line of fire around them. The startled Midianites must have thought that countless thousands of angry Israelites were upon them. Panic-stricken, they *ran, crying out as they fled.* No one paused to light a lamp; no one took time to pack his belongings. Some did pick up their swords.

Charging out of their tents, the Midianites saw dark figures coming swiftly toward them. Swinging their swords in blind horror, they cut down their own comrades. In darkness and terror they ran screaming until they were out of breath and only faintly could hear the sound of the three hundred trumpeters, each of whom remained steadfast in his place. With scarcely a pause for rest, the Midianites pushed on toward the Jordan River and their homeland to the east of it (v. 22).

The rout of Midian was under way. Probably those men who had left the camp of Israel earlier now returned to chase the fleeing enemies, and other men of Israel joined in the pursuit (v. 23). Men from the tribe of Ephraim were alerted to intercept the fugitives (vv. 24, 25). Gideon then led his troops across the Jordan and defeated the Midianite army that remained there (Judges 8:10-12).

TOO MUCH LIGHT

Most people enjoy the added brightness that Christmas lights bring to December evenings. Many Christians see in the myriad of lights a symbol, not only of the season, but of Jesus, the "light of the world."

Some, however, don't quite see it that way. In Little Rock, Arkansas, Jennings Osborne's Christmas lights reached three million bulbs a few years ago. It was then that his neighbors claimed, "That's too much light!" They filed a lawsuit to make him turn off some of his lights. Osborne fought the suit all the way to the Arkansas State Supreme Court. Alas, he lost, and the December nights became a bit darker in his part of Little Rock.

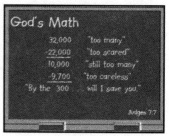

The visual that corresponds to this lesson illustrates God's ability to do much with little. Discuss contemporary illustrations of the same concept.

When Gideon's three hundred men had surrounded the Midianites in the dark of night, they blew their trumpets and lit their torches. This sudden "light show" caused the Midianites to panic, and they fled in fear of a vastly greater army than was really there. Three hundred torches may not provide a lot of light (at least by our standards), but they were too much for the enemies of God's people. On the other hand, those who are on God's side of the battle against evil never have to fear the light!   —C. R. B.

CONCLUSION

We're very blessed, aren't we? Nomads never bring their sheep and cattle across the river to devour our growing crops. What, then, does this lesson mean to us? Let's think about some things that do happen here.

A. EXAMPLES

Cora had never been in the room where the men's class met, but through the open door she saw the torn shade at the window. It looked disgraceful. A month later the door was open again. Cora looked, and that window shade still looked disgraceful.

After church Cora stood on a chair and lifted the shade with its roller off the brackets. On Monday she took it to the hardware store and got a new one just like it. On Wednesday she went early to midweek Bible study and put the new shade in its place.

On Sunday the men were delighted. Happily they commented, "They finally did something about that shade!"

Dave was unhappy because his daughter didn't like Sunday school. The high school kids met with the adults, and they were bored. So Dave took it up with the teacher, who was also the preacher.

"Sam, how about starting a separate class for the high school kids?"

"Great idea," said Sam. "But a class needs two things: a teacher and a room."

"Couldn't we meet in the auditorium and let them have our room?"

"Maybe. How about a teacher?"

"There's Bill. He's both a teacher and a football coach. The kids think he's great."

Sam nodded. "OK. You get Bill to teach the kids, and I'll see what I can do to get our class to move."

Bill frowned at first, but on second thought he began to smile. "I'd really like to teach some Bible to those kids. In Sunday school I'd be free to shoot down some of the nonsense we read in the textbooks."

Not all the older folks like the auditorium, but they don't complain much because the high school class is growing every week.

B. THE PROCESS

You see the process, don't you? It goes something like this:

See the Problem. That isn't much, but it's a start.

Do Something. That's what Cora did about the window blind. There are other things that can be done single-handedly.

Get Help. Dave couldn't teach a high school class, but he knew who could.

Solve Problems. Moving the older adults' class may have been difficult, but it could be done once the benefits were clearly seen.

So what need do you see in your church? What can you do about it? Who can help? What problems will arise? How can they be solved?

Discovery Learning

This page contains an alternate lesson plan emphasizing learning activities. Classes desiring such student involvement will find these suggestions helpful. The next page is a reproducible activity page to further enhance discovery learning.

LEARNING GOALS

After this lesson each student will be able to:

1. Recount the story of the unusual way in which God used Gideon to rescue Israel from the Midianites.

2. Explain why one's reluctance to serve the Lord should not keep him or her from such service.

3. Seek an opportunity to encourage an individual who has been rather timid in serving the Lord to use his or her talents in his service.

INTO THE LESSON

Write on the chalkboard the word *reluctant* without the vowels: R _ L _ C T _ N T. Ask the class to fill in the blanks to discern a key word for today's lesson. Once the class identifies the word, ask, "Why are people sometimes reluctant to serve God?" (*They are uncertain of their talents or anxious about failure; they feel inadequate; they think they are too busy, that they don't have time.*)

State: "Our text today describes one who was reluctant to serve God. He gave some of the same reasons reluctant people today give for their unwillingness to be used by God. Let's turn to Judges 6 and find the reasons he gave and how he overcame them to become obedient to God."

INTO THE WORD

Ask the students to read Judges 6:11-16 to see what excuses Gideon gave for his reluctance to do the Lord's work. Have each student discuss these reasons with one person sitting next to him or her. Allow about three minutes; then restate the question and write the suggested answers from the class on the chalkboard under the heading, "Excuses." (*He questioned whether the Lord was really with the Israelites, v. 13; he cited the absence of God's miracles, v. 13; he said the Lord had abandoned Israel, v. 13; his clan was the weakest in Manasseh, v. 15; he was the least in his family, v. 15*).

Summarize: "Basically, Gideon's excuses could be condensed to two: he doubted God's presence and he doubted his own ability." Write these two excuses on the chalkboard.

Ask the class to notice how God responded to Gideon's excuses. The Lord reassured Gideon that he should go and save Israel from the Midianites (cite verses 14 and 16). But Gideon wanted some signs. Divide the class into four groups, asking each to read one of the following passages and to prepare a summary: 1. Judges 6:17-24; 2. Judges 6:25-32; 3. Judges 6:36-40; 4. Judges 7:9-14. After three to five minutes, ask the first three groups to summarize the signs the Lord gave to Gideon.

Read Judges 7:1-7 aloud. Ask, "Why did the Lord reduce Gideon's army from 32,000 to 300 men?" (*So Israel would not boast that they had saved themselves.*) To reassure Gideon once he had only 300 men, the Lord gave the sign of a dream. Ask the fourth group above to summarize this reassurance for the class. Conclude this Bible study with a brief summary of Israel's defeat of the Midianites (cite Judges 7:20, 21).

INTO LIFE

Photocopy the reproducible activity "Reassurance for the Reluctant" from the next page. Move the class into triads (groups of three) and give one copy to each person. State: "Gideon was reluctant because he doubted God's presence and doubted his own ability. What type of reassurance can we give someone today who is reluctant to get involved and serve the Lord?" (*Affirm that God is present and has not abandoned us; share God's Word—e.g., Philippians 4:13; affirm the person's giftedness and abilities; encourage the person to try.*)

State: "We may not be controlled by the army of the Midianites today, but churches are often ravaged and robbed of potential growth by the lack of programs or workers. What lack of programs or personnel robs our church's growth today?" (Note: make an overhead transparency sheet of the reproducible activity "The Reassured Reluctant Servants Respond.") Brainstorm the needed programs or those needing workers and write them on the transparency sheet under "Programs Needed."

Divide the class into the number of groups equal to the number of needed programs. Assign each group one program. Ask the groups to identify some individuals who have the gifts and abilities to serve in that particular program. Give the class five to seven minutes for this discussion. Finally, ask each group member to select one individual from the list to encourage and to share with the members of the group the selected ways he or she can reassure that person. Ask each group to pray together for the opportunity to encourage the selected individuals.

(Be sure to coordinate your efforts with those who are responsible for recruiting various workers. Check with them before approaching any potential workers.)

Reassurance for the Reluctant

Gideon was reluctant because he doubted God's presence and doubted his own ability. What type of reassurance can we give someone today who, for either of these reasons, is reluctant to get involved and serve the Lord? List as many ideas as you can under each category below.

DOUBT GOD'S PRESENCE   *DOUBT PERSONAL ABILITY*

The Reassured Reluctant Servants Respond

To the left of the cross below list some of the programs or ministries needed in your church. To the right list the names of some people you think can help launch those programs or ministries. Discuss your ideas with the staff or other people responsible for the programs, and see what gets accomplished!

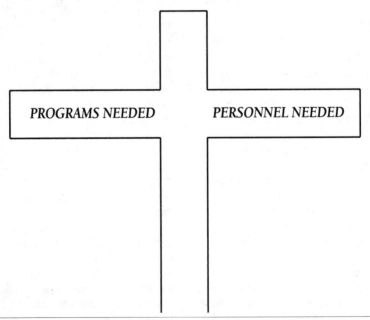

PROGRAMS NEEDED   *PERSONNEL NEEDED*

SAMSON

LESSON 3

WHY TEACH THIS LESSON?

The Bible is full of surprises. The more I read it, the more it amazes me. Shortly after I had heard a sermon about Lot and the compromises he made with evil—drifting farther and farther from God as he moved close to Sodom and then moved *into* Sodom—I was reading the book of 2 Peter. In the second chapter the big fisherman described Lot in a very different way from the way the preacher had! Three times in verses 7 and 8 Peter refers to Lot as "righteous." I thought, "If he was so 'righteous,' what was he doing in Sodom?"

We are similarly surprised by Samson. Sermons today describe him as the "Weakest Strong Man" or some similar oxymoron. But open Hebrews 11, and there is his name, along with faithful Noah and Abraham and Moses! With all his faults, he was still a man of faith. Peter might even have called him "righteous"!

If your learners have trouble identifying with some of the giants of the faith, perhaps they can identify with the "weak" and temptable Samson. And perhaps they can be encouraged that God can use them, too, if they will just seek to be faithful in spite of their flaws!

INTRODUCTION

Carson was an ordinary town. It had an ordinary high school and an ordinary church that most people ignored. Then Weber came to town.

A. A Town Transformed

Weber became janitor at the high school. He was an ordinary man who could do extraordinary things. When a student couldn't get his car started after school, Weber fixed it. Rejecting pay, he said, "Helping is more fun when you don't get paid. That's the way Jesus did it." The student wanted to know more about Jesus, and Weber took him to Sunday school. Because the student was a popular boy, friends started going with him.

Weber turned down overtime pay with the same kind of response when he worked all night to replace a broken pipe so that school could open in the morning. Impressed with Weber's dedication, the principal started going to church. Many of the teachers followed his example and took their families with them.

In his own neighborhood, Weber was everyone's helper. He led in making his block the neatest one in town. Happy neighbors responded by going to church with him, and they brought others. Soon the church had to build a bigger house.

That, in brief, is the story of a town that was changed because an ordinary man had an extraordinary talent for helping people and making friends. This week's lesson brings us a different story: the story of an extraordinary man who had an extraordinary talent for making enemies. But his enemies were God's enemies, and thus his story has a place in God's Word.

B. Lesson Background

Today's lesson background describes a time when Israel forgot God and fell into idolatry and other sins. Where have we heard that before? In the two lessons

Devotional Reading:
Psalm 145:14-21

Background Scripture:
Judges 13–16

Printed Text:
Judges 16:4, 5, 16, 17, 19-22, 28-30

Sep 17

Lesson Aims

After this lesson students will be able to:

1. Give the details of Samson's demise and how God used it for good.

2. Tell why using God's gifts to promote his agenda rather than ours is the path to genuine fulfillment.

3. Tell how their own talents can be better used for God.

Key Verse

"O Sovereign LORD, remember me. O God, please strengthen me just once more."

—Judges 16:28

HOW TO SAY IT

Antioch. AN-tee-ock.

Apollos. Uh-PAHL-us.

Aquila. ACK-wih-luh.

Barnabas. BAR-nuh-bus.

Dagon. DAY-gon.

Delilah. Dih-LYE-luh.

Dorcas. DOR-cus.

Gaza. GAY-zuh.

Joppa. JOP-uh.

Joses. JO-sez.

Mediterranean. MED-uh-tuh-
    RAY-nee-un.

Nazirite. NAZ-uh-rite.

Philistines. Fuh-LISS-teens or
    FILL-us-teens.

Priscilla. Prih-SIL-uh.

Sorek. SO-rek.

Tabitha. TAB-ih-thuh.

prior to this one, of course, and at many other places in the Old Testament. It was a pattern of behavior that was common during the period of the judges.

On this occasion the Lord delivered his sinful people to the Philistines, who lived along the southern Mediterranean coast. These oppressors harassed Israel, stealing the people's livestock and harvests for forty years (Judges 13:1).

Once more God set in motion a plan to rescue his people from their enemies. This plan, however, was quite different from what he had done in previous instances. He sent his angel to tell a childless couple that they would have a son who would be a Nazirite all his life. This meant that he would remain dedicated to the service of God. The sign of his dedication would be that his hair must never be cut. (Read more about the Nazirite vow in Numbers 6:1-21.) When the promised baby was born, he was named Samson (Judges 13:2-25).

As he grew to manhood, Samson began to demonstrate incredible strength. On one occasion, when a lion was about to attack him, Samson tore the beast apart with his bare hands (Judges 14:5, 6). In spite of Samson's failure to demonstrate a wisdom to match his strength, God repeatedly used his recklessness to punish the Philistines. During a conflict that followed Samson's marriage to a Philistine girl, he twice put to death some of the Philistines and set fire to their ripened grain fields (Judges 14:10—15:8). When the Philistines came in great numbers to capture Samson, he picked up the jawbone of a donkey and killed a thousand of them (Judges 15:9-20).

Today's lesson text brings us to the final chapter of the story of Samson—perhaps the most noteworthy of the judges.

I. SAMSON TRAPPED (JUDGES 16:4, 5, 16, 17)

It seems that Philistine women held a "fatal attraction" for Samson, but in the providence of God this proved fatal to his enemies. As noted above, when Samson married a Philistine girl, the resulting conflict brought death to Philistines, not Samson. When he visited another Philistine girl in Gaza, the Philistines shut and locked the gates of the city, planning to trap and kill him. But Samson simply pulled up the gates with the gateposts and carried them away (Judges 16:1-3).

Now we come to Samson's pivotal encounter with the infamous Delilah.

A. EVIL PLOT (vv. 4, 5)

4. *Some time later, he fell in love with a woman in the Valley of Sorek whose name was Delilah.*

The *Valley of Sorek* extended from near Jerusalem to the Mediterranean Sea, about eight and a half miles south of Joppa. From the little that is told of *Delilah*, we suppose that she was a Philistine woman of charming personality and pagan moral standards. Some students think that Samson married her. Whether he did or not, it seems clear that he often came to spend time with her, but was away long enough to let the Philistines plot with her in his absence.

5. *The rulers of the Philistines went to her and said, "See if you can lure him into showing you the secret of his great strength and how we can overpower him so we may tie him up and subdue him. Each one of us will give you eleven hundred shekels of silver."*

The phrase *rulers of the Philistines* describes the five men (Judges 3:3) who ruled the key cities situated in different parts of the Philistines' territory. They wanted to find out two things: what gave Samson his *great strength* and how that strength could be overcome.

Vengeful as they were, these angry men did not want to kill Samson. They wanted to *tie him up and subdue him*: they wanted to see him suffer in retaliation for all the suffering that he had brought upon the Philistines. The bribe they offered Delilah totaled fifty-five hundred *shekels of silver.* The fact that during the time of the judges someone could be hired at a salary of ten shekels a year (Judges 17:10) indicates the enormous sum that was being offered to Delilah. That the Philistine rulers were willing to pay it shows their determination to rid themselves of Samson.

It appears that Samson, despite his unruly behavior, was something of a joker and a maker of riddles (see Judges 14:10-14). Here he teased Delilah three times, pretending to reveal to her the secret of his strength. Delilah tried each way and found it would not work (Judges 16:6-15). Urged on by thoughts of a lucrative reward, she kept on trying.

B. ENDLESS NAGGING (v. 16)

16. With such nagging she prodded him day after day until he was tired to death.

Delilah had reproached Samson for lying to her (vv. 10, 13) and had complained that he did not love her (v. 15). Now she resorted to ceaseless *nagging* until Samson could stand it no more.

C. EARNEST ADMISSION (v. 17)

17. So he told her everything. "No razor has ever been used on my head," he said, "because I have been a Nazirite set apart to God since birth. If my head were shaved, my strength would leave me, and I would become as weak as any other man."

Finally Samson gave in. He *told* Delilah the simple truth: if his hair was cut, his tremendous *strength* would be gone. Three times this woman had revealed her purpose to turn Samson over to the enemy (vv. 6-14), and now he was letting her know how it could be done. How could he be so blind to her intentions?

Apparently Samson had become accustomed to irresistible power. It seems that he really could not imagine himself weak and powerless, even when he divulged how he could be reduced to that state. At the moment, he could think only of putting an end to Delilah's continual nagging. That was the part of Samson's character that constantly led him into trouble: his desire to live for the moment and satisfy the desires of the flesh.

GIVING IN TO PRESSURE

An old story tells about Jim, a soldier who was sent off to battle. He left behind a wife whose talent seemed to be advising him about what he ought to do, how he ought to do it, and berating him if he didn't do it (or do it in the way she had suggested). It was what some call "nagging." Secretly Jim felt good about getting away from her barrage of counsel.

While Jim was at the battlefront, he received letter after letter from his wife advising him, "Try to get assigned away from the front lines," "Be sure you don't get captured," "Watch out so that you don't get shot," and so on. Finally, when Jim had become fed up with all of this advice from someone who had no idea what life in combat was like, he wrote his wife a letter. It contained two sentences: "Please stop sending me these nagging letters. Just let me enjoy this war in peace."

Samson's relationship with Delilah may have resembled the story of Jim. However, during a time of war with the Philistines, Delilah's nagging was not to assure Samson's safety, but to find a way to destroy him. When he finally gave in to her, the results were disastrous.

Like Samson, we face pressure from evil forces on a daily basis. And, like Samson, when we give in to the pressure to do wrong, the consequences can be devastating.
                                                          —C. R. B.

WHAT DO YOU THINK?

Samson illustrates the wisdom of Paul's warning, "If you think you are standing firm, be careful that you don't fall!" (1 Corinthians 10:12). When we read of Samson's dealings with Delilah, we are amazed at his foolish overconfidence. Apparently he fancied that he was powerful enough that, even with his hair cut, he was more than a match for the Philistines. Sadly, he learned otherwise. How do people in our own time demonstrate a similar arrogance?

II. SAMSON SUBDUED (JUDGES 16:19-22)

At last Delilah had the truth! Once more she sent word to the Philistine conspirators, confident that she could now deliver Samson into their hands (v. 18).

A. LOST STRENGTH (v. 19)

19. Having put him to sleep on her lap, she called a man to shave off the seven braids of his hair, and so began to subdue him. And his strength left him.

Now the woman displayed nothing but tender affection for her man. She stroked and soothed him until he fell asleep *on her lap*. There he lay undisturbed, oblivious to what proceeded to take place. Long and flowing, Samson's *hair* had been tied or woven into *seven braids. A man* was summoned to remove them all. Thus Delilah *began to subdue* Samson, for *his strength*, which had kept him from being subdued, *left him*.

WHAT DO YOU THINK?

Poor Samson! He had no idea that the Lord was no longer with him! How might a leader today get himself in a position where he is not following the Lord, but does not even know it? What can be done to help such a person return to the Lord?

B. HELPLESS CAPTIVE (vv. 20, 21)

20. Then she called, "Samson, the Philistines are upon you!"

He awoke from his sleep and thought, "I'll go out as before and shake myself free." But he did not know that the LORD had left him.

Samson expected to overcome his attackers as he had always done before, for *he did not know that the Lord had left him*. Samson's strength was not really from his hair; it was from the Lord (Judges 14:6, 19; 15:14, 15). Samson had been devoted to the Lord by his parents' vow before he was born. His uncut hair was the sign of that vow (Judges 13:3-5). When Samson recklessly let the sign be removed, the Lord departed. Samson was now "as weak as any other man" (v. 17).

THE PRICE OF A HAIRCUT

Back in the 1940s, a man could get a haircut for a dollar or less. Of course, it didn't take much time for a barber to run a pair of electric clippers over a fellow's head. The "G.I." haircut went by various names: crewcut, buzz, butch, etc. And because American fighting men were heroes in those days, their hairstyle was very popular even among civilians.

How things have changed since then! Hair styles and lengths differ widely today. And so do the prices. Today a haircut may cost five or ten dollars at a small-town barber or upwards of fifty dollars at a salon in a bigger city. One barber reportedly charged Bill Clinton $200 to give the President a haircut aboard *Air Force One*. But the most expensive haircut of all time was the one into which Delilah lured Samson. That haircut cost Samson his dignity and strength as well as his locks. Ultimately it cost him his life.

It may be argued that our society makes too much out of how a man cuts his hair. But it's hard to overstate the cost to Samson of his haircut. Hairstyle (as well as most other issues of style) may be irrelevant, except when—as in Samson's case—it reflects a change in our relationship with God.   —C. R. B.

21. Then the Philistines seized him, gouged out his eyes and took him down to Gaza. Binding him with bronze shackles, they set him to grinding in the prison.

Imagine the delight of the Philistines. Samson was in their power, and they lost no time in adding to his misery. First, they *gouged out his eyes*. Then they *took him down to Gaza*, one of their principal cities, and bound him *with bronze shackles*. His superhuman power was gone; his human power was put to work turning a heavy millstone in order to grind wheat for his captors' food. That was a task sometimes given to an ox or a donkey.

C. NEW HOPE (v. 22)

22. But the hair on his head began to grow again after it had been shaved.

The sign of the vow was returning. Would Samson renew the vow itself? Would the Lord come back to him? Would Samson be strong again?

III. SAMSON AVENGED (JUDGES 16:28-30)

The capture of Samson called for a celebration. The Philistines gathered to rejoice and to give thanks to Dagon, their supposed god. When the hearts of the revelers were merry, Samson was brought from the prison to entertain them (vv. 23-25). We can only guess what cruelties were involved in this "entertainment."

It is hard for us to imagine the shape of the "temple" (v. 29) in which the celebration was held. Probably it was dedicated to the worship of Dagon, in whose honor the Philistines had assembled. Verse 27 tells us that about three thousand people were gathered on the roof of the structure to watch Samson.

At some point Samson asked to be led to the pillars that supported the temple so that he could lean against them (v. 26). The stage was set for the final scene.

A. PRAYER FOR STRENGTH (v. 28)

28. Then Samson prayed to the LORD, "O Sovereign LORD, remember me. O God, please strengthen me just once more, and let me with one blow get revenge on the Philistines for my two eyes."

Blinded by his enemies and abused to amuse them, Samson thirsted for vengeance as he once had thirsted for water: *please strengthen me . . . and let me with one blow get revenge on the Philistines for my two eyes.* However, though Samson was making a request for himself, the vengeance that answered his prayer gave Israel freedom from Philistine oppression for some time.

B. VICTORY IN DEATH (vv. 29, 30)

29. Then Samson reached toward the two central pillars on which the temple stood. Bracing himself against them, his right hand on the one and his left hand on the other,

As noted earlier, the design of this *temple* is not made clear to us in the biblical record. What is clear is that Samson was guided to *the two central pillars on which the temple stood.* The stability of the entire structure depended on those two. In some way Samson braced *himself against them.*

30. . . . Samson said, "Let me die with the Philistines!" Then he pushed with all his might, and down came the temple on the rulers and all the people in it. Thus he killed many more when he died than while he lived.

Blinded, imprisoned, and tormented, Samson no longer cared to live. He wanted only for the Philistines to *die,* too. In answer to Samson's prayer, God gave him the strength he needed. With one great final effort he pushed (or pulled) the two main pillars out of place, and the building came tumbling down. *Thus he killed many more when he died than while he lived.* The five *rulers* of the Philistines died in that catastrophe, and probably their subordinates as well. Eventually, however, the Philistines regained strength and again became a force capable of threatening Israel, which they did during the reigns of Saul and David.

The Bible adds a touching postlude in verse 31. Members of Samson's family came to dig his body from the rubble and take it home for an honored burial. More important, the inspired writer gives Samson an honored place in God's Book. With all his faults and follies, this man is worthy of honor. Among the heroes of Israel he stands alone. In the New Testament, the writer of Hebrews cites Samson as an example of faith in action (Hebrews 11:32).

The visual for today's lesson pictures Samson's final act by which he avenged himself and became God's instrument of judgment on the pagan Philistines.

WHAT DO YOU THINK?

Samson prayed for strength so that he could gain revenge on his enemies. That may seem to us a selfish prayer. What, if anything, can we learn from Samson's prayer?

WHAT DO YOU THINK?

Samson is one of the Old Testament heroes of the faith cited in Hebrews 11. Does that surprise you? What of Samson's life do you think earned him a place in the "roll call of the faithful"? What can we learn from his example?

THOUGHT TO REMEMBER

My talent is not really mine; it's God's.

WHAT DO YOU THINK?

Some church members have unique talents that they utilize in their work, but seldom if ever employ in the betterment of the church. How can we challenge them to offer those talents freely in the cause of Christ?

PRAYER

How richly you have blessed our minds and our hands, our Father! What myriad ways you have set before us to make a living and to make our living happy! As we manage those gifts you have given, may we remember always that they come from you. In Jesus' name. Amen.

CONCLUSION

Samson might be called a two-talent man. He was gifted with enormous physical strength and with courage to use it against overwhelming odds. Beyond these, we see nothing to distinguish him. He did not have the moral purity we expect in a man of God. We see no wisdom in Samson's dealings with Philistine women, but God used even Samson's folly in this area to accomplish his purpose.

A. OTHER ANCIENT TALENTS

Apollos was a talented preacher, but his understanding of God's plan was incomplete. After receiving further instruction from Aquila and Priscilla, he continued using his talents and "was a great help to those who by grace had believed" (Acts 18:24-28).

Joses had such a talent for encouraging others that the apostles named him *Barnabas*, which means "Son of Encouragement." Note how he encouraged the poor believers at Jerusalem (Acts 4:36, 37), Saul (Acts 9:26-28), the believers in Antioch (Acts 11:19-26), and faltering John Mark (Acts 15:36-39).

Tabitha, also known as Dorcas, had a talent for needlework, and widows in Joppa treasured the coats and garments that she made for them (Acts 9:36-39).

Wonderful things happen when God's people use their talents to enrich one another and to hold forth the Word of life to all the world.

B. TODAY'S TALENTS

Tom was a "natural" at salesmanship. Back in 1936, when people were still feeling the effects of the Great Depression, his income averaged five hundred dollars a week. But Tom would have no part in evangelistic calling for the church. "That's not my responsibility," he said.

Mark is one of the most popular and most effective teachers in the local high school, while the little high-school class at church struggles along with a series of untalented and ineffective teachers. Mark turns a deaf ear to pleas that he teach that class. "I live with those kids five days a week," he explains. "Don't you think I deserve the weekend off?"

Marilyn has a big home and provides expert day care for babies, but she never works in the church nursery. Stewart is a landscape architect, but he can't find time to landscape the church lot. Mel is a building contractor. His new roof for the church was expertly done, but the price was high. The Merry Minstrels are so busy with weddings and parties that they turn down every invitation to bring special music at the church.

But the picture has a brighter side. Many talents are hard at work for the Lord. Laura works five days a week at Marilyn's day care center, but her chief joy is Sunday morning in the nursery at church. Annie teaches music and directs several singing groups in the high school, but she finds time to work with both the choir and the youth choir at church. Don's business is heating and air conditioning. He keeps the church's equipment in top condition, but laughs off every suggestion of payment. Mack's little truck farm produces mostly vegetables for the dinner table, but his little flower garden by the church door is a thing of beauty and a joy forever. And how the church is filled with food and gladness when the ladies combine their talents to produce a fellowship dinner!

What is your talent, your ability, your special gift from God? Is the Great Giver receiving any return?

Discovery Learning

This page contains an alternate lesson plan emphasizing learning activities. Classes desiring such student involvement will find these suggestions helpful. The next page is a reproducible activity page to further enhance discovery learning.

LEARNING GOALS

After participating in this lesson, your students will be able to:

1. Give the details of Samson's demise and how God used it for good.

2. Tell why using God's gifts to promote his agenda rather than ours is the path to genuine fulfillment.

3. Tell how their own talents can be better used for God.

INTO THE LESSON

Write on the chalkboard the following list of places: Zorah, Timnah, Lehi, Gaza, and Valley of Sorek. Ask whether any in the class can guess which judge of Israel is the subject of today's study, based on these place names.

It would take a very well-versed student to identify Samson from this list, so be generous in your praise if anyone comes up with that answer. If not, give the following list and let them try again: jawbone of a donkey, unusual birth, gates of the city, Delilah, foxes and fire-brands. This time nearly everyone should recognize that Samson is the subject.

If there is time, have the students try to match the items on the second list with the places in the first. Afterward, or instead, quickly summarize the information to provide some background. Samson's birth was to a couple from Zorah (Judges 13:2). At Timnah Samson tied firebrands to the tails of three hundred foxes and destroyed Philistine grain (14:1—15:5). It was at Lehi that Samson slew a thousand Philistines with the jawbone of a donkey (15:9-15). Samson carried the gates of Gaza off when the Philistines tried to trap him in that city (16:1-3). And Delilah lived in the Valley of Sorek (16:4). She is a key player in today's lesson text.

INTO THE WORD

Assign the members of your class the following roles: Samson, Delilah, Narrator, Rulers of the Philistines (there were five but use at least two people for this role), Philistine People (Judges 16:24, 25).

1. *Samson Trapped, Judges 16:4-17.* Using the assigned roles, ask the class members to read this section of the text. Ask the class to answer the following questions. How did the rulers persuade Delilah to find out the secret of Samson's strength? (See verse 5.) What three unsuccessful methods did Delilah try to subdue Samson? (See verses 7-9, 11 and 12, 13 and 14.) Why did Samson finally reveal the truth about his strength? (See verses 15, 16.) What was the significance of Samson's uncut hair? (See Judges 13:3-5.)

2. *Samson Subdued, Judges 16:18-21.* Ask the class members to read their assigned words of the text. Then ask: What was the real source of Samson's great strength? *(The Lord's presence, v. 20.)* What did the Philistines do to Samson after capturing him? (See v. 21.)

3. *Samson Avenged, Judges 16:22-30.* Once again have the class members read their assigned words. Ask: What led to Samson's renewed strength? *(Hair began to grow; he prayed to the Lord for strength one more time.)* State: "So Samson died using God's gift of strength to deliver Israel from the hand of the Philistines."

INTO LIFE

Samson broke his vow of devotion to the Lord and the Lord departed from him. As a result of his failure, he was physically abused, disabled, and humiliated. How do some people respond to personal failure? (Give up and quit; try again and again.) If Samson had died in the prison, how would he have viewed his life before God? (Unfulfilled; did not live up to God's purpose for his life.) Let's draw forth some principles from his life that we can apply to us today. What principles do we find in the life of Samson? Use the activity from the reproducible page that follows. Make a copy for each person. Briefly go over each principle. *(Personal failure did not cause him to give up on God. He did not allow physical hardship, disability, or humiliation to keep him from serving God. He took advantage of the opportunity he had to use his gift from God. He asked the Lord for strength to use his talent. He was true to God's calling and purpose for his life.)*

Tell the class members to evaluate how closely each principle is followed in their own lives. Ask each person to read each principle and evaluate himself or herself on how closely it is followed by placing an "x" on each line. Next, ask the learners to think about the gifts and abilities God has given them. Ask the class to move into groups of three and have each member share how his or her own talents can be better used for God. Lead the class in a prayer of commitment to use God's gifts for him.

Following Samson Today

The following principles are taken from the life of Samson (Judges 16:4, 5, 16, 17, 19-22, 28-30). Evaluate how well you follow each principle; mark an "x" on the line below each principle to indicate your evaluation. Then identify some way you can improve your performance in one of these areas.

PRINCIPLE #1:

*PERSONAL FAILURE
DOES NOT CAUSE YOU TO GIVE UP ON GOD.*

Seldom Followed _____ Regularly Followed

PRINCIPLE #2:

*PHYSICAL HARDSHIP, DISABILITY, OR HUMILIATION
DOES NOT KEEP YOU FROM SERVING GOD.*

Seldom Followed _____ Regularly Followed

PRINCIPLE #3:

*YOU TAKE ADVANTAGE OF OPPORTUNITIES
TO USE YOUR GIFTS FROM GOD.*

Seldom Followed _____ Regularly Followed

PRINCIPLE #4:

*YOU ASK THE LORD FOR STRENGTH
TO USE HIS TALENT IN SERVICE TO HIM.*

Seldom Followed _____ Regularly Followed

PRINCIPLE #5:

*YOU ARE TRUE TO GOD'S CALLING
AND PURPOSE FOR YOUR LIFE.*

Seldom Followed _____ Regularly Followed

I plan to improve my performance in following Principle # ____ by doing the following:

SAMUEL

LESSON 4

WHY TEACH THIS LESSON?

Does your church have one of those new hymnals—one that "updates" many of the old hymns? Gone are the *thees* and the *thous*, unless one is needed for rhyming purposes. Other terms that the editors felt were used nowhere except in church have been replaced with newer, more contemporary, terminology.

One of the words that is missing from our hymnal is in today's text: *Ebenezer*. I think that's too bad. Meaning "stone of help," it identifies the monument Samuel raised to acknowledge Israel's dependence on the Lord (1 Samuel 7:12).

Today's lesson will give you a chance to enlighten your students on what the strange word in the hymn "Come, Thou Fount" means—if you don't have one of those hymnals with the updated language. More importantly, it will provide an opportunity to remind your class once again that we are what we are only by God's help, God's grace. Whatever words you use, it is a needed reminder.

INTRODUCTION

The agnostic and the preacher were having a friendly argument:

Agnostic: If God wants me to believe in him, he's got to let me know he's there.

Preacher: Look at the sun. Did you put it in place?

Agnostic: Maybe it's always been in place. Maybe it's eternal, as you say God is.

Preacher: Then take a look at yourself, or a mouse, or a bug. Surely, you're not going to say that living things have been on earth forever, are you?

Agnostic: No. Scientifically speaking, the earth once was too hot to support life.

Preacher: And, scientifically speaking, every living thing comes from something that was living before. The living God put life on earth.

Agnostic: But you're assuming God exists. No one knows how life originated. One theory is as good as another. I'm not going to believe in God until I see some evidence I can accept.

Preacher: In other words, you will believe in God if he takes orders from you.

Agnostic: How's that again?

Preacher: You will believe in God if he obeys you, if he gives the kind of evidence *you* demand. Who do you think you are—some kind of "supergod"?

A. WHO IS NUMBER ONE?

How many human beings want to be "number one"! Like the agnostic, some of them will believe in God only if he provides the kind of evidence they demand.

Samuel had a better idea. Instead of trying to shape God according to his own wishes, he said, "Speak, for your servant is listening."

B. LESSON BACKGROUND

Hannah had no children. In the time and place in which she lived, this was thought to be a terrible hardship. More than that, some believed that it was a disgrace, a reproach, even a punishment or curse from God. To make matters worse for Hannah, her husband's other wife did have children, and she taunted Hannah unmercifully (1 Samuel 1:1-8).

DEVOTIONAL READING:
GALATIANS 6:7-10

BACKGROUND SCRIPTURE:
1 SAMUEL 3:1—4:1; 7:3-17

PRINTED TEXT:
1 SAMUEL 3:2-10, 19-21; 7:3-5, 12

Sep
24

LESSON AIMS

After participating in this lesson, each student will be able to:

1. Relate the account of how God called Samuel, then used him to deliver Israel from the Philistines.

2. Explain the role of the Bible in providing us with a means of "hearing God's voice."

3. Develop or maintain a pattern of regular Bible study in order to stay sensitive to God's will.

KEY VERSE

"Speak, for your servant is listening." —1 Samuel 3:10

Desperately Hannah prayed for a son; fervently she promised that she would give him to the Lord and signify his dedication by leaving his hair uncut (1 Samuel 1:9-11).

Finally Hannah did have a son, whom she named Samuel (1 Samuel 1:20). Unlike some who make promises to the Lord while in difficult circumstances, Hannah took her vow seriously. When the child was weaned (probably around the age of three), she left him with Eli the priest to be brought up in the service of God (1 Samuel 1:25-28; 2:11).

I. GOD'S UNEXPECTED CALL (1 SAMUEL 3:2-10)

As the years passed, this special child "continued to grow in stature and in favor with the Lord and with men" (1 Samuel 2:26). Our text takes up the story while Samuel was still a boy (1 Samuel 3:1), but we are not told how old he was. Josephus, a noted Jewish historian who lived during the first century, says that he was twelve.

A. ASLEEP IN THE TEMPLE (vv. 2, 3)

2. One night Eli, whose eyes were becoming so weak that he could barely see, was lying down in his usual place.

Eli was "very old" (1 Samuel 2:22). Perhaps the weakness of his *eyes* is mentioned at this point to explain why the boy Samuel was constantly at his call, night or day. Now it was *night*, and Eli had gone to bed.

3. The lamp of God had not yet gone out, and Samuel was lying down in the temple of the LORD, where the ark of God was.

The tabernacle had been set up at Shiloh soon after Israel had conquered the promised land and had divided it among the twelve tribes (Joshua 18:1). But here we read of the *temple* rather than the tabernacle, and verse 15 mentions "the house of the Lord." These differences in terminology should not confuse us. In our own time a historic building is sometimes enclosed within a larger structure to protect it from the weather. Perhaps something similar had been done for the tabernacle.

Inside the tabernacle itself was *the lamp of God*, the seven-branched golden lampstand that gave light to the Holy Place (Exodus 25:31-40). In the Holy of Holies rested *the ark of God*, often called the ark of the covenant. Of course, Eli and Samuel did not sleep in the Holy of Holies or even in the Holy Place, where the lampstand was. They must have had bedrooms elsewhere in the larger (perhaps enclosed) structure that is here called *the temple of the Lord*.

The golden lampstand was replenished with oil every morning, for it was against the regulations of the law of Moses to allow the light to go out (Exodus 27:20, 21; 30:7, 8). That the incident recorded in our text is said to have occurred before *the lamp of God* went out indicates that it took place in the early morning hours, before all the oil was consumed.

B. A VOICE IN THE NIGHT (vv. 4-7)

4. Then the LORD called Samuel. Samuel answered, "Here I am."

In the darkness *Samuel* heard his name *called*. The voice probably awakened him from his sleep. Promptly he responded so that whoever had spoken would know that his words had been heard.

5. And he ran to Eli and said, "Here I am; you called me."

But Eli said, "I did not call; go back and lie down." So he went and lay down.

Naturally the boy thought the person speaking was Eli. What else could he think? But Eli *did not call*, nor had he heard anyone speak. Probably supposing that Samuel had been dreaming, Eli sent him back to bed.

6. *Again the LORD called, "Samuel!" And Samuel got up and went to Eli and said, "Here I am; you called me."*

"My son," Eli said, "I did not call; go back and lie down."

Again came the call, too plain to be unheeded. Samuel could only respond as he had done before, and Eli could only send him *back* to bed again.

7. *Now Samuel did not yet know the LORD: The word of the LORD had not yet been revealed to him.*

Of course, Samuel had been taught about *the Lord*. He must have known that his mother had dedicated him to the Lord's service; he must have known that Eli was training him for that service. But he was not yet personally acquainted with the Lord; that is, the Lord had never spoken to him before. He must have been puzzled by the repeated sound of his name, but he had no reason to think that the Lord was speaking.

C. THE RIGHT ANSWER (vv. 8-10)

8. *The LORD called Samuel a third time, and Samuel got up and went to Eli and said, "Here I am; you called me." Then Eli realized that the LORD was calling the boy.*

At last Eli *realized* the truth. It was not that his young helper was dreaming; it was that *the Lord was calling the boy.*

9. *So Eli told Samuel, "Go and lie down, and if he calls you, say, 'Speak, LORD, for your servant is listening.'" So Samuel went and lay down in his place.*

Throughout this text, the word *Lord* is used to translate God's personal name, the name that is often rendered in English as "Jehovah" or "Yahweh." That name in later centuries was considered so sacred that Jews refused to speak it at all, lest they use that holy name in vain. Whenever they read the Scriptures and came to that name, they read "adonai," *the Lord,* instead. Many English translations use the name they read instead of the name that was written; but they print LORD in small capitals to let us know that it represents the more personal name.

10. *The LORD came and stood there, calling as at the other times, "Samuel! Samuel!" Then Samuel said, "Speak, for your servant is listening."*

This time Samuel answered according to Eli's instructions—almost. Eli had told him to say, "Speak, Lord [Yahweh], for your servant is listening." Perhaps the boy was afraid to utter the sacred name. He said, *"Speak, for your servant is listening."*

The Lord then told Samuel that he would carry out his judgment against Eli and his family because Eli had failed to restrain the reckless wickedness of his sons (vv. 11-14). Eli had heard that before from another prophet (1 Samuel 2:27-36). Hearing it again from Samuel confirmed that the Lord had indeed spoken to him. The old man accepted his punishment with resignation (1 Samuel 3:15-18).

II. GOD'S ESTABLISHED PROPHET (1 SAMUEL 3:19-21)

A. GOD BLESSES SAMUEL (v. 19)

19. *The LORD was with Samuel as he grew up, and he let none of his words fall to the ground.*

As Samuel *grew up*, he continued in the service of God to which his mother had dedicated him (1 Samuel 1:11). *The Lord was with Samuel*, guiding his speech so that *none of his words* could *fall to the ground*; that is, nothing he said was false or mistaken. What he said about the past or present was true; what he said about the future came true in the proper time.

B. SAMUEL'S REPUTATION GROWS (v. 20)

20. *And all Israel from Dan to Beersheba recognized that Samuel was attested as a prophet of the LORD.*

Speak; for thy servant heareth.

1 Samuel 3:10

Today's visual reminds us that the Lord still speaks if we will but listen. He speaks to young and old alike through his Word.

WHAT DO YOU THINK?

Eli told Samuel to say, "Speak, Lord, for your servant is listening." Certainly we do not expect to receive revelation in the same manner as the inspired prophets. Otherwise, our "revelations" would be as authoritative as the Bible (2 Timothy 3:16; 2 Peter 1:20, 21). Still, God does speak to us through the Word. What relevance do you see for us today in Samuel's prayer? What do you think would happen if we had Samuel's prayer on our lips whenever we read the Bible?

WHAT DO YOU THINK?

"All Israel from Dan to Beer-sheba recognized that Samuel was attested as a prophet of the Lord." What do all your neighbors know about you and your relationship with the Lord? What can or should you do to have a greater testimony in your community?

Samuel's reputation spread *from Dan* in the far northern part of Israel *to Beer-sheba* in the far south. The truth of his teaching and the accuracy of his predictions convinced *all Israel* that he was *a prophet of the Lord*.

PROPHETS, TRUE AND FALSE

In March of 1997, thirty-nine members of the "Heaven's Gate" cult committed mass suicide. Their leader had told them that by this means they were preparing themselves to be transported to a spaceship that would fly them to Heaven on the tail of a comet.

William Proctor claims that these people were mistaken. The truth—according to Proctor—is that in 2001, thirty-three spaceships will land on top of one another on the San Diego property owned by Proctor's cult, the Unarius Academy of Science. Each of these ships will carry one thousand "space brothers" who will come to teach us how to live peaceably on earth. Unarius stands for Universal Articulate Interdimensional Understanding of Science, which claims to have five thousand members and asserts that nearly half a million people have read their books and seen their videos.

There is no end to the parade of misguided souls who seek enlightenment from mistaken and (often) unscrupulous people who claim to have secret knowledge. Time will prove William Proctor wrong soon enough, as it has every other prophet with fanciful ideas.

On the other hand, Samuel spoke the truth: his words were the words of the Lord. "All Israel" recognized that Samuel was a true prophet. As false prophets vie for our attention today, those who are wise will listen only for the words that come from God.   —C. R. B.

C. GOD'S REVELATION CONTINUES (v. 21)

21. The LORD continued to appear at Shiloh, and there he revealed himself to Samuel through his word.

The Lord appeared not just once to Samuel; he *continued to appear* to him *at Shiloh*. The last part of the verse explains that the Lord did not appear in a visible form to be seen by Samuel or anyone else; *he revealed himself to Samuel through his word*. Such a word was desperately needed in all Israel, for the nation was sinking into sin and idolatry.

III. ISRAEL'S RETURN TO GOD (1 SAMUEL 7:3-5, 12)

Here we see an occasion where Israel's trouble came once more from the Philistines. As we saw in last week's lesson, Samson had won a significant victory over the Philistines; but they had recovered their power and now began once more to oppress Israel. Read about this in 1 Samuel 4. Israel was then under the dominance of the Philistines for twenty years, "and all the people of Israel mourned and sought after the Lord"; that is, in their suffering and misery they turned to him for help (1 Samuel 7:2).

WHAT DO YOU THINK?

Samuel showed the Israelites that deliverance would come when they obeyed the word of the Lord. What are some examples of how deliverance comes to people today when they obey God's Word?

A. APPEAL AND RESPONSE (vv. 3, 4)

3. And Samuel said to the whole house of Israel, "If you are returning to the LORD with all your hearts, then rid yourselves of the foreign gods and the Ashtoreths and commit yourselves to the LORD and serve him only, and he will deliver you out of the hand of the Philistines."

The law required the men of Israel to gather three times a year for the great national festivals of Passover, Pentecost, and Tabernacles (Exodus 23:14-17). Perhaps such a gathering provided an opportunity for Samuel to speak to *the whole house of Israel*. Mourning over their oppression and appealing to God for help (v. 2) was good, but it was only a first step. The people needed to do more. If they were sincere in their appeal to God, they needed to get rid of the idols that offended him.

Foreign gods were the imaginary gods of the pagans. The term *Ashtoreths* describes imaginary goddesses supposed to be associated with the imaginary gods (usually as their lovers). The presence of such supposed gods in Israel showed how far the people had drifted from worship of the one true God. The first of his Ten Commandments was, "You shall have no other gods before me" (Exodus 20:3). If the people would obey that command, said Samuel, the true God would *deliver* them *out of the hand of the Philistines.*

4. So the Israelites put away their Baals and Ashtoreths, and served the LORD only.

Samuel's recommendation made sense, and the people followed it. *Baals* was a general name for all the false gods, even as the term *Ashtoreths* included all the false goddesses.

CLEANING OUT THE GARBAGE

The man who had lived in apartment 21 for eleven years drove a shiny new BMW sedan and wore nice clothes. He never spoke to neighbors, and no one knew what his living quarters looked like. Then one day he drove away with just a few boxes in his car. That's when the building manager discovered a literal garbage dump. Countertops were piled high with beer bottles, empty microwave dinner boxes, and assorted junk. The bathtub was covered with black mold except for where the tenant stood to take a shower. The bedroom was piled high with clothes except for the spot on the bed where he had slept. Perhaps the man figured it was easier to move and leave everything behind than to clean up the mess on a regular basis, as most folks do.

On a spiritual level, Israel had a similar problem. They had brought the gods of the pagans into their spiritual "house," polluting the land in which they lived and making it a spiritual garbage dump. However, since this was the land God had given them, they couldn't just move away and leave it all behind. Samuel called on them to do a thorough housecleaning, and they followed his command.

Housecleaning, whether physical or spiritual, is always hard work, but it pays the dividend of a more satisfying life. How many of us have learned the lesson the Israelites learned? —C. R. B.

B. PRAYER AND VICTORY (v. 5)

5. Then Samuel said, "Assemble all Israel at Mizpah and I will intercede with the LORD for you."

If Samuel's recommendation was given at one of the major national festivals, the people needed to return home in order to obey his words and get rid of their idols. Perhaps some time later, when Samuel was convinced that the idols were gone, he sent messengers throughout the villages inviting the people to *assemble . . . at Mizpah* for prayer. Mizpah was a town in Benjamin, about seven and a half miles north of Jerusalem. Its central location made it an appropriate place at which to hold a national gathering. The people gathered as Samuel asked, and, with penitent fasting, they confessed their sins (v. 6).

The Philistines soon became aware of the gathering. Since this was not taking place at the time or the location of one of the national festivals, it must have appeared as if the Israelites were plotting a rebellion. The Philistines gathered their troops and determined to put a stop to that (v. 7). They arrived just as Samuel was offering a sacrifice and praying for Israel. The Lord answered his prayer with a terrific thunderstorm that threw the Philistines "into such a panic that they were routed before the Israelites" (vv. 8-10). (Recall a similar strategy that we saw God use in a previous lesson, in Judges 4:15; 5:4, 5, 21.) The Philistines took to their heels, and the men of Israel chased them back home (v. 11).

WHAT DO YOU THINK?

The stone called Ebenezer would remind the Israelites of how the Lord had helped them. Why is it important that we frequently remind ourselves of how the Lord has helped us? What are some appropriate occasions for engaging in this exercise of reminding ourselves?

C. MONUMENT IN MEMORY (v. 12)

12. Then Samuel took a stone and set it up between Mizpah and Shen. He named it Ebenezer, saying, "Thus far has the LORD helped us."

To commemorate Israel's triumph, *Samuel took a stone* and placed it as a monument to mark the occasion. The location of *Shen* is not certain; the word means "tooth" and may designate a sharp or pointed rock near the battle site. *The Lord* had *helped* his people at that spot. Samuel called the stone *Ebenezer,* which means "stone of help."

CONCLUSION

A. GOD'S ANCIENT SPEAKING

Over many centuries God spoke to his people through the prophets (Hebrews 1:1). Samuel is an example, but God spoke to his people through all the other prophets whose words are recorded in the Old Testament.

Then came the time when God spoke through his Son. Some editions of the New Testament have the words of Jesus printed in red, as if to set them apart and give them supreme importance. But much as we treasure those words, they are not all that God has said through his Son. Since the Holy Spirit inspired the writers of the New Testament (John 14:15-17, 26; 16:12-15), the teaching of those writers is the teaching of Jesus as truly as are the words printed in red.

B. GOD'S SPEAKING TODAY

WHAT DO YOU THINK?

How can we best use the Bible to allow God to speak to us in our homes? How can we best use it to hear God's voice in our worship services?

Today we do not expect to hear our names called in the night by the audible voice of God. However, through the pages of the New Testament, God *is* speaking to us. Listen . . . .

At Home. "Wives, submit to your husbands as to the Lord. . . . Husbands, love your wives, just as Christ loved the church and gave himself up for her. . . . Children, obey your parents in the Lord, for this is right. . . . Fathers, do not exasperate your children; instead, bring them up in the training and instruction of the Lord" (Ephesians 5:22—6:4).

At Work. "Slaves, obey your earthly masters with respect and fear, and with sincerity of heart, just as you would obey Christ. . . . Masters, treat your slaves in the same way. Do not threaten them, since you know that he who is both their Master and yours is in heaven, and there is no favoritism with him" (Ephesians 6:5-9).

In the Community. "Everyone must submit himself to the governing authorities, for there is no authority except that which God has established. The authorities that exist have been established by God" (Romans 13:1).

In the Church. "To the elders among you, I appeal. . . . Be shepherds of God's flock that is under your care. . . . Young men, in the same way be submissive to those who are older. All of you, clothe yourselves with humility toward one another" (1 Peter 5:1-5).

PRAYER

Great God in Heaven, we know that your ways are above our ways and your thoughts are above our thoughts, as far as Heaven is above the earth. Thank you for talking to us through your holy Word. May we listen with alert minds and eager hearts. May we be quick not only to hear, but also to obey. In Jesus' name. Amen.

Why should we listen to God? Let's note a few good reasons:

1. God knows more than we do. Unless we acknowledge this in our actions as well as our words, we will be in trouble.

2. God loves us and wants us to do what is best for us. Unless we accept his direction, we will have to settle for less than the best.

3. No other advice is as good as God's advice. Unless we believe this, how can we say we believe in God at all?

So what are we waiting for? Let's be listening to God today.

When we say, "Speak, Lord, for your servant is listening," we need to sit down with the Bible and listen—listen intently, listen for a long time, listen not only for what happened long ago, but especially for what God is saying to us today.

THOUGHT TO REMEMBER

Listen to the Lord.

Discovery Learning

This page contains an alternate lesson plan emphasizing learning activities. Classes desiring such student involvement will find these suggestions helpful. The next page is a reproducible activity page to further enhance discovery learning.

LEARNING GOALS

After participating in this lesson, each student will be able to:

1. Relate the account of how God called Samuel, then used him to deliver Israel from the Philistines.

2. Explain the role of the Bible in providing us with a means of "hearing God's voice."

3. Develop or maintain a pattern of regular Bible study in order to stay sensitive to God's will.

INTO THE LESSON

Write on the chalkboard the phrase, "Hearing God's Voice." When the students arrive they will read the phrase and begin to focus their thoughts on the lesson theme. Begin the class by asking, "What are the ways that people today claim to hear God's voice?" As answers are suggested, write them on the chalkboard.

State, "As you can see, people *claim* to hear God's voice in a variety of ways. But in the Bible, who actually heard God's voice?" (*Examples include Adam, Abraham, Moses, Noah, Samuel, Elijah, Elisha, Peter, James, and John.*) "Our text today centers on Samuel and his experience of hearing God's voice. God used Samuel to deliver Israel from the Philistines. Turn to 1 Samuel 3, and let's see how God called Samuel."

INTO THE WORD

Read 1 Samuel 3:2-10, and give a brief lecture describing God's call of Samuel. Use the information in the lesson commentary. Make certain that you explain the following terms: *lamp of God, ark of God, temple of the Lord,* and LORD (*i.e., Yahweh*). Then ask, "Why did Samuel not immediately recognize the Lord's voice?" (*the word of the Lord was rare in those days, v. 1; Samuel did not yet know the Lord, and the word of the Lord was not yet revealed to him, v. 7.*)

Ask someone in the class to read 1 Samuel 3:19-21, and then ask the following questions: "What is meant by the phrase, 'let none of his words fall to the ground' in verse 19?" (*Samuel did not speak anything false or misleading; all his predictions came true.*) What led to Israel's conclusion that Samuel was a prophet? (*The Lord revealed himself to Samuel; his words were truthful and reliable; even his personal integrity was a contrast to Eli's sons.*) How did the Lord reveal himself to Samuel in Shiloh? (*By the word of the Lord, v. 21.*)

Read 1 Samuel 7:3-5, 12, and then ask the following questions: "What were the Israelites supposed to do to be delivered from the Philistines?" (*Put away the foreign gods and Ashtoreths; commit themselves to the Lord; serve him only.*) Next, give a summary lecture over the events in 1 Samuel 7:6-11 that led to the setting up of the stone monument mentioned in verse 12. State: "So the Lord delivered Israel from the Philistines. But note the order. First the Lord revealed himself to Samuel by the word of the Lord, 3:21. Then the word of the Lord through Samuel went to all Israel, 4:1. Next, Israel obeyed the word of the Lord, 7:4. Finally, the Philistines were subdued, 7:13. Hearing and obeying the word of the Lord were the key."

INTO LIFE

Say, "Today we hear God's voice through the Bible. Our ability to hear God's voice and to stay sensitive to God's will increases the more we read, hear, and understand the Word of God."

Divide the class into three equal parts. Distribute copies of the reproducible page that follows. Then ask the students to look up the passages listed and tell what each passage suggests we should do to hear God's voice and stay sensitive to God's will. (They should write these in the "Helpful Suggestion" column.) Then ask the students to consider each suggestion and decide how it could be integrated into their lives. Ask them to write in the "My Personal Plan" column what they will do to tune in God's voice through his Word. (If time is short, ask each group to take just two of the passages.)

After several minutes, ask the groups to share their plans with the class. Allow a few minutes; then ask for the results. (*Suggested answers for column 1 may include daily Bible reading and meditation; regular, ongoing study of the Word; hearing and obeying the Word. Suggested answers for column 2 may include setting a definite time; a definite place; a specific process; a specific study topic; a specific person to study with; etc.*) Note how the lower section of the reproducible page gives an opportunity for the learners to write their commitment to regular Bible study. Encourage each one to write the time, place, process, and specific study he or she will use to spend time each day seeking to hear God's voice.

Lead the class in prayer to develop and maintain a pattern of regular Bible study.

Tuning In God's Voice

Look up and read the verses listed on the chart below. Then write a suggestion for how to hear the voice of God based on each verse. Write these in the "Helpful Suggestion" column. In the last column write some ideas about how to implement each suggestion.

SCRIPTURE VERSE	HELPFUL SUGGESTION	MY PERSONAL PLAN
Psalm 1:1, 2		
2 Timothy 2:15		
1 Peter 1:22-25		
Hebrews 4:12		
Luke 11:28		
Romans 15:1-4		

Commitment to Tuning In

Knowing that we hear "God's Voice" through the Word of God, the Bible, and that our ability to hear God's voice and stay sensitive to God's will increases the more we read, hear, study, and understand the Word of God, I commit to the Lord:

A Definite Daily Time: _____   A Definite Daily Place: _____

A Definite Specific Study: _____

A Definite Specific Process: _____

Date: _____   Signature: _____

SAUL BECOMES KING

LESSON 5

WHY TEACH THIS LESSON?

Our lesson writer for the current quarter is a remarkable man. At ninety-five years of age, he generates more written material than many writers supposedly in the "prime" of their lives. He lives in a retirement home where close to a third of the residents are also ninety years old or older.

Imagine what these senior saints have seen in their lifetimes! Cars have replaced horses. Aerospace has leaped from the pages of science fiction to real life. Telephones, fax machines, and the Internet have revolutionized communication.

In today's lesson, Israel was beginning a new era as well. A monarchy was replacing the old system of government. It would require faithfulness on the part of the new king as well as God's people to make it work. Were they up to the task?

Many of your students face new challenges as well. This lesson will give you the opportunity to encourage them to face the challenges with faith!

INTRODUCTION

From his infancy, Dave spent Sunday mornings in the church house: first in the nursery, then in the toddlers' room, and on through each grade of the Sunday school. In the high school class he was a leader among the church youth and a second baseman on the softball team. No one was better known to church members young and old.

Then Dave went to college far from home. He stayed until his name was adorned with several degrees; then he became a professor and stayed on in that capacity. Only seldom did he visit his old home.

When Dave's son Joel graduated from high school, he too went to college far from home. From time to time, he took part of his weekend to stop by and visit Grandpa. When Grandpa and Joel stepped into the older adults' Sunday school class, the members greeted Joel with joy; but they called him Dave. Anyone could see that he was the "spitting image" of his father.

From such similarity comes the old saying, "Like father, like son." It comes from more important similarities too—similarities of character, purpose, and action. We expect the son of a good man to be a good man, and the son of a rascal to be a rascal. But it is not always so.

A. LIKE FATHER, UNLIKE SON

In real life, "Like father, *unlike* son" seems to be the principle at work sometimes. Last week we read of Eli, who brought up young Samuel as a wise and godly man. But Eli's own sons were scoundrels (1 Samuel 2:12-17).

The same tragedy was repeated in the next generation. Samuel became judge of all Israel. He was a prophet of God as well, and his judgments were always just and right. However, like Eli's sons, Samuel's sons were scoundrels. Samuel appointed them judges in Beersheba, but they "accepted bribes and perverted justice" (1 Samuel 8:1-3). The situation was so bad that it became a national scandal.

DEVOTIONAL READING:
PSALM 119:1-8

BACKGROUND SCRIPTURE:
1 SAMUEL 9, 10

PRINTED TEXT:
1 SAMUEL 9:1, 2a; 10:17-26

**Oct
1**

LESSON AIMS

After this lesson each student will be able to:

1. Summarize what today's text says about Saul and about the Israelites' acceptance of him as their first king.

2. Describe some of the ways in which God's rule over our lives today is threatened.

3. Pinpoint an area where God's authority as King needs to be allowed to have a greater impact.

KEY VERSE

Samuel said to all the people, "Do you see the man the LORD has chosen? There is no one like him among all the people."
—1 Samuel 10:24

B. LESSON BACKGROUND

The elders of Israel were concerned about this turn of events, as they should have been. Samuel was old; he could not judge Israel much longer. If his evil sons succeeded him, there would likely be little or no justice in the nation. Something had to be done, and the elders proposed what they thought was the best solution. They asked Samuel to appoint a king over Israel (1 Samuel 8:4, 5).

Samuel did not like that suggestion, and neither did God. Samuel even warned the people of all the negative consequences that would accompany having a king. But the people insisted, and God told Samuel to let them have their way. They would have to learn from their own mistake (1 Samuel 8:6-22).

I. INTRODUCING SAUL (1 SAMUEL 9:1, 2a)

After God instructed Samuel to let the people have a king, Samuel told the assembled people to return home (1 Samuel 8:22). They did not need to have a king named immediately. The biblical writer then introduces Saul, the man who became Israel's first king.

A. SAUL'S FAMILY (v. 1)

1. *There was a Benjamite, a man of standing, whose name was Kish son of Abiel, the son of Zeror, the son of Becorath, the son of Aphiah of Benjamin.*

First to be introduced is Saul's father, *Kish*. He was a *Benjamite* (a member of the tribe of *Benjamin*). Several generations of his ancestors are named, but we know nothing more about any of them. Kish is described as *a man of standing*. Other versions read "power" or "valor" or "wealth" instead of *standing*. Apparently Kish was a very prominent citizen, respected by his peers.

B. SAUL HIMSELF (v. 2a)

2. *He had a son named Saul, an impressive young man without equal among the Israelites.*

The word *impressive* probably refers to Saul's appearance. Apparently he was a strikingly handsome fellow, a fine figure of a man—so much so that Saul was *without equal among the Israelites.*

The rest of chapter 9 and the first part of chapter 10 record a meeting of Samuel and Saul. At God's direction, Samuel anointed Saul to be king, but he did this privately. No one else knew about it.

II. DEMAND FOR A KING (1 SAMUEL 10:17-19)

At an earlier time, the elders of Israel had come to Samuel to demand a king, as we have noted in the introduction to this lesson. Now Samuel knew whom God had chosen to be that king. He therefore called a meeting of the people to let them know who would be their king and that God had chosen him. Samuel began by recalling the demand for a king that the people had expressed to him.

A. GOD'S FAITHFULNESS (vv. 17, 18)

17. *Samuel summoned the people of Israel to the LORD at Mizpah. . .*

Meeting at *Mizpah* would have reminded the people of the decisive victory over the Philistines God had given them there a few years earlier (1 Samuel 7:5-14).

18. *. . . and said to them, "This is what the LORD, the God of Israel, says: 'I brought Israel up out of Egypt, and I delivered you from the power of Egypt and all the kingdoms that oppressed you.'*

In these few words spoken by Samuel, God reminded the people of all the blessings and help he had given them in the past. He had rescued them from

The visual for today's lesson will help your students locate where the events of this lesson, and the other lessons of this quarter, took place.

their bitter bondage under *the power of Egypt.* He had *delivered* them from *all the kingdoms* that had opposed their march toward the promised land (Numbers 21:21-35). Once the people had taken possession of the promised land, the Lord had rescued them from all who had *oppressed* them.

B. ISRAEL'S UNFAITHFULNESS (v. 19)

19. *"But you have now rejected your God, who saves you out of all your calamities and distresses. And you have said, 'No, set a king over us.' So now present yourselves before the LORD by your tribes and clans."*

Yes, *God* had been faithful to his people, rescuing them from every difficulty. But they had not been faithful to him. In demanding a *king,* they were forgetting that God himself was their real King. He had given them their law—a law that provided no central government to enforce it. Each person was responsible for his own obedience; each parent was responsible for teaching his children to obey.

Now, however, the people were asking for a king to enforce the law. In so doing, they were bypassing their own personal responsibility to obey and teach that law. They also wanted the king to be responsible for the national defense, to go out before them and fight their battles (1 Samuel 8:19, 20). What they failed to discern was that, if they had fulfilled their own responsibility by obeying the law, no battles would have been needed! The Lord would have given them victory over every foe.

The people had made their choice. Disregarding the warnings of God and Samuel, they had persisted in demanding a king. Therefore, said Samuel, they should prepare to *present* themselves *before the Lord* so he could designate the one from among them who should be their king. They should present themselves first by *tribes* and then by the smaller groups of *clans.*

DREAMS OF PERFECTION

Most people have dreams of what life would be like if some part of it were "perfect" (whatever that means). For Gordon and Mary Aughinbaugh, the dream was a house with a spectacular ocean view in a very upscale community southwest of Los Angeles. It was to be a "perfect" $1.5 million, French-style manor that would "stand 900 years" (so the owners envisioned it).

But fifteen years after construction began, the house was still unfinished and the dream had turned into a nightmare. The couple became involved in lawsuits with three different contractors. The local homeowners' association sued to have the house torn down because it had been an eyesore for more than a decade. In fact, Mr. Aughinbaugh died before the house was finished, and it was sold to someone else, who completed the project.

Like many others since who have seen what their neighbors possessed and have dreamed of possessing it as their own, the Israelites saw that the nations about them had kings. They assumed that a king would be the "perfect touch" that would complete their struggle toward nationhood. And so, turning aside from the God who had been their flawless leader, they determined to be led by men who were flawed in sometimes serious ways.

Any "perfection" we seek in this world—without God and his help—is sure to disappoint us.   —C. R. B.

III. KING AND KINGDOM (1 SAMUEL 10:20-26)

Though the people had rejected God in their demand for a king, Samuel wanted their first king to be God's choice; and he wanted the people to understand that God was making this choice.

DAILY BIBLE READINGS

Monday, Sept. 25—Saul Searches for the Man of God (1 Samuel 9:1-10)

Tuesday, Sept. 26—Samuel Recognizes Saul (1 Samuel 9: 11-16)

Wednesday, Sept. 27—Saul Meets Samuel (1 Samuel 9: 17-21)

Thursday, Sept. 28—Saul Anointed King (1 Samuel 9: 22—10:1)

Friday, Sept. 29—Samuel Directs Saul (1 Samuel 10:2-8)

Saturday, Sept. 30—Saul Prophesies (1 Samuel 10:9-16)

Sunday, Oct. 1—Saul Proclaimed King (1 Samuel 10: 17-26)

WHAT DO YOU THINK?

Saul hid himself while he was being selected as king. It is generally believed that this was an indication of modesty or humility on his part. In his later years, however, Saul was proud, arrogant, and jealous. How can a person elevated to a place of leadership and influence maintain his initial humility?

A. THE CHOICE (vv. 20, 21a)

20. When Samuel brought all the tribes of Israel near, the tribe of Benjamin was chosen.

We need not suppose that entire *tribes* paraded before Samuel and the Lord. Perhaps one man was called forward to represent each tribe. We are not told exactly how *the tribe of Benjamin was chosen* from the rest. Possibly the Urim and Thummim, which the high priest was to use in making important decisions (Exodus 28:30; Numbers 27:21), were used to help make this choice (though we do not know exactly what the Urim and Thummim were or what using them involved).

Another suggestion is that a "casting of lots" of some kind was used and that God was asked to guide the result. For example, a white pebble might be placed in a jar with eleven dark ones. A man of each tribe would reach into the jar without looking and take a pebble. The tribe whose representative drew out the white pebble would be taken as the chosen tribe. Or, each tribe might mark a small stone with the name or symbol of that tribe. The stones would be put in a jar. Samuel, as God's prophet, would select one without looking, and the tribe indicated by that stone would be the chosen tribe. Whatever the procedure, Benjamin was revealed to be the chosen tribe.

21a. Then he brought forward the tribe of Benjamin, clan by clan, and Matri's clan was chosen. Finally Saul son of Kish was chosen.

Perhaps by the same procedure previously used, *Matri's clan was chosen* from all the families of the tribe of *Benjamin*. By a final step, *Saul son of Kish was chosen* from all the men of Matri's family.

B. THE BASHFUL KING (vv. 21b, 22)

21b. But when they looked for him, he was not to be found.

Saul's absence here tells us that a man could be included among the candidates without even being present. Perhaps an elder of Matri's family wrote the names of the men of that family on separate stones, and Samuel or someone else randomly selected the stone with Saul's name on it. Whatever the process was, it is clear that all Israel was convinced, and rightly so, that God was making this choice.

When Saul's name was announced, of course, everyone began looking for him. But *he was not to be found.*

22. So they inquired further of the LORD, "Has the man come here yet?" And the LORD said, "Yes, he has hidden himself among the baggage."

Saul was not in the crowd. Was it possible that he had not arrived at Mizpah yet? That question was put to the Lord, and he answered it plainly: Saul was hiding *among the baggage.* The Hebrew word rendered *baggage* seems to describe supplies of some kind. People who walked two or three days to get to Mizpah would have brought a lot of such items, including clothing, blankets, food, and cooking utensils. Perhaps a particular area (possibly a large tent) had been designated as a place to keep such items—a "baggage depot" of sorts. There Saul had *hidden himself.*

The question of Saul's whereabouts was not so easily answered by a procedure such as "casting lots." That is one reason for putting a "perhaps" with the above suggestions of the procedure used to select who would be Israel's first king. We do not really know how the selection was made, and likewise we do not know how the Lord responded to this question. The most likely suggestion for the latter is that he inspired his prophet Samuel with the answer. At any rate, by some clear and unmistakable means, God revealed the truth to Samuel and the Israelites.

We need to remember that Saul knew in advance that he would be chosen as Israel's king. (See 1 Samuel 9:1—10:16.) Why, then, was he hiding? Was he bashful, afraid to face the stares of the crowd? Was he modest, shrinking from the praise that would be heaped upon him? Was he frightened by the responsibility he was being given? Keep in mind that this was something new for both him and the nation: Saul had never been a king, and Israel had never had a king.

RELUCTANT HEROES

Some people intentionally become heroes: in warfare, in scientific endeavors (such as becoming astronauts), and in the field of sports. Marty Hornick, a U.S. Forest Service trails ranger, is one such intentional hero. He is a self-acclaimed "peak bagger" who has climbed Mt. Whitney hundreds of times.

But one day in 1991, Hornick proceeded on what became a record-setting climb. In just two hours, eight and a half minutes, he covered six miles of trail and gained 6,200 feet in elevation. And then, just three hours and twenty-three minutes after he started his climb, he was back at the Whitney Portals trailhead. His feat is significant because it was the fastest Whitney ascent ever—a notable achievement, given the fact that the mountain (at 14,494 feet) is the highest in the contiguous United States.

Saul apparently did not want to "set a record" as the first king of Israel. He hid "among the baggage," even though he already knew that God had chosen him to lead Israel as her king. Perhaps he was being genuinely humble, or perhaps he was stricken with a sense of the monumental task that lay before him.

Whatever Saul's motives for hiding himself, he was like many of us—reluctant to act when challenged to perform some significant task for the Lord. We never know how that challenge may be presented or how heroic our task may be. But God helps even reluctant heroes to find the strength to do what he asks of them.

—C. R. B.

C. THE KING IS ACCEPTED (vv. 23, 24)

23. They ran and brought him out, and as he stood among the people he was a head taller than any of the others.

Eager men *ran* to where the baggage was and escorted the reluctant king to the throng of his waiting *people*. Instantly everyone noticed that he was *a head taller than any of* them! He looked like a king!

24. Samuel said to all the people, "Do you see the man the LORD has chosen? There is no one like him among all the people."

Then the people shouted, "Long live the king!"

Samuel made two observations. First, *the Lord* had *chosen* this man to be their king. *All the people* had seen that no man or group of men had made the choice. If it was made by casting lots, they had asked God to determine the outcome; and they believed that he had done so.

Second, Saul's appearance seemed to verify the choice. Like a royal figure, he towered above the common people. Saul's fellow Israelites responded to Samuel's words with a roar of approval: *Long live the king!*

D. THE KINGDOM IS DESCRIBED (vv. 25, 26)

25. Samuel explained to the people the regulations of the kingship. He wrote them down on a scroll and deposited it before the LORD. Then Samuel dismissed the people, each to his own home.

Having a king brought a new kind of government to Israel. Thus Samuel's next step was to tell *the people* what *the regulations of the kingship* should be. No

HOW TO SAY IT

Abiel. AY-be-el.
Aphiah. Uh-FYE-uh.
Becorath. Be-KO-rath.
Beersheba. Beer-SHE-buh.
Benjamite. BEN-juh-mite.
Gibeah. GIB-ee-uh.
Matri. MAY-try.
Mizpah. MIZ-pah.
Thummim. THUM-im.
Urim. YOU-rim.
Zeror. ZEE-ror.

WHAT DO YOU THINK?

Some have suggested that the people of Israel let their emotions get away from them when they saw how impressive Saul's appearance was. What do you think? What can we learn from this event?

portion of this lecture has been preserved for us, but we can easily imagine some of its main points. First, God's law was still the law of the land. Second, each person still was responsible for his own obedience to the law. Third, the king also was to be bound by the law. He must not become an arbitrary tyrant. Emphasizing this would make it clear that kingship in Israel was to be significantly different from kingship in surrounding nations (even though one reason the people had demanded a king was a desire to be like "all the other nations," 1 Samuel 8:5).

After giving this instruction to the assembled people, Samuel sent them *home*. He also *wrote* his words concerning the kingdom *on a scroll* (probably at a later time) and *deposited* it in the tabernacle *before the Lord*. There it would be available for future reference as needed.

26. Saul also went to his home in Gibeah, accompanied by valiant men whose hearts God had touched.

What does a new king do in a country that never had a king before? This one simply *went* back *home* to the farm, as other people did. (*Gibeah* was located about four miles southeast of Mizpah.) Still, his life was not quite the same, for he went *accompanied by valiant men whose hearts God had touched*. Perhaps he touched their hearts with sincere concern for the king and the kingdom. As a result they volunteered to assist the new king in any way they could.

The record adds that Saul wisely ignored the dissidents who sneered at him (v. 27); and when a national emergency arose, this new king knew what a king must do. In fact, he did it so well that the people enthusiastically reaffirmed their allegiance to him (1 Samuel 11).

CONCLUSION

In recent centuries, kings have lost some of the sense of "enchantment" that at one time surrounded them. Some monarchies have become democracies; in others, kings are nothing more than figureheads. This change seems to be approved by nearly everyone (except the deposed kings).

Although a democracy can provide many freedoms and opportunities not available under a monarchy, many people today ignore the laws of democracies. Worse still, many renounce the rule of God. This seems to be the prevailing trend in our society, where a man will accept no king but himself. Proudly he announces that *he* will decide what is right for him.

God's Word teaches us to be obedient to the government we have, because it is ordained of God (Romans 13:1, 2). How many ordinary citizens ignore laws they consider trivial—traffic regulations, for example? How many of us are proud of our cleverness in avoiding the taxes that God's Word teaches us to pay (Romans 13:6, 7)? God's law said, "You shall not steal" (Exodus 20:15). Still, many citizens prefer their own rule: "I'm going to take care of myself." Our neighborhood supermarkets lose surprising sums to shoplifters, and some of them lose as much to pilfering employees.

God's law said, "You shall not murder" (Exodus 20:13), and Jesus' apostle teaches us not even to hate (1 John 3:15). Yet our morning paper reports a murder in our town, and probably your paper reports another in your town.

God's law said, "You shall not commit adultery" (Exodus 20:14). Yet adultery is shown once or twice during a thirty-minute TV show that is supposed to portray real life. How often does it occur in life that is truly real?

How much better it would be if no man would think himself a king and no man would think any other man a king, but every man would bow in humble obedience to the King of kings and Lord of lords!

WHAT DO YOU THINK?

How can you tell when God has touched a person's heart today?

PRAYER

Forgive us, Father, when we have turned aside from your commands to follow our own inclination. Forgive us when we have ignored your leading to follow human leaders. As we read your Word, may our minds be keen to see your will; may our hearts be strong to cherish it; may our bodies be quick to obey it. In Jesus' name, amen.

THOUGHT TO REMEMBER

Christ is King!

Discovery Learning

This page contains an alternate lesson plan emphasizing learning activities. Classes desiring such student involvement will find these suggestions helpful. The next page is a reproducible activity page to further enhance discovery learning.

LEARNING GOALS

After this lesson each student will be able to:

1. Summarize what today's text says about Saul and about the Israelites' acceptance of him as their first king.

2. Describe some of the ways in which God's rule over our lives today is threatened.

3. Pinpoint an area where God's authority as King needs to be allowed to have a greater impact.

INTO THE LESSON

Use the reproducible page that follows to make an overhead transparency of the puzzle entitled, "Possible 'Gods' People Worship Today." Begin the class by projecting the transparency of the puzzle and asking the class to read the four clues. As class members call out the correct words, fill in the blanks on the puzzle (*possessions, money, pleasures, fame*).

State: "People today worship possessions, money, pleasures, and fame. In reality, *self* sits on the throne as one's king, and people worship self instead of God." (Note the word *self* in the highlighted spaces.) "In the same way, the children of Israel rejected God as their true King and demanded an earthly king. Let's turn to 1 Samuel 9 and 10 for our lesson today."

INTO THE WORD

The Israelites wanted to be like all the other peoples of the world with a king. They failed to realize that as God's people, they were to be different! First Samuel 9 introduces the man God chose to be king. Read 1 Samuel 9:1, 2 and ask the following questions: (1) What is meant by the description of Kish as a "man of standing"? (*Probably someone noted for his financial success; wealthy.*) (2) Describe the physical stature of Saul. (*A head taller than other Israelites; handsome; "impressive."*)

Make a transparency of the reproducible activity called "How God Arranged the Meeting" from the next page. Divide the class into three groups and assign each group one of the three passages on the handout. Ask each group to identify the events that led to Samuel's meeting with Saul to anoint him as king. After several minutes have each group report its findings to the class. Write in the space provided the specific ways God arranged for Samuel and Saul to meet. (*Group 1: Donkeys became lost, and Saul was sent to look for them; servant told Saul about the man of God and suggested they see him. Group 2: Girls

came out of the city and told Saul where to find Samuel; Samuel came up to Saul and his servant as they entered the city. Group 3: The Lord told Samuel the day before that a man from Benjamin would come to him; the Lord told Samuel when he saw Saul that he was the one to be king.*) Read 1 Samuel 9:25—10:1. State: "So Samuel anointed Saul privately to be the leader of God's people. The remainder of our text tells of Saul's public coronation."

Ask a volunteer to read 1 Samuel 10:17-26, and then ask the following questions:

1. Why was the Israelites' demand for a king a rejection of their God? (*God was their King who had brought them out of Egypt and delivered them from all the kingdoms that oppressed them. This was just one more way they had forsaken God to serve themselves, 1 Samuel 8:8.*)

2. Saul knew in advance that he would be chosen. Why do you think he had "hidden himself among the baggage," 1 Samuel 10:22? (*Perhaps he was frightened by the responsibility, uncertain as to how the people would accept him, or maybe just bashful!*)

3. What was the people's response to God's selection of Saul as king? (*People readily accepted Saul as king.*)

4. Why did Samuel take the time to give all the instructions about the kingdom to the people and write them in a scroll? (*Israel had never had an earthly king, and instructions were needed now.*)

State: "Just as the people of Israel rejected God's rule over their lives, people today reject God's rule over their own lives. When we confess Jesus as Lord, we are saying that Christ is King of our lives."

INTO LIFE

Ask the class to brainstorm some possible answers to this question: "What are some ways that God's rule over our lives today is threatened?" Write the suggested answers on the chalkboard or overhead transparency. After you have compiled a good-sized list, ask, "What are some areas where God's authority as King needs to have a greater impact in Christian lives today?" Write the suggested answers on the board. State: "In the final analysis, we either worship self by allowing personal desires, things, or people to control us, or we worship God."

Distribute copies of the activity at the bottom of the reproducible page. Ask the learners to complete the activity and to keep the page as a reminder for the next several days. Then close with a prayer of commitment.

Possible "Gods" People Worship Today

Read the clues below to determine some of the "gods" that people worship today. Write them in the spaces provided.

1. Things that you own are called _____.
2. That which you spend to buy things is called _____.
3. Moses did not "enjoy the _____ of sin" even for "a short time" (Hebrews 11:25).
4. Seek "_____ and fortune."

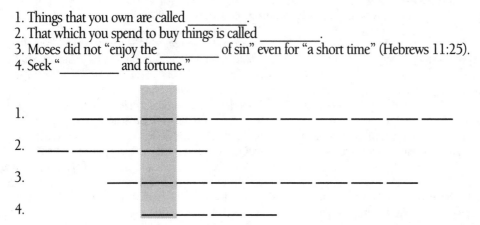

The highlighted area reveals the name of the "chief god" of our age. What is it?

How God Arranged the Meeting

God arranged for Samuel to meet Israel's first king and to anoint him privately before announcing the new king to the nation. Read the following passages and summarize what each says about how this meeting came about.

1 Samuel 9:3-10

1 Samuel 9:11-14

1 Samuel 9:15-17

"Christ Is King" Commitment!

Father, I no longer want your rule over my life to be threatened. I want you to be King over every area of my life. I want your kingship and authority to have a greater influence in the following area of my life:

I surrender my will to you and ask you to strengthen me by your Spirit. In Jesus' name I pray, amen.

SAUL REJECTED AND DAVID ANOINTED

LESSON 6

WHY TEACH THIS LESSON?

"Who would have thought it?" That old expression did not originate as long ago as the events of today's lesson, but it certainly could have been applied to them. Samuel tells Jesse one of his sons will be chosen for a position of leadership, so Jesse parades the boys before the prophet, starting with the impressive-looking oldest son. But he and six more are rejected, and someone has to fetch the youngest from the field. "Who would have thought it?" It is the youngest who is selected!

Some of your students would be equally surprised to learn what God would like to do with them. If their hearts are given wholly to the Lord, then he can "do immeasurably more than all we ask or imagine" (Ephesians 3:20). That is the challenge of today's lesson.

INTRODUCTION

A. USE AND ABUSE OF POWER

"Power tends to corrupt, and absolute power corrupts absolutely." So wrote a British historian in 1887. History furnishes many examples, from King Ahab in the ninth century B.C. to corrupt Communist dictators in the twentieth century A.D.

Some men of power, however, are incorruptible. History tells us of Cincinnatus, a Roman general and statesman of the fifth century before Christ. Having led his people to victory, he resigned his office and went back to his farm. Americans honor George Washington. After he had led an infant nation in war and peace and served two terms as president, he declined a third term and went back to his plantation. Citizens lauded him as "the first, the last, the best; the Cincinnatus of the West."

B. LESSON BACKGROUND

Last week we read of Saul, a modest man who hid from public acclaim on the day he was declared king of Israel. He then went back to the family farm; but when a national emergency came, he was ready. Boldly he raised an army and rescued a city of Israel that was being threatened by foreigners (1 Samuel 11). The new king went on to subdue other enemies of Israel (1 Samuel 14:47, 48), and Israel became an international power. At that point, having a king seemed to be yielding all the positive results for which Israel had hoped.

Tragically, Saul's humble and unpretentious spirit did not last. Success seemed to go to his head, and he began to revel in his power. Once Saul took priestly prerogative and offered sacrifices rather than wait for Samuel. The prophet warned the king, "Your kingdom will not endure" (1 Samuel 13:14) because of his rash act. Later the Lord sent Saul to exterminate the nation of Amalek. Because of the wickedness of that nation, it was to be wiped out—men, women, children, even animals. But Saul thought he had a better plan. He spared the life of the Amalekite king and the best of the Amalekites' livestock.

DEVOTIONAL READING:
ISAIAH 55:6-11
BACKGROUND SCRIPTURE:
1 SAMUEL 15:10—16:13
PRINTED TEXT:
1 SAMUEL 16:1-13

Oct
8

LESSON AIMS

After this lesson students will be able to:

1. Describe the process by which Samuel was led to anoint David as Israel's king.

2. Explain the importance of having one's heart wholly committed to the Lord.

3. List actions and attitudes they can cultivate in seeking to serve the Lord wholeheartedly.

KEY VERSE

The LORD does not look at the things man looks at. Man looks at the outward appearance, but the LORD looks at the heart.
—1 Samuel 16:7

This act marked the beginning of the end for Saul. The Lord rejected the disobedient king and sent Samuel to tell him so—confirming the Lord's earlier warning. Saul's rule must end; the Lord had found a better man to take his place (1 Samuel 15:28).

I. SEARCH FOR A KING (1 SAMUEL 16:1-5)

Saul had rejected the Lord, and the Lord had rejected Saul. God's prophet Samuel came no more to counsel the king; nevertheless, "Samuel mourned for him" (1 Samuel 15:35). What a sad turn of events! Saul had begun his reign so nobly, wisely, heroically, and successfully. But now the disobedient king was doomed, and Samuel grieved for him.

A. GOD'S PROPHET SENT (v. 1)

1. *The LORD said to Samuel, "How long will you mourn for Saul, since I have rejected him as king over Israel? Fill your horn with oil and be on your way; I am sending you to Jesse of Bethlehem. I have chosen one of his sons to be king."*

The time to *mourn for Saul* was over. The Lord's prophet must be about the Lord's business, and that was the anointing of a man to replace Saul as *king*. This did not mean that the new king would take office soon. Saul himself had been anointed in private, when no one but he and Samuel knew about it (1 Samuel 9:27; 10:1). This new king's anointing would be known to only a few; Saul would remain king for several years to come. Samuel did not yet know whom he was to anoint, but it would be one of the *sons* of *Jesse*, a citizen of *Bethlehem*.

B. SAFETY PROMISED (vv. 2, 3)

2. *But Samuel said, "How can I go? Saul will hear about it and kill me."*
    The LORD said, "Take a heifer with you and say, 'I have come to sacrifice to the LORD.'

Modest Saul had been tolerant of those who had opposed his kingship (1 Samuel 10:27; 11:12, 13). But Saul was no longer modest and no longer tolerant. He had shown himself arrogant enough to go his own way in defiance of God's order. Now God was telling Samuel to anoint another man to replace Saul. If Saul heard about that, he would call it treason. It is likely that Samuel would be punished by death.

But the Lord had a ready answer for Samuel's dilemma. Saul need not know about the anointing. Samuel could take a *heifer* (young cow) to Bethlehem and offer a *sacrifice* there. It was not necessary that Saul be informed about the other purpose of the trip.

3. *Invite Jesse to the sacrifice, and I will show you what to do. You are to anoint for me the one I indicate."*

Samuel was to *invite Jesse to the sacrifice*. Later verses indicate that he was to invite Jesse's sons as well. In many sacrifices, only a small part of the sacrificed animal was actually burned on the altar. In this case, probably a part of the meat of the sacrificed heifer would provide a feast for the guests.

By this time, Samuel had been known as a judge of Israel for many years. It was not likely that any of the Israelites would have declined an invitation from him to attend a sacrifice. Once those invited were assembled, God would give Samuel further instructions. Most important, he would tell him whom to *anoint*.

C. SACRIFICE ARRANGED (vv. 4, 5)

4. *Samuel did what the LORD said. When he arrived at Bethlehem, the elders of the town trembled when they met him. They asked, "Do you come in peace?"*

WHAT DO YOU THINK?

Samuel had been mourning over Saul's failure as king, but God told him it was time to take action. We also may be mourning over certain circumstances when God wants us to take action. Some leaders mourn over the church's failure to grow when they ought, instead, to inaugurate some new means of outreach into the community. Some mourn over the fact that young people in town are getting into serious trouble with drugs, alcohol, and sex, but they do nothing to launch a ministry that will provide those young people with positive direction. Many mourn over the immoral content of television programs today without so much as writing a letter to a television network or station, or to an advertiser, to voice their concerns.

Can you think of some other examples? What specifically can we do to address these issues rather than just mourn over them?

The elders of the town trembled. Perhaps they had heard of Samuel's recent execution of the king of the Amalekites (1 Samuel 15:33). Had he come to *Bethlehem* to accuse the elders or the people of some terrible wrong? Or had he *come in peace?* The elders were frightened.

5. Samuel replied, "Yes, in peace; I have come to sacrifice to the LORD. Consecrate yourselves and come to the sacrifice with me." Then he consecrated Jesse and his sons and invited them to the sacrifice.

Samuel reassured the elders: he had come *in peace.* His purpose was *to sacrifice to the Lord.* The text seems to indicate that he invited the elders to be present as well as Jesse and his sons, but in the following verses only Jesse and his sons are mentioned. Possibly the events recorded from verse 6 on involved a private meeting of only Samuel and Jesse and his sons, at some time during the proceedings.

A few generations ago in rural America, it was customary for farmers to take a bath on Saturday night. Then on Sunday morning they put on clean clothes to go to church. In a somewhat similar manner, the ancient Israelites *consecrated* themselves before meeting the Lord in a special way. Exodus 19:10-14 tells of an occasion when such ceremonial cleansing included putting on clean clothes. *Jesse and his sons* received special treatment as they were prepared by Samuel himself.

II. REJECTED CANDIDATES (1 SAMUEL 16:6-10)

We are not told exactly when the sacrifice occurred following Samuel's arrival in Bethlehem. Our text proceeds to the primary reason for which the Lord had sent Samuel to Bethlehem.

A. THE LORD'S INSIGHT (vv. 6, 7)

6. When they arrived, Samuel saw Eliab and thought, "Surely the LORD's anointed stands here before the LORD."

Jesse and his sons met with Samuel at the place of sacrifice. Samuel first *saw Eliab,* probably because he was the oldest of Jesse's sons (1 Samuel 17:28); and Samuel liked what he saw. *Surely* this fine-looking young man was to be Israel's next king!

7. But the LORD said to Samuel, "Do not consider his appearance or his height, for I have rejected him. The LORD does not look at the things man looks at. Man looks at the outward appearance, but the LORD looks at the heart."

People like to have a leader who looks the part—one who is tall and handsome and stands out from his peers. But other qualifications are more important. Samuel thought that no one could be a more capable king than Eliab, but the Lord knew better. He was looking for a man after his own *heart* (1 Samuel 13:14).

B. PARADE OF POSSIBILITIES (vv. 8-10)

8. Then Jesse called Abinadab and had him pass in front of Samuel. But Samuel said, "The LORD has not chosen this one either."

Apparently Samuel had made known to Jesse his purpose to appoint a king as well as to offer a sacrifice. Jesse was presenting his sons one by one, probably in order of their ages. The Lord rejected the second as he had rejected the first.

9. Jesse then had Shammah pass by, but Samuel said, "Nor has the LORD chosen this one."

The third son likewise was rejected. It seems that the Lord, without words, made his will known to Samuel's mind, and Samuel conveyed that message to Jesse. From Samuel's youth he had thus been revealing the will of God, so that "all Israel from Dan to Beersheba recognized that Samuel was attested as a prophet of the Lord" (1 Samuel 3:20).

10. *Jesse had seven of his sons pass before Samuel, but Samuel said to him, "The LORD has not chosen these."*

No longer naming the *sons* one by one, the record adds that four more of them were presented *before Samuel.* Most likely they were presented one by one, and one by one *the Lord* rejected them.

FAULTY EXPECTATIONS

At 2:25 A.M. on February 25, 1942, the "Great Los Angeles Air Raid" began. Sirens sounded the alarm, searchlights swept across the sky to find invading Japanese warplanes, and anti-aircraft shells were fired into the darkness.

Later that morning, the *Los Angeles Times* gave a detailed account of the attack, but also mentioned (strangely) that "no bombs were reported dropped." Nevertheless, there were casualties. Two people died of heart attacks during the excitement, and three died in traffic accidents during the blackout that occurred. The following day, however, the Secretary of the Navy admitted that the entire raid had been a mistake: there had been no enemy attack. Because of the tension surrounding World War II, people had been so certain that Japan would attack California that someone mistook weather balloons released that night for enemy aircraft!

Samuel discovered that faulty expectations can be misleading. None of the stalwart, older sons of Jesse was God's choice for the next king of Israel. Like Samuel, we tend to judge people by outward appearances, which often tell us nothing about their moral fiber. Our political (and even some religious) leaders have demonstrated this time and again. By now we should have learned our lesson.   —C. R. B.

III. THE ONE CHOSEN (1 SAMUEL 16:11-13)

Samuel must have been puzzled. God had sent him to anoint one of Jesse's sons, but he had rejected each one Samuel had seen. What could that mean?

A. YOUNGEST SON (v. 11)

11. *So he asked Jesse, "Are these all the sons you have?"*

"There is still the youngest," Jesse answered, "but he is tending the sheep."

Samuel said, "Send for him; we will not sit down until he arrives."

Did *Jesse* have any other sons? That was Samuel's first question. Yes, said Jesse, but only one—*the youngest.* It had not seemed necessary to have him present. Surely *he* would not be chosen to rule his older brothers and the entire nation of Israel. Someone was needed to take care of the *sheep,* and naturally that duty had fallen to the "kid brother." But now all the other brothers had been rejected. There was nothing to do but send for the one who remained.

Note that the sacrifice that Samuel had come to offer has not been mentioned since verse 5. Perhaps at that point (when Jesse and his seven sons "arrived," verse 6) the sacrifice was offered. The meat for the family feast would then have been cooking while Samuel was searching for the chosen king. Perhaps Samuel now said, *We will not sit down* (to the feast) *until he arrives.* Or possibly *we will not sit down* merely means that we will not rest—we will not end the search for God's chosen king—until the youngest son has been included.

B. ANOINTED KING (vv. 12, 13)

12. *So he sent and had him brought in. He was ruddy, with a fine appearance and handsome features.*

Then the LORD said, "Rise and anoint him; he is the one."

We can only guess how far away the young man was with the sheep, or how long it took him to join the family. But when he came, Samuel noticed his *fine appearance and handsome features.* Perhaps he looked as good as the oldest son who had impressed Samuel at the beginning of his search (v. 6). Some students take *ruddy* to mean that the young man had a healthy outdoor complexion; others take it to indicate that he had red hair. The Lord saw the young man's heart as well, and he gave Samuel a quick and clear message: *Rise and anoint him; he is the one.*

THE "KID BROTHER" SYNDROME

The youngest child in a family often gets viewed with a certain amount of disdain. While older children in the family often think that the youngest child gets "babied" and catered to, psychologists tell us that the oldest child frequently enjoys advantages of parental attention that diminish as other children are born into the family. In some cases youngest children sometimes find that they are never quite recognized as having grown up, even when they reach adulthood.

However that might be, history has shown that oldest children are disproportionately represented among the kings and leaders of societies around the world. Thus it is not too shocking that Samuel was doubly surprised in his search for Israel's new king: first, that Eliab, Jesse's oldest son, was not the choice; and second, that David, the "kid brother" in a family of eight boys, was the choice.

David would prove that birth order has no bearing on God's call to service. Far more important than where we fit in our own families is where we fit in God's family. This is determined by our faithful response to God's will—and by nothing else.

—C. R. B.

The visual for today's lesson contrasts David's appearance in the eyes of his family with the potential God saw in him, and which he realized.

13. So Samuel took the horn of oil and anointed him in the presence of his brothers, and from that day on the Spirit of the LORD came upon David in power. Samuel then went to Ramah.

On an earlier occasion, Samuel had anointed Saul in private (1 Samuel 9:27; 10:1). Only Samuel and Saul knew about this until the time came to reveal the choice and let all Israel know that God had made it (1 Samuel 10:17-24). In the same way, the anointing of this new king was known only to his family (unless the elders of Bethlehem were also there). Undoubtedly any who were present were warned not to tell what had happened. If arrogant King Saul heard about it, surely he would want to kill both Samuel and the son of Jesse who was anointed (and probably any others who were witnesses).

The Spirit of the Lord came upon David. Now at last we are given the name of this youngest son of Jesse, who was anointed to be king. He was *David.* After becoming king, he would subdue enemy nations and build Israel into an empire. He would also become known as "Israel's singer of songs" (2 Samuel 23:1), writing many of the songs we treasure in the book of Psalms.

Samuel then went to Ramah, which was his home (1 Samuel 7:17). For a long time the anointing of David seemed to make no difference. In fact, David did not become king until Saul was dead. In the meantime he served King Saul in several ways. His music subdued an evil spirit that troubled Saul (1 Samuel 16:14-23). He killed the giant Goliath, and the invading Philistines fled (1 Samuel 17:49-51). He led Saul's troops in battle so successfully that the king became jealous of his popularity (1 Samuel 18:5-9). When Saul determined to murder him, David fled instead of fighting (1 Samuel 19:8-18). Not until Saul was dead did David become king of Judah (2 Samuel 2:1-4), and then seven and a half more years passed before he became king of all Israel (2 Samuel 5:4, 5).

CONCLUSION

A. HUNTING HIDDEN HEARTS

Kings generally inherit their positions, but those who live in democratic societies have a voice in choosing the people who make their laws and enforce them.

DAILY BIBLE READINGS

Monday, Oct. 2—Attack Against the Amalekites (1 Samuel 15:1-9)

Tuesday, Oct. 3—A New Word (1 Samuel 15:10-16)

Wednesday, Oct. 4—The Confrontation (1 Samuel 15:17-23)

Thursday, Oct. 5—God Rejects Saul as King (1 Samuel 15:24-29)

Friday, Oct. 6—Saul's Confession and Samuel's Departure (1 Samuel 15:30-35)

Saturday, Oct. 7—Samuel Is Sent to Bethlehem (1 Samuel 16:1-5)

Sunday, Oct. 8—David Is Anointed as King (1 Samuel 16:6-13)

PRAYER

Father, we know that you have given us every talent, every ability, every usefulness we have. Help us to understand what we are and what we ought to be. For every work we do with joy we give you thanks. If we must do what we do not like, help us to do it with all our heart, remembering that we are doing it for you and not just for an employer. In Jesus' name. Amen.

THOUGHT TO REMEMBER

"Whatever you do, work at it with all your heart, as working for the Lord, not for men" (Colossians 3:23).

WHAT DO YOU THINK?

How can we find the kind of work for the Lord that we can do wholeheartedly? Why is this important?

Like Samuel, we tend to look on the outward appearance; but the man with the handsome face and glib tongue is not necessarily the best. How can we know what is in his heart?

Alas, we often fail to do our homework. To take time to examine a candidate's positions would be a long and arduous task, and we have other things to do. So we vote blindly for our party's candidate. Then who is to blame if we are not well represented on a local, state, or national level?

B. HELPLESS HASTY HEARTS

The prettiest girl in town may not become the best wife. The popular college football star, when he gets married, may forget all he ever learned about teamwork. Too many people choose their mates by outward appearance because that is all they can see. Worse yet, they choose when their own hearts are helpless—blinded by infatuation and incapable of sober thought. How can a boy or girl in love know anything about the heart of the beloved?

It takes time. It takes attention. But there are signals to look for. If a girl takes delight in teaching little ones in Sunday school, if she turns down a date with her boyfriend to go with them on an outing, if she happily washes dishes after a fellowship dinner at church, if she is considerate of her parents and careful not to worry them, if she is courteous and helpful to other adults—all of these provide glimpses of her heart. If a boy teases little children unmercifully and upsets a smaller child on a bicycle, if he scorns work day at church and cleanup day in the community, if he takes delight in disobeying his parents and makes fun of people feeble with age—watch out!

Whatever actions a boy or girl consistently demonstrates are an indicator of the contents of his or her heart.

C. WHOLEHEARTED OR HALFHEARTED?

Some of us don't even know our own hearts. In choosing a career, it is important to get acquainted with your heart and find a work you can put that heart into. Consider two examples.

At the age of five, Eddie announced his intention: "I'm going to be a preacher just like Ralph." Ralph was a young man who recently had become a preacher. Church members were proud of him. No one could remember when that church had sent out a preacher before. Happy Christians praised Ralph with enthusiasm. They expected great things from him.

Eddie never faltered in his determination. On "Youth Sunday" at his church, he always delivered better sermons than anyone else because he worked harder in preparation. He went to Bible college, graduated with honors, and became the minister of a large and growing church. He is happy, his family is happy, and his church is happy because Eddie's heart is in his work.

Meanwhile Ralph was failing in the ministry. He tried to put his heart into it, but his heart rebelled. He had a daily battle with himself, and it broke him down. He just didn't have the heart of a "people person." Finally he gave up the battle. He found an editorial job, working with words instead of people. He loved it with all his heart and did it with joy until he retired at eighty.

How do you feel about your job? Are you doing it with all your heart? Or are your heart and your work a bad match? If they are, maybe you can change your work. If that is impractical, maybe you can change your heart. Give it some thought. You don't want to be unhappy all your life. Can't you learn to love your work because it provides your daily bread, or because it provides a needed product for many people, or because it does some good in the world?

Discovery Learning

*This page contains an alternate lesson plan emphasizing learning activities. Classes
desiring such student involvement will find these suggestions helpful. The next page
is a reproducible activity page to further enhance discovery learning.*

LEARNING GOALS

After this lesson students will be able to:

1. Describe the process by which Samuel was led to anoint David as Israel's king.

2. Explain the importance of having one's heart wholly committed to the Lord.

3. List actions and attitudes they can cultivate in seeking to serve the Lord wholeheartedly.

INTO THE LESSON

Bring to class a bag of balloons of different colors and shapes. Inflate one balloon with air, another with water, and, if possible, a third with helium. Ask each student to take a balloon from the bag for use later in the class. Begin the class by asking for various ways to use these balloons when filled with air, water, or helium. As ideas are mentioned, write them on the chalkboard (*decorations, playing games, water bombs, to carry a message to someone*). State, "By filling these balloons with air, water, or helium we can use them in different ways. Helium-filled balloons wouldn't work very well as water bombs! So what matters is what's inside! In the same way, God tells us in 1 Samuel 16 that it's what's inside that counts!"

INTO THE WORD

Make a transparency of the reproducible activity "Saul's Rejection." Begin the background Bible study by dividing the class into three groups, asking them to read the assigned passage and answer their particular question.

Group 1: Read 1 Samuel 15:1-9; tell why Saul was rejected as king. (*He did not obey God and destroy all the Amalekites and their animals.*)

Group 2: Read 1 Samuel 15:11, 19-23; tell how Saul's failure was described by God and by Samuel. (*God: "He has turned away from me and has not carried out my instructions." Samuel: He did not obey the Lord; he did evil in the eyes of the Lord; he rejected the word of the Lord.*)

Group 3: Read 1 Samuel 15:13, 20, 21, 24, 30; describe Saul's difficulty in accepting personal responsibility for his sin. (*First, he claimed to have "carried out the Lord's instructions," v. 13. Second, he blamed the people for taking from the plunder, vv. 20, 21. Third, he admitted that he had sinned but blamed the people for his sin, v. 24. Finally, he confessed that he had sinned, v. 30.*)

After five minutes, have each group report to the class. Write the answers on the transparency.

Have a volunteer read 1 Samuel 16:1-13 aloud. Ask the following questions: (1) Why did the Lord send Samuel to Bethlehem? (*The Lord wanted Samuel to anoint the next king.*) (2) Why did the Lord instruct Samuel to take a heifer to Bethlehem? (*Samuel was fearful of Saul's finding out; the heifer was to be offered as a sacrifice to the Lord.*) (3) By what process did Samuel select the next king to anoint? (*Samuel invited Jesse and his sons to the sacrifice. As the sons passed by, the Lord would tell him which one to anoint.*) (4) Why was Samuel's initial choice of Eliab wrong? (*He looked at his outward physical stature and appearance, but the Lord looked on his heart and refused him.*) (5) Why was David selected to be the next king? (*Because his heart was wholly committed to the Lord, Acts 13:22.*)

INTO LIFE

State: "David was selected because he was a man after God's own heart. He was wholly committed to the Lord. Why is it important to have one's heart wholly committed to the Lord?" As answers are suggested, write them on the chalkboard or an overhead transparency sheet so all can see. Then read aloud 1 Chronicles 28:9, David's instruction to Solomon.

Distribute copies of the reproducible activity "Serving Wholeheartedly" from the next page. Also make a transparency to project on the screen or wall. Ask the class to move into groups of three and to come up with suggested "Attitudes" and "Actions" that Christians need to serve the Lord wholeheartedly. After several minutes, call for suggestions, writing them under the respective headings. (*Attitudes: humility, obedience, surrender, esteem others, love people. Actions: serve or minister to others, daily read/study the Word, pray daily, faithfully attend worship services, promote unity. Refer to Philippians 2:1-11 for help.*)

State: "If we are truly honest before God, each of us has some growing to do to serve the Lord wholeheartedly. Look at these lists and select one attitude and one action that you *most need to cultivate.* Now take the balloon you picked earlier and blow it up partially. Write that attitude and action on the balloon and let the air out. Carry this balloon around all week in your pocket or purse to remind you each day that it's what's inside that counts.

Close the session with a prayer of commitment. Or form a prayer circle and encourage each one who is willing to offer such a prayer.

Saul's Rejection

Read 1 Samuel 15:1-9; tell why Saul was rejected as king.

Read 1 Samuel 15:11, 19-23; tell how Saul's failure was described by God and by Samuel.

Read 1 Samuel 15:13, 20, 21, 24, 30; describe Saul's difficulty in accepting personal responsibility for his sin.

Serving Wholeheartedly

What are some of the attitudes and actions that Christians need to serve the Lord wholeheartedly? List as many as you can think of on the chart below. Then choose one or two from each column that you will give greater attention to this week to develop those attitudes and actions in your own life.

ATTITUDES	ACTIONS

DAVID MOURNS SAUL AND JONATHAN

LESSON 7

WHY TEACH THIS LESSON?

In today's lesson we see David at his best. In our own time many have struggled to give proper honor to certain national leaders because of improper behavior on the part of the office holder. The integrity of the office has been sullied by the person. But whatever we have seen in our own day is paltry compared to Saul's abuse of his office—and David was the object of Saul's abuse. But when Saul died, David was genuinely grieved.

We hardly understand it, but we cannot help but admire it. It goes beyond protocol; it is what the New Testament writers call *agape*. If your students need a good model for loving one's enemies—and who doesn't—then this lesson is just what they need.

INTRODUCTION

Marty and Mary were made for each other. Anyone could see that. They suspected it themselves the first time their eyes met. Enrolling as college freshmen when they were nearing thirty years of age, they felt worlds apart from their younger classmates but blissful with each other. In weeks they were thinking of marriage; in months they were talking about it.

But there was a problem—money, or the lack of it. Both of them were working their way through school, supplementing their earnings with student loans. Reluctantly they agreed that marriage must wait until one of them was earning a living wage. Work and studies left little time for dating, so four years dragged by with long waits between happy dates.

Then came graduation. Mary took a job in town; Marty took one a thousand miles away. For nearly two years they endured separation, but they paid off their loans. Then Marty made a down payment on a car, drove a thousand miles, was married, and took his bride home in celebration. Like characters in a storybook romance, Marty and Mary lived happily ever after.

A. WAITING—AND WAITING

Haven't we all been dismayed by delay? Haven't you yourself had to wait and wait for an opportunity, a job, a promotion, a home, or something else that you desired and felt you deserved? Imagine how David felt when he knew that the Lord had chosen him to be king of Israel, yet year after year the throne remained in the control of a king whom the Lord had abandoned.

David had one great advantage. The Spirit of the Lord was with him (1 Samuel 16:13). Thus guided, he provides an admirable example for all of us who have to learn the difficult art of waiting. David became a loyal servant of the reigning king and learned to wait patiently for God's timing. He steadfastly refused to take any action against the king who was so eager to kill him (1 Samuel 24:2-7; 26:6-12).

DEVOTIONAL READING:
PSALM 77:1-9

BACKGROUND SCRIPTURE:
1 SAMUEL 31:1—2 SAMUEL 1:27;
1 CHRONICLES 10

PRINTED TEXT:
2 SAMUEL 1:17-27

LESSON AIMS

After participating in this lesson, each student will be able to:

1. Summarize David's lament for Saul and Jonathan.

2. Tell how the expression of grief helps one to cope with a great loss.

3. Express his or her hope in Christ and how that hope helps in times of grief.

Oct 15

KEY VERSE

Your glory, O Israel, lies slain on your heights. How the mighty have fallen!   —2 Samuel 1:19

LESSON 7 NOTES

The beauty of Israel is slain upon thy high places: how are the mighty fallen!
2 Samuel 1:19

Today's visual shows Mount Gilboa, where Saul and his sons died. Locate the site on a map. (See the visual for lesson 5.)

WHAT DO YOU THINK?

David mourned over Saul's death, primarily because the king was God's anointed. But he must surely have been troubled also over the manner of Saul's death. The king had perished in battle with pagans! While Saul's death cleared the way for David to assume his rightful place on the throne, it also gave the ungodly reason to rejoice and to dishonor the name of the Lord. How can we develop a sense that sees beyond personal benefit or loss in each situation to see also how the Lord's kingdom is affected? How can we make the kingdom our priority even over our own interests?

B. LESSON BACKGROUND

A band of Amalekites had invaded the southern part of Israel, burning a city and taking its people as captives. David and his men pursued the invaders, defeated them, and brought back the captives and the spoil (1 Samuel 30:1-20). Meanwhile the Philistines invaded farther to the north. Saul and his troops met them in a fierce battle in which Israel was soundly defeated. During the fighting, Saul was killed, along with Jonathan and two other sons of Saul (1 Samuel 31:1-7).

When David heard of this, did he rejoice in the death of the king who had been trying to kill him? No, he mourned; and we find a very touching expression of his grief in today's text.

I. LAMENT FOR SAUL (2 SAMUEL 1:17-21)

Poets sometimes puzzle us with their figurative language. Sometimes they abandon the ordinary practices of grammar for the sake of meter and rhyme. For the same reason, they sometimes find and use words we never heard of before; or they use them in ways with which we are unfamiliar. We have to guess at the meaning or use a dictionary. In other cases they include a word that has more than one meaning, and again we have to guess at which meaning the poet is using.

The Hebrew poetry found in the Old Testament exhibits these same qualities. In addition, the poets sometimes abbreviate, and a translator has to add certain words to make sense in English. However, not all translators add the same words. Thus, if we read David's lament in two or more versions, we may find some puzzling differences. But regardless of the version used, the message of this text is unmistakably clear: David is expressing heartfelt grief at the deaths of Saul and Jonathan.

A. PRELUDE (vv. 17, 18)

17. David took up this lament concerning Saul and his son Jonathan,

We can understand why David felt grief for *Jonathan*, the dear friend who had turned against his own father and had risked his own life to save David from death (1 Samuel 20:30-34). More surprising is David's grief over *Saul*, the vindictive king who had pursued David relentlessly in order to kill him. But David's grief for Saul was real, too. Saul was God's anointed ruler, and for a time he had served God's people well. David loved and respected him for that.

18. . . . and ordered that the men of Judah be taught this lament of the bow (it is written in the Book of Jashar).

Now our difficulty begins. Translating the Hebrew words as literally as possible, we read, "And he said to teach the children of Judah bow." The *King James Version* says David instructed some unnamed persons to teach the men of the tribe of Judah "the use of the *bow.*" The translators of our text took this reference to the bow to indicate that the lament that follows was known as *lament of the bow* (which perhaps eventually became its title), because it praises the bow of Jonathan (v. 22). Apparently David wanted his own tribe (the tribe of Judah) to learn the lament and thus commemorate the loss of Saul (even though Saul was of the tribe of Benjamin, not Judah).

The *New American Standard Bible* reads, "the song of the bow" instead of "the lament of the bow." This may have the same meaning, but some students believe it means that the following lament is to be sung to the tune of another song called "the Song of the Bow."

Whatever meaning we give to the first part of verse 18, the latter part tells us that the following lament, or else another song sung to the same tune, *is written in the Book of Jashar.* The Hebrew word *Jashar* means straight, upright, or righteous. The book is also mentioned in Joshua 10:13, where it is said to contain the account of how the sun stood still to allow the Israelites to win an important battle during the time of Joshua. Apparently the book was a record of some of the significant people and events in Israel's history. At some point it was lost or destroyed.

B. ISRAEL MOURNS (v. 19)

19. *"Your glory, O Israel, lies slain on your heights. How the mighty have fallen!*

What does the phrase *your glory, O Israel* describe? It may refer to King Saul or to both Saul and Jonathan, who are the primary subjects of the lament. Or, it may refer to all the men of Israel *slain* in the battle with the Philistines—praising them as the finest men in Israel's army. Possibly a combination of both concepts is meant. The term *heights* apparently describes Mount Gilboa and the highlands around it (1 Samuel 31:1).

C. ENEMIES REJOICE (v. 20)

20. *"Tell it not in Gath, proclaim it not in the streets of Ashkelon, lest the daughters of the Philistines be glad, lest the daughters of the uncircumcised rejoice.*

Gath and *Ashkelon* were two of the Philistines' chief cities. David was wishing that the news of Saul's death could never be told there. His wish was in vain, of course. First Samuel 31:9, 10 tells how the news was heralded in every Philistine town.

D. MOUNTAINS ARE BARREN (v. 21)

21. *"O mountains of Gilboa, may you have neither dew nor rain, nor fields that yield offerings [of grain]. For there the shield of the mighty was defiled, the shield of Saul—no longer rubbed with oil.*

Mountains of Gilboa describes the highlands running southeast and south of the valley of Jezreel. These were verdant in spring. The steeper slopes were usually covered with woodlands, while on the level places one could produce fields of grain, some of which would be used as *offerings* to the Lord. In David's grief he longed for all that region to be desolate—a waterless desert—because of the tragedy that had taken place there; *for there the shield of the mighty* King Saul was *defiled.* The king's honored shield was disgraced by defeat, soiled by blood and by the dirt of the ground, and abandoned on the battlefield of defeat.

The final part of the verse presents another puzzle to the translator. Rendered word for word, it says, "the shield of Saul, not anointed with oil." *The New International Version* says that *the shield of Saul* was *no longer rubbed with oil.* Many students think that a warrior's shield was rubbed with oil to make it bright and shining. Others believe that the oil was meant to serve as a kind of lubricant, making arrows and spears glance off the shield more readily. But after the tragic battle on Mount Gilboa, Saul's shield was neither bright nor lubricated; it was defiled with blood and dirt—and David mourned.

GRIEVING FOR A FALLEN LEADER

"The president has been shot!" Most of us who were teens or adults in the United States on November 22, 1963, can remember where we were when we heard those fateful words about President John F. Kennedy. A man who was then a seminary student recalls that he was approaching the classroom building where two other students were discussing what had taken place. Just then a professor known for his partisan politics came out the door and asked what had happened. On hearing the news, his unthinking response was to utter words he would later

WHAT DO YOU THINK?

David's lament seems to have been not only for Saul and Jonathan, but for all the Israelite warriors who had fallen in battle with the Philistines. He recognized that everyone is important, not just those with rank and recognition. How well do we demonstrate appreciation for the unknown many who support the work of the Lord and who serve behind the scenes today? How can we do better at that?

HOW TO SAY IT

agape (Greek). uh-GAH-pay.
Amalekites. AM-uh-leh-kites or
    Uh-MAL-ih-kites.
Ashkelon. ASH-keh-lon.
Gilboa. Gil-BO-uh.
Jashar. JAY-shar.
Jezreel. JEZ-ree-el or JEZ-reel.
Philistines. Fuh-LISS-teens or
    FILL-us-teens.

regret: "Someone should have done it a long time ago!" As you might expect, news of his crass remark spread across the campus like wildfire. The following day he was forced to make a public apology.

One of the blessings of living in a democratic society is that we can have a part in choosing our political leaders and can criticize them without fear of reprisal when they do not conduct themselves or the affairs of state as we think they should. Sometimes we find it difficult to honor the office while criticizing the person who holds it. But David's grief at the death of Saul provides a helpful model for us. Even though Saul had tried to kill David, David made his personal concerns subservient to the greater importance of his nation's well-being. Whenever our political leaders disappoint us, David's example is worth remembering.

—C. R. B.

II. PRAISE FOR SAUL AND JONATHAN (2 SAMUEL 1:22-24)

From a wail of grief, David's song now turns to a eulogy for the dead. Three of Saul's sons had been killed in the horrible battle (v. 2), but Jonathan had been David's special friend. The eulogy centers on Saul and Jonathan.

A. THEIR COURAGE (v. 22)

22. *From the blood of the slain, from the flesh of the mighty, the bow of Jonathan did not turn back, the sword of Saul did not return unsatisfied.*

Jonathan and *Saul* had been both valiant and victorious in battle. *The bow of Jonathan* refers to Jonathan's distinguished activity in warfare. He had never turned back, retreated, or been frightened by the prospects of combat. The references to *blood* and *flesh* call to mind the language of animal sacrifices, which is sometimes used in describing battles (cf. Isaiah 34:6, 7; Jeremiah 46:10). *The sword of Saul* likewise highlights Saul's activity in battle. It had not returned *unsatisfied*; that is, it had been successful and had accomplished its purpose.

These declarations of courage and success were no empty tributes. Remember how Saul had left the family farm to raise an army and win a dramatic victory (1 Samuel 11:1-11). Remember how Jonathan, with only one companion, had attacked a Philistine garrison and put it to flight (1 Samuel 14:1-23). Saul and Jonathan truly had been successful before that battle in which they died, and even in that fatal fight their courage had not weakened.

B. THEIR CHARACTER (v. 23)

23. *"Saul and Jonathan—in life they were loved and gracious, and in death they were not parted. They were swifter than eagles, they were stronger than lions.*

Perhaps when we think of Saul we remember the insane jealousy that moved him to try to kill David, who had done him nothing but good. David, however, remembered how *loved and gracious* Saul had been before that. Saul had received a shepherd boy into the royal court and had promoted him to a place of command over many older men.

Meanwhile, David and Jonathan had become the best of friends (1 Samuel 18:1-5). Jonathan disagreed vocally with his father's treatment of David (1 Samuel 20:32) and even helped David escape Saul's wrath (vv. 35-42). Yet he continued to serve faithfully in Israel's army under the command of his father. Together they died bravely on the field of battle.

C. SAUL AS PROVIDER (v. 24)

24. *"O daughters of Israel, weep for Saul, who clothed you in scarlet and finery, who adorned your garments with ornaments of gold.*

WHAT DO YOU THINK?

David seemed to have the ability to focus on the good things he had experienced with Saul. How can we learn to concentrate on the good in people who treat us badly?

Here David called the women of *Israel* to join him in mourning for Saul. Israel's first king had done much for them. They were able to wear fine clothing and golden jewelry because the nation had prospered during his administration. Some of these costly clothes and jewels were likely among the spoils of Saul's successful wars (1 Samuel 14:47, 48).

III. LAMENT FOR JONATHAN (2 SAMUEL 1:25-27)

The last stanza of David's lament expresses his grief over the loss of Jonathan, his dearest friend (1 Samuel 18:1).

A. JONATHAN'S DEATH (v. 25)

25. "How the mighty have fallen in battle! Jonathan lies slain on your heights.

How the mighty have fallen! This cry of grief introduced the lament for Saul (v. 19); now it introduces the lament for Jonathan. But the Hebrew word for *mighty* is plural. The mourning is for both Saul and Jonathan, yes, and perhaps includes the warriors of Israel who died in the battle with the Philistines. However, the latter line of the verse centers attention on *Jonathan*. Along with the other heroes of Israel, he was *slain* in that fierce battle on the *heights* of his homeland—the elevated terrain on and around Mount Gilboa.

B. DAVID'S GRIEF (v. 26)

26. I grieve for you, Jonathan my brother; you were very dear to me. Your love for me was wonderful, more wonderful than that of women.

I grieve for you. This line may also be translated "distress is mine" or "grief is mine." The basic Hebrew verb means to be narrow or confining. David felt pressed and burdened by an overwhelming sense of grief over the death of his dearest friend. Many of us know that feeling, for we too have lost loved ones. Added to the crushing weight of sorrow is the feeling of utter helplessness. The dear one is dead. Nothing can be done about that. David's dear one was so close that he was more than a friend. David calls him *Jonathan my brother.*

There is no suggestion of a homosexual relationship in the closing line of this verse. David is simply stating that the strength of the bond between him and Jonathan was not one commonly found among men. First Samuel 18:1 describes this bond as follows: "Jonathan became one in spirit with David, and he loved him as himself."

A MAN'S TEARS

The Persian Gulf War of 1991 was carried off with such finesse that it seemed to be the product of cold, calculated military planning devoid of any humane considerations. However, President George Bush later revealed that it was not so. With uncharacteristic lack of guile for a politician, Bush said that he had broken into tears while praying the night before giving the command to go to war.

In speaking of the event, tears again came to his eyes. Later, when asked by reporters about the matter, he told of how he had been torn by the decision that had the potential to bring death in battle to thousands of enemies and allies alike. And once again, his eyes grew moist.

For many generations in Western culture, masculine tears have been thought of as a sign of weakness. Tears aren't part of the image of a "real man." But David was not ashamed to grieve publicly over the death of his beloved friend, Jonathan. Stern resolve in the face of danger may be a sign of manliness, but so are tears for the untimely end of a good person's life.
                                                                              —C. R. B.

THOUGHT TO REMEMBER

"Christ Jesus . . . has destroyed death and has brought life and immortality to light through the gospel" (2 Timothy 1:10).

DAILY BIBLE READINGS

Monday, Oct. 9—The Battle of Mount Gilboa (1 Samuel 31:1-7)

Tuesday, Oct. 10—The Rescue of Saul's Body (1 Samuel 31:8-13)

Wednesday, Oct. 11—The Amalekite Messenger (2 Samuel 1:1-16)

Thursday, Oct. 12—David's Lament (2 Samuel 1:17-27)

Friday, Oct. 13—Comfort in Times of Distress (Psalm 77:1-9)

Saturday, Oct. 14—Death of Saul and His Sons (1 Chronicles 10:1-7)

Sunday, Oct. 15—Burials and a Judgment Against Saul (1 Chronicles 10:8-14)

WHAT DO YOU THINK?

Both the Christian and the non-Christian experience real sorrow over the separation from their loved ones that comes with death. What comparisons and contrasts can we draw between the grief a Christian feels when a loved one dies and the grief of an unbeliever in a similar situation?

C. CLOSING WORDS OF SORROW (v. 27)

27. "How the mighty have fallen! The weapons of war have perished!"

How the mighty have fallen! This cry was the introduction of the lament for Saul (v. 19) and the lament for Jonathan (v. 25). Now it becomes the sorrowful conclusion of the entire elegy. How great and how sad is the contrast between mighty and fallen!

Obviously *the weapons of war* could not perish as the warriors themselves did, but the Hebrew word for *perished* can sometimes mean *lost*. (It is thus translated in 1 Samuel 9:3 and Ezekiel 34:16, for example.) Perhaps the weapons left on the battlefield were gathered up by the Philistines who came back to steal the clothing of the dead (1 Samuel 31:8). Thus the dead warriors and their weapons were both lost to Israel.

CONCLUSION

A. LOVE YOUR ENEMIES

Jesus said, "Love your enemies" (Matthew 5:44). Long before he said it, David was demonstrating what it means. The word *love* is used so loosely today that we hardly know what it means when we hear it, for there are many kinds of love.

Jesus was talking about the most unselfish kind of love—the kind called *agape*. It is a love that is seen in the life as well as felt in the heart. Jesus explained it thus: "Love your enemies and pray for those who persecute you" (Matthew 5:44).

How do you feel toward those who mistreat you, slander you, insult you, abuse you? If you examine your heart and find no love for them, then fill your life with loving deeds. Do good to them at every opportunity you see, and make some opportunities that you do not yet see. If you do this earnestly and conscientiously, you will be surprised by the love that begins growing in your heart.

B. SORROW AND HOPE

"How the mighty have fallen!" That refrain in our text sets the tone of the entire lament. We are hearing a wail of sorrow untouched by hope. Saul and Jonathan were lovely and pleasant in their lives, but now they are dead. They were swifter than eagles and stronger than lions, but now they are dead. They were benefactors of Israel, but now they are dead.

In other Scriptures, however, we see indications that David expressed a clear hope of life after death. Mourning for his own young son, he said, "I will go to him" (2 Samuel 12:23). Was he not hoping for a living reunion with his dead son? Then there is the triumphant conclusion of the best-loved of all David's songs: "I will dwell in the house of the Lord forever" (Psalm 23:6). Surely David did not think that *forever* would end with his death, did he?

Today, because of Jesus' resurrection, Christian teaching is bright with the hope, not only that the dead bodies will rise at the last day (1 Thessalonians 4:16, 17), but also that death brings the Christian into the presence of Jesus. Contemplating the possibility of his own death, Paul longed "to depart and be with Christ, which is better by far" (Philippians 1:23). He knew that to be absent from the body is to be present with the Lord (2 Corinthians 5:6-8).

When we lay our Christian loved ones in the grave, we grieve as David grieved for Saul and Jonathan; but we do not sorrow as others who have no hope (1 Thessalonians 4:13). Our grief is lightened because we know those loved ones are living now with Jesus, and we know that one day those bodies we lay in the graves will be raised alive, changed, and glorified to live forever with their spirits and with the Lord.

Discovery Learning

*This page contains an alternate lesson plan emphasizing learning activities. Classes
desiring such student involvement will find these suggestions helpful. The next page
is a reproducible activity page to further enhance discovery learning.*

LEARNING GOALS

After this lesson each student will be able to:

1. Summarize David's lament for Saul and Jonathan.

2. Tell how the expression of grief helps one to cope with a great loss.

3. Express his or her hope in Christ and how that hope helps in times of grief.

INTO THE LESSON

Write the following on a poster: "When loved ones die unexpectedly, people react with. . . ." Place the poster on the wall with a couple of markers nearby. Encourage each person to write on the poster a completion to the partial statement. When class starts, call attention to the statement as completed by the students. (*Possible answers include shock, anger, weeping, grieving, blaming God, feelings of hopelessness or helplessness.*) State: "Our hearts respond with many emotions when we face the loss of loved ones. Some of these David experienced, as we see in our lesson today. But he also responded in ways that we have not mentioned. Let's see how he reacted to the loss of two friends, Saul and Jonathan."

INTO THE WORD

Background. Begin the Bible study section of the lesson with a brief three- to five-minute lecture from 2 Samuel 1:1-16. State: "What is very interesting in this account is the totally unexpected response from David to the news of Saul's death. There was no rejoicing or celebrating now that he could officially become the king. There was no vindictiveness in spite of all that Saul had done to try to kill him. How did David respond to the news of Saul's death?" (*Tore his clothes, mourned, wept, fasted, and wrote a lament about his loss; he grieved.*) Summarize by saying, "David carried no grudge, no bitterness, no revengeful spirit toward Saul."

Distribute copies of the reproducible activity "Opportunities for Revenge" from the next page. Allow a few minutes for the learners to work through the activity, either individually or in small groups. Then ask, "Why did David refuse to try to kill Saul?" (*Saul was the Lord's anointed; David trusted the Lord to give him the kingdom in his own time and in his own way.*)

Lament for Saul and Jonathan. Prior to class prepare a summary on the chalkboard or a poster of David's lament for Saul and Jonathan. Use the three-section lesson outline: "Lament for Saul, 1:17-21"; "Praise for Saul and Jonathan, 1:22-24"; and "Lament for Jonathan, 1:25-27." Call attention to the outline as you summarize David's lament.

Ask a volunteer to read aloud 2 Samuel 1:17-27. Using the lesson commentary, identify the following terms or phrases: "Your glory, O Israel," "heights," "Book of Jashar."

What praises for Saul did David emphasize in his lament? (*Mighty, v. 19; successful warrior, v. 22; loved and gracious, swifter than eagles, stronger than lions, v. 23; increased the wealth of Israel, v. 24*) What praises for Jonathan did David emphasize in his lament? (*courageous, v. 22; swift and strong, v. 23; loving friend, v. 26*) State: "We've seen David's grief at the death of Saul. What we need to see is that his expression of grief in this lamentation helped him to cope with this loss."

INTO LIFE

When people today suffer the loss of a loved one, what do they often remember and talk about in their grief? (*They remember the things the loved one said or did and the good times that were shared together.*) State: "By remembering and talking about what our loved ones did or said, we express our grief over the loss. Such expression of grief helps us to cope with loss."

Have a volunteer read 1 Thessalonians 4:13-18 aloud. Ask the following questions: "How should Christians respond to the loss of loved ones?" (*We have sorrow and grief, but not in the same way as those who have no hope.*) "How does this passage help Christian people in their times of grief?" (*See v. 17.*) "How does the apostle Paul say to use this teaching?" (*See v. 18.*) State: "Death comes, but Christ overcomes!"

Give a copy of the reproducible activity "Paul's Memo Reminder" to each person. (See page 72.) Say, "Suppose the apostle Paul has found out that you have suffered the loss of a loved one and are grieving. So he writes a memo to you encouraging you to express your grief and your hope in Christ to help you in your time of grief. Use this sheet to write his memo to you."

Allow about five minutes for this activity. Then ask for volunteers to read their memos to the class. After several have done so, encourage all to keep their memos in their Bibles for future times of grief. Close the class in prayer, thanking God for the hope that we have in Christ.

Opportunities for Revenge

Twice David had an opportunity to kill Saul himself and to seize the throne. Look up the following Scripture passages and tell how each situation came about and how David responded in each case.

SCRIPTURE	SITUATION	RESPONSE
1 Samuel 24:1-22		
1 Samuel 26:1-25		
Why did David refuse to kill Saul?		

Paul's Memo Reminder

Memo

To: _____
(Write your name here)

From: Paul the Apostle

Re: Coping with loss

_____

_____

_____

_____

DAVID BECOMES KING OF ALL ISRAEL

LESSON 8

WHY TEACH THIS LESSON?

From the time Samuel anointed him as the next king of Israel, David must have longed for the promise to become reality. No doubt he first envisioned a peaceful transfer of power, perhaps working alongside Saul as a member of the royal court to "learn the ropes" before assuming the throne at Saul's death. When Saul turned hostile, that idea quickly proved untenable. So how would David become king? Only God knew, and David was content with that.

It is David's calm patience, even when the throne was in sight, that is most instructive to us. Like so many others, we are prone to run ahead of God's timing and to try to engineer an outcome to our liking. David waited on the Lord, and he became Israel's greatest king. If your learners would be great in God's kingdom, the path David took is still the best way.

INTRODUCTION

A. POWER STRUGGLES

Every four years the United States engages in a presidential election with much sound and fury, but the issues are decided by ballots, not bullets. It has been nearly a century and a half since America has experienced a bloody civil conflict. Some nations have survived much longer without civil war, but others have not been so fortunate. Early in the twentieth century, the bloody Bolshevik revolution was in the news; and now the Soviet empire that resulted has been broken up, though not without bloodshed. Most everyone who watches TV or reads the papers is aware of how civil war has engulfed several African nations in recent times.

Ancient Israel had its share of civil strife. Not long ago one of our lessons dealt with the judge named Gideon. When he died, one of his sons seized control by murdering seventy of his brothers and half brothers (Judges 9:1-6). But that was not the end of civil strife. It continued until the murderous son himself was killed in battle (Judges 9:50-56). Another civil war erupted when Israelites undertook to punish the men of Gibeah for an evil deed. Thousands of men were slain (Judges 19, 20).

Israel became a monarchy by popular demand and without a battle; but when the first king died, it took a long war (at least two years, according to 2 Samuel 2:10) before the next one was securely on the throne.

B. LESSON BACKGROUND

When Saul died in battle, along with three of his sons and numerous soldiers in his army, Israel suddenly found itself without a king. Apparently distressed over being without a leader, the rest of Saul's army fled. Civilians living near the battlefield also vacated their towns. Philistines moved in and took possession of that section of Israel (1 Samuel 31:1-7).

DEVOTIONAL READING:
PSALM 78:67-72
BACKGROUND SCRIPTURE:
2 SAMUEL 2–5; 1 CHRONICLES 11:1-3
PRINTED TEXT:
2 SAMUEL 2:1-7; 5:1-5

LESSON AIMS

After participating in this lesson, each student should be able to:

1. Tell how David became king of all Israel after Saul's death.

Oct 22

2. Explain how David's reliance on the Lord's leading was key to his becoming king.

3. Suggest a means by which to determine the Lord's leading in an area of his or her interest.

KEY VERSE

The LORD said to (David), "You will shepherd my people Israel, and you will become their ruler." —2 Samuel 5:2

Meanwhile David and his men were warring with Israel's enemies in the south (1 Samuel 30:1-20). Returning in victory to Ziklag, they were greeted by the news of Saul's defeat and death. David's lament for Saul and Jonathan formed the text of our lesson last week (2 Samuel 1:17-27). In today's lesson we consider events that transpired following Saul's death.

I. KING OF JUDAH (2 SAMUEL 2:1-4a)

David had been sincerely loyal to Saul even when the king had hated him and wanted to kill him. Now the king was dead; yet David still desired to determine God's will before he made any move to claim the throne.

A. CONSULTING THE LORD (v. 1)

1. *In the course of time, David inquired of the LORD. "Shall I go up to one of the towns of Judah?" he asked.*

The LORD said, "Go up."

David asked, "Where shall I go?"

"To Hebron," the LORD answered.

When we pray, we do not expect an instant answer in plain words. We wonder how David was able to get such a response. Our question is not answered in this text, but from other Scriptures we can suggest a possibility. On another occasion when David inquired of God, he asked the priest to bring the ephod (1 Samuel 30:7, 8). The ephod was a kind of jacket. The elaborate one worn by the high priest is described in Exodus 28:5-14. Attached to the ephod was the breastplate of judgment (Exodus 28:15-30), and in the breastplate were the Urim and the Thummim (Exodus 28:30). Israel's leaders were to receive answers from God by means of these (Numbers 27:21; Ezra 2:63; Nehemiah 7:65).

The words *Urim* and *Thummim* may be literally translated *lights* and *perfections*. We do not, however, know exactly what these objects were; and we do not know how they conveyed God's answer to a specific question. Still, it seems probable that David often inquired of the Lord with the aid of the priest and received the Lord's answer by means of the Urim and Thummim.

In any case, the main point of this verse is that David sought the Lord's will, accepted it, and followed it. Do we sometimes fail because we proceed in our own way without even looking for leading from the Lord? Even when we see his way, do we sometimes think we can improve on it? Or do we, like David, look for the Lord's will, find it, and follow it?

David was living in the territory held by the Philistines, where he had gone to escape the fury of King Saul. He had made peace with the Philistine king of Gath and had been permitted to live in Ziklag (1 Samuel 27:1-7). Now the Lord told him to go back to Israel—to the city of *Hebron*, which belonged to the tribe of *Judah*.

B. SETTLING AT HEBRON (vv. 2, 3)

2. *So David went up there with his two wives, Ahinoam of Jezreel and Abigail, the widow of Nabal of Carmel.*

Several years (perhaps as many as fifteen) had passed since David had been anointed to be king. His heart must have leaped with eagerness when the Lord told him to make his move and claim the kingship.

Also noted is the fact that when David moved to Hebron, he took his two wives, *Ahinoam* and *Abigail*, with him. Ahinoam is identified as being from *Jezreel*, probably to distinguish her from the wife of Saul (1 Samuel 14:50). Abigail had become David's wife following the death of her wicked husband Nabal (1 Samuel 25:39-42).

WHAT DO YOU THINK?

The lesson writer observes, "David sought the Lord's will, accepted it, and followed it." We cannot use the Urim and Thummim to do that, but how can we follow David's example?

Some may question how David's having two wives could square with the description of him as a man after God's own heart (1 Samuel 13:14). Although polygamy was not God's intention for man (Genesis 2:24), it was a common practice in the ancient Near East (other notable examples are Abraham and Jacob). It should be noted, however, that such polygamous situations in Scripture are always accompanied by strife and turmoil in the home.

3. David also took the men who were with him, each with his family, and they settled in Hebron and its towns.

When David was a fugitive, hiding in the desert to elude Saul, he was joined by other *men* who were discontent or dissatisfied for some reason (1 Samuel 22:1, 2). Eventually their number grew to about six hundred (1 Samuel 23:13). These men followed David during his flight from Saul, and now they and their families returned with him to *Hebron* and the smaller *towns* around it.

C. ANOINTED BY JUDAH (v. 4a)

4a. Then the men of Judah came to Hebron and there they anointed David king over the house of Judah.

In the last part of our text we shall see reasons why all Israel later accepted David as king (2 Samuel 5:1, 2). Those reasons must have seemed even more compelling to the *men of Judah*, David's own tribe; and those men likely saw other reasons as well. As Saul had become more and more unjust and cruel, they must have taken pleasure and pride in the clever way David was able to avoid the vindictive king. The farmers of Judah must have been grateful, because David and his six hundred men protected their flocks and herds by destroying their enemies in the south (1 Samuel 27:8, 9; 30:1-20). So it was likely with enthusiastic support that the *men of Judah came to Hebron and there they anointed David king over the house of Judah*. However, they could not speak for all the other tribes of Israel.

II. GRATITUDE EXPRESSED (2 SAMUEL 2:4b-7)

David's first act as king was not to fortify the city of Hebron or to increase the size of his army. It was to send a message of thanks to the brave men who had been devoted to Saul.

A. REASON (v. 4b)

4b. When David was told that it was the men of Jabesh Gilead who had buried Saul,

Gilead included the land east of the Jordan River that became Israel's possession. *Jabesh* was a town in that territory. In his first major military endeavor as king of Israel, Saul had saved this town from savage treatment by hostile neighbors (1 Samuel 11:1-11). At Hebron David learned that heroic men of that town had taken Saul's mangled body from the vindictive Philistines and had given it an honorable burial. (See 1 Samuel 31:8-13.)

B. BLESSING AND PRAYER (vv. 5, 6)

5. . . . he sent messengers to the men of Jabesh Gilead to say to them, "The LORD bless you for showing this kindness to Saul your master by burying him.

In last week's lesson we studied David's lament for Saul. It showed that David loved and respected Saul for what he had been and what he had done for Israel. Now once more David showed his admiration for Saul by his sincere pronouncement of blessing on the brave men who had risked their lives to show *kindness* to the dead king.

6. May the LORD now show you kindness and faithfulness, and I too will show you the same favor because you have done this.

WHAT DO YOU THINK?

David waited quite a long time after his anointing before he actually became king. How would you advise a person who expressed frustration over a long wait for God to answer a prayer or to fulfill a promise? How are Psalm 90:4 and Isaiah 26:8 helpful in this discussion?

DAILY BIBLE READINGS

Monday, Oct. 16—The Rival Kings (2 Samuel 2:1-11)

Tuesday, Oct. 17—Abner Defects to David (2 Samuel 3:6-21)

Wednesday, Oct. 18—Joab Murders Abner (2 Samuel 3:22-27)

Thursday, Oct. 19—David Mourns Abner (2 Samuel 3:28-39)

Friday, Oct. 20—The Death of Ish-Bosheth (2 Samuel 4:1-12)

Saturday, Oct. 21—David, King of Israel, Captures Jerusalem (2 Samuel 5:1-12)

Sunday, Oct. 22—David Rules Israel From Jerusalem (1 Chronicles 11:1-9)

David then asked that the Lord would reward those brave men by showing them *kindness and faithfulness*, or by dealing kindly and justly with them. David added that he too would *show* them *favor*, though he said nothing about how or when he would do so.

C. CHALLENGE (v. 7)

7. Now then, be strong and brave, for Saul your master is dead, and the house of Judah has anointed me king over them."

The king so respected among those in Jabesh was *dead*; David was now *king* of *Judah*. There seems to be here an implied plea for the people of Jabesh to support him in his kingship because he also respected Saul. Later, when David did become king of the entire nation, he would be in a position to reward Jabesh as he was promising to do (v. 6).

DEATH WITH DIGNITY

One of the results of the many twentieth-century advances in medical science has been a dramatic increase in life expectancy. New vaccines, medications, vitamins, surgeries, and therapies have been developed to treat ailments and diseases ranging from arthritis to heart disease to cancer. Millions of people have benefited.

There has also been what many call a "downside" to these advances. We can now extend a person's life into a weakened old age that may last for years. We are able to keep a body "alive" on life support systems long past the point at which he or she otherwise would have died.

One of the reactions to this has been a so-called "death with dignity" movement. Many people now write "living wills" to instruct family and physicians how they wish to be treated in the case of a terminal illness. They want to "die with dignity."

In our text, David commended the people of Jabesh Gilead for giving the body of Saul a dignified burial. While Saul's actions had often threatened David, he recognized that dignifying King Saul in his burial also dignified the kingship that David eventually assumed.

There is also a lesson here about treating the past in the "dignified" way God wants us to treat it. To minimize or detract from the work of our predecessors in our jobs or ministries minimizes us as well. God's kingdom is better served by letting the past "die with dignity."

—C. R. B.

III. KING OF ALL ISRAEL (2 SAMUEL 5:1-5)

During Saul's reign, his second in command was Abner, who served as general of the army. Following Judah's declaration of David as king, Abner proclaimed that Saul's son, Ish-Bosheth, was king "over . . . all Israel" (2 Samuel 2:8, 9). Abner's army soon clashed with David's army, led by Joab (2 Samuel 2:12-32). Thus began a "war between the house of Saul and the house of David" which "lasted a long time. David grew stronger and stronger, while the house of Saul grew weaker and weaker" (2 Samuel 3:1).

Eventually Abner must have realized that he was on the losing side of this war; nevertheless, the conflict continued. Then a quarrel took place between Abner and Ish-Bosheth. Abner decided to desert Ish-Bosheth and turn his support over to David. He urged the elders of Israel to do the same, and he himself went to David to express his personal support and his desire to "assemble all Israel" to "make a compact," or agreement, with David (2 Samuel 3:6-21).

Not long afterward, both Abner and Ish-Bosheth were killed by assassins. The nation was now leaderless (except for Judah); however, Abner had already persuaded most of its elders that it was in their interest to endorse David. Thus the stage was set for the events recorded in the last part of our text.

WHAT DO YOU THINK?

A cynic might accuse David of merely trying to "butter up" the men of Jabesh Gilead in order to gain their support for his rule over all Israel. But the biblical account indicates that David's message of thanks was a genuine reflection of his feelings. Why is it important to be sincere in our gestures of praise and gratitude?

HOW TO SAY IT

Abishai. Uh-BISH-ay-eye.

Ahinoam. Uh-HIN-o-am.

Calebite. KAY-leb-ite.

Carmel. CAR-mul.

ephod. EE-fod.

Gibeah. GIB-ee-uh.

Gideon. GID-ee-un.

Hebron. HEE-brun or HEB-run.

Ish-Bosheth. Ish-BO-sheth.

Jabesh Gilead. JAY-besh-GIL-ee-ud.

Jezreel. JEZ-ree-el or JEZ-reel.

Joab. JO-ab.

Macedonia. Mass-eh-DOE-nee-uh.

Nabal. NAY-bull.

Philistines. Fuh-LISS-teens or FILL-us-teens.

Thummim. THUM-im.

Urim. YOU-rim.

Ziklag. ZIK-lag.

A. TRIBES SPEAK (vv. 1, 2)

1. All the tribes of Israel came to David at Hebron and said, "We are your own flesh and blood.

All the tribes of Israel were David's kinsmen; all were one family; all were descended from Jacob, whose other name was Israel. Therefore it was fitting for David to be king over all of them.

2. In the past, while Saul was king over us, you were the one who led Israel on their military campaigns. And the LORD said to you, 'You will shepherd my people Israel, and you will become their ruler.'"

The people of Israel stated three reasons for making David king of the entire nation: he was "kin" to the people whom he would be ruling (v. 1); he had proved competent when he was a general in Saul's army and *led Israel on their military campaigns*; and most important, *the Lord* had designated him to be king.

B. ELDERS ANOINT (v. 3)

3. When all the elders of Israel had come to King David at Hebron, the king made a compact with them at Hebron before the LORD, and they anointed David king over Israel.

The reasons listed in verses 1 and 2 seemed compelling (of course, at this point there was no other candidate for the throne). Gladly *David . . . made a compact* (the Hebrew word is the word usually translated "covenant") with *all the elders of Israel*, thus ending the long war. The elders then *anointed David king over Israel*.

TWO KINGDOMS OR ONE?

On November 27, 1941, the State of Jefferson officially seceded from both Oregon and California. The secessionists blocked Highway 99 (the main north-south highway in California at the time) and announced that they would "secede each Thursday until further notice." Their agenda was to force the leadership in California into building some good roads in what was then a largely undeveloped part of the state. On December 4, 1941, a Crescent City judge was inaugurated as acting governor of the new "state." However, three days later the Japanese attacked Pearl Harbor; and California and the entire nation turned their attention to more important matters that affected a much larger number of people.

When David became king in Judah, the nation of Israel was divided. Conflict between supporters of David and supporters of Saul escalated. Eventually Abner and Ish-Bosheth, two leaders who could have created a separate kingdom, met violent deaths, and all Israel came to realize that David was the Lord's choice to rule all his people.

Sometimes, in both church and society, selfish concerns so grasp our attention that only a momentous or disastrous event can bring us to our senses. Then we may realize that a greater cause is more important than one that pleases only ourselves. —C. R. B.

C. DAVID REIGNS (vv. 4, 5)

4, 5. David was thirty years old when he became king, and he reigned forty years. In Hebron he reigned over Judah seven years and six months, and in Jerusalem he reigned over all Israel and Judah thirty-three years.

David was king of *Judah seven years and six months* before becoming king of all Israel; but that does not mean that the war mentioned in 2 Samuel 3:1 was that long. Ish-Bosheth was king only two years (2 Samuel 2:10). The time of fighting would have been at least that, and probably not much longer. Thus the seven and a half years includes time both before the fighting started and after it ended.

CONCLUSION

No one can doubt that David was a remarkable young man. It seems that his every effort was crowned with success. Whether it was to conquer a well-armed

WHAT DO YOU THINK?

One reason the people of Israel were willing to make David their king was the military leadership he displayed while serving under King Saul. How important is it, when selecting leaders for the church, to examine previous leadership experience?

[See 1 Timothy 3:1-7, especially verses 4 and 5.]

Today's lesson is illustrated by the same poster as was used for lesson 6. The shepherd boy, by the grace of God, has become king!

giant with a single stone or become king of all Israel, David did it. How could he be so successful all the time? Several factors can be cited.

A. GOOD GUIDANCE

There is a clue in the first verse of our printed text for today: "David inquired of the Lord." That same statement appears again and again in the record. When faced with some difficult enterprise, David asked for instructions, got them, and obeyed them. That may leave us feeling deprived. We have no high priest with Urim and Thummim to obtain God's instructions for us. We have no inspired prophet to tell us exactly what God says.

Yet how well do we follow the instructions we do have? Consider just one example. Jesus said, "Love your enemies and pray for those who persecute you" (Matthew 5:44). That is as plain as the instructions given to David, but how many Christians ignore it completely!

B. COURAGE TO ACT

If a lion or a bear threatens my sheep, I may be brave enough to wave something and yell. I am sure I will not catch the animal by the beard and kill him! But David did (1 Samuel 17:34-36).

If our church house is too small, or if one of our members is unemployed and hungry, or if we are not winning people to Christ, or if we have no positive influence in community affairs, is it because we do not know what is needed? Or is it because we are not daring and vigorous enough to do what needs to be done?

C. DETERMINATION TO DO RIGHT

It was right to protect a sheep from a lion and a bear. It was right to pursue a troop of raiders and rescue the captives they had taken (1 Samuel 30:1-20). It was not right to assassinate the man whom God had chosen as king, not even when he threatened David's life. On one occasion, King Saul led his troops out in the desert to catch David and kill him. In the darkness of a desert night, David and Abishai sneaked past the sentries and found Saul sleeping on the ground. "Let me pin him to the ground with one thrust of my spear," whispered Abishai. "I won't strike him twice." But David said no. It would not be right (1 Samuel 26:1-12).

When you are threatened, cheated, mistreated, injured, or insulted, you may hear an "Abishai" whispering, "Get even!" The Lord says, "It is mine to avenge; I will repay" (Romans 12:19). What do you say?

D. TRUST IN GOD

We ought to trust in God, but a word of caution is needed. Trust in God does not mean that we ought to be foolish. It was the devil who urged Jesus to jump from a pinnacle of the temple, trusting God to keep his promise that angels would bear him up. Jesus answered with another word from God: "Do not put the Lord your God to the test" (Matthew 4:5-7). To test God is to make him prove what he has said. It would be wrong for Jesus to make that wild leap just to prove that angels would bear him up—or just to draw a crowd.

How do we know what God wants us to do? We have the written Word that God has given, and we have the minds that God has given. With these we must discover what God wants us to do—and we must take care not to equate our own selfish desires with God's will.

Do you remember the praise given to the Christians in Macedonia who gave all they could, and even more than they could (2 Corinthians 8:1-3)? Many of us can do more than we think we can.

WHAT DO YOU THINK?

David's courage was one of his outstanding attributes. How can we develop courage?

PRAYER

Almighty God, we know your way is always right. Thank you for the Bible that reveals your way to us; thank you for minds to understand it. Father, we do want to do your will. Empower our minds to understand it rightly, we pray; and empower both minds and bodies to obey it faithfully. In Jesus' name. Amen.

THOUGHT TO REMEMBER

"Do not merely listen to the word, and so deceive yourselves. Do what it says" (James 1:22).

Discovery Learning

This page contains an alternate lesson plan emphasizing learning activities. Classes desiring such student involvement will find these suggestions helpful. The next page is a reproducible activity page to further enhance discovery learning.

LEARNING GOALS

After participating in this lesson, each student will be able to:

1. Tell how David became king of all Israel after Saul's death.

2. Explain how David's reliance on the Lord's leading was key to his becoming king.

3. Suggest a means by which to determine the Lord's leading in an area of his or her interest.

INTO THE LESSON

Prior to class draw a shield on a sheet of paper with a magic marker. Divide the shield into four sections and make enough copies for each person in the class. Begin this week's class by passing out one copy of the shield and a colored marker to each person. State: "To introduce today's lesson, I would like you to sketch in three sections of the shield your answers to three questions. Your sketches will portray various occupations. Here are the three questions: In section 1, when you were a child, what did you want to be when you grew up? In section 2, when you were older, what did others want you to be when you grew up? In section 3, as an adult, what have you become? You have three minutes to sketch your answers." When time is up, ask for volunteers to show their sketches and explain them to the class.

State: "Some of you decided to enter an occupation because that is what you wanted to do. Others chose a job because that is what someone else wanted you to do. Today's lesson centers on David's decision to go to Hebron to become king of Judah. Turn to 2 Samuel 2 to find out what guided his decision-making."

INTO THE WORD

Ask a class member to read 2 Samuel 2:1-7 and 5:1-5 aloud. To help students work through the lesson text and understand how David became king of all Israel, use the reproducible activity, "King of All Israel," from the next page. Make copies of the crossword puzzle and give one to every student. Allow ten minutes to complete the puzzle. Then go over each question to verify

answers located in the references at the end of the questions. State: "We've seen how David became king of all Israel after Saul's death. But what guided David's decision-making to go into Judah and become king?" (*The Lord's leading*)

INTO LIFE

Say, "After Saul died, David knew he was to be the next king. He had been anointed by Samuel in the midst of his brothers (1 Samuel 16:13). Rightfully, he could have gone up immediately to claim his position as king. But he chose not to do so. He would not take matters into his own hands. Instead, David relied on the Lord to guide his life. How did David's reliance on the Lord's leading affect his becoming king of all Israel?" (*He waited for the Lord to direct his life, telling him when to go and where to go. He trusted God's timing, waiting for the elders of Israel to come to him.*)

Ask, "What are some ways to determine the Lord's leading in our lives today?" (*Search Scripture for principles to apply; seek counsel and advice from godly Christians; pray for guidance of the Holy Spirit and submission to his will.*)

Write on the chalkboard the following general areas of life: Spiritual Life; Emotional Life; Social Life; Moral Life; Family Life; Church Life; Witnessing; Work/job. State: "As we look at these general categories, take a few moments to reflect on how regularly you follow the Lord's leading in these areas of your life. On a scale of 1 (never) to 5 (daily), rank how you regularly follow the Lord."

After a few moments, ask whether every answer were a "5." State: "All answers below '5' indicate a need for a greater sensitivity to following the Lord's leading. Now think of a specific example in one of these areas where you especially need the Lord's leading in your life. Take the shield you used at the beginning of the lesson. In section 4 sketch the answer to this question: 'What does God want you to become or do in that specific area where the Lord's leading is needed?'"

Allow a couple of minutes for reflection and for sketching. Then ask the class to form groups of three to share their sketches and to close the class in prayer for each other. Encourage them to pray for the Lord's leading and for their willingness to recognize and respond to his leading. (If you don't want to try to draw a shield, use the reproducible activity "Where He Leads Me" from the next page for this application point.)

"King of All Israel"

Read 2 Samuel 2:1-7 and 5:1-5 to help you fill in the blanks and complete the crossword puzzle below.

ACROSS

1. David was ____ years old when he became king. (5:4)
5. David was told to go to the city of ____. (2:1)
8. ____ were sent to convey David's blessing. (2:5)
12. The ____ of Israel anointed David king. (5:3)
13. The men of Judah ____ David king of Judah. (2:4)
14. Men of Jabesh ____ buried Saul. (2:4)

DOWN

2. All the ____ of Israel came to David. (5:1)
3. As king over Israel, David lived in ____. (5:5)
4. David blessed the men of Jabesh Gilead for their act of ____. (2:5)
6. David made a ____ with the leaders of Israel. (5:3)
7. David ____ of the Lord. (2:1) *
9. When Saul was king, the Lord said that David would become ____ over Israel. (5:2)
10. David ____ forty years. (5:4)
11. Ahinoam and ____ went with David. (2:2)

Where He Leads Me

In what specific area of your life do you think you need to pay closer attention to the Lord's leading? Suggest some specific action you can take this week to follow the Lord more closely than you have been doing.

GOD'S COVENANT WITH DAVID

WHY TEACH THIS LESSON?

"Great Is Thy Faithfulness" is my wife's favorite hymn. It's a good choice, and its title is the theme of our lesson today. In response to David's desire to build a temple for the Lord, God tells David that he himself will build David's house. He rehearses his faithfulness over the centuries and promises continued faithfulness to David's faithful house.

Ah, there's the rub. God's great faithfulness puts a demand on people. It made demands of David's house, and it makes demands on us. This lesson will encourage your students to remain faithful to the God whose great faithfulness they praise.

INTRODUCTION

The election season is quite a time for those of us who live in democratic societies. Candidates are seen everywhere—debating in town meetings, making promises on television, and flaunting their names on billboards. Nearly all of them want to improve public education, stop the flow of illegal drugs, and reduce taxes. And when we elect the people who have clamored for change, isn't it amazing to see how few changes occur?

What would you do if you became king? Imagine you were living back in the time when the king's word was law, when he had a powerful army to back him, and when there was no opposition party. What would you do first? Most likely you would do none of the things that David did.

A. WHAT DAVID DID

One of King David's first acts was to capture Jerusalem (or Zion, as it is also called) and make it his capital city. That city had been captured and burned long before by members of the tribe of Judah (Judges 1:8); however, Joshua 15:63 notes that they were unable to drive out the Jebusites who were inhabiting the city.

Jerusalem's location on a hill made defending the city much easier; in fact, the Jebusites living there when David captured Jerusalem had felt confident that he would never enter the city (2 Samuel 5:6, 7). In addition, Jerusalem was located near the border of Judah and Benjamin; thus David did not appear to be favoring either Judah (which had earlier made him its king) or the remainder of his kingdom to the north.

Another noteworthy achievement in the early stages of David's reign was not of his choosing; it was forced on him. The Philistines who had defeated King Saul gathered their forces in order to let the new king know that they were still the dominant people of the region. But David twice defeated them, and for a time they gave Israel no more trouble (2 Samuel 5:17-25).

DEVOTIONAL READING:
1 KINGS 8:15-21

BACKGROUND SCRIPTURE:
2 SAMUEL 7; 1 CHRONICLES 17

PRINTED TEXT:
2 SAMUEL 7:1-13, 16

LESSON AIMS

After participating in this lesson, students should be able to:

1. Recount the covenant that God made with David and the circumstances under which he made it.

2. State how this covenant is fulfilled in Jesus and in the covenant he has established.

3. Praise God for the blessings of grace given in the New Covenant.

Oct
29

KEY VERSE

Your house and your kingdom will endure forever before me; your throne will be established forever. —2 Samuel 7:16

B. LESSON BACKGROUND

Once David had gained firm control of his kingdom, he began to think about the ark of the covenant. For many years it had been separated from its original home in the tabernacle. The Philistines had captured it and taken it away (1 Samuel 4:1-11). But the ark brought only trouble to them, so they returned it to Israel. There it was kept in a private home (1 Samuel 5:1—7:2).

After becoming king, David wanted to bring the ark to Jerusalem. The first attempt ended in disaster because it was not carried properly (2 Samuel 6:1-11), but a second attempt was successful. The ark was then placed inside a tent that David provided for it (2 Samuel 6:12-19).

There was great rejoicing when Israel brought the ark to Jerusalem. David himself "danced before the Lord with all his might" (2 Samuel 6:14, 15) on this occasion. But soon the king began to have second thoughts. A portable tabernacle had been an appropriate place for the ark when Israel was traveling in the desert. It had been God's tent in the midst of the tents of his people. But now his people were living in houses. David himself was residing comfortably in a new palace in Jerusalem (2 Samuel 5:11). Shouldn't God's house be superior to David's?

I. PLANS FOR GOD'S HOUSE (2 SAMUEL 7:1-7)

A. DAVID'S THOUGHTS (vv. 1-3)

1. After the king was settled in his palace and the LORD had given him rest from all his enemies around him,

With God's help, David had become undisputed king of all Israel. He had defeated, not only the Philistines, but any other *enemies* that had threatened the nation. Eventually a point was reached where no immediate military action was required. David was able to relax *in his palace*.

2. . . . he said to Nathan the prophet, "Here I am, living in a palace of cedar, while the ark of God remains in a tent."

David's palace was probably of stone on the outside, but on the inside it was covered with *cedar* brought from faraway Lebanon with the help of King Hiram of Tyre (2 Samuel 5:11). No doubt David's house was among the finest in Jerusalem, yet God's house in the same city was only a *tent*!

3. Nathan replied to the king, "Whatever you have in mind, go ahead and do it, for the LORD is with you."

Without any additional words from David, *Nathan* knew what was in the king's *mind*. David wanted to build a house for the Lord—a house finer than the king's to serve as a fitting place for the ark of God. That sounded reasonable, so Nathan said, *Go ahead and do it.*

B. GOD'S THOUGHTS (vv. 4-7)

4. That night the word of the LORD came to Nathan, saying:

Without waiting to be asked, Nathan had given an uninspired opinion to David. Without waiting to be asked, *the Lord* now gave his own *word* to *Nathan*.

5. "Go and tell my servant David, 'This is what the LORD says: Are you the one to build me a house to dwell in?

The Lord spoke to Nathan, but the message was for *David*. The question sounds as if he were saying, "Not so fast! Let's think this over."

6. I have not dwelt in a house from the day I brought the Israelites up out of Egypt to this day. I have been moving from place to place with a tent as my dwelling.

Approximately four and a half centuries had passed since the Lord had *brought the Israelites up out of Egypt*. Through most of those centuries the people had been living in houses rather than in tents, but the Lord had never had a

WHAT DO YOU THINK?

According to 1 Kings 8:18, God was pleased with David's intention to build the temple even though he rejected David's offer. He told David, "You did well to have this in your heart." Why do you think God was pleased? How is David's desire a good example for us to follow?

WHAT DO YOU THINK?

In giving David an affirmative answer, Nathan gave what he assumed would be God's answer to David's request. He was right that God was pleased with David's heart, but he was wrong about God's intention for the temple. What can we learn from Nathan's mistake?

house of his own; that is, the ark that was the symbol of his presence had never been kept in a house built and dedicated for that purpose. Its home was in *a tent*—the tabernacle, which had been specially made for it and which had moved *from place to place* at the Lord's direction.

7. *Wherever I have moved with all the Israelites, did I ever say to any of their rulers whom I commanded to shepherd my people Israel, "Why have you not built me a house of cedar?"'*

Wherever . . . the Israelites went in their travels, the Lord had never *commanded* anyone in *Israel* to build a *house of cedar* for him. That was David's idea, not God's. That is not to say it was a bad idea. Later in this text we shall see that it was a good one, and acceptable; but its time had not yet come.

II. GOD'S BENEFITS (2 SAMUEL 7:8-11a)

As he often did when asking his people to obey him, God now paused to remind them that they were indebted to him for benefits many and great. In this case he spoke of benefits to David personally as well as those to the nation as a whole.

A. TO DAVID (vv. 8, 9)

8. *"Now then, tell my servant David, 'This is what the LORD Almighty says: I took you from the pasture and from following the flock to be ruler over my people Israel.*

David's rise from shepherd to king was not his own accomplishment; it was God's doing.

9. *"'I have been with you wherever you have gone, and I have cut off all your enemies from before you. Now I will make your name great, like the names of the greatest men of the earth.*

The Lord had been *with* David every step of the way from following sheep to leading people; the Lord had given him victory over *all* his *enemies*; the Lord had made him as famous as any of *the greatest men of the earth.*

COMMONERS OR ROYALTY?

In Scotland several years ago, a baby girl born to a poor family of tenant farmers was given the name "Princess." But five months after her birth, the Registrar General in Edinburgh told her parents that the British Crown possessed a sole right to use the name, and that the little girl's name would have to be changed.

The family appealed to Queen Elizabeth, who replied through an aide that she took no offense at the choice of name. However, the bureaucracy still denied the family the use of the name. Finally, when the girl was two and a half years old, the government relented and notified her grateful parents that Princess would be allowed to keep her name.

David also came from a humble background. God took this shepherd boy and called him to be "ruler over . . . Israel." In similar fashion, he took a nation of slaves and made them his "treasured possession" (Exodus 19:5). Today God can turn a person from the most humble of origins into a member of Heaven's royal family. He will do so for any who will turn to him through Jesus, the royal Son of David. —C. R. B.

B. TO ISRAEL (vv. 10, 11a)

10. *"And I will provide a place for my people Israel and will plant them so that they can have a home of their own and no longer be disturbed. Wicked people will not oppress them anymore, as they did at the beginning. . .*

This repeats the promise God had given long before, beginning with Abraham (Genesis 12:1; 17:8). He would give his *people* a land of their own; he would establish them securely in that land; he would protect them from their pagan neighbors. Of course, this abbreviated form of the promise did not cancel the

HOW TO SAY IT

Babylon. BAB-uh-lun.

Cyrus. SIGH-russ.

Hiram. HIGH-rum.

Jebusites. JEB-yuh-sites.

Philistines. Fuh-LISS-teens or FILL-us-teens.

Tyre. Tire.

WHAT DO YOU THINK?

God reminded David of how far he had brought him, from the humble life of a shepherd to the throne of Israel. God has brought some Christians from a life ravaged by alcoholism to one characterized by productive service to others. Some believers with musical talent once employed that talent in bars and nightclubs, but now they use it to lift fellow believers in worship to God. Other saints can testify that they were foul-mouthed and abusive, but they have learned to use their tongues to praise God and edify their fellow human beings. In these and countless other ways God has brought his people from wasted, selfish, purposeless lives into dynamic service for him. How worthwhile do you think it is to ponder occasionally how far God has brought us? Why?

conditions that were attached to it. The people of Israel were to have the promised land and its abundant blessings as long as they obeyed God. If they disobeyed, they would forfeit those blessings and would lose possession of the land. This is stated at length in Deuteronomy 28:15-68.

11a. "'. . . and have done ever since the time I appointed leaders over my people Israel. I will also give you rest from all your enemies.

God's *people Israel* had been afflicted by pagan tribes both before and during the time when God had appointed *leaders* in Israel, but now God had given David and his people *rest* from such affliction. This peaceful rest would continue if both the king and the people obeyed God's law.

III. TWO HOUSES (2 SAMUEL 7:11b-13, 16)

David was thinking about building for the Lord a house—a magnificent temple that would stand through centuries of time. The Lord was steering David away from that plan because he had a better plan. The Lord promised to build a house for David—not a building of stone and wood, but a household, a family, a dynasty that would rule forever!

A. DAVID'S HOUSE (v. 11b)

11b. "'The LORD declares to you that the LORD himself will establish a house for you:

David should give up the idea of building a house for the Lord; instead, he should consider the different kind of *house* the Lord was going to build for him.

B. DAVID'S SON (v. 12)

12. "'When your days are over and you rest with your fathers, I will raise up your offspring to succeed you, who will come from your own body, and I will establish his kingdom.

When David's life on earth was over, his son would take his place as king, and God would *establish his kingdom* as he had David's. Thus David's house, or family, would continue to rule.

C. GOD'S HOUSE (v. 13)

13. "'He is the one who will build a house for my Name, and I will establish the throne of his kingdom forever.'"

This verse makes it clear that God did not forbid the building of a temple, but he wanted it to be done by David's son. Another passage tells us the reason for this: David was a "warrior" who had "shed blood" (1 Chronicles 28:2, 3). This is not to say that David's activity in those battles was wrong. God approved David's wars and gave him victory in them, but still he preferred to have his temple built by Solomon, a man of peace. (The name Solomon means "peaceful.")

David himself was at peace when he considered building a temple: "The Lord had given him rest from all his enemies" (v. 1). David had subdued many nations around Israel (2 Samuel 8:1-14; 10:1-19; 12:26-31). Under his leadership, Israel reached great prominence, but not without a significant amount of fighting.

This helps us to see a practical reason for postponing the temple building until the reign of Solomon. Senior citizens in Europe and America can remember the troubled years of World War II. Hardly anything was built unless it was needed in the war effort. Most available material and manpower were directed to that cause. So it was during the years of David's wars, and for that reason the building of the temple was left for a man of peace to undertake during a time of peace. At that point, Israel's men could be released from any military duty, and Solomon could assemble an army of workers to help with the temple (1 Kings 5:13-16).

WHAT DO YOU THINK?

God promised David an everlasting kingdom, and David was awed by the promise. (See vv. 18ff.) What promises similarly bring you to respond with awe to God's wonderful nature?

David accepted God's decision without complaint. Later he received plans for the temple from the Lord, and then passed them on to Solomon to use in carrying out the task (1 Chronicles 22:2-5; 28:11-19).

Then the Lord added, *I will establish the throne of his kingdom forever*, thus adding *forever* to the promise of verse 12. Certainly Solomon would not last forever, but the throne of his kingdom would. Because of the sins of the people, there were times when that promise seemed uncertain. At one point the people of Israel were captives in Babylon, having no king of their own. Then they were ruled by the Persians and later by the Romans.

"But when the time had fully come" (Galatians 4:4), Jesus was born. He was a son of David, but, more importantly, he was the Son of God. He rules a kingdom "not of this world" (John 18:36), "that will never be destroyed, . . . but . . . will itself endure forever" (Daniel 2:44).

And thine house and thy kingdom shall be established for ever before thee: thy throne shall be established for ever.

D. DAVID'S KINGDOM (v. 16)

16. "'*Your house and your kingdom will endure forever before me; your throne will be established forever.*'"

David's little *kingdom* of Israel would one day culminate in the great eternal kingdom of Jesus Christ. David's descendants would rule over the land of Israel; David's descendant, Jesus, would rule *forever* over the eternal kingdom—the "Israel of God" (Galatians 6:16).

Today's visual illustrates verse 16 of the printed text. Discuss how Jesus is the ultimate fulfillment of this promise to David.

AN EVERLASTING EMPIRE

In 1968 Mohammed Reza Pahlavi (Mo-*ham*-id Rih-*zah* Pah-luh-vee), the Shah of Iran, proclaimed himself "King of Kings, Light of the Aryans." In 1971 he declared a celebration of the twenty-five hundredth anniversary of the Persian Empire. The festivities lasted four days and cost one hundred million dollars! The guest list included six hundred dignitaries from sixty-nine nations.

Only eight years later, the fabled empire and the reign of this "King of Kings" lay in ruins. Muslim fundamentalists overthrew the Shah in 1979 and installed their religious leader, Ayatollah Khomeini (Eye-uh-*toll*-uh Ko-*may*-nee), as the sole ruler of their nation. The Shah had fancied himself to be ruler of an empire that had begun with Cyrus the Great in the sixth century B.C. (although he would have been hardpressed to prove that connection). At any rate, the "timeless empire" that he envisioned came crashing down, and the nation was thrown into chaos.

This has been the fate of most of the world's kingdoms. Regardless of the pretensions of their leaders, nations rise and then fall, and other governments supersede them. So the promise to David that his throne would be established *forever* was startling news indeed. The New Testament reveals to us that Jesus Christ was the Son of David who has established this everlasting empire—a spiritual kingdom that is not of this world. What a privilege is ours to be citizens of such a kingdom!   —C. R. B.

CONCLUSION

This week we are thinking of "God's Covenant With David." In our time the word *covenant* is not used very much, except in religious contexts. It means an agreement, a contract. Usually a contract between two persons confers certain benefits on each and makes certain demands of each. The Bible records several contracts between God and man. God has a glorious record of keeping every contract; man has a dismal record of breaking every one.

A. GOD'S COVENANTS

God's covenant with Adam provided a beautiful garden home with abundant food. It required Adam to dress and keep the garden and to abstain from

WHAT DO YOU THINK?

Human beings falter in living up to their responsibilities according to God's covenants, but he has always been and always will be faithful. "If we are faithless, he will remain faithful, for he cannot disown himself" (2 Timothy 2:13). How does it help you to meditate on the fact of God's faithfulness?

PRAYER

Almighty God, we are grateful for your grace. We were lost and helpless on the way of death until you found us, holding out your New Covenant and offering to forgive our iniquities and to remember our sins no more. With full hearts we praise you, Father. With all our hearts we promise to walk in your way, and with all our hearts we plead that you will forgive our failures. In Jesus' name, amen.

THOUGHT TO REMEMBER

We can choose death—or life.

eating the fruit of one certain tree. Adam broke the covenant and lost his home in the garden.

God's covenant with Noah offered safety in a devastating flood and the assurance that there would never be such a flood again. Noah kept this covenant. He believed God, obeyed him, and praised him.

The covenant with Abraham required him to trust God, to leave home and family, and to journey to an unknown land. It promised a great nation of descendants who would have a permanent home in that unknown land. Abraham was one of the better human covenant keepers; however, his record was not flawless. (See Genesis 12:10-20; 16:1-12.)

The covenant with the people of Israel promised them a permanent home in that same land that had been promised to Abraham. It promised abundant harvests, healthy livestock, and prosperity. It promised divine protection from enemies. But it also required them to obey the law that God gave at Sinai. In past lessons we have seen how abysmally the people failed in keeping that law, and how terribly they suffered from the invasions of enemies when divine protection was withdrawn. We shall see still more of their covenant breaking in lessons to come.

Why did all of those ancient covenants fail to produce the desired results? God was not at fault: he has never failed to keep a covenant. Every one of those covenants was shattered by the sins of men. History verifies the words of Scripture: "All have sinned" (Romans 3:23). Our own experience verifies it as well.

What we need, then, is a covenant that can overcome sin—one by which sinners can be forgiven, come into God's kingdom, and enjoy the blessings he is longing to give. That is exactly what God promised through his prophet Jeremiah (Jeremiah 31:31-34). And that is exactly what God now offers through Jesus, the Son of David and the Son of God.

B. GOD'S NEW COVENANT

"The wages of sin is death" (Romans 6:23). Therefore all mankind was doomed to die, from Adam down to me. That doom was of man's own doing, but God was not content to have it so. "For God so loved the world that he gave his one and only Son, that whoever believes in him shall not perish but have eternal life" (John 3:16).

To put it in simple terms, Jesus died in my place, in your place, and in the place of all the sinners of the world. So you and I and all the sinners of the world can escape the death we deserve and have everlasting life.

That does not mean that every sinner will automatically live forever. No one is saved from death against his will. Each person still can choose, and most people choose to die (Matthew 7:13, 14).

That seems absurd, doesn't it? Why would anyone choose to die? One reason is that the same covenant that offers everlasting life to us also makes some demands on us. If we want Jesus to be our Savior, we must also take him as our Lord. In the everyday language of our time, we must make him our boss, we must obey him, we must do his will rather than our own. Some people balk at that.

What happens if we disobey God after we have accepted his covenant and promised to obey him? That depends on our attitude. "If we confess our sins, he is faithful and just and will forgive us our sins and purify us from all unrighteousness" (1 John 1:9). But if we arrogantly cling to our own way when we know it is contrary to God's way, "no sacrifice for sins is left, but only a fearful expectation of judgment and of raging fire that will consume the enemies of God" (Hebrews 10:26, 27).

The choice is ours.

Discovery Learning

This page contains an alternate lesson plan emphasizing learning activities. Classes desiring such student involvement will find these suggestions helpful. The next page is a reproducible activity page to further enhance discovery learning.

LEARNING GOALS

After this lesson students will be able to:

1. Recount the covenant that God made with David and the circumstances under which he made it.

2. State how this covenant is fulfilled in Jesus and in the covenant he has established.

3. Praise God for the blessings of grace given in the New Covenant.

INTO THE LESSON

Begin this week's lesson by projecting an overhead transparency sheet made from the reproducible activity "Contract" from the next page. Say: "In the next minute and a half, please brainstorm as many different types of contracts that you can." As suggested contracts are called out, write them down to form a list under the word "kinds." (*Purchase of house or car; loan at the bank; marriage; job contract; remodeling contract; selling of a bond; U.S. savings bond; will; IRA.*) State: "We are all very familiar with contracts. Many of us have signed contracts before. Now, I'd like us to think about the various parts of a contract. As you think of the parts that make up a contract, call them out and we'll put them under the word, "Parts." (*Names; date; time frame; signatures; promise or benefit; responsibility or conditions; an agreement.*)

State: "A contract is a binding agreement between two or more parties. Normally it contains promises and responsibilities made and accepted by all the participants. One party promises to provide certain goods or services when the other party fulfills certain responsibilities. Our lesson today centers on a contract or covenant made by God as the party of the first part with David and Israel as the parties of the second part. Let's turn to 2 Samuel 7 to see what promises and responsibilities are included."

INTO THE WORD

Ask a volunteer to read aloud 2 Samuel 7:1-13, 16. Ask the following questions.

1. What were the circumstances that led to God's covenant with David? (*It was a time of peace, during which David could "rest from all his enemies." David had built a palace for himself, but the ark of God was still in a tent. David wanted to build a house for the ark of God.*)

2. Why did Nathan initially encourage David to build a house for the Lord? (*God had been with David, delivering him from all his enemies.*)

3. Describe the transition that the Lord brought about in David's life. (*From following sheep to being the ruler of God's people, Israel.*)

State: "Now that we've understood a little of the background of God's covenant with David, let's focus on the promises that the Lord gave David in this covenant." For this next question, divide the class into groups of three. Give to each group a large sheet of blank newsprint from an easel pad, along with a marker. Ask, "What promises did the Lord give to David in this covenant?" Allow about seven minutes for the groups to locate the promises and to write them on the paper.

When each group is finished, ask a member of the group to stick the paper on the wall so all can see. (*Possible answers: provide a permanent dwelling for Israel free from wickedness and affliction, vv. 10, 11; establish David's house forever, vv. 11, 16; give David a son who would build the temple after David's death, vv. 12, 13; David's son's kingdom and throne would endure forever, v. 16.*) State: "David accepted these promises without complaint. They had an immediate, contemporary application through David's son Solomon. But they also spoke of an eternal kingdom, an eternal throne, a house that would last forever—a partial glimpse of the New Covenant that Jesus established."

INTO LIFE

Read Luke 1:31-33 and ask, "How is God's covenant with David fulfilled in Jesus and the New Covenant?" (*Jesus is a Son of David; he inherits the throne of David; his kingdom is forever.*) Divide the class into three groups of equal size. Assign one of the following passages of Scripture to each group: Matthew 26:28; Romans 11:27; Hebrews 9:15. Ask each group to tell how its passage describes this New Covenant. Allow ten minutes for discussion; then ask for answers to be reported to the class. (*Jesus' blood sealed the New Covenant; he is its mediator; the key provision is the forgiveness of sins.*)

Make a transparency of the reproducible activity "New Covenant Blessings" from the next page. Assign the passages evenly to the students and have them read the verses and answer this question within their groups: "What are the blessings of grace given in the New Covenant?" Write suggested answers on the transparency. (*Laws in their minds and on their hearts; all will know the Lord in this covenant; wickedness is forgiven; sins remembered no more.*)

"Contract"

List as many kinds of contracts as you can think of in the left column below. In the right column list the various parts of a contract. How are these like the covenant God has given us? How are they different?

KINDS OF CONTRACTS   PARTS OF A CONTRACT

New Covenant Blessings

What are the blessings of grace given in the New Covenant? Look up the following Scriptures and list as many blessings as these verses suggest to you.

Luke 22:20 _____

1 Corinthians 11:25 _____

2 Samuel 23:5 _____

Hebrews 8:6-13 _____

Jeremiah 31:31-34 _____

Jesus Loves Me

Write a new stanza for the song "Jesus Loves Me." Each line has seven syllables; the last syllables of lines 1 and 2 rhyme, and the last syllables of lines 3 and 4 rhyme. Paraphrase some of the blessings cited above to come up with your stanza.

DAVID AND BATHSHEBA

LESSON 10

WHY TEACH THIS LESSON?

Why is it that so much good in a person's life can be blotted from memory because of one bad deed? Think of the politicians whose careers have been wrecked by revelations of personal indiscretions. Think of Christian leaders whose ministries have been obliterated because of some moral wrong. Or think of David, a man after God's own heart, whose reputation is forever tarnished because of his affair with the beautiful Bathsheba.

Everyone, it seems, knows about this event from David's life—even those who know little else about him. When a television movie was made of his life, was it: "David, a Man After God's Own Heart" or "David, Sweet Psalmist of Israel"? No, it was "David and Bathsheba"! Sinners use the event to excuse their own sins. Saints are troubled by its sullying of an otherwise noble reputation.

This lesson has many points of application. Perhaps one of its most powerful is the reminder of how much harm one bad decision can create. If your students remember that in the throes of temptation, your time today will have been well spent.

INTRODUCTION

A. LEARNING THE HARD WAY

Summer vacation was in full swing. Sammy, Joe, and Mike were fishing in a little creek under tall sycamore trees, but the fish showed no interest in their worms. The boys were bored and ready for some other way to pass the time.

Then the Smoot boys came down the road. They were men, really, but everyone called them boys. On horseback, they were driving a small herd of cattle to the north range. Suddenly the three fishermen thought of something more exciting to do. They knew where the Smoot watermelon patch was, screened from the road by a patch of tall corn. Quickly they brought a big melon to the shade of a tree by the road. Opening it with a pocket knife, they scooped out the insides with grimy fingers until they were "full up to the ears," as Sammy put it. Then they stretched out on the ground for a nap.

Suddenly they were roused by the sound of hooves. The Smoot boys were coming back. The kids started to hurry back to the creek, but the riders pricked their horses into a gallop. "Split up!" yelled Sammy. "They can't catch us all."

The three ran in three different directions, but two were quickly overtaken. Mounted behind an older rider, each was taken to his home, where his father found a big switch and used it. (This was many years ago, when a switch was the accepted way of teaching a boy not to steal.)

Meanwhile, Sammy had escaped and headed straight for home, but he was nervous. He had no appetite for supper. Mom put a hand on his forehead to see if he had a fever. All night Sammy was restless. In the morning he only picked at his breakfast. Mom talked about taking him to town to see the doctor. At that point, Sammy burst into tears and sobbed out the story of the stolen watermelon. Dad found a big switch. After a painful whipping, Sammy felt better. At noon he was ready for a hearty meal.

DEVOTIONAL READING:
NUMBERS 15:30, 31

BACKGROUND SCRIPTURE:
2 SAMUEL 11:1—12:25

PRINTED TEXT:
2 SAMUEL 11:2-5, 14-18, 26, 27;
12:13-15

LESSON AIMS

After participating in this lesson, each student will be able to:

1. Give the details of David's adultery and cover-up, as well as the terrible consequences that followed.

2. Explain the lessons that this account teaches us about the nature of temptation and the consequences of sin.

3. Suggest a specific step that he or she can take to resist a particular temptation.

NOV
5

KEY VERSE

Why did you despise the word of the LORD by doing what is evil in his eyes? —2 Samuel 12:9

Did an act of secret wrongdoing ever make you miserable? Did you feel better after the wrong became known? David had such an experience. It was so memorable that he wrote an account of it in one of his songs (Psalm 51). Now, some three thousand years later, his sin and his song are before us still.

B. LESSON BACKGROUND

After David became king of all Israel, the Philistines assembled their forces in order to challenge his rule. David soundly defeated them (2 Samuel 5:17-25). Later victories over enemy nations are recorded in 2 Samuel 8:1-14. Then the Ammonites (to the east of Israel) enlisted the help of Arameans from the north to fight against Israel, but David's forces routed both Ammonites and Arameans until the Arameans were afraid to help the Ammonites any more (2 Samuel 10).

The war with the Ammonites was put on hold through the winter months, but resumed in the spring. This time David stayed in Jerusalem, putting Joab in command of the army. Again Joab defeated the Ammonites, who took refuge in their chief city, Rabbah, where Joab initiated a siege (2 Samuel 11:1).

I. ADULTERY (2 SAMUEL 11:2-5)

During this time David lived at ease in his palace in Jerusalem. It is certainly worth observing that in the past David had gone to battle with his men, as noted in the previous section. Now he was relaxing in Jerusalem "at the time when kings go off to war" (2 Samuel 11:1). Had David been where he was supposed to be, and had he been doing what he was supposed to be doing, perhaps the following sorry incident never would have occurred.

A. TEMPTATION (v. 2)

2. *One evening David got up from his bed and walked around on the roof of the palace. From the roof he saw a woman bathing. The woman was very beautiful . . .*

In the crowded city of Jerusalem, every house, including the king's *palace*, had a flat *roof* that could be used as we use a porch or patio—as a pleasant place to relax in the open air. Perhaps David had just awakened from a nap. As he *walked* across the *roof*, he caught sight of a *beautiful* neighbor taking her bath. She may have been in an enclosed courtyard of the house where she lived, with walls around her but no roof overhead. David found the sight very attractive.

B. INVESTIGATION (v. 3)

3. *. . . and David sent someone to find out about her. The man said, "Isn't this Bathsheba, the daughter of Eliam and the wife of Uriah the Hittite?"*

Who was that lovely lady next door? David *sent someone to find out about her.* The investigator came back with the lady's name, her father's name, and her husband's name. Perhaps he also brought the information that her husband was miles away east of the Jordan, serving in the army that was besieging Rabbah.

C. SIN (v. 4)

4. *Then David sent messengers to get her. She came to him, and he slept with her. (She had purified herself from her uncleanness.) Then she went back home.*

This time *David sent* more than one messenger. If the woman seemed reluctant to come, they could bring her anyway. The text gives no hints about her willingness or reluctance. Some students suppose that she was a virtuous woman who objected vigorously, though she was too dignified to be dragged kicking and screaming to the king. Others believe that she staged her bath with the deliberate purpose of seducing the king. Either explanation is mere speculation, however.

WHAT DO YOU THINK?

The sight of Bathsheba either undressed or nearly so was the beginning of David's problems. Today nudity or scanty attire is common in our society. How can Christians avoid the potential temptations to lust and adultery?

The text focuses on David, and as for him, the record is clear. While for most of his life he did what was right in God's eyes, what he did on this occasion was wrong. "The thing David had done displeased the Lord" (v. 27).

We are told that before committing this act, Bathsheba *purified herself from her uncleanness*. This indicates that she had just become ceremonially clean, according to the law of Moses, following the time of uncleanness associated with the menstrual cycle (Leviticus 15:19-30). This also makes it clear that she was not already pregnant by Uriah when David *slept with her*.

LUST AND POWER

Former U. S. Secretary of State Henry Kissinger was once asked how a man of his rather plain appearance could date so many beautiful women. He replied, "Power is the ultimate aphrodisiac." Power seems to make many men feel as if they are invulnerable, and, in keeping with Kissinger's observation, many women seem to be drawn to men of power like moths to a flame. When those two forces come together, sin is frequently the result.

So it was with David. He reigned as king of Israel during a time when rulers could command absolute obedience from their subjects. We should not be surprised that he was tempted to use his position of power to satisfy his own lusts or that Bathsheba—if she acted willingly—responded to his invitation.

More important to us is how *we* conduct ourselves when opportunity and desire coincide. God still expects us—whether king or commoner—to exercise control over both our position and our passion.   —C. R. B.

D. CONSEQUENCE (v. 5)

5. The woman conceived and sent word to David, saying, "I am pregnant."

Bad news! Bathsheba was *pregnant*. Her adultery could not be denied. According to the law of Moses, both she and David should be put to death for this act (Leviticus 20:10). She simply relayed the news to the king without further comment. Now the matter was his to deal with. What would he do?

II. MURDER (2 SAMUEL 11:14-18, 26, 27)

David's first thought was to make it appear that Bathsheba's baby belonged to her husband, Uriah. So he sent for Uriah and encouraged him to go home to his wife. If he spent a night with her, everyone would assume that he was the father of Bathsheba's child.

But Uriah was a loyal soldier. He thought it was not right for him to enjoy a night with his wife while his comrades were risking their lives on the field of battle. He spent two nights with David's men in Jerusalem, then returned to the siege (2 Samuel 11:6-13). So David was still left with his dilemma.

A. PLANNED (vv. 14, 15)

14. In the morning David wrote a letter to Joab and sent it with Uriah.

This was the *morning* after Uriah's second night with the king's men. He was now going back to take his place with the troops besieging Rabbah. David gave him *a letter* to carry *to Joab*, commander of those troops.

15. In it he wrote, "Put Uriah in the front line where the fighting is fiercest. Then withdraw from him so he will be struck down and die."

It was murder that David ordered—murder disguised to look like death in battle, but still murder. Both David and his commander Joab were battle-hardened veterans. The loss of a few soldiers seemed to them a small thing. It happened in every conflict; it was the price of victory. Now it was to be the price of hiding the king's adultery. *Uriah*, who had shown such devotion to the king,

---

HOW TO SAY IT

Absalom. AB-suh-lum.
Ammonites. AM-un-ites.
Arameans. Air-uh-ME-uns.
Bathsheba. Bath-SHE-buh.
Eliam. Ih-LYE-am.
Hittite. HIT-ite.
Joab. JO-ab.
Philistines. Fuh-LISS-teens or
    FILL-us-teens.
Rabbah. RAB-buh.
Uriah. You-RYE-uh.

WHAT DO YOU THINK?

David hoped to make Bathsheba's pregnancy appear legitimate by calling Uriah home to spend a night or two with his wife. What are some devices people use today to cover up sin?

was to be assigned to a place of intense *fighting* and then abandoned during the fighting to increase the likelihood of his death.

B. Accomplished (vv. 16, 17)
16. So while Joab had the city under siege, he put Uriah at a place where he knew the strongest defenders were.

Joab had *had the city under siege* long enough to know that the *strongest defenders* were posted in a certain place, probably to guard an important gate leading into the city. Israel's troops were all around the city so that no one could go out or come in; but they were too far away to be reached by arrows from the wall. Now Joab sent *Uriah* and some other men nearer the wall at the point where those defenders were stationed. We are not told what the mission of the little group was supposed to be. Possibly they were to draw the defenders out from the city so that the other troops could swarm in and overpower them.

17. When the men of the city came out and fought against Joab, some of the men in David's army fell; moreover, Uriah the Hittite died.

Those *men of the city* whom Joab knew about did venture out to fight with the small detachment of his troops that had approached the wall. During the fighting *some of the men* of Israel were killed, and *Uriah* was one of them.

C. Reported (v. 18)
18. Joab sent David a full account of the battle.

Joab promptly *sent David a full account of the battle*. He thought the king would be angry when he learned that some men had been killed because they had recklessly ventured near the wall; but he knew what would soothe that anger. The messenger must report, "Also, your servant Uriah the Hittite is dead." That, after all, was the king's objective. So King David sent back to Joab a message of assurance, telling him not to feel badly about the loss (vv. 19-25).

D. Hidden (vv. 26, 27)
26. When Uriah's wife heard that her husband was dead, she mourned for him.

Bathsheba's mourning could not have been very long (we may wonder how sincere it was), but she did go through the motions.

27. *After the time of mourning was over, David had her brought to his house, and she became his wife and bore him a son. But the thing David had done displeased the LORD.*

David's scheme seemed to have succeeded: he had a beautiful *wife* to add to those he already had, and soon she *bore him a son.* In fact, Bathsheba seems to have become David's favorite wife. He even bequeathed his kingdom to one of her sons (not the one mentioned here). Was she really the true love of his life? Or did he feel obligated to favor her because he had killed her husband? We do not know.

But the thing David had done displeased the Lord. Thus David's scheme yielded a greater harvest of grief than of joy. We shall see a bit of that before we finish this lesson. Besides that, David himself was displeased with what he had done. We shall see a bit of that as well.

III. PARDON AND PUNISHMENT (2 SAMUEL 12:13-15)

The Lord sent Nathan the prophet to rebuke David's sin. The prophet came with a parable. He told of a rich man who had plenty of lambs in his flock, but stole the one pet lamb of a poor man to prepare for dinner. When David angrily declared that such a man ought to be put to death, Nathan turned that judgment back on the king himself: "You are the man!" David had wives enough of his own, yet he had stolen the one wife of poor Uriah. To make matters worse, he had murdered Uriah himself. King though he was, David would not escape punishment. From his own family evil would rise against him, and his own wives would be stolen (2 Samuel 12:1-12). That startling condemnation brought forth David's confession that we see in the last section of our text.

A. CONFESSION AND PARDON (v. 13)

13. *Then David said to Nathan, "I have sinned against the LORD."*

Nathan replied, "The LORD has taken away your sin. You are not going to die."

An evil king might have had Nathan beheaded, but David was a good king who had done an evil deed. When the fact of David's sin was plainly set before him, he humbly confessed it. Nathan then gave the welcome news: *The Lord has taken away your sin.* What that meant is explained in the next statement: *You are not going to die*; that is, David was not to be put to death immediately, as he himself had said he ought to be (v. 5).

B. PUNISHMENT PROMISED (v. 14)

14. *But because by doing this you have made the enemies of the LORD show utter contempt, the son born to you will die."*

God's forgiveness does not remove all the evil consequences of an evil deed. David would not die immediately, but *the son* of his adultery would. The reason for this is given: *because by doing this you have made the enemies of the Lord show utter contempt.* David had tried to hide his sin, but in time it would become known. The Lord's people would grieve (as we do upon reading of this incident) because the good king had done such a terrible deed. But the Lord's enemies would sneer. They would say, "What kind of a god is your God, that he blesses a king who does such a wicked thing?" However, when the child died, everyone would realize that the Lord was not blessing David's adultery. Thus the blasphemy of the enemies would be stopped.

C. PUNISHMENT GIVEN (v. 15)

15. *After Nathan had gone home, the LORD struck the child that Uriah's wife had borne to David, and he became ill.*

"Why did you despise the word of the Lord by doing what is evil in his eyes?"

Today's visual cites 2 Samuel 12:9. This verse reminds us that the Lord sees our sin, even as he saw David's, no matter how well we cover it up.

DAILY BIBLE READINGS

Monday, Oct. 30—David and Bathsheba's Affair (2 Samuel 11:1-5)

Tuesday, Oct. 31—David's Plot (2 Samuel 11:6-13)

Wednesday, Nov. 1—Uriah's Murder (2 Samuel 11:14-27)

Thursday, Nov. 2—The Prophet Nathan's Story (2 Samuel 12:1-6)

Friday, Nov. 3—The Judgment on David (2 Samuel 12:7-15)

Saturday, Nov. 4—Death of One Son, Birth of Another (2 Samuel 12:16-25)

Sunday, Nov. 5—Atonement for Sins (Numbers 15:27-31)

PRAYER

Thank you, Father, for the sobering lesson we have learned today. How often a wrong that seems trivial leads to another wrong, and thus wrong follows wrong until the throng of wrongs yields disaster! Thank you for the Holy Bible that shows us the right way. May we have clear eyes to see that way and stout hearts to follow it. In Jesus' name. Amen.

THOUGHT TO REMEMBER

Do right.

So ends our printed text, but verse 18 adds that *the child* died after a week of sickness. Of course, that was not the end of David's punishment. The dire prediction of verses 11 and 12 remained to be fulfilled.

CONCLUSION

The record of David's sin comes to us from centuries past, but it bristles with warnings for the present. Let's note some of them.

A. WRONG LEADS TO WRONG

David committed adultery, and then he tried to hide his guilt by committing murder. That was some thousand years ago, but only a few years ago a robber ran into the woods with a policeman in hot pursuit. The robber stopped behind a big tree until the pursuer came close, then shot him at point-blank range.

Very few of us have committed murder, but how many of us have done some trivial wrong and then lied about it? Whatever happened to the honest practice of admitting your wrong and taking the consequences?

B. WRONG IS HARD TO HIDE

Perhaps you have heard the saying, "Murder will out." It may not prove to be true in every case; however, on the day these lines were written, authorities in our area announced the solution of a murder committed eighteen years ago.

The messengers who took Bathsheba to David must at least have suspected his adultery. Joab knew about Uriah's murder, and perhaps some other soldiers did as well. Surely someone would talk, and the wrongs of the king would become so widely known that they would give the Lord's enemies an excuse to sneer both at David and at the Lord. Isn't it better to admit your wrongdoing than to have it exposed by others? Of course, it is better still not to do wrong.

"You may be sure that your sin will find you out." That is an oft-quoted saying from God's Word (Numbers 32:23). If we do manage to take some dark secrets with us to our graves, "we must all appear before the judgment seat of Christ" (2 Corinthians 5:10).

C. WRONG HAS LONG-TERM RESULTS

When David was guilty of adultery, how could he be stern with a son who raped his half-sister (2 Samuel 13:1-19)? When he failed to punish that crime, how could he be stern with the girl's full brother when he killed the rapist (2 Samuel 13:20-29)? The killer did flee to a foreign land for a while (2 Samuel 13:37-39), but then was received back into the family (2 Samuel 14).

That killer was Absalom, a wild and willful young man who loved to be the center of royal attention (2 Samuel 15:1). He wanted to be king. It seems that he had a charming personality and no regard for truth or right. Secretly he won the hearts of many people and turned them against the king. When he thought he had followers enough, he led them in armed revolt, and David had to flee from Jerusalem (2 Samuel 15–17).

But David was still masterful in warfare. Though driven from his capital, he marshaled his loyal troops for a counterattack. The revolt was crushed. Twenty thousand men were killed, and Absalom was among them. Victory was complete, but the death of Absalom made David's triumph hollow (2 Samuel 18).

Thus Nathan's words in 2 Samuel 12:10-12 began to be fulfilled—and there was more to come. How many times David must have wished he had never seen that woman taking a bath!

Discovery Learning

This page contains an alternate lesson plan emphasizing learning activities. Classes desiring such student involvement will find these suggestions helpful. The next page is a reproducible activity page to further enhance discovery learning.

LEARNING GOALS

After this lesson each student should be able to:

1. Give the details of David's adultery and cover-up, as well as the terrible consequences that followed.

2. Explain the lessons this account teaches us about the nature of temptation and the consequences of sin.

3. Suggest a specific step that he or she can take to resist a particular temptation.

INTO THE LESSON

Secure a video tape of the popular Disney film *Pinocchio*. Play a segment of the tape to begin your class session. Begin at the point where Pinocchio is sent to school. Show Pinocchio's meeting with the fox "Honest John" and his sidekick. See how they lure Pinocchio off the right path and into "show business." Stop the tape at the point where Jiminy Cricket sees Pinocchio perform and decides the puppet has done all right for himself.

Discuss how we are all tempted in similar ways. We intend to do right, but something or someone distracts us. We might even think we have done all right—for a while. Then turn the tape on again. Play it until Pinocchio is locked into a cage by his new owner. Point out that sin eventually shows itself to be a trap or prison.

Say, "In our lesson today we will consider the actions of one whom God considered exceptional but who gave in to temptation and committed a grievous sin. From this tragic chapter in David's life we will learn how we can seek righteousness and be careful in our actions and thoughts.

INTO THE WORD

Ask a volunteer to read aloud 2 Samuel 11:2-5. Write the words *Sight, Search, Summons,* and *Surrender* on the chalkboard. (Or use the reproducible activity from the next page. You may choose to photocopy it on to an overhead transparency and project it, make handouts to distribute to your students, or both.) Discuss how David fell into temptation and how there were deliberate steps taken. *Sight:* Do you think David just happened to be at that place at that time? Why or why not? *Search:* While "sight" may have been an accident, David did not stop the situation there. *Summons:* David found out Bathsheba was someone's wife but he sent for her anyway. *Surrender:* The last step in this sequence was adultery resulting in pregnancy. How might the story have been different had Bathsheba not conceived? Discuss, "At what point did 'temptation' become 'sin?'"

Summarize the events of 2 Samuel 11:6-13. Uriah, Bathsheba's husband, became an innocent victim in the next set of steps. Ask a volunteer to read aloud 2 Samuel 11:14-18, 26, 27; then give a brief lecture, noting the following three points. *Deception:* Discuss David's plan to set Uriah up to be killed. *Description:* Discuss Joab's report. Note the involvement of other innocent parties. *Displeasure of God:* God does not condone sin—even from favorite children. Note that not much is given along the way concerning God's displeasure—just a short statement. However, David's actions resulted in more grief than joy.

Finally David woke up. Summarize the events of 2 Samuel 12:1-12; then ask a third volunteer to read aloud 2 Samuel 12:13-15. Discuss the following steps in the conclusion of this situation. *Contrition:* Before confession was made, there had to be a realization that wrong had been done. With this realization David felt remorse. *Consequences:* Every sin has consequences. In this case the son conceived would die. Discuss the severity of this consequence.

INTO LIFE

Remind the students that David was a good person, but he was not perfect. Discuss how we may be like David or different from him.

Ask, "How does modern culture provide for the 'sight' step in various forms and various media?" When confronted with tempting sights or other tempting situations, we may react in different ways. Discuss how we exercise our will compared to the pull or influence of Satan.

Ask the students to list ideas that might help them to avoid temptation and sin. These might include the following:

1. Be more discerning in what we watch or read. Remember the little song that says, "Be careful little eyes what you see. . . ."

2. Be aware of seemingly innocent circumstances that lead to more serious consequences.

3. Pray for God's constant care.

4. Develop a habit of thinking through our actions to their conclusions.

5. Develop associations to help us avoid temptations.

In conclusion, urge the students to give careful thought to their actions, realizing that there are consequences to everything we do, and resolve to apply God's guidance.

Step by Step

Read 2 Samuel 11:2-5. Tell how David's sin grew with each step listed on the chart below. In the right column, tell how one today might similarly be tempted and/or commit sin. (The sin you cite may not be sexual in nature but grows progressively even as David's sexual sin grew.)

STEP	DAVID'S SIN	CONTEMPORARY SIN
Sight		
Search		
Summons		
Surrender		

Now read 2 Samuel 11:14-18, 26, 27. Tell how David's sin grew even more with the involvement of other parties, either as victims or as unwitting accomplices.

STEP	DAVID'S SIN	CONTEMPORARY SIN
Deception		
Description		
Displeasure of God		

Finally, read 2 Samuel 12:13-15. Tell how David's situation was resolved, and how our sins today might similarly find resolution.

STEP	DAVID'S SIN	CONTEMPORARY SIN
Contrition		
Consequences		

SOLOMON SUCCEEDS DAVID

LESSON 11

WHY TEACH THIS LESSON?

Near the end of last week's text we read the sad words, "But the thing David had done displeased the Lord." What a refreshing contrast to see at the conclusion of today's text, "The Lord was pleased."

That, in a nutshell, is the reason we teach any lesson, the reason we study the Bible at all—to learn, and thus to do, what pleases the Lord.

The occasion for the Lord's pleasure in today's lesson is Solomon's seeking God's wisdom as he begins to reign as king. Seeking God's wisdom is always appropriate—whether one is launching a new career or enterprise, or continuing in one in which he or she has been involved for many years. Encouraging your learners in that pursuit is your goal in this lesson today.

INTRODUCTION

"The king is dead. Long live the king." When I first noticed that expression in my reading, it seemed silly. If the king was dead, he could not live at all. But Dad explained that this was an actual saying from history.

In a country that has a king, said Dad, almost everyone knows who the next king will be. Usually he is the oldest son of the present king. They call him the crown prince. Some time after a king dies, a ceremony takes place during which the crown prince receives the crown; but in reality he is king as soon as his predecessor dies. When a herald goes out to announce the death of the king, he also shouts good wishes to the new king: "The [old] king is dead. Long live the [new] king."

A. ISRAEL'S NEW KING

In the early years of Israel's experience with kings, the transition from king to king was not so smooth. The first king was Saul. After he died in battle, the general of his army attempted to make Saul's son Ish-Bosheth the next king. But the tribe of Judah made David their king, and war ensued between Judah and the other tribes. Not until seven and a half years later, when Ish-Bosheth and his general were dead, did David become king of all Israel (2 Samuel 5:5).

It appears that at some point during his reign, David's desire for his son Solomon to succeed him became known; however, not everyone was pleased with that choice. An older son, Absalom, gathered followers enough to stage a powerful revolt in an attempt to make himself king. But the revolt failed, and Absalom died during the conflict (2 Samuel 15–18).

Then a man named Sheba led another revolt, but he failed to gather enough followers to start a war. When Joab led his troops out to capture him, he took refuge in a walled city. Far from providing a refuge for him, the people of the city cut off his head and threw it over the wall to Joab (2 Samuel 20:1-22).

B. LESSON BACKGROUND

When David was feeble with age, there was yet another attempt to take the throne by force. It was led by Adonijah, another son older than Solomon. He even enlisted the help of Joab, longtime general of David's army. They staged a

---

DEVOTIONAL READING:
PSALM 119:10-19

BACKGROUND SCRIPTURE:
1 KINGS 2:1-4; 3:1-15; 1 CHRONICLES 29:22-25; 2 CHRONICLES 1:1-13

PRINTED TEXT:
1 KINGS 2:1-4; 3:3-10

LESSON AIMS

After participating in this lesson, each student will be able to:

1. Tell about David's final counsel to Solomon and of Solomon's discerning request of the Lord.

2. Explain why God's wisdom is needed regardless of one's stage in life.

3. Make a commitment to pray daily for wisdom to live a life that honors the Lord.

Nov
12

KEY VERSE

So give your servant a discerning heart to govern your people and to distinguish between right and wrong. —1 Kings 3:9

celebration and announced that Adonijah was king. But David, though old, was not too feeble to respond to this challenge. Before Adonijah's celebration was over, David's supporters staged a similar celebration and announced that Solomon was king. Adonijah's supporters then deserted him. (Perhaps they remembered what had happened to Absalom's revolt!) So Adonijah's effort failed, and Solomon became king while David was still living (1 Kings 1:5-53).

I. ADVICE FOR A KING (1 KINGS 2:1-4)

We are not told how old Solomon was when he became king. David called him "young and inexperienced" (1 Chronicles 22:5). He called himself "a little child" (1 Kings 3:7). Some Bible students think he was no more than twenty, perhaps even younger. But Solomon was not a "spoiled brat" like Adonijah, who had always been allowed to do as he pleased (1 Kings 1:5, 6). Solomon himself tells of how he had been taught to follow the path of wisdom by his father David (Proverbs 4:3-9). Our text includes some of David's final instructions to Solomon.

A. BE STRONG (vv. 1, 2)

1. When the time drew near for David to die, he gave a charge to Solomon his son.

David's body was weakened by age (1 Kings 1:1), but his mind was alert, well informed, and capable of responding to a challenge, as Adonijah quickly learned (1 Kings 1:5-53). After officially making Solomon king, David realized he would not live much longer. He therefore gave Solomon some final words of advice.

2. "I am about to go the way of all the earth," he said. "So be strong, show yourself a man. . .

Older opponents of young Solomon might look on him as a mere boy; but he must *be strong* and *show* himself *a man*, taking the responsibility of government and ruling well. David had foiled Adonijah's attempt to seize the throne, but Solomon would have to deal with his continued plotting (1 Kings 2:13-25).

Solomon would also have to deal with Joab. This man, who was David's nephew, had long been a loyal and capable general of Israel's army; but he had killed Absalom in open defiance of David's order (2 Samuel 18:5, 9-15). He had murdered two capable military men who were his rivals for the position of commander (2 Samuel 3:22-27; 20:4-10). He had supported Adonijah, thus giving Solomon reason to question his loyalty. It was time for him to pay for his crimes (1 Kings 2:5, 6, 28-34).

B. OBEY GOD (v. 3)

3. ". . . and observe what the LORD your God requires: Walk in his ways, and keep his decrees and commands, his laws and requirements, as written in the Law of Moses, so that you may prosper in all you do and wherever you go . . .

The first responsibility of a strong king must be to obey *the Lord*, who is far stronger and wiser. We need not pause to look for fine distinctions among the words *decrees, commands, laws,* and *requirements.* All of these are *written in the Law of Moses,* and all of that law must be obeyed. Only by obeying it faithfully could the king hope to *prosper* in everything he did.

C. THINK OF THE FUTURE (v. 4)

4. "And that the LORD may keep his promise to me: 'If your descendants watch how they live, and if they walk faithfully before me with all their heart and soul, you will never fail to have a man on the throne of Israel.'"

The Lord had promised David that his *descendants* would rule in *Israel* forever (2 Samuel 7:8-16). David understood that to mean that they would continue to

WHAT DO YOU THINK?

David's exhortation to Solomon, "Be strong," is an exhortation that Paul frequently directed to his readers. (See 1 Corinthians 16:13; Ephesians 6:10; 2 Timothy 2:1.) In one of these cases the exhortation was, "Be strong in the Lord," and in another it was, "Be strong in the grace that is in Christ Jesus." Why do Christians need to take this exhortation to heart?

[Encourage your students to suggest specific challenges for which divine strength is needed, and discuss ways to encourage and build up one another in the face of such challenges.]

rule *if* they obeyed God, not if they disobeyed. Fresh in his memory were the disasters that had followed his own disobedience, and he warned Solomon to avoid such disasters by faithful obedience.

GOOD ADVICE

Robert Fulghum has been called America's most popular philosopher. He is perhaps best known for his book, *All I Really Need to Know I Learned in Kindergarten*. A book reviewer called Fulghum's advice "as universal as air." *All I Really Need to Know. . .* has been followed by several bestsellers, including one with the catchy title, *It Was on Fire When I Lay Down on It.*

Fulghum's fame apparently started with a simple list of advice from his kindergarten days. "Share everything. Play fair. Don't hit people. Put things back where you found them. Clean up your own mess. Don't take things that aren't yours. Say you're sorry when you hurt somebody," etc. The list was widely reproduced; a kindergarten teacher sent it home with her students, and the mother of one of them sent it to a New York literary agent. The agent asked Fulghum for more and sent all of the material to Random House. Within a decade, Fulghum had become a literary success on the basis of his homespun (and very practical) advice.

David's advice to Solomon was more profound than any we may get from the pop philosophers of our time. His counsel came, not from kindergarten, but from a lifetime of walking with God (and sometimes *not* doing so!). He had learned that godliness is the only sure way to succeed in the areas of life that really count.   —C. R. B.

II. SOLOMON'S DEVOTION (1 KINGS 3:3, 4)

The rest of chapter 2 records the death of David and the vigorous way in which Solomon secured his kingship, executing the treasonous Adonijah and Joab. Now we consider Solomon's attitude as he began his reign.

A. LOVING OBEDIENCE (v. 3)

3. Solomon showed his love for the LORD by walking according to the statutes of his father David, except that he offered sacrifices and burned incense on the high places.

Solomon showed his love for the Lord. At this point his heart was committed to obeying and serving God. He showed his love by living according to the *statutes* given him by *his father David, except that he offered sacrifices and burned incense on the high places.* God's law was given before Israel reached the promised land, but it prescribed that any sacrifices and incense offered in the promised land should be offered in the place where God would "choose . . . to put his Name there" (Deuteronomy 12:5-7). The *high places* were places of worship scattered throughout the country. This one exception to Solomon's devotion is a foreshadowing of the more grievous errors that would mar his later reign.

At this time the ark of the covenant (the special symbol of God's presence) was in Jerusalem, while the tabernacle, with the altar on which God had prescribed that all sacrifices be made, was located at Gibeon. It is unclear to us now which of those sites was the proper location for sacrifices. The lack of a central place of worship seems also to have left some question in the minds of the Israelites about the proper place for offering sacrifices (1 Kings 3:2). Even Samuel offered sacrifices at a high place (1 Samuel 9:11-14, 19, 25). It appears that the use of these high places was tolerated by God as long as such locations had no ties to pagan worship.

Later Solomon would build a temple in Jerusalem, and God would clearly designate it as the central place of worship. That will appear in our lesson next week. Once the temple was completed, worship at the high places was no longer tolerable. Even so, the practice persisted. Several of the later kings of

HOW TO SAY IT

Absalom. AB-suh-lum.
Adonijah. Ad-o-NYE-juh.
Amaziah. Am-uh-ZYE-uh.
Azariah. Az-uh-RYE-uh.
Gibeon. GIB-ee-un.
Ish-Bosheth. Ish-BO-sheth.
Jehoash. Jeh-HOE-ash.
Joab. JO-ab.
Jotham. JO-tham.
Sheba. SHE-buh.

Today's visual illustrates Solomon's opportunity while it challenges students to consider their own priorities and opportunities.

WHAT DO YOU THINK?

Solomon observed that God had shown kindness to his father David. What are some lessons in wisdom that he could have learned from David's example—both good and bad?

[Discuss the value of imitating the lives of the faithful who have gone before us, perhaps even noting specific individuals in your church who can serve as examples. (See 1 Corinthians 11:1; Hebrews 13:7.) If you have mature adults in your class, you should challenge them to consider the impact of their own example on younger believers.]

WHAT DO YOU THINK?

Solomon referred to himself as "a little child." The prophet Jeremiah later referred to himself as "a child" (Jeremiah 1:6). But while the Lord was pleased with Solomon's prayer, he was displeased with Jeremiah's. Why do

Judah are noted as faithful except for their failure to remove the high places (e.g., Jehoash, 2 Kings 12:2, 3; Amaziah, 2 Kings 14:1-4; Azariah, 2 Kings 15:1-4; and Jotham, 2 Kings 15:32-35).

B. GENEROUS OFFERINGS (v. 4)

4. The king went to Gibeon to offer sacrifices, for that was the most important high place, and Solomon offered a thousand burnt offerings on that altar.

Probably the *high place* at *Gibeon* was considered *most important* because the tabernacle was there. The proper procedure for making *burnt offerings* is described in Leviticus 1. Such an offering might be a bull, a sheep, or a goat. Presenting *a thousand* of them was generous—even for a *king*.

III. GOD'S GIFT TO SOLOMON (1 KINGS 3:5-10)

The value of Solomon's gift to God was great, but the value of what God was about to give to Solomon was beyond any counting or measuring. As is often said, "You can't outgive God."

A. UNIQUE OPPORTUNITY (v. 5)

5. At Gibeon the LORD appeared to Solomon during the night in a dream, and God said, "Ask for whatever you want me to give you."

Fiction abounds in stories of a fairy, genie, or other imaginary creature who offers to grant one wish to a fortunate mortal. But we are reading factual history, and it records that *the Lord appeared to Solomon . . . in a dream* and told him to make one request.

B. PAST GIFTS ACKNOWLEDGED (v. 6)

6. Solomon answered, "You have shown great kindness to your servant, my father David, because he was faithful to you and righteous and upright in heart. You have continued this great kindness to him and have given him a son to sit on his throne this very day.

Before voicing any request, Solomon expressed his appreciation for what God had done for *David* his *father*. With rare exceptions, David had been *faithful . . . and righteous and upright in heart.* Because of this, God had *shown* to him *great kindness.* The word rendered *great kindness* here is a rich Hebrew word, sometimes translated *mercy, loving-kindness, goodness,* or *favor.* Each of these words is an apt description of what God had shown toward David.

God's own summary of what he had done for David is found in 2 Samuel 7:8, 9: God had raised David from a shepherd to a king; God had been with him continually; God had given him victory over his enemies; and God had made him famous. Furthermore, God had promised that David's descendants would rule after him and that David's house and his kingdom would be established forever (2 Samuel 7:12, 16). Here Solomon acknowledged that God was beginning to keep that promise by giving the *throne* to him, David's *son.*

C. SOLOMON'S SMALL ABILITY (v. 7)

7. "Now, O LORD my God, you have made your servant king in place of my father David. But I am only a little child and do not know how to carry out my duties.

The phrase *a little child* reflects Solomon's awareness of his inadequacy to rule Israel. At the same time, he came to the throne well prepared: undoubtedly his natural talent was great, and the teaching David had given him was no small thing. It included general instruction about doing right (Proverbs 4:3-9), and it provided practical advice for dealing with specific cases (1 Kings 2:1-9). Still,

Solomon was right in recognizing that his ability was not enough to *carry out* the formidable challenge before him.

D. SOLOMON'S BIG TASK (v. 8)

8. *"Your servant is here among the people you have chosen, a great people, too numerous to count or number.*

Some students estimate that there were more than six million *people* in Israel at this time. How could a new king know the needs of all of them, much less their wants? There were twelve tribes, every one of them motivated to some degree by tribal pride and jealousy. How could a king mold them into one nation under God? Solomon was wise enough to know that he was facing a fearsome task.

E. SOLOMON'S REQUEST (v. 9)

9. *"So give your servant a discerning heart to govern your people and to distinguish between right and wrong. For who is able to govern this great people of yours?"*

A *discerning heart!* Living in the royal palace, Solomon needed heartfelt sympathy to appreciate the concerns of the millions of Israelites who lived in ordinary houses and toiled at ordinary tasks. He needed wisdom enough to understand the many regulations written in the law. He needed the practical good sense to apply those regulations fairly in all circumstances.

Who is able to govern this great people of yours? No one is able to do that; it is too much for any human being. Desperately the king needed wisdom from above, and it was to his credit that he realized what he needed.

THE RIGHT KIND OF HEART

A relatively few people with severe heart disease are fortunate enough to receive a heart transplant—one of the most remarkable achievements of modern medicine. But Greg Hamilton is one of very few people around the world who have had *two* heart transplants. It was not by design—several hours into the first operation it was discovered that Hamilton's blood type had been misidentified. Thus he was receiving a heart of the wrong blood type, which created a strong likelihood of his body's rejecting the new heart. So the surgeons finished the job, and Hamilton was placed at the top of the list to receive another new heart. A week later he got it, and less than two weeks after the second surgery he walked out of the hospital on the road to recovery.

When Solomon became king of Israel as a young man, he had much going for him. Not the least of his blessings was God's gift of the right kind of heart. While we know that "a discerning [or understanding] heart" does not refer to the literal heart that beat within Solomon's chest, it is a phrase that is pregnant with meaning. An attitude that reacts to every situation by first turning to God for wisdom is a blessing that all of us should seek.

No matter how low or high our station in life, such a "heart" should be among our deepest desires. This is all the more true if we are placed in positions of leadership in society or in the church. —C. R. B.

F. THE LORD'S PLEASURE (v. 10)

10. *The Lord was pleased that Solomon had asked for this.*

A selfish man in Solomon's position might have asked for long life for himself and sudden death for his enemies or for riches that would astound the world. But Solomon was not selfish. His request was not for himself; it was for the multitude of Israelites who depended on him for good and just government. Gladly the Lord gave Solomon what he *asked*: Solomon's wisdom became the wonder of the world and of the ages. There had never been, and never would be, anyone like him.

you think God did not respond in the same way to these two incidents, and what lessons can we learn from the two of them?

WHAT DO YOU THINK?

Solomon asked for a discerning heart. We, especially if we are in positions of leadership, should offer a similar prayer. What can we do to prepare ourselves for God's answer? How can we prepare ourselves for wisdom concerning God's will? How can we prepare ourselves for wisdom concerning the needs of people?

WHAT DO YOU THINK?

One of the most striking aspects of Solomon's prayer at Gibeon is its unselfishness. He asked for help in serving his people, not for personal advantages. One of the titles that has been given to Jesus is, "the Man for others." He lived his life in total unselfishness. He refused to employ his miraculous powers to benefit himself but ministered with them to the blind, the lame, the lepers, and others in need. As John 17 demonstrates, he gave priority to praying for others. Each of us should aim to be "a man for others" or "a woman for others." How can we gain the wisdom to lead a totally unselfish life—to be a man or woman "for others"?

And the Lord gave to Solomon what he had not requested: riches and honor unmatched among the kings of the world. Long life? That depended on Solomon. He could have it if he would continue to obey God and his law (vv. 11-14).

CONCLUSION

We have been reading of Solomon the young king. We have seen how he pleased God with a choice he made. But what about us? Can we apply this lesson to ourselves? Can we please God as Solomon did?

A. UNSELFISHNESS

God was pleased with Solomon's unselfish request. True, he asked for wisdom for himself, but he did so for the benefit of his people. He wanted to be wise enough to govern them well.

Unselfishness is one of the cardinal principles of Christian living. "Nobody should seek his own good, but the good of others" (1 Corinthians 10:24). If I work for wages, I am concerned about getting enough pay to live on; but I am no less concerned about the good of my employer, giving him the full value of every dollar he pays me. If I am in a business of buying and selling, I am eager to make a profit; but I am no less eager to see that the transaction is good for the buyer. This is also true if I am engaged in manufacturing. Every good business transaction is good and profitable both to seller and to buyer. With such business God is pleased.

B. OBEDIENCE

Solomon understood that God had given David great mercy and kindness because David had made obeying God a priority (1 Kings 3:6). Likewise Jesus urges us not to be overly anxious about such items as food, clothing, and shelter. These will be provided for us if we give first priority to seeking God's kingdom and his righteousness—that is, making him our King, being obedient subjects, and doing his will (Matthew 6:25-33).

Our obedience will not earn our place in Heaven, but it will please God and bring us a reward. Obeying Jesus is like building a house on the rock. Such a house will stand through all the storms that may come (Matthew 7:24, 25).

C. KEEPING ON

Looking at the paragraph in the Bible following our printed text, we see God's warning to Solomon. The king could have a long life if he kept on obeying God (1 Kings 3:14). But God's great kindness is withdrawn from one who turns away and stops obeying him. In just two weeks we shall see how horribly Solomon failed to "keep on keeping on."

This emphasis on faithfulness is just as clear in the New Testament. Jesus said that one who fails to keep on in the Christian way is not fit for the kingdom of God (Luke 9:62). James said, "Blessed is the man who perseveres under trial, because when he has stood the test, he will receive the crown of life that God has promised to those who love him" (James 1:12). The writer of the letter to the Hebrews urged us to "hold unswervingly to the hope we profess" and to "run with perseverance the race marked out for us" (Hebrews 10:23; 12:1). The apostle Paul wrote, "Stand firm. Let nothing move you. Always give yourselves fully to the work of the Lord, because you know that your labor in the Lord is not in vain" (1 Corinthians 15:58).

"Let us not become weary in doing good, for at the proper time we will reap a harvest if we do not give up" (Galatians 6:9).

PRAYER

Our Father and our God, we are humbled by the responsibilities you have given to us as your people. We ask of you the wisdom we need to do our task well, and we pledge our best efforts to follow your leading now and always. In Jesus' name. Amen.

THOUGHT TO REMEMBER

Keep on keeping on.

Discovery Learning

This page contains an alternate lesson plan emphasizing learning activities. Classes desiring such student involvement will find these suggestions helpful. The next page is a reproducible activity page to further enhance discovery learning.

LEARNING GOALS

After this lesson each student will be able to:

1. Tell about David's final counsel to Solomon and of Solomon's discerning request of the Lord.

2. Explain why God's wisdom is needed regardless of one's stage in life.

3. Make a commitment to pray daily for wisdom to live a life that honors the Lord.

INTO THE LESSON

Distribute copies of the reproducible activity "Wise or Otherwise" from the next page. Allow students three or four minutes to mark their responses. Ask them to share some of the wise things they did in their youth. If they are willing, ask them to tell about some of the foolish things they did when they were young. Ask them to tell about some of the more humorous foolish things they have done as adults. Finally, ask them to report on the wise things they have done as adults.

In studying this lesson, we should learn that we do make wise decisions and that the greatest of these is to devote our lives in unselfish obedience to God.

INTO THE WORD

Briefly describe the lesson background; then read the printed text. Divide the class into three groups and provide each group with its assignment. Have each group select a spokesperson who will report back to the class. (Answers are provided below for teacher's assistance.)

Group 1: Advice Given (1 Kings 2:1-4)

1. Who is giving advice? (*David.*)

2. What are the relative ages of the one giving advice and the recipient? (*David is very old, and Solomon is very young.*)

3. Why was the advice being given? (*To encourage obedience.*)

4. What advice was given? (*Be strong; obey God; think of the future.*)

Group 2: Advice Followed (1 Kings 3:3, 4)

1. To whom did Solomon show respect? (*David, God.*)

2. Did Solomon follow advice precisely? (*No; he sacrificed and burned incense on the high places. Discuss how Solomon may have been trying to show love to God but was falling short. Note the influence of social pressure.*)

3. How generous were Solomon's offerings? (*A thousand was very generous, even for a king.*)

4. This occasion happened before Solomon received a special measure of wisdom from God. How would you evaluate the wisdom he showed? (*Solomon displayed a mature wisdom in listening to David and seeking to honor the Lord.*)

Group 3: God's Gift (1 Kings 3:5-10)

1. What was the gift? (*Wisdom.*)

2. Even before God granted his wish, Solomon showed wisdom. How? (*a. followed David's advice, b. expressed appreciation to God for blessings to David, his father, c. humbly asked God for the greatest gift possible.*)

3. Was the request selfishly motivated? Why or why not? (*There is no hint that it was. God would not likely have honored a selfish request.*)

Allow about ten minutes for the groups to work; then have each group share its responses. Discuss the answers given and be sure adequate information is reported on each.

INTO LIFE

Ask these groups to consider the need for wisdom in present-day situations. Ask group 1 to defend the proposition, "Young people need God's wisdom to get along in life more than any other age group." Group 2 is to suggest reasons to support the idea that "Adults in the twenty- to fifty-year-old age range need God's wisdom to get along in life more than any other age group." And group 3 is to support the notion, "Older adults need God's wisdom to get along in life more than any other age group."

Give the groups three or four minutes to come up with a few arguments to support their positions. Summarize by saying, "Obviously we need God's wisdom no matter what age we are. Each phase of life offers its own challenges, but God gives us the wisdom to handle each one."

Ask, "How do we get such wisdom?" Distribute copies of "Sources of Wisdom" from the reproducible page that follows. Ask the students to complete the activity; then discuss the results briefly. Ask the students to reflect on their own lives—do they show a commitment to the ideal standards or a tendency to follow the world's standards?

Read James 1:5, 6. Close with a time of silent prayer in which students are encouraged to make a commitment to seeking God's wisdom on a daily basis and to reject worldly standards of wisdom.

Wise or Otherwise

If you are like most of us, you have done some wise—and some not-so-wise—things in your life. Reflect on your life to date. What were the wisest and the most foolish things you can recall doing in the first eighteen years of your life?

Divide the number of years you have lived since you were eighteen by three. (If you are 45, you have lived 27 years beyond 18; 27 divided by 3 is 9.) What are the wisest and most foolish things you have done in each third of your life since you were eighteen?

First third (e.g., ages 19–27)

Second third (e.g., 28–36)

Most recent third (e.g., 37–45)

Sources of Wisdom

Rank the following sources of information from 1 (best) to 9 (least value) for shaping wisdom. In the left column mark the world's standard. In the right, mark the ideal (godly) priorities.

World's Ideal

World's	Ideal	
____	____	Advertising
____	____	Books
____	____	Church experiences
____	____	Media (radio/TV/newspapers)
____	____	Education/schools
____	____	Friends
____	____	God's Word
____	____	Parents
____	____	Prayer

Are you more often following the world's standards or the ideal? What can you do to follow the ideal standards more consistently?

SOLOMON BUILDS THE TEMPLE

LESSON 12

WHY TEACH THIS LESSON?

With a pure heart David had desired to build a temple for the Lord God of Israel, but he was not permitted to do so. We wonder whether he would even have wanted to if he could have known how later generations would treat it. Could he have imagined idols within the temple courts, disobedient people chanting "the temple of the Lord, the temple of the Lord" for good luck, or weak kings robbing its treasuries to bribe foreign kings?

David's heart was pure, and he worshiped God even without a temple. It is the purity of heart that is important to God, not the structure in which worship takes place. Even as you study the dedication of the temple, that is a fact you will want your learners to know.

INTRODUCTION

A. A PALACE FOR KING DAVID

No visit to London is complete without a stop at Buckingham Palace, the residence of the royal family. Anyone who visits there gazes with respect at the magnificent edifice. When it was built, the king of England was James I, the same monarch to whom the famous *King James Version* of the Bible was dedicated. That version was published in 1611, just four years after the first British colony was established in North America.

In contrast, the United States seems like only a "beginner" nation. The first part of its president's home was not completed until 1800, but from the start that house has been a national landmark. It seems that a king or a president cannot be allowed to live in an ordinary house. That would reflect badly on the entire nation.

After David became king of Israel, he conquered Jerusalem and made it his capital city (2 Samuel 5:6-9). He was then blessed with expert help in building a royal palace. King Hiram of Tyre not only supplied cedar from the northern mountains for timber; he also sent skilled builders to make for David what was likely the finest house in Israel (2 Samuel 5:11).

B. A TENT FOR THE LORD?

David also wanted the new capital city to be the home of the ark of the covenant, the visible earthly symbol of God's presence. At one point the Philistines had captured the ark, but had soon returned it to Israel (1 Samuel 5:1—6:16). For years it had then been kept in a private house. Now David brought it to Jerusalem with fanfare and rejoicing and set it in a tent that he had prepared for it (2 Samuel 6).

So the king of Israel had a palace, but the King of Heaven and earth had only a tent. That didn't look right to David. He wanted to build for the Lord a temple finer than his own palace.

DEVOTIONAL READING:
PSALM 84:1-4

BACKGROUND SCRIPTURE:
1 KINGS 5:1-12; 6:1-38; 8:1—9:5

PRINTED TEXT:
1 KINGS 6:37, 38; 8:22, 23, 27-30; 9:1-5

LESSON AIMS

After participating in this lesson a student should be able to:

1. Recall key points from Solomon's prayer of dedication for the temple and from the Lord's response.

2. Tell why obedience to God's commands was important in Solomon's day and why it remains important today.

3. Suggest one act of obedience he or she can perform in the next seven days.

KEY VERSE

Will God really dwell on earth? The heavens, even the highest heaven, cannot contain you. How much less this temple I have built!   —1 Kings 8:27

Nov 19

LESSON 12 NOTES

However, the Lord's plan was not quite the same. He did not forbid building the temple, but he postponed it. David was a man of war. That in itself was not wrong. God approved his wars, but it was more appropriate for the Lord's temple to be built by a man of peace. David, said the Lord, should leave it for his son Solomon to do (1 Chronicles 22:6-10).

David humbly accepted God's will. Then, to help prepare Solomon for the work that he himself was not allowed to do, he began gathering various materials to be used in the project (1 Chronicles 22:2-5). In fact, 1 Chronicles 22:5 notes that David "made extensive preparations before his death." He did all he could to make sure this task would go smoothly for his son.

C. LESSON BACKGROUND

The temple that Solomon built is described in chapter 6 of 1 Kings. God himself was its architect. He revealed his plans to David, and David passed them on to Solomon (1 Chronicles 28:11, 12). The heart of the temple had the same sacred rooms as the tabernacle: the Holy Place and the Most Holy Place. The latter, which housed the ark of the covenant, was a cube—thirty feet long and wide and high. The Holy Place next to it was the same in width but was twice as long.

The height of the structure was notable—forty-five feet, rising like a tower above the court around it. Thus there must have been a large space under the roof of the temple and above the ceiling of the Most Holy Place. Across the front of the temple was a porch fifteen feet wide. Inside the temple the stone walls were covered with cedar, which was intricately carved and then overlaid with gold. Against the outside of the walls, three stories of side rooms were built. Above these side rooms, the temple walls had narrow windows that allowed some light to enter.

I. BUILDING THE TEMPLE (1 KINGS 6:37, 38)

Our printed text begins with a brief description of the time it took to build the temple.

A. ITS BEGINNING (v. 37)

37. The foundation of the temple of the LORD was laid in the fourth year, in the month of Ziv.

Solomon began to build the temple *in the fourth year* of his reign. *The month of Ziv* was the second month of the Hebrew year. It was a springtime month, corresponding to the latter part of April and the first part of May on our calendar. The name *Ziv* means splendor or beauty—most likely a reference to the growing and blooming that occurred during the month. In later years (following the return from captivity in Babylon) the same month was called *Iyar*, which has the same meaning.

B. ITS COMPLETION (v. 38)

38. In the eleventh year in the month of Bul, the eighth month, the temple was finished in all its details according to its specifications. He had spent seven years building it.

Counting only complete years, it took *seven years* to finish the temple. Being a little more accurate, it took seven and a half years; for the work began in the second month of the fourth year of Solomon's reign and ended in the *eighth month* of the *eleventh year*. That month corresponds to the last part of October and the first part of November on our calendar. It brought the beginning of the rainy season, and so it was named *Bul*, meaning rainy.

WHAT DO YOU THINK?

Solomon's temple was a magnificent structure. The length of time required for its construction speaks volumes about the splendor of it. Today many people feel that church buildings should be similarly ornate, while many others believe that spending money on aesthetics is wasteful. After all, they say, the true temple of God today is the heart of the believer (1 Corinthians 6:19). What do you think? Why?

II. SOLOMON'S PRAYER (1 KINGS 8:22, 23, 27-30)

First Kings 7:1-12 describes other buildings in the vicinity of the temple. It notes that Solomon's palace took thirteen years to build. It must have been grand!

The structure known as "the Palace of the Forest of Lebanon" probably had that name because its many pillars were made of cedar wood from Lebanon. No doubt they stood as majestically as the trunks of a forest. The purpose of this house is not stated. Perhaps it served as a guest house and reception area, for Solomon was visited by some of the great men and women of his time (1 Kings 10:24). The queen of Sheba is perhaps the most famous example (1 Kings 10:1-13).

First Kings 7:13-22 records that Solomon commissioned an expert metal worker from Tyre to make two massive pillars of brass for the porch of the temple. The rest of that chapter describes the furnishings of the temple, and chapter 8 records the installation of the ark of the covenant and the temple dedication. Particularly noted is the cloud of divine glory that filled the temple—clear evidence that the Lord accepted it as his dwelling place among his people (1 Kings 8:10, 11).

At this point our printed text includes some excerpts from Solomon's prayer.

A. PRAISE TO THE LORD (vv. 22, 23, 27)

22. Then Solomon stood before the altar of the LORD in front of the whole assembly of Israel, spread out his hands toward heaven . . .

Solomon had been speaking to the *assembly* (vv. 14-21). Now his upraised arms made it plain that he was speaking in prayer to God.

23. . . . and said: "O LORD, God of Israel, there is no God like you in heaven above or on earth below—you who keep your covenant of love with your servants who continue wholeheartedly in your way."

The *Lord*, Yahweh, stands alone as the one and only *God*. In all creation there is none to be compared with him. One evidence of that is seen in the way he kept his *covenant*. He had made that covenant at Sinai when his people left Egypt. He had promised to bless them with prosperity and happiness if they would walk before him *wholeheartedly*—that is, if they would obey his law sincerely and gladly. God's promise had been kept faultlessly for nearly five hundred years (1 Kings 6:1). The same covenant had promised disaster to the people if they did not obey, and that promise had also been kept.

Solomon then prayed that God would keep his recent promise that David's descendants would continue to rule (vv. 24-26); but our text omits that and goes on to the climax of Solomon's praise in verse 27.

27. "But will God really dwell on earth? The heavens, even the highest heaven, cannot contain you. How much less this temple I have built!

God is great beyond our comprehension. All of outer space is too small to *contain* him. How absurd it would be to think that he could be found only in that tiny *temple* that Solomon had just completed!

B. PLEA FOR MERCY (vv. 28-30)

28. "Yet give attention to your servant's prayer and his plea for mercy, O LORD my God. Hear the cry and the prayer that your servant is praying in your presence this day.

Understanding that God was not confined to the temple, Solomon nevertheless pleaded that God would *give attention* to the *prayer* that he was about to speak as that temple was being dedicated.

29. "May your eyes be open toward this temple night and day, this place of which you said, 'My Name shall be there,' so that you will hear the prayer your servant prays toward this place.

Use today's visual to encourage your students to share the awe expressed by Solomon at the greatness of our God, who cannot be confined or limited.

WHAT DO YOU THINK?

It was fitting that Solomon emphasized the fact that God was not confined to the temple, but is greater than the expanse of the heavens. How can we overcome the tendency to confine our recognition of God to the church building?

HOW TO SAY IT

Babylon. BAB-uh-lun.
Bul. Bool.
Hiram. HIGH-rum.
Iyar. EE-yar.
Sheba. SHE-buh.
Ziv. Ziv.

Though God lived in the distant Heaven, Solomon prayed that he would give special attention to the *temple night and day.* Before Israel reached the promised land, God had promised that he would put his name at a specific *place* in that land. That place was to be a special place of contact with God: people of Israel were to present their offerings there (Deuteronomy 12:10, 11). Then God had promised David that Solomon would build a place for God's name (2 Samuel 7:13). Now Solomon had completed the temple and placed in it the ark of the covenant, the visible symbol of God's presence. God had signaled his acceptance of the temple by filling it with his glory (1 Kings 8:10, 11). Surely this was the place of which God could say, *My Name shall be there.*

True, God could not be confined to the temple; yet in a special sense he was there, as he had demonstrated by filling that place with his glory. Solomon asked for God's special attention, not only to the *prayer* he was making before the temple that day, but also to whatever prayer he later would make *toward this place.*

WHERE CAN YOU FIND GOD?

What would you say is the most awe-inspiring place on earth? Certainly one possibility would be Glacier Point in Yosemite National Park. There one can look straight down more than three thousand feet to the floor of Yosemite Valley, or north across the valley to Yosemite Falls (the highest falls in North America), or eastward toward the great monolith of Half Dome standing out against the backdrop of the snow-covered Sierra Nevada Mountains. Many people feel close to God in such a setting.

Another person might choose Victoria Falls in Africa as a place that declares the mighty power of God. Someone else might say, "Just let me sit in a peaceful garden. I can feel God's presence there." Still others have been known to claim that they can worship God better with a fishing pole in their hands than in any cathedral ever built. (We should be skeptical about this one!)

Obviously, as Solomon observed, no building—not even the heavens themselves—can contain the God we worship. However, he can and does inhabit both the world he made and the buildings we erect to aid us in worshiping him. The issue is not so much *where* we find God, but *whether* we find him. Private worship has its place, but God also commands us to join with others in seeking his presence. He promises to be there with us when we do so.   —C. R. B.

WHAT DO YOU THINK?

Suppose a Christian brother or sister said to you, "Solomon asked the Lord to give heed to the prayers for forgiveness of sin that were offered in connection with the temple. But we do not have a temple! How can I know that God hears my prayers for forgiveness?" How would you answer?

[Consider Hebrews 4:16, all of Hebrews 9, and 1 John 1:9 in your discussion.]

30. "Hear the supplication of your servant and of your people Israel when they pray toward this place. Hear from heaven, your dwelling place, and when you hear, forgive."

Now Solomon pleaded that the Lord would hear not only his prayers, but the prayers that all Israel would *pray toward* this special *place* of God's presence—especially prayers for pardon. Read on in verses 31-40 to see this verified. Solomon foresaw the time when the people of Israel would fall into idolatry and other sins, as they had often done before. God would punish their sinning with national disaster, as he had often done before. In misery they would repent of their sins and plead for forgiveness, as they had often done before. Solomon prayed that God would be merciful and forgive them yet again.

III. THE LORD'S ANSWER (1 KINGS 9:1-5)

The latter part of chapter 8 records what happened after Solomon finished his lengthy prayer. Though he foresaw times when Israel would turn from God, the king urged the people to avoid such times by careful obedience to God. The completion of the temple was celebrated with a two-week festival; then the people were dismissed to go home, still rejoicing in the blessings the Lord had given them.

Now we turn to the Lord's answer to Solomon's prayer. Whether it was given during the two weeks of celebration or later, it is recorded in chapter 9 of 1 Kings.

A. THE LORD'S APPEARANCE (vv. 1, 2)

1. When Solomon had finished building the temple of the LORD and the royal palace, and had achieved all he had desired to do . . .

This makes it clear that we are now looking at a time not only after Solomon completed the *temple*, but also after he completed such buildings as the *royal palace* and the Palace of the Forest of Lebanon (1 Kings 7:1, 2). In fact, *all* that Solomon *had desired to do* he *had achieved*. Some have suggested that this was a kind of crossroads in Solomon's reign and that God was appearing to him to remind him of his responsibility to be faithful as David his father had been.

2. . . . the LORD appeared to him a second time, as he had appeared to him at Gibeon.

At Gibeon the Lord had *appeared* to Solomon in a dream by night and had said, "Ask for whatever you want me to give you" (1 Kings 3:5). Now he appeared again in a similar way.

B. THE LORD'S ACCEPTANCE (v. 3)

3. The LORD said to him:

"I have heard the prayer and plea you have made before me; I have consecrated this temple, which you have built, by putting my Name there forever. My eyes and my heart will always be there.

The Lord had *heard* Solomon's *prayer*, parts of which have been included in our printed text (1 Kings 8:22, 23, 27-30). In response he had *consecrated* the new *temple*: he had made it holy, set it apart, dedicated it as the place foretold in Deuteronomy 12:10, 11. It was to be the national worship center of Israel—the place where sacrifices and offerings would be made. God's *eyes* and *heart* would be there: he would be watching and cherishing that temple *always*.

TRUE SIGNIFICANCE

Mickey's Dining Car has been located on Seventh Street in St. Paul, Minnesota, for some sixty years. For more than twenty of those years, city officials tried in vain to convince Eric Mattson, the owner of this old-fashioned eatery, that he ought to accept the inevitable and move his business elsewhere. Finally, the insurance firm that owned the surrounding property put up a seventeen-story, nearly one-half million square foot building that dwarfs the diner.

The dining car is officially known as an Art Deco Streamline Moderne-style car. That's important because this simple structure, originally one of thousands across America, is now one of only a few left. And because of its style and historic significance, Mickey's has been officially listed on the National Register of Historic Places. Neither the insurance company nor the city—which tried to move the diner so it could widen the street in front of it—can touch it.

The temple that Solomon built was never at the mercy of city bureaucrats or big business, since Solomon was both the king and the richest man around. However, the most important fact about the temple was that God had hallowed it with his presence—a fact far more significant than being listed on any "national register."

No matter how famous or important we may become, what matters most is whether our lives have been hallowed by the presence of God.   —C. R. B.

C. SOLOMON'S RESPONSIBILITY (v. 4)

4. "As for you, if you walk before me in integrity of heart and uprightness, as David your father did, and do all I command and observe my decrees and laws . . .

With only a few exceptions, *David* had obeyed God with wholehearted devotion and upright living. If Solomon would do the same, he could be sure that God would keep the promise found in the next verse.

WHAT DO YOU THINK?

God's promises to Solomon were clearly conditional ones: "If you [will] . . . I will" (1 Kings 9:4, 5). What are some conditional promises that God has made to human beings in the New Covenant age?

[If you need to "prime the pump" for this discussion, refer to some examples: Romans 10:9; Hebrews 3:14; 1 John 1:9.]

PRAYER

Father in Heaven, how kind you are, and how limitless is your love, reaching out to all the sinners in the world! Grateful for your gracious forgiveness, grateful for the unfailing leading of your Word, we pledge ourselves anew to seek your way and to follow it. In our Master's name, amen.

THOUGHT TO REMEMBER

Obey God.

WHAT DO YOU THINK?

Some have claimed that the passages quoted in the conclusion to today's lesson are contradictory. How would you reply to such a charge?

D. THE LORD'S PROMISE (v. 5)

5. ". . . I will establish your royal throne over Israel forever, as I promised David your father when I said, 'You shall never fail to have a man on the throne of Israel.'"

God had promised that David's *royal throne* would last *forever*, and that one of David's descendants would always be king—but only if those descendants would obey him sincerely (1 Kings 2:4). Now the Lord made the same promise to Solomon: his descendants would rule over Israel forever. Again the Lord stated the condition: the rule of Solomon's descendants would not be continuous unless their obedience to God was continuous (v. 4).

This same warning is emphasized strongly in the verses that follow our printed text (6-9). If Israel turned to idolatry and wickedness, it would lose the promised land; and that magnificent temple would be destroyed. Sadly, this is eventually what happened (2 Kings 24:10-13; 25:8, 9, 13-17).

CONCLUSION

What is so attractive about doing wrong? All history proves that it is destructive; so why do most people still choose it (Matthew 7:13, 14)? Nothing could be plainer than the warning of 1 Kings 9:6-9. How could Solomon ever ignore it? He was gifted with more wisdom than any other man, yet even he played the fool. He disobeyed God and brought his magnificent empire to the brink of disaster. We shall read about that in next week's lesson.

A. THE FACT OF SIN

This series of lessons has shown us how often and how dismally Israel failed to obey God, and thus forfeited his blessing. Wise King Solomon commented, "There is no one who does not sin" (1 Kings 8:46). Thus he echoed the sad song of his father David: "All have turned aside, they have together become corrupt; there is no one who does good, not even one" (Psalm 14:3). Centuries later Paul added this confirmation: "All have sinned and fall short of the glory of God" (Romans 3:23).

B. DEALING WITH SIN

"The wages of sin is death," wrote Paul in Romans 6:23, but that is not the entire story. He continues: "but the gift of God is eternal life in Christ Jesus our Lord." All the sinners in the world were doomed to die, but Jesus died in their place.

Does that mean that all sinners are automatically saved from death? No, each person can still choose, and many still choose the road that leads to destruction.

If I choose to live rather than to die, what can I do about it? Paul told the jailer in Philippi, "Believe in the Lord Jesus, and you will be saved" (Acts 16:31). To the Romans he wrote, "If you confess with your mouth, 'Jesus is Lord,' and believe in your heart that God raised him from the dead, you will be saved" (Romans 10:9). Sending other apostles to give doomed sinners his offer of life, Jesus said, "Whoever believes and is baptized will be saved, but whoever does not believe will be condemned" (Mark 16:16). Giving instructions to convicted sinners, Peter said, "Repent and be baptized, every one of you, in the name of Jesus Christ for the forgiveness of your sins. And you will receive the gift of the Holy Spirit" (Acts 2:38). Saul of Tarsus was agonizing in repentance when God's messenger told him, "Get up, be baptized and wash your sins away, calling on his name" (Acts 22:16).

Are all these quotations confusing? Are you wondering just what a person should do for his salvation? Then search the Scriptures. Search especially the New Testament, because it testifies most clearly about the New Covenant. Consider all the Scriptures that tell what one should do to be saved, and take them in their context. Then do *everything* they say you should do.

Discovery Learning

This page contains an alternate lesson plan emphasizing learning activities. Classes desiring such student involvement will find these suggestions helpful. The next page is a reproducible activity page to further enhance discovery learning.

LEARNING GOALS

After this lesson a student should be able to:

1. Recall key points from Solomon's prayer of dedication for the temple and from the Lord's response.

2. Tell why obedience to God's commands was important in Solomon's day and why it remains important today.

3. Suggest one act of obedience he or she can perform in the next seven days.

INTO THE LESSON

Distribute copies of the reproducible page that follows. Ask students to complete the activity; then discuss the results. Since the church is the people, obviously it is more important to have a great church than a great church building. (The first-century church had no buildings!) Note how often our buildings consume a large portion of our time and resources. Discuss ways to keep the building in perspective: it's a tool to help the church to be what God wants it to be.

In today's lesson we will see how important it was for Israel to have a temple, and Solomon's temple was truly grand. More importantly we will see the need for faithful obedience to the Lord's commands.

INTO THE WORD

Read 1 Kings 6:37, 38; 8:22, 23, 27-30; 9:1-5. Ask the students the following questions.

1. How long did it take to build the temple? (*Seven years; 6:38*)

2. In Solomon's prayer, how was God described? (*Unique in heaven and on earth, Keeper of covenants; 8:22, 23*)

3. With whom did Solomon say the Lord kept his covenants? (*God's "servants that walk before [him] with all their heart"; 8:23*)

4. For what particular blessing on God's people did Solomon ask if they would pray toward the temple? (*forgiveness; 8:28-30*)

5. How did God affirm his pleasure at what Solomon had done? (*Appeared to Solomon the second time, as he had done at Gibeon [see lesson 11]; 9:1, 2*)

6. On what condition did God say he would establish Solomon's throne "over Israel forever"? (*If Solomon would walk as David did, in integrity of heart, in uprightness, and in obedience to God's commands; 9:4, 5*)

Ask the students to list and discuss significant elements of Solomon's prayer. Some of them follow:

1. Solomon recognized God's majesty and recounted God's consistent promises and blessings.

2. Solomon sought God's continued blessing for the people and acceptance of the temple as a place of special contact with him.

3. The temple was important, but God's presence is even more important and is not limited to the temple.

4. Solomon sought God's grace for future generations, who were sure to err.

Ask the students to list and discuss the main points in God's answer.

1. God acknowledged Solomon's prayer and gave his blessing to the temple.

2. God confirmed his earlier promises with another, promising that David's kingdom would last forever if his descendants obeyed sincerely.

INTO LIFE

Reflecting on Solomon's prayer we can see many parallels to everyday life. Ask the class to comment on the following statements. How does today's lesson text instruct us about the issues raised in these statements?

1. Many associate their religious life with a specific place and/or time of worship.

2. Many associate worship with specific days or seasons.

3. We seek immediate results or gratification rather than exercise patience.

Comment on the following principles from God's response to Solomon.

1. God and his promises are everlasting.

2. Man will always be imperfect on his own. God has the perfect solution through his perfect Son.

3. The new covenant with Christ continues God's promises.

4. Obedience to God and his commands is paramount among God's concerns for us.

If we would obey God, then we must know what he has commanded. Ask the class to suggest commands of God to which we need to give careful obedience. List these on the chalkboard. Then ask each student to choose one that he or she needs to be more diligent in obeying and to make a silent commitment to do so in the coming week.

A Building or a Church?

Think about what you would like in a church building. What would make for a great church building? Then consider what makes a great church.

GREAT CHURCH BUILDING	GREAT CHURCH

Which is more important, having a great church building or a great church? Why?

Which gets more attention, a great church building or a great church? Why?

Which has the higher priority in your own church, the building or the church? What evidence can you cite to support your answer?

Which has the higher priority in *your* own life, the building or the church? What evidence can you cite to support your answer?

SOLOMON'S MISTAKES

LESSON 13

WHY TEACH THIS LESSON?

"Don't bring that into the living room," I said.

"Why not?" my preschool son whined.

"Because you might spill it."

"Oh, I'll be careful," he vowed. "I won't spill it."

Against my better judgment I relented. And you *know* what happened! My son demonstrated once again the futility of the "it-can't-happen-to-me" philosophy.

Sometimes it's a spilled drink on the carpet. Sometimes, it's much more serious. I still remember sitting on that same carpet weeping after my brother called and reported that he had resigned his ministry position because he had had an affair with a woman in his church. I wept at the heartache he had brought to himself, his wife, and the rest of the family. I wept at the lost potential for ministry.

And I wept, I think, over my own loss of innocence. Up until then I had believed that adultery was a sin that "could not happen to me." I no longer believe that, and many times since I have prayed for protection from the kind of temptation that might lead to infidelity. God has honored that request—partly, I think, because I have been more alert and less complacent.

Solomon knew better. But he must have thought, "It can't happen to me!" Probably there are some in your class who think the same thing. Use this lesson to warn them. It can!

INTRODUCTION

A. ISRAEL KNEW BETTER

Over the last three months our lessons have reminded us again and again of the misdeeds of Israel's people and of the punishment that followed. Their sin was the more shameful because the people knew better. At the beginning of their life as a nation, God had given them his law. He had assigned parents the duty of teaching it to their children—teaching it earnestly and constantly (Deuteronomy 6:6, 7). Priests had the duty of teaching the parents (Leviticus 10:8-11). When both parents and priests neglected their duty, God sent prophets to point out the misdeeds of the people.

In all of this, however, the people could not see the sorrowing face of their Father in Heaven. They saw the face and heard the voice of his prophet, so they tried to silence the prophet instead of correcting their way of living. Nothing but punishment could bring them to their senses. Oppressed by the various invaders whom God sent, they finally realized that their misery was the result of their sin. Prepared again to obey God, they pleaded with him for mercy; and he rescued them from their misery.

B. LESSON BACKGROUND

Our lesson title is "Solomon's Mistakes." That is a charitable way to put it. We might fittingly say, "Solomon's Sins," for surely Solomon knew better. We do not know how much he was schooled by faithful priests or tutored by Nathan the prophet; but we know that he recalled the teaching of his father David, a man

DEVOTIONAL READING:
NAHUM 1:2-8

BACKGROUND SCRIPTURE:
1 KINGS 11

PRINTED TEXT:
1 KINGS 11:1-13a

LESSON AIMS

After this lesson a student should be able to:

1. Tell what contributed to Solomon's demise and how God disciplined him.

2. Compare Solomon's sin with that of those who try to compromise faith in Christ.

3. Make a statement of uncompromising faith in Jesus Christ as the only Son of the one true and living God.

KEY VERSE

The LORD became angry with Solomon because his heart had turned away from the LORD, the God of Israel. —1 Kings 11:9

after God's own heart (Proverbs 4:3, 4). In addition, he possessed a special gift of wisdom from God (1 Kings 3:11, 12). He himself became a noted teacher. "The whole world sought audience with Solomon to hear the wisdom God had put in his heart" (1 Kings 10:24). "He spoke three thousand proverbs" (1 Kings 4:32), many more than we see in the book of Proverbs.

Looking at the proverbs written in that book, we soon read, "The fear of the Lord is the beginning of knowledge" (Proverbs 1:7). Looking at the conclusion of one of Solomon's other books, we read, "Fear God and keep his commandments, for this is the whole duty of man" (Ecclesiastes 12:13). Surely, we would think, so wise a man should never let himself be ensnared in wrongdoing. But he did—even though without doubt he knew better.

I. SOLOMON'S WOMEN (1 KINGS 11:1-3)

God's law did not forbid polygamy, but it did command that Israelites marry only other Israelites (Deuteronomy 7:1-4). Early in his reign, however, Solomon ignored that law, primarily for political reasons. He made an alliance with Pharaoh, king of Egypt, and strengthened the bond by taking that ruler's daughter as his wife (1 Kings 3:1). But that was only the beginning.

A. FOREIGN WOMEN (v. 1)

1. King Solomon, however, loved many foreign women besides Pharaoh's daughter—Moabites, Ammonites, Edomites, Sidonians and Hittites.

The *foreign women* whom Solomon *loved* included *many . . . besides Pharaoh's daughter*. The *Moabites* lived east of the Dead Sea. The *Ammonites* lived east of Israel and north of Moab. The *Edomites* lived south of the Dead Sea. The *Sidonians* took their name from Sidon, a city of Phoenicia north of Israel on the Mediterranean coast. The *Hittites* were prominent in Syria and Palestine for centuries. At this time they probably were strongest in the territory east of Phoenicia.

David had subdued these smaller nations and made them part of his empire, which was now ruled by Solomon. Each nation managed its own affairs but paid tribute to Israel. Since Solomon was respected and admired throughout the known world, there was a certain prestige in being associated with him. A foreign ruler might consider it a privilege to be a father-in-law to such a man. Also, if one of the subject kings ever thought of rebelling and refusing to pay tribute to Israel, he might be restrained by remembering that his daughter was in Jerusalem. She easily could be made a prisoner or a slave instead of a wife.

B. FORBIDDEN WOMEN (v. 2)

2. They were from nations about which the LORD had told the Israelites, "You must not intermarry with them, because they will surely turn your hearts after their gods." Nevertheless, Solomon held fast to them in love.

God *had told the Israelites* to destroy the pagan *nations* that inhabited the promised land. His people were not to associate with them; specifically, they were not to marry pagans (Deuteronomy 7:1-5). The reason was very simple: *they will surely turn your hearts after their gods.*

Solomon, however, became engrossed in preserving the stability of his empire. For political expediency he ignored God's law. He spoke affectionately to pagan kings; he took their daughters into his harem.

C. A THOUSAND WOMEN (v. 3)

3. He had seven hundred wives of royal birth and three hundred concubines, and his wives led him astray.

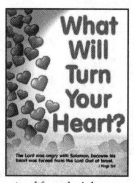

What Will Turn Your Heart?

The Lord was angry with Solomon, because his heart was turned from the Lord God of Israel.
1 Kings 11:9

The visual for today's lesson challenges us to learn from Solomon's tragic error. Discuss what turns people's hearts today and how the church can encourage faithfulness.

Israel had no king but God when the law was given, but the law included some specific regulations for the king who was to come later. One regulation forbade the king to "take many wives" (Deuteronomy 17:17). Solomon violated that one extravagantly!

It seems hard to believe that Solomon accumulated seven hundred princesses from the five small nations mentioned in verse 1. We know he made an alliance with Egypt and cemented it by marrying that king's daughter (1 Kings 3:1). Perhaps he did the same with countries west and south of Egypt, with the kingdoms in Arabia, in Asia Minor north of the Mediterranean, and even in Mesopotamia. Even so, it appears that a smaller country must have had several of its princesses in Solomon's harem. Solomon was the greatest and most feared king on earth. It was an honor to be allied with him—and it was politically prudent as well.

Concubines have been described as "second-class wives." They had no royal fathers; they were not chosen for political purposes, and so their status was inferior. We wonder, then, why they were chosen. When Solomon saw an extremely beautiful woman, did he simply take her home to keep for his own? We wonder if these *three hundred* were the prettiest, the most vivacious, the most interesting, and the best loved of the thousand. We have no way to be certain. The record simply notes that the king had three hundred concubines.

Ominously the record adds that the warning of Deuteronomy 17:17 proved to be well founded: *his wives led him astray*.

SIMPLE PLEASURES

Some teenage boys from the Los Angeles area were looking for some "innocent fun." They began playing with bulldozers at a construction site during the evenings after the work crews had gone home. Apparently some of the boys knew how to "hot wire" the big diesel engines to start them without ignition keys.

One evening, one of the boys lost control of the bulldozer he was driving. The huge machine left the construction site and destroyed a major portion of a nearby church building before being stopped. Fortunately, this happened on one of the few nights when the building was not being used; so no one was injured or killed. One church member saw a positive side to the incident: with the publicity the church got, the whole community now knows about the church!

Solomon's dalliance with evil probably began innocently enough—at least in his opinion. He discovered that it was politically astute to marry the daughters of kings whose kingdoms were subject to Israel. No doubt Solomon also found the practice quite enjoyable as well. What harm could there be in such "simple pleasures"?

Through Solomon's "pleasure," however, he learned a hard lesson. What was formerly unthinkable became a fact of life: his idol-worshiping wives turned his heart to other gods. What the world calls expedient often leads to grievous sin.   —C. R. B.

II. SOLOMON'S IDOLATRY (1 KINGS 11:4-8)

God had said, "You shall have no other gods before me" (Exodus 20:3). Perhaps Solomon had no intention of breaking that law when he let his Egyptian wife bring her religion with her to the palace in Jerusalem. But Solomon's tolerance of false religion led to support, and his support eventually resulted in actual worship.

A. HIS WANDERING HEART (v. 4)

4. *As Solomon grew old, his wives turned his heart after other gods, and his heart was not fully devoted to the LORD his God, as the heart of David his father had been.*

Who would have thought that the wisest man on earth would play the fool? Perhaps during the early years of his reign, when the words of *David his father* were still fresh in his mind, Solomon made an effort to distance himself from the

WHAT DO YOU THINK?

Solomon must have known what God's law said. Still, he took foreign wives. He must have thought, "They won't turn *my* heart away." And we do the same thing! We really believe that our love for God will keep us faithful in spite of the things we add to our lives that will eventually pull us away from him. So a young Christian girl begins to date a non-Christian boy. At first she remains faithful, but then she drifts away. A businessman tunes into adult entertainment while on business trips—and then one day he wonders what happened to his marriage. What are some other examples? Why is it that we so often think, "It won't happen to me," and refuse clear warnings of Scripture or helpful friends? How can we prevent such errors?

[Consider Romans 12:3; 1 Corinthians 10:12; Galatians 6:3.]

pagan idols and practices of his many wives. But as he *grew old*, his will to resist seems to have weakened. In time, *his wives turned his heart after other gods*.

B. His False Gods (vv. 5-8)

5. He followed Ashtoreth the goddess of the Sidonians, and Molech the detestable god of the Ammonites.

Ashtoreth was a *goddess* worshiped by many pagans along the Mediterranean coast. She was portrayed in somewhat different ways in different towns and territories. Solomon followed the Sidonian version, probably because a wife from Sidon brought this goddess to Jerusalem.

As noted earlier, the *Ammonites* lived east of Israel. Different groups of them worshiped different versions of their so-called god, *Molech*. The name is derived from a word that means *king*. This deity was especially *detestable* because some of his worshipers burned their children in sacrifice to him, which Israelites were forbidden to do (Leviticus 18:21). Solomon did not go that far, but one of his descendants (approximately two centuries later) did (2 Kings 16:1-3).

6. So Solomon did evil in the eyes of the Lord; he did not follow the Lord completely, as David his father had done.

Any involvement with false gods was *evil*. Solomon knew that, but for the sake of his wives he drifted into idolatry of various kinds. *David* in his later years was guilty of adultery and murder, but never of idolatry.

7. On a hill east of Jerusalem, Solomon built a high place for Chemosh the detestable god of Moab, and for Molech the detestable god of the Ammonites.

A *high place* describes a place of worship. They were called high places because many of them were located on hilltops; but the name came to be given even to shrines that were set up in the valleys. The sites mentioned here most likely were situated on the Mount of Olives, which is a *hill east of Jerusalem*.

To the south of the Ammonites lived the people of Moab, and it seems that the Moabite god *Chemosh* was similar to the false deity the Ammonites called *Molech*. Second Kings 3:26, 27 records that the king of Moab offered his son as a burnt offering, and a Moabite record (known as the Moabite Stone) adds that he made the offering to Chemosh.

Solomon's support of the high places helps us understand why God's plan was for Israel to worship him at the one place that he would choose (Deuteronomy 12:10, 11). While worship at the high places was tolerated (1 Samuel 9:25), God knew that it also had the potential to open the door to the actual worship of false gods. This is exactly what happened in the case of Solomon.

8. He did the same for all his foreign wives, who burned incense and offered sacrifices to their gods.

This does not mean that Solomon made seven hundred worship places for his seven hundred *wives*. Perhaps dozens of wives worshiped at each place he built. Still, there must have been a bewildering number of shrines in and near Jerusalem. Probably none of them was as big as the temple of the Lord, and none was as richly adorned with gold and silver; but a visitor in the area would not conclude that the Lord was the one and only God worshiped in Jerusalem.

The Influence of "Outsiders"

North America has always been a land of immigrants. In prehistoric times, they were apparently Asians who came across a "land bridge" between what is now Siberia and Alaska. At the beginning of the modern era of history, the immigrants were Europeans and Africans, the latter brought against their will. As the end of the twentieth century approached, the newcomers were primarily from Asia and Latin America.

As each wave of immigrants arrived, previous residents resisted yielding a measure of control over the land, the culture, and the social and governmental structures. This has been true whether the immigrants to an area were of a different race or nationality, or whether they were simply "outsiders" who didn't understand the customs of the places where they moved. "City folks" moving to small towns, "Yankees" moving to the South, or Southerners moving to New England have all found difficulty fitting in with their new environments.

Israel's problem in Solomon's time was that the immigrants (Solomon's wives) and their pagan culture (especially their worship) were readily accepted. Where Solomon should have resisted change, he gave in all too easily to his wives' pagan practices.

God's people are called to influence their surroundings, not to be influenced by them. Our contacts with "outsiders" should be designed to improve them, not to impair us. —C. R. B.

III. SOLOMON'S PUNISHMENT (1 KINGS 11:9-13a)

Solomon had been doing just as he pleased for some time, and thus far his reign had been successful. That was true because he pleased to please God by worshiping him and obeying him. But now the voices of his wives seemed nearer, louder, and more insistent than the voice of God. So Solomon pleased to please his wives, and God was displeased.

A. THE LORD'S ANGER (vv. 9, 10)

9. The LORD became angry with Solomon because his heart had turned away from the LORD, the God of Israel, who had appeared to him twice.

The Lord is rightly *angry* with wrongdoing, and Solomon's conduct was clearly wrong. With his great wisdom, he should have managed his own *heart* better; he should have kept it faithful to the Lord. His turning away was the more inexcusable because the Lord *had appeared to him twice.* The first time he had granted Solomon's request for wisdom and had added a bonus of riches and honor (1 Kings 3:5-14). The second time he had promised continued success to Solomon if Solomon remained faithful to him and disaster if Solomon did not (1 Kings 9:4-9). With that promise as plain as words could make it, how could Solomon turn from God? But he did. See the next verse.

10. Although he had forbidden Solomon to follow other gods, Solomon did not keep the LORD's command.

The law forbade idolatry (as clearly stated in the first two of the Ten Commandments). The Lord had appeared to Solomon and *had forbidden* him *to follow other gods* (1 Kings 9:6, 7). But Solomon had disobeyed.

B. PUNISHMENT PROMISED (v. 11)

11. So the LORD said to Solomon, "Since this is your attitude and you have not kept my covenant and my decrees, which I commanded you, I will most certainly tear the kingdom away from you and give it to one of your subordinates.

With all his wisdom Solomon must have known that Israel had turned away from God time after time and that disaster had followed every instance of turning away. How could Solomon think that he could turn to idols without escaping punishment? Most likely he simply stopped thinking about pleasing God and thought only of pleasing his wives.

The punishment prescribed by God must have hurt Solomon deeply. The *kingdom* that David his father had left him to rule and had prepared him to rule and that represented Israel at the height of its glory was to be taken from Solomon and given to one of his *subordinates.*

WHAT DO YOU THINK?

Solomon seems to have become more interested in pleasing his wives than in pleasing God. How can a Christian balance faithfulness to God with pleasing his or her spouse?

C. PUNISHMENT POSTPONED (v. 12)

12. "Nevertheless, for the sake of David your father, I will not do it during your lifetime. I will tear it out of the hand of your son.

Solomon certainly deserved punishment, but it was postponed—not for his *sake*, but for *David's*. *David* had served God heroically many years. God would not let his empire collapse so quickly. That would happen after Solomon's *son* came to power. At that time, the kingdom divided and the "subordinate" mentioned in verse 11 (Jeroboam) became king of the northern part (1 Kings 11:26-31; 12:20).

Did this mean that Solomon himself would escape punishment? No. God had promised long life to Solomon if he would be obedient to him (1 Kings 3:14). But disobedient Solomon died rather young, probably no more than sixty years of age.

D. PUNISHMENT MODIFIED (v. 13a)

13a. "Yet I will not tear the whole kingdom from him, but will give him one tribe. . . ."

In addition to declaring that Solomon's punishment would be postponed, God also modified the punishment by stating that Solomon's son, Rehoboam, would not lose *the whole kingdom*. He would continue to rule the *one tribe* of Judah (1 Kings 12:17, 20), though some from the tribe of Benjamin also chose to support Rehoboam (1 Kings 12:21).

In the remainder of this verse, God repeated that he would allow Solomon's son to keep one tribe for David's sake and, in addition, "for the sake of Jerusalem, which I have chosen." God had a great plan for David's kingdom, and his plan would not be frustrated by Solomon's sin.

CONCLUSION

Since this is the final lesson of this series, let's leap over the centuries when David's descendants ruled in Jerusalem. Let's look briefly at the kingdom that will "endure forever" (Daniel 2:44).

A. THE KING ETERNAL

There came a time when God's promise seemed to have failed: no man of David's family ruled in Jerusalem. But God's promise did not fail. During that time there was born a son of David who is also the Son of God. He is the King eternal.

This King "went around doing good" (Acts 10:38). The power of God was in his voice and in his fingertips. He gave hearing to the deaf, sight to the blind, health to the sick, and life to the dead. He shed no blood but his own, and by his death he conquered death. He rose triumphantly from the tomb; he soared beyond the skies to sit down at the right hand of God; he rules forevermore.

B. THE KING'S PEOPLE

If we are citizens of the kingdom eternal, our duty is basically the same as the duty of David and Solomon: *we ought to obey God*. This does not mean that we are under the law God gave at Sinai. With us God has made a New Covenant (Jeremiah 31:31-34). His supreme spokesman is not Moses but Jesus (Hebrews 1:1-4). What Jesus said is the supreme guide for our living. When Jesus went away, he sent the Holy Spirit to guide his apostles into all truth and to teach them the word and will of Christ (John 16:12-15). Therefore the inspired writings of those apostles are the teachings of Christ just as much as the words he spoke with his own mouth.

Through the open pages of the New Testament, God's Son speaks to us day by day. Let's listen. Let's allow nothing to keep us from time with God's Word, lest we become like Solomon—with a heart that is "turned away from the Lord."

WHAT DO YOU THINK?

God's purposes were not frustrated by Solomon's sin. While God allows us to make our own choices, he is still in control. He even uses our mistakes to accomplish his purposes. How have you seen God work to accomplish his will in spite of errors made by humans? What kind of encouragement does this truth give you?

PRAYER

We plead for mercy, Father, for we have disobeyed you. Please forgive us, and help us to bring under your control all that we do, all that we say, all that we think, and all that we feel. In our Master's name. Amen.

THOUGHT TO REMEMBER

Christ is King; obey him.

Discovery Learning

*This page contains an alternate lesson plan emphasizing learning activities. Classes
desiring such student involvement will find these suggestions helpful. The next page
is a reproducible activity page to further enhance discovery learning.*

LEARNING GOALS

After this lesson a student should be able to:

1. Tell what contributed to Solomon's demise and how God disciplined him.

2. Compare Solomon's sin with that of those who try to compromise faith in Christ.

3. Make a statement of uncompromising faith in Jesus Christ as the only Son of the one true and living God.

INTO THE LESSON

Write the following scrambled word on the chalkboard or on a large poster: MORPOSCIME. As the students arrive, ask them to try to unscramble the word. When it is time for the session to begin, see how many determined that the word is *compromise.* You might award a small token prize to all those who correctly unscrambled the word.

Ask, "Is compromise good or bad, and why do you think so?" In your discussion you should note that there are times when compromise is good. When issues like personal tastes and preferences are all that are at stake, compromise can be a means of making peace. But when the issue is a matter of right and wrong, compromise is a prescription for disaster. Solomon illustrates that sad fact in our lesson today.

INTO THE WORD

Review the lesson background; then ask a volunteer to read the printed text, 1 Kings 11:1-13. Provide the students with copies of the following questions (they are in the student book) and ask them to write an answer for each one.

1. Who were some of the wives of Solomon? (*Daughter of Pharaoh, Moabites, Ammonites, Edomites, Sidonians, and Hittites, v. 1.*)

2. What had God said about marrying foreign women? ("*You must not intermarry with them, because they will surely turn your hearts,*" v. 2.)

3. What happened when Solomon was old? (*His heart was turned away after other gods, v. 4.*)

4. How did Solomon show that his heart was turned to false gods? (*He "followed" Ashtoreth and Molech, and he built high places for Chemosh and Molech, as well as the other gods worshiped by his wives, vv. 5, 7, 8.*)

5. What was God's reaction to Solomon's sin? (*He was angry, v. 9.*)

6. What would God do because of Solomon's sin? (*He would take the kingdom from Solomon's family and give it to his servant, v. 11.*)

7. When was God going to do this? (*When Solomon's son was king, v. 12.*)

8. How much was he going to take away? (*All but one tribe, v. 13.*)

Allow about five minutes for the class to work; then compare answers. Note information from the commentary pages that will enhance the students' understanding of these verses. Discuss how compromise led to Solomon's downfall.

INTO LIFE

Distribute copies of the case studies from the next page. Have students work in small groups to suggest biblical advice for the persons involved in each case.

After about eight or ten minutes, ask the groups to report. Note the dangers of compromise in each case. Consider the following:

1. If Randy compromises his honesty to pad the time sheets, how will he have any credibility to resist suggestions of wrongdoing in the future? What will it do to his ability to testify of his faith? What if Randy's boss is merely testing him rather than really wanting him to cheat?

2. If Brenda sleeps with her fiancé, how will she encourage her daughter—now eighteen—to remain sexually pure? What will happen to her already strained relationship with the church if she compromises her sexual purity? Will she be better off *eternally* to give in to her boyfriend—whether or not she might benefit in the short term? How often has a man promised he will marry a woman, and then backed out—especially if he has not even committed to a specific date?

3. If Ed and Mary lie for their son, what will happen if other witnesses are found who can establish Tom's actual whereabouts on that date? If Tom is guilty, could his parents be charged as accomplices after the fact? If Tom is really wanting to renew his faith, shouldn't a commitment to honesty be part of that? Can he trust God with his future?

After discussing the three case studies, have the students look at the "Fourth Case." Tell them they will not have to reveal what they write to anyone else, and encourage them to respond frankly in the exercise. Close with a prayer of uncompromising commitment to the Lord.

Difficult Cases

FIRST CASE: THE ALTERED TIME SHEETS

Randy is a service technician. His job is to repair small appliances brought to him by customers. The customers leave the appliances and come back at a later date to pick them up, at which time they pay for parts and labor.

Randy is new at the job, so he has no close friends. His boss has come to him and said, "No one knows how much time you really spend on a job. If you pad your time sheet a little, we'll take in more money and reach our sales goal. Then we'll all get bonuses from corporate headquarters. We're all counting on you, Randy. Don't let us down."

What would you advise Randy to do?

SECOND CASE: THE GENEROUS LOVER

Brenda's husband died three years ago, leaving her a minimal insurance benefit and three children, a fifteen-year-old daughter and two boys, nine and twelve. At first she remained very active with the church, and the church benevolence ministry has even helped her a couple of times. More and more, however, she finds she has no time for extra activities and even misses Sunday mornings occasionally.

For the past six months she has been dating a very kind and generous man, and he has helped her pay some of her bills. They plan to get married, but they have not set a date. Recently, however, he has been insisting that he be allowed to spend the night with her. He says it's only right after all he's done to help her—and, besides, they are going to get married.

What would you advise Brenda to do?

THIRD CASE: THE PRODIGAL SON

Ed and Mary's son Tom was always popular in school. A talented athlete and a bright student, he went to college on a scholarship. At the university, however, his faith began to waver. Ed and Mary prayed fervently for him, but he eventually dropped out of church and began to pursue material wealth with an almost religious fervor. His relationship with his parents also cooled. He hardly ever visits, and sends cards only on Mother's Day and Christmas.

Last month, however, he showed up at their home. He claims he wants to renew his faith, and he has been attending worship services with his parents. However, he is suspected of embezzling $50,000 from his former place of work, and he has asked his parents to say he was at their house on a certain date two weeks before he arrived. He claims he is innocent but cannot prove it, so he needs their help to avoid being falsely accused.

How would you advise Ed and Mary?

FOURTH CASE: YOU!

How is Satan trying to get you to compromise your faith?

List some specific consequences that could result if you do.

List some specific measures you can take to strengthen your resolve to remain faithful to the Lord.

Winter Quarter, 2000-2001

Good News of Jesus

(The Gospel of Luke)

Special Features

Lessons

Unit 1: A Savior Is Born

Unit 2: Mission and Ministry

Unit 3: Cross and Resurrection

About These Lessons

These lessons comprise the first section of a two-part study of the writings of Luke, the beloved physician. Taken from the Gospel of Luke, the lessons will remind us once again of the good news of Jesus—his miraculous birth, his powerful life, his challenging teachings, and his victorious death, burial, and resurrection. Do you know someone who needs some "good news"? Invite that one to study with you this quarter!

Dec 3
Dec 10
Dec 17
Dec 24
Dec 31
Jan 7
Jan 14
Jan 21
Jan 28
Feb 4
Feb 11
Feb 18
Feb 25

Timeless Truths

by Johnny Pressley

Why do we have four Gospel accounts of the life of Jesus? Isn't this just the same story being repeated? It is true that there is much overlap in material within the books of Matthew, Mark, Luke, and John, but it would be a mistake to think that the Gospel writers simply repeat each other. Each author uses a distinctive style and emphasizes certain themes for his readers. Thus our understanding of the life of Jesus has a richness that no single account could provide.

Matthew, for example, wrote primarily to Jewish readers. His Gospel cites a significant number of Old Testament messianic prophecies in order to show how Jesus fulfilled the promises that God's people had relied on for ages. Mark, on the other hand, seems to address a Gentile culture. By focusing on the miracles of Jesus, he demonstrates the powerful manner in which Jesus carried out his ministry. John adopts a more reflective manner and challenges philosophical minds with a portrait of Jesus as the true source of divine knowledge and wisdom.

Luke makes his distinctive contribution to our knowledge of Jesus by operating from a historian's perspective. It is Luke's intent to establish the historical reality of the life of Christ and to present the relevant historical facts. Thus he explains to his reader: "Therefore, since I myself have carefully investigated everything from the beginning, it seemed good also to me to write an orderly account for you, most excellent Theophilus, so that you may know the certainty of the things you have been taught" (Luke 1:3, 4).

The lessons for this quarter are all drawn from the Gospel of Luke. Taken as a whole, they will serve to summarize the life of Jesus from his birth in Bethlehem, to his teaching ministry, and then to the climax of his suffering on the cross and resurrection from the grave. It is a familiar story, but it is one that deserves to be reviewed again and again. Each time we do, we discover a new perspective that deepens our understanding of, and our appreciation for, our Lord and Savior.

A GIFT TO MANKIND

The first unit of five lessons is entitled, "A Savior is Born." Here we shall see the very first "Christmas gift," presented as God gives his beloved Son to mankind. A spirit of celebration and gratitude should spring from our study of the opening chapters of Luke as we are reminded of the angel's words to the shepherds: "I bring you good news of great joy that will be for all the people. Today in the town of David a Savior has been born to you; he is Christ the Lord" (Luke 2:10, 11).

DECEMBER

Lesson 1, "Preparing the Way," will highlight the ministry of John the Baptist as he made ready for the arrival of the promised Messiah. John's task was to create a climate of expectation in which Jesus could teach and minister effectively. His theme was repentance, something that is still required of any who wish to know Jesus as Lord and Savior.

Lesson 2, "Responding to God," will focus on the humility and trust of Mary as she welcomed the opportunity to fulfill God's role for her in bringing forth the long-awaited Messiah. This lesson will remind us of the kind of spirit that should characterize each of us, as seen in Mary's words: "I am the Lord's servant. . . . May it be to me as you have said" (Luke 1:38).

Lesson 3, "Praising God," will illustrate the nature of worship as we hear praise flow from the heart of the mother of Jesus. One of the most beloved prayers in Scripture is that spoken by Mary as she anticipates the birth of the Savior. *The Magnificat*, as Mary's praise is commonly called today, has been a source of inspiration for many and will move us to consider appropriate ways by which to exalt the name of the Lord and to express our gratitude for the "great things" he has done (Luke 1:49).

Lesson 4, "A Savior Is Born," will review what may be the most familiar chapter in the entire Bible—the Christmas story of Luke 2. We never tire of hearing about the baby Jesus' being born in humble surroundings and placed in a manger, or of the angel's announcing good news to the shepherds as they watched their flock by night. A devotional spirit will be most appropriate for the classroom, for this year the nativity story will be taught on a Christmas Eve Sunday.

Lesson 5, "Presented in the Temple," will focus on one of the lesser known events surrounding the birth of Jesus. As Mary and Joseph took their holy child into the temple shortly after his birth, they were confronted by an old man (Simeon) and an aged prophetess (Anna). Each acknowledged the significance of the child and expressed praise to God. This lesson will provide a final occasion to celebrate the birth of Christ as the holiday season draws to a close.

A CALL TO SERVICE

The second unit of study, "Mission and Ministry," presents four lessons drawn from the teaching ministry of Jesus. In the texts selected for study, we shall see how Jesus revealed the nature of his ministry while urging his disciples to follow his example. Our goal will be to learn more about how we can be faithful servants of Christ in our world today. *JANUARY*

Lesson 6, "Jesus in Nazareth," will give an example of the kind of opposition Jesus often confronted during his ministry. The occasion was Jesus' initial announcement to his hometown that he was, in fact, the fulfillment of the messianic prophecies. What should have been a cause for celebration turned into the first of many attempts on Jesus' life. Jesus' example shows us the kind of perseverance and determination needed when difficulties threaten to undermine our Christian service.

Lesson 7, "The Cost of Discipleship," will be one of the more challenging lessons in this quarter. It will remind us that Jesus' teaching on discipleship emphasizes a very demanding and rigorous commitment, comparable to what he himself gave in his service to God. This lesson should call forth reflection and self-evaluation as we consider how well we are living up to the calling we profess.

Lesson 8, "Lost and Found," will highlight one of the best-known parables of Jesus—the parable of the "prodigal son." How well we remember the story of the foolish young man who left the comfort of his father's home and then squandered his inheritance! In this lesson we shall celebrate the grace of our Father, who continues to love us even when we have disappointed him. But we shall also be challenged to develop the kind of repentance and humility that teaches us to appreciate God's grace.

Lesson 9, "Threat of Riches," will make a specific application of the discipleship theme to the way we manage our money and possessions. Worldly wealth can easily distract us from godly concerns, so much so that Scripture repeatedly cautions us to be wary of its appeal. In fact, our attitude toward worldly things is a good test of how much we are truly disciples of Christ.

THE WAY TO GLORY

The final unit of lessons, "Cross and Resurrection," focuses on the climax of the life of Christ—his death at Calvary and his resurrection from the dead. Of *FEBRUARY* the four Gospels, Luke in particular develops the theme of Jesus' focus on the cross (Luke 9:51) and how an ever-present anticipation of his suffering and death carried him to the completion of his ministry.

Lesson 10, "Going to Jerusalem," will provide an example of the clear perception Jesus had of the suffering that lay ahead of him. It will also take us back to the favorite childhood story of Zaccheus, the little man in the sycamore tree. Here we shall explore again the biblical themes of forgiveness and acceptance by God.

Lesson 11, "One Who Serves," will survey some of the events on the night when Jesus observed the Passover with his apostles and instituted the Lord's Supper. The truths regarding discipleship and service that were emphasized in our second unit of lessons were exemplified by the One who told his followers, "I am among you as one who serves" (Luke 22:27).

Lesson 12, "Dying on a Cross," will focus on Luke's account of the greatest act of love in history. The lesson will give us another opportunity to reflect on Jesus' suffering at Calvary for the sins of the world.

Lesson 13, "Witnesses to the Resurrection," will serve as a fitting conclusion to our study of the life of Christ. Jesus' resurrection confirms that a complete atonement for sins was accomplished on the cross. It is his resurrection that gives us hope of our own resurrection to eternal life with him.

The life, death, and resurrection of Jesus Christ do not belong in the realm of myth or legend; these are events that are firmly established in history. They are timeless truths to be cherished with all our hearts and to be proclaimed unashamedly to a lost world.

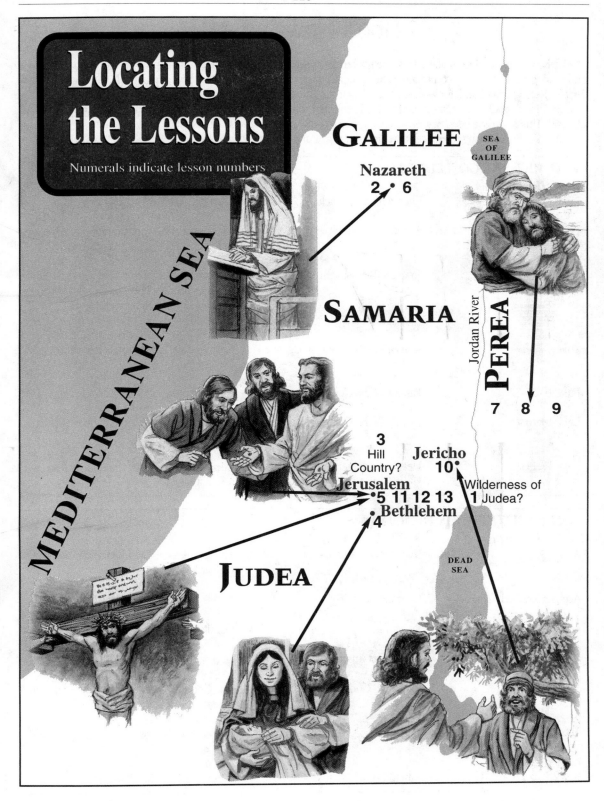

Good News for All

Matthew, Mark, and John all make some references to the impact of the gospel on all peoples. Consider Matthew's and Mark's record of Jesus' command to his disciples to go to "all nations" (Matthew 28:19) and "all creation" (Mark 16:15). Recall John's familiar words that "God so loved the world" (John 3:16).

Luke, however, demonstrates a particularly keen interest in God's concern for those considered outside the nation of Israel. This may have been of special significance to Luke since he himself, most likely, was a Gentile.

Consider the following references that are unique to Luke's writings:

VOLUME I: THE GOSPEL OF LUKE

REFERENCE	INCIDENT	SIGNIFICANCE
Luke 2:10	Shepherds in the field	"good news . . . for all the people"
Luke 2:29-32	Simeon in the temple	Jesus is described as a "light for revelation to the Gentiles"
Luke 3:6	John the Baptist's preaching	"all mankind" shall see God's salvation (all four Gospel writers quote from Isaiah; only Luke includes the reference to "all mankind")
Luke 4:25-27	Jesus in the Nazareth synagogue	God's special care for a Gentile widow and for Naaman (a Syrian)
Luke 10:25-37	Parable of the Good Samaritan	A Samaritan is commended for his kindness
Luke 14:15-24	Parable of the Great Supper	Those in the "roads and country lanes" represent the Gentiles
Luke 17:11-19	Healing of the ten lepers	The only healed leper who thanks Jesus is a Samaritan

VOLUME II: THE BOOK OF ACTS

REFERENCE	INCIDENT	SIGNIFICANCE
Acts 1:8	Jesus' Great Commission	The apostles are told to go to the "ends of the earth"
Acts 9:15; 22:21; 26:16-18	Commission to Paul	Paul is sent to the Gentiles
Acts 10:45; 11:18	Preaching to Cornelius	Gentiles accept the gospel
Acts 14:27	End of first missionary journey	God opens the "door of faith to the Gentiles"
Acts 15:12-19	Jerusalem Conference	The Gentiles' reception of the gospel is encouraged
Acts 20:21	Paul addresses Ephesian elders	Paul stresses his ministry to both Jews and Greeks
Acts 28:23-28	Paul in Rome	Gentiles' faith is highlighted

PREPARING THE WAY

LESSON 1

WHY TEACH THIS LESSON?

I am amazed at what passes for "news" these days! So much of the evening news concerns what used to be called trivia—interesting, if useless, information that seems more amusing than helpful. Some of it seems more like free advertising for certain businesses—especially if the establishment is disreputable!

I live in an area that has worked hard to get rid of sleazy, sexually oriented businesses. Hard-core pornography is hard to come by here, in spite of the recent efforts of one particular pornographer to bring his special brand of immorality to town. So every time he or some other promoter of illicit titillation makes a move or suggests opening a store or nightclub, that gets plenty of coverage at four, five, five-thirty, and six! Some of the news anchors seem almost apologetic that these so-called defenders of first-amendment rights have had such a rough time here. So much for objective reporting!

What we need is some good news, and today's lesson has it. John the Baptist was the first to break the news, in the Desert of Judea. And while it seems like anything that was news two thousand years ago could not still be news, in fact, it is. And your students need to be among the reporters who tell the good news. John is their example, as you will soon help them to see.

INTRODUCTION

A. "ALLOW ME TO INTRODUCE . . ."

Public speaking is a great challenge under any circumstance, but many speakers will tell you that one of the greatest challenges is to introduce someone else. How do you prepare an audience for what the speaker is going to say? How much do you tell the people about the speaker? How much do you say about the subject?

John the Baptist was given a similar assignment: he was to introduce the Messiah. How was he to prepare the people for such an individual? How much should he tell them about him? How much of the attention should he draw to himself? Judging from the Messiah's own words, John did a superlative job in preparing the way for Jesus. Jesus once said, "Among those born of women there has not risen anyone greater than John the Baptist" (Matthew 11:11).

John kept the primary focus of his ministry as "preparer" in mind, even when some of his own disciples expressed concern that Jesus was starting to gain a greater following than his. John was not jealous or upset to hear this; his response left no doubt that he was content to be what God had called him to be. "He must become greater; I must become less," said John of the Messiah (John 3:30).

John the Baptist was willing to take second place—to tell others, "Allow me to introduce you to Jesus"—and then to slip into the background. That's not a bad description of our responsibility as disciples of Jesus today.

B. LESSON BACKGROUND

Even though John the Baptist was content to take a back seat to Jesus, his ministry had a significant impact. At one point in Jesus' ministry Herod Antipas speculated that he might be John the Baptist returning from the dead (Matthew

DEVOTIONAL READING:
ISAIAH 40:1-5
BACKGROUND SCRIPTURE:
LUKE 1:5-25; 3:1-22
PRINTED TEXT:
LUKE 3:2b-18

LESSON AIMS

After participating in this lesson, each student will be able to:

1. Summarize what Luke says about the message of John the Baptist.

2. Tell why some of the specific applications in John's message are important to a demonstration of repentance.

3. State one action he or she will take this week as a demonstration of repentance from past sins and commitment to the Lord.

KEY VERSE

"A voice of one calling in the desert, 'Prepare the way for the Lord, make straight paths for him.'"
—Luke 3:4

HOW TO SAY IT

Antipas. AN-tih-pus.
Essenes. EH-seenz.
Gabriel. GAY-bree-ul.
Herod. HAIR-ud.
Isaiah. Eye-ZAY-uh.
Pharisees. FAIR-ih-seez.
Sadducees. SAD-you-seez.
Zaccheus. Zack-KEE-us.
Zechariah. Zek-uh-RYE-uh.

14:2). During Jesus' final week of ministry the Jewish leaders did not want to appear critical of John lest they offend the crowds in Jerusalem (Matthew 21:23-27). Some of the men who became part of Jesus' twelve disciples were originally disciples of John the Baptist (John 1:35-42). John was also a man of godly courage, who was not afraid to tell a king the truth even though it cost him his life (Matthew 14:3-11).

Today's lesson serves not only as the introductory lesson to our studies from Luke's Gospel but also as the first in a unit of lessons that will take us through the Christmas season. This unit will focus on some of the unique contributions that Luke makes to our understanding of the birth of Christ and the events surrounding it. Some might question why we should pay attention to John the Baptist during the season when we celebrate the birth of Jesus. Just as John prepared people for the arrival of the Messiah on the stage of history, he can prepare us to celebrate the true meaning of the Christmas season.

I. JOHN AND HIS MINISTRY (LUKE 3:2b-6)

A. HIS BAPTISM (vv. 2b, 3)

2. The word of God came to John son of Zechariah in the desert.

John the Baptist was a prophet (Luke 7:26), cast in the same mold as the prophets of the Old Testament. When the text says *the word of God came to John*, it is using words that remind us of the kind of call that summoned those men who proclaimed God's message fearlessly to his people Israel. Prophets did not invent their own messages; they were ministers of the oracles of God.

John is described as the *son of Zechariah*. Zechariah, whose name means "God remembers," was a priest. Luke is the only Gospel writer to mention him. Earlier Luke tells of how, when Zechariah was taking his turn of service in the temple, the angel Gabriel appeared to him and announced that he and his wife Elizabeth would have a son in their old age (Luke 1:5-23).

We may wonder why John conducted his ministry *in the desert*. Perhaps he was distancing himself from the religious establishment that resided in the cities. Some have speculated that John may have been a member of the Essenes, a sect of the Jews known for its simplicity and strictness of lifestyle. But there is no biblical evidence to support such a notion.

3. He went into all the country around the Jordan, preaching a baptism of repentance for the forgiveness of sins.

John's ministry took him *into all the country around the Jordan*. Matthew says John preached "in the Desert of Judea" (Matthew 3:1). Most likely Luke's words describe John's preaching in the wilderness areas on both sides of the Jordan River.

The reason John became known as "John the Baptist" (or "Baptizer") was his distinctive message and practice. He came *preaching a baptism of repentance for the forgiveness of sins*. This explains why John stayed near the Jordan River: he wanted to remain close to a body of water in which to perform baptisms.

Christian baptism would later build on the concepts of repentance and remission of sins, adding a connection with the death, burial, and resurrection of Jesus and with the gift of the Holy Spirit (Acts 2:38). Thus John's baptism looked forward to the time when remission of sins could be offered as a result of Jesus' death and resurrection, just as the Old Testament sacrifices looked forward to Jesus' perfect sacrifice.

Was the idea of baptism totally contrary to Jewish thinking and experience? First-century Judaism did include a "proselyte baptism" to bring Gentile converts into the Jewish faith, but there is no clear evidence that this preceded John's baptism. John's baptism was unique in its form and, more significantly, in its purpose.

B. HIS MISSION (vv. 4-6)

4. As is written in the book of the words of Isaiah the prophet: "A voice of one calling in the desert, 'Prepare the way for the Lord, make straight paths for him.

Here Luke quotes from *Isaiah* 40:3. The prophet's language describes what happened whenever a king prepared for a journey. Workers and soldiers would proceed in advance to make sure that the road on which the king would travel was smooth and safe. John saw himself as engaged in a similar task on behalf of the Messiah.

How were John's listeners to *prepare the way for the Lord* and *make straight paths for him?* By turning the people's attention to spiritual concerns, John was seeking to heighten their receptiveness to the Messiah's message of a spiritual kingdom. John had no desire to further his own agenda; "he himself was not the light; he came only as a witness to the light" (John 1:8).

5. "'Every valley shall be filled in, every mountain and hill made low. The crooked roads shall become straight, the rough ways smooth.

The figure of speech continues with a description of the process involved in preparing the Messiah's way, making it both smoother and straighter. John's preaching was aimed at encouraging his hearers to clear away any obstacles in their thinking and living that could cause them to miss "God's salvation" (v. 6).

6. "'And all mankind will see God's salvation.'"

When the Messiah arrives, *all mankind will see God's salvation.* While all four Gospel writers refer to Isaiah's prophecy (Matthew 3:3; Mark 1:3; John 1:23), only Luke includes this emphasis that Jesus came for all mankind, not just for the Jewish nation. This is one of Luke's major themes in both Luke and Acts (cf. Luke 2:10, 29-32; 13:29; 17:11-19; 24:47; Acts 1:8; 11:18; 13:41-48; 15:12-19). It was probably of special significance to him, since he himself, most likely, was a Gentile.

II. JOHN AND HIS MESSAGE (LUKE 3:7-14)

A. STERN WARNINGS (vv. 7-9)

7. John said to the crowds coming out to be baptized by him, "You brood of vipers! Who warned you to flee from the coming wrath?

The use of the word *crowds* indicates a diverse group of people. Luke's emphasis is more inclusive than that of Matthew, who calls attention to the Pharisees and Sadducees who came to John's baptism (Matthew 3:7). John's message would have been particularly irritating for the Jewish leaders to hear, but it was intended for everyone in his audience.

John's message was uncompromising, and his rhetoric was strong. He described the crowd as a *brood of vipers.* Later Jesus would use the same figure of speech to portray the Pharisees (Matthew 12:34). John's question, *Who warned you to flee from the coming wrath?* may have been tinged with sarcasm (particularly toward the Pharisees and Sadducees), indicating that they had heard numerous warnings concerning God's *wrath.* They simply refused to listen.

8. "Produce fruit in keeping with repentance. And do not begin to say to yourselves, 'We have Abraham as our father.' For I tell you that out of these stones God can raise up children for Abraham.

John urged his hearers to *produce fruit in keeping with repentance.* It is important for every Christian to bear fruit. No one can see another person's heart. The only way to tell whether genuine repentance has occurred is by examining the deeds, or fruit, of someone's life. It has been said that while works do not justify us, they do identify us.

John also urged his audience not to depend on their ancestry to save them. There was no security in saying, *We have Abraham as our* genealogical *father.* John

WHAT DO YOU THINK?

What kind of "fruit" is "in keeping with repentance"?

[Consider the difference between sorrow for sin and genuine repentance—i.e., a "turning around," a "change of course." The truly repentant will replace certain elements of their lives with positive alternatives—encourage your learners to suggest some of these alternatives.]

DAILY BIBLE READINGS

Monday, Nov. 27—The Prophecy of John's Birth (Luke 1:5-17)

Tuesday, Nov. 28—Too Good to Be True (Luke 1:18-25)

Wednesday, Nov. 29—John the Baptist's Birth (Luke 1:57-66)

Thursday, Nov. 30—Prophetic Words of Hope (Isaiah 40:1-5)

Friday, Dec. 1—John's Proclamation (Luke 3:1-6)

Saturday, Dec. 2—Baptism, Repentance, and Change (Luke 3:7-14)

Sunday, Dec. 3—The Truth Hurts (Luke 3:15-20)

declared that God could make *children* of Abraham out of *stones* if he so desired. Clearly the One who created man from the dust of the earth could also make people from stones; John's audience would have admitted that. That these new creations could be children of Abraham foreshadowed the Christian message that all people can by faith be children of Abraham (Romans 4:11, 12).

9. *"The ax is already at the root of the trees, and every tree that does not produce good fruit will be cut down and thrown into the fire."*

Here John used a figure of speech to illustrate impending judgment. He pictured a farmer cutting down a lifeless, fruitless *tree* and casting it into the *fire* to be burned. Why is it burned? Because it is useless. Recall words similar to these in John 15:6.

B. PRACTICAL APPLICATIONS (vv. 10-14)

10. *"What should we do then?" the crowd asked.*

The crowd responded to John's appeal in a way strikingly similar to the response to Peter's sermon in Luke's sequel, the book of Acts (2:37). They asked, *What should we do then?*

11. *John answered, "The man with two tunics should share with him who has none, and the one who has food should do the same."*

To the crowd in general, John suggested a very practical application of his message: he urged compassion on the needy. In John's day, most people had no need of *two tunics*, so John recommended sharing with anyone who had none. (The *tunic* was worn by both men and women under one's outer garment or robe.)

John urged the sharing of *food* with those who have none. If this spirit of kindness characterized disciples of John, how much more should it be the trademark of followers of Jesus!

WEARING AND SHARING

When the Communists controlled Eastern Europe, Christians in those countries came from time to time to Vienna, Austria, to a mission called Haus Edelweiss (House Ay-del-vice). In addition to offering Bible classes, the mission kept a used clothing room. Each guest was given an opportunity to spend a couple of hours there and take anything that he or his family could use. During one conference the weather turned rather cool, so my wife suggested some might want to make a second visit to the clothing room to get a sweater. Later a man from Estonia came to her with a sweater and said, "I would like to donate this to the clothing room. I already have a sweater."

This man's attitude toward his possessions reminded us of John the Baptist's challenge: "The man with two tunics should share with him who has none." We live in a world where many are poorly clothed. The need is so enormous that we cannot clothe them all. But if we can clothe one, we should. Likewise, we live in a world where millions are hungry. We cannot personally feed them all. But if we can feed one, we should.

We need to take John's teaching out of the realm of theory and put it into action. How many times do we look into our closets and say, "I don't have a thing to wear!" Wouldn't it be more accurate to say that we do not have anything we *want* to wear, or that we cannot decide what to wear?

Let's keep our eyes open to the blessings we have and to the needs of those around us. Many would dearly love to have what we often consider "nothing" to wear or "nothing" to eat.   —R. C. S.

12. *Tax collectors also came to be baptized. "Teacher," they asked, "what should we do?"*

Luke notes that even *tax collectors also came to be baptized*. Tax collectors have never been popular, but in Jesus' day they were especially despised as thieves and traitors. They were viewed as traitors because of their cooperation with the Romans. They were regarded as thieves because many of them were! The Roman system of collection encouraged them to use strong-arm tactics and take more than was required, allowing them to pocket the surplus. Recall that Jesus made a great impact on two tax collectors in particular—Matthew and Zaccheus.

13. "Don't collect any more than you are required to," he told them.

John commanded the tax collectors that they should not *collect any more than* what was *required* by law. Zaccheus, following his encounter with Jesus, was so concerned about his own practices that he gave half of his wealth to the poor and offered four-fold restitution to those whom he had cheated (Luke 19:8).

14. Then some soldiers asked him, "And what should we do?"

He replied, "Don't extort money and don't accuse people falsely—be content with your pay."

Even *soldiers* were attracted to John's message. We do not know what kind of soldiers these were. Limited numbers of them were available to guard the king, to monitor the temple, and to escort tax collectors. Soldiers also served as a kind of police force. John urged these men to be ethical in their dealings with people. They were not to *extort money* or lie in making accusations.

John did not recommend that either tax collectors or soldiers resign from their positions. He told them to demonstrate integrity in everything they did, thus showing "fruit in keeping with repentance" (v. 8).

PREACHER PIERCE

He was a bi-vocational minister whom everyone called "Preacher Pierce." His full-time job was running a collection station for cream brought in by the local farmers. He owned the small building and all the equipment, and he had a contract with a company to collect and store the cream for a percentage of the money paid to the farmer. On one occasion, at the end of the month he kept the check that he received from the company and did not cash it. When the representative of the firm came by, Preacher Pierce told him, "This check is wrong, and I won't accept it."

The representative said, "That is the amount we agreed to pay you, and we will not pay you one penny more."

"You misunderstand," Pierce replied. "It's not that the check is too small. It's too big. I don't think I earned this much, and I won't accept it!"

Consider this man's attitude in light of John the Baptist's challenge to "be content with your pay." Most people are discontent, not because they are paid too much, but because they believe they are paid too little! A great deal of envy, bitterness, anxiety, and frustration could be avoided if people took to heart the words of "Preacher John."

As for "Preacher Pierce"—what became of him? By refusing to accept what he thought he had not earned, he earned the respect of the entire community; and his ministry had an impact that it probably would not have had otherwise. —R. C. S.

III. JOHN AND THE MESSIAH (LUKE 3:15-18)

A. JOHN'S NOTORIETY (v. 15)

15. The people were waiting expectantly and were all wondering in their hearts if John might possibly be the Christ.

Some among the crowds were *wondering* privately *if John might possibly be the Christ*. It is clear, especially from the apostle John's account, that John the Baptist was not the Messiah and never claimed to be (John 1:8, 19-27; 3:28). He was true to his role as forerunner, calling attention only to his successor, never to himself.

WHAT DO YOU THINK?

What if your occupation were represented in the crowd? If someone with the same job as you asked John, "What should we do?" what do you think John would have said?

PRAYER

Father, I come to you for mercy, and I present to you my desire for a changed life. May it be evident to all that I am serving you. Strengthen me for the crucial task of being fruitful in a rotting world. In Jesus' name and for his sake, amen.

B. JOHN'S HUMILITY (vv. 16-18)

16. John answered them all, "I baptize you with water. But one more powerful than I will come, the thongs of whose sandals I am not worthy to untie. He will baptize you with the Holy Spirit and with fire.

To illustrate the superiority of the Messiah, John referred to his own baptism and compared it with the baptism that Jesus would institute. (Since John was known primarily for his baptism, this served as an especially effective comparison.) John said, *I baptize you with water.* He then noted that the Messiah would administer a superior baptism: *he will baptize you with the Holy Spirit and with fire.*

Some believe that the baptism with the Spirit refers to what happened on the day of Pentecost when the Holy Spirit came upon the apostles (Acts 2:1-4). Others maintain that this baptism with the Spirit is identical to what is called the gift of the Holy Spirit—that is, the promise that the Holy Spirit will dwell in all Christians (Acts 2:38; 5:32; 1 Corinthians 12:13). Luke himself seems to indicate the former when he quotes the resurrected Christ telling the apostles to "wait for the gift my Father promised" and adding, "For John baptized with water, but in a few days you will be baptized with the Holy Spirit" (Acts 1:4, 5). The baptism *with fire* most likely describes God's judgment, given the reference to fire in verse 17.

Once again, John's humility is demonstrated in his acknowledgment that he was not *worthy to untie* the *sandals* of the Messiah. John refused to receive any acclaim that should go to the One whose way he was preparing.

17. "His winnowing fork is in his hand to clear his threshing floor and to gather the wheat into his barn, but he will burn up the chaff with unquenchable fire."

In continuing his description of judgment, John announced that the Messiah will come with a *winnowing fork*—a farm implement that was used on the *threshing floor* after *wheat* was cut during the harvest. First, the grain was separated from the straw, often by having oxen trample it. Then, in order to separate the kernel of wheat from the lighter shell or *chaff*, the grain was scooped up with a wide fork and tossed into the air. The wind separated the light chaff from the heavier grain, which was then stored in a *barn.* In a similar way, the Messiah will separate the truly repentant from the wicked, gathering the former to be with him and destroying the latter (Matthew 13:41-43).

18. And with many other words John exhorted the people and preached the good news to them.

We can only speculate about the content of these *other words* that John *preached.* About the purpose of this exhortation there need be no speculation. John's words were meant to point away from himself and toward Jesus.

WHAT DO YOU THINK?

John's task is our task—to point people toward Jesus. How are we tempted to draw attention to ourselves? How can we more effectively point people to Jesus?

CONCLUSION

John the Baptist's message speaks powerfully to Christians today. He taught that the process of preparing the way for the Messiah was to prepare one's heart through repentance and visible evidence of a reformed life.

How much more is this an appropriate way to prepare for Jesus' second coming! The world often associates repentance with an "old-fashioned" religion that has no relevance whatever to modern times. It will be more likely to understand the concept if it can see "fruit in keeping with repentance" in the lives of God's people.

Most are acquainted with the Boy Scout motto: *Be prepared.* That's the substance of what John told people in his day; it describes the attitude of Christians as we consider the promised return of Jesus. And, like those in John's audience, we should look at our lives, take stock of our level of preparation, and ask ourselves the question, *What should we do?*

THOUGHT TO REMEMBER

Repentance and reformation bring restoration.

Discovery Learning

This page contains an alternate lesson plan emphasizing learning activities. Classes desiring such student involvement will find these suggestions helpful. The next page is a reproducible activity page to further enhance discovery learning.

LEARNING GOALS

After this lesson each student will be able to:

1. Summarize what Luke says about the message of John the Baptist.

2. Tell why some of the specific applications in John's message are important to a demonstration of repentance.

3. State one action he or she will take this week as a demonstration of repentance from past sins and commitment to the Lord.

INTO THE LESSON

Ask class members to imagine that the President of the United States (substitute the appropriate title and country if you live outside the U.S.) is coming to your town in one month. Discuss what would be done (and by whom) to prepare for this event. Encourage the class members to be as detailed as possible.

Tell the students, "When someone important is expected to arrive on the scene, there is always considerable preparation. Let's look at how the way was prepared for Jesus' ministry."

INTO THE WORD

Examine the character of John the Baptist in parallel texts—Matthew 3:1-6; Mark 1:1-8; John 1:19-27. Assign each text to one third of the class for reading and thinking. Instruct the students to look for characteristics of John because they will be telling you what to list on the chalkboard. They may suggest *humble, obedient, simple, bold, rugged,* or *biblically literate.* Read the list and comment on his obedience, sense of duty, and responsibility.

With this background understanding of John, ask a volunteer to read Luke 3:2b-18. Form groups of four or five and distribute copies of the reproducible activity page that follows. Ask the students to use the top activity and summarize the significance of each of the sections of text. Discuss the responses as a class. Emphasize the following areas of significance:

Verses 2b-6: John's heritage (son of Zechariah, a Levite), his prophetic role (the word of God came to him; fulfilled the prophecy of Isaiah 40:3-5).

Verses 7-9: the view of repentance as action.

Verses 10-14: specific applications.

Verses 15-18: preparation for the incarnation of God: Jesus.

Class members may ask some of the following questions or you may raise them.

"Why would the people wonder if John were the Christ?" (*The religious establishment was seeking a Messiah. The incorporation of Israel into the Roman Empire caused some to expect the coming of the Messiah.*)

"What is the difference between the baptism of John and Christian baptism as we know it today?" (*The baptism of John was in accordance with repentance and forgiveness of sins; Christian baptism builds on this—cf. Acts 19:4, 5. In addition, Christian baptism is intimately bound with the death, burial, and resurrection of Jesus Christ, which had not yet taken place.*)

Observe, "Many types of people were asking the same question of John that day: 'What should we do?'" Discuss what the various responses that John gave have in common. Ask the students to suggest how we can act in the same spirit even if our specific actions may differ.

INTO LIFE

Instruct the students to look at the activity at the bottom of the activity page. Then ask them to use each letter of the word to begin a word or phrase that describes a specific action one might take today in demonstration of true repentance. Ask, "If we could bring John the Baptist back to life and have him visit our class, what might he say to us? If we asked, 'What should *we* do?' how might he answer us?" Use the acronym to suggest some answers. As appropriate, have class members tell how they completed the acronym.

Observe, "We know Jesus is coming, and we often speak of being 'ready' for his return. How is preparation for Jesus' return similar to and different from the preparations for his first coming?" (*In each case the exact time of his coming was/is unknown. In both cases repentance was/is appropriate. In preparing for his first coming, John was preparing the people to hear and believe the message that was yet to be delivered. In our preparation, we want people to accept the truth already available. John prepared for Jesus to **begin** his work; we prepare for Jesus to **complete** his work.*)

Point out that John the Baptist fulfilled his responsibility in preparing the way for the coming of Jesus. Discuss, "What is our responsibility in preparing for the return of Jesus? What shall we do?" Close the lesson with a prayer for each class member to repent.

Areas of Significance

How would you summarize the significance of each of the following sections of our text?

Luke 3:2b-6

Luke 3:7-9

Luke 3:10-14

Luke 3:15-18

What Shall *We* Do?

This question is repeated by different groups of people in the text. Using the letters of the word REPENT, write different aspects of repentance that are needed in your life.

R _____

E _____

P _____

E _____

N _____

T _____

RESPONDING TO GOD

LESSON 2

WHY TEACH THIS LESSON?

We often speak of a child's "taking after" one of his or her parents. What we mean, of course, is that the child displays a character trait or personality feature similar to that parent. In many ways, Jesus "took after" his Father because of the unique oneness they shared (John 10:30).

But Jesus took after his mother as well. When Jesus said he "did not come to be served, but to serve" (Matthew 20:28), he echoed his mother's response to Gabriel, "I am the Lord's servant" (Luke 1:38). If your students would take after Jesus, they can start in no better place than with Mary. You will help them do that in today's lesson.

INTRODUCTION

A. THE IMPORTANCE OF MOTHERHOOD

While both parents of a child are important, there has always been a special emphasis placed on motherhood. This remains true even in our day, in spite of efforts by some to downplay the significance of motherhood. But no one can discount what it means when a woman bears in her own body the life of a growing baby. Her body sustains the very life of that child. Nor can anyone discount the pain involved in childbirth.

Clearly great sacrifices are made by a woman in order to bring a child into the world. Because of this and many other reasons, there is a unique bond between mother and child. This was particularly true in the ancient world, where the mother was the first and usually only teacher and caregiver for a child. What a humbling responsibility it was, then, for Mary to carry within her body the Messiah! Such a holy privilege had to be given to someone who could bear both the blessings and the burdens that accompanied the honor. Surely God found that kind of person in Mary of Nazareth.

B. BABIES CHANGE EVERYTHING

Every family has discovered that the addition of a baby changes everything— immediately! Everyone's schedule must be altered to accommodate the baby's needs. Not only will there be the new experience of midnight feedings, but regular meal times will never be the same—in fact, nothing will ever be the same.

Certainly the addition of a baby changed everything for Mary and Joseph. Along with the changes to which all parents must adjust, they faced additional burdens from raising such an extraordinary child in extraordinary circumstances.

Of course, there is another higher sense in which Mary and Joseph's baby has changed everything—for all people. Our world has never been the same since Jesus came. He has changed the way we look at God, ourselves, and the world. He continues to change individuals who come to him in faith and obedience.

C. LESSON BACKGROUND

Today's lesson forms an interesting kind of "package" with last week's and next week's. Last week we considered the impact of the ministry of John the Baptist.

DEVOTIONAL READING:
MATTHEW 1:18-25
BACKGROUND SCRIPTURE:
LUKE 1:26-38
PRINTED TEXT:
LUKE 1:26-38

LESSON AIMS

After participating in this lesson, each student will be able to:

1. Give the important details of Gabriel's message to Mary and her response to it.

2. Tell why Mary's response to God's will is an appropriate model for Christians.

3. Think of a difficult decision or issue he or she is facing, and commit that matter to God in simple faith.

KEY VERSE

"I am the Lord's servant," Mary answered. *"May it be to me as you have said."* —Luke 1:38

Next week we shall look at Mary's visit to Elizabeth, who was the mother of John the Baptist. This week we examine the announcement to Mary (described as a "relative" of Elizabeth in Luke 1:36) that she would give birth to the Messiah.

Luke provides some significant details surrounding the birth of Jesus that are not found in the other Gospels. His account of what happened on the night of Jesus' birth is the fullest account of what we call the "Christmas story." Luke supplies information about the conception and birth of John the Baptist that no other writer does. We are also given a personal glimpse into the thoughts of Mary as she first became aware of her special role in God's plan.

In some ways, the account of the announcement to Mary resembles the account of the announcement to Zechariah concerning John the Baptist. Indeed, the same angel (Gabriel) appears to the individuals involved to tell them the startling news.

I. THE ANGEL'S MESSAGE (LUKE 1:26-33)

A. THE MOTHER GOD CHOOSES (vv. 26-28)

26. In the sixth month, God sent the angel Gabriel to Nazareth, a town in Galilee.

Our text describes events that took place *in the sixth month*. This does not refer to the sixth month of the year, but to the sixth month of Elizabeth's pregnancy with John the Baptist. This is clear from the description of how Elizabeth "remained in seclusion" for five months in Luke 1:24 and from the angel's words concerning Elizabeth in verse 36 that she was "in her sixth month." The mention of Elizabeth's pregnancy indicates that Jesus was about six months younger than John the Baptist.

God's message to Mary was sent by way of *the angel Gabriel*. The name Gabriel can mean "mighty man of God" or "God is my hero." He was *sent* to the town of *Nazareth*, a small *town in Galilee* that covered approximately seven acres in New Testament times.

The designation *Galilee* means "the circle," indicating that the name must have referred originally to a group of towns that formed a rough circle in northern Palestine. By living this far north, the Jews in Galilee came into more frequent contact with Gentiles than did the Jews in Judea to the south. No doubt the distance to Jerusalem prevented many Galileans from attending some of the annual feasts in Jerusalem. These factors and others caused the Jews in Judea to consider Galileans inferior to themselves. Nazareth itself was held in such contempt that Nathanael, on hearing that Jesus was from Nazareth, wondered if any good could come from there (John 1:45, 46).

27. . . . to a virgin pledged to be married to a man named Joseph, a descendant of David. The virgin's name was Mary.

Even before we learn the name of the person to whom Gabriel was sent, we learn something more significant about her: she was a *virgin*. Matthew notes that the virgin birth fulfilled a prophecy spoken by Isaiah (Isaiah 7:14; Matthew 1:22, 23).

The virgin birth of Christ has troubled some people, for the very idea goes against the normal manner by which children are born. But this is to be expected in someone who was not a "normal" human being. If Jesus is the unique Son of God and Messiah, and one whose life was characterized by the miraculous, should it be any great surprise that he would come to the earth in a miraculous manner?

At this time, *Mary* was *pledged to be married* to Joseph. This pledge, called "betrothal," involved a step that was short of actual marriage but much stronger than our idea of engagement. If a girl's betrothed died, for example, she was

WHAT DO YOU THINK?

Nazareth was perhaps the last place anyone would expect to produce a leader of any kind. It was not a center of commerce, politics, education, or religion. What significance, if any, do you see in the fact that God chose a woman of Nazareth, an obscure little Galilean village, to be the mother of Jesus?

considered a widow. In fact, a betrothal could be abolished only by an act of divorce. Betrothal was considered a legal contract for a future marriage, but sexual relations between the couple were not permitted until after the marriage ceremony. At the same time, sexual relations between one of the parties and someone other than the betrothed was considered adultery. This explains why, according to Matthew's Gospel, Joseph at first planned to divorce Mary upon learning of her pregnancy (Matthew 1:19).

Joseph was *a descendant of David*. In Luke 2 we are told that this was the reason he went to Bethlehem, in obedience to the emperor's decree (Luke 2:1-4). Chapter 3 of Luke's Gospel includes a genealogy of Jesus (vv. 23-38), which is generally considered to trace his ancestry on Mary's side. Since this mentions David (v. 31), it appears that she also was a descendant of David.

28. The angel went to her and said, "Greetings, you who are highly favored! The Lord is with you."

The angel Gabriel began his message with *Greetings*, followed by the declaration that Mary was considered *highly favored* by God. Gabriel's words indicate that Mary was a person of unique piety. We could expect no less for the mother of Jesus.

Mary was also informed that *the Lord is with you*. She would need that comfort, not only on this day, but in the difficult days that lay ahead. Such comfort was frequently offered to God's servants when they faced a particularly daunting task (Moses in Exodus 3:12; Joshua in Joshua 1:5; Gideon in Judges 6:12; Jeremiah in Jeremiah 1:8).

B. THE COMFORT GOD BRINGS (vv. 29, 30)

29. Mary was greatly troubled at his words and wondered what kind of greeting this might be.

As we might expect, Mary at first was fearful of this messenger. Any angelic visitation usually produced great anxiety (Judges 6:22; Mark 16:5, 6; Luke 1:11, 12). In Mary's case, it was not just the appearance of the angel that caused concern; she also *wondered* about the meaning of the words that the angel had spoken. Humble people are always uneasy with high praise, and what higher praise could have been accorded Mary than this? No wonder she *was greatly troubled!*

30. But the angel said to her, "Do not be afraid, Mary, you have found favor with God.

The angel's next words, *Do not be afraid*, are the same words the shepherds would hear outside of Bethlehem (Luke 2:10). As noted above, fear is a normal response to seeing an angel.

Not only did Mary have nothing to fear; she had much for which to be grateful. Once again she was told that she had *found favor with God*. What a compliment! This angelic visit was not to pronounce judgment; it was to announce God's choice of Mary for a special purpose.

C. THE CHILD GOD SENDS (vv. 31-33)

31. "You will be with child and give birth to a son, and you are to give him the name Jesus.

Even though Jesus' *birth* was miraculous in that he was conceived in the womb of a virgin, it was in every other respect a normal human pregnancy and birth. The Son of God did not spring from the head of a god or grow from a flower or appear from the water. The accounts in the four Gospels exhibit none of the markings of ancient myths. Jesus entered the world as all human beings have—by birth. His coming to our world was characterized by a wonderful combination of the supernatural and the natural.

How to Say It

Gabriel. GAY-bree-ul.
Gideon. GID-ee-un.
Isaiah. Eye-ZAY-uh.
Jeremiah. Jair-uh-MY-uh.
Nathanael. Nuh-THAN-yull.
Nazareth. NAZ-uh-reth.
Zechariah. Zek-uh-RYE-uh.

WHAT DO YOU THINK?

The angel Gabriel told Mary that she was "highly favored" and that she had "found favor with God." What does it mean to find favor with God? How does knowing that the word for favor is often translated "grace" or "gift" influence your thinking on this issue? Consider that the gospel story is about God's showing favor (grace) to those who do not deserve it. "While we were still sinners, Christ died for us" (Romans 5:8). How do we, like Mary, find favor with God?

[Consider Ephesians 2:8, 9; Hebrews 4:16; and James 4:6 in your discussion.]

The *name* chosen for the child was *Jesus,* which is the Greek form of the Old Testament name *Joshua.* While this was a very common name, it was particularly appropriate for the Messiah, since it means, "The Lord is salvation." Just as Joshua led the children of Israel into the freedom of the promised land, so this new Joshua will lead his people from the slavery of sin into the freedom of eternal life.

COMMON NAME, UNCOMMON CHILD

Two boys, Joe and Max, were talking at the local playground one day. Max, who came from a well-to-do family and whose father was a prominent businessman, was bragging about all the nice things his family owned. Repeatedly he belittled Joe and his family in the process. Finally Joe said, "I've got something you don't have and probably never will have."

"Like what?" asked Max.

"The name Joe," replied Joe. Then he walked off, leaving Max standing speechless.

Jesus was a common name in the first century. Thus the designation "Jesus of Nazareth" was used to distinguish Mary's son from others of the same name. There is even another Jesus mentioned in the New Testament (Colossians 4:11).

Such a common name reflects the purpose for which Jesus came to earth. He was like us in so many ways: he was born; he grew from infancy to adulthood; he was hungry (Matthew 4:2) and tired (John 4:6); he was "tempted in every way, just as we are" (Hebrews 4:15).

And yet he was *un*common—*un*like us in so many ways. The most important of these was that, though tempted like us, he "was without sin" (Hebrews 4:15). This fact leads us to the heart of the gospel: the uncommon, sinless Son of God died in the place of common sinners.

Jesus was known by a common name, but he lived up to the meaning of that name—Savior—in a way that no one else could. —R. C. S.

32. "He will be great and will be called the Son of the Most High. The Lord God will give him the throne of his father David,

While Jesus was a descendant of *David* and even though his reign was described as occurring on David's *throne,* he was not to be a king exactly like David. Jesus' kingdom was not political or earthly at all; it was a spiritual and heavenly kingdom, "not of this world" (John 18:36). The nature of Jesus' messiahship was a frequent source of contention among Jews in trying to evaluate him. No one doubted that the Messiah would be a king, but they often assumed that he would rule according to the world's definition of "king," not God's.

Gabriel also referred to Jesus as *the Son of the Most High,* indicating his deity. (This is also emphasized in verse 35.) Later Zechariah spoke of John the Baptist as a "prophet of the Most High" (Luke 1:76). John was a spokesman for God; Jesus was the Son of God.

33. ". . . and he will reign over the house of Jacob forever; his kingdom will never end."

Crowns and thrones of this earth will perish. How different is the *kingdom* of Jesus, which *will never end!* These words call to mind the promise that God gave to David, found in 2 Samuel 7:16: "Your house and your kingdom will endure forever before me; your throne will be established forever." (See also Daniel 2:44; 7:14.)

II. MARY'S RESPONSE (LUKE 1:34-38)

A. HER QUESTION (vv. 34, 35)

34. "How will this be," Mary asked the angel, "since I am a virgin?"

Mary's initial reaction was to question *how* the promised birth could occur outside of normal sexual relations with a man. Such a birth seemed to defy all

WHAT DO YOU THINK?

Mary was confused. So she asked, "How will this be, since I am a virgin?" How can we encourage young people and others to ask questions freely when they do not understand theological issues?

logic. While many today find the virgin birth a difficult truth to accept, we must keep in mind that this was no less true for Mary. Her response to Gabriel's message was different from Zechariah's unbelief (Luke 1:18-20). Her question indicated acceptance, but she was perplexed with a natural bewilderment.

35. *The angel answered, "The Holy Spirit will come upon you, and the power of the Most High will overshadow you. So the holy one to be born will be called the Son of God.*

In answer to Mary's inquiry, Gabriel declared that the *Holy Spirit* would be responsible for the conception of the promised child. A veil of privacy continues to hide the mechanics of the act of conception and how God accomplished it. This is as it should be. Even a normal conception is filled with mystery and wonder and is most difficult to describe. Gabriel's words simply state that the entire process would be miraculous and that the child would not be the offspring of any earthly father. He *will be called the Son of God.*

B. HER SIGN (vv. 36, 37)

36. *"Even Elizabeth your relative is going to have a child in her old age, and she who was said to be barren is in her sixth month.*

Mary did not ask Gabriel for any kind of confirming sign, yet one was offered: the pregnancy of *Elizabeth*, her *relative*. Elizabeth's conception, despite the fact that she had been childless and that both she and Zechariah were "well along in years" (Luke 1:7), was a sign that God could do whatever he wished.

This calls to mind women such as Sarah (Genesis 18:9-15), the mother of Samson (Judges 13:2, 3), and Hannah (1 Samuel 1:11), all of whom were considered barren. Yet God overruled their condition and gave them the privilege of becoming mothers. (In Sarah's case, her age also appeared to prevent her from having children.)

We can understand why Mary "hurried" to visit Elizabeth (vv. 39, 40). God had done something "impossible" for both of them!

37. *"For nothing is impossible with God."*

This statement (or one similar in meaning to it) is made in more than one place in Scripture (Genesis 18:14; Jeremiah 32:17; Matthew 19:26), but here it is especially appropriate. The virgin birth is unique. To believe it, one must affirm that God is not limited by the so-called "laws of nature." Since he is the one who put those laws into effect, he can set them aside or override them at any time to accomplish his purposes. Thus *nothing is impossible with God.*

SPECIALIZING IN THE IMPOSSIBLE

The songs and choruses that are sung in Christian youth camps change over the years—just as the songs we sing in worship services change over the years. One that was popular years ago, but is seldom heard today, is a chorus with these words: "God specializes in things thought impossible. He does the things others cannot do."* It's a lovely little song, and it speaks a great truth.

We are not told *how* the Holy Spirit accomplished the conception of Jesus within Mary's womb. If Gabriel's explanation had been phrased according to our modern understanding of genetics, it would have baffled men in the succeeding centuries and would have produced confusion instead of a sense of wonder. It was not considered necessary for Mary (or for us) to understand completely the ways of God.

Mary's task was, and ours is, simply this: to "walk by faith"—faith in a God who "specializes in things thought impossible" and "does the things others cannot do."

—R. C. S.

*"Got Any Rivers," by Oscar C. Eliason. © 1945, Benson Music Group. Used by permission.

WHAT DO YOU THINK?

How would the news that Elizabeth had conceived be an assurance to Mary that Gabriel's message to her was true? What particular act of God gives you reassurance that his promises to you are true?

[In addition to citing biblical promises, encourage your students to cite answers to prayer or dramatic changes of lifestyle in themselves or people they know. These testify that God is still at work.]

WHAT DO YOU THINK?

Mary had to believe that "nothing is impossible with God." How has God accomplished some blessing in your life in a surprising or even "impossible" way? Can you trust him to do the impossible again?

Today's lesson visual reminds us that we, too, can serve God as Mary did. Adopting her attitude is the key to faithful service.

C. HER SUBMISSION (v. 38)

38. "I am the Lord's servant," Mary answered. "May it be to me as you have said." Then the angel left her.

Mary's submission is a model for all Christians. She agreed to be God's *servant*, to do whatever he asked. This responsibility was not a burden, but a blessing.

At this point Mary could not have been aware of all that she would have to face in fulfilling this extraordinary role. She would endure the gossips in Nazareth (speculating as to the *real* father of her child), the long trip to Bethlehem, the birth of her child in less than ideal conditions, the threat from jealous King Herod, and another long trip to Egypt and then back to Nazareth. She would watch as Jesus left the family circle to minister to people all over Galilee and Judea. Ultimately—and worst of all—she would watch as her son was crucified.

While Mary could not have anticipated most of this, the biblical record indicates that she fulfilled all that was asked of her. This is not to say that her understanding of Jesus and his ministry was flawless. At times she did not grasp the full significance of who he was or what he had come to do (Luke 2:48-50; John 2:1-4). Still, her faithfulness is exemplary.

CONCLUSION

A. "WHATEVER"

It has become a common practice whenever one wants to dismiss a comment or an opinion simply to shrug one's shoulders and say, "Whatever. . . ." In that context, the word is not an expression of commitment but of apathy.

There is, however, a better way to use this word. When we submit ourselves to Christ we say, "Whatever . . ." with an entirely different tone of voice and a different meaning. In using that word, we express our acceptance of *whatever* the Lord would have us do—not only whatever, but wherever, whenever, and however.

When one surrenders himself to God, he commits himself to a life of both responsibility and privilege. It may be said that there can be no privilege without responsibility. The real joys of Christian living come to those who are willing to do "whatever"—great or small, public or private—to the glory of the One we love.

B. SOMETHING SPECIAL

There is something special about Christmas because there is something special about the first Christmas. Jesus was born into a special heritage, born to special parents, born in a special way, and born to fulfill a special purpose. The special heritage was the lineage of David. The special parents were Joseph, a man of righteousness and compassion, and Mary, a woman of singular virtue and commitment. Jesus was born in a special way through the virgin birth: a spiritual and biological miracle. Most of all, he was born to fulfill a special purpose—to save his people from their sins (Matthew 1:21) and to establish "a kingdom that will never be destroyed" (Daniel 2:44).

C. ONE GRAND PACKAGE

During December it is appropriate to emphasize Jesus' birth. But in so doing, we should not overlook the impact of all of Jesus' life, including his teachings, miracles, death, resurrection, and promised return. One can imagine how odd it would seem to observe the birthday of any famous individual by focusing only on his birth and childhood and ignoring all the achievements of his adult life. The same is true of Jesus. At Christmas we should recognize that God has given us one grand package—one matchless life. This gift is ours to open and to treasure—not only at Christmas, but throughout the year.

PRAYER

Father, help me, like Mary, to accept whatever task you give me. My task will certainly not be as great as hers, but that is all right. It is a privilege to serve you. Whether my task be great or small, may I say with a willing heart, "Yes, Lord." In Jesus' name, amen.

THOUGHT TO REMEMBER

What is the best way to respond to God? As Mary did—with simple, trusting faith.

Discovery Learning

*This page contains an alternate lesson plan emphasizing learning activities. Classes
desiring such student involvement will find these suggestions helpful. The next page
is a reproducible activity page to further enhance discovery learning.*

LEARNING GOALS

After participating in this lesson, each student will be able to:

1. Give the important details of Gabriel's message to Mary and her response to it.

2. Tell why Mary's response to God's will is an appropriate model for Christians.

3. Think of a difficult decision or issue he or she is facing, and commit that matter to God in simple faith.

INTO THE LESSON

As students arrive, give each one a copy of the reproducible activity "Varied Responses" from the following page. Ask the students to write how they would respond to each of the messages. (If any message on the list might prove difficult for your class because of recent events, you might want to prepare your own handout without some of the items listed here and/or with some different ones. For example, if your church has just lost one of its young people in a tragic accident, feel free to omit the second message.)

After a few minutes, ask volunteers to report some of their responses. Discuss why some messages get an action response and other messages are dismissed. After a brief discussion, you can probably make the observation that we respond to messages we believe. Then discuss what makes some messages believable and others not.

Make the transition to the lesson by noting that Mary received a seemingly incredible message. She could have passed it off as "too good to be true," but she believed it and responded in faith.

INTO THE WORD

Ask a volunteer to read Luke 1:26-38 aloud. Then form groups of three or four students each and instruct the groups to list the main points of Gabriel's message. Give the students copies of the reproducible activity "Stages of Response" from the next page. Using these handouts, the students should outline the main points of the message in the left column and the stages of Mary's response in the right. It might be said that Mary's response to this incredible news was to experience some inner turmoil (v. 29a), consider the situation (v. 29b), gather appropriate information (v. 34), proclaim her primary role (v. 38a), and submit to the will of God (v. 38b).

Let the class discuss the main points of the message and the stages of Mary's response. Ask, "What factors would make this task difficult for Mary?" (*Social stigma, youth, uncertainty about whether Joseph would believe her, the importance of the task, etc.*) Note that Mary had already demonstrated a sense of duty and responsibility by submitting to the pledge to be married. These character traits continue to show in her faithful response to God's message that was delivered to her by Gabriel. While we will not have the same kind of task as Mary did, her faithful response to a difficult duty is worthy of our imitation.

INTO LIFE

Tell students to recall four or five of the most difficult situations they have faced in their lives. Encourage them to recall events from different time periods in life and then to write these down on the back of the handout on which the previous activity was printed.

When everyone has a list, ask students to choose situations that they are willing to discuss with their small groups (the same groups that were formed earlier). Encourage them to consider all that was involved in dealing with their situations and compare theirs with Mary's. Ask them to make a list of their typical stages of response to difficult situations, based on the way they handled the ones they have been thinking about.

Then tell students to return to their small groups. Have the groups consider the typical responses, suggesting some better ways to handle some of the situations and affirming the positive responses. Have each group come up with a list of wise, helpful, and godly stages in a plan for responding to difficult situations.

Then ask students to think of some difficult decisions or duties that they are currently facing. Ask each to consider what has already been discussed and to write out a plan for addressing the issue he or she is facing (even if it is only a first step and not the entire process).

Remind the class of Mary's sense of duty and responsibility: "When a plan of response is prepared, a person of duty will follow that plan even when it is difficult. Like Mary, our life of responsible faith includes turmoil, thoughts, questions, and submission."

Close by asking the students to commit their situations to God in silent prayer while you play a recording of the song, "Mary, Did You Know?"

Varied Responses

Look at the list of messages below. If someone were to give you each message, how would you respond? Write your response on the chart below.

MESSAGE	RESPONSE
Mommy, there's a monster in my closet!	
There's been an accident; you need to come to the hospital with me.	
Schools are closed today because of the inclement weather.	
If you'll invest just $5,000 in my new invention, you can double your money in a month!	
Mom, Dad, I'm getting married!	
If you will accept a transfer, we can offer you a position at the home office at twenty percent more than your current salary.	
The world will end at midnight on December 31!	

Stages of Response

Read Luke 1:26-38. On the chart below list the significant details of Gabriel's message to Mary. Alongside each detail, list the stages of Mary's response to the message.

DETAILS OF GABRIEL'S MESSAGE   STAGES OF MARY'S RESPONSE

Now imagine (or recall) a trying situation that you might face (or have faced). On a separate sheet of paper (or the back of this one) list the stages of your typical or likely response (perhaps your actual response). Then list the stages of your desired response—the way you think you ought to respond to such a situation.

PRAISING GOD

LESSON 3

DEVOTIONAL READING:
PSALM 34:1-3
BACKGROUND SCRIPTURE:
LUKE 1:39-56
PRINTED TEXT:
LUKE 1:39-55

Dec
17

WHY TEACH THIS LESSON?

Jesus once said that, if the people would not voice their praise, then "the stones will cry out" (Luke 19:40). Some actions are not only appropriate in certain situations, they are demanded. And praise is one of those imperatives.

Elizabeth and Mary sensed it. When they came together, each of them anticipating the birth of a wondrous child, they broke out in praise. Your students not only anticipate the Messiah, but they know of his birth and his life and his atoning death and his resurrection. If they do not sense and respond to the moral imperative of praise, then this lesson will not have been a success.

INTRODUCTION

A. WHO UNDERSTANDS?

If you are having a problem in your profession, who can understand that problem better than another person in the same profession? Physicians understand the problems of other physicians, while teachers can appreciate the problems of other teachers. That is the reason, among others, that there is a peer association for nearly every major profession.

If you are going through a trial of some kind—a sickness or some other personal crisis—who can understand your situation better than someone who has already been through it? Only an alcoholic can truly understand the struggles of an alcoholic. Only the widowed understand the special heartaches of widowhood. Only parents understand both the joys and frustrations that can make parenthood a joy one minute and an absolute nightmare the next. That is why there are so many effective support groups to help people cope with various crises.

As Mary faced the pressures and responsibilities accompanying her special pregnancy, with whom could she discuss her concerns? No one had ever gone through (or would ever go through!) what she would experience. The person whose situation most resembled hers was Elizabeth. She, too, was in the midst of an unusual pregnancy with an unusual child. She, too, was deeply committed to the Lord (Luke 1:5, 6). Even though there were differences in their respective situations, only Elizabeth could really understand what Mary was facing. Elizabeth would also believe Mary's explanation of what had happened. After all, the same angel who had visited Mary had also appeared to Elizabeth's husband Zechariah.

Also worth noting is the age difference between Mary and Elizabeth. Mary was quite young, perhaps in her early teens; Elizabeth was quite old, well past childbearing years. No doubt it was a comfort to Mary to have an older woman in whom to confide and from whom to receive advice. In addition, as noted in last week's lesson, Mary and Elizabeth were relatives (Luke 1:36).

Given all of these factors, it is not difficult to see why Mary wanted to visit Elizabeth and talk with her about the extraordinary news that Gabriel had brought.

B. LESSON BACKGROUND

Today's lesson text immediately follows last week's text (from Luke 1:26-38). It ushers us into the private meeting that took place between Mary and Elizabeth.

LESSON AIMS

After participating in this lesson, students will be able to:

1. List the elements of praise included in the songs of Elizabeth and Mary.

2. Explain how these songs highlight the unique way in which God works.

3. Express their personal praise to God for his work in their lives.

KEY VERSE

"My soul glorifies the Lord and my spirit rejoices in God my Savior, for he has been mindful of the humble state of his servant."
—Luke 1:46-48

Both of them break forth in praise to God for his wondrous working in their lives. While their words are not actually called *songs* in the Scriptures, they resemble the songs of praise found in the Psalms of the Old Testament. Mary's praise in particular exhibits the characteristics of a poem that could be (and has been) set to music.

In addition, Mary's tribute displays a keen knowledge of the Old Testament Scriptures, especially of Hannah's words of praise uttered in gratitude to God for her son Samuel (1 Samuel 2:1-10). Since from early childhood boys and girls were taught the Scriptures, it would have been natural for Mary to recall some phrases from Hannah's poem and to use them in expressing her own gratitude to God for the special son she would bear.

I. THE SONG OF ELIZABETH (LUKE 1:39-45)

A. MARY'S ARRIVAL (vv. 39, 40)

39. At that time Mary got ready and hurried to a town in the hill country of Judea,

The angel Gabriel had told Mary of Elizabeth's miraculous pregnancy (Luke 1:36), perhaps to let her know that she was not alone in her extraordinary condition. Here was someone else with a seemingly impossible pregnancy. Mary's pregnancy was miraculous because she was a virgin; Elizabeth's, because she had always been infertile and was now beyond the age of childbearing.

It appears that as soon as she could do so, Mary *hurried* to go to see Elizabeth. We are not given the name of the *town in the hill country of Judea* where Elizabeth lived. Mary's journey likely covered from sixty to seventy miles—quite a distance for her to travel. But such was the importance of visiting and talking with Elizabeth that distance was of little concern to Mary.

40. . . . where she entered Zechariah's home and greeted Elizabeth.

A guest's greeting a hostess when she entered a *home* was a common practice, but it was to be followed by an uncommon reaction.

B. THE BABY'S REACTION (v. 41)

41. When Elizabeth heard Mary's greeting, the baby leaped in her womb, and Elizabeth was filled with the Holy Spirit.

It is not unusual for babies in the *womb* to kick, but Elizabeth could tell that these movements of the child inside her were out of the ordinary. Luke (a physician) uses the word *leaped* to describe what took place. This leaping was done with joy (v. 44), apparently because of what Mary's presence as the mother of the Messiah signified. Elizabeth's response to Mary's greeting was prompted by her being *filled with the Holy Spirit.*

C. ELIZABETH'S RESPONSE (vv. 42-45)

42. In a loud voice she exclaimed: "Blessed are you among women, and blessed is the child you will bear!

The sheer excitement of Elizabeth is seen in the fact that she cried *in a loud voice.* Empowered by God's Spirit, she acknowledged Mary's unique status *among women* and the uniqueness of the *child* she would *bear.*

While not of major significance, it is interesting that the word *blessed* used here is not the same Greek word that is rendered *blessed* in the Sermon on the Mount. The word in the Sermon on the Mount has the connotation of happiness or satisfaction. The word used by Elizabeth combines the Greek words for "good" and "word," resulting in the term we transliterate as "eulogy." This is not only a "good word" spoken of the deceased at a funeral. It is often used in the sense of speaking praise or pronouncing a blessing.

WHAT DO YOU THINK?

Why do you think Mary made the long trip to see Elizabeth? How do you choose someone to confide in? What do you gain from that kind of relationship?

HOW TO SAY IT

Gabriel. GAY-bree-ul.
Immanuel. Ih-MAN-you-el.
Jeremiah. Jair-uh-MY-uh.
Magnificat. Mag-NIF-ih-cot.
Nazareth. NAZ-uh-reth.
Simeon. SIM-ee-un.
Zechariah. Zek-uh-RYE-uh.

43. "But why am I so favored, that the mother of my Lord should come to me?

In describing Mary as *the mother of my Lord*, Elizabeth humbly recognized the superiority of the one for whom her son would prepare the way. In the same way, John one day would draw attention away from himself to his far more worthy successor. (See John 1:29-34; 3:26-30.) Even though Elizabeth was joyous about her own pregnancy, it did not prevent her from being excited and happy about Mary and about the nature of the child she would bear. While Elizabeth felt a sense of honor, she acknowledged that Mary had been given an even greater honor. Like John, she was content to serve the Lord in a secondary role.

44. "As soon as the sound of your greeting reached my ears, the baby in my womb leaped for joy.

Elizabeth was filled with wonder at the *joy* represented by her child's reaction to the *sound* of Mary's voice. It is interesting to compare this verse with John's later words in describing his joy at fulfilling his God-given assignment: "The bride belongs to the bridegroom. The friend who attends the bridegroom waits and listens for him, and is full of joy when he hears the bridegroom's voice" (John 3:29).

JOY IN BELIEVING

There's a lot of wisdom to be found on the bumper stickers that people put on their cars. One declares that April 1 is National Atheists' Day. When you remember that April 1 is April Fool's Day, you understand the message: "The fool says in his heart, 'There is no God'" (Psalm 14:1).

The wise individual recognizes that faith in God makes life fit together and gives it meaning. The great British writer G. K. Chesterton once said that when he was an atheist, there was a large hole in his thinking that he could not fill. He discovered that it was a God-shaped hole, and he became a devout believer and a staunch defender of the Christian faith.

Atheism is not only foolish; it is futile. Ultimately it leaves one utterly hopeless in the face of death. In contrast, the two women in today's lesson, Mary and Elizabeth, found great joy in their faith in God and their acknowledgment of his power and presence. The apostle Paul writes of "joy . . . in believing" (Romans 15:13, *New American Standard Bible*). Jeremiah said that God's words "were my joy and my heart's delight" (Jeremiah 15:16). Peter tells Christians that believing in Jesus causes them to be "filled with an inexpressible and glorious joy" (1 Peter 1:8).

You can buy a bottle of dish soap called "Joy," but real joy does not come in a bottle. Real joy comes only by believing God and trusting his promises. Such faith brought joy to Mary and Elizabeth and will bring lasting joy into the life of every believer.

If April 1 is National Atheists' Day, then every day is Believers' Day. Every day the person of faith can say, "This is the day the Lord has made; let us rejoice and be glad in it" (Psalm 118:24).   —R. C. S.

45. "Blessed is she who has believed that what the Lord has said to her will be accomplished!"

Elizabeth pronounced an inspired blessing on Mary, who *believed* Gabriel's message to her in spite of its "impossible" promise (Luke 1:37). Elizabeth also expressed an assurance that everything that Gabriel spoke would come to pass. Certainly she was the right person to offer such assurance. After all, she too had experienced the faithfulness of God in honoring his promises concerning an unusual conception.

Here the Greek word translated *blessed* is the same word as that used in the Beatitudes. It describes a blessing that is applicable to all Christians, who can

WHAT DO YOU THINK?

Have you noticed that some people—very unlike Elizabeth—do not share the joy of others? Instead, they often feel diminished by another's success, good fortune, or recognition. Why is that? How can we respond more like Elizabeth in those situations?

DAILY BIBLE READINGS

Monday, Dec. 11— *Gratitude (Psalm 34:1-4)*

Tuesday, Dec. 12—It Is Good *to Give Thanks (Psalm 92:1-4)*

Wednesday, Dec. 13—Mary *Visits Elizabeth (Luke 1:39-45)*

Thursday, Dec. 14—Mary's *Song of Praise (Luke 1:46-56)*

Friday, Dec. 15—Sing to the *Lord (Psalm 96)*

Saturday, Dec. 16—Bless the *Lord (Psalm 103:1-5, 19-22)*

Sunday, Dec. 17—Daniel's *Prayer and Praise (Daniel 2: 17-23)*

take comfort in the assurance that God will keep his "very great and precious promises" (2 Peter 1:4).

II. THE SONG OF MARY (LUKE 1:46-56)
A. GOD'S BLESSINGS (vv. 46-48)
46. And Mary said: "My soul glorifies the Lord.

We come now to what is considered the song of Mary. Note that similar expressions of praise are recorded in the early chapters of Luke's Gospel. These include the words of Zechariah (Luke 1:67-79), of the angels who announced Jesus' birth (Luke 2:13, 14), and of Simeon in the temple (Luke 2:28-32).

Mary's song is often called *The Magnificat*, a title derived from the first word in the Latin translation. It is filled with words and phrases from the Old Testament. One commentator has counted twelve separate Old Testament references in it. We have already noted its similarity to Hannah's song of praise, found in 1 Samuel 2:1-10.

The word *glorifies* is rendered "magnifies" in some versions. We often think of magnifying as enlarging (which is what happens to an image when we use a magnifying glass). Certainly we cannot make the Lord larger, but we can enlarge his "image." The actual print on the page remains the same size even when we use a magnifying glass, but it appears larger. Even so our praise acts as a magnifying glass to others—God is seen more clearly, though he himself remains unchanged. From the depths of her *soul* Mary was giving to the Lord a greater measure of reverence in expressing her awe at who he is and what he had done.

MAGNIFICENT MUSIC

Every writer wants his last book to be his best book. Every artist wants his last painting to be his best painting. Every composer wants his last piece of music to be his best. Thus, for his final composition, the great composer Heinrich Schütz chose to write music to the words of Mary found in today's text. Her song is often called *The Magnificat*. Many composers before and after Schütz have written music for it. It is quite remarkable to think that these words, first spoken by a peasant girl from Galilee in the isolated Judean hill country of the first century, have been set to music and heard by millions. Truly God has "lifted up the humble" (Luke 1:52).

But the lovely words of these verses deserve music—and the finest music. They are poetry at its best. They are theology of the highest caliber, describing God's marvelous ways. Let us not discount the guidance of the Holy Spirit in all of this. If the Spirit could create the child in Mary's womb (Luke 1:35), the same Spirit could create the poetry in Mary's mind.

These words of Scripture are called *The Magnificat* because the first word in the Latin translation is *magnificat*. They could also be called *The Magnificat* simply because they are magnificent words!   —R. C. S.

47. ". . . and my spirit rejoices in God my Savior.

Together, verses 46 and 47 provide a good illustration of what is called *parallelism* in biblical poetry. Quite simply this means that the same idea in one verse or part of a verse is repeated in a slightly different form in the next verse or part of the verse. *My spirit rejoices in God my Savior* is saying essentially the same thing as *my soul glorifies the Lord*. Both phrases refer to praise that is not shallow or thoughtless, but originates from deep within one's being.

The word *Savior* draws attention to the purpose that Mary's child was coming to fulfill—a purpose that is reflected in his name. An angel told Joseph, "You are to give him the name Jesus, because he will save his people from their sins" (Matthew 1:21). That God would be so committed to saving sinful, rebellious

WHAT DO YOU THINK?

Mary was eager to glorify the Lord. How do believers today glorify the Lord? How is that important? What is the value of our praise to God? to us? to others—including unbelievers—who hear our praise?

Mary's praise might easily have been a song, as illustrated by today's visual. Ask the class, "If you were to write a song of praise for what God has done for you, what would you include?"

humanity that he would sacrifice his own Son is something that should prompt us to praise him as well.

48. ". . . for he has been mindful of the humble state of his servant. From now on all generations will call me blessed.

Mary's *humble state* describes her position in the social order of that day. There is no doubt that she and Joseph were rather poor. Recall that the offering they made at the temple for Mary's purification consisted of a "pair of doves" (Luke 2:24)—the approved substitute for the more costly lamb (Leviticus 12:6-8). Carpenters in Jesus' day were not well paid. No doubt, this was especially true in a small town such as Nazareth. Since families contracted marriages and usually tried to select spouses who came from the same social strata, then most likely Mary's family also was not wealthy. Nevertheless, God chose the Messiah's mother from the ranks of the poor and lowly.

Mary and Joseph thus illustrate the beauty and wonder of the incarnation—that Immanuel ("God with us") would come to dwell with lowly, impoverished (not only physically, but also spiritually) humanity. Such are the surprising ways of the Lord. He "chose the foolish things of the world to shame the wise; God chose the weak things of the world to shame the strong . . . so that no one may boast before him" (1 Corinthians 1:27-29).

Mary's declaration that future *generations* would call her *blessed* was not an arrogant boast. She spoke out of a sense of genuine humility that God would use her in such a wonderful way.

B. GOD'S CHARACTER (vv. 49, 50)

49. ". . . for the Mighty One has done great things for me—holy is his name.

The *Mighty One* is God. He had *done great things* for a humble peasant girl from an obscure Galilean village. Mary understood that the privilege of being the mother of the Messiah was something truly *holy*. We are reminded of the words at the beginning of the Lord's Prayer: "Hallowed be your name" (Matthew 6:9). In biblical thought, the *name* of a person represented the person. Thus to hallow a name is to hallow or revere a person. When Mary says that God's name is holy, she is declaring God himself as holy.

50. "His *mercy* extends to those who fear him, from generation to generation.

While God's *mercy* receives particular emphasis in the New Testament because of its expression through Jesus Christ, mercy has always been part of God's character. Mary's statement resembles several Old Testament declarations of God as merciful (Exodus 20:6; 34:6, 7; Psalm 103:17; Micah 7:18).

To *fear* God is not to cringe before him in cowering terror. It means to acknowledge his holiness and purity and to recognize how unworthy we are of the mercy that he shows (Isaiah 6:1-5).

C. GOD'S WAYS (vv. 51-53)

51. "He has performed mighty deeds with his arm; he has scattered those who are proud in their inmost thoughts.

God's *arm* is a symbol of his strength. (Some of the many passages that use this term include Exodus 15:16; Deuteronomy 4:34; 1 Kings 8:42; and Psalm 98:1.) His power is so far beyond human capabilities that for us to become *proud* in our *thoughts*, words, and actions should be out of the question. Pride blinds us to what God, whose ways are so different from man's, is doing. For example, few could have imagined that here in the seclusion of the hill country of Judea, God's redemptive plan was unfolding. Likewise, most of those crowded into Bethlehem on the night Jesus was born had no idea that the Messiah was in their midst.

WHAT DO YOU THINK?

What does it mean to fear God? What is likely to be true of those who fear God?

WHAT DO YOU THINK?

What does God have against rulers (v. 52)? Does this mean that we should shun all positions of power and influence? Why or why not?

52. "He has brought down rulers from their thrones but has lifted up the humble.

This verse and the next highlight how God's ways amount to a complete reversal of the world's standards. God humbles those who think they are secure in their position (think of wicked King Herod), and he elevates those from lower stations in life (think of Mary). As Jesus later taught, "Whoever exalts himself will be humbled, and whoever humbles himself will be exalted" (Matthew 23:12).

53. "He has filled the hungry with good things but has sent the rich away empty.

Certainly those who hungered for physical food were fed during Jesus' ministry (Luke 9:16, 17). And Jesus issued a solemn warning to those who are *rich* (Luke 6:24). However, it may be more appropriate to view this verse in spiritual terms. Those who "hunger and thirst for righteousness" will find themselves *filled* (Matthew 5:6), while those who consider themselves in good standing with God are often blind to their desperate need for him (Luke 18:9-14). This verse calls to mind Jesus' story of the rich man and Lazarus (Luke 16:19-31) with its vivid illustration that this life does not reveal the complete truth about riches and poverty.

D. GOD'S CARE FOR ISRAEL (vv. 54, 55)

54. "He has helped his servant Israel, remembering to be merciful.

God's help for *Israel* had been exhibited in numerous ways: the exodus, the provision for Israel's needs through forty years of wandering in the desert, deliverance from oppression by means of the judges, the prosperity during the reigns of godly kings, and the restoration after the Babylonian captivity to name just a few. Israel did not always deserve God's favor, as the Old Testament record clearly shows, yet he continued to be *merciful* to his chosen people.

Here, Mary's words point to the fact that the ultimate help to Israel is coming in the form of God's chosen Person—the Messiah. He is the ultimate sign of God's mercy, not only to "Abraham and his descendants" (v. 55), but to all of sinful humanity.

55. ". . . to Abraham and his descendants forever, even as he said to our fathers."

The term *fathers* describes the patriarchs (such as *Abraham*) and other men of faith in the Old Testament. God had promised to bless the entire world through Abraham's *descendants* (Genesis 12:3). As Paul notes, that promise of a seed is fulfilled in Jesus Christ (Galatians 3:16). The child whom Mary was carrying thus fulfilled not only Gabriel's words to her (Luke 1:26-38), but a plan that God had "chosen before the creation of the world" (1 Peter 1:20).

Luke 1:56 tells us, "Mary stayed with Elizabeth for about three months and then returned home." Apparently Mary remained with Elizabeth until John's birth and then returned to Nazareth. Eventually she traveled southward once more, this time to Bethlehem with Joseph. There she saw that what the Lord had promised her was indeed "accomplished" (Luke 1:45).

PRAYER

Dear Father, as both Elizabeth and Mary did, I lift my voice in praise because of your many blessings to your people. I want to thank you because you have been so gracious to me personally. I may not be able to compose a song to your glory, but there is a song in my heart. In Jesus' name, amen.

CONCLUSION

The humility demonstrated by both Elizabeth and Mary should stir all of us to ask the question, "Do we deserve God's mercy and grace?" The answer is a clear *no*. What is the difference between mercy and grace? Some have stated it this way: mercy is not getting the punishment you deserve, and grace is getting something good you don't deserve. Thus they may be viewed as two sides of the same coin. Mercy is for the guilty; grace is for the undeserving.

From time to time people say something like, "I wish I could get what I deserve." But would we *really* want what we deserve—in the spiritual realm? Elizabeth and Mary both saw themselves as undeserving of God's great blessings. Shouldn't we all?

THOUGHT TO REMEMBER

You will never run out of reasons to praise God.

Discovery Learning

This page contains an alternate lesson plan emphasizing learning activities. Classes desiring such student involvement will find these suggestions helpful. The next page is a reproducible activity page to further enhance discovery learning.

LEARNING GOALS

After this lesson students will be able to:

1. List the elements of praise included in the songs of Elizabeth and Mary.

2. Explain how these songs highlight the unique way in which God works.

3. Express their personal praise to God for his work in their lives.

INTO THE LESSON

Tell the class to imagine that they just received an incredible challenge. Ask, "With whom would you want to talk about this challenge, and why?" Allow a little time for the students to think, and then ask for volunteers to give answers. As they do, gently prod the students to examine their connection with the people they mention.

Comment appropriately about the students' answers. Then say, "When we are facing a challenge, we often want to talk to someone who has faced the same challenge. In our Bible study today, a young woman goes to a godly older woman who will understand her circumstances."

INTO THE WORD

Read Luke 1:39-55. Using information from the commentary and your own study, present a lecture on the relationship between Elizabeth and Mary. Include Mary's willingness to travel sixty or seventy miles (three to four days) for this counsel. Describe Elizabeth's circumstances, pointing out that she had experienced the faithfulness of God in honoring his promises and was quietly carrying out her responsibility to bear a promised special son. Here she rejoiced with Mary, who had received a similar promise. Her praise is instructive to us, both for its content and for the attitude that it suggests.

Note that Mary was also prepared. Even though she experienced some turmoil, she submitted to the will of God. (Refer to last week's lesson.) Today we see that she knew her Scriptures so well that she could incorporate up to twelve separate Old Testament references in her praise. Mary's praise is poetic in form.

Divide the class into two groups. Ask one group to study Elizabeth's praise (vv. 41-45) and the other to examine Mary's (vv. 46-55). Have each group make a list of the elements of praise found in each expression of praise. After a few minutes ask the groups to report. Write their suggestions on the chalkboard, an overhead transparency, or a chart tablet. Students should discover the following elements, or similar ones.

Elizabeth: Praise for what God was doing in Mary's life (v. 42); praise for being associated with his work (vv. 43, 44); confidence in God's continued working (v. 45).

Mary: God's blessings to her (vv. 46-48); God's superlative character (vv. 49, 50); God's concern for the downtrodden (vv. 51-53); God's concern for Israel (vv. 54, 55).

INTO LIFE

Observe that Ken Medema, a Christian vocalist and pianist, urges people to use the history of their church to write a congregational song of praise. Say, "First, let's identify God's work in the life of this congregation, and then we will praise him. Think of prayers that have been answered, people who have been won to Christ, spiritual growth, people sent out into ministry, and the like." Encourage students to talk about one or two of the significant events. Ask, "What did you experience when these events happened?"

As students list significant events in the life of the congregation and identify ways that God has cared for them, write their contributions on the chalkboard so that it will be available for reference. Be ready to add ideas that you have learned from your own research.

If your students are comfortable with creative writing assignments, invite them as individuals or small groups to prepare one of the following.

• Use the congregation's history to write lyrics to the tune of a well-known song.

• Write a poem of praise.

• Pen a letter of praise.

If your class is not ready for such creative writing assignments, lead them in writing an original responsive reading. Use the reproducible activity page that follows to prepare an overhead transparency (or handout) that allows space for students to dictate statements about God, with each one followed by this statement from Mary's song: "His mercy extends to those who fear him, from generation to generation."

Read the responsive prayer together to close your class session.

Responsive Praise Reading

Mary said of God, "His mercy extends to those who fear him, from generation to generation" (Luke 1:50). In the spaces between that repeated expression of praise below, write several statements of praise to God. Use the resulting page to participate in a responsive praise reading with your class or to meditate on the goodness of God in your private devotions.

His mercy extends to those who fear him, from generation to generation.

His mercy extends to those who fear him, from generation to generation.

His mercy extends to those who fear him, from generation to generation.

His mercy extends to those who fear him, from generation to generation.

His mercy extends to those who fear him, from generation to generation.

His mercy extends to those who fear him, from generation to generation.

His mercy extends to those who fear him, from generation to generation.

A SAVIOR IS BORN

LESSON 4

WHY TEACH THIS LESSON?

"Jesus is the reason for the season!" You've probably heard that at least once in the past few days or weeks. It is an important reminder that Christmas is not just a holiday, not just an excuse for a party, and not just a time for gift-giving. It is the birthday of a real person—Jesus of Nazareth!

Technically, however, the statement is not correct. Jesus' birth is what we might call the "occasion" for the season. In truth, *we* are the "reason for the season," for we are the reason Jesus was born. Had we not needed a Savior, Jesus would not have come.

But we did—we do—and so he came. Our need for the Savior is the reason to teach this lesson as well.

INTRODUCTION

A. SOMETHING TO SING ABOUT

There is a legend concerning a little brown bird that lived in the stable where Jesus was born. According to this legend, the bird had never sung before. That night, hearing the angels' song to the shepherds, he learned to sing. In fact, the music that came from the little bird was the most beautiful and heavenly music anyone had ever heard. From that day forward people have listened to and enjoyed the nightingale, never realizing that it was imitating the angels' song.

This is only a legend, of course, and yet there is some truth in it. Because of what happened that night in Bethlehem, we have a reason to sing. Before Christ came, we had nothing to sing about. Because of Christ, that has changed. Let this story put a song in your heart this season.

What is it about Christmas that gives most people a lift? What makes them kinder and gentler? There is an extraordinary power in the story of the birth of Jesus, even for those who don't believe all of it. We have all seen some of the most secular people manifest a bit of the attitude of Jesus at Christmas, if only for a short while. For those who believe in him as Savior, there is an abundance of joy that does not come and go with the season because they have come to know personally the purpose for which the baby was born.

B. LESSON BACKGROUND

Luke provides more details about Jesus' birth than Matthew, Mark, or John do. At the beginning of his Gospel, Luke tells us that many other accounts of Jesus' life had been written (Luke 1:1, 2). It is interesting to speculate what these other accounts were like or what happened to them. Of far greater significance is the fact that the four we have in the New Testament are those Spirit-inspired records that are meant to lead the reader to faith in Jesus as God's Son (John 20:30, 31). Each Gospel tells the same story, but each has its own unique features. One of Luke's distinctive features is his account of the events surrounding Jesus' birth, which is the source of many of the readings traditionally used during the Christmas season.

DEVOTIONAL READING:
MATTHEW 16:13-16
BACKGROUND SCRIPTURE:
LUKE 2:1-20
PRINTED TEXT:
LUKE 2:4-20

Dec
24

LESSON AIMS

After this lesson each student will be able to:

1. Retell Luke's account of the birth of Jesus.

2. Contrast the humble scene of the nativity with the commercialism of the current celebration of Christmas.

3. Express a commitment to celebrating Christ's birth with a "spiritual pilgrimage" to Bethlehem to worship the Savior.

KEY VERSE

Today in the town of David a Savior has been born to you; he is Christ the Lord. —Luke 2:11

LESSON 4 NOTES

Today's lesson may suffer somewhat from "over-familiarity." To gain a genuine appreciation of this lesson requires the desire to approach these words with a willingness to see their power afresh. This willingness will allow the reader to capture a bit of the excitement and wonder experienced by the original participants.

I. BIRTH OF THE CHRIST CHILD (LUKE 2:4-7)

A. THE TOWN (vv. 4, 5)

4. So Joseph also went up from the town of Nazareth in Galilee to Judea, to Bethlehem the town of David, because he belonged to the house and line of David.

The Greek word rendered *town* is used to describe villages as well as major cities. *Nazareth* was a small town in *Galilee* that was held in little regard by the people of Jesus' day (John 1:46). Nonetheless, it was situated close to several main trade routes, so it was not completely removed from the outside world.

The town of *Bethlehem* was a small village located just a few miles south of Jerusalem. Bethlehem held a special place in the heart of every Jew, for it was the hometown of King *David* (1 Samuel 16:1, 13). The name itself means "house of bread." Joseph and Mary would have traveled approximately eighty miles to go there—no easy journey for anyone, especially a pregnant woman.

5. He went there to register with Mary, who was pledged to be married to him and was expecting a child.

This particular taxation (which affected the entire empire, according to verse 1) does not appear in Roman records. But this is no reason to conclude that it never took place. It was a common practice for the Romans to conduct such a tax or census in occupied territory. In fact, Luke records a similar census, taken later than the one mentioned here, in Acts 5:37. Luke's writing consistently reflects a careful attention to historical detail, and we can trust that this is the case here.

Mary is described as *pledged to be married to* Joseph. This seems to suggest that they embarked on the journey to Bethlehem before they had completed their marriage ceremony. But Matthew tells us that Joseph "took Mary home as his wife. But he had no union with her until she gave birth to a son" (Matthew 1:24, 25). It is more likely, then, that they had had their wedding ceremony and even lived together as husband and wife. Technically, however, they would not have become husband and wife until their union was consummated—after Jesus was born. Matthew addresses the legal issue while Luke is more technical.

B. THE TIME (vv. 6, 7)

6. While they were there, the time came for the baby to be born.

We do not know exactly how far along Mary was in her pregnancy when she and Joseph reached Bethlehem, nor do we know how much time passed after their arrival before the delivery occurred. We are simply told that, at some point during their stay in Bethlehem, *the time came for the baby to be born.*

At this point, it was also true that "the time had fully come" for God to send his Son (Galatians 4:4). With Jesus' birth, two of the most notable of Old Testament prophecies were fulfilled: that he would be born of a virgin (Isaiah 7:14) and that he would be born in Bethlehem (Micah 5:2).

7. . . . and she gave birth to her firstborn, a son. She wrapped him in cloths and placed him in a manger, because there was no room for them in the inn.

It is commonly assumed that Jesus was born in a stable because of the word *manger.* That term simply describes a feeding place for the animals. In the time of Jesus, animals were sometimes kept near a house in a separate space. Thus Mary and Joseph may have been taken to an area that belonged to the inn, but was not the portion where guests usually stayed.

HOW TO SAY IT

Gabriel. GAY-bree-ul.
Isaiah. Eye-ZAY-uh.
Micah. MY-kuh.
Nazareth. NAZ-uh-reth.
Simeon. SIM-ee-un.
Zechariah. Zek-uh-RYE-uh.

WHAT DO YOU THINK?

We might think that Mary had every right to expect God to provide royal accommodations for his Son. But if she expected such an advantage, she surely did not receive it. Although she was pregnant with the Son of God, Mary was not spared difficulty, discomfort, or frustration. Do you find that encouraging, discouraging, or neither? What does it tell you about your own difficulties?

[Conclude your discussion with a reference to Galatians 6:9.]

Others have proposed that the birth of Jesus happened in a cave, which is also a place where animals were often kept. Wherever Jesus was born, it is clear that the event took place in very humble circumstances. Perhaps being away from the noise and confusion that probably characterized the inn during the time of taxation was, in some respects, to Mary and Joseph's advantage; at least it offered some privacy.

That Jesus is referred to as Mary's *firstborn* implies that she had other children later. We know that Jesus had brothers (or more accurately, half-brothers) named James, Joseph, Simon, and Judas, and that he had sisters (Matthew 13:55, 56). There is no reason from the Scriptures to assume anything other than that these were children of Mary and Joseph.

This verse also mentions the *cloths* in which Mary *wrapped* Jesus. Wrapping an infant in such cloths was the ordinary way to care for a newborn. They were folded around a baby to make him or her feel more comfortable, warm, and secure. The way in which they were wrapped made the baby look almost like a small mummy.

II. ANNOUNCEMENT OF THE BIRTH (LUKE 2:8-14)

A. THE ANGEL'S APPEARANCE (vv. 8, 9)

8. And there were shepherds living out in the fields nearby, keeping watch over their flocks at night.

Even though much has changed around Bethlehem since the first century, *shepherds* still *watch over their flocks* in the vicinity as these did. What time of year might this have been? We celebrate Christmas on December 25, but there is nothing in our text to indicate any specific season. Some argue that since winter is the rainy season in Israel and that shepherds would not have been in the fields during the rainy season, Jesus could not have been born in the winter.

Others propose, however, that the shepherds in Bethlehem may have provided lambs for the temple sacrifices in Jerusalem, which was only a few miles away. Thus these shepherds would have been *in the fields* throughout the year. Though we cannot know with certainty exactly when Jesus was born, this should not be allowed to affect our understanding of why he was born. There is no doubt whatsoever about that!

Why did the announcement of Jesus' birth come to shepherds? Was it because they raised the animals used in temple sacrifices—making them an appropriate group to welcome the Lamb of God? Was it because Jesus was a descendant of David, who was a shepherd? Was it because Jesus would one day describe himself as "the good shepherd," who "lays down his life for the sheep" (John 10:11)?

Most likely shepherds were given this honor because they were among the humblest and most scorned individuals in the society of that time. Luke demonstrates a special interest in outcasts and in Jesus' concern for them (Luke 5:12-14, 27-32; 7:36-50; 10:25-37; 14:12-14; 15:11-24; 19:1-10), so he was likely impressed with the fact that the news of Jesus' birth first came to lowly shepherds.

9. An angel of the Lord appeared to them, and the glory of the Lord shone around them, and they were terrified.

What an interruption to an otherwise ordinary evening! Nothing could have prepared these simple shepherds for what they would experience. The wording in the Greek text literally reads, "They feared a great fear." This emphasizes even more the terror that filled the shepherds at the sight of *an angel of the Lord*.

WHAT DO YOU THINK?

Why do you think the appearance of angels announcing Jesus' birth was given to only a few shepherds and not to crowds of people or to more influential people? Why not announce it in Jerusalem—in Herod's court or to the Pharisees and Sadducees in the temple?

Brighter than the light of the angelic messengers was the "Light of the world" whose birth they announced. Display this visual as you discuss verse 11.

B. THE ANGEL'S MESSAGE (vv. 10-12)

10. But the angel said to them, "Do not be afraid. I bring you good news of great joy that will be for all the people.

Since the immediate reaction of the shepherds was fear, it was appropriate for the *angel* to begin his message with the words, *Do not be afraid*. The reason that fear was not necessary was that the angel had come to convey a message of *good news*, not of judgment. The Greek phrase rendered "good news" is closely related to a word that gives us our word "evangelism." The gospel is God's good news to a fallen world. Its product is *great joy* and its scope is universal—*all the people*. The apostle John tells us that Jesus died for "the sins of the whole world" (1 John 2:2).

The angel who uttered these words is not named in the text. Could it have been Gabriel, whose appearances to Zechariah and Mary are recorded earlier by Luke? We are not told.

11. Today in the town of David a Savior has been born to you; he is Christ the Lord.

Let us focus on the three words used to describe Jesus: *Savior, Christ*, and *Lord*. Jesus is *Savior* because he came to be the atoning sacrifice for our sins. He is Messiah (*Christ*) because he is the "anointed" or "chosen one" who fulfills Old Testament prophecy. The term *Lord* calls attention to his authority over all things "in heaven and on earth" (Matthew 28:18). The verse is a comprehensive statement of who Jesus is and what he came to do.

"TODAY"

The angel announced, "Today in the town of David a Savior has been born to you" (Luke 2:11). Of course, we do not know exactly what day *today* was. We are not certain that Jesus was born on December 25—or, for that matter, in the month of December. And that, of course, is not really important. We have set aside a day to honor Christ's birth. What is important is that we use the day to honor him.

We call this particular day *Christmas*; however, British writer Dorothy Sayers once suggested that we should call it *Wishmas*. She claimed that in fact this had already occurred and that Wishmas had superseded the commemoration of Christmas. It was marked, she said, by "the exchange of cards, bearing wishes for the recipients' material prosperity and frequently adorned with ice, snow, holly, and other polar symbols." She also noted that the day was characterized by "factitious heartiness and family friction."

Is it really true that the holiday known as Christmas is more correctly described as Wishmas? Has it lost its spiritual and Christian significance? No doubt it has for many. One liquor company erected a huge billboard at Christmas time right across the street from a church. The billboard showed the picture of a bottle of whiskey and declared, "The Spirit of Christmas!"

If we cannot turn Wishmas back into Christmas nationally, or even locally, we can certainly do so in our own hearts and homes. We can make certain that, at least for us and our families, "today"—indeed, every day—will always honor Christ.

—R. C. S.

12. This will be a sign to you: You will find a baby wrapped in cloths and lying in a manger."

As noted in the comments under verse 7, it would not have been unusual to see *a baby wrapped in cloths*. What was remarkable was that the baby would be found *lying in a manger*.

C. THE ANGELS' PRAISE (vv. 13, 14)

13. Suddenly a great company of the heavenly host appeared with the angel, praising God and saying,

---

WHAT DO YOU THINK?

The angel used the terms *Savior, Christ*, and *Lord*. Do you think these terms are understood by the average person today? Why or why not? If not, what can we do to help such a person understand?

DAILY BIBLE READINGS

Monday, Dec. 18—The Future King (Isaiah 9:1-7)

Tuesday, Dec. 19—The Ruler From Bethlehem (Micah 5:2-5)

Wednesday, Dec. 20—The Birth of Jesus (Luke 2:1-7)

Thursday, Dec. 21—The Ancestors of Jesus (Luke 3:23-38)

Friday, Dec. 22—The Shepherds and the Angels (Luke 2:8-14)

Saturday, Dec. 23—The Adoration of the Shepherds (Luke 2:15-20)

Sunday, Dec. 24—Sons and Daughters, Not Slaves (Galatians 4:1-7)

First there was just one *angel*; now *suddenly* there was a *great company*. Again, as with the words of Elizabeth (Luke 1:41-45) and Mary (Luke 1:46-55), the words of these angels are often considered to comprise a song, although the text simply records that the angels were *saying* them.

14. *"Glory to God in the highest, and on earth peace to men on whom his favor rests."*

This account from Luke illustrates the two ways in which *glory* is used in Scripture. There is the *glory of the Lord* (v. 9), which is the radiant light that shone from the angel; and there is the *glory to God*, which describes the praise spoken by the multitude of angels.

The final phrase in this verse calls attention to the *peace* that Jesus came to bring. While there is always much talk of peace during the Christmas season, it remains true that the world will never know real and lasting peace until people acknowledge Jesus as the Prince of peace and come to know peace with God through him.

CHOIR PRACTICE

We would assume that a choir of angels should never need rehearsals. But just for a moment, try to imagine that it does. You are a member of the choir, and you are on your way to choir practice. "Where are we going to sing? It must be an important place for us to be rehearsing like this."

Another angel responds, "Earth."

"What? That disgusting little planet? Then surely we must be preparing to visit an important city on earth!"

"No, actually it's a rather small town—a town called Bethlehem."

"Well, then it must be an important audience—possibly kings or queens!"

"No, we're going to sing for shepherds out in a field!"

Of course, this is all imaginary, but such a hypothetical conversation can help us appreciate the wonder of what did take place on the night Jesus was born. To put it in a modern setting, what if the Mormon Tabernacle Choir were sent to sing in a remote country town? What if the Metropolitan Opera put on a performance in a town so small that they had to sing in a pasture because there was no auditorium?

Note the dramatic contrast portrayed in Luke 2: singers sent from Heaven and shepherds out in the field. Why did God choose to make the announcement of his Son's birth in this manner? Surely it calls attention to the essence of the "good news" of which the angel spoke. The sinless Son of God came to this "disgusting" world to save sinners. The Son of the Highest came to rescue the lowest.

True, the shepherds were not worthy to be the first to hear the good news. That is just the point—no one is worthy to hear it.   —R. C. S.

III. RESPONSE OF THE SHEPHERDS (LUKE 2:15-20)

A. THE SHEPHERDS' VISIT (vv. 15, 16)

15. *When the angels had left them and gone into heaven, the shepherds said to one another, "Let's go to Bethlehem and see this thing that has happened, which the Lord has told us about."*

Immediately the *shepherds* decided to travel to *Bethlehem* and to *see* for themselves the scene just described for them by the angel. Theirs is the kind of enthusiasm that we associate with people who become aware for the first time of what Jesus has done for them.

16. *So they hurried off and found Mary and Joseph, and the baby, who was lying in the manger.*

The shepherds *hurried off*, signifying the urgency of responding to the angel's message. Recall how Mary "hurried" to see Elizabeth following Gabriel's message to her (Luke 1:39). Do we treat the Lord's work with a similar sense of urgency?

PRAYER

Father, help me to move beyond what the world tells me Christmas is all about, for the world is often too busy and loses sight of the true meaning of Christmas. Help me to appreciate its real significance: You sent your Son to save us from our sins. Having grasped that message, may I, like the shepherds, want to tell everyone I meet. Help me to have the courage to do that, in Jesus' name. Amen.

THOUGHT TO REMEMBER

Jesus' coming changed an ordinary night into something extraordinary. He can do the same with our lives.

WHAT DO YOU THINK?

Unfortunately, Christmas for many is the glorification of an out-of-control materialism, or it is a secularized holiday for promoting personal peace and goodwill. Even Christians can get caught up in the frenzy. How does your observance of Christmas glorify and praise God? How could you make it an even more God-glorifying event?

B. THE SHEPHERDS' WITNESS (vv. 17-20)

17. When they had seen him, they spread the word concerning what had been told them about this child.

Instantly these shepherds became evangelists and witnesses as they *spread the word* about what they had *seen* and what they *had been told*. With Jerusalem being as close as it was to Bethlehem, it is possible that word of the *child* reached the people there. If not, the news would be spread by way of Simeon and Anna (whom we shall consider in next week's lesson).

18. . . . and all who heard it were amazed at what the shepherds said to them.

Should any of us be surprised that *all who heard it were amazed at what the shepherds* described to them? It must have seemed unbelievable. Angels do not appear every day—but then, neither does the Messiah.

19. But Mary treasured up all these things and pondered them in her heart.

Mary remained quiet through all of this. She did not go around town bragging about the identity of her child. Most likely she displayed the normal pride that any mother would demonstrate regarding her newborn. Although the shepherds must have told her what they had experienced, even these wondrous *things* she also kept within herself and *pondered . . . in her heart*. There is a time when the good news must be told to others, but there must also be moments for private reflection on what the Lord has done in our lives.

20. The shepherds returned, glorifying and praising God for all the things they had heard and seen, which were just as they had been told.

We have already noted that the *shepherds* were in a sense evangelists, telling the news of Jesus' birth to others. Our lesson ends, however, with the shepherds' returning to their fields, *glorifying and praising God for all the things they had heard and seen*. Just as Mary felt humbled to bear the Messiah, the shepherds must have felt humbled to be the first recipients of the news concerning the Messiah's birth. Moreover, they had opportunity to verify the angel's words and to see the Christ for themselves. They knew that all they had been *told* was true. Their lives would never be the same.

What about us and our witness today? Some who follow Jesus answer the call to vocational service in his name. That is, their vocation—what they do to earn a living—is itself related to the spread of the gospel. Most of us, however, serve Christ in more "secular" settings. Just as the shepherds *returned* to their fields, so we return to our occupations each day. In so doing, however, we also return to our "fields," for the places where we work are often fields "ripe for harvest," as Jesus described them (John 4:35). There is a great need in these places for the faithful, consistent testimony of a dedicated Christian. Wherever we work, whether it be an office, an assembly line, a restaurant, a department store, or a farm, let us be committed to making a difference for Christ.

CONCLUSION

During the Christmas season, many people desire to travel to Bethlehem. They want to visit the site that has been traditionally identified as the birthplace of Jesus. Certainly there is something special and unforgettable about such an experience. However, far more important than visiting Bethlehem in that way is to visit it through a "spiritual pilgrimage" and to understand personally the significance of what took place there.

Have you *really* been to Bethlehem in this sense? If you embark on such a pilgrimage, you will find, as so many others have found, that it will change, not only your celebration of Christmas, but your life—forever.

Discovery Learning

This page contains an alternate lesson plan emphasizing learning activities. Classes desiring such student involvement will find these suggestions helpful. The next page is a reproducible activity page to further enhance discovery learning.

LEARNING GOALS

After participating in this lesson, each student will be able to:

1. Retell Luke's account of the birth of Jesus.

2. Contrast the humble scene of the nativity with the commercialism of the current celebration of Christmas.

3. Express a commitment to celebrating Christ's birth with a "spiritual pilgrimage" to Bethlehem to worship the Savior.

INTO THE LESSON

Prepare a video tape of the sights and sounds of Christmas around your community. Record activity at the mall, a program rehearsal, people's comments, and anything else you can think of. (If you do not have access to a video camera, you can still discuss the issues in the next paragraph. A video like the one described here would generate interest and enhance your discussion, but it is not vital to your discussion of these issues. Simply modify some of the instructions as needed.)

Begin the session by playing the video and asking, "What are some of the common images or concepts of Christmas? Which impressions would you label as Christian? Biblically accurate?" Allow answers. Then ask, "So does that mean that the people in the video were not Christians?" Allow response. Note, "It is possible that some of these people are Christians who have allowed modern Christmas celebration practices to invade their personal celebration, so that they have lost sight of the Christ, whose birth they are supposed to celebrate."

INTO THE WORD

Ask a volunteer to read aloud Luke 2:4-20. Distribute copies of the reproducible page that follows and form groups of no more than four students. Give half the groups the first assignment on the reproducible page and half of the groups the second one.

Give each group doing the movie poster assignment a poster board and some colored markers. If you think your students will be hesitant to be artists, provide magazines, old Christmas cards, scissors, and glue sticks. Explain that each group is to make an imaginary movie poster for the birth of Jesus. (You could show them a movie poster ad out of a magazine to stimulate their thinking.) Tell the students to base their posters on today's text.

Provide the "songbook" groups a number of hymnals, Christmas carol books, or other available songbooks. Have them list at least six songs that are very faithful to the Scripture, especially the text from today's lesson. Have them keep track of why certain songs were rejected. Provide poster board and markers to these groups also so they can make their lists large enough to be seen by the rest of the class.

When work is completed, display the posters. Ask a representative from each group to explain his or her group's poster. Be sure each reporter points out the connection between the group's work and details of Luke 2.

After the reports, ask the class, "As you have worked on your posters, you have been forced to rediscover the excitement of the birth of Jesus. What are you already planning to do, or could you do, this evening or tomorrow to inject that excitement into the Christmas celebration of which you will be a part?" If you have a large class, let students share their thoughts and plans in pairs. This allows everyone the opportunity to speak in a non-threatening atmosphere.

Conclude this section by reading the text once again and by using material in the commentary to contrast Jesus' humble birth with the commercialization that surrounds Christmas today.

INTO LIFE

Observe that even Christian families can get caught up in the commercialization of Christmas. It often takes a deliberate decision and plan to change such practices. Ask all the small groups (from the earlier exercise) to work on the third assignment from the reproducible page. Students should consider personal experiences, things they have read, and ideas prompted by brainstorming in their groups. Some suggestions might include attending a Christmas Eve worship service, serving Christmas dinner in a homeless shelter, inviting a person who lives alone to join one's family on Christmas Day, or giving anonymous gifts to people with notes saying that the gifts are given because of Christ's love. Let pairs pray together for each other's plans.

Close the session by singing one or more Christmas carols that hold no major errors. Suggested are "God Rest Ye Merry, Gentlemen," "Joy to the World," "O Come, All Ye Faithful," "O Little Town of Bethlehem," or "What Child Is This?"

Celebrate Jesus' Birth

Choose one or more of the following activities and work with three or four others from your class to complete the assignment(s).

MOVIE POSTER

All of us have seen at some time a poster advertising a movie. A good one catches the essence of the story through picture. It may be a montage of pictures or one bold or poignant picture. Many have become collectors' items.

You have been commissioned to design a movie poster for the birth of Jesus. Talk together to determine the key idea or theme that you want to portray with your poster. Think about the facts of the event and its purpose. Then use the materials supplied to you to tell the world your message.

SONGBOOK

You are on the music committee for the Christmas presentation to the community. The emphasis this year is the simple, humble account of Jesus' birth. With so many misconceptions about the facts, it has been decided this year to emphasize the simplicity and humility of Jesus' birth. To support this emphasis, you have been asked to select songs that are as accurate as possible.

Using the song books provided and your Bible, evaluate the Christmas songs to see which ones you will recommend to the executive committee.

BOOKLET

There has been a lot of discussion about losing Christ in the Christmas celebration. You have been asked to prepare a booklet to be distributed to families and friends of the congregation. You have been charged to gather practical suggestions for how a Christian individual, couple, or family could break away from the commercialization of the season to focus this year's Christmas celebration more on the true meaning of Christmas.

You have been reminded that the market is broad: single adults, families with young children, families with teenagers, couples whose children are grown, and couples who have retired to smaller quarters. Brainstorm ideas from your own experiences, friends' experiences, and tips read in articles or books.

PRESENTED IN THE TEMPLE

LESSON 5

WHY TEACH THIS LESSON?

The writer of Hebrews tells us that Moses' parents "saw he was no ordinary child" (Hebrews 11:23). By what revelation or inspiration they saw that we do not know, but surely Mary and Joseph could see that the child Mary had borne was "no ordinary child." Predicted by angels, virgin born, and then heralded by angels and visited by shepherds, this was one incredible baby!

If Mary and Joseph thought that things would become "normal" after the shepherds left, they were mistaken. On a routine trip to the temple to fulfill the ceremonial rites of purification and dedication, the uniqueness of Jesus was affirmed once—even twice—again. And if your students are ever tempted to think of Jesus as ordinary or "normal," this lesson will dispel such thoughts.

INTRODUCTION

A. THE DIGNITY OF AGE

Today's lesson focuses on the faith of two elderly saints. The Bible holds elderly people in high regard and teaches that they should be treated with respect (Leviticus 19:32; 1 Timothy 5:1). It tells us that God's care for individuals never diminishes, regardless of their age (Psalm 71:9, 18-21; Isaiah 46:3, 4).

For decades now people have talked about the "generation gap." Admittedly there is often tension between the generations. But while some of their interests and concerns may differ, the young and the elderly often find reason to display genuine respect for one another. Each has much to offer the other: the young have energy and enthusiasm; the elderly, experience and wisdom.

One of the ways in which a society can be judged is by how it treats its elderly. Are they considered a burden or a blessing? How foolish to discount years of experience and the resultant wisdom of those years!

Today we will consider two elderly saints who are certainly worthy of honor. They met a young couple and their infant child in the temple in Jerusalem, and both young and old benefited. The young couple received additional confirmation of their child's importance in the plan of God. The elderly saints were rewarded for their years of faithful service and patient waiting on the Lord by being granted the privilege of seeing the fulfillment of their hopes—the Lord's Messiah.

B. LESSON BACKGROUND

The occasion that brought Jesus and his parents to the temple involved the fulfillment of responsibilities prescribed by the law of Moses. Three duties were expected of the parents of a firstborn son: circumcision of the child, dedication of the child, and purification of the mother. Luke 2:21 tells us that Jesus was circumcised on the eighth day (no doubt while the family was still in Bethlehem). Also on this occasion he was officially given the name *Jesus*, although an angel had already instructed both Mary and Joseph as to what his name would be (Luke 1:31; Matthew 1:21).

Another responsibility concerned the mother. According to Leviticus 12, a woman was considered ceremonially unclean for a specified period of time

DEVOTIONAL READING:

ISAIAH 52:7-10

BACKGROUND SCRIPTURE:

LUKE 2:21-40

PRINTED TEXT:

LUKE 2:25-38

Dec
31

LESSON AIMS

After participating in this lesson, each student will be able to:

1. Summarize the reactions of Simeon and Anna upon seeing the Christ child.

2. Tell how these reactions reflected a hope based on the faithfulness of God and his promises.

3. Identify one person who does not have hope in Christ, and suggest a specific way to share with that person the good news of Jesus.

KEY VERSE

My eyes have seen your salvation, which you have prepared in the sight of all people, a light for revelation to the Gentiles and for glory to your people Israel.

—Luke 2:30-32

following childbirth. During this time, she was not to participate in public worship services or other activities outside the home. This period of uncleanness was not intended to be a negative reflection on women or on childbearing; it was essentially a time of recuperation for the mother.

In order for the new mother to be able to return to her normal activities, including worship, she had to go through a ceremony of purification following the time specified in the law. This period of time was forty days in the case of a male child. Approximately one month later, the firstborn was presented for dedication. While this was the general practice, it appears that Mary and Joseph combined the purification act with the dedication, making them part of one visit to the temple.

Luke 2:24 tells us that Joseph and Mary offered a sacrifice of two birds for Mary's purification. The law of Moses actually preferred a lamb and a bird, but allowed a couple to substitute a second bird if they could not afford a lamb (Leviticus 12:6-8). A couple with limited means could do as Joseph and Mary apparently did and let the bird offerings satisfy both the purification and dedication requirements.

It is interesting to consider where the incident studied today fits in relationship to the visit of the wise men and to the journey of Joseph, Mary, and Jesus into Egypt (Matthew 2:1-14). Probably these events followed this incident in the temple (though we cannot be sure how much time elapsed). It does not seem likely that Joseph and Mary's offering would have been a pair of birds if they had just received the treasures from the wise men. In addition, since Herod and "all Jerusalem" were "disturbed" by the word of a new king (Matthew 2:3), the presentation of Jesus in the temple at that time would have been extremely risky. Some students are uncomfortable with this harmony because Luke says the couple and Jesus "returned to Galilee to their own town of Nazareth" after performing these things (2:39), not to Bethlehem (where the wise men would find them). But Luke chose not to include the visit of the wise men or the flight to Egypt at all, so it was proper for him simply to mention the return to Nazareth here.

We noted last week that Jesus' birth was witnessed by humble shepherds. Today we see how two humble and devout individuals—Simeon and Anna—rejoiced in his coming. Just as few realized what was happening in Bethlehem on the night Jesus was born, so did few probably notice what happened when a simple peasant couple entered the temple to fulfill the law.

I. SIMEON (LUKE 2:25-35)

A. HIS CHARACTER (v. 25)

25. Now there was a man in Jerusalem called Simeon, who was righteous and devout. He was waiting for the consolation of Israel, and the Holy Spirit was upon him.

Simeon is not identified with any particular group, such as the Pharisees or Sadducees, but his reputation for integrity and righteousness is noted. It has generally been assumed from the context that Simeon was an elderly man. There is, however, nothing in the text that explicitly mentions his age.

The phrase *consolation of Israel* refers to the messianic hope. To many, this hope carried political overtones. They believed that the Messiah would come and throw off the yoke of Roman rule, thus providing *consolation* to Israel and relief from the tyranny of pagans. Of course, Jesus' style of Messiah was quite different and was quite problematic for some.

Simeon is also described as someone *upon* whom was the *Holy Spirit*. This is important since, as the next verse states, the Holy Spirit was the source of a special revelation given to Simeon.

WHAT DO YOU THINK?

The description of Simeon as righteous and devout tells us much about his character. Since he was devout toward God, we may assume he was a student of the Scriptures and morally scrupulous. Synonyms for just are fair, upright, and impartial.

Whom have you known personally whom you would describe as "righteous and devout"? How does his or her example influence you and others?

B. HIS HOPE (v. 26)

26. It had been revealed to him by the Holy Spirit that he would not die before he had seen the Lord's Christ.

The Holy Spirit had assured Simeon that he would live to see *the Lord's Christ*. We can only wonder how long Simeon had waited and when he first received this promise. Perhaps day after day—for weeks and months and years—he had scanned the crowds that passed through the temple area and wondered if this would be the day he would see the Messiah.

LIVING IN HOPE

Simeon is described as "waiting for the consolation of Israel" (Luke 2:25). He was sustained by hope—a hope that was finally realized when he saw the infant Jesus. We, too, are sustained by hope. The novel *Zorba the Greek* was written by Níkos Kazantzákis (*Nick*-oss Kah-zahn-*tsah*-kis). When Kazantzákis died in 1957, his philosophy of life was engraved on his tombstone: "I hope for nothing. I fear nothing. I am free." What a sad (and wrong) view of life! Lack of hope does not make us free. Hope makes us free. We cannot live without hope.

If you look up the word *hope* in Stevenson's *Home Book of Quotations*, you will read the entry "see also Optimism." But hope and optimism are not the same thing. Optimism is natural. Hope is spiritual. Optimism comes from a sunny disposition. Hope comes from faith. Optimism can fade with the passing years. Hope is eternal. We will not see our hope realized on earth as Simeon did. But our hope is no less real.

It was the blind songwriter Fanny Crosby who wrote the words, "And I shall see him face to face, And tell the story—Saved by grace." Both Simeon and Fanny Crosby saw their hope fulfilled by seeing Jesus. Our hope assures us that we too "shall see him as he is" (1 John 3:2). —R. C. S.

C. HIS PRAISE (vv. 27-33)

27. Moved by the Spirit, he went into the temple courts. When the parents brought in the child Jesus to do for him what the custom of the Law required.

Simeon was prompted *by the Spirit* to go to the *temple* on this day. There he would meet Mary, Joseph, and the infant *Jesus*.

The *custom of the Law* mentioned here refers to the purification service for the mother and to the dedication service of the firstborn son. Though Luke's Gospel is characterized, as we have noted, by an emphasis on Jesus' concern for different groups of people, he notes that Jesus followed the important Jewish customs of his day (Luke 2:41; 4:16; 5:12-14; 17:11-14).

28. . . . Simeon took him in his arms and praised God, saying . . .

What an amazing sight it must have been for Mary and Joseph to see aged Simeon lift up *in his arms* the infant Messiah! Just as God had impressed on Simeon that he would see the Messiah, so he impressed on him that Joseph and Mary's child was that special individual for whom he had been waiting so patiently.

29. "Sovereign Lord, as you have promised, you now dismiss your servant in peace.

Simeon's words have come to be called the *Nunc Dimittis*, which is Latin for "you now dismiss." Having seen the promised Christ, Simeon knew that he could face death with *peace*. This is the reason it is assumed that Simeon was an old man. Now that the Lord's promise to him had been fulfilled, Simeon felt his life was complete. He did not mean that he longed for death, but that now he could die content with the knowledge that the Messiah had come!

The word translated *Lord* in this verse is not the word by which God is usually addressed. Instead, it is the word from which our word *despot* comes. It describes

---

WHAT DO YOU THINK?

Simeon was promised that he would see the Messiah in his lifetime. How do you suppose that promise affected him? How would your life be different if you knew the Lord would return in your lifetime?

HOW TO SAY IT

Arimathea. AIR-uh-muh-THEE-uh.
Assyria. Uh-SEAR-ee-uh.
Mediterranean. MED-uh-tuh-RAY-nee-un.
Nunc Dimittis. Nunk Dih-MIT-us.
Phanuel. FAN-you-el.
Pharisees. FAIR-ih-seez.
Sadducees. SAD-you-seez.
Simeon. SIM-ee-un.

Today's visual illustrates the vision of Simeon, who by the Spirit saw God's "salvation," which Jesus brought by the power of the same Spirit.

WHAT DO YOU THINK?

The Jews in Simeon's day would have agreed that the Messiah would be the glory of Israel. They believed the Messiah would restore independence to Israel and reestablish the throne of David in Jerusalem. The Gentiles were not included, except as objects of judgment and wrath.

Simeon saw Jesus as a "light for revelation to the Gentiles" as well as "for glory to . . . Israel." How does his statement speak to the mission of the church today?

WHAT DO YOU THINK?

"This child is destined to cause the falling and rising of many in Israel, and to be a sign that will be spoken against." How do these words continue to apply wherever Christ is proclaimed?

---

a sovereign master or owner. Simeon saw himself as a slave who was prepared to depart, or be dismissed from, this life because his goal had been reached. He "had seen the Lord's Christ" (v. 26). Nothing else in the world held any attraction for him. He was satisfied.

30. "For my eyes have seen your salvation.

Simeon's *eyes* had *seen [God's] salvation* in that he had looked upon the one who had come to bring salvation. Simeon probably did not grasp the full significance of his statement or comprehend just how that salvation would be provided (although later, as recorded in verse 35, he did hint at the suffering that Christ would experience).

31. ". . .which you have prepared in the sight of all people.

Simeon gave thanks that the Messiah's salvation was being *prepared* with *all people* in mind. While many did not notice the humble birth of Jesus or this incident in the temple, the impact of his extraordinary birth and life was meant to be felt by succeeding generations of peoples around the world. In the early chapters of his Gospel, Luke's interest in all people is seen in the words of the angels to the shepherds (Luke 2:10) and in the preaching of John the Baptist (Luke 3:6), as well as here.

32. ". . . a light for revelation to the Gentiles and for glory to your people Israel."

Luke often records events in which *Gentiles* or other outcasts were included in or affected by the ministry of Jesus. (See "Good News for All" on page 126, as well as comments under Luke 2:8 on page 153, for examples.) Here Jesus is called *a light for . . . the Gentiles* as well as to *Israel*. This emphasis, however, is not exclusively Luke's. Even Matthew, the most "Jewish" of the Gospels, includes indications that Jesus came to bless Gentiles (the visit of the wise men is a good example).

Luke's second book, the book of Acts, shows how the gospel message was first proclaimed among the Jews and eventually came to be preached among the Gentiles. Such an outreach did not come easily for the church. It is one thing to quote Jesus' Great Commission and quite another to practice it.

33. The child's father and mother marveled at what was said about him.

Both Joseph and Mary had already seen and heard more than enough concerning Jesus to cause them to marvel; yet Simeon's words on this occasion produced a similar effect.

D. HIS PROPHECY (vv. 34, 35)

34. Then Simeon blessed them and said to Mary, his mother: "This child is destined to cause the falling and rising of many in Israel, and to be a sign that will be spoken against.

Simeon's welcome was also filled with words of warning. That Jesus would *cause the falling and rising of many in Israel* indicates how Jesus would become a kind of "watershed." Some would believe in him and find eternal life; others "did not receive him" (John 1:11). Some experienced his "consolation" (v. 25); others rejected it.

Simeon further warned that Jesus would face stern opposition. While Jesus was extremely popular at times, certain individuals or groups, unhappy with him or jealous of his success, spoke *against* him and his teachings.

Even today, the idea of rising or falling is an apt way to describe how there is no middle ground concerning Jesus. It is impossible to remain neutral about him.

35. ". . . so that the thoughts of many hearts will be revealed. And a sword will pierce your own soul too."

The previous verse noted that Simeon's warning was directed specifically to Mary. These are not exactly the kind of words that a young mother wants to hear. The opposition against Jesus would become so pronounced, said Simeon, that it would wound Mary, piercing her very *soul*. No doubt it was difficult for Mary when the religious and political leaders began their verbal attacks against Jesus. Most agonizing of all, of course, was the pain she endured in watching her son die the humiliating death of crucifixion. The fact that Jesus himself would be pierced is clear from the word *too*. Thus, even at this early stage in the life of Christ, we see the foreshadowing of the cross.

How are *the thoughts of many hearts . . . revealed* through Jesus? They are revealed by the person's response to him. What Jesus said and what he did, particularly in his death and resurrection, challenges individuals to look at themselves and to confront the questions of eternal significance. Thus you can tell what a person is really like by his view of Jesus and his teachings.

During his earthly ministry, Jesus possessed special insight into the thoughts of people (John 2:24, 25). Even now, whenever we read his teachings and consider his example, we see his unique insight into the human condition.

II. ANNA (LUKE 2:36-38)

A. HER IDENTITY (v. 36)

36. *There was also a prophetess, Anna, the daughter of Phanuel, of the tribe of Asher. She was very old; she had lived with her husband seven years after her marriage.*

Simeon was not identified as a prophet, yet he, through God's Spirit, prophesied on this day. *Anna*, on the other hand, is called a *prophetess*. Her name is essentially the same as the Old Testament character Hannah, and it means "grace."

Anna is described as *the daughter of Phanuel*. We know nothing else about this man, but he was probably well known at the time for his name to be mentioned here.

Anna is also described as a member *of the tribe of Asher*. When the promised land had been divided among the twelve tribes, Asher was assigned an area along the Mediterranean coast north of Mount Carmel. Although many of the people of this northern tribe had been carried away by the Assyrians (following the conquest of the northern kingdom by Assyria in 722 B.C.), the tribe had not completely lost its identity.

Luke also mentions that Anna was widowed *seven years* into her marriage and never remarried. Life could be very difficult for widows in the ancient world. They were often poverty stricken and the targets of unscrupulous practices, sometimes from supposedly religious individuals (Luke 20:45-47). Luke's unique references to widows (here; 4:25, 26; 7:12; 18:1-8) comprise another indication of his Gospel's concern for those considered outcasts by society.

B. HER CHARACTER (v. 37)

37. . . . *and then was a widow until she was eighty-four. She never left the temple but worshiped night and day, fasting and praying.*

Anna's devotion to God was such that *she never left the temple*. This may simply mean that she stayed there all day, not that she lived there. It is possible, however, that she lived in one of the rooms adjoining the temple and did volunteer service there. The depth of her spiritual commitment is clear from the statement that she *worshiped night and day, fasting and praying*.

There is some disagreement among Bible students regarding Anna's age. According to our text, Anna was currently a *widow* and currently *eighty-four* years

DAILY BIBLE READINGS

Monday, Dec. 25—*The Consecration of the Firstborn (Exodus 13:11-16)*

Tuesday, Dec. 26—*According to the Law (Luke 2: 21-24)*

Wednesday, Dec. 27—*Our Love for God (Deuteronomy 6: 1-9)*

Thursday, Dec. 28—*Adoration and Prophecy of Simeon (Luke 2:25-35)*

Friday, Dec. 29—*The Good News of Peace (Isaiah 52:3-10)*

Saturday, Dec. 30—*Adoration of Anna (Luke 2:36-38)*

Sunday, Dec. 31—*Honor Widows Who Hope in God (1 Timothy 5:3-8)*

PRAYER

Dear Father, thank you for sending us light. Thank you for sending us salvation. We recognize that these have come to us through a person—Jesus. He gives us reason to raise our voices in praise, just as Simeon and Anna did. In his dear name we pray. Amen.

THOUGHT TO REMEMBER

No matter what your age may be, God always gives you reason to hope and to look forward to tomorrow.

old. The text is ambiguous enough, however, that it could mean that she had been widowed for eighty-four years. If so, then Anna was over a hundred years old. Such a scenario, though unusual, would not have been impossible.

C. HER TESTIMONY (v. 38)

38. Coming up to them at that very moment, she gave thanks to God and spoke about the child to all who were looking forward to the redemption of Jerusalem.

Anna's testimony concerning the child was far more public than Simeon's was. Like the shepherds, she too was a kind of evangelist, telling people who *were looking forward to the redemption of Jerusalem* that their looking was over; the Messiah had come! It appears that her proclamation concerning Jesus was not limited to the people in the temple. She conveyed the news wherever she could find an interested hearer.

REST STOP

The minister arrived early for the morning service, but one person was already seated in the sanctuary. She was sitting in the back, at the end of the pew, half asleep. The minister walked over and teased her about getting her nap finished before he began to preach. "This is the only place I can get any rest," she said. At first he thought that she had back trouble and that the contour of the padded pew gave her relief. But as they talked on, he realized she meant something else. She worked a full-time job outside the home and cared for all the household duties in the home. When she came to the church building, it was the only time she could get any rest.

Many have experienced rest in the church—not physical rest, but spiritual and emotional rest. Guilt-laden people say, "This is the only place I can get any rest." Sorrow-laden people say, "This is the only place I can get any rest." Worried people say, "This is the only place I can get any rest." Even people in physical pain can find relief in worship. As an old hymn says, "O Love that wilt not let me go, I rest my weary soul on Thee."

Both Simeon and Anna found peace and rest in the place that had been dedicated to the worship and service of God. Many today will testify that there is something about the atmosphere of a modern house of worship that brings a sense of contentment and rest to their bodies, their minds, and their souls. —R. C. S.

CONCLUSION

One of the toughest things to do in life is to wait. When we are children, we think that Christmas will never come or that the school year will never end. When we are waiting for news from a medical test, the minutes seem like days.

In the time in which Simeon and Anna lived, there was a general hope and expectation in Israel that God was about to do something. Along with these two, we know that Joseph of Arimathea also possessed such a hope (Luke 23:50, 51). People were praying for and watching for a Messiah. They took a new interest in the promises of the prophets. They held tightly to every hint in the Scriptures of the Messiah's coming. There must have been times when they thought this event would never happen, yet they continued to trust God's promises.

On the day that Joseph and Mary entered the temple with the infant Jesus, two faithful saints of God—Simeon and Anna—learned that the long wait was over. God was acting. God was coming in the form of a baby to meet human need. No wonder these devout believers lifted their voices in praise.

Today people are still in need of the light and salvation that Jesus came to bring. Like Anna, we must tell everyone we can about this good news.

Discovery Learning

This page contains an alternate lesson plan emphasizing learning activities. Classes desiring such student involvement will find these suggestions helpful. The next page is a reproducible activity page to further enhance discovery learning.

LEARNING GOALS

After this lesson each student will be able to:

1. Summarize the reactions of Simeon and Anna upon seeing the Christ child.

2. Tell how these reactions reflected a hope based on the faithfulness of God and his promises.

3. Identify one person who does not have hope in Christ, and suggest a specific way to share with that person the good news of Jesus.

INTO THE LESSON

Before the class arrives write, "Promises! Promises!" on the chalkboard or on a large poster. Below that write, "How promises affect my behavior." As students enter the room, direct their attention to what you have written. Allow some time for the students to think, and then ask for responses. Ask for volunteers to tell about times they have said—or wanted to say—"Promises! Promises!" Why did they doubt? Were they right about the promises' not being kept, or were they surprised? How do we respond to promises that we believe?

Make the transition to Bible study by saying, "In our lesson today we will meet two people who believed God's promise to send a Messiah. Their faith led them to dramatic encounters with baby Jesus in the temple."

INTO THE WORD

Ask a volunteer to read Luke 2:25-38. Then divide the class into two groups. Ask the first group to consider Simeon and the second to consider Anna. Each group should determine how belief in God's faithfulness had guided Simeon's or Anna's life until the important day recorded in our text. The groups should also tell how these two saints displayed their faith in God's keeping his word when they saw Jesus.

After ten minutes, ask a reporter from each group to stand and summarize the group's findings. Some suggested discoveries follow.

Simeon: His "waiting for the consolation of Israel" (v. 25) is evidence that Simeon trusted God to keep his word. Probably his presence at the temple was additional evidence. His prayer that he could depart in peace was a prayer of triumph and anticipation of God's putting into place his plan of salvation. His prophecy, while troubling, was a confident expression of hope that God would work out his plan even through distress.

Anna: Her continual presence at the temple was, no doubt, a demonstration of her faith and hope in God to provide a Redeemer. Her fastings and prayers also demonstrated her faithfulness. She gave thanks to God for the Christ child, and spoke of him "to all who were looking forward to the redemption of Jerusalem" (v. 38). Comment on how our willingness to talk to others about Jesus shows our own faith.

INTO LIFE

Comment on how Simeon and Anna demonstrated their hope in God's salvation even without knowing all the details. Jesus was but a baby and was probably but a youth when these two saints died. But we know the rest of Jesus' life. We know the convincing proofs he gave to show that he was sent by God, that he is "the Christ, the Son of the living God" (Matthew 16:16). We know of his death, burial, and resurrection. How much more ought we to be confident of his identity and of his ability to provide salvation!

But many today do not know him. Distribute copies of the reproducible page that follows; then ask the learners to write the names of the people they think of. Ask them to think about which of these they can talk with this week about the Lord—as Anna told all those looking for redemption. Are there individuals on your students' lists who are seeking the Lord? Have some of them expressed interest in your students' faith or in the church? Have they visited the worship service? Have some of them had recent experiences that may serve to awaken spiritual interest or desire?

Ask the students also to think about the people with whom they have the most credibility. Are there coworkers with whom they have a closer relationship than with others? Are there people on their lists who seek them out for advice?

Have the students consider practical matters such as how often they see the people they listed. Are there some they know they will see every day this week, or at least once during the week?

Have the students evaluate all the information; then ask each one to choose one person from his list with whom he will share the good news of Jesus this week. Brainstorm some specific ways of doing that, and then ask each student to choose one of the methods discussed and make plans to share the gospel this week.

Spread the Word

Think of five non-Christians whom you know. Write their names below.

1.

2.

3.

4.

5.

Think about which of these you can talk with this week about the Lord—as Anna told all those looking for redemption. Are there individuals on your list who are seeking the Lord? Have some of them expressed interest in your faith or in the church? Have they visited the worship service? Have some of them had recent experiences that may serve to awaken spiritual interest or desire? Write the names of those who have shown some interest below.

With which of these people do you have the most credibility? Are there coworkers with whom you have a closer relationship than with others? Are there people on your list who seek you out for advice? Write their names below.

How often do you see the people listed? Are there some you know you will see every day this week, or at least once during the week? Write the name(s) below.

Evaluate all the information; then choose one person from your list with whom you will share the good news of Jesus this week. Think of some specific ways of doing that, and then choose a specific method and make plans to share the gospel this week.

This week I will share the gospel with _____

Some specific ways I can do that are. . . .

JESUS IN NAZARETH

LESSON 6

WHY TEACH THIS LESSON?

Ours is a culture that does not know how to handle rejection. It is fear of rejection that puts teeth into peer pressure. It is fear of rejection that keeps timid boys from asking popular girls for dates. And it is the abhorrence of rejection that makes the label "intolerant" so intolerable. We want the people around us to like us, to accept us as one of them, to make us feel that we belong. Rare is the man or woman who can defy public opinion and take a stand simply on the rightness or wrongness of the issue endorsed or opposed.

More and more, however, it is just that type of independence of popular opinion that is needed. As biblical values are more and more marginalized in our culture, Christians find they are increasingly called on to find their values outside the mainstream. And the price they pay for doing so goes up every day.

This lesson will show them how Jesus handled rejection. It's a lesson whose value is sure to increase.

INTRODUCTION

A. GOING HOME

Students of American literature are familiar with the works of Thomas Wolfe, a novelist who lived during the first half of the twentieth century. One of his best-known novels is entitled *You Can't Go Home Again*. Certainly there is a measure of truth to that. Going home can be difficult if an individual left home amidst a flurry of high expectations but then fell flat on his face in failure.

On the other hand, going home can be one of the most thrilling, rewarding experiences of a person's life if the individual lived up to, or even exceeded, the expectations surrounding him. And if he left home with few thinking that his chances for success were very great, going back home to headlines of "Local Boy [or Girl] Makes Good" would be especially satisfying.

In today's lesson we consider what happened when Jesus made his first visit back to his hometown of Nazareth after he had begun his messianic ministry. One would think, given the excitement over Jesus' ministry to this point, that the reception of the townspeople would have been most favorable. But such was not the case; in fact, the residents of Nazareth became not only unfriendly, but hostile.

B. LESSON BACKGROUND

From the story of the presentation of Jesus in the temple (the subject of last week's lesson), our study of the Gospel of Luke moves forward to Jesus at age thirty (Luke 3:23). It was then that he initiated his ministry as Messiah by means of his baptism in the Jordan River (Luke 3:21, 22).

From the river to the wilderness, the Holy Spirit led Jesus to a confrontation with the devil. This time of temptation tested the resolve of the Messiah. Though physically weakened by forty days of fasting (Luke 4:1, 2), Jesus proved to be stronger than any scheme of the tempter. He was now ready to pursue his ministry in earnest.

DEVOTIONAL READING:
ISAIAH 61

BACKGROUND SCRIPTURE:
LUKE 4:14-30

PRINTED TEXT:
LUKE 4:16-30

LESSON AIMS

After this lesson each student will be able to:

Jan 7

1. Tell what happened in Nazareth when Jesus identified himself as the fulfillment of one of Isaiah's prophecies of the Messiah.

2. Compare the prophesied role of the Messiah with Jesus' ministry and with that of the church today.

3. Give a specific example of how the church can continue the messianic ministry Isaiah prophesied and Jesus fulfilled.

KEY VERSE

"The Spirit of the Lord is on me, because he has anointed me to preach good news to the poor. He has sent me to proclaim freedom for the prisoners and recovery of sight for the blind, to release the oppressed, to proclaim the year of the Lord's favor."
—Luke 4:18, 19

After first spending some time in Jerusalem and the surrounding vicinity, Jesus led his disciples north to Galilee (Luke 4:14), where together they ministered for nearly two years. There he began to visit some of the synagogues in Galilee, where "everyone praised him" (Luke 4:15). Eventually he came to his hometown of Nazareth.

I. A GOSPEL MISSION (LUKE 4:16-21)
A. Announced in the Synagogue (vv. 16, 17)
16. He went to Nazareth, where he had been brought up, and on the Sabbath day he went into the synagogue, as was his custom. And he stood up to read.

Though Jesus had been born in Bethlehem, not far from Jerusalem, he was *brought up* in the town of *Nazareth*. We have noted in previous lessons that in Jesus' day Nazareth was a small village of little notoriety. It was considered by many to be too remote and uncultured to produce anything good, let alone a Messiah (John 1:46). Yet Jesus was respectful enough of his hometown to give its residents the opportunity to hear the good news of his appointment by God as the Messiah.

It was Jesus' *custom* to attend worship services in a Jewish *synagogue* every Sabbath day (i.e., Saturday). It is important to note that, while on the one hand Jesus did not consider himself to be bound by man-made traditions such as not healing on the Sabbath (Luke 6:6-10), he was nevertheless fully committed to the letter and spirit of God's Word. The consistent picture throughout all four Gospels is that Jesus was faithful in observing the requirements of the Old Testament law. The seriousness with which he pursued the religious practices of his day serve to inspire us in our walk with the Lord today.

THE WORTH OF WORSHIP
Some time ago a lady by the name of Mary Ellen Benson was fined five dollars for not attending meetings of Local 356 of the United Papermakers Union. The reason she did not attend was that the meetings were held on Sunday mornings during the time of her church's worship services. She refused to pay the fine, so the union took her to court. The court ordered her to pay and added court costs of $5.40. So skipping the union meetings cost Mrs. Benson $10.40. But the worth of worship is much, much more than that!

Jesus recognized the priority of worship. It was his "custom" to be present at the services held each Sabbath at the synagogue in Nazareth (Luke 4:16).

Many today object, "Look at all the problems in the church! It's full of hypocrites! I can live a life just as good and as pleasing to God without the church as I can with the church." But does today's church have any more problems than the synagogues did in Jesus' day? (Think of the "hypocrites" whom Jesus often confronted who were in regular attendance at the synagogues!)

If Jesus recognized the necessity of regular worship—if he saw the value of observing this "custom" faithfully—what about us? The writer of Hebrews says it well: "Let us not give up meeting together, as some are in the habit of doing, but let us encourage one another—and all the more as you see the Day approaching" (Hebrews 10:25).   —R. C. S.

17. The scroll of the prophet Isaiah was handed to him. Unrolling it, he found the place where it is written:

It was a common synagogue practice in first-century Judaism to show respect to visiting teachers by inviting them to read Scripture aloud and then give their exposition of the passage read. This custom afforded Jesus a ready opportunity to proclaim his gospel message in every city and village that he visited on a Sabbath day. The apostle Paul later made it "his custom" to turn this tradition into an evangelistic opportunity as he traveled about (Acts 17:2).

The *scroll* that was handed to Jesus contained the writings of *the prophet Isaiah.* We are not told whether Jesus requested this particular scroll or simply accepted whatever book of Scripture was currently being used in this synagogue's rotation of Bible reading. No doubt he knew, whether by his own request or by divine foreknowledge, what scroll he would be reading. Immediately Jesus sought out a well-known messianic text—Isaiah 61:1, 2. By careful design Jesus turned that day's reading into an extraordinary event. A familiar prophecy was read aloud by the one who had come to fulfill it!

B. FORETOLD IN PROPHECY (vv. 18, 19)

18. "The Spirit of the Lord is on me, because he has anointed me to preach good news to the poor. He has sent me to proclaim freedom for the prisoners and recovery of sight for the blind, to release the oppressed.

The prophecy that Jesus chose to read was clearly a reference to the Messiah, which means *anointed* one. The Messiah of Jewish expectation was not merely one who was anointed with oil, but anointed with the *Spirit of the Lord.*

Having identified the source of power for the Messiah, the prophet then set forth a summary of God's agenda for the Messiah. It was not exactly what the first-century Jews were hoping for. They wanted a deliverer to destroy the hated Romans—or at least to banish them from the Jewish homeland—and reestablish the political empire that David and Solomon ruled.

Isaiah's picture was quite different. First, the Messiah was appointed *to preach good news* of God's salvation. The Greek verb used in this text is one from which we get the term "evangelist." It literally refers to proclaiming aloud good news.

It is difficult to know whether we should interpret the next portion of Isaiah's prophecy in literal terms or in a way that applies the language to spiritual concerns. Certainly we can acknowledge the fact that Jesus' ministry did reach out to both the spiritual and physical needs of the people he met. His "good news" made a difference in peoples' lives in more than one way, and his work serves to remind us that we too need a view of ministry that is broad enough to respond to both spiritual and physical needs.

19. ". . . to proclaim the year of the Lord's favor."

Here the term *year* is not describing a calendar year. It refers instead to the era when all of the above actions would take place—in other words, the messianic age. Many Bible students have seen a reference in Jesus' words to the Old Testament Year of Jubilee (Leviticus 25:8-55). At that time, which was to occur once every fifty years, slaves were freed, debts were canceled, and ancestral property that had been sold during the previous fifty years (because of poverty) was returned to the family that originally owned it. Whereas Isaiah first uttered these words to promise Israel deliverance from captivity in Babylon and repossession of her "property" in the promised land, Jesus used it to announce deliverance from sin and its consequences.

THE YEAR OF THE LORD'S FAVOR

Jesus told those who had gathered in the synagogue in Nazareth that he had come to proclaim "the year of the Lord's favor" (Luke 4:19). While Jesus was not referring to a calendar year when he spoke of "the year of the Lord's favor," the phrase should merit special consideration as we embark on the year 2001. Will this be "the year of the Lord's favor," in the sense that we will become more firmly committed to living under the lordship of Jesus in our daily lives and spreading the

WHAT DO YOU THINK?

How do those who minister in the name of Jesus continue to "preach good news to the poor . . . proclaim freedom for the prisoners and recovery of sight for the blind, [and] release the oppressed"?

Display the poster from last week's lesson. Note how Jesus' claim fulfilled not only Isaiah's prophecy, but the prophecy of Simeon as well.

HOW TO SAY IT

Babylon. BAB-uh-lun.
Capernaum. Kuh-PER-nay-um.
Elijah. Ee-LYE-juh.
Elisha. Ee-LYE-shuh.
Isaiah. Eye-ZAY-uh.
Mediterranean. MED-uh-tuh-RAY-nee-un.
messianic. mess-ee-AN-ick.
Kerith. KEY-rith.
Naaman. NAY-uh-mun.
Nazareth. NAZ-uh-reth.
Sidon. SIGH-dun.
synagogue. SIN-uh-gog.
Syrian. SEAR-ee-un.
Tyre. Tire.
Zarephath. ZAIR-uh-fath.

WHAT DO YOU THINK?

The people in Nazareth were amazed at the "gracious words" that Jesus spoke. Do people consider your words "gracious"? Why or why not? How can we speak "gracious words"?

[Consider Colossians 4:5 and 6 and James 1:5 and 6 in your discussion.]

message of his grace to others? Could this *really* be the year of the Lord's favor, in that it will be the year the Lord "favors" us with his return?

Whatever the year is, it ought to be "the year of the Lord's favor" in the sense that we seek his favor through an increase in our faith in the Lord and in yielding our lives more completely to his service.
—R. C. S.

C. FULFILLED BY JESUS (vv. 20, 21)

20. Then he rolled up the scroll, gave it back to the attendant and sat down. The eyes of everyone in the synagogue were fastened on him.

Jesus followed the customary practice for speaking in a synagogue. Out of respect for the Word of God, a speaker would stand while reading aloud a Scripture text (v. 16), but then it was acceptable to sit down while speaking and teaching. On this occasion of Jesus' first sermon in his hometown, *the eyes of everyone . . . were fastened on him* as they listened intently to see what he would say regarding his ministry of preaching and healing that had caused such a stir throughout Galilee (v. 14).

21. . . . and he began by saying to them, "Today this scripture is fulfilled in your hearing."

Today this Scripture is fulfilled in your hearing. This was a bold statement to make. Jesus was doing significantly more than simply claiming to be a new kind of prophet or rabbi. The Messiah held a one-of-a-kind position rooted in the hopes of the Jewish faith—hopes that were especially intense at this time. By identifying himself with this prophecy, Jesus provided both an announcement of his ministry plans and a means for the people to measure whether or not he lived up to the divine standard for the Messiah.

II. A SKEPTICAL RESPONSE (LUKE 4:22-27)

A. THE CROWD'S REACTION (v. 22)

22. All spoke well of him and were amazed at the gracious words that came from his lips. "Isn't this Joseph's son?" they asked.

It is probable that the words recorded in verse 21 do not comprise all that Jesus said before the crowd responded. Matthew and Mark both note that Jesus taught at Nazareth (Matthew 13:54; Mark 6:1, 2), which most likely included additional words beyond those recorded by Luke.

Reaction from the crowd appears to have been mixed. On the one hand, *all spoke well of him*: they seemed to enjoy Jesus' style and delivery and to relish the messianic possibilities within his *gracious words*. On the other hand, the people found it hard even to imagine that one of their own—from their insignificant town—could actually turn out to be someone as profoundly important as the Messiah. *Isn't this Joseph's son?* they asked. As they did so, they must have spoken with a certain measure of skepticism or even derision. After all, a lowly carpenter's son is not a likely candidate to become a royal, messianic figure. This latter view seems to have been more commonly held; both Matthew and Mark note that the audience "took offense" at Jesus' words (Matthew 13:57; Mark 6:3).

B. JESUS' DEFENSE (vv. 23-27)

23. Jesus said to them, "Surely you will quote this proverb to me: 'Physician, heal yourself! Do here in your hometown what we have heard that you did in Capernaum.'"

Jesus perceived the crowd's growing skepticism. He knew that they were expecting him to defend his messianic claim by producing supernatural manifestations before their eyes. After all, they had *heard* reports of Jesus' performing miracles *in Capernaum* prior to his arrival in Nazareth. The Gospels do not record any details from this preliminary work in Capernaum, but it must have been impressive enough that rumors had spread all the way out to Nazareth. Now the townspeople wanted to see some of these wonders for themselves.

24. "I tell you the truth," he continued, "no prophet is accepted in his hometown.

Throughout his preaching ministry, Jesus often noted the tragic irony that the very nation that claimed to be devoted to Jehovah God had a long history of killing his messengers (Luke 11:49-51). False prophets had always been welcomed because they preached what the people wanted to hear. But a genuine *prophet* with a challenging message from God was usually not *accepted in his hometown*.

The phenomenon Jesus described has its parallel in our experiences today. It is often quite difficult for someone to be taken seriously by the people who have known him the longest and the best. Images from their past often shape their perception of the present, not allowing them to see individuals in a new and different light. Apparently the memories of Jesus growing up in Joseph's humble home kept the people of Nazareth from accepting Jesus as someone to listen to and heed. Today we sometimes quote the saying, "Familiarity breeds contempt." This is in essence the idea Jesus was expressing in his words, *No prophet is accepted in his hometown.*

25. "I assure you that there were many widows in Israel in Elijah's time, when the sky was shut for three and a half years and there was a severe famine throughout the land.

The tone of Jesus' remarks in the synagogue had taken a decisive turn. Whereas he began with "gracious words" (v. 22) about the fulfillment of messianic prophecy, the predominantly skeptical reaction of his audience prompted him to speak words of rebuke. Using illustrations from the lives of two great Old Testament prophets, Jesus told how a hostile reception to a messenger of God can result in blessings being taken away and given to others more receptive.

The prophet Elijah pronounced a drought upon *Israel* that lasted for *three and a half years* (1 Kings 17:1; James 5:17). This resulted in a *severe famine throughout the land.* But Elijah did not provide supernatural relief for the hungry of Israel, in large part because they were under God's discipline. They had failed to heed the preaching of Elijah and other prophets of God, and they were suffering the consequences.

26. "Yet Elijah was not sent to any of them, but to a widow in Zarephath in the region of Sidon.

After Elijah hid himself for a while on the east side of the Jordan near the little brook of Kerith (1 Kings 17:3), God instructed him to relocate to the small town of *Zarephath.* This was located on the Mediterranean coast in the region of *Sidon,* approximately fourteen miles north of Tyre. There Elijah was to seek out the hospitality of a particular *widow.* Though her food supply was almost exhausted, she shared what little she had with this prophet of God, and was thereby blessed with sufficient food for the duration of the drought (1 Kings 17:8-16).

27. "And there were many in Israel with leprosy in the time of Elisha the prophet, yet not one of them was cleansed—only Naaman the Syrian."

Like his predecessor Elijah, *Elisha* worked in an environment of hostility, experiencing rejection by both the king of *Israel* and the people. Thus his miracle-working power was allowed to bless someone outside of Israel—*Naaman,* whose account is told in 2 Kings 5:1-19.

Naaman was a captain in the army of the neighboring country of Syria (Aram), which was at odds with Israel during the ministry of Elisha. He had some form of

DAILY BIBLE READINGS

Monday, Jan. 1—*Tempted As We Are (Luke 4:1-13)*

Tuesday, Jan. 2—*A Mission to the People (Luke 4:14-21)*

Wednesday, Jan. 3—*The Good News of Deliverance (Isaiah 61)*

Thursday, Jan. 4—*His Own Received Him Not (Luke 4:22-30)*

Friday, Jan. 5—*The Healing of Naaman (2 Kings 5:1-14)*

Saturday, Jan. 6—*The Rejection of Jesus (Matthew 13:54-58)*

Sunday, Jan. 7—*Whoever Does the Will of God (Mark 3:31-35)*

WHAT DO YOU THINK?

Jesus cited examples of blessings that went to those outside Israel because they had a simple trust in God. Matthew notes that Jesus *"did not do many miracles [in Nazareth] because of their lack of faith"* (Matthew 13:58). Who knows how many sick or disabled or demon-possessed continued to suffer there because of their lack of faith? Listen to the testimonies of the faithful today, at what God has done in their lives. These are the blessings that would be lacking if those saints had no faith.

What blessings do you think you, your church, or your community may have missed because of skepticism and doubt?

leprous skin disease, which, though apparently not contagious (since he was still on "active duty"), was nevertheless serious enough that he desired relief. He was instructed by Elisha to dip seven times in the Jordan River, and upon his obedience to the word of God he was healed (2 Kings 5:14).

Jesus' point in calling attention to this story was to emphasize that there were *many* lepers *in Israel* that Elisha could have healed; however (as was shown in the preceding example from Elijah's ministry), blessings of God are often withheld from those who reject the preaching of God's servants. Nazareth was being warned in no uncertain terms that it was headed down a similar path of disaster.

III. A DETERMINED SPIRIT (LUKE 4:28-30)

A. FACING HOSTILITY (vv. 28, 29)

28. All the people in the synagogue were furious when they heard this.

The majority of the people who *heard* Jesus speak reacted with anger at his rebuke. Their earlier anticipation at seeing one of their own return home was now replaced with a violent rage.

29. They got up, drove him out of the town, and took him to the brow of the hill on which the town was built, in order to throw him down the cliff.

There is not enough information here to know exactly what the crowd intended to do with Jesus. Their plan to *throw him down the cliff* could be read as an attempt to kill him by throwing him from a precipice. However, the topography of Nazareth resembles a sloping hill more than a mountainous cliff. What Luke may be describing here is the preliminary steps to a stoning. It was common practice among the Jews to cast a person to be stoned down into an area below the crowd, where they could then throw stones from above.

B. PRESSING FORWARD (v. 30)

30. But he walked right through the crowd and went on his way.

Luke does not explain exactly how Jesus survived this threat. Perhaps he used his supernatural power to shield himself from the crowd and then passed *right through the crowd* unharmed. Or it may be that he challenged their intimidation with a powerful presence and an unyielding resolve, thereby defusing the situation before it could get further out of hand.

Regardless of how Jesus escaped from this scene, he was not moved from the mission he had announced in the synagogue. Jesus *went on his way* and immediately proceeded to carry out the gospel agenda prophesied in Isaiah 61, undaunted by this or any other opposition he would encounter.

CONCLUSION

What a frustrating thing it is to attempt to get people to try something that we know will be good for them, only to have them say, "I'll try it, but I know I'm not going to like it." Sometimes they are pleasantly surprised, and our pleas and assurances are vindicated. But too often our good intentions are wasted as a biased attitude refuses to give the item a fair chance. "How can anyone be so closedminded?" we wonder—that is, until we recall those occasions when our preconceived notions turned out to be just as mistaken.

The gospel of Jesus Christ deserves a fair hearing, with no bias or prejudice, lest a truly good thing be lost. At the same time, we who are followers of Jesus should determine that nothing we say or do will cause others to be biased against him. We must, by our conduct, lead others closer to Jesus, not drive them farther away from him.

WHAT DO YOU THINK?

The people of the Nazareth synagogue reacted to Jesus' message with rage. How do you normally respond to a convicting message or a rebuke? What determines whether a person responds with anger or with grace?

PRAYER

Father, thank you for sending your Son Jesus Christ to be our Savior and Lord. May we always be receptive to his words. May we continue to carry out his mission of proclaiming "the year of the Lord's favor." In Jesus' name. Amen.

THOUGHT TO REMEMBER

Jesus came to fulfill the Scripture; the church is to proclaim that fulfillment.

Discovery Learning

This page contains an alternate lesson plan emphasizing learning activities. Classes
desiring such student involvement will find these suggestions helpful. The next page
is a reproducible activity page to further enhance discovery learning.

LEARNING GOALS

After this lesson each student will be able to:

1. Tell what happened in Nazareth when Jesus identified himself as the fulfillment of one of Isaiah's prophecies of the Messiah.

2. Compare the prophesied role of the Messiah with Jesus' ministry and with that of the church today.

3. Give a specific example of how the church can continue the messianic ministry Isaiah prophesied and Jesus fulfilled.

INTO THE LESSON

People have many roles in their lives. Our roles often define who we are or what we will do. These roles are also used by others to determine their acceptance or rejection of us. Ask, "What are some of the roles you play in life?" In groups of four have the students tell about their roles—e.g., parent, plant supervisor, Little League coach, deacon, etc.

Continue with this activity by asking the groups to discuss the following questions:

• "Which role provides you the most fun?"
• "Which role do you find the most rewarding?"
• "Which role provides the most challenge?"
• "Which role gives you the most frustration?"

Ask whether anyone has ever been rejected in any role. Have volunteers to tell how they have experienced rejection and how they responded. Then say, "Today we will examine an episode in which Jesus revealed his identity and work in Nazareth. Within that revelation was a challenge of ministry to his followers. We will see how a similar challenge is given to us today."

INTO THE WORD

Prepare a three- to five-minute lecture using material from the lesson commentary's Introduction section. Have a student read Luke 4:16-30 aloud. Then appoint at least three groups of four students. If you have more students, give the assignments to more than one group. Each group should appoint a reporter to write answers on a poster you have mounted on the wall and to explain the group's answers to the class.

Group 1: Responses of People

1. What positive responses to Jesus are seen in this passage?

2. What negative responses to Jesus are seen here?

3. What changes are recorded in this passage to bring forth these different responses?

Group 2: The Roles of the Messiah

1. List the five roles of the Messiah presented in this passage.

2. Give examples from Jesus' ministry that fulfilled these roles.

3. What do you think the people expected from Jesus after he read these words?

Group 3: Handling Rejection

1. What kind of rejection did Jesus face here?

2. How did Jesus handle this rejection?

3. What does this passage teach us about handling rejection?

OPTION

Distribute copies of the reproducible activity "Headline News" from the next page. Have students work in small groups to write newspaper headlines that summarize today's text. Then use the activity at the bottom of the page to encourage application of the lesson.

INTO LIFE

Draw attention to the answers on Group 2's poster. Be sure to highlight the five points that Jesus made about his ministry: preach the good news, proclaim freedom to prisoners, perform acts of mercy, pursue release for the oppressed, proclaim God's grace to sinners.

Discuss the following questions.

1. How do these five points compare with the role that the church is to play in the world today?

2. What response should we expect from the world if we are involved in such a task?

3. What would it cost the church to perform these roles in the community?

Discussion should reveal that the church is to fulfill these tasks today, and that the same responses can be expected: praise, amazement, disbelief, anger, and rejection.

Bring enough bulletins or calendars from your church for each group. Using the five areas of mission delineated by Group 2, evaluate your church's schedule. Place each scheduled activity in an area of mission. Ask, "After checking our church's activities, in which area of mission do you believe we are the strongest? In which area are we the weakest? What activities should we consider to better fulfill the messianic ministry Jesus has given us?"

Headline News

Read Luke 4:16-30. Write two newspaper headlines concerning the events in this passage.

Mission Statement

"The Spirit of the Lord is on me, because he has anointed me to preach good news to the poor. He has sent me to proclaim freedom for the prisoners and recovery of sight for the blind, to release the oppressed, to proclaim the year of the Lord's favor" (Luke 4:18, 19).

The church is to continue the messianic ministry prophesied by Isaiah and fulfilled by Jesus. Taking the printed text, write a mission statement for your church. Detail two activities that would help fulfill this mission statement and that would be "headline" events at your church.

Our church exists to

We will accomplish this by

1.

2.

THE COST OF DISCIPLESHIP

WHY TEACH THIS LESSON?

We call him the "rich young ruler"—that wealthy young man who approached Jesus and asked what good thing he could do to inherit eternal life. Matthew, Mark, and Luke all include his story in their Gospels—though our study of Luke this quarter will not deal with the account. Jesus told the young man to sell all he had and give to the poor; then he could follow Jesus.

We are usually quick to point out that this was a special case! Jesus saw that the man's wealth was a stumbling block to discipleship, so Jesus told him to get rid of it. "Jesus never told anyone else to do the same," we always say.

Today's lesson will challenge that thought. Our text concludes with these words from the Master: "In the same way, *any of you* who does not give up everything he has cannot be my disciple." This lesson will challenge your students' understanding of the rich young ruler—and of their own commitment to discipleship.

INTRODUCTION

A. "A FEW GOOD MEN"

The recruitment posters for the Marine Corps make a powerful statement. The Corps is not for everyone—only for the best among recruits. As their motto says, they want only "a few good men." Now, on the one hand, we like an open policy that allows anyone who wishes to participate in a program to do so. For some activities that may be the only way we will get in. On the other hand, we admire programs that operate with tough admission standards, that bring together the best and most talented people they can find, and then put out a "product" that is a cut above the rest. And while the latter approach may discourage some, for others it is the kind of challenge that draws them in.

Although the invitation to be a disciple of Christ is open to all, the standards set forth by the Master are rather demanding. Our Lord is not as interested in the numbers he recruits as he is in the quality of service we give. Only those who are ready to give Jesus their best need apply.

B. LESSON BACKGROUND

Luke 9:51 is an important transitional statement in Luke's account of the life of Jesus. It may be considered a framework for viewing the remainder of his Gospel. It reads, "As the time approached for him to be taken up to heaven, Jesus resolutely set out for Jerusalem." This shows Jesus' awareness that the time of his death, by which he would fulfill his Father's plan, was approaching. However, Luke does not say that this was Jesus' final journey to Jerusalem. It appears that this journey marked the beginning of a time of ministry in Judea, during which, according to John's record, the Feast of Tabernacles was observed (John 7:1-10). This ministry is recorded in Luke 9:51—13:21. It was during this trip toward Jerusalem that Jesus encountered the would-be disciples mentioned in the first part of today's printed text. This probably occurred about six months prior to the Lord's crucifixion.

The second portion of our text comes from Luke 14:25-33. By this time, Jesus' ministry had moved into Perea—the territory located across the Jordan River

DEVOTIONAL READING:
MATTHEW 10:34-39
BACKGROUND SCRIPTURE:
LUKE 9:18-25, 46-62; 14:25-35
PRINTED TEXT:
LUKE 9:57-62; 14:25-33

LESSON AIMS

After this lesson the students will be able to:

1. Summarize Jesus' teaching about the demands of discipleship according to today's text.

Jan 14

2. Tell why encouraging people to "count the cost" should be an integral part of evangelism.

3. Pinpoint an excuse that they have been using to avoid a deeper commitment to Christ, and express a commitment to strengthen their discipleship.

KEY VERSE

Anyone who does not carry his cross and follow me cannot be my disciple. —Luke 14:27

LESSON 7 NOTES

from Samaria and Judea. Here, where "large crowds" were following Jesus (v. 25), he gave one of his most straightforward descriptions of what it really means for a person to follow him. This incident must have taken place sometime following the observance of the Feast of Tabernacles (John 10:40 records Jesus' movement "across the Jordan"). The cross was now only three to four months away.

I. DECISIVE ACTION (LUKE 9:57-62)

A. NO HESITATION (vv. 57, 58)

57. As they were walking along the road, a man said to him, "I will follow you wherever you go."

Earlier we called attention to Luke 9:51, where Jesus "resolutely set out for Jerusalem," as a framework for viewing the second half of Luke's Gospel. Whatever Jesus said or did from this point on was keenly focused on his impending death. Thus, when Luke says *as they were walking along the road* toward Jerusalem, he may intend us to think not only of literal walking, but also of Jesus' resolute purpose: as Jesus anticipated the cross that lay ahead, he spoke of the cost of being his disciple.

We can certainly commend the enthusiasm for service expressed in the words, *I will follow you wherever you go*. Indeed, discipleship does require a "wherever you want me" attitude. But Jesus was well aware that words of commitment are more easily spoken than acted on. Sometimes we say the right words without giving thought to their implications. Thus Jesus responded with a challenge that may be summarized as, "Do you really understand what you are getting yourself into?"

58. Jesus replied, "Foxes have holes and birds of the air have nests, but the Son of Man has no place to lay his head."

The path of service and ministry for God often requires some personal sacrifices of us, as demonstrated by the one who went before us on this same path. *The Son of Man has no place to lay his head*. Jesus' fulfillment of his messianic ministry did not allow him to settle down with a house, a family, and a regular paying job. He was constantly on the move—living a modest lifestyle and depending on the generosity and hospitality of others.

WHAT DO YOU THINK?

Jesus had very little in the way of material goods—not even a place "to lay his head" (Luke 9:58). As a disciple of Jesus, what do you expect in the way of material security?

[Consider Matthew 6:31-33.]

HOMELESS

In 1970 Jim Vernon founded a ministry in Atlanta, Georgia, known as "Jesus Place Inner City Mission." His primary purpose was to serve the homeless people who lived under the bridges and viaducts of the city. Initially the ministry was conducted out of a storefront; it now operates from a donated church building.

For a period of time in between those two locations, the ministry of "Jesus Place" actually operated out of Jim Vernon's van. The ministry had lost the lease to the storefront, and the church building had not become available. During these uncertain days, Jim drove down an Atlanta street and picked up a homeless man. Seeing the words "Jesus Place" on the side of the van, the man asked, "Where is this Jesus Place?"

"You're sitting in it," said Vernon.

"Oh, I guess that makes sense," said the man, "because Jesus was homeless, too."

We sometimes forget that Jesus was accustomed to homelessness. He began his earthly life homeless in Bethlehem. As G. K. Chesterton wrote, Bethlehem was the place "where the Son of Man was homeless and where all men are at home."

Sometimes people identify Jesus with settled, secure middle-class homeowners. In fact, we should identify him with the rootless, homeless people of society and of the world. It is not surprising that the church has often been the only agency that shows any real compassion for homeless people. The church helps them because their need is so great—but also helps in the name of the one who became homeless that we may one day live in his home!   —R. C. S.

B. NO CONDITIONS (vv. 59, 60)

59, 60. He said to another man, "Follow me."

But the man replied, "Lord, first let me go and bury my father."

Jesus said to him, "Let the dead bury their own dead, but you go and proclaim the kingdom of God."

On the surface it appears that this man was simply asking for time to provide a proper burial for his *father*. It is not readily evident how a few days' delay for a funeral would interfere with Jesus' ministry plans.

Perhaps what the man actually desired was to remain at home and care for his father until after he had died and was buried, whenever that might be. After all, in that time and place burials were virtually immediate after a death. If the man's father were already dead, he should have been at home making the arrangements for the burial even then.

We can see, then, why Jesus rejected his proposal. Caring for one's parents can last several years, but Jesus had only a few months (approximately six) remaining in his ministry on earth. He needed this man's help right then, not several years down the road. The immediate urgency of his mission called for disciples who were ready to serve immediately.

With this understanding in mind, it seems most likely that Jesus was making a play on words when he spoke of *the dead* in verse 60. He was suggesting to this man that he leave his father in the care of family members who were "spiritually dead" and had no interest in serving Jesus to the extent that this man did. We can learn a lesson for our own situation from Jesus' wise counsel. It is still true today, for some of us, that we could decide to put aside our earthly interests and actively pursue Christian service; and someone would be available to take over what duties we left behind. (This is true whether the people we would leave behind were Christians or "spiritually dead.") Most parents will not suffer if left in the immediate care of our siblings who do not share our interest in leaving home in order to serve the Lord. Community programs and activities will still continue even if we are no longer involved. Rarely would a business shut down because one employee decided to quit and go to Bible college.

When we realize that most people will not answer the call to vocational service for Christ, then those of us who are considering such service should determine whether or not our earthly concerns should be allowed to outweigh the opportunities that God has placed before us.

C. NO REGRETS (vv. 61, 62)

61. Still another said, "I will follow you, Lord; but first let me go back and say good-by to my family."

This request to *say good-by* to one's *family* before setting out to *follow* Jesus sounds very similar to what Elisha asked of the prophet Elijah when he was summoned to leave home and become his disciple (1 Kings 19:19, 20). However, there is a difference. In the case of Elisha, when he went home to say good-by to his father and mother, he went with a heart that was ready and willing to leave everything and follow the prophet. His attitude is evidenced in his sacrificing two oxen to celebrate his prophetic call and then immediately leaving to follow after Elijah (1 Kings 19:21).

But the attitude of the man who approached Jesus was apparently not as eager as Elisha's. Judging by Jesus' response, this man seems to have had some misgivings about leaving his home and family, and thus may have had an attachment that would interfere with his ability to give full attention to the service that Jesus would require of him.

DAILY BIBLE READINGS

Monday, Jan. 8—On the Master's Mission (Luke 9:1-9)

Tuesday, Jan. 9—Hospitality Refused (Luke 9:51-56)

Wednesday, Jan. 10—The Christ and His Suffering (Luke 9:18-27)

Thursday, Jan. 11—The Would-be Followers of Jesus (Luke 9:57-62)

Friday, Jan. 12—Warnings and Encouragements (Luke 12:4-12)

Saturday, Jan. 13—Guilt by Association (Luke 22:54-62)

Sunday, Jan. 14—The Cost of Being a Disciple (Luke 14:25-33)

HOW TO SAY IT

Elijah. Ee-LYE-juh.

Elisha. Ee-LYE-shuh.

Malachi. MAL-uh-kye.

Perea. Peh-REE-uh.

Samaria. Suh-MARE-ee-uh.

WHAT DO YOU THINK?

When confronted with a choice, loyalty to Jesus as Lord may be at stake. Caring for an aging parent is a good thing, but according to our text the call of discipleship requires something different. What difficult choices have you had to make to maintain following Jesus as the first priority in your life?

[This can be a time of helpful affirmation of some who have struggled financially or socially but remained faithful to the Lord through their difficulties. Let their testimonies be an encouragement to all, but be careful that the discussion does not become a "Can-you-top-this?" exercise.]

62. Jesus replied, "No one who puts his hand to the plow and looks back is fit for service in the kingdom of God."

This imagery speaks clearly to each one of us, even if one has never used a horse or mule to drag a *plow* through a field. We know from other experiences what is the best strategy for making a straight line, whether we are putting down white chalk on a baseball field, dragging a stick on the ground to make a line in the dirt, or just trying to walk a straight path through an open field. If, as we walk, we have our head turned around watching the line behind us, the twist of the body will throw off our sense of balance, and we will digress from the straight line we intended. To stay on course, we must set our sights ahead on a distant object and let it serve as a bearing that keeps us on a straight path.

The man in this story apparently did not yet have his sights fully set on Jesus. He was looking *back* on something that still held his attention—in this case, family and home life. His divided interests threatened any long-term commitment that he might make to the Lord's work.

For this reason, Jesus warned him (and warns us) that he must first determine if in fact he is ready to make *service* for Jesus his first priority before he even starts down that pathway. To begin with only a half-hearted interest is to run the later risk of frustration and disappointment. Both the disciple and the work of the *kingdom* are thereby harmed.

NO TIME FOR GOOD-BYES

Does it ever seem to you that Jesus was the most unreasonable man who ever lived? What harm could there be in wanting to go home and say good-bye to one's family? However, keep in mind that saying good-bye can take a long time. Some couples will recall a time, before they were married, when it took half an hour just to say good night! Farewells can take time.

Remember also that Jesus could read the heart of the man who asked to return home; we can read only his words. Perhaps Jesus knew that the young man's parents would try to persuade him not to go after Jesus if he went back home to see them.

The encounters described in Luke 9:57-62 reveal an urgency about the work of the kingdom that must not be missed. It is easy for us to forget that urgency. Not a moment of time should be wasted. The return of Christ may be nearer than we think. Our opportunities may be fewer than we think. The one we hope to win to Christ may not have many years, or even days, ahead of him or her. (We may not have many years, or even days, ahead of us!)

The novelist Rebecca West once observed that we cannot imagine Jesus hurrying—yet there was always an urgency about his efforts. While we should never be frantic about our work, we should certainly be urgent.   —R. C. S.

II. FULL DEVOTION (LUKE 14:25-27)

A. SETTING PRIORITIES (vv. 25, 26)

25. Large crowds were traveling with Jesus, and turning to them he said:

Throughout his ministry Jesus attracted *large crowds* of people. Had he been interested in sheer numbers of followers, he could have achieved his goal very easily. However, the commitment found within these large crowds was always mixed. Many of them had no interest in Jesus beyond his ability to perform dramatic miracles. Now, with the cross just a few months away, Jesus wanted the multitudes to realize what being identified with him was going to cost.

26. "If anyone comes to me and does not hate his father and mother, his wife and children, his brothers and sisters—yes, even his own life—he cannot be my disciple.

Here is one of the most puzzling statements made by Jesus in the Gospels—we must *hate* those we love the most if we are to be disciples of Jesus. Given

WHAT DO YOU THINK?

Can you give an example of an instance when loyalty to Christ must take precedence over family members or even your own life?

[Consider the "sacrifices" of a Christian family as well as those by a believer with non-Christians in his or her family. Examples may be hypothetical or they may be actual, but encourage wide participation.]

Jesus' frequent emphasis on love, it is hard to imagine that he would ever encourage hatred, especially toward our own families.

Jesus' meaning is better understood when we take into consideration that he was using a figurative expression from the ancient world. When contrasting one's feelings toward two different persons or objects, to say that you *love* one and *hate* the other simply means that you have a preference for the former over the latter. In this usage, the word *hate* really means "to love less than" something else. Thus when the Mosaic law (Deuteronomy 21:15-17) refers to a man who loved two women enough to marry them both but had a preference for one over the other, it speaks of "the wife he loves" and "the wife he does not love" (or, the one that is "hated" in some versions). This love/hate language is even used of God's attitude toward Jacob and Esau (Malachi 1:2, 3).

Thus we can see that Jesus was emphasizing the superior love and devotion that he deserves over any other person or object. Jesus was not promoting feelings of hatred toward family and friends; he was setting forth the degree of commitment required of anyone who aspires to be his disciple. This interpretation is confirmed by Jesus' words on another occasion: "Anyone who loves his father or mother more than me is not worthy of me; anyone who loves his son or daughter more than me is not worthy of me" (Matthew 10:37).

The cross demanded all that Jesus had, and the Lord asks no less of his disciples. Use today's visual poster to remind your class of that fact.

The standard of priority commitment to Jesus Christ lends itself to many applications. For example, as Christians we are to be respectful to all in authority over us, including *father and mother*. But if ever told to do something that is clearly a sin, our first priority is to honor the will of God (Acts 5:29). Furthermore, serving Christ will not necessarily require that we forego marriage or a family, or that we move away from our parents and siblings. But a committed disciple is willing to do so if that would best serve the kingdom.

A disciple must likewise be willing to give up personal comfort and worldly gain for the sake of serving the Lord. And, if called upon to make the ultimate sacrifice, a true disciple is willing even to die for the cause of Christ.

B. CARRYING THE CROSS (v. 27)
27. And anyone who does not carry his cross and follow me cannot be my disciple.
At that time, Jesus' audience did not yet understand the theological implications that we see in the word *cross*. For them, a cross would bring to mind a slow, torturous death—the most horrible way to die that they could imagine. It was this level of suffering that Jesus said his followers must be willing to endure if they were to be true disciples. If we say that we want to follow Jesus, then we should not be surprised if our path leads us through opposition and hardship (1 John 3:13); for that is exactly the kind of path that our Master himself had to walk.

III. CAREFUL THOUGHT (LUKE 14:28-33)
A. FINISH WHAT YOU START (vv. 28-30)
28. Suppose one of you wants to build a tower. Will he not first sit down and estimate the cost to see if he has enough money to complete it?
In biblical times a landowner would often *build a tower* in order to keep an eye on his fields and, especially, his vineyards (Mark 12:1). A wise landowner would first take inventory of his time, laborers, and finances to determine whether or not he had *enough money to complete* the project in a reasonable amount of time.
29, 30. For if he lays the foundation and is not able to finish it, everyone who sees it will ridicule him, saying, 'This fellow began to build and was not able to finish.'
The gospel invitation to follow Christ carries with it a warning: a person must first "count the cost" before he responds. Thus our evangelistic efforts should not

WHAT DO YOU THINK?

No one can predict what suffering or sacrifice may be required in order to follow Christ for the rest of one's life. Without that information, how can anyone commit to discipleship?

only show people the benefits and joys of becoming a Christian, but also the expectations and difficulties that accompany this decision. This is not to say that discipleship is optional. The one who "counts the cost" and determines that he cannot pay it does so to his own peril. Rather, he must count the cost and determine to pay it!

Furthermore, as each of us considers what types of service and ministry we will pursue in behalf of our Lord and Savior, we should carefully assess our abilities and opportunities and our strengths and weaknesses, lest we take on a task of service that we are not able to complete. Again, this does not suggest that ministry is optional. Rather, it is a challenge to consider the cost of ministry and make preparations to pay it. And once we have made a commitment to serve, we must resolve not to allow any discouragement or distraction to pressure us to quit before we have given our best effort to accomplish what we said we would do.

B. DO WHATEVER IS NEEDED (vv. 31-33)

31. "Or suppose a king is about to go to war against another king. Will he not first sit down and consider whether he is able with ten thousand men to oppose the one coming against him with twenty thousand?

Whether the party involved be a nation or an individual, we do not regard lightly any offense or threat by our enemies. The impulse to fight and to defend our honor and our lives comes from a strong inner passion. These emotions can serve to sustain us through the duration of a conflict, but they can also cloud our judgment if we impulsively take on a battle for which we are not prepared. A wise leader holds his emotions in check while he assesses the prospects for victory.

32. "If he is not able, he will send a delegation while the other is still a long way off and will ask for terms of peace.

A king who foresees unacceptable losses or certain defeat in battle would be wise to send a delegation to attempt to negotiate a peaceful solution to the conflict. Though this will likely require giving away something to the enemy, that is preferable to a humiliating defeat.

The choice to follow Jesus should be based not on the emotions of the moment, but on careful reflection regarding the demands of discipleship. Only those who are prepared to do "whatever it takes" to serve Christ should sign on for duty.

33. "In the same way, any of you who does not give up everything he has cannot be my disciple."

What an excellent summary of all that Jesus had taught regarding discipleship! Commitment to Christ requires nothing less than everything we can give him. It is truly "all or nothing."

CONCLUSION

Are you familiar with the expression, "Don't bite off more than you can chew"? We can imagine a person stuffing his mouth with so much food that he cannot easily chew or swallow. As a result, it is impossible for him to gain any enjoyment or satisfaction from what he is eating. And, of course, we can understand the point that it is foolish to say "yes" to more responsibilities than we can realistically manage. We who are disciples of Jesus need to weigh carefully the many opportunities for service and to choose the one that best matches our gifts and abilities. Jesus deserves only our best and will settle for nothing less.

"Counting the cost" is also imperative for those who are not yet disciples. And as they weigh that choice, they must consider not only what it costs to follow, but what it means to reject Christ's call. Yes, it costs to follow Jesus—some even lose their lives in his service. But the cost of not following, of remaining lost for eternity, is far greater!

Discovery Learning

This page contains an alternate lesson plan emphasizing learning activities. Classes desiring such student involvement will find these suggestions helpful. The next page is a reproducible activity page to further enhance discovery learning.

LEARNING GOALS

After this lesson the students will be able to:

1. Summarize Jesus' teaching about the demands of discipleship according to today's text.

2. Tell why encouraging people to "count the cost" should be an integral part of evangelism.

3. Pinpoint an excuse that they have been using to avoid a deeper commitment to Christ, and express a commitment to strengthen their discipleship.

INTO THE LESSON

Every day people use excuses to explain the lack of follow-through on projects, commitments, and relationships. Hang a large sheet of paper on the classroom wall or use an overhead projector transparency. Write the word *EXCUSES* vertically. Students are to think of words that they might use as excuses for lack of following through on something. Words could include: Education, eXtra work, Cost, not Understanding, Schedule, Entertainment, and lack of Skills.

Say, "Often we are excited about new opportunities that look too good to be true. What scheme has been attractive to you? Perhaps you wanted a new car, an addition to your house, or a college education. Each of those comes with hidden price tags." Distribute copies of the reproducible activity "Hidden Price Tags" from the next page. Ask the students to work on these individually. After a few minutes compile a list of some of the "hidden costs" by asking volunteers to report what they wrote. (*Examples may include less money for other activities, loss of free time, dust and mess around the house, etc.*)

Perhaps you have had class members who remarked, "I thought becoming like Jesus and following him would be simple. It seems that I have struggled from day one!" Discuss why that expectation is not warranted.

Then say, "Today we are going to explore the challenges put forth by Jesus concerning the cost of following him. We will be asked to evaluate our willingness to pay the cost of discipleship."

INTO THE WORD

Ask a volunteer to read Luke 9:57-62 and another to read Luke 14:25-33. Then provide copies of the following questions and allow students several minutes to answer them. Use these as a guide to discussion in studying the passage. (You will want to be familiar with the commentary material for difficult questions that may arise during the study.)

1. What is the most important thought in this passage?

2. What is the key verse in this passage?

3. Why did Jesus need to teach this lesson?

4. What is the most practical teaching in this passage for you?

5. If you had been in the crowd before Jesus, what would you have asked him?

After discussing students' findings ask, "What do each of these teachings tell us about giving our lives to Jesus?" Students should see that there is a cost to following Jesus, a cost that is too seldom emphasized.

INTO LIFE

Prepare a chart with the following headings: "Benefits" and "Costs." Say, "Suppose that you are asked to develop a brochure for our evangelism program here at church to help people understand the cost of following Jesus. Using this chart, what would you include?" Answers should include promises Jesus made concerning the new life, as well as the things that would need to be given up as the Christian becomes more like Jesus.

Discuss how such a tool would be helpful for a person making a decision for Christ. Would it help a person not to be too hasty, but also give a realistic picture of the cost of discipleship?

Most of us began following Jesus with the best of intentions. Just as the people in the text today, we would follow Jesus anywhere. However, we too can make excuses. Prepare three posters with the following headings: "Comfort," "Social Concerns," and "Family Concerns."

Have your students gather in three groups. Ask each group to write on one of the posters excuses that the group members have heard people use to keep from developing stronger discipleship. Some might include: "I really don't have time for devotions. I need to get a lot of sleep." "You don't understand; I am involved in so many community events." "My family wouldn't understand my being at Bible study on a weeknight."

Distribute copies of the second reproducible activity from the next page ("What Causes Your Heart to Be Divided?"). Allow a few minutes for the learners to work on these privately. Then form a circle and close by having each group member pray for greater resolve on behalf of the member on his or her right.

Hidden Price Tags

In many of today's decisions there is often a hidden price tag. This may include money, time, comfort, or options. On the tags below, write some potential hidden prices.

Clothing   House

Car   College

What Causes Your Heart to Be Divided?

Read Luke 9:57-62 and Luke 14:25-33. In these passages, Jesus asks us to count the cost to wholeheartedly follow him. On the broken heart below, write some of the things that keep you from following wholeheartedly. After you have written, write the name of Jesus over the heart for healing and recommitment.

LOST AND FOUND

LESSON 8

WHY TEACH THIS LESSON?

"Ziggy," the quintessential comic-strip loser, was walking by a poorly dressed man who was begging in the street. "There, but by the grace of God, go I," Ziggy thought. Unknown to him, the beggar looked at Ziggy and thought the same thing!

It seems we can all pick out someone who is "worse" than we are. We can sometimes feel pretty smug about it. Today's lesson is designed to get each of your learners to identify with a loser—not a comic-strip loser like Ziggy, but a real loser, a sinner: himself without Christ! Each of us can look at our lives outside of Christ and see a hopeless condition. And there, but by the grace of God, go I!

INTRODUCTION

A. WHAT A WASTE!

"What a waste!" we often say when we hear about an athlete suspended for drug use, a good student who drops out of school, or a teen who runs away from home and gets caught up in the dangers of life on the streets. And how easy it is for us to write off such people, assuming that they will never amount to anything.

But the good news of Jesus Christ is that by God's grace there is always room for repentance, for forgiveness of the past, and for a new beginning. Lost lives—even those believed to be "too far gone"—can be reclaimed, if they can be led to a humble repentance before God. Jesus' classic story of the prodigal son serves to remind us of this important biblical truth.

B. LESSON BACKGROUND

Today's text follows where last week's study left off (14:25-33). Luke 15 is well-known for its three parables about lost items—a lost sheep, a lost coin, and a lost son. However, the emphasis in these parables is not only on the word *lost*, but also on the *joy* that results from finding what was lost. And just as Heaven rejoices each time a person comes to know Jesus Christ as Lord and Savior (Luke 15:7, 10), so likewise we should be filled with excitement and appreciation whenever a lost person "comes home" to the Father.

I. SINFUL ATTITUDES (LUKE 15:1, 2, 11-13)

A. BITTER SPIRIT (vv. 1, 2)

1. Now the tax collectors and "sinners" were all gathering around to hear him.

Throughout his ministry Jesus reached out to all people, particularly those commonly rejected as society's outcasts. Perhaps the most notable example of this was the *tax collectors*. This group was viewed with special scorn, for reasons that went beyond the fact that people naturally resist paying taxes. Because the tax collectors acted as agents of the Roman Empire, they were judged as "traitors," working in league with those considered oppressors of Israel. In addition, the power given to tax collectors easily lent itself to abuse, serving to increase the hatred of the general populace toward all tax collectors.

In addition to the tax collectors, other groups were looked down upon by many of the Jews. These disfranchised people included "the poor, the crippled,

DEVOTIONAL READING:
EPHESIANS 1:15—2:5
BACKGROUND SCRIPTURE:
LUKE 15
PRINTED TEXT:
LUKE 15:1, 2, 11-24

LESSON AIMS

After participating in this lesson, the students will be able to:

1. Tell how the prodigal son in Jesus' parable left his father's home and was later reconciled to his father.

2. Tell how this parable pictures our heavenly Father's compassion for repentant sinners.

3. Acknowledge that they are represented by the prodigal son, and give thanks for the Father's stubborn love for them.

Jan
21

KEY VERSE

This son of mine was dead and is alive again; he was lost and is found. —Luke 15:24

WHAT DO YOU THINK?

If unbelievers or lapsed believers feel comfortable meeting with our church, they probably do so because of some intentional effort that we put forth to make them feel welcome. Are we attracting a large number of "sinners" who want to inquire about Christian teaching? Why or why not? How can our church become more appealing to "sinners"?

WHAT DO YOU THINK?

In what situations do you associate with unbelievers? How may Christians associate with unbelievers and not compromise their witness?

the blind and the lame" (Luke 14:21). Also included were those with disreputable lifestyles, such as prostitutes, thieves, and swindlers. All such people were commonly lumped together in the category of *sinners*.

While neither tax collectors nor other sinners were welcome in respectable groups of that day, they were always treated in a gracious manner by Jesus. Note that these people *were all gathering around* Jesus *to hear him*. Earlier Jesus had concluded his teaching on discipleship with the words, "He who has ears to hear, let him hear" (Luke 14:35). While the religious leaders dismissed Jesus' teaching, the tax collectors and sinners gladly listened to and carefully considered his message.

2. But the Pharisees and the teachers of the law muttered, "This man welcomes sinners and eats with them."

Jesus often faced complaints and criticisms from *the Pharisees and the teachers of the law* (or scribes), two of the ruling classes within the Jewish community. They considered it a violation of Mosaic law to associate with people who did not live up to their high moral standards. They possessed no evangelistic vision of reaching out to the lost or of joyfully receiving *sinners* who chose to draw near to God. The gracious manner of Jesus stood in sharp contrast to their bitter spirit, which was later illustrated by the attitude of the prodigal's older brother (vv. 25-32).

EATING WITH SINNERS

Lawrence of Arabia was one of the most adventurous personalities of World War I. During his travels through the Middle East, he found hospitality in the home of a desert sheik who was thought to be on the side of the enemy. After they had eaten together, the sheik told Lawrence that he would no longer be in any danger. According to the social customs of the Middle East, once two men had eaten together there was a bond between them. This custom is still observed. An Arab bus driver for a Holy Land tour bought bread and gave some to every tourist. "Now we are friends," he told them, "because we have eaten together."

Such a perspective helps us understand the Pharisees and scribes' evaluation of Jesus: "This man welcomes sinners and eats with them." Jesus is a friend of sinners! How appalling!

Of course, we realize that if Jesus had not eaten with sinners, he would always have eaten alone. There was no one else with whom he *could* eat! True, he was eating with sinners, but his critics were sinners, too—as are we all. In fact, Jesus came to our world not only to eat with sinners, but to *die for* them. He is a friend of sinners! How amazing!   —R. C. S.

B. SELFISH LIFESTYLE (vv. 11-13)

11. Jesus continued: "There was a man who had two sons.

Jesus did not give names to the characters in this parable, nor did he indicate whether or not it was taken from a real life situation. Nevertheless, the circumstances Jesus described would have seemed quite realistic to his audience.

12. "The younger one said to his father, 'Father, give me my share of the estate.' So he divided his property between them.

The law of Moses established some basic guidelines regarding a family *estate* (Deuteronomy 21:15-17). The oldest son was to receive a majority *share* of money and *property*, at least two times as much as the other brothers and sisters received. In the situation described by Jesus, the process of dividing the goods was fairly simple: two-thirds would go to the older son and one-third to the *younger*.

Though as a general rule inheritances were not distributed until after the death of a father, they could be disbursed at any time the father wished. For instance, a man growing old and feeble might choose to go ahead and invest his oldest son in his position as chief heir and then live under his care. Likewise, a father could give permission to his younger children to go ahead and try to establish themselves in the world with their smaller portions.

13. *"Not long after that, the younger son got together all he had, set off for a distant country and there squandered his wealth in wild living.*

The description of the *younger son* gathering up all his money and taking off to *a distant country* has a modern ring to it. It sounds like the son or daughter who can hardly wait to get as far away from parental oversight as possible. Didn't this father realize what his son would do with the money he received? Perhaps he did, but this is not indicated in the parable. Every parent, however, has wrestled with the decision to give a child freedom and responsibility when he or she is not certain how the child will handle it.

Sadly (and with a folly not uncommon when young people first step out on their own) the younger son *squandered his wealth in wild living*. We can imagine what this involved—perhaps an abundance of eating, drinking, and entertaining friends and female companions—the lure of "wine, women, and song." Note the older brother's complaint to his father that "this son of yours" had "squandered your property with prostitutes" (v. 30).

It is this young man's selfish and foolish spending spree that has earned him the title "the prodigal (wasteful) son." And in this behavior his true character was revealed. He exhibited no thought of acting with prudence and discretion, and showed no concern for honoring his father and his family. He was simply focused on himself and his desire to enjoy all the worldly pleasures that money could buy.

II. HUMBLE REPENTANCE (LUKE 15:14-19)

A. HITTING BOTTOM (vv. 14-16)

14. *"After he had spent everything, there was a severe famine in that whole country, and he began to be in need.*

Eventually an extravagant and wasteful lifestyle takes its toll on a young man's financial resources. Running out of money is a problem under any circumstances, but it is even more serious when *a severe famine* has struck the *whole country*.

15. *"So he went and hired himself out to a citizen of that country, who sent him to his fields to feed pigs.*

The younger son *hired himself out to a citizen,* meaning that he agreed to work for a man who offered him employment. His employer was a resident of the unnamed *country* to which the young man had traveled. Judging from the brief references to this land and the presence of *pigs*, it seems that the young man was no longer among his fellow Jews but was in Gentile territory. Working for a Gentile master would likely disturb the conscience of many a Jew, since the law of Moses discouraged any intimate association with Gentiles (Acts 10:28). However, during a famine one must seek wages wherever he can find someone willing to pay them.

How this young man's pride must have taken a beating throughout this disheartening turn of events! Not only did he have to deal with the loss of all his money (and thus the loss of all the companions whom his money had attracted), but now he was forced to accept the terms of a Gentile master. And that was not the end of the indignities he experienced. For in his fall from what he had once perceived as the good life, there would be no "modest setbacks," as we like to say. His life came crashing down to "rock bottom." He was hired to *feed pigs*.

Pigs were among the animals that, according to the law of Moses, were to be considered "unclean" by the Jews (Leviticus 11:7; Deuteronomy 14:8). These ritualistic distinctions of "clean" and "unclean" formed much of the basis of the ethnic identity of the Jewish people. Yet in his abject desperation, with starvation looming before him, the young man forced himself to violate his conscience and

HOW TO SAY IT

Bathsheba. Bath-SHE-buh.
Pharisees. FAIR-ih-seez.

WHAT DO YOU THINK?

In circumstances of severe suffering, the prodigal repented of his ways. What are some of the circumstances that are likely to be turning points for people today?

[If you have students who came to the Lord as adults, perhaps they can relate what situations became turning points for them.]

WHAT DO YOU THINK?

The prodigal found courage to return home because his father had a reputation as kind and generous. How can we convince spiritual prodigals that the heavenly Father is kind and generous?

his heritage, thus destroying whatever self-respect and dignity he may have had left. And even this was not the full extent of his downfall.

16. "He longed to fill his stomach with the pods that the pigs were eating, but no one gave him anything.

In his masterful telling of this story, Jesus brought his Jewish audience to a point where their hearts would have ached for this young man. For no matter how foolish he had been, no Jew deserved this fate: *he longed to fill his stomach with the pods that the pigs were eating.* Apparently he was so hungry that he longed to eat the food that he was putting out for the pigs. These *pods* were likely what are called carob pods. This crop was specifically grown for feeding livestock, but it was sometimes eaten by the poor during times of severe hardship. Such was the plight of the prodigal. For a Jewish man to be envious of pigs indicates what little self-respect remained in him.

To emphasize further the young man's sorry condition, Jesus then added, *but no one gave him anything.* No doubt the prodigal could not help but notice that there was no help forthcoming from the "friends" who had helped him spend his money. He was truly alone and helpless—quite a contrast from the cocky young man who had so rudely demanded his father's inheritance.

As completely hopeless as this situation might have seemed, such was not the case. God always holds before us a hope for recovery and renewal, even in our darkest moments. However, we cannot see it, nor can we pursue it, until first our pride has been broken and our spirit has been humbled. For it is in our times of failure that we finally see our foolish and sinful choices for what they truly are. It is in our deepest despair that we realize the need to approach our Father with the humility to admit that we were wrong and to seek his grace and mercy.

B. CONFESSING SIN (vv. 17-19)

17. "When he came to his senses, he said, 'How many of my father's hired men have food to spare, and here I am starving to death!

Deep despair can either break a man down to the point of giving up on life, or it can challenge him to fight back and consider all his options, no matter how unpromising they might be. The latter was the case with our young man, as in the field with the pigs *he came to his senses.* This phrase meant much more than regaining a level of mental composure that would enable him to assess his situation and form a plan of action. Primarily it indicated the young man's repentance, which is a common theme linking all three of the parables in this chapter of Luke (15:7, 10). The young man was now beginning to see the reason for his troubles and was on the verge of accepting responsibility for his own foolish mistakes.

During this process, the young man began to reflect on the status of the *hired men* in his *father's* household. They received a fair wage for their labor, along with sufficient *food* to eat. Their condition, compared with his own sorry existence, led the young man to devise a plan where moments before all had seemed hopeless.

18. "'I will set out and go back to my father and say to him: Father, I have sinned against heaven and against you.

The words of repentance are short and simple, yet so difficult to say: *I have sinned.* None of us likes to admit that we were wrong. But genuine repentance requires that we set aside any defense of our actions and honestly admit our sin.

This young man's sin was both *against heaven* and *against* his *father.* Certainly his conduct had shown disrespect to his father. But first and foremost, he had sinned against God. All of our wrongful actions against others are ultimately sins against God. After all, our misdeeds are a violation of the instructions God has clearly revealed to us in his Word; thus they are a resistance to the will of God over our lives. For example, David's adultery with Bathsheba was certainly a departure from the fidelity he owed to his family, and it was a despicable treatment of one of his most loyal officers and that man's wife. And yet, behind all of this was a blatant sin against God himself. As David put it, "Against you, you only, have I sinned and done what is evil in your sight" (Psalm 51:4).

19. "'I am no longer worthy to be called your son; make me like one of your hired men.'

I am no longer worthy to be called your son, the young man intended to say to his father. While he was still physically and legally the man's son, he did not feel that he deserved to be treated as a son after what he had done. Living as one of the *hired men* under his own father's roof would be a fitting punishment, or so he thought. His public humiliation would serve to vindicate his father, to declare that he had been right all along.

The spirit of humility and repentance was now running so deep within the soul of the young man that he was willing to do anything he must in order to make things right again with his father and thereby save himself from complete ruin. Note how his attitude had changed from "give me" (v. 12) to *make me.*

III. GRACIOUS WELCOME (LUKE 15:20-24)

A. LOVING FATHER (vv. 20, 21)

20. "So he got up and went to his father.

"But while he was still a long way off, his father saw him and was filled with compassion for him; he ran to his son, threw his arms around him and kissed him.

The *father saw* his returning son *while he was still a long way off.* Perhaps he just happened to look out on the horizon at the time his son was approaching, or possibly he had been watching and hoping for his son's safe return. The latter is certainly appropriate when this story is applied to our Father in Heaven.

As for the traditional protocol of that era, the father tossed aside all formalities. He *ran* to greet his son, *threw his arms around him and kissed him.* The reason for this dramatic reception: the father's heart *was filled with compassion* for his errant son. Perhaps, for the sake of emphasis, it would be better not to title this story "the Prodigal Son," but to call it instead "the Gracious Father."

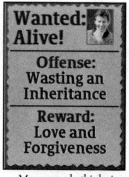

Wanted: Alive!

Offense:
Wasting an Inheritance

Reward:
Love and Forgiveness

Many people think sin makes us "unwanted" by God. The theme of today's text, illustrated by the lesson visual, is that even though we sin, God **wants** *us!*

HOLY LOVE

One evening Richard Wurmbrand, who ministered for many years in lands under the control of Communism, was talking with a man from Romania. The man did not know that Wurmbrand, a Christian, was also a former Jew. The man boasted of killing Jews during the Holocaust. Then Wurmbrand told him that he himself was a Jew and so was his wife. He said that his wife was sleeping in the next room. He then proposed an experiment. The two men would go in and tell Wurmbrand's wife the man's story and see what she would do.

So the men did this. Wurmbrand told his wife, "This man is the murderer of your sisters, your brother, and your parents. What do you have to say to him?" In response Wurmbrand's wife put her arms around that man's neck. Both wept. It was a scene of holy love. Wurmbrand then said to the man, "If my wife, who is only human, can do this—if she can love you like this, knowing what you have done, and can forgive you—then how much more will God, who is love!"

As instructive as it is for us to see ourselves in the prodigal son, it is also important that we see God in the forgiving father. The parable shows us a God who is not distant and far removed from us—even when we have treated him with the utmost contempt. He is ever and always the compassionate Father, longing for us to come home.
                                                  —R. C. S.

21. *"The son said to him, 'Father, I have sinned against heaven and against you. I am no longer worthy to be called your son.'*

The son immediately began the repentance speech that he had rehearsed in the field with the pigs. But before he could complete it, the father interrupted his words and chose to disregard any thought of humiliating his son. He had more noble plans in mind.

B. JOYOUS RECEPTION (vv. 22-24)

22. *"But the father said to his servants, 'Quick! Bring the best robe and put it on him. Put a ring on his finger and sandals on his feet.*

The *father* called for his *best robe* and bestowed on his son a treatment reserved for honored guests. He offered full admission back into his home by giving his son *a ring,* perhaps a signet ring that symbolized authority (cf. Genesis 41:42). He rejected the idea of his son's showing penance as a household servant. Instead, he had him fitted with leather *sandals*—a luxury not often enjoyed by mere *servants.* The reception of the son back into the home he had abandoned was complete and uninhibited, and it was founded entirely on the grace of the father.

23. *"'Bring the fattened calf and kill it. Let's have a feast and celebrate.*

Fresh meat was not a regular part of meals in that day and culture. Grains and fruit were the norm. A *fattened calf* was used for special occasions, and today was such. The joy of the father at receiving back his lost son was similar to that portrayed in the other two parables in this chapter—when a shepherd found his lost sheep (Luke 15:5, 6) and a woman found her lost coin (v. 9).

As it is in Heaven (Luke 15:7, 10), so should it be on earth among God's people. All of us should rejoice at seeing lost souls rescued and saved. The callous attitude of the Pharisees and scribes in this regard had initiated this series of parables (v. 2). May it not be our attitude as well. We should practice an evangelism that shares the gospel with all creation (Mark 16:15), offer a Christian hospitality that gladly welcomes all repentant sinners into our fellowship (James 2:1-9), and envision an assembly both on earth and in Heaven that encompasses "every nation, tribe, people and language" (Revelation 7:9).

24. *"'For this son of mine was dead and is alive again; he was lost and is found.' So they began to celebrate."*

When the son chose to abandon his home, his family relationship was *dead.* But more to the point for us, he had been spiritually dead because of the sinful lifestyle he pursued. The message of Jesus' parable is that an enthusiastic "welcome home" is always available for each one of us through the grace and mercy of our loving heavenly Father.

CONCLUSION

"Amazing grace! how sweet the sound, That saved a wretch like me! I once was lost, but now am found, Was blind, but now I see." Perhaps no song is more cherished among Christians than this old hymn. Certainly no message is any dearer to our hearts than the story of our Father's amazing grace for sinners such as ourselves. The thought should fill us with an "inexpressible and glorious joy" (1 Peter 1:8).

Moreover, what God has done for us should prompt us to show kindness and compassion to others, even as we have received it ourselves. Once we realize what it means to "come home" to the Father, we are to search for those still wandering, who need to know that they can stop running. The Father longs for them to come home.

WHAT DO YOU THINK?

In Jesus' story the father threw a huge party at the return of his son who had been "lost." How can Christians add more celebration when modern prodigals turn to God?

PRAYER

Father, we thank you for the grace you have shown to us in spite of our failings before you, and we thank you for your Son Jesus, in whose name we pray. Amen.

THOUGHT TO REMEMBER

"I tell you, there is rejoicing in the presence of the angels of God over one sinner who repents" (Luke 15:10).

Discovery Learning

This page contains an alternate lesson plan emphasizing learning activities. Classes
desiring such student involvement will find these suggestions helpful. The next page
is a reproducible activity page to further enhance discovery learning.

LEARNING GOALS

After this lesson the students will be able to:

1. Tell how the prodigal son in Jesus' parable left his father's home and was later reconciled to his father.

2. Tell how this parable pictures our heavenly Father's compassion for repentant sinners.

3. Acknowledge that they are represented by the prodigal son, and give thanks for the Father's stubborn love for them.

INTO THE LESSON

Begin the lesson by putting your students into groups of three. Prepare the following questions on paper for each student. Ask the students to choose to answer the question with which they are most comfortable.

1. If you could wave a magic wand and make your life perfect, how would it be different from the way it is now?

2. If you could rewind the "tape" of your life and live a year over again, which one would it be? Why?

3. What was your most embarrassing moment?

Allow ten minutes for people to think about their answers and respond. This introduction will prepare them for identifying with the prodigal in today's lesson.

Say, "Each of us has issues in which he has not lived up to God's standard. Sometimes we have been willful about it, other times ignorant. In today's lesson we shall see just how far God's grace goes in reaching us when we need him."

INTO THE WORD

Select someone early in the week to review the lesson commentary and other materials concerning Luke 15:1, 2 and prepare a five-minute report on the crowd to which Jesus spoke. Contrast the ones who gathered around Jesus with the ones who murmured against him.

Create three groups of up to six students each, and give them the following assignments. (If you have more than eighteen students, create more groups and repeat assignments.)

Group 1. Use a concordance to find Old Testament verses with references to God as "Father"—especially from Psalms and Isaiah. List as many as you can, and be prepared to report on these verses to the class.

Group 2. Read Luke 15:11-24. Prepare a short drama on the events told here. You will present this drama to the class.

Group 3. Read Luke 15:11-24. Prepare a short drama putting the events in terms of a "sinner" and God rather than a son and a father. Decide what characters need to be present; then write the dialog. You will present this drama during the session.

After fifteen minutes call the groups together. Have Group 2 present its drama. If any questions arise from the presentation, refer to the commentary for answers.

Ask Group 1 to present the results of its Scripture search. Ask the class, "In this parable, who is the father?" Then say, "By our Scripture search, it is reasonable to assume that the Pharisees and the teachers of the law understood Jesus' point. God is gracious toward those who stray from his way."

OPTION

If you prefer to have all your students work on the same activity, distribute copies of the reproducible activity "The Father's Traits" from the next page. (*Suggested traits for each section are as follows: vv. 11-15: willing to let his son make mistakes; vv. 16-19: able to wait for change in his son; vv. 20-22: full of grace and forgiveness; vv. 23, 24: quick to celebrate life.*)

INTO LIFE

Ask Group 3 to present its drama; then ask, "How do you think most people would have felt when they first saw the father again? How do you think most people would have reacted had they *been* the father? What does this passage tell us about repentance?" (See the commentary section, "Humble Repentance," pages 185-187.) "What does this passage tell us about God's grace?" (See "Gracious Welcome," pages 187, 188.)

As a result of this lesson, each student should identify with the prodigal. Distribute copies of the reproducible activity "He Forgives My Past" from the next page. Ask each student to complete the exercise privately. You might want to suggest some categories for the students to consider, such as family, finances, friends, faithfulness, business, emotions, self-discipline, sexual issues, etc. Remind believers of the promise of forgiveness in 1 John 1:9. If you have non-Christians in the class, invite any who wish to do so to remain after class to talk about the forgiveness available through Jesus' blood.

Close the class with a prayer of confession and of thanksgiving for God's forgiveness.

The Father's Traits

Read Luke 14:11-24, and focus on the father. What traits in the father can you discern from each of the following sections of the text?

vv. 11-15

vv. 16-19

vv. 20-22

vv. 23, 24

These traits are also the traits of our Heavenly Father. For which of the Father's traits are you most thankful? Why?

He Forgives My Past

On the "rear-view mirror" below, draw or list some of the things that you have left behind you, or should have left behind you, that God has forgiven.

"If we confess our sins, he is faithful and just and will forgive us our sins and purify us from all unrighteousness" (1 John 1:9).

THREAT OF RICHES

LESSON 9

WHY TEACH THIS LESSON?

One of the subtle dangers of the modern television drama or action film is the glorification of bad behavior. In many of these stories the hero is something of a "loose cannon"—breaking the rules, disobeying his supervisors, and ignoring the niceties of protocol. But it's all for a good cause, we're led to believe, so we cheer for the rogue hero in spite of his flaws.

Even more troubling, for many believers, is the anti-hero in today's lesson text, who is a dishonest manager. When he is exposed as incompetent—if not actually a crook—the manager secures his future by cheating his employer to ingratiate himself with the employer's debtors. How can such a man be worthy of imitation?

This lesson provides an important reminder and caution. A parable generally has one main point. Other details are for the sake of the story, not for application. We can learn the lesson of priorities without making a hero of a villain.

INTRODUCTION

A. NO REGRETS?

One of Frank Sinatra's most popular songs was entitled "My Way." In it he mentioned that he'd had a few regrets, but not enough of them to mention. Part of his statement is true. We do not care to mention our regrets about the past, though not because they are "too few." The truth is that all of us have made many, many mistakes of which we do not wish to be reminded. And the more we grow spiritually, the more sensitive we become regarding the sinful and foolish things we have done—and still do.

What a blessing it is that God allows "second chances"—not that we can undo the past, but we can put it behind us and move ahead. Through Christ we can be forgiven of the sins of yesterday and resolve to be better and to do better by the power of his Spirit in us. Although we cannot look back and honestly say "no regrets," we must not allow ourselves to be burdened with guilt about the past; for we are strengthened and encouraged by the abundant grace of God.

B. LESSON BACKGROUND

Jesus' parables, taken as a whole, reveal his extensive knowledge of the variety of life experiences within his age and culture. He could tell stories about children playing in the marketplace and about a housewife baking bread or searching a room for a missing coin. He could paint verbal pictures of a fisherman with his net, a farmer sowing seed or pruning his vineyards, and a shepherd seeking a lost lamb. He could draw imagery from a king preparing for battle or planning a royal wedding feast. And, as will be seen in today's text, Jesus could draw an important spiritual lesson from an individual's management (or more accurately, mismanagement) of an estate. His teaching ministry demonstrates that much of life readily lends itself to spiritual parables and analogies well suited for our edification.

The text for today's lesson follows the passage from which last week's study was drawn. Jesus was still in Perea, east of the Jordan River from Samaria and Judea. Approximately three to four months remained until his crucifixion.

DEVOTIONAL READING:
LUKE 12:13-21
BACKGROUND SCRIPTURE:
LUKE 16
PRINTED TEXT:
LUKE 16:1-13

LESSON AIMS

After this lesson each student will be able to:

1. Recount Jesus' parable of the dishonest manager.

2. Tell how a story about a person's unethical behavior can serve as an example to Christians.

3. Pinpoint an area where he or she has been trying to "serve two masters," and suggest ways to put God first.

Jan
28

KEY VERSE

You cannot serve both God and Money. —Luke 16:13

LESSON 9 NOTES

I. WASTED OPPORTUNITIES (LUKE 16:1-3)
A. FALLING SHORT (vv. 1, 2)

1. Jesus told his disciples: "There was a rich man whose manager was accused of wasting his possessions.

The responsibilities of the *manager* of a wealthy man's estate varied. For instance, he could serve as a household manager, supervising the various servants (cf. Matthew 24:45) and overseeing the household budget and all expenditures. Or, as in the case of the individual in this parable, he could be the equivalent of our modern business manager. With the estate of a landowner, that role would involve selling the goods produced from the land—seeking the best price and maximum profit for the owner. Such a manager would also need to purchase whatever supplies were needed for further production.

A household manager was typically a slave trained in management. A business manager could likewise be a slave, but it was not uncommon for this to be a hired position. The latter appears to be the case with the manager in our parable, who was facing accusations of mismanagement. Had he been a slave, he could have anticipated a severe beating, if not death. But the punishment that this man faced was the loss of his job (v. 2)—the appropriate penalty for a hired employee.

The accusation was that of *wasting* the owner's *possessions*. Perhaps he had made some careless transactions or failed to take advantage of some profitable opportunities. It may be that his weakness was in record keeping, and that inventory and receipts were not being fully accounted.

Whatever the problems, the manager was not accused of dishonesty or embezzlement. The same Greek word used for the prodigal son when he "squandered" his inheritance (Luke 15:13) is applied to this man as well. Of course, it is little consolation to be spared a charge of criminal misconduct in favor of being branded incompetent. For a business manager, either charge could ruin a career.

2. "So he called him in and asked him, 'What is this I hear about you? Give an account of your management, because you cannot be manager any longer.'

In the process of having his employee *give an account of* his *management*, the owner would usually want to conduct what we call an "audit" of the ledger books. This accounting would serve to confirm whether or not the accusations of poor management were true. However, apparently enough was already known or assumed by the owner that the fate of the *manager* was already determined: he was to be dismissed from his employment.

Truly this story is a parable with applications to many of us as we reflect on the personal stewardship of our lives. It is with deep regret that we look back and acknowledge our careless mistakes, our halfhearted efforts, and our wasted opportunities. And there is one more thing we share in common with this manager—the mistakes of the past often catch up with us, threatening our present security and our future prospects. How much better we would be now if only we had made better choices in our past!

B. FILLED WITH DESPAIR (v. 3)

3. "The manager said to himself, 'What shall I do now? My master is taking away my job. I'm not strong enough to dig, and I'm ashamed to beg—

Were the charges of mismanagement actually true? Apparently so. An audit of the ledgers could have exonerated an innocent man, but the manager had already accepted the inevitable. His initial reaction to the prospect of dismissal from his *job* was a deep sense of despair.

I'm not strong enough to dig, the manager lamented. He seems afraid to face a type of employment for which he may have had no training or experience. Perhaps

WHAT DO YOU THINK?

The manager was called to "give an account" of his management. How would you fare if called to "give an account" of your management of the resources God has made available? How does knowing that you will someday be asked for such an accounting affect the decisions and choices that you make each day?

[Consider the management of money, time, talent, potential for influence, and any other kind of resources.]

he wondered whether or not he possessed the stamina to keep up with a more physically demanding job. For many a modern "desk jockey," the prospects of an abrupt switch to manual labor could produce similar feelings of apprehension. Furthermore, this manager would probably need to adjust to the loss of a level of income to which he had grown accustomed.

If the manager was not willing to do any of the lesser jobs that were available, his only other option might be *to beg*. That, however, was unacceptable, for he was *ashamed* to stoop to such tactics. Indeed, begging for a handout by its very nature assaults one's self-esteem and dignity. This manager would have none of that. And yet, with either of the options before him, pride would take a beating. When someone in a professional career deliberately chooses to give up the "rat race" for a simpler lifestyle, we admire the person. But when someone is fired for incompetence and is forced to abandon his career and aspirations and settle for something less, we pity him.

Consider the depth of despair being experienced by the manager in this parable. Some of us have "been there," and we have felt our world come crashing in on us; we feared that life would never be the same again. Even if we have not felt such despair personally, we have seen it in others and have witnessed its demoralizing and debilitating effects. The situation Jesus portrayed is unfortunately all too real in our time.

II. SWIFT RECOVERY (LUKE 16:4-8)
A. THE MANAGER'S PLAN (vv. 4-7)
4. "'I know what I'll do so that, when I lose my job here, people will welcome me into their houses.'

Deep despair over a set of circumstances can often lead to inactivity and thus to further problems. Not so with this manager. He took control of his emotions, thought carefully about his situation, and resolved to initiate a plan of action. It is this determination and willpower in the face of certain failure that will later serve as the manager's redeeming quality in the lesson to be learned from this parable.

The manager's scheme was designed to win the favor of the businessmen with whom he been dealing on behalf of the landowner. He hoped that placing before them an exceptionally good financial opportunity would ingratiate himself with them, thereby setting himself up for future employment options.

5. "So he called in each one of his master's debtors. He asked the first, 'How much do you owe my master?'

In his position, the manager would have regularly set up buying and selling transactions and would have been responsible for calling in debts on behalf of the landowner. To put it in contemporary terms, his "signature" would have been as good as the owner's. Thus the manager was taking advantage of his position of authority while it still remained intact in order to carry out his plan.

6. "'Eight hundred gallons of olive oil,' he replied.

"The manager told him, 'Take your bill, sit down quickly, and make it four hundred.'

The first businessman owed the landowner's estate *eight hundred gallons of olive oil*. This would have been a large transaction in that day, likely to be paid off in increments over a period of time. Here was the manager's offer: he would discount the debt by half if the businessman would act *quickly* and pay in full right then. This would amount to such a tremendous savings that anyone with the resources to pay would leap at the opportunity.

It is not likely, as some assume, that this offer was based on the manager's cutting out his commission on the transaction. Fifty percent is much too large a figure

HOW TO SAY IT
Perea. Peh-REE-uh.
Samaria. Suh-MARE-ee-uh.

DAILY BIBLE READINGS
　　Monday, Jan. 22—The Dishonest Manager (Luke 16:1-8)
　　Tuesday, Jan. 23—Faithful Stewardship (Luke 16:10-13)
　　Wednesday, Jan. 24—Give to God (Deuteronomy 14:22-26)
　　Thursday, Jan. 25—The Law and God's Kingdom (Luke 16:14-18)
　　Friday, Jan. 26—Rich Man, Poor Man (Luke 16:19-26)
　　Saturday, Jan. 27—Warnings About Riches (Luke 16:27-31)
　　Sunday, Jan. 28—Respect the Great King (Psalm 24)

for a commission. It is more likely that the manager was undercutting the real value of the original deal simply to buy the good favor of this businessman. In any event, one who had been filled with desperation over his plight was now moving swiftly with a strategy to ensure his survival.

7. "Then he asked the second, 'And how much do you owe?'
"'A thousand bushels of wheat,' he replied.
"He told him, 'Take your bill and make it eight hundred.'

The *second* businessman received an offer comparable to that given to the first man. Instead of paying the landowner for *a thousand bushels of wheat*, he would pay for only *eight hundred*. While not the fifty percent reduction the first debtor received, the twenty percent discount would represent a substantial savings and make for an attractive offer. The parable records only two transactions by the manager, but the implication is that there were as many others as he could arrange.

WHAT DO YOU THINK?

The manager in Jesus' story is commended for his shrewd plan of action. What kind of actions characterize the wise Christian "manager" today?

B. THE OWNER'S PRAISE (v. 8)

8. "The master commended the dishonest manager because he had acted shrewdly. For the people of this world are more shrewd in dealing with their own kind than are the people of the light.

With this verse we can see why most Bible students consider this parable to be a tricky passage to interpret. The actions of the manager in offering these "discounts" were clearly unethical. He is referred to as a *dishonest manager*. He had not acted in the best interest of the landowner; his actions were focused purely on his own self-preservation.

It is not that the manager acted illegally, for as manager he had full authority to make any deal that he wanted to make. Certainly we would expect him to know better than to cross the line into criminal mischief, knowing that he was currently under close scrutiny. But in the business world, legal is not necessarily the same as ethical. Thus, while the original charge against him was that he had been wasteful and had poorly managed his duties (v. 1), here he had pushed the boundaries of ethical responsibility and was declared *dishonest*.

So how can a dishonest character such as this manager serve as the main character in a parable intended to teach positive spiritual lessons? Actually, Jesus did this more than once in his teaching. Consider, for example, his parable of the "unjust judge" in Luke 18:1-8. Jesus described this judge as one who "neither feared God nor cared about men" (v. 2). He responded to a widow's plea for justice only because her persistent appeals wearied him. And yet this "unjust judge," as he is called, was used to teach us a lesson regarding prayer. Obviously Jesus was not saying that God is unjust or that he does not care about our needs and concerns. No, the lesson in this parable is in the widow's persistence, not in the moral character of the judge (or of the widow, for that matter).

Even granting that Jesus could use a dishonest character in a parable, why did *the master* commend this manager, and how can he serve as an example for us? First, he was not commended for his unethical conduct, but for having *acted shrewdly*. This means that the manager had carried out his scheme with great craft and cunning. When his life was unraveling before him, he refused to be defeated. His actions themselves were not commendable, either to the landowner or to Jesus. And he is not to be respected by us for his motives of self-interest, for he showed little regard for the best interests of the man whose property he managed. But his ability to devise a prudent plan in the midst of professional and emotional turmoil was impressive even to the landowner who was firing him.

It is the manager's refusal to be defeated and his dogged determination to succeed that are commended to Jesus' followers, that is, to *the people of the light*. Of course, Jesus expects our actions to be more honorable than those of the manager; but our resolve to succeed should be no less intense than was his. Believers are encouraged to act as *shrewdly* with spiritual matters as unbelievers do with earthly ones. We are urged to make present investments in future, and eternal, "securities."

III. FAITHFUL SERVICE (LUKE 16:9-13)

A. RESPONSIBLE IN EVERYTHING (vv. 9-11)

9. "I tell you, use worldly wealth to gain friends for yourselves, so that when it is gone, you will be welcomed into eternal dwellings.

Worldly wealth refers to material possessions. There is nothing inherently evil about such wealth, but there is nothing inherently righteous about it either. *To gain friends for yourselves* means to make friends by means of, or by using, such wealth.

But how and why are we to make friends through our worldly possessions? Perhaps Jesus is offering practical advice for our interaction with people on earth; that is, good deeds and acts of kindness in sharing worldly goods toward others will often "come back" to bless those who do them. This may have been what the manager had in mind when he reduced the indebtedness of his master's debtors. Perhaps he hoped that, once he was out of work, they would repay his kindness by assisting him with food or housing.

However, Jesus' statement that we *will be welcomed into eternal dwellings* suggests a loftier idea. It may be that he is challenging us to use our material wealth in ways that will win us "friends in Heaven"—that is, in ways that will encourage the spread of the gospel and will win people to Christ. In other words, Jesus is saying that our wealth should always be used in a manner that pleases God and advances his cause. We should be as shrewd in using wealth in this honorable manner as the manager was in promoting his self-serving agenda.

FRIEND OR FOE?

Several years ago a wealthy automobile dealer in Tampa, Florida, got into an argument with his wife. This was not an infrequent event for the couple, but on this occasion the wife shot and killed her husband. Later, when she was being interviewed by the press, she said, "It's all because of the money. I wish there had never been any money at all!" No doubt many others have expressed the same wish, after coming to realize that the money they had thought would bring them happiness brought nothing but misery.

Jesus encouraged us to "use worldly wealth to gain friends for yourselves" (Luke 16:9). Many have found mammon to be a foe more than a friend, a hindrance more than a help, a curse more than a blessing. Some make a living stealing money, but money is itself a thief—robbing people of genuine peace and happiness and, in many cases, destroying their most important relationships.

Jesus counsels us to use money in a wise way, not to let money use us in a wasteful way. —R. C. S.

10. "Whoever can be trusted with very little can also be trusted with much, and whoever is dishonest with very little will also be dishonest with much.

This verse states a most valuable rule for daily life. How well we handle current tasks and decisions implies how well we would manage greater responsibilities, if given the opportunity to do so. Unfortunately, many people put forth a halfhearted effort in some of their current work, while maintaining that they would surely do better if they had better work to do. Consider responses to each of the following hypothetical situations.

"If I were promoted to manager of this store, I would really put forth my best effort." *But then, why aren't you giving your best effort now?*

WHAT DO YOU THINK?

What kind of behavior demonstrates a faithfulness that suggests that one can be trusted to be faithful with greater things?

WHAT DO YOU THINK?

What are the "true riches" to which Jesus refers (verse 11)? Why are they more valuable than money?

"If I were alone on a trip and approached by a prostitute, I would surely say no." *But then, how well are you resisting the lustful images that come your way each day?*

"If I were a millionaire, I would give away a lot of money to Christian work." *But then, how generous are you now in what you give from your current income?*

"If I were an overseas missionary, I would evangelize as many people as I could." *But then, to how many of your friends and neighbors did you witness today?*

"If I were facing a martyr's death, I would boldly testify to my faith." *But then, how boldly do you speak the name of Jesus even now among friends and colleagues?*

If we are not doing our best with what we have been given now, we are only kidding ourselves to imagine that we would do better if given greater opportunities.

11. *"So if you have not been trustworthy in handling worldly wealth, who will trust you with true riches?*

Here Jesus mentions once again the specific issue of *worldly wealth*. His words indicate that how we handle these riches determines whether God will commit to our care *true riches*. Consider a similar principle stated by Paul concerning leadership: "If anyone does not know how to manage his own family, how can he take care of God's church?" (1 Timothy 3:5).

The right use of wealth is certainly not a condition of salvation, but a wrong use of it indicates that one's life is not under the lordship of Christ as much as it ought to be. As Jesus pointed out, "Where your treasure is, there your heart will be also" (Matthew 6:21). Much of the spiritual riches that could be ours (in areas such as faith and love) often go unclaimed because we are selfish with our material wealth.

B. DEVOTED TO THE MASTER (vv. 12, 13)

12. *"And if you have not been trustworthy with someone else's property, who will give you property of your own?*

WHAT DO YOU THINK?

What are some decisions or choices that you have made because you serve the Lord—and what different choices or decisions do you think you would have made if money were your god?

This verse restates the lesson of the previous verse. The true and eternal wealth (which is really our *own* and which the world cannot take away) will not be ours at all if we cling selfishly to worldly wealth (which was never ours to begin with but came from someone else—and ultimately from God).

13. *"No servant can serve two masters. Either he will hate the one and love the other, or he will be devoted to the one and despise the other. You cannot serve both God and Money."*

Here is the crux of the matter: who is really in control of your life? A life dedicated to accumulating *Money* will time and again run into conflicts with the demands of serving *God*. The more the pursuit of earthly things becomes a priority, requiring our time and energy, the more our devotion to Christ and his ministry will diminish. And what is said about money could be said just as well about anything in this life that we value: nothing should ever be permitted to stand in the way of our commitment to Jesus Christ.

CONCLUSION

How satisfying it is to be commended for our efforts by our peers—to receive awards and commendations, or a promotion and a raise. But none of this compares with the commendation that awaits us at the final judgment if we have been faithful in all things in the sight of Jesus. The world may scoff at our devotion to the cause of Christ and our disdain for the pleasures it counts dear. To hear these words from the Master will be worth whatever ridicule or opposition we have had to endure:

"Well done, good and faithful servant! You have been faithful with a few things; I will put you in charge of many things. Come and share your master's happiness!" (Matthew 25:23).

Today's visual reminds us that we cannot go two ways at once. Discuss some of the choices that have to be made in order to serve God and not money.

Discovery Learning

This page contains an alternate lesson plan emphasizing learning activities. Classes desiring such student involvement will find these suggestions helpful. The next page is a reproducible activity page to further enhance discovery learning.

LEARNING GOALS

After this lesson each student will be able to:

1. Recount Jesus' parable of the dishonest manager.

2. Tell how a story about a person's unethical behavior can serve as an example to Christians.

3. Pinpoint an area where he or she has been trying to "serve two masters," and suggest ways to put God first.

INTO THE LESSON

Search newspapers, newsmagazines, or business papers for articles concerning "good" and "bad" managers. Place the chairs of the room in circles of four with an article in each circle. Students will summarize the article, identifying the positive or negative nature of the person.

You may also introduce this lesson by asking, "If you could have any job in the world right now, what job would you like to have? Don't let issues related to changing jobs affect your answer—issues like changing your kids' schools, moving, and the like. Simply consider the job itself—what is your dream job? Why?" Allow the groups a few minutes for discussion.

Make the transition to today's Bible study by saying that we will be looking at a story about a man who was on the verge of losing his "dream" job and what he decided to do about it.

INTO THE WORD

Begin with a brief lecture using the lesson commentary's introductory materials and the following statement: "Today's lesson encourages us to look beneath the surface a bit. We are challenged by Jesus' commendation of someone who was dishonest. Our study is designed to uncover this mystery. What we have here is a person who has made mistakes and needs a second chance."

Distribute copies of the reproducible activity page that follows. Give the learners time to complete the activity, either individually or in small groups. Then review the page to be sure everyone got the correct answers. Discuss issues from the text as they come up in the review. Then discuss the following questions:

1. Why does Jesus need to tell this story to his disciples? (*Perhaps he is indicating that planning and possessions can be important for the kingdom. The disciples could see wealth as evil, or they could become preoccupied with amassing wealth, as the Pharisees were—see v. 14.*)

2. What surprises you most about this story?

3. Name one other parable where Jesus uses a dishonest character to teach a spiritual lesson. (*Luke 18:1-8.*) What is the lesson we should learn here? (*It is the refusal of the manager to be beaten down and his dogged determination to succeed.*)

4. What is the meaning of Jesus' words "trustworthy in handling worldly wealth"?

5. What does this passage teach about handling money?

6. What's the problem in trying to serve two masters?

Allow ten minutes for research, and then call for reports. Observe that some difficult questions are raised by this passage.

1. Jesus said, "You will be welcomed into eternal dwellings." We cannot earn or buy our salvation; what does this mean? (*Use commentary notes under verse 9.*)

2. Some say that in this passage Jesus condones greed and dishonesty. What is wrong with that view? (*See verses 10-13.*)

These difficult verses force us to determine whom we shall serve. Jesus leaves no "wiggle room" for his disciples. "Choose," he says.

INTO LIFE

There are three areas that this parable challenges us to evaluate. The first is our trustworthy character. Use the lesson commentary material under verse 10 to challenge students to greater commitment in what they are presently doing.

Second, prepare a short checklist concerning the students' relationship with money. Ask each student to check the most appropriate statement.

__ God wants me to be trustworthy in my use of money.

__ I must stop serving money and serve God.

__ I need to use my money to help others.

__ I need to make wise, honest business decisions.

Third, while money may have been a focus of this lesson, there are other "masters" that compete with our allegiance to God. Say, "On the back of the sheet used for the checklist, list some of the 'masters' you have served in the past. List some that tug for your allegiance now. Write one practical change you can make in your life so that you can serve God more completely."

Close with this prayer, "Lord, I cannot serve two masters. Help me to value what you value. Today, I choose you! Amen."

Choose This Day!

From the time of Joshua, God's people have been challenged to serve him and no other master (Joshua 24:15). Fill in the blanks below from Luke 16. Check the shaded area for our challenge today.

1. The rich man accused the manager of "wasting his _____." (v. 1)
2. The rich man said, "Give an account of your _____." (v. 2)
3. The manager "called in each one of his master's _____." (v. 5)
4. What kind of oil was owed? (v. 6)
5. One thousand _____ of wheat was owed. (v. 7)
6. "People of the _____" are less shrewd than they of the world. (v. 8)
7. "Use worldly wealth to gain friends for yourselves, so that when it is gone, you will be _____ into eternal dwellings." (v. 9)
8. If you can be trusted with little, you can be _____ with much. (v. 10)
9. "No servant can serve two _____." (v. 13)
10. "Either he will hate the one and _____ the other. . . ." (v. 13)
11. ". . . or he will be devoted to the _____ and despise the other." (v. 13)
12. "You cannot serve both God and _____." (v. 13)
13. "You are the ones who justify yourselves in the eyes of men, but God knows your _____." (v. 15)

From the letters in the shaded boxes complete the following:

Our challenge today is to _____ _____ _____

GOING TO JERUSALEM

LESSON 10

WHY TEACH THIS LESSON?

Do fire departments still send out rescue teams to rescue lost kittens from trees? I can't imagine that happening in large cities anymore—they have more important things to do—but perhaps in some smaller communities it still takes place. It's a touching sight when a big, strong fireman pulls the frightened feline from her perch and returns her safely to the little child who has been watching with anxiety ever since the fire department was summoned.

Well, it wasn't a lost kitten in a tree, but a lost tax collector. And it wasn't that Jesus didn't have important things to do. He was on his way to Jerusalem, where "everything that [was] written by the prophets about the Son of Man [would] be fulfilled" (Luke 18:31). Still he stopped, and he invited himself to lunch. Zaccheus and the poor of Jericho were glad he did!

This lesson reminds us of the important mission we share with Jesus, and it demonstrates how to accomplish it. We, like Jesus, want to seek and to save the lost. We do it, one lost person at a time.

INTRODUCTION

A. THE LAZARUS MAN

In October of 1975 a man in our congregation proposed that we reach out to the less fortunate in our community in a very special way. He suggested that the families in our church sacrifice their usual Thanksgiving celebrations and prepare a Thanksgiving meal for people in a part of town that was far removed from our nice suburbs. The proposal was met with genuine enthusiasm, and we began making preparations.

When Thanksgiving came, we gathered in a rented storefront. We did all the cooking and set tables for seventy-five people. We had distributed flyers for several days, and our efforts at publicity were very successful. Before long, we realized that we were going to have to buy more food and get more people to cook. Some stood as they ate their meals because there were not enough chairs.

After the meal, we conducted a Thanksgiving service with music and preaching. One man had come in to eat toward the end of the meal. He had not received as much to eat as some others, but he did not complain. It appeared that he had been drinking. His clothes were little more than rags. He clung tenaciously to his one valued possession—a heavy winter coat.

As we began our Thanksgiving service, the man wandered to a metal chair in the back row. As we began to sing one of the traditional Thanksgiving hymns, one of our men noticed that the man did not have a hymnal. He went over and sat down beside him. He moved his chair close to the man and wrapped his arm around the back of the man's chair so that they could share a hymnal. After the service the two men stood and talked for a long time. They were an odd sight— one was a pathetic alcoholic; the other was a highly respected educator.

Later I questioned my friend about his encounter with the man. When I asked about his name, my friend said that he thought he should be named, "Lazarus." I asked why, and he replied, "Because he stinketh." We laughed a little about

DEVOTIONAL READING:

MATTHEW 10:32-39

BACKGROUND SCRIPTURE:

LUKE 18:15—19:10

PRINTED TEXT:

LUKE 18:31-34; 19:1-10

LESSON AIMS

After this lesson each student will be able to:

1. Tell how Jesus met and accepted Zaccheus.

2. Explain why Zaccheus is a good illustration of Jesus' mission "to seek and to save what was lost."

3. Identify a "Zaccheus" among his or her own acquaintances and suggest one means of reaching this person with the gospel.

Feb
4

KEY VERSE

The Son of Man came to seek and to save what was lost.

—Luke 19:10

that, but it was a laugh tinged with sadness. My friend had told the man how much Jesus loved him and wanted to free him from his bondage to sin. The man then began to cry and promised to think about the things he had been told. He also promised to read the Bible my friend had given him.

We never heard from that man again. He had gladly received food for his body. Our prayer is that he also received food for his soul.

B. LESSON BACKGROUND

Our final unit of study from the Gospel of Luke focuses on the death and resurrection of Jesus. Jesus tried several times to prepare his followers for the horrible ordeal that awaited him in Jerusalem. (Luke records warnings in Luke 9:22, 44, 45; 12:50; 13:33; and 17:24, 25.) At the time of today's text, Jesus had met with little success in making them understand what was about to happen.

Embarking on a pivotal journey to Jerusalem, Jesus would try once again to prepare the disciples for the events that would happen there. As the group passed through Jericho, he illustrated for his followers, in an unforgettable manner, the true nature of his mission: "to seek and to save what was lost" (Luke 19:10).

I. THE MEANS ANNOUNCED (LUKE 18:31-34)

In the time of Jesus, Israel was waiting and longing for the Messiah to come. To many, the need for the Messiah had never been more urgent: the Romans had conquered much of the world, and Israel had not been spared their tyranny.

Jesus of Nazareth, while he appeared to do and to say much that seemed messianic, did not meet many of the popular expectations. He did not assemble an army or wield mighty weapons. He did not talk of overthrowing Rome or of delivering Israel. In fact, he later encouraged people to "give to Caesar what is Caesar's" (Luke 20:25). However, none of this was as astonishing as the fact that Jesus proposed to "deliver" his people and fulfill his Father's will by means of a cross.

WHAT DO YOU THINK?

Jesus knew that going to Jerusalem would result in suffering and death for him, but still he went there. The suffering that awaited him was a necessary part of God's plan for our redemption. What about us? Should we walk into situations we know will result in confrontation? How do we know when to stand against opposition and when to walk away?

A. DELIVERED AND DEGRADED (vv. 31, 32)

31. Jesus took the Twelve aside and told them, "We are going up to Jerusalem, and everything that is written by the prophets about the Son of Man will be fulfilled.

As Passover approached and Jesus and the disciples made their last trip to Jerusalem, the Lord tried again to prepare his followers for the horrible events that lay ahead. Here he introduced an element he had not mentioned in earlier predictions of his death: it would accomplish what the *prophets* had *written . . . about the Son of Man*. Thus, while Jesus' death would be tragic and shameful, it would be no accident. It would mark the fulfillment of a plan, revealed by God to his spokesmen of the past (1 Peter 1:10-12).

From our vantage point, many of these prophecies are obvious; they include Psalm 22:1-31; Isaiah 52:13—53:12; and Daniel 9:24-27. But as we shall see, the disciples did not yet grasp what Jesus was telling them.

32. "He will be handed over to the Gentiles. They will mock him, insult him, spit on him, flog him and kill him.

Contrary to the popular opinion of the time, the Messiah was not going to be welcomed with open arms and treated as a V.I.P. He was going to be *handed over to the Gentiles*. His own people (John 18:35) would deliver him to the people whom they hated so deeply—the Romans. That is how intense the religious leaders' hatred of Jesus had become.

We may become angry when we read about Jesus' unjust treatment at the hands of the Roman soldiers: they would *mock him, insult him, spit on him, flog him and kill him*. But let us never forget that our sin was the reason he endured that suffering. Such was the depth of his love for lost humanity. We must never take that love for granted.

The most unthinkable part of Jesus' description of his future treatment was that he would be killed. Peter told his audience on the Day of Pentecost, "Jesus of Nazareth . . . was handed over to you by God's set purpose and foreknowledge; and you, with the help of wicked men, put him to death by nailing him to the cross" (Acts 2:22, 23). Yes, wicked men had crucified Jesus; but it was according to God's plan. Jesus was a volunteer on a rescue mission. It is not entirely correct to say that men took the life of Jesus; he gave his life to save mankind (John 10:18).

B. DEAD, THEN ALIVE (v. 33)
33. "On the third day he will rise again."

Had Jesus spoken only of his death, his disciples would have been left without hope. But Jesus never leaves his followers hopeless. He assured them that death would not triumph. He would *rise again* on the *third day* after being crucified.

C. DEAF TO JESUS' WORDS (v. 34)
34. The disciples did not understand any of this. Its meaning was hidden from them, and they did not know what he was talking about.

It is easy for us to look back on this scene and wonder how the *disciples* could have been so ignorant. However, let us remember that we have twenty centuries of hindsight that the disciples did not have!

That the *meaning* of Jesus' words *was hidden from them* does not imply that God was doing the hiding. The meaning was hidden from the disciples because of their own preconceived ideas and motives concerning the Messiah's mission. When Jesus first spoke plainly of being killed, Peter chastised him for suggesting such foolishness (Matthew 16:21, 22). The disciples soon became preoccupied with planning their own places in the kingdom that they believed Jesus would rule (Matthew 18:1). Even on the night before he died, they argued about their position in Jesus' kingdom (Luke 22:24). Like many in their day, they rejected the idea of a Messiah who would suffer and die. That was not what they wanted to hear, so they simply refused to accept it. They apparently thought Jesus was using figurative language that they could not understand (cf. Mark 9:10).

We may view the disciples' shortcomings with a critical eye, but are we not like them? Jesus spoke many difficult truths. Do we accept them all or just what we want to hear? Do we turn the other cheek? Do we pray for those who persecute us? Do we love our enemies? Do we love the lost? Do we invest in God's kingdom rather than in earthly wealth? We may think that the disciples were deaf to Jesus' words, but are we qualified to claim that we have been model followers of Jesus?

II. THE METHOD APPLIED (LUKE 19:1-7)
A. BEING SEEN (vv. 1-4)
1. Jesus entered Jericho and was passing through.

On their way to Jerusalem, *Jesus* and his disciples were *passing through* the town of *Jericho*, approximately twelve miles northeast of Jerusalem. It was located on one of the lowest points in the Jordan valley, some eight hundred fifty feet below sea level. Jerusalem, by contrast, was situated in the Judean hills at about twenty-six hundred feet above sea level.
2. A man was there by the name of Zacchaeus; he was a chief tax collector and was wealthy.

Zacchaeus collected taxes for the Romans. The Jews who performed that service for the Romans were hated for two reasons: first, they were considered traitors

WHAT DO YOU THINK?

From our vantage point, it seems preposterous that the disciples could misunderstand what Jesus was telling them. But the disciples pictured Jesus reigning over a kingdom in which they would enjoy privileged positions of power. This concept was so firmly planted in their minds that they literally could not conceive of Jesus' being put to death in Jerusalem. What truths have some people today "misunderstood" because the truth is contrary to their preferred ideas?

WHAT DO YOU THINK?

Zaccheus was rich, but his wealth did not bring him contentment. In what do people today wrongly seek to find contentment? How can we help them to find true joy in Jesus?

(since they were employed by the people who were considered Israel's oppressors); and second, they were usually wealthy because Rome cared little if they overcharged the people and kept some of the money for themselves. As *a chief tax collector* Zaccheus was hardly the most popular man in Jericho; but being *wealthy* may have made up for not having a lot of friends.

3. He wanted to see who Jesus was, but being a short man he could not, because of the crowd.

We do not know why Zaccheus was interested in Jesus, but, like many others, he wanted *to see* him. This was an important first step. Perhaps Zaccheus's riches had left him feeling spiritually empty. But a *crowd* had gathered, which posed a problem for Zaccheus. He was *a short man*; he *could not* see over the people.

4. So he ran ahead and climbed a sycamore-fig tree to see him, since Jesus was coming that way.

Zaccheus was not easily discouraged. He *ran ahead* to a spot where a *sycamore-fig tree* stood beside the road, and he *climbed* up into the tree so that he could *see* Jesus as he passed by. When it comes to spiritual matters, how easily do you give up? If something takes time, effort, and sacrifice, do you bail out? Zaccheus is a great example of perseverance in the face of obstacles.

The tree that Zaccheus climbed was a wide, sturdy tree with low limbs that allowed even a short man like Zaccheus to climb into it. It was also well-known for the shade it provided from the heat.

B. BEING KNOWN (vv. 5, 6)

5. When Jesus reached the spot, he looked up and said to him, "Zacchaeus, come down immediately. I must stay at your house today."

Zaccheus caught Jesus' eye, and Jesus immediately responded to the obvious eagerness of this man in the tree. Jesus knew Zaccheus's name, but more important he knew what was in his heart. Jesus quickly and lovingly responded to the longing of Zaccheus by inviting himself to Zaccheus's *house*.

It is God's desire to know us. He created us in order to have an intimate fellowship with us. Sin ruined that fellowship, but God wants it restored. That is the reason Jesus came. Is it not amazing to think that the Creator of the universe desires such intimacy with us?

KNOWN BY NAME

It has been said that nothing sounds sweeter to any man or woman than the sound of his or her own name. That is the reason motivational speakers urge their audiences to learn people's names. They even suggest certain techniques for remembering names, such as repeating a person's name while we are conversing with him or her. Perhaps we have heard a person say, "Your face is familiar, but I can't recall your name." Some people might be offended at hearing that.

A. B. "Happy" Chandler served as governor of Kentucky, as a United States senator, and also as the commissioner of baseball. It was said that, because of his phenomenal memory and a real effort he made to remember names, he never forgot the name of any person he met.

When Jesus met Zaccheus, he did not say, "Hey, you—you, up in the tree there—get down!" He called Zaccheus by name. Such are God's dealings with his creation. Recall his speaking by name to Abraham (Genesis 22:11), Moses (Exodus 3:4), and Samuel (1 Samuel 3:4-10).

It is not at all hard to believe that the very hairs of our head are numbered by such a God. He who created us in his image knows each one of us personally and individually, and he sent his Son to die for each one of us. We are never simply "John Doe" or "Jane Doe" to the Christ!   —R. C. S.

WHAT DO YOU THINK?

How can we tell who is interested in the gospel today when nobody is climbing trees to see Jesus? Of course, the gospel is for all, and we want to proclaim the gospel to everyone we can. But there are times when taking one course of action will, of necessity, eliminate other possible courses. As we plan our outreach, how do we know how to target our message?

HOW TO SAY IT

Jericho. JAIR-ih-co.
Lazarus. LAZ-uh-rus.
messianic. mess-ee-AN-ick.
Zaccheus. Zack-KEE-us.

6. So he came down at once and welcomed him gladly.

Zaccheus must have been ecstatic to hear Jesus' words. Not only was he going to get to see Jesus, but he was going to have him as a guest in his home! Such an enthusiastic response should cause us to ask ourselves just how welcome we have made Jesus feel in our own homes.

C. BEING JUDGED (v. 7)

7. All the people saw this and began to mutter, "He has gone to be the guest of a 'sinner.'"

Everywhere Jesus went there was a critic, or so it seemed. Here in Jericho his intention to go home with Zaccheus confounded and disturbed the crowd that had gathered. Wasn't he aware of Zaccheus's position and reputation? How could he socialize with such a man? But Jesus was often criticized for making friends with the wrong people. Instead of cultivating the companionship of the pious, he associated with prostitutes, lepers, and tax collectors. Yes, the people were right about Zaccheus: he was indeed a *sinner*—but so was each of them.

In Jericho Jesus showed his disciples the nature of his mission. Despite the judgmental attitude of others, Jesus extended his love and grace to any who wanted to know him. That invitation is still open: he still welcomes those who want to know him and to learn about him because he is so eager to know us and fellowship with us. Do we as Christ's people communicate that truth in our outreach? If not, why not?

III. THE MISSION ACCOMPLISHED (LUKE 19:8-10)

A. REPENTANCE (v. 8)

8. But Zacchaeus stood up and said to the Lord, "Look, Lord! Here and now I give half of my possessions to the poor, and if I have cheated anybody out of anything, I will pay back four times the amount."

We do not know what Jesus and Zaccheus discussed in Zaccheus's home. At some point, Zaccheus was apparently challenged to follow a new Master. He responded by making a radical pledge *to the Lord*: he would *give half* of all he had *to the poor* and offer a quadruple repayment to anyone he had *cheated*. This fourfold return went far beyond the requirements of the law of Moses, which stipulated that one restore twenty percent more (one-fifth) than he had wrongfully taken (Leviticus 6:1-5; Numbers 5:5-7).

It is easy to express repentance in words. To follow up with action is more difficult. True sorrow for sin manifests itself in a change of direction that is reflected in a desire to make amends for one's wrong actions wherever possible. Zaccheus went from being a taker to being a giver! Which category describes you?

THE EXECUTION OF RESTITUTION

Wedding Nurseries is a well-known business in St. Petersburg, Florida. It has supplied ornamental plants to the city for a long time. As is the case with most nurseries, this one discovers from time to time that some of its plants have been stolen. In fact, one young man stole plants repeatedly and was never caught. But then he became a Christian. To demonstrate his repentance and his commitment to his new way of living, he brought back *three truckloads* of plants that he had stolen from the nursery. (He even brought back plants that he had raised from the stolen plants!) Clearly this man wanted to make restitution for what he had done in his past.

While we often talk about repentance, we seldom discuss restitution. Of course, in some situations restitution for past wrongdoing cannot be made. If we have ruined someone's reputation, we cannot easily make restitution. And there are cases where even an attempt at restitution would only make matters worse.

DAILY BIBLE READINGS

Monday, Jan. 29—The Coming of the Kingdom (Luke 17:20-30)

Tuesday, Jan. 30—Keep On Praying (Luke 18:1-8)

Wednesday, Jan. 31—The Pharisee and the Publican (Luke 18:9-14)

Thursday, Feb. 1—Innocence and Humility (Luke 18:15-17)

Friday, Feb. 2—The Rich Ruler (Luke 18:18-30)

Saturday, Feb. 3—Join the Procession (Luke 18:31-43)

Sunday, Feb. 4—Jesus and Zaccheus (Luke 19:1-10)

WHAT DO YOU THINK?

Being in the company of Jesus had a profound effect on Zaccheus. How could you increase the power of your example and your witness to the lost people you meet?

PRAYER

Father, help us to see the lost through your eyes. Remind us that we once were separated from you, and may this motivate us to reach out to the least and the last and the lost. We thank you for sending Jesus on his marvelous rescue mission. May his love be in our hearts and his truth be on our lips as we seek to be lights in a dark world. In Jesus' name. Amen.

Today's lesson visual illustrates verse 10 of our Scripture text. Discuss how we today can participate in seeking and saving the lost.

However, there are situations where it is possible to make restitution; and where that is possible, it needs to be done. A teenage girl told her minister that as a child she had stolen candy from a store. But that was in another city, and the store was no longer in business. The minister told her that her forgiveness did not depend on restitution, but that she might feel better if she did such an act. So he told her to buy some candy of equal value and give it to a poor child. She did this and felt immeasurably better.

Zaccheus did not buy his forgiveness, nor did this teenage girl. But an act of restitution can express how grateful we are to be forgiven and how much we love the One who has forgiven us.   —R. C. S.

B. REDEMPTION (v. 9)

9. Jesus said to him, "Today salvation has come to this house, because this man, too, is a son of Abraham.

Jesus knew the content of Zaccheus's heart and the genuineness of his repentance. He saw that Zaccheus's god of money had been dethroned. Faith in earthly riches had been replaced by faith in the living God. It is by faith that we come to God (Hebrews 11:6). It is by faith that we become children of Abraham (Romans 4:13-16; Galatians 3:29). Zaccheus, a descendant of Abraham in the flesh, was now also a *son of Abraham* by faith.

C. REMINDER (v. 10)

10. "For the Son of Man came to seek and to save what was lost."

Son of Man was Jesus' most commonly used title for himself. (In the Gospels it is never used by anyone except Jesus.) Its messianic significance is clear from its use in Daniel 7:13, 14. Here the Son of Man responded to the faith of Zaccheus by proclaiming that his mission was *to seek and to save what was lost*—in other words, people just like Zaccheus.

We have seen in a previous lesson (lesson 8) how Jesus used parables to illustrate God's desire to reclaim that which was lost (Luke 15). Zaccheus provided a personal and dramatic illustration of this desire. As Jesus approached Jerusalem (and therefore Calvary), he wanted to impress on his disciples what his ministry was all about. He had come to change people's lives by bringing them from darkness to light, from slavery to freedom, from sin to salvation. In Zaccheus his followers could see a living example of "mission accomplished."

CONCLUSION

Jesus came from Heaven to earth on a rescue mission. He came to reunite sinners with a perfect, holy God by means of his atoning death. Jesus' love for sinners is illustrated by his compassion for Zaccheus. Man's greatest need is still the restoration of fellowship with God, but we can never accomplish that ourselves. God, in love and mercy, reached out and, in Christ, did for us what we could not do for ourselves.

Anyone who has played baseball knows that to be a successful batter, you must keep your eye on the ball. Sometimes in the church we get sidetracked. We take our eyes off the ball. The gospel is about salvation. That is its focus.

The church can put its time, energy, and financial resources into many good causes. We can work to help the poor. We can work to stop abortion. We can try to help young people stop the violence in their schools and neighborhoods. All of those are good things to do. But the church must never get so busy doing good things that it forgets the main thing—the purpose for which Jesus came and the mission he left to his followers: "to seek and to save what was lost."

THOUGHT TO REMEMBER

God's love for the lost is beyond our ability to understand. But we know it is real because of Jesus.

Discovery Learning

This page contains an alternate lesson plan emphasizing learning activities. Classes desiring such student involvement will find these suggestions helpful. The next page is a reproducible activity page to further enhance discovery learning.

LEARNING GOALS

After this lesson each student will be able to:

1. Tell how Jesus met and accepted Zaccheus.

2. Explain why Zaccheus is a good illustration of Jesus' mission "to seek and to save what was lost."

3. Identify a "Zaccheus" among his or her own acquaintances and suggest one means of reaching this person with the gospel.

INTO THE LESSON

To begin the class, distribute copies of a handout containing the following information:

"In a rural midwestern community, a toddler has fallen down a newly dug well, twenty feet deep. The well is only two feet wide—too narrow for an adult to climb down. The child is wedged in head first, near the bottom of the well, too far down to reach by hand through the opening. Rescuers fear that pulling the child out with a rope will seriously hurt him. Widening the well could cause a mud slide that would bury him. How can they rescue him?"

Ask students to suggest ways to save the child, writing their advice on a chalkboard. When they finish making suggestions, tell them the child was actually rescued by digging a shaft beside the well, then tunneling beneath him. Then tell your class that this lesson will provide an opportunity to discuss strategies for saving the lost.

INTO THE WORD

Choose five to seven students to do a dramatic reading based on today's text and found on the reproducible page that follows. You will need a narrator, two disciples, Jesus, two from the crowd, and Zaccheus. (The disciples could also play the crowd.)

Next, divide your class into an equal number of groups composed of four to six students per group. Half of your groups will do Study A, below. The other half will do Study B. After they finish their studies, have each group report its findings to the class.

Study A: Compare Luke 18:31-34 with Luke 5:35; 9:22, 44, 45; 12:49, 50; 13:32, 33; 17:22-25. Then answer the questions below.

1. How many times did Jesus warn his disciples that he had to die?

2. How did the disciples react to his predictions? Why didn't the disciples understand Jesus' warnings?

3. Luke 18:34 says the meaning of Jesus' explanation was hidden from the disciples. What or who was responsible for hiding the truth?

4. In 1 Corinthians 15:3-8, Paul lists what he calls matters of "first importance" for the Christian. Compare his listing with Luke 18:31-33. Why are these truths so important?

Study B: Provide copies of the chart below (without the material that appears in parentheses). Give the class the following instructions: "Read Luke 19:1-10 and complete this chart, indicating how Zaccheus and the crowd in the story reacted to Jesus. Answer the discussion questions that follow."

Verses	What Jesus Did	Zaccheus's Response	The Crowd's Response
1-4	(Came to Jericho)	(Eager to see Jesus)	(Flocked to see Jesus)
5-7	(Asked to stay with Zaccheus)	(Received Jesus joyfully)	(Murmured against Jesus)
8-10	(Taught and forgave him)	(Repented and made amends)	(No reaction)

1. Why was there such a difference between the crowd's reaction to Jesus and Zaccheus's reaction?

2. Summarize Jesus' techniques for evangelizing Zaccheus. Which of them can we use today?

INTO LIFE

Discuss the following scenarios with your class. If time is short, divide the class into three groups and give one scenario to each group. The groups can summarize their findings for the class.

1. Steve has always been a follower. He is a kind-hearted person, but he has allowed bad friends to get him into trouble with drugs and alcohol. What can be done to lead him to Christ?

2. Jennifer has a drive to succeed in business. She has devoted her life to success. Everything else, including family, friends, and God, is secondary. What strategy would you develop to present the gospel to her?

3. Michael is an intellectual. His college studies in science and philosophy have convinced him that God does not exist. How would you penetrate his wall of unbelief?

To close the study, urge each student to pick some unsaved person—a Zaccheus—to reach with the gospel and to develop a strategy for leading that person to Christ.

On the Jericho Road: A Dramatic Reading

Optional Props: A stepladder for Zaccheus's sycamore-fig tree.

Characters: Narrator, two of Jesus' disciples, Jesus, Zaccheus, the crowd (perhaps the same people who play the two disciples or two others).

Narrator: *(While Jesus and the disciples walk along)* As Jesus and his disciples were on their way to Jerusalem, Jesus took them aside from the crowd and said . . .

Jesus: *(Stops and speaks)* We are going up to Jerusalem, and everything that is written by the prophets about the Son of Man will be fulfilled. He will be handed over to the Gentiles. They will mock him, insult him, spit on him, flog him, and kill him. On the third day he will rise again.

Narrator: But the disciples did not understand any of this. Its meaning was hidden from them, and they did not know what he was talking about.

Disciple 1: Do you understand what the Master is talking about?

Disciple 2: Not me! All this talk about dying in Jerusalem scares me. I thought we were on our way there to crown Jesus king!

Narrator: *(Jesus and the disciples walk toward Zaccheus)* And Jesus entered Jericho and was passing through.
(The crowd forms a line between Jesus and Zaccheus)
A man was there by the name of Zaccheus; he was a chief tax-gatherer and was wealthy. He wanted to see who Jesus was, but being a short man he could not, because of the crowd.
(Zaccheus climbs the ladder)
So he ran ahead and climbed a sycamore-fig tree to see him, since Jesus was coming that way. When Jesus reached the spot, he looked up and said to him . . .

Jesus: Zaccheus, come down immediately. I must stay at your house today.

Narrator: *(Zaccheus climbs down and he and Jesus walk away together)* So he came down at once and welcomed him gladly. But all the people saw this and began to mutter . . .

Crowd 1: Can you believe that? Jesus is going to be the guest of a sinner.

Crowd 2: I thought he was a prophet or something. Maybe even the Messiah. But if he can't spot a tax collector when he sees one. . . . I just don't know.

Narrator: But Zaccheus stood up and said to the Lord . . .

Zaccheus: Look, Lord! I know my life needs a major change of direction. Here and now I give half of my possessions to the poor, and if I have cheated anybody out of anything, I will pay back four times the amount.

Jesus: Today salvation has come to this house, because this man, too, is a son of Abraham. For the Son of Man came to seek and to save what was lost.

ONE WHO SERVES

LESSON 11

WHY TEACH THIS LESSON?

Scholars debate the chronology of the events in the upper room on the night Jesus was betrayed. The Gospel accounts have the details arranged differently, so it is hard to determine the actual order. Luke, it seems, had a more topical approach than chronological, and we are the richer for it.

In today's lesson we see how Luke presented Jesus' lesson on service in the context of the Lord's Supper. The disciples could not have appreciated the significance at the time, but surely we can. What a grand illustration of Jesus' coming "as one who serves." What a perfect demonstration that Jesus "did not come to be served, but to serve, and to give his life as a ransom for many" (Matthew 20:28). May we be challenged also to serve, and to serve in that same spirit.

INTRODUCTION

A. "I AM THE GREATEST"

The young boxer from Louisville, Kentucky, had lightning quick hands and feet. He was equally quick with a quote or a quip. When he entered the ranks of professional boxing and began to make his mark, he soon became associated with a slogan that is readily recalled nearly forty years later: "I am the greatest!" While few could argue with Cassius Clay (later Muhammad Ali) in his assessment of his boxing skills, many were offended by such brashness. In those days, humility was a quality that most people admired.

Today the lack of humility seems to be more highly valued. Humility is equated with weakness or the lack of "self-esteem." Elevation of self to a place above others (at any cost) is considered part of getting ahead in the world. In the days when beepers were in frequent use, I remember being told by one man (seeking to impress me with his status) that he was not a person to be beeped. He was the one to do the beeping!

Jesus, the Creator of the universe, the King of kings and Lord of lords, never spoke a word of self-adulation. He refused to be governed by the world's standard of greatness. He knew that greatness in God's eyes comes through humble service.

B. LESSON BACKGROUND

Jesus and his disciples had come to Jerusalem for the Passover feast. His enemies had anticipated his arrival for this occasion. They had spent months scheming to kill Jesus and thought that the Passover might provide them the opportunity. They also knew, however, that Jesus was very popular (Luke 22:2). He had been teaching in the temple, where many gathered to hear him speak (Luke 21:37, 38). The religious leaders were fearful of the turmoil that could erupt if the populace became aware of their intentions concerning Jesus.

None of this caught Jesus by surprise. He knew what was being planned. He had come to Jerusalem to offer himself as a sacrifice for the sins of the world. Recall the words of Luke 9:51, which tells us that "as the time approached for him to be taken up to heaven, Jesus resolutely set out for Jerusalem." He alone recognized the eternal significance of the events that were about to unfold in Jerusalem.

DEVOTIONAL READING:
MARK 10:35-45
BACKGROUND SCRIPTURE:
LUKE 22:1-30
PRINTED TEXT:
LUKE 22:14-30

LESSON AIMS

After this lesson each student will be able to:

1. Give the details surrounding Jesus' institution of the Lord's Supper.

2. Contrast the attitude required for a proper observance of the Lord's Supper with the attitude that the disciples displayed on this occasion.

3. Write a Communion meditation that incorporates Jesus' call to humility in discipleship.

Feb
11

KEY VERSE

The greatest among you should be like the youngest, and the one who rules like the one who serves. —Luke 22:26

LESSON 11 NOTES

By the time of the events recorded in today's printed text, preparations already had been made for the Passover meal. A place had been secured. A lamb had been slain. All other necessary arrangements had been made. Despite the numerous warnings of Jesus, his disciples did not seem to appreciate the gravity of this observance of the Passover, as we shall see.

Luke's account of these events differs somewhat from that of the other Gospel writers. He includes material that other writers omit and omits information that others include. (Similar variations can be seen when comparing the records of almost any incident in the life of Christ.) When all four Gospels are harmonized, the Bible student is presented with a more complete picture of the events. The differences do not weaken or destroy the integrity of any of the accounts. The differences most difficult to harmonize concern the arrangement of the material. In these we are forced to conclude that not all the accounts are given in chronological order. While that may seem strange in our time-bound culture, topical or other arrangements of historical information were common in the first century.

I. THE PASSOVER (LUKE 22:14-20)

A. EAGERNESS EXPRESSED (vv. 14-16)

14. When the hour came, Jesus and his apostles reclined at the table.

Jesus *reclined at the table* with *his apostles* to observe the Passover. Passover marked the remembrance of God's salvation of his people on that night when all the firstborn in Egypt were killed (Exodus 11:4—12:30). Even though this feast of remembrance had been celebrated for centuries, it still held great significance in teaching the young and refreshing the memory of the old. The Jews were not to forget what God had done in delivering their ancestors from cruel bondage in Egypt. While this feast was usually observed in families, Jesus chose to observe it with the people closest to him.

15. And he said to them, "I have eagerly desired to eat this Passover with you before I suffer.

In this verse we are given a glimpse into the heart of Jesus, for he *eagerly desired to eat* the *Passover* with his disciples. Jesus was always eager to do what God had asked his people to do. But this night was special, and Jesus had been looking forward to it with anticipation.

For Jesus, *this Passover* was meaningful, not only as a means of looking back but also as a way of looking ahead. He was eating this meal *before* he would endure his suffering on behalf of those enslaved to sin, in order to "free those who all their lives were held in slavery by their fear of death" (Hebrews 2:15).

Jesus was also eager to be *with* those whom he loved. Jesus had chosen these twelve men, had invested much of his life in them, and had come to love them in spite of their many weaknesses. As John notes, "Having loved his own who were in the world, he now showed them the full extent of his love" (John 13:1). The work of his kingdom would be placed in their hands. Even though they had failed him at times and would desert him this very night, we should not forget that he wanted to be with them at this Passover.

WHAT DO YOU THINK?

The expression Jesus used to explain that he "eagerly desired" to eat the Passover with his disciples (v. 15) is a very intense one, but Luke does not tell us why Jesus was so eager to do this. Why do you think it was so important to Jesus to share this "Last Supper" with his disciples? What significance is there for us in Jesus' desire?

THE LOVING CUP

In medieval times, on the twelfth night after Christmas, people gathered to celebrate the conclusion of the Christmas season. During the meal, all who were present drank from a two-handled cup. Since this cup was intended to be shared, it came to be known as a "loving cup."

Today a "loving cup" refers to a trophy that one receives after winning a contest. But on the night *before* the cross, at the *beginning* of his anguish over the sins of the world, Jesus sat down to share a cup with his closest followers. It would be proper to refer to this as a "loving cup" because Jesus loved these men so deeply (John 13:1). He had looked forward "eagerly" to celebrating with them (Luke 22:15).

Today the Communion cup is always a shared cup. This is true even if a church uses individual cups, as most congregations do. Though each of the people who partakes has a cup, each cup is shared with Christ. And each cup is a loving cup, pledging our love for Christ and for his people even as we celebrate his love for us. It is no wonder that John Brokhoff entitled his book about Communion, *A Table for Lovers*. At the Lord's table, we renew our love for Jesus and for one another.   —R. C. S.

16. "For I tell you, I will not eat it again until it finds fulfillment in the kingdom of God."

Jesus knew that this was the last Passover meal that would ever be necessary. There was one final Passover Lamb to be slain—"the Lamb of God, who takes away the sin of the world" (John 1:29; cf. 1 Corinthians 5:7). Once he had been slain, there would be no more need for animal sacrifices (Hebrews 9:11-15).

Jesus had spoken often of the *kingdom of God*, or the kingdom of Heaven (Matthew 4:17; Mark 1:14, 15). Most of his listeners did not understand what he meant. They expected the Messiah to sit on a physical throne and restore the political nation of Israel to its past glory. But Jesus knew the true nature of the kingdom of God: it is radically different from all earthly kingdoms. Jesus is its King, and his throne is within the hearts of those who acknowledge his kingship. The kingdom could not be inaugurated until after Jesus' death and resurrection.

Jesus' statement that he would *not eat it again until it finds fulfillment in the kingdom of God* is taken by some to mean that he will not share in this feast again until the "wedding supper of the Lamb" in the heavenly kingdom (Revelation 19:9). Others believe that Jesus was referring to the spiritual union that Christians enjoy with him whenever they celebrate the Lord's Supper. If that is so, then this union was experienced just a few weeks later when the church began on the Day of Pentecost and began to observe the "breaking of bread" (Acts 2:42). Perhaps one should accept a combination of these views: the spiritual union here on earth will be consummated by the visible presence of Jesus in Heaven.

B. OLD MEAL OBSERVED (vv. 17, 18)

17. After taking the cup, he gave thanks and said, "Take this and divide it among you.

The fact that Luke mentions another cup later in connection with the "new covenant" (verse 20) indicates that the *cup* that Jesus took at this point was one of the cups included in the Passover observance. In a traditional Passover meal, there were four occasions when the participants would drink a cup of the fruit of the vine. Each cup had a distinctive theme, often accompanied by prescribed words, songs, and prayers. The first two cups were taken prior to the main meal, and the latter two cups were taken after the meal. The third cup was called the Cup of Redemption, which celebrated Israel's redemption from bondage in Egypt.

This third cup may have been the cup that Jesus now told his disciples to *divide* among themselves. He would then have used the fourth and final cup to institute a new kind of memorial to a new kind of redemption (verse 20). However, others believe that the cup of this verse was the final cup and that the cup of verse 20 was a different cup to mark a new and different memorial.

18. "For I tell you I will not drink again of the fruit of the vine until the kingdom of God comes."

Jesus' promise that he would *not drink . . . until the kingdom of God comes* is similar to his promise about eating, explained under verse 16.

C. NEW MEAL INSTITUTED (vv. 19, 20)

19. And he took bread, gave thanks and broke it, and gave it to them, saying, "This is my body given for you; do this in remembrance of me."

The coming of the kingdom was contingent on the willingness of the King of kings to become the sacrificial Lamb of God, an atoning sacrifice for the sins of all humanity (1 John 2:2). This sacrifice was what Jesus proceeded to call attention to by instituting a new kind of memorial feast. He *took bread* (the unleavened bread that remained from the Passover observance), once again *gave thanks*, *broke it*, and *gave it to* his disciples. He stated that the bread was his *body given for* them. Previously Jesus' followers had heard him refer to himself as the "bread of life" (John 6:48). They had heard him tell a great crowd that they should eat his flesh (John 6:53-58). Although the disciples probably did not grasp the true significance of Jesus' words, they knew that he was speaking metaphorically and not advocating cannibalism. What they did not realize was how quickly that body would be taken from them and be torn and broken—at the cross.

Jesus has instructed his followers to remember him by means of breaking bread and drinking of the fruit of the vine. This act is not magical or mystical. It simply uses common—yet significant—items to remind us of Jesus and his love.

20. In the same way, after the supper he took the cup, saying, "This cup is the new covenant in my blood, which is poured out for you.

Jesus then gave a *cup* to his disciples, instructing them to use it to remember his *blood*, which would be *poured out* for them. That cup and its contents represented a *new covenant*—a new stage in God's dealings with humanity. People would no longer anticipate the coming of the Messiah. They would look back on his coming as a historical event and celebrate his death. The blood of Jesus, having the power to cleanse from sin (1 John 1:7), must not be forgotten. The fruit of the vine forever serves as an apt reminder.

II. THE BETRAYER (LUKE 22:21-23)

A. WARNING (v. 21)

21. "But the hand of him who is going to betray me is with mine on the table.

Jesus knew of Judas's treachery. At this point he told the disciples that one of them would *betray* him; but in the tension and confusion of the hour, the disciples did not discern the identity of the schemer. Imagine the sorrow in Jesus' heart as he spoke of how one who was eating with him would soon betray him!

Here is where it is apparent that Luke's account of the events in the upper room is not chronological. The other Gospels give the indication that Judas was not present at the institution of the Lord's Supper (in other words, that the act of identifying the betrayer occurred before the institution of the Supper). It seems that Luke's record is topical and that he placed the institution of the Supper at the beginning for emphasis.

B. WOE (v. 22)

22. "The Son of Man will go as it has been decreed, but woe to that man who betrays him."

Jesus' death was part of a plan set in place by his Father, and this plan was about to come to fruition. But Jesus made it clear that this did not excuse the actions of his betrayer. Betraying the *Son of Man* was not an act to be taken lightly.

C. WORRY (v. 23)

23. They began to question among themselves which of them it might be who would do this.

Immediately the disciples expressed their dismay over Jesus' unexpected announcement. None of them believed himself capable of such a hideous act. Judas, of course, knew he was "that man" (v. 22), though none of the other disciples realized the significance of his sudden departure (John 13:21-30).

III. THE DISPUTE (LUKE 22:24-30)

A. CONFUSION (v. 24)

24. Also a dispute arose among them as to which of them was considered to be greatest.

Even now, with the cross just hours away, Jesus' disciples still had their heads in the clouds. They were still being influenced by the notion that Jesus would overthrow the Romans, sit on a throne in Jerusalem, and rule the nation of Israel. Then they, his loyal followers, would have positions of power and prestige in his kingdom. Because they were confused about the nature of Jesus' kingdom, they were confused also about the path to greatness in that kingdom.

B. COMPARISON (v. 25)

25. Jesus said to them, "The kings of the Gentiles lord it over them; and those who exercise authority over them call themselves Benefactors.

Jesus tried to show the disciples a different way to greatness by contrasting his way with the world's concept of greatness. The disciples knew how the *Gentiles* (or pagan peoples) became powerful: they would *exercise authority over* their subjects by forcing them into submission. Sometimes they tried to compliment themselves for their treatment of their subjects by referring to themselves as *Benefactors* of the poor and underprivileged. Such self-promoting leadership was the very type exhibited by the disciples as they bickered over who was the greatest.

C. CHALLENGE (vv. 26, 27)

26. "But you are not to be like that. Instead, the greatest among you should be like the youngest, and the one who rules like the one who serves.

Jesus rejected the worldly path to greatness and instructed the disciples in a better, godly way. In the Jewish home, the oldest son inherited a larger portion of the father's estate than any of the younger children. The disciples were all acting like oldest sons, each claiming that he should have the most prominent position in Jesus' kingdom. Jesus told them to begin thinking like *youngest* sons—those considered least worthy of honor. If any wanted to sit in a chief position, he must become *one who serves.* That is what greatness means in Jesus' kingdom!

27. "For who is greater, the one who is at the table or the one who serves? Is it not the one who is at the table? But I am among you as one who serves.

Here Jesus used another illustration to make his point about greatness. Most people consider the master of the house more important than the one who *serves* him his meals. Such thinking is not the rule in Jesus' kingdom. There the virtue is in serving, not in being served. Jesus himself lived by this principle: *I am among you as one who serves.* John tells how Jesus, on this night, washed the feet of his disciples (John 13:1-15). And in just a few hours he would "give his life as a ransom for many" (Matthew 20:28) in the ultimate act of service.

HERE TO HELP

Near the end of the nineteenth century a New York newspaperman named Jacob Riis (*Rees*) wrote a book entitled *How the Other Half Lives.* It described the deplorable conditions in the slums of New York City, including the vice and crime that occurred there. The book was read by future U.S. President Theodore Roosevelt, who went

WHAT DO YOU THINK?

When Jesus said that one of the Twelve would betray him, Matthew tells us that they all began to ask, "Surely not I, Lord?" (Matthew 26:22). None pointed a finger at another, but instead each looked at himself. We should similarly examine our own lives for evidence of betrayal (1 Corinthians 11:28). How can we do that?

WHAT DO YOU THINK?

Jesus claimed that true greatness is measured in the number you serve, not in the number you command. How have you seen the truth of Jesus' words displayed in life?

[The answer to this question may be generic, focusing on occupations or callings, or your class may be specific. Use each example as motivation to the class to think first of serving, not of being served.]

Borrowing an image from John 13, today's visual suggests one means by which Jesus might have ended the disciples' dispute about greatness.

Who Is the Greatest?
Luke 22:26

PRAYER

Father, help us to reject the standards of the world and to seek to be great in your eyes. Help us to remember Jesus' death when we observe the Lord's Supper, and help us to remember his life and example when we get too wrapped up in becoming great in the eyes of men. Humble us, and remind us how to attain greatness in your kingdom. Thank you for loving us. We ask all things in the name of our King. Amen.

immediately to the newspaper office. When he found out that Riis was not in his office, Roosevelt left a note: "I have read your book, and I have come to help."

It is easy to complain about conditions in society, in the world at large, or in our own city or community. And there are plenty of people who will agree with our pessimistic assessment. But finding the people who are willing to work personally for a better world or a better community is another matter. Only a few are willing to say, "I have come to help."

Jesus did not come to our world simply to point a finger and cite all the wrongs we had done. He came to help. He told his disciples, "I am among you as one who serves." Although Luke does not mention it, by this time in the evening Jesus probably had washed his disciples' feet. It was an act of service that stunned the disciples, but it was only a precursor to his greatest act of service—his death on the cross.

Jesus did more than just lecture about service: he truly *served*. He practiced what he preached.   —R. C. S.

D. COMMENDATION (vv. 28-30)

28. "You are those who have stood by me in my trials.

Jesus spoke of the disciples' devotion to him during his *trials*. He knew that they would soon disappoint him by fleeing from the garden, but in this moment he spoke in gentle, affectionate terms of appreciation.

29. "And I confer on you a kingdom, just as my Father conferred one on me.

The disciples would not sit on earthly thrones, wear crowns, or hold scepters. Instead, they would have the grand privilege of being the first to proclaim the story of Jesus and his glorious *kingdom*. They would tell of the life, death, and resurrection of the King of kings. Yes, they would be great, but on Jesus' terms, not theirs.

30. ". . . so that you may eat and drink at my table in my kingdom and sit on thrones, judging the twelve tribes of Israel."

Jesus' commendation of his disciples concluded with a stirring pronouncement. They would be privileged to *eat and drink* with him in his *kingdom* as he had promised earlier (vv. 16, 18). In addition, they would *sit on thrones* and judge *Israel* in a way they had never imagined. By the preaching of the gospel of Christ, these same men who had gathered with Jesus at this Passover celebration would set a standard by which all people—both Jews (those of Israel) and Gentiles—will be judged. They, through the proclamation of the gospel, would open the doors to the kingdom of Heaven (Matthew 16:18, 19). That took place for the first time on the Day of Pentecost, and it continues today through the preaching of the apostolic message by the church.

CONCLUSION

What makes a person great? In our culture we often equate greatness with being a celebrity. We idolize sports figures and entertainers. Even in the church we can fall into this trap. Everyone knows who the soloist was in the morning worship. How many people know who stayed in the nursery and changed diapers?

No one would deny that we live in a me-first, blow-your-own-horn, climb-over-others-to-get-to-the-top world. Humility is scoffed at; arrogance is admired. Heroic figures are those who tell us how great they are rather than prove it by their lives. Style is more important than substance. Public relations is the name of the game.

John tells us of another event that happened in the upper room. During the evening, Jesus took a towel and a basin of water and performed the most menial task of a household servant. He washed the feet of the disciples (John 13:4, 5). Think of it: the most powerful person ever to walk on earth was kneeling to wash the dirty feet that would soon carry away the men who would desert him when he needed them most. Such is the nature of true greatness.

THOUGHT TO REMEMBER

True greatness is attained by following Jesus.

Discovery Learning

This page contains an alternate lesson plan emphasizing learning activities. Classes desiring such student involvement will find these suggestions helpful. The next page is a reproducible activity page to further enhance discovery learning.

LEARNING GOALS

After this lesson students should be able to:

1. Give the details surrounding Jesus' institution of the Lord's Supper.

2. Contrast the attitude required for a proper observance of the Lord's Supper with the attitude that the disciples displayed on this occasion.

3. Write a Communion meditation that incorporates Jesus' call to humility in discipleship.

INTO THE LESSON

Distribute copies of the following agree-disagree exercise, and ask your students to circle the response that best reflects their opinion for each statement.

1. The Lord's Supper is primarily a remembrance of Christ's death. Agree or disagree?

2. The Lord's Supper reminds us to be like Christ in our daily lives. Agree or disagree?

3. A servant's attitude is necessary to observe the Lord's Supper properly. Agree or disagree?

4. Few Christians exhibit a proper attitude when they observe the Lord's Supper. Agree or disagree?

5. It is impossible for a person to take the Lord's Supper properly if he is conceited or hates another person. Agree or disagree?

Discuss your students' answers briefly. Then tell your class that today's lesson will deal with the attitude required to observe the Lord's Supper properly.

INTO THE WORD

Hand out copies of the matching test below. Instruct your students to match each event with its corresponding Scripture reference by looking up the references in the Bible. Correct answers are indicated in parentheses.

____ 1. Peter and John prepare an upper room and the Passover meal. (c)

____ 2. Jesus and the Twelve observe the Passover. (f)

____ 3. Jesus washes the disciples' feet. (b)

____ 4. The traitor is identified. (d)

____ 5. The disciples argue over greatness. (g)

____ 6. Jesus predicts Peter's denial. (e)

____ 7. Jesus institutes the Lord's Supper. (a)

a. Luke 22:17-20   b. John 13:1-20   c. Luke 22:7-13
d. Luke 22:21-23   e. Luke 22:31-34   f. Luke 22:14-16
g. Luke 22:24-30

When your students complete the test, review the correct answers. As you do, you will want to discuss the circumstances and chronology of the events (they are listed in chronological order) surrounding the inauguration of the Lord's Supper. Discuss the following questions.

1. Luke indicates that Jesus made extensive preparations for this special supper. How should we prepare to take the Lord's Supper? *(Focus on preparing one's heart.)*

2. Read 1 Corinthians 5:7. How is Jesus "our Passover lamb"? What was the purpose of his suffering? *(Jesus delivered us from bondage to sin, as God delivered the Israelites from Egyptian bondage at the first Passover.)*

3. What lesson did Jesus teach by washing the disciples' feet? *(Humility.)* Who usually performed such a task? (See 1 Samuel 25:41.) *(The lowest servant.)* What does that tell us about the nature of leadership in God's kingdom? *(Leadership is best exercised through service.)*

4. How could the disciples argue over greatness after Jesus washed their feet and after he announced that one of them was a traitor? Contrast their attitudes with Jesus'.

5. What is the purpose of the Lord's Supper? *(Jesus said it was to be done in remembrance of him, v. 19. It is an expression of love and gratitude to him and an expression of unity with his body.)*

INTO LIFE

Ask each student to write a brief Communion meditation, using Luke 22:14-30; John 13:1-20; 1 Corinthians 11:20-32; and Philippians 2:1-11 as source material, on the general subject of discipleship. Students may wish to focus on one of the following themes:

1. It is impossible for a person to take the Lord's Supper properly if he is conceited or hates another person (Luke 22:24-27; 1 Corinthians 11:22; Philippians 2:3).

2. A servant's attitude is necessary to observe the Lord's Supper properly (Luke 22:24-27; John 13:12-17; Philippians 2:1-8).

3. The Lord's Supper reminds us to be like Christ in our daily lives (Luke 22:24-27; John 13:14-16).

Students may work in pairs, if desired. When they have finished, ask volunteers to share their work with the class. Collect the completed meditations for possible use in your congregation's worship services.

Alternatively, you can distribute copies of the reproducible page that follows and have students complete the exercise there.

Your Version of the Last Supper

In Leonardo da Vinci's famous painting, *The Last Supper*, the artist portrays the reaction of the disciples to Jesus' announcement that one of them would betray him. There are, however, many other things about the Last Supper that da Vinci could have emphasized. In the space below, draw your own rendition of *The Last Supper* (you need not be an artist), emphasizing some important point of today's lesson.

DYING ON THE CROSS

LESSON 12

WHY TEACH THIS LESSON?

"Father, forgive them, for they do not know what they are doing" (Luke 23:34). Who was the "them" for whom Jesus prayed? Was it the Roman soldiers, who did not know they were pawns being manipulated by the jealous priests and Pharisees who had demanded Jesus' execution? Was it the Jewish leaders themselves, who did not know they were murdering their own Messiah?

You can debate that issue today if you want—this verse is part of our text. But your lesson will be a success only if your students are led to answer the question as Pogo did in the old comic strip: "We have met the enemy, and he is us." We crucified Jesus, for he died for each one of us. None of us can plead "not guilty." That is what this lesson is all about.

INTRODUCTION

A. THE MAN IN THE WATER

In January of 1982 an Air Florida aircraft taking off from Washington, D.C., on a cold, snowy day crashed into a bridge and plunged into the Potomac River. As television reporters with their camera crews arrived and began to cover the tragedy, they broadcast an event on live television that few who witnessed will ever forget.

By the time rescue efforts could be organized, the plane had virtually disappeared beneath the surface of the Potomac. Most of the passengers either had been killed already or were trapped in the wreckage beneath the water. At the surface of the water, a handful of survivors were in immediate peril of freezing or drowning. It was clear that both the location of the crash and the bitter winter weather were going to make rescue efforts difficult.

Soon a helicopter flew above the survivors bobbing in the icy water. The helicopter crew dropped a flotation device on a tether. Those in the water were either too weak or confused to be lifted into the helicopter, so they were dragged to shore where they were met by medics and others involved in the rescue operation.

As millions watched on live television, a true hero emerged. Whenever the helicopter returned to the survivors and the flotation device was lowered, a man in the water would gather in the device, hand it to another survivor, and help him or her attach it properly. Finally, the only person left in the water was the man himself, who had been so willing to make sure that everyone else was rescued. But when the helicopter returned to get him, he had slipped beneath the surface of the water. This man had died saving the lives of several other people.

B. LESSON BACKGROUND

Jesus' mission was coming to its climax. He had celebrated the Passover with his disciples. He had washed their feet to illustrate the path to greatness in God's kingdom. He had agonized in the garden of Gethsemane, pondering the awful weight of man's eternal destiny. He had suffered the humiliation of illegal trials throughout the night. He had been mocked and spit on. A crown of thorns had been jammed onto his head. He had struggled under the weight of the cross until a man named Simon was pressed into service to carry it to the place of execution.

DEVOTIONAL READING:
LUKE 23:50-56

BACKGROUND SCRIPTURE:
LUKE 23:13-56

PRINTED TEXT:
LUKE 23:33-49

LESSON AIMS

After this lesson each student will be able to:

1. Relate the details of the crucifixion of Christ, according to Luke's account.

2. Explain the significance of the cross in the redemptive plan of God.

3. Praise God for Jesus' atoning death at Calvary.

Feb
18

KEY VERSE

Jesus called out with a loud voice, "Father, into your hands I commit my spirit."

—Luke 23:46

As these events unfolded, Jesus' enemies must have rejoiced. Finally, they thought, they would be rid of the man who had been a thorn in their sides for far too long. In contrast, those who had been followers of Jesus now followed at a distance, viewing the macabre scene and wondering if God would intervene. They did not realize that what was about to transpire just outside Jerusalem was, in fact, God's intervention: Jesus was fulfilling the plan of his Father by giving himself to die for the sins of the world. The world has never seen another such compelling demonstration of love.

I. THE CHRIST (LUKE 23:33-38)

Many kings in history have been willing to put their subjects to death in order to save themselves. King Jesus was willing to be put to death in order to save his subjects. Such is the depth of God's love for us!

A. CRUCIFIED (v. 33)

33. *When they came to the place called the Skull, there they crucified him, along with the criminals—one on his right, the other on his left.*

The Roman soldiers and the men who were to be *crucified* arrived at the *place* of execution, which was known as *the Skull* (Matthew 27:33; Mark 15:22; John 19:17). Matthew, Mark, and John (in the references cited above) also note the Aramaic term for the place, which is "Golgotha." It is unclear whether the name derived from the appearance of the place (perhaps it looked something like a skull) or from the presence of skulls and other bones from the many executions. Both explanations have been suggested.

Crucifixion was a gruesome, torturous way to kill a person. The Romans had "perfected" it to make it especially so. They knew how to carry out a crucifixion so that death came slowly—usually by suffocation as the body sagged beneath its own weight and compressed the lungs. Shock, fatigue, and blood loss complicated the respiratory problem. Death would finally come only when a person could no longer lift himself by pushing on the nails in his feet to straighten his body and thus expand his lungs. To this agony the Son of God submitted himself for you and me.

Jesus was not alone at Calvary. Two other men were also crucified that day. We do not know their names. We know only that they were *criminals*. Matthew and Mark call them robbers (Matthew 27:38; Mark 15:27). Thus the Romans added to Jesus' humiliation by crucifying him between two lawbreakers. The only perfect person in history was treated as a common criminal. This calls attention to the purpose of Jesus' death: to die in the place of sinners. As Paul says, "God made him who had no sin to be sin for us" (2 Corinthians 5:21).

Calvary. CAL-vuh-ree.

centurion. sen-TURE-ee-un.

Gethsemane. Geth-SEM-uh-nee.

Golgotha. GAHL-guh-thuh.

Hades. HAY-deez.

Ishmael. ISH-may-el.

kranion (Greek). kruh-NEE-on.

Magdalene. MAG-duh-leen or
   Mag-duh-LEE-nee.

Pharisees. FAIR-ih-seez.

THE HONOR GUARD

In Greece the Orthodox Church has an interesting custom that it observes on the Saturday before Easter Sunday. A picture of Christ is brought into the church building and used as a symbol of the tomb of Jesus. It is placed in a prominent part of the building and surrounded by flowers. Then four soldiers stand as an honor guard, each at a corner of the picture. Other soldiers take their places when their shift is completed. All day Saturday the honor guard stands at attention beside the picture. Then at midnight there is a great celebration, and early on Easter Sunday morning the same picture is carried through the streets in a great procession accompanied by joyful worshipers.

Jesus, of course, was assigned no "honor guard" when he died. Instead, he was crucified between two robbers. Yet it was actually a mark of honor for Jesus that he should be flanked by sinners in his death, for he came to the world to die for sinners.

While the presence of the robbers may have been intended to shame and degrade Jesus, it was something foreseen hundreds of years earlier: "he . . . was numbered with the transgressors," said Isaiah (Isaiah 53:12). This was just one instance of how, at the cross, the enemies of Jesus engaged in actions and spoke words that were, unintentionally, most appropriate. It was fitting that Jesus should die *between* sinners, for he came to die *for* them.   —R. C. S.

B. COMPASSIONATE (v. 34)

34. Jesus said, "Father, forgive them, for they do not know what they are doing." And they divided up his clothes by casting lots.

We do not know the precise moment at which Jesus spoke these words. Many believe that *Father, forgive them; for they do not know what they are doing* was the first of the seven sayings uttered by Jesus at the cross. It is often assumed that he said this after the cross had been raised. It is possible, however, that these words were spoken even as Jesus was being nailed to the cross.

Whatever the timing, there may be no greater expression of compassion known to man than these words of Jesus. Jesus wanted the men responsible for his present agony to be forgiven—to have the opportunity to repent of their sin and experience his love. Concerning the Jewish leaders, Acts 6:7 records that "a large number of priests became obedient to the faith." Some of the Pharisees became Christians (Acts 15:5), the most notable example being Paul (Philippians 3:5).

The callousness of the Roman executioners is evident from their activity amidst the suffering going on around them. They were playing a game, *casting lots* for Jesus' *clothes*, specifically for his seamless "garment" or tunic (John 19:23, 24). Crucifixion was "business as usual" for them; they hardly noticed the agony of their victims. Their actions, however, fulfilled an Old Testament prophecy (John 19:24; cf. Psalm 22:18).

C. CURSED (vv. 35-37)

35. The people stood watching, and the rulers even sneered at him. They said, "He saved others; let him save himself if he is the Christ of God, the Chosen One."

Some of the Jewish *rulers* journeyed to the site of the crucifixion. They were delighted to see that their strategy for getting rid of Jesus had worked. They *sneered at him* with taunts, implying that if he were the true Messiah, he could *save himself* from this injustice (if it really was injustice). Surely if he were the *Christ of God, the Chosen One*, God would intervene and rescue him. These men did not understand that the very act they were witnessing was what the chosen of God had come to do. *Others* would never be *saved* if Jesus decided to *save himself* from the cross.

36. The soldiers also came up and mocked him. They offered him wine vinegar . . .

Once the crosses had been erected, the job of the *soldiers* was simply to watch the crowd and make sure order was maintained. To pass the time, the soldiers engaged in activities like gambling for the victims' clothes (as we have seen). Sometimes they made sport of those who were dying by playing little jokes on them, and some students believe Luke's mention of offering Jesus *wine vinegar* at this point—soaking a rag or sponge with vinegar and raising it to his mouth on a spear or pole—indicates it was part of the soldiers' mocking. Other students believe that a consideration of all four Gospel accounts suggests that there may have been mixed motives involved in offering the vinegar to Jesus. The vinegar itself appears to have been the same cheap wine used by the soldiers for their own refreshment.

37. . . . and said, "If you are the king of the Jews, save yourself."

WHAT DO YOU THINK?

The Roman soldiers displayed a callous disregard for life when they gambled for the clothing of Jesus. What evidence of a similar callousness do you see in our own society? How can we appeal to such a culture with the love of Christ?

WHAT DO YOU THINK?

Many people taunted Jesus while he hung on the cross, including curious onlookers, religious leaders, and soldiers. Which do you think hurt the most, and why? Whose rejection and/or taunts hurt you the most? What can you do about it?

WHAT DO YOU THINK?

From Matthew 27:44 we know that both robbers at first mocked Jesus. One of them, however, apparently had a sudden change of heart. What do you think changed his mind about Jesus? How can we help hardened unbelievers to make such a dramatic turn?

The soldiers did not concern themselves with Jesus' claim to be the Messiah. They were aware of the title he had been given—*king of the Jews.* They knew something of kings and royalty, and they could see that the man on the cross before them bore none of the usual marks of royalty. To the soldiers Jesus was just another rabble-rouser who ran into trouble with the authorities. That some considered him a king only served as fodder for their mockery.

D. CONFIRMED (v. 38)

38. There was a written notice above him, which read: THIS IS THE KING OF THE JEWS.

The charges against a crucified person were often *written* on a board and placed at the top of the victim's cross. No legal charge had been made against Jesus, so Pilate ordered that the charge presented by the Jews themselves be displayed. This also gave Pilate an opportunity to ridicule the Jews by proclaiming a tortured, dying man to be their king. What Pilate failed to comprehend was that by posting this sign, he was declaring a glorious truth. He had unwittingly confirmed the royal status of Jesus, who was not only the *King of the Jews,* but the "KING OF KINGS AND LORD OF LORDS" (Revelation 19:16).

II. THE CRIMINALS (LUKE 23:39-43)

A. RUDE (v. 39)

39. One of the criminals who hung there hurled insults at him: "Aren't you the Christ? Save yourself and us!"

The selfish motives of this robber are evident. He had heard the claims that Jesus was the *Christ.* His concern, however, was not in acknowledging Jesus as the Anointed One of God; all he wanted was to be freed from the agony of the cross.

B. REPENTANT (vv. 40-42)

40. But the other criminal rebuked him. "Don't you fear God," he said, "since you are under the same sentence?

The other criminal did not share the cynicism of the first one. He *rebuked* the first robber for his words and attitude, asserting that he was hardly in a position to be condemning someone else.

41. "We are punished justly, for we are getting what our deeds deserve. But this man has done nothing wrong."

What did this robber know about Jesus? Judging from his words in verse 42, it is clear that he knew something about Jesus' kingdom. Apparently he was aware also of Jesus' righteous character. He recognized that Jesus was being executed unjustly, whereas he and the other robber were receiving exactly what they deserved.

42. Then he said, "Jesus, remember me when you come into your kingdom."

There is an obvious tone of humility and repentance in the words of this robber. He asked that Jesus *remember* him when his *kingdom* was established. Again, we do not know exactly what concept of the kingdom this man had, but he knew that he wanted to be where Jesus was.

C. REWARDED (v. 43)

43. Jesus answered him, "I tell you the truth, today you will be with me in paradise."

Many have tried to use this robber as an example of how a person today can be saved. All that an individual needs to do, so these students say, is to appeal to Jesus to save him. But we must keep in mind that at this point Jesus was still alive. Hebrews 9:15-17 is quite clear that the will or "new covenant" established by Jesus did not go into effect until his death (as is true of any will). While Jesus was living, he, as the "testator," had every right to declare someone saved since he could read the hearts of men (John 2:25). Thus Jesus could declare that the robber would be with him in paradise. Today our situation is quite different; with Jesus' death, burial, and resurrection having occurred, it is our responsibility as Christians to declare the "terms of pardon" as recorded in the New Testament.

Paradise refers to the temporary abode of the righteous dead. It was a portion of Hades to which Jesus went during the time between his death and resurrection (1 Peter 3:18-20).

III. THE CLIMAX (LUKE 23:44-49)

A. DARKNESS (vv. 44, 45)

44. It was now about the sixth hour, and darkness came over the whole land until the ninth hour.

As noon (*the sixth hour* by Jewish reckoning) approached, *darkness came over the whole land.* It remained until three in the afternoon (*the ninth hour*). It was as if God drew a curtain of darkness to conceal his Son from the evil eyes of those who would torment his body and soul.

45. . . . for the sun stopped shining. And the curtain of the temple was torn in two.

Another astonishing occurrence took place in the *temple.* The *curtain* separating the Most Holy Place from the Holy Place was suddenly *torn in two.* It tore from the top to the bottom, indicating that this was an act of God, not of man (Matthew 27:51). This act symbolized the new accessibility of God to man, for Jesus, by his death, was opening the way for all men to approach God (Hebrews 9:1-8; 10:19-22).

B. DEATH (v. 46)

46. Jesus called out with a loud voice, "Father, into your hands I commit my spirit." When he had said this, he breathed his last.

With one last burst of strength, Jesus *called out with a loud voice,* entrusting his spirit to the *Father.* The dramatic events of that pivotal day had come to a climax. Under a darkened sky, the Son of God had paid the penalty for mankind's sin. The world would never be the same!

STEERING BY THE CROSS

The only constellation that appears on a national flag is a group of stars called the Southern Cross. (You can see it on the flags of Australia and New Zealand.) It is not there just because the constellation is so prominent in their skies, though absent from the skies in the northern hemisphere. It is also there because early explorers in the South Pacific navigated by those stars. They determined the direction that their ships should take by following the Southern Cross.

Like these explorers, we who are Christians navigate our lives by a cross—the cross of Christ. Some choose to steer their lives away from the cross. They find it offensive, irrelevant, or meaningless. But we steer our lives by the cross. We see in the sacrifice of the Lord Jesus a nobility that we try to emulate in our daily living. He died for others; we try to live for others. We steer by the cross, for we see it as God's "plus sign."

Just as the Southern Cross pointed explorers and sailors to a safe harbor, the cross of Christ guides our way to the only truly safe haven—Heaven. As long as we navigate by the cross, we are guaranteed to arrive home safely.   —R. C. S.

C. DECLARATION (v. 47)

47. The centurion, seeing what had happened, praised God and said, "Surely this was a righteous man."

WHAT DO YOU THINK?

Whatever Jesus meant by quoting Psalm 22:1 (see Matthew 27:46; Mark 15:34), he was not left alone by his Father. We know that because he was praying to the Father ("into your hands I commit my spirit") at the moment of his death. What does this say to you about God's presence in your own life during trying times?

Today's visual reminds us that Jesus was in his Father's hands, even at the moment of his awful death.

The *centurion* (a Roman) was probably the man in charge at the crucifixion. He *praised God* and acknowledged that Jesus was *a righteous man*. At what point had the centurion become aware of this truth? We do not know. Perhaps the inexplicable darkness made a convincing impact on him. Perhaps the exchange of words between Jesus and the robber was persuasive. Or perhaps this centurion, who may have seen hundreds or even thousands of men die, took note of Jesus' words and actions and realized that this was no ordinary man.

D. DISTRESS (vv. 48, 49)

48. When all the people who had gathered to witness this sight saw what took place, they beat their breasts and went away.

All crucifixions were gruesome. The crucifixion of Jesus had been accompanied by a series of highly unusual circumstances. Perhaps the sum total of events persuaded some who were present that a terrible injustice had been committed. They *beat their breasts*, or chests, which was a sign of fear, anguish, and grief (Luke 18:13). Then they *went away*—either to their daily activities or, perhaps, to their homes. One wonders how they could return to routine matters after such a spectacle. They knew that the events they had witnessed were unlike any they had ever seen before.

49. But all those who knew him, including the women who had followed him from Galilee, stood at a distance, watching these things.

We know from John's Gospel that some of Jesus' closest followers and his mother stood near the cross as he was dying (John 19:25-27). Others, however, *stood at a distance*. These included some of the *women . . . from Galilee*, one of whom was Mary Magdalene (Matthew 27:55, 56). They were probably among those mentioned in Luke 8:2 and 3, who supported Jesus' ministry.

Most of us have lost loved ones. We know how difficult this is. Try to imagine what it would be like to see a loved one unjustly accused, denied justice, subjected to whipping and mocking, and finally nailed to a cross and displayed before the public. We cannot begin to know the anguish in the hearts of those followers of Jesus who saw these events unfold. The one on the center cross was not just a casual acquaintance. He was their friend. They had seen him gather little children into his lap. They had seen him cry with friends at the death of a loved one. They had witnessed his concern over the hunger of large crowds of people. They knew him as a compassionate, generous, kind, gentle man. Now he was dead, and for many, their hopes and dreams died with him that day. However, as we know, this was only a temporary setback. Three days later the gloom of the cross would be erased by the glory of the empty tomb.

CONCLUSION

The story of the Old Testament patriarch Abraham is familiar to many. Not as familiar, however, is an event that took place after Abraham's death. When Abraham died, a reunion took place. Genesis 25:9 tells us that Isaac and Ishmael buried their father. These men had been separated for approximately seventy-five years (cf. Genesis 17:17; 21:8-14; 25:7). It took their father's death to bring them back together!

God and man are separated by sin. Man is incapable of bridging this enormous gap by himself. But God, in his infinite mercy and grace, sent his own Son to do for us what we could never have accomplished for ourselves. It took a death to bring us together! What happened on Calvary two thousand years ago is still touching lives every day and for all of eternity. "God demonstrates his own love for us in this: While we were still sinners, Christ died for us" (Romans 5:8).

WHAT DO YOU THINK?

Some who witnessed the crucifixion "beat their breasts," presumably in fear or grief. Perhaps these realized the gravity of what they had done. If Jesus was in fact the Christ, what hope could there now be for a world that put him to death? What kind of judgment might God bring on them? For whom is Jesus' crucifixion a fearful thing? Why?

PRAYER

Heavenly Father, keep us mindful of the price of our salvation. May our every word, thought, and action express to you our gratitude for what Jesus has done for us. Rekindle our passion for lost souls. Energize us through the Holy Spirit so that we may be ambassadors for Christ, telling all we meet of the love, compassion, mercy, and grace of him who willingly went to Calvary to die for our sins. In his glorious name we pray, amen.

THOUGHT TO REMEMBER

It took Jesus' death to bring God and us together.

Discovery Learning

This page contains an alternate lesson plan emphasizing learning activities. Classes desiring such student involvement will find these suggestions helpful. The next page is a reproducible activity page to further enhance discovery learning.

LEARNING GOALS

After participating in this lesson, each of your students will be able to:

1. Relate the details of the crucifixion of Christ, according to Luke's account.

2. Explain the significance of the cross in the redemptive plan of God.

3. Praise God for Jesus' atoning death at Calvary.

INTO THE LESSON

Distribute these open-ended statements on paper and instruct your students to complete them.

1. When I think of Jesus dying on the cross, I. . . .

2. If I had been present at Christ's crucifixion, I. . . .

3. If Jesus had not died on the cross, I. . . .

When they finish, ask volunteers to share their work. Tell your class that today's lesson will deal with the significance of Christ's death on the cross.

INTO THE WORD

Give a brief lecture to provide some background, using information in the commentary section and other sources available to you. Note *why* crucifixion was used as a form of execution (to humiliate the victim and deter others from breaking the law) and *how* crucifixion was carried out (several types of crosses were used; the most common was probably the "T" shaped cross; the victim was tied or nailed to the cross). Observe also that victims could survive for days before suffocating or dying of exposure and shock. Emperor Constantine finally ended the practice in the fourth century because of its cruelty.

To explore today's text, divide the class into small groups. Each group is to examine how some of those present at the crucifixion of Jesus reacted to his execution. After reading Luke 23:33-49, each group should write a brief description of the crucifixion from the point of view of one of the following: Jesus, the Jewish people, the religious rulers, the Roman soldiers, Jesus' disciples, and the crucified robbers. After a few minutes have each group report its findings to the class.

Distribute the outline below (if you use the student quarterly, use the proper page in that book for this activity). Use the outline to discuss the reasons for Jesus' death. (Leave blanks in place of the boldfaced words.) Students should fill in the blanks during the discussion.

A. What Did Sin Do to Man?

1. It made him **guilty** of breaking God's law. So, man owed God **payment** in penalty for every sin (Ezekiel 18:20; Romans 2:5-11; 5:12-14; 6:23; James 2:10).

2. It placed a **barrier** between man and God, disrupting **fellowship** between the two (Isaiah 59:2).

3. It left man unable to save himself from the penalty for **sin**. Unless his sins are paid for by someone else, he is **doomed** (Romans 2:12-25; 3:19-26).

B. What Did Jesus' Death Accomplish?

1. His death was an *atoning* or *substitutionary sacrifice.* He took the **punishment** man deserved because man's **guilt** was transferred to him (Romans 3:25; 5:6-8; 2 Corinthians 5:21; 1 Timothy 2:6; Hebrews 2:9; 1 Peter 2:24; 3:18; 1 John 2:2).

2. His death *redeemed* man from **bondage** to sin and paid the penalty owed God (Matthew 20:28; Luke 24:21; Romans 3:24; 8:23; Galatians 3:13; 1 Timothy 2:6).

3. His death *reconciled* man to *God* by breaking down the sin barrier between the two (Romans 5:8-11; 2 Corinthians 5:18-21; Ephesians 2:16; Colossians 1:21, 22).

4. His death *justified* man, so God could declare him *"not guilty"* even though man deserved to die for his sins (Romans 3:26; 5:9, 19).

INTO LIFE

How can we express our thanks for all Christ has done for us? For one thing, we can praise the Father and the Son for their gracious love. For this activity, distribute a hymnal to every student. Ask each group to write its own "Easter cantata," based on the outline above, by selecting a different hymn stanza to illustrate each point, then writing a brief narration to explain the stanza's significance. So, to illustrate Christ's sacrificial death, students might use the second stanza of "Beneath the Cross of Jesus." When the groups finish, ask each to share its work with the class (singing is optional).

OPTION

Distribute copies of the reproducible page that follows. Use one or both of the activities there, either in addition to the activities described here or instead of one or more of them.

Psalm Writing

Using Psalm 100 as a model, write your own psalm praising God for what Jesus accomplished at Calvary.

PSALM 100	YOUR PSALM
1 Shout for joy to the Lord, all the earth. **2** Worship the Lord with gladness; come before him with joyful songs. **3** Know that the Lord is God. It is he who made us, and we are his; we are his people, the sheep of his pasture. **4** Enter his gates with thanksgiving and his courts with praise; give thanks to him and praise his name. **5** For the Lord is good and his love endures for- ever; his faithfulness continues through all genera- tions.	

Nailed to the Cross

Colossians 2:13, 14 says, "When you were dead in your sins and in the uncircumcision of your sinful nature, God made you alive with Christ. He forgave us all our sins, having canceled the written code, with its regulations, that was against us and that stood opposed to us; he took it away, nailing it to the cross."

On the "sign" below, write down some of the sins from your life that God has nailed to the cross. Then praise God in prayer for the forgiveness you have received.

WITNESSES TO THE RESURRECTION

LESSON 13

WHY TEACH THIS LESSON

As a teacher, you share a grand mission with Jesus himself. After his resurrection, he met with the apostles, and "he opened their minds so they could understand the Scriptures" (Luke 24:45). That is what you do each time you teach your class.

The subject today is the resurrection. It is the single most important fact for a Christian to understand and believe. If you can help your class members to be assured of that—even as the apostles were finally led to be—then this class time will have been one of the finest hours you and your class have ever spent!

INTRODUCTION

A. THE NATURE OF CHRISTIAN FAITH

Why do you believe that Jesus of Nazareth is the promised Messiah, the Son of God? Why do you believe that he came forth from the tomb to live again? You may have a hereditary faith—"Grandma believed it, and so do I." You may have a "substitutionary confidence" faith—"the preacher believes it, and if it's good enough for him, it's good enough for me." You may have an uninformed faith—"I don't know why I believe; I just do."

We owe the world something better than such inferior brands of faith as these. The apostle Peter gave this charge to all believers: "In your hearts set apart Christ as Lord. Always be prepared to give an answer to everyone who asks you to give the reason for the hope that you have" (1 Peter 3:15). If we are going to persuade others of the truth of the gospel, our faith needs to be capably defended. We must know what we believe and *why* we believe it.

The resurrection of Jesus is the central event of the Scriptures. Thus our ability to defend that event is of paramount importance. Fortunately, God did not leave us in the dark. He gave us abundant evidence on which our trust can be built. Christian faith is not, as some have suggested, a leap in the dark. Faith is, by God's provision, a walk in the light!

B. LESSON BACKGROUND

The reality of Jesus' death (our topic last week) had settled in on his followers. His body had been hastily laid in a tomb. The burial procedures were not completed because of the time of Jesus' death and the need to place his body in a tomb before the Sabbath began at sundown.

Early on the first day of the week, after the Sabbath had passed, some women went to the tomb to finish the burial procedures. When they arrived, the tomb was opened and empty, and Jesus was not there (Luke 24:1-3). Two angels told the women that he was alive (vv. 4-6). Later Jesus himself appeared to Mary Magdalene (Mark 16:9-11; John 20:11-18) and then to the rest of the women (Matthew 28:9, 10). At some point he also appeared to Peter (Luke 24:34).

DEVOTIONAL READING:
MATTHEW 28:16-20
BACKGROUND SCRIPTURE:
LUKE 24:13-53
PRINTED TEXT:
LUKE 24:33-49

LESSON AIMS

After this lesson the students will be able to:

1. Describe what happened when Jesus appeared to his disciples after his resurrection and how he proved to them that he was alive.

2. Explain why the resurrection of Jesus is crucial to our faith in him as Lord and Savior.

3. Develop a plan (or involve themselves in a program) that will help them become better prepared to present a witness to the risen Christ.

KEY VERSE

And repentance and forgiveness of sins will be preached in his name to all nations. . . . You are witnesses of these things.
—Luke 24:47, 48

Feb
25

LESSON 13 NOTES

That same day two men walked from Jerusalem to the little village of Emmaus, located about seven miles northwest of Jerusalem. As they walked, Jesus joined them, but they did not recognize him. They explained the events that had transpired in Jerusalem over the past few days (Luke 24:14). They told Jesus of the reports of the empty tomb (vv. 22-24). Jesus then explained to the men the Old Testament Scriptures about the suffering and resurrection of the Messiah (v. 27).

When the three men arrived at Emmaus, the two whom Jesus had joined extended their hospitality to him and asked him to join them for a meal. As he broke the bread that they shared, his true identity was revealed to them; then "he disappeared from their sight" (vv. 30, 31).

I. THE MEETING (LUKE 24:33-35)

The events of that first day of the week were, without doubt, confusing and distressing for Jesus' disciples. Were the reports true? The tomb was indeed empty, but did that mean that Jesus was alive? Perhaps his body had simply been stolen. Perhaps all of this was a plot by the Jews to ferret out the true followers of Jesus, arrest them, and charge them with some crime. The disciples desperately needed some firm assurance that the reports they were hearing were true. As they gathered together in secret, they did so in fear (John 20:19).

A. WITNESSES GATHER (v. 33)

WHAT DO YOU THINK?

Following Jesus' death, the eleven and others of Jesus' followers were gathered together in Jerusalem. How does being with other Christians help us in times of grief?

33. They got up and returned at once to Jerusalem. There they found the Eleven and those with them, assembled together.

The two men from Emmaus were so excited about Jesus' appearance to them that they immediately hurried back to Jerusalem. On arriving, they *found* the place where Jesus' followers had *assembled together.*

The Eleven is how the closest disciples of Jesus were known at this point, for Judas had hanged himself (Matthew 27:3-5). The remaining group of eleven is identified by that number, even though Thomas was not with them on this occasion (John 20:24). Jesus would appear to them all a week later and assure Thomas that the testimony of the other disciples was true (John 20:25, 26).

The men from Emmaus apparently knew the place where the disciples were meeting. We can imagine that they could hardly contain their excitement as they hurried to Jerusalem. They knew that rumors were circulating rapidly within the company of Jesus' followers. They could add another piece of evidence to the testimony of those who claimed Jesus was alive!

B. WITNESSES TESTIFY (vv. 34, 35)

WHAT DO YOU THINK?

Read Luke 24:30, 31 to see how Jesus "was recognized by [the men from Emmaus] when he broke the bread" (v. 35). Why do you think this act was significant in their recognition of Jesus? How can people "recognize" Jesus today?

34. And saying, "It is true! The Lord has risen and has appeared to Simon."

The men from Emmaus quickly discovered that others, such as *Simon* Peter, had seen the risen Christ just as they had.

35. Then the two told what had happened on the way, and how Jesus was recognized by them when he broke the bread.

Now it is *the two* from Emmaus who proceeded to tell their exciting news. Yes, they know Jesus is alive, and not just because they have already heard a report of his resurrection. They themselves have seen him! He has walked with them, talked with them, and eaten with them!

Imagine the scene as the disciples looked at each other in wide-eyed wonder. Here was further proof of what had seemed too good to be true. One might suspect the assertions of only one or two people who claimed that they had seen Jesus alive. Now, however, the testimony from credible witnesses was becoming more and more persuasive.

II. THE MASTER (LUKE 24:36-46)

A. DECLARATION (vv. 36-38)

36. While they were still talking about this, Jesus himself stood among them and said to them, "Peace be with you."

With beautiful simplicity the Scripture states that *Jesus himself stood among them.* There is no explanation of how this was done. Most important is the fact that Jesus was there! He addressed his disciples with the usual greeting of *peace.*

37. They were startled and frightened, thinking they saw a ghost.

To say that the men in that room were surprised would be a significant under-statement! Jesus was dead; they had seen him die. They had watched as he was carried to Joseph's tomb and placed in it. Despite reports that he was alive again, to witness his sudden appearance in the middle of a group of people and in a room where the doors were shut (John 20:19) was startling to say the least. Luke tells us that the disciples *were startled and frightened*—so taken aback that they thought they were seeing a *ghost.*

38. He said to them, "Why are you troubled, and why do doubts rise in your minds?

Jesus mildly rebuked the disciples for being *troubled.* Had he not told them on previous occasions that he would be killed and would rise from the dead (Luke 9:22, 44; 18:31-33)? Jesus knew their thoughts and the questions and *doubts* that flooded their *minds.* He attempted to calm their fears even as he had done prior to his death when he told them, "Do not let your hearts be *troubled*" (John 14:1).

B. DEMONSTRATION (vv. 39-43)

39. "Look at my hands and my feet. It is I myself! Touch me and see; a ghost does not have flesh and bones, as you see I have."

To allay the fears of his disciples, Jesus instructed them to examine him closely. They had seen him with their eyes and heard him with their ears; now he told them to use another of their senses—*touch.* No, their eyes and ears were not playing tricks on them. This was not a *ghost* standing before them. A ghost might be seen or even heard, but everyone knew that a ghost had no *flesh and bones.*

40. When he had said this, he showed them his hands and feet.

Jesus also offered the disciples the opportunity to examine *his hands and feet.* There they would find the flesh wounds made by the nails that held Jesus to the cross. John notes that Jesus also permitted them to examine the wound that the spear had made in his side (John 20:20). He wanted the disciples to be com-pletely convinced of his identity. The proclamation of the gospel was going to be entrusted to them. They must be absolutely certain of Jesus' bodily resurrection!

41. And while they still did not believe it because of joy and amazement, he asked them, "Do you have anything here to eat?"

In spite of the evidence before them, the disciples *still did not believe it because of joy and amazement.* We usually think of Thomas as the "doubting disciple," yet certainly the rest of the group required some convincing as well! Perhaps the dis-ciples' joy was tempered by a fear that something might happen to "burst the bubble" and bring them back to reality.

Then Jesus spoke again. He asked for something *to eat.* This provided further proof that he was not a ghost or an illusion. He was there with them in the body that they recognized, and he was hungry.

42. They gave him a piece of broiled fish.

Despite the excitement of the day, the disciples were still in need of nourish-ment. Thus there was food present in this room. The men *gave* Jesus *a piece of broiled fish.*

43. . . . and he took it and ate it in their presence.

WHAT DO YOU THINK?

The disciples "did not believe [that Jesus was alive] because of joy and amazement" (v. 41). In other words, they thought Jesus' presence among them was just "too good to be true"! People may feel the same way about the claims of the gospel. Why? How can we convince them that the claims of the gospel—as great as they are—really are true?

WHAT DO YOU THINK?

The resurrection was confirmed to the disciples a number of times and in a number of ways. For you, which is the most compelling reason to believe in the risen Lord?

Jesus *took* the food that was offered and *ate it in* the disciples' *presence.* (Ghosts could not do this!) What an encouragement to these men to see Jesus eating with them just as he had before!

MEETING FOR EATING

If you ever visit a congregation when the people are having a church dinner, you will often hear someone say, somewhat apologetically, "One thing for sure about this church—we're good eaters." Someone even went so far as to poke fun at such events in a little poem written in fractured English:

> We met and we et.
> And if we hadn't have et,
> We wouldn't have met.

But no one should criticize meeting for eating. Consider how often we find the risen Christ eating with his disciples. He did it at Emmaus. He did it in Jerusalem. He did it when he cooked breakfast by the Sea of Galilee for seven of his followers (John 21:9-13).

Certainly such incidents prove the reality of the resurrection, but they teach us much more than that. Whenever a congregation comes together to eat a meal, something happens that is not visible. There is a spiritual dimension to such gatherings that should never be overlooked.

Compare the church family with the human family. Family mealtimes are important; when families are too hurried to eat together, something important is lost. Opportunities for talking, laughing, and dreaming are wasted. One cannot imagine a family reunion without a time for eating together. One cannot imagine a holiday family gathering without a meal being shared. It expresses togetherness and solidarity.

So it is with the church family. When Jesus ate with his disciples, he underscored the spiritual blessings that come when Christians eat together. Is it any wonder that the most important time in our worship is when we observe the Lord's *Supper* in remembrance of Jesus and with others in God's family?   —R. C. S.

C. DISCOURSE (vv. 44-46)

44. He said to them, "This is what I told you while I was still with you: Everything must be fulfilled that is written about me in the Law of Moses, the Prophets and the Psalms."

As the Master Teacher, Jesus saw this as a teachable moment. He reminded the disciples that he had talked to them about the things that would happen to him. In addition he noted that none of this had happened by accident; all of it was prophesied in what we know as the Old Testament. Here Jesus mentions the three main sections of the Scriptures as first-century Jews divided them—*the Law of Moses* (the Pentateuch), *the Prophets,* and *the Psalms*. The disciples were seeing events that *fulfilled* prophecies that had been *written* hundreds of years before.

45. Then he opened their minds so they could understand the Scriptures.

Jesus knew that there was far more to be done with the disciples than simply validating his resurrection. They needed to *understand* the Old Testament prophecies about him in order to appreciate how the resurrection was God's supreme act of authenticating Jesus as the Messiah.

So Jesus continued to teach his disciples, helping them to *understand the Scriptures* and the plan of God recorded in them. At times it appears that these men did not pay adequate attention to Jesus while he walked the dusty roads of Palestine with them. Now, however, they must have been listening with "new ears." Just a few hours earlier, their Instructor had been lying in a tomb. Now he was with them, enjoying their food and fellowship. He had their undivided attention!

HOW TO SAY IT

Emmaus. Em-MAY-us.
Isaiah. Eye-ZAY-uh.
Magdalene. MAG-duh-leen or
   Mag-duh-LEE-nee.
Pentateuch. PEN-tuh-teuk.

Understanding the Bible is vital to the life of every Christian. By it we learn of God's special interest in mankind. By it we learn about sin and our condemnation because of sin. By it we learn of Jesus and his death for our sins. By it we learn of God's promise of his Spirit to live in us. By it we learn of our eternal home—the place God himself has prepared for his people. Never let your Bible gather dust on a shelf or a coffee table. It is God's love letter to you!

46. He told them, "This is what is written: The Christ will suffer and rise from the dead on the third day.

It was necessary for *Christ* to *suffer*. It had been prophesied in Scriptures such as Psalm 22:1-21 and Isaiah 53. But so had the fact that he would *rise from the dead on the third day*; see Psalm 16:9-11; Isaiah 53:10, 11; and Jonah 1:17 (cf. Matthew 12:40). Jesus had clearly fulfilled these prophecies.

TO BE CONTINUED

Many of us have become deeply involved in watching a television program, hardly aware of the passing of time. Just when it seems that we are reaching a pivotal moment in the action, the TV picture freezes, and at the bottom of the screen appear the words: *To Be Continued*. We realize, to our dismay, that we are going to have to wait another week to find out what happens.

As Jesus was dying on the cross, one of the statements he uttered was, "It is finished" (John 19:30). And certainly that was true in that he had paid the price "in full" for the sins of the world. But there was more to come. The resurrection of Jesus tells us that his death on the cross was not the conclusion of God's work. His plan was "to be continued"—and so it was three days later when Jesus arose.

We are reminded that it is only when we look back at the cross from the vantage point of the resurrection that the cross makes any sense at all. Few people doubt that Jesus died on the cross. Many doubt that he rose from the dead. It is amazing that those who doubt can see any value in Jesus, any helpful lessons from his life, or any relevance in his teachings. But when you include, as you must, the resurrection, then and only then does the story of Jesus become truly good news. Only then do we share in the victory that Jesus secured. We realize that death is not the end for those who trust Jesus; life is "to be continued"—with him!   —R. C. S.

III. THE MISSION (LUKE 24:47-49)

A. MESSAGE (v. 47)

47. ". . . and repentance and forgiveness of sins will be preached in his name to all nations, beginning at Jerusalem.

In addition to predicting events such as the life, death, and resurrection of the Messiah, the Scriptures foretold that these redemptive acts of God were to be accomplished on behalf of *all nations*—not just the Jews. We can see evidence of God's interest in all peoples as early as his promise to Abram: "All peoples on earth will be blessed through you" (Genesis 12:3). The book of Isaiah is full of such prophecies (Isaiah 2:1-4; 19:16-24; 25:6-9; 42:1-4; 49:5-7; 51:4-6; 55:5; 60:1-3; 61:1-9).

B. MESSENGERS (v. 48)

48. "You are witnesses of these things.

Not everyone could know Jesus as those gathered in that room knew him. They had heard his teachings. They had seen him command the forces of nature. They had watched as he brought healing to lives ravaged by disease and affliction, causing the deaf to hear, the blind to see, the lame to walk, and the lepers to be made whole. They had seen Jesus bring the dead back to life. Then they had seen him die. Now they beheld him alive again.

Today's visual recalls some of the events in Jesus' life of which we are "witnesses." Discuss ways to give testimony of Jesus to your community.

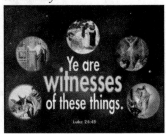

WHAT DO YOU THINK?

What obligation, if any, do believers today have for being witnesses to the resurrection, preaching "repentance and forgiveness of sins . . . to all nations"?

PRAYER

Father, may the testimony of those who saw the resurrected Christ stir us as we read it today. May we appreciate the reality of that miracle more than ever before. Use us to tell others of the joy of new life in Christ. Compel us to proclaim our faith boldly and to touch the lives of others. In Jesus' wonderful name we pray. Amen.

THOUGHT TO REMEMBER

Faith is not a leap in the dark—it is a walk in the light!

To all of these wonderful works—and more—these men were *witnesses*. They would bear the responsibility of telling the world what they had seen and heard.

C. MIGHT (v. 49)

49. "I am going to send you what my Father has promised; but stay in the city until you have been clothed with power from on high."

Jesus knew that he would not be able to stay with his followers indefinitely. He would appear to them a few more times, but forty days after his resurrection he would leave them. He would ascend to his *Father*, as he said he would do (John 20:17), and would return at a time known only to the Father (Matthew 24:36; Acts 1:7, 11). He knew that the instructions he was giving his disciples at this point were crucial to their future success in taking his message to the world.

Jesus' departure was necessary in order for him to *send* the promise of the Father to the disciples. This promise referred to the prophecy of Joel regarding the coming of the Spirit upon God's people (Joel 2:28-32), which would be fulfilled seven weeks later on the Day of Pentecost (Acts 2:1-4). During the night before his death, Jesus had spoken to the disciples of the Spirit's coming (John 14:15-26; 16:7-15). Now he assured them again that, although he would be leaving them, they would never be alone. The Father would empower them through the Spirit to face the exciting, but challenging, days ahead.

Jesus also instructed his followers to *stay in the city* until the Spirit had *clothed* them *with power*. Apparently this did not mean that they could never travel beyond Jerusalem at this point, because Jesus later met with some of his disciples in Galilee (Matthew 28:16-20; John 21:1-3). They were, however, back in Jerusalem by Pentecost.

CONCLUSION

A. EXCLAMATION POINT

The resurrection is God's "exclamation point" in verifying Jesus' identity. The resurrection is proof positive that Jesus is exactly who he said he was. Paul tells us that Jesus was "declared with power to be the Son of God by his resurrection from the dead" (Romans 1:4).

In 1 Corinthians 15 Paul again addresses the importance of the resurrection. There he points out that the resurrection of Jesus is central to the Christian faith. Without it we have no assurance and no hope. If Christ is not alive, death retains its sting. The grave is still frightening. Life after death remains forever in the realm of the unknown. Christian faith becomes an exercise in futility.

B. "I SERVE A RISEN SAVIOR"

These words are taken from a well-known hymn: "I serve a risen Savior, He's in the world today." Part of the words in the chorus of that hymn are as follows: "You ask me how I know he lives? He lives within my heart." While that is a wonderful thought, we need to remember that our faith is not founded on emotional experience. It is based firmly on facts. These facts are clear. Jesus of Nazareth claimed to be the Son of God and did many mighty works to substantiate that claim. He died on a cross. He rose from the dead. Eyewitnesses spoke and wrote of all these events.

We believe in a risen Savior because we have abundant eyewitness testimony on which to base our belief. We serve that Savior because the persuasive testimony of the eyewitnesses has convinced us of the truth of their message. Jesus lived, died, and by the power of God lives again.

We, too, "are witnesses of these things."

Discovery Learning

This page contains an alternate lesson plan emphasizing learning activities. Classes desiring such student involvement will find these suggestions helpful. The next page is a reproducible activity page to further enhance discovery learning.

LEARNING GOALS

After this lesson your students will be able to:

1. Describe what happened when Jesus appeared to his disciples after his resurrection and how he proved to them that he was alive.

2. Explain why the resurrection of Jesus is crucial to our faith in him as Lord and Savior.

3. Develop a plan (or involve themselves in a program) that will help them become better prepared to present a witness to the risen Christ.

INTO THE LESSON

Frank Capra's classic movie *It's a Wonderful Life* concerns a well-intentioned but disillusioned character, George Bailey, who decides to end his life. To convince George not to commit suicide, an angel grants George's wish that he never had been born. Once George sees how many lives are changed for the worse because he was not there to help, he decides that life is worth living after all.

Ask your class to imagine what the world would be like—religiously, morally, politically, and socially—if Jesus had not risen from the dead. Give them paper to record their answers or refer them to the student book, where this exercise is printed.

Option. Distribute copies of the reproducible page that follows, and ask the learners to complete the first exercise.

When the class is finished, discuss the learners' answers or articles, then tell your class that today's lesson will deal with the impact of Christ's resurrection on the world.

INTO THE WORD

You will need to provide some background for today's lesson text. These details are rather familiar to most Christians, so perhaps a question-and-answer session will help you bring out the necessary details. Ask the following questions and see whether members of the class can answer. If not, provide the Scripture references and let the class search out the answers. Provide the Scripture references also when the questions are answered correctly so that those who did not know the answers can look up the Scriptures and read the information for themselves.

1. How do we know that Jesus really died on the cross? (*A soldier pierced his side with a spear, John 19:33, 34; a centurion confirmed his death, Mark 15:44, 45.*)

2. What happened to Jesus' body after he died? (*It was buried in a tomb [Luke 23:50-53] with a stone rolled across the entrance [Matthew 27:60] and a detachment of soldiers guarding it [Matthew 27:62-66].*)

3. Who first saw Jesus after his resurrection? (*Mary Magdalene, Mark 16:9; John 20:11-18.*)

4. Who saw him next? (*The other women who had come to the tomb, Matthew 28:9, 10.*)

5. Two unnamed disciples walked with Jesus to Emmaus, not recognizing him at first. Describe this encounter. (*See Luke 24:13-32.*)

Point out that when we read, "They got up and returned at once to Jerusalem" in our text, the *they* are these two disciples from Emmaus. They arrived back in Jerusalem in time to be present for Jesus' first appearance to the apostles as a group (except for Thomas—see John 20:19-24). Then have a volunteer read Luke 24:33-49.

Ask, "What evidence do you find in this text for the resurrection of Jesus?" Have students call out answers while you write them on the chalkboard. The following should be included: a reported appearance to Simon (i.e., Peter or Cephas, v. 34; see 1 Corinthians 15:5); the witnesses saw and heard Jesus (v. 36); they were invited to see his wounds and touch him to prove he was not a ghost (vv. 37-40); he ate physical food (vv. 41-43); he taught them insights from the Scriptures (vv. 44-47); he commissioned them as witnesses (vv. 48, 49).

Read 1 Corinthians 15:1-19; then ask someone to summarize what Paul says about the significance of Jesus' resurrection. (*It is the foundation of our faith and hope. Without it our faith is useless and we are still lost!*)

INTO LIFE

Ask, "What can we do to share this knowledge with the lost?" Distribute a handout titled, "Action Plan," with two columns marked below the heading. Ask students to list in the first column what your congregation is doing to evangelize the lost. Then ask them to brainstorm other ways to evangelize. Write these suggestions in the second column. Allow learners to choose what they think is the most promising method and make definite plans to carry it out.

If using tracts or brochures is part of your plan, refer students to the second activity on the reproducible page. Work together to make a tract to share the gospel.

Close with a prayer for boldness in telling of Jesus.

Newspaper Article

Imagine the headline below appearing in the *Jerusalem Times* the day after Jesus' resurrection. In the space provided (or on a separate piece of paper), write a brief article to go along with the headline.

Jesus' Tomb Empty! Body Missing!

Officials speculate that disciples stole body.

Why We Believe

Using material from today's lesson, write a tract (a small brochure) to convince an unbeliever of the truth of the resurrection. Use the space below, plus the back of this page, for your work.

Spring Quarter, 2001

Continuing Jesus' Work

(The Book of Acts)

Special Features

Lessons

Unit 1: Beginning in Jerusalem

Unit 2: Witnessing in Judea and Samaria

Unit 3: Spreading the Gospel Into All the World

About These Lessons

The book of Acts, or "The Acts of the Apostles," is the focus of this quarter's lessons. It has also been called "The Acts of the Holy Spirit," for it is clearly the Spirit who is driving the action and not the apostles themselves. One teacher always added a "Chapter 29" to his syllabus. That was the chapter not yet written, for the Spirit is still driving the church to fulfill the mission given by Christ—and he is not finished with us yet.

Mar 4

Mar 11

Mar 18

Mar 25

Apr 1

Apr 8

Apr 15

Apr 22

Apr 29

May 6

May 13

May 20

May 27

Unfinished Business

by Edwin V. Hayden

"Before we proceed with your new proposal, Brother Jones, we need to act on an item of business left over from our previous meeting. We have a motion before us—properly made, seconded, and discussed at some length—but neither accepted nor rejected by a determinate action of the body. We may approve, reject, or table the motion. But we must deal with it in some way before we go on."

The rules of order call for finishing what you have started before you start something else.

WHAT JESUS DID

When God sent his Son into the world, he provided the way to finish what he had started in creation—to bring into fellowship with himself those whom he made in his own likeness and image. Jesus recognized an unchanging responsibility to pursue that purpose to its end: "'My food,' said Jesus, 'is to do the will of him who sent me and to finish his work'" (John 4:34). Within hours of his crucifixion he prayed, "I have brought you glory on earth by completing the work you gave me to do" (John 17:4).

Forty days after that work was completed, Jesus ascended into Heaven. From his exalted position as Lord and Christ, he sent the Holy Spirit to lead and empower his chosen apostles to convey his message, directly and indirectly, to the entire inhabited earth. The book of Acts describes the way in which Jesus' ministry became the ministry of the Spirit-empowered apostles. Our studies for this quarter provide highlights from that account of the Lord's ongoing ministry to all mankind.

BEGINNING IN JERUSALEM

Our four lessons in March develop the theme introduced by Jesus in a final conversation with the apostles and recorded in Luke 24:47: "Repentance and forgiveness of sins will be preached in [Christ's] name to all nations, *beginning at Jerusalem.*"

MARCH

Lesson 1, from Acts 1, deals with "The Promise of the Spirit's Power." This promise was very specific, given to the apostles who remained after the death of Judas. The promise was to be fulfilled "a few days" after it was spoken (Acts 1:5). We can accept, then, with the utmost confidence the record of the words and deeds of the apostles on and after the fulfillment of Jesus' promise at Pentecost. Their teachings must remain the standard by which all other teachings and truth claims are measured.

Lesson 2, "The Holy Spirit Comes in Power," focuses on the opening and closing portions of Acts 2. These tell how the Holy Spirit came upon the apostles in dramatic fashion. They also show the Spirit's power in working through Peter's message (vv. 14-36) to convince and convict sinners. As a result, three thousand hearers were baptized.

Lesson 3, "The Holy Spirit Works With Power," deals with the Spirit's working through the apostles Peter and John, as seen in Acts 3 and 4. First, we read of a miracle of healing in the case of a lame man at the temple gate. Then noted is the response of the "unschooled" and "ordinary" apostles to an official order that they soft-pedal their insistence that the Lord Jesus was not only the source of the healing miracle, but also the only source of salvation for all mankind.

Lesson 4, "Obedient to the Spirit," from Acts 5, reveals an increasing level of opposition to Jesus from the Jewish leaders. Failing in their efforts to silence the apostles by threats and commands, the authorities added imprisonment and beatings. The apostles responded that they were committed to obeying God rather than men. They rejoiced in being counted worthy to suffer shame for the sake of their Lord.

WITNESSING IN JUDEA AND SAMARIA

The lessons for the first four weeks in April follow the pattern of Jesus' directive in Acts 1:8: "You will be my witnesses in Jerusalem, and in all Judea and Samaria."

Lesson 5, "Empowered to Serve," is taken from portions of Acts 6 and 7. It calls attention to the church's care for the needy folk in its midst. As that need grew with the growing church, so did the apostles' need for helpers to relieve them of having to address material concerns. Seven carefully selected men were ordained for the work with the laying on of the apostles' hands. One of them, Stephen, was finally stoned to death following his bold rebuke of the Jews for their rejection and slaying of Jesus.

APRIL

Lesson 6, "Witnessing Beyond Jerusalem" (from Acts 8), follows the preaching of Philip to the people of Samaria and to an Ethiopian on his way home from worshiping in Jerusalem. Philip heard the Ethiopian reading Isaiah's prophecy of God's Suffering Servant. Philip explained the application to Jesus, and when the traveler pointed out available water, Philip baptized him.

Lesson 7, "Proclaiming the Risen Lord," provides a suitable study for our annual celebration of Jesus' resurrection. Part of the printed text comes from Luke 24, where angels at the empty tomb announced the historic event. The other part of the printed text is taken from Acts 9. It highlights the testimony that Saul of Tarsus bore concerning the risen Lord after encountering him on the way to Damascus and being baptized by a disciple named Ananias. Saul astonished observers at Damascus by boldly preaching Jesus as the Christ.

Lesson 8, "Gentiles Receive the Spirit," draws from a part of Acts 10 to tell how the gospel was first proclaimed to Gentiles. As Peter presented the gospel in the house of Cornelius, the Holy Spirit came upon these Gentiles; and they spoke in languages that they had never studied or learned, just as the apostles had done on the Day of Pentecost. Thus assured that these Gentiles were acceptable with God, Peter commanded that they be baptized.

SPREADING THE GOSPEL INTO ALL THE WORLD

Our lessons for the last week in April and the four weeks in May build on Jesus' promise that the Spirit-empowered apostles would become his witnesses "to the ends of the earth" (Acts 1:8).

Lesson 9, "The Church in Antioch," draws from Acts 11 and 13 to tell of the church that was established in Antioch of Syria, where Christ's followers were first called Christians. The church received encouragement from Barnabas, who came from Jerusalem and later brought Saul from Tarsus to join in the work. Eventually, the Holy Spirit directed the church to send Barnabas and Saul to preach in areas not yet reached with the gospel.

Lesson 10, "Mission to Gentiles," draws from Acts 13 to tell of evangelizing done by Saul (now called Paul) and Barnabas in Cyprus and in Antioch of Pisidia. They preached first in synagogues to Jews and to proselytes to Judaism. When certain Jews resisted and opposed the gospel, Paul and Barnabas took their message to Gentiles in the city with such success that Jewish

MAY

jealousy finally drove them to other communities. Believers were left rejoicing in the Spirit.

Lesson 11, "The Jerusalem Conference," is taken from Acts 15. There we read of a problem that arose from the missionaries' work among the Gentiles. Certain Jewish Christians insisted that Gentiles could not be saved without first having been circumcised according to the law of Moses. Paul and Barnabas were asked to discuss the problem with the apostles and elders in Jerusalem, and they did so. After hearing testimonies of the Holy Spirit's work among the Gentiles through the gospel, the gathering concluded that circumcision should not be required of Gentile converts.

Lesson 12, "Responding to Need," draws from Acts 16 and tells of events in Philippi of Macedonia during Paul's second missionary journey. Notable was the conversion of a businesswoman, Lydia, and her household. Also recorded was the conversion of a jailer whom Paul and Silas taught and led to Christ following a dramatic midnight earthquake.

Lesson 13, "Serving With Humility," includes a text from Acts 20. There Paul summarizes his ministry among the Ephesians as he addresses the elders of that church at the close of his third missionary journey. Paul had endured many hardships (and he expected others even more severe), but he desired only to finish the ministry that Jesus had assigned to him. He urged the elders to exercise a similar faithfulness in the face of coming dangers and difficulties.

When Jesus departed this earth, he conveyed his ongoing ministry to the Spirit-led apostles. When the apostle Paul neared the conclusion of his third missionary journey, he conveyed the ongoing responsibility to the elders with whom he had labored. The fulfillment of Jesus' Great Commission—the unfinished business of worldwide evangelism—continues to be conveyed to generation after generation of committed, Spirit-filled Christians, including us.

THE
NEW TESTAMENT WORLD

The Arrangement of Acts

Many outlines have been suggested for the study of the book of Acts. C. H. Turner's suggestion of six chronological "panels" in the book may actually come the closest to Luke's own plan as he laid out the material. Each "panel" covers a particular time and focuses on (though not exclusively) one geographical area. In addition, each one concludes with a distinct summary statement in the text.

Panel One   Acts 1:1—6:7

Location: Jerusalem

Summary: "So the word of God spread. The number of disciples in Jerusalem increased rapidly, and a large number of priests became obedient to the faith."   —Acts 6:7

Panel Two   Acts 6:8—9:31

Location: Judea and Samaria (and Galilee)

Summary: "Then the church throughout Judea, Galilee and Samaria enjoyed a time of peace. It was strengthened; and encouraged by the Holy Spirit, it grew in numbers, living in the fear of the Lord."
          —Acts 9:31

Panel Three   Acts 9:32—12:24

Location: Syria; Gentiles included

Summary: "But the word of God continued to increase and spread."   —Acts 12:24

Panel Four   Acts 12:25—16:5

Location: Asia Minor

Summary: "So the churches were strengthened in the faith and grew daily in numbers."   —Acts 16:5

Panel Five   Acts 16:6—19:20

Location: Gospel introduced in Europe; churches strengthened in Asia Minor

Summary: "The word of the Lord spread widely and grew in power."   —Acts 19:20

Panel Six   Acts 19:21—28:31

Location: The church reaches Rome

Summary: "Paul . . . welcomed all who came to see him. Boldly and without hindrance he preached the kingdom of God and taught about the Lord Jesus Christ."   —Acts 28:30, 31

THE PROMISE OF THE SPIRIT'S POWER

LESSON 1

WHY TEACH THIS LESSON?

While all Scripture has the same stamp of divine inspiration and authority, some texts are more significant in that they are pivotal to our understanding. John 3:16, often called the gospel in a nutshell, is one. Another is Matthew 28:19, 20—the Great Commission.

Today's text contains another such pivotal passage. Another expression of the Great Commission, Acts 1:8 gives the strategy for world evangelism. It will challenge your students to be involved at every level of evangelism and missions: local, regional, and worldwide.

INTRODUCTION

A. EVIDENCE FOR THE DEFENSE

Suppose a friend told you that last year an alien spaceship flew over his house and landed in a nearby field. You are naturally skeptical and begin to ask him some important questions. "What specifically did you see? Who else saw it? Do all the witnesses' stories agree? What evidence do you have? I've never seen a flying saucer, so why should I believe you? And if this thing landed, where is it now?"

Tough questions . . . questions similar to those that Christians sometimes face when they share with others the good news of Jesus Christ. Quite often today, a skeptical world demands that believers have more to offer than just a nice story. Can a person living in the twenty-first century really believe that Jesus of Nazareth is the Son of God who died for our sins and was raised from the dead to ascend to the right hand of Almighty God? The answer is, "Yes, you can believe—and you don't have to abandon your rational mind."

Jesus was well aware of how difficult it can be to lead people to faith, so he prepared a group of specially instructed and empowered men to be his official witnesses to their world and to ours. Today's lesson describes the last stage of that training before the apostles would embark on their worldwide task.

B. LESSON BACKGROUND

Our printed text includes the opening verses of the book known as "The Acts of the Apostles." That title, however, is somewhat misleading. The "acts" and words of only two apostles dominate the book: Peter in the first twelve chapters and Paul in the last sixteen. However, the focus on their ministries gives us an accurate representation of the general witness and preaching of all the apostles.

The author of Acts is Luke, the beloved physician and a co-worker of Paul. Judging from the events recorded at the end of the book (Paul's journey to Rome and his imprisonment there), Luke probably wrote Acts around A.D. 62. Luke's Gospel and Acts form a two-volume presentation of the life of Christ and the first years of Christ's church. In fact, Acts forms a kind of "bridge" from the Gospels

DEVOTIONAL READING:
JOHN 16:7-14
BACKGROUND SCRIPTURE:
ACTS 1
PRINTED TEXT:
ACTS 1:1-14

LESSON AIMS

After this lesson each student should be able to:

1. Describe how Jesus prepared his apostles to be his witnesses.

2. Tell how Acts 1:8 can serve as a model for evangelistic efforts today.

3. Suggest a specific way to act as a witness for Jesus in the coming week.

KEY VERSE

"You will receive power when the Holy Spirit comes on you; and you will be my witnesses in Jerusalem, and in all Judea and Samaria, and to the ends of the earth." —Acts 1:8

to the epistles. Without it, the letters of Paul, James, Peter, John, and Jude would be far more difficult to understand.

I. A PERIOD OF PROOFS (ACTS 1:1-5)

Luke begins by connecting the book of Acts with his Gospel. He takes the last major event in his Gospel (the ascension of Jesus into Heaven, Luke 24:50-53) and expands on it in the opening verses of Acts.

A. INTRODUCTION TO THE BOOK (vv. 1, 2)

1, 2. In my former book, Theophilus, I wrote about all that Jesus began to do and to teach until the day he was taken up to heaven, after giving instructions through the Holy Spirit to the apostles he had chosen.

The *former book* refers to Luke's Gospel. Both the Gospel and Acts are addressed to the same individual, *Theophilus*. Who was he? Since Luke describes him by the title "most excellent" in Luke 1:3, Theophilus was probably a Gentile who was a high official in the service of Rome. He may have been Luke's "patron" in writing these books. Apparently he had received some instruction about Jesus, and Luke's carefully researched Gospel reinforced the reliability of all he had heard (Luke 1:1-4). Perhaps Theophilus was considering becoming a Christian or was a new believer whom Luke wanted to encourage in the faith.

Luke says his Gospel told how Jesus' ministry *began* until he ascended into *heaven;* Acts tells how Jesus' ministry continued after his ascension through his *apostles* and his church. Notice that Luke emphasizes Jesus' actions by putting *to do* before *to teach.* The apostles' preaching in Acts focused on Jesus' miracles, including his death for us and his resurrection, rather than his ethical teaching. The gospel that saves us centers on what Jesus did (1 Corinthians 15:1-4).

B. EVIDENCE OF THE CHRIST (v. 3)

3. After his suffering, he showed himself to these men and gave many convincing proofs that he was alive. He appeared to them over a period of forty days and spoke about the kingdom of God.

One matter about which the apostles had to be utterly convinced was that Jesus had overcome death. In fact, Jesus went out of his way to make sure that the apostles had all the *proofs* they needed. So he invited them to look at his nail marks and spear wound, to touch him, to give him food to eat, and even to thrust their hands into his wounds (Luke 24:37-43; John 20:27). With such a continual stream of evidence that Jesus was alive again, the apostle John could say that the apostles' message was based on what they had heard, seen, and handled concerning the "Word of life"—that is, Jesus (1 John 1:1-3).

The subject of Jesus' post-resurrection teaching was the *kingdom of God,* just as that had been the subject of his public ministry before (Luke 4:43). As described in the Lord's prayer, God's kingdom is present when those who are his subjects do his will here on earth as it is done in Heaven (Matthew 6:10). With the establishment of Jesus' church on the Day of Pentecost, the *kingdom of God* describes both the church's present identity and its future goal.

C. BAPTISM OF THE SPIRIT (vv. 4, 5)

4. On one occasion, while he was eating with them, he gave them this command: "Do not leave Jerusalem, but wait for the gift my Father promised, which you have heard me speak about.

On one occasion, Jesus *was eating with* his apostles. He warned them not to go their separate ways, as they may have done earlier during this forty-day period

(John 21:1-14). Instead, they were to stay together in *Jerusalem* and *wait for the gift his Father promised*, which, as the next verse shows, referred to the coming of the Holy Spirit. The Spirit was not a new subject to the apostles; they had *heard* Jesus *speak* of him on the night before his crucifixion (John 14:16, 17, 26; 15:26, 27).
5. For John baptized with water, but in a few days you will be baptized with the Holy Spirit."

This verse calls to mind *John* the Baptist's prophecy of how Jesus' ministry would supersede his own (Luke 3:16). People can administer water baptism— whether John, the apostles, or any Christian. But only Jesus can immerse (the meaning of the word *baptize*) people *with* (or "in") *the Holy Spirit.*

Baptism in the Holy Spirit is mentioned only seven times in the Bible. The first four are the Gospel accounts of John the Baptist's prediction that the one coming after him would baptize with the Holy Spirit (Matthew 3:11; Mark 1:8; Luke 3:16; John 1:33). The next occurrence is our text in Acts 1:5. Jesus' comment here points directly to the Spirit's filling of the apostles at Pentecost (Acts 2:4). The sixth reference is found in Acts 11:16, where Peter connects the Lord's promise of the Spirit's filling with events at the household of Cornelius as well as with the filling of the apostles "at the beginning" (Acts 11:15). Thus the baptism in the Spirit is historically connected with just two events—the filling of the apostles at Pentecost and the filling of Cornelius's household. These two events mark the first gospel presentations to the Jews and then to the Gentiles.

The seventh and final verse describing a Spirit baptism is found in 1 Corinthians 12:13. Here Paul notes that all Christians have been baptized "by one Spirit into one body." (The Greek word that is translated "by" is the same word that is used in the other six passages, where it is translated "with.") Here, however, Paul is not discussing the Spirit baptism that Jesus administered. Instead, he is talking about the unity of the church based on the fact that all Christians have been "baptized . . . into one body." Given the fact that there is only "one baptism" (Ephesians 4:5), it seems best to understand 1 Corinthians 12:13 as a reference to the "gift of the Holy Spirit" that accompanies the baptism in water that all Christians are to experience (Acts 2:38). Biblically, then, the promise of Jesus' baptizing in the Spirit is applied to only two important occasions in the book of Acts.

The apostles had to wait ten days for the Spirit's coming. We know this because Jesus was with them after his resurrection for forty days (v. 3) and the Spirit came at Pentecost—a feast held fifty days after the Passover celebration during which Jesus died and rose again.

II. A PROMISE OF POWER (ACTS 1:6-11)

A. TIME OF THE KINGDOM (vv. 6, 7)

6. So when they met together, they asked him, "Lord, are you at this time going to restore the kingdom to Israel?"

The apostles' question was not unreasonable. Jesus had been teaching them about the *kingdom* of God (v. 3) and he had promised the coming of the Holy Spirit, which Israel had always associated with the restoration of its greatness as an independent nation (Ezekiel 36:22-28). In the first century, many believed that this restoration would be accompanied by the overthrow of the Roman forces who occupied the country.

Throughout Jesus' ministry the apostles had been interested in becoming leaders in the restored kingdom of which he spoke (Matthew 20:20-28; Luke 22:24-30). Their interests, however, had been tainted by the popular thinking. Even now, with Jesus' death and resurrection having taken place, the apostles'

what promises do you await fulfillment with the assurance that the promises came from Jesus?

WHAT DO YOU THINK?

The lesson writer says the apostles' understanding of the kingdom "had been tainted by the popular thinking." In what ways are modern Christians' ideas "tainted by the popular thinking" of our day? How can we prevent such influence from corrupting our views?

question revealed that they still held certain misunderstandings about what Jesus had taught them.

7. He said to them: "It is not for you to know the times or dates the Father has set by his own authority.

Jesus told the apostles that information about God's timetable was not meant for them. Such knowledge was not necessary for the apostles to have in order to complete their mission. In fact, such knowledge is reserved by God *the Father* for himself (Mark 13:32). The focus of Jesus' teaching about the end *times* is not to provide us with a handy chart outlining when and how he will return to reign over all; his main concern is that we be active and faithful servants, ready for the Master to return at any moment (Mark 13:33-37).

B. POWER OF THE WITNESSES (v. 8)

8. But you will receive power when the Holy Spirit comes on you; and you will be my witnesses in Jerusalem, and in all Judea and Samaria, and to the ends of the earth."

Instead of giving the apostles a timetable, Jesus gave them a task: he told them that they were to be his *witnesses* to the entire world. He also assured the apostles that the Spirit's coming would give them the *power* that they would need to be effective witnesses.

What power did Jesus mean? At least three types are indicated in the Bible. One power that the Spirit gave the apostles was the ability to accurately recall and proclaim all that Jesus taught them during his three and a half years of public ministry. Furthermore, the Spirit would reveal to them any additional truths as they would need them (John 14:26; 15:26, 27; 16:13-15). A second witness power given to the apostles was the ability to perform attesting signs and wonders to confirm that their message came from God and was true (Acts 2:43; 5:12; 2 Corinthians 12:12).

The third power that accompanied the apostles' preaching was the working of the Holy Spirit on the hearts of the hearers of the gospel to convict them of their sin and of their need for a Savior (John 16:7-11). This power is still available whenever we share the gospel with others.

This verse may be considered a "key" that "unlocks" the development of the rest of the book of Acts. Jesus told his disciples to fulfill their task in three stages: in *Jerusalem* (as told in Acts 1-7), in *Judea and Samaria* (chapters 8-12), and throughout the known world (chapters 13-28). This pattern for evangelism is one that all of us can use; we can begin with reaching those close to us even as we keep *the ends of the earth* as our ultimate goal.

SHARING GOOD NEWS

Where should a single, eighty-one-year-old man go in search of a wife? Apparently it depends on what his mother thinks! An Associated Press story datelined in Corbeil, Ontario, a few years ago offered an interesting perspective on how to find a suitable marriage partner.

At the time the story was printed, the gentleman in question had a 117-year-old mother who believed it was important for her son to have a good wife and some kind of social life. "Mom" lived in a home for senior citizens. She made sure that all the "younger" women in the home were aware of some good news: her son was a fine man who would make some woman an excellent husband!

You have to admire this woman's zeal. She had some good news, and she began spreading it to anyone who would listen. She started where she was and took the message to the ends of her limited universe!

Jesus directed his apostles to take much the same approach in spreading the gospel. They were to start where they were and not stop until they had spread the

WHAT DO YOU THINK?

Acts 1:8 is frequently used as a model for evangelism. Suggest some specific strategies for testifying of Christ in each of the four levels mentioned: local (Jerusalem), regional (Judea), national (Samaria), and global (the ends of the earth).

[Here is a chance to get very practical with the lesson. What specific needs can your class address in your community? What about the larger region around you—can you support a new church nearby, perhaps in the inner city, or maybe in a fast-growing suburb? Can you sponsor evangelistic efforts on foreign soil? How about a mission trip by your class or some members of your class and others in the church?]

This map in the Adult Visuals kit will give your students a visual representation of the spread of the gospel in the book of Acts.

message to "the ends of the earth." We Christians, both individually and collectively (as the church), have not really fulfilled the Great Commission until we have evangelized our own "Jerusalems" and have also found some means of helping to spread the gospel to the far corners of the earth.   —C. R. B.

C. CERTAINTY OF JESUS' RETURN (vv. 9-11)

9. After he said this, he was taken up before their very eyes, and a cloud hid him from their sight.

As he had foretold, Jesus now left the earth to return to his Father (John 16:28). The *cloud* into which he ascended may have been simply an ordinary cloud that finally *hid him from* the apostles' view. However, it is also possible that this was the cloud of glory associated with the presence of God in the Old Testament and with Jesus at his transfiguration (Exodus 40:34; Mark 9:7).

10. They were looking intently up into the sky as he was going, when suddenly two men dressed in white stood beside them.

The *two men* who *stood beside* the apostles are not specifically identified, but their sudden appearance and the fact that they were *dressed in white* (cf. Matthew 28:3; John 20:12) leave little doubt that they were angels.

11. "Men of Galilee," they said, "why do you stand here looking into the sky? This same Jesus, who has been taken from you into heaven, will come back in the same way you have seen him go into heaven."

The gentle angelic rebuke seems to say, "Why are you staring at the sky? Unlike what happened at his transfiguration, Jesus will not rejoin you when the clouds roll back. But he will return! Until he does, remember: you have his orders to carry out!"

The promise to the apostles (and to us) is that *this same Jesus* will return *in the same way* he left: personally, visibly, bodily, unexpectedly, and gloriously. The early Christians lived with a joyous expectation of Jesus' imminent return. This promise encouraged them as they moved out to win as many as possible to his kingdom before he came again. Our expectation of Jesus' coming should do the same for us, for this is certain: every day we are closer to his return.

"BECAUSE IT IS THERE"

Many will recognize the words, "Because it is there," as the answer given by George Mallory, the famous English mountain climber, when he was asked why he wanted to climb Mount Everest. On his third attempt to scale the mountain, in 1924, Mallory was last seen moving toward his goal before a cloud enfolded him about eight hundred feet below the summit.

It is not known whether Mallory conquered Everest before Sir Edmund Hillary and Tenzing Norgay (who succeeded in 1953). The latter pair can prove their feat by documentary evidence, including the photographs they took while on the peak. Even when the remains of Mallory were found in 1999 approximately two thousand feet below the summit of Everest, the question remained unanswered. A broken rope about his waist and a fractured leg indicate that he died in a fall. His camera (which might have provided evidence of his having reached the summit) was never found.

Jesus has not been seen since he ascended into a cloud in the Judean sky nearly two thousand years ago. However, unlike George Mallory, the fact of Jesus' success in achieving his life's mission is attested to by a host of eyewitnesses whom he had instructed in the meaning of his life, death, and resurrection. Their testimonies, recorded in Scripture, give us assurance of the trustworthiness of the Christian message. We can trust what those witnesses say "because they were there."

—C. R. B.

HOW TO SAY IT

Alphaeus. Al-FEE-us.
Bartholomew. Bar-THAH-luh-mew.
Cornelius. Cor-NEEL-yus.
Matthias. Muh-THIGH-us.
Samaria. Suh-MARE-ee-uh.
Theophilus. Thee-AHF-ih-luss.
Zealot. ZEL-ut.

VISUALS FOR THESE LESSONS

The small visual pictured in each lesson (e.g., page 240) is a small reproduction of a large, full-color poster included in the Adult Visuals packet for the Spring Quarter. The packet is available from your supplier. Order No. 392.

THOUGHT TO REMEMBER

Christian witnesses confirm their testimony by the way they live and by the way they die.

WHAT DO YOU THINK?

Early disciples "joined together." How can such unity be achieved today? What can you do to promote it?

DAILY BIBLE READINGS

Monday, Feb. 26—The Promise of the Holy Spirit (Acts 1:1-5)

Tuesday, Feb. 27—The Ascension of Jesus (Acts 1:6-11)

Wednesday, Feb. 28—Jesus Appoints the Twelve (Mark 3:13-19)

Thursday, Mar. 1—The Acts of the Apostles Begin (Acts 1:12-20)

Friday, Mar. 2—The Voice of the Lord (Psalm 29)

Saturday, Mar. 3—The Suicide of Judas Iscariot (Matthew 27:3-10)

Sunday, Mar. 4—Matthias Chosen to Replace Judas Iscariot (Acts 1:21-26)

III. A PRAYER OF PREPARATION (ACTS 1:12-14)

A. RETURNING TO THE CITY (v. 12)

12. Then they returned to Jerusalem from the hill called the Mount of Olives, a Sabbath day's walk from the city.

Luke's Gospel records that the apostles had followed Jesus out of Jerusalem toward Bethany, which is just over the crest of the Mount of Olives (Luke 24:50, 51). After Jesus ascended to Heaven, the disciples returned to the city with great joy and anticipation (Luke 24:52, 53). Their journey was no farther than Jews were allowed to travel on a Sabbath—about three quarters of a mile.

B. GATHERING TO PRAY (vv. 13, 14)

13. When they arrived, they went upstairs to the room where they were staying. Those present were Peter, John, James and Andrew; Philip and Thomas, Bartholomew and Matthew; James son of Alphaeus and Simon the Zealot, and Judas son of James.

This "witness list" includes those who had once fled into the night when Jesus was arrested. Now they waited eagerly to proclaim publicly their Lord and Savior. Soon the name of Matthias will be added to this list to replace the betrayer, Judas (Acts 1:26).

14. They all joined together constantly in prayer, along with the women and Mary the mother of Jesus, and with his brothers.

Besides the apostles, the women who had followed Jesus during his ministry and Jesus' brothers are mentioned. This is the last New Testament reference to Mary the mother of Jesus. Just as she appeared at the beginning of Luke's Gospel (Luke 1:26, 27), she appears here at the beginning of the church. Jesus' brothers (more accurately, half-brothers) were James, Joseph, Simon, and Judas (Matthew 13:55). They had not believed in their brother before he was crucified (John 7:5). But apparently, when the resurrected Jesus appeared to one of them (James, 1 Corinthians 15:7) their doubts were transformed into faith. James became an important leader in the Jerusalem church (Acts 15:13; cf. Galatians 2:9).

As Luke leaves this group of believers waiting for the promise of the Spirit, he notes that they all joined together (they were united in a common purpose) constantly in prayer. Their attitude does not appear to be one of agonizing and pleading for the Spirit to come. Instead, they appear certain that Jesus' promise would be fulfilled, leaving them filled with courage, expectancy, and joy. Christ's witnesses could hardly wait to begin the grand task of proclaiming the living Lord.

CONCLUSION

While none of us can be witnesses of the resurrection in the same way that the apostles could, each of us can give a testimony for Jesus in other ways. We can share with those who do not know Jesus the good news based on the apostles' witness. We can also share how Jesus has changed our lives and given us new hope and joy in his grace and forgiveness. We can show how Jesus can change a person's character to become like his own by demonstrating the fruit of the Spirit.

What all of this comes down to is this: we witness of Christ through the total commitment of our lives to serve him and further his kingdom wherever we are. It is interesting that by the end of the New Testament, the word for "witness" had taken on an additional meaning: it described a person willing to give up his life for his faith in Jesus (Revelation 2:13). This has come into our language as the word martyr—one whose witness to Jesus is signed in blood.

Whether or not we are called to give testimony in this way, may we all be faithful witnesses of Jesus as we await his return.

Discovery Learning

This page contains an alternate lesson plan emphasizing learning activities. Classes desiring such student involvement will find these suggestions helpful. The next page is a reproducible activity page to further enhance discovery learning.

LEARNING GOALS

After this lesson each student will be able to:

1. Describe how Jesus prepared his apostles to be his witnesses.

2. Tell how Acts 1:8 can serve as a model for evangelistic efforts today.

3. Suggest a specific way to act as a witness for Jesus in the coming week.

INTO THE LESSON

To introduce today's lesson, use the true-false quiz below. Allow a few minutes for the learners to complete the quiz; then discuss their answers. (Two of these statements will require more information than can be gleaned from the Bible text alone—numbers 5 and 7. Use the commentary section to answer these, as they provide helpful background for the students.)

1. Jesus told his disciples not to leave Jerusalem until the Day of Pentecost. *(False, v. 4.)*

2. The Great Commission is given in Acts 1:8. *(True.)*

3. God selected Matthias to replace Judas as one of the twelve apostles. *(True, vv. 24-26.)*

4. Luke identifies himself as the author of Acts. *(True, v. 1.)*

5. Theophilus may have been the patron who sponsored the writing of Luke and Acts. *(True.)*

6. The names of the twelve apostles are given in Acts 1. *(True, v. 13—plus Matthias, v. 26.)*

7. "The Acts of the Apostles" is a good title for Luke's second book. *(False, see p. 237.)*

8. After the resurrection, the apostles finally understood the kingdom of God. *(False, v. 6.)*

9. There were three thousand disciples with the Twelve in Acts 1. *(False, v. 15.)*

10. Jesus appeared after his resurrection over a period of fifty days. *(False, v. 3.)*

INTO THE WORD

Have your students work in small groups to outline the first fourteen verses of Acts. Encourage each group to read the text at least twice, list the main idea in each verse or paragraph, and then try to connect the ideas with an acrostic (the first letter of each point spells a word) or an alliteration (each title begins with the same letter). For example, steps 2 and 3 might produce:

1-3	Acts Introduced
4-6	Await the Holy Spirit
7, 8	All the World
9	Ascension
10, 11	Angelic Message
12-14	Apostles at Prayer

OPTION

Use the reproducible activity "Newspaper Article" from the next page to explore the details of the lesson text. Actually, this could be a continuing project throughout the quarter to help learners explore the text in a fun and refreshing way.

INTO LIFE

OPTION 1: LETTER WRITING

Almost every church has members who are living away from home attending a college or university. A letter from a concerned Christian back home would be welcome mail.

Bring paper, envelopes, stamps, and addresses to class. (The church secretary or the students' mothers can help with the addresses.) Ask each class member to write a letter to a college student explaining why the testimony of God's chosen witnesses is a better foundation for our faith than an individual believer's personal religious experience.

OPTION 2: MEMORIZATION

Encourage the learners to memorize Acts 1:8 during the class period. Select one of the following methods or use another of your own choosing.

1. Read the verse aloud several times. Then have all Bibles closed and ask each person to take a turn saying one word of the verse until the whole has been recited.

2. Write the verse with the reference on a chalkboard or marker board. Have the class read the verse aloud together a couple of times; then erase one or two words. Continue erasing words one or two at a time until nothing remains and everyone is quoting the verse from memory.

OPTION 3: MOST WANTED LIST

Use the reproducible activity "Witnessing Project" from the next page to encourage learners to get personally involved in sharing the gospel with those closest to them. Once they identify those who need the gospel, encourage them to pray for opportunities to share it.

Newspaper Article

The book of Acts is a historical narrative that is ideal for a newspaper as an ongoing project, possibly continuing the entire quarter. You probably have frustrated newspaper reporters in your class that would enjoy releasing their creative energy by writing a weekly edition of *The Jerusalem Herald* as it might have appeared in the days of the apostles. News articles can be written for each lesson's text. An artist's sketch of the lead story would add eye appeal. Editorials and letters to the editor could provide for various points of view. Recruit your staff for the first four lessons and then continue if there is sufficient interest. A bulletin board could display the weekly issues, or current issues could be copied and distributed in class.

When Paul and Barnabas begin their journeys, you could receive weekly reports from your staff on the road with Paul and his companions. Other features could appear from time to time, such as classified ads like this one: "For Sale: one used set of crutches. Owner no longer needs them, thanks to the name of Jesus Christ! 2 shekels or best offer."

Cut out the masthead below and attach it to the top of a blank sheet of paper. Use that new paper as your master to make copies for each week that you use this activity.

THE JERUSALEM HERALD

The City of David's First Voice in News Today That Affects Tomorrow's World

Witnessing Project

The message of the book of Acts is the account of Spirit-empowered witnessing for Jesus Christ. (See Acts 1:8.) Are there some people that God would want you to witness to in the next few days or weeks? Make a list of people that need your testimony. Include family, neighbors, work companions, service people, shut-ins, and those away from home for military service or college. Pray daily for this list and keep track of the results.

NAME	RESULTS
1.	
2.	
3.	
4.	
5.	

THE HOLY SPIRIT COMES IN POWER

Mar
11

LESSON 2

WHY TEACH THIS LESSON?

It has already been noted that the book of Acts might well be called "The Acts of the Holy Spirit." The book is full of amazing deeds done by Spirit-filled individuals. Many are miraculous—the lame are made to walk, the sick are healed, the dead are raised—all by the power of the Spirit. Today we will see the spectacular beginning of that divine empowering, as the Spirit comes on the apostles.

Some of your students may think the Spirit's role was confined to the book of Acts. Not seeing spectacular works like the raising of Dorcas, they assume the Spirit is not active today. For these students, the promise of Acts 2:38 must not be missed—forgiveness of sins *and* the gift of the indwelling Holy Spirit! The Spirit's work may not be as spectacular to the casual observer, but the transformation he brings to lives and families is just as amazing as anything that happened through Peter or Paul.

INTRODUCTION

A. FINDING THE POWER TO CHANGE

Even the most attractive celebrity has some physical attributes that are less than perfect in someone's eyes. That is the reason plastic surgeons have waiting lists of hopeful people longing to change for the better. However, the most difficult task on the face of the earth has to be the permanent and positive transformation of the human soul. Thousands of self-help books, programs, and organizations have claimed to have the power to make lasting and beneficial changes in people. Yet whatever temporary improvements occur tend to be followed by long-term failures.

Jesus claimed that he had come to bring us life "more abundantly" (John 10:10, *King James Version*). He insisted that real change comes only "from the inside out" (Mark 7:21-23). Such change requires a special kind of power.

On the Day of Pentecost, when the church began, Jesus sent the Holy Spirit to enter obedient believers and to begin building new lives. Those new lives made up the new body of Christ, his church. Today's lesson focuses on how God brought the church into being.

B. LESSON BACKGROUND

According to Acts 1, following Jesus' ascension into Heaven the apostles were guided by God in selecting a replacement for Judas. This man, Matthias, most likely joined the other apostles during the time that "they stayed continually at the temple, praising God" (Luke 24:53). There must have been tremendous excitement among the apostles. They could hardly wait to share the good news of Christ's resurrection. Still, they followed Jesus' instructions and remained together until they were "clothed with power from on high" (Luke 24:49).

DEVOTIONAL READING:
JOHN 3:5-8
BACKGROUND SCRIPTURE:
ACTS 2
PRINTED TEXT:
ACTS 2:1-4, 37-47

LESSON AIMS

After this lesson each student should be able to:

1. Describe the events of Pentecost and the earliest days of the church.

2. Explain the importance of each element of worship cited in Acts 2:42.

3. Consider one of the elements cited in Acts 2:42 and suggest some specific steps he or she can take to grow in maturity in that area.

KEY VERSE

Peter replied, "Repent and be baptized, every one of you, in the name of Jesus Christ for the forgiveness of your sins. And you will receive the gift of the Holy Spirit." —Acts 2:38

I. THE SPIRIT DESCENDS (ACTS 2:1-4)

A. WONDROUS WIND (vv. 1, 2)

1. When the Day of Pentecost came, they were all together in one place.

The feast of *Pentecost* was one of the three great sacred assemblies of the Jewish religion. The word *Pentecost* means *fifty*, as the observance of the feast fell fifty days after the Passover Sabbath. That means that Pentecost would have occurred on the first day of the week. The church was born on the day we call Sunday.

Although Luke does not mention it, Pentecost was a harvest feast that celebrated the end of the barley harvest. Out of all the days that God could have chosen to begin his church, he chose a harvest celebration to plant the seed of the gospel and reap his first crop of souls.

When Luke says *they were all together,* what group does he mean by *they?* Some students believe the pronoun refers to the one hundred twenty disciples mentioned in Acts 1:15. This is suggested primarily because that group included both men and women, and Peter linked the events of Pentecost with Joel's prophecy that the Spirit of God would be poured out on both men and women (Acts 2:16-21; cf. Joel 2:28-32). But this prophecy can also be understood to refer to all the work of the Holy Spirit from that first day (when the church began) until the day when Christ comes again—a period of time when many men and women would be filled with the Spirit.

It is better to understand the word *they* as a reference to the apostles. The pronoun's immediate antecedent—the group named in the previous verse—is the apostles (1:26). The group consisted only of Galileans (2:7). The group consisted only of men (2:13). And the group is specifically identified as Peter and the other eleven apostles—twice (2:14, 37).

If the *one place* where the apostles were gathered was the upper room mentioned in Acts 1:13, then they must have left that place as the crowd began to gather. Otherwise they could not have addressed so large a crowd that three thousand could respond to their message. For that reason, many students believe that the *one place* was somewhere around the temple courts—perhaps near the Court of the Gentiles. Such a place would have been large enough to accommodate the thousands who convened to hear the apostles' preaching. That the place is called a "house" in verse 2 is not a problem, since the temple—or even the tabernacle—is also called a house (Matthew 21:13; Mark 2:26; John 2:16, 17; Acts 7:47).

2. Suddenly a sound like the blowing of a violent wind came from heaven and filled the whole house where they were sitting.

The first of a cluster of four events described is a *sound*—a sudden noise that resembled the echoing roar of a *violent wind*. Note that Luke does not say that an actual wind was present, only the sound that a wind would make. He seems to have been using a play on words, for the Greek word that is translated *wind* is also the word that is translated, on some occasions, as *spirit*. Like the wind, the Holy Spirit is unseen but not unnoticed: his movement is mysterious and powerful, and the effects of his working are undeniable (John 3:8).

B. TESTIFYING TONGUES (vv. 3, 4)

3. They saw what seemed to be tongues of fire that separated and came to rest on each of them.

Here Luke tries to describe the second event, which was something the apostles *saw.* The shape of what they saw resembled a group of *tongues*, apparently similar to human tongues. The brightness of the tongues was like flickering *fire*. The movement of the tongues was to divide from a central point; they *separated* until one bright shape *came to rest on each* apostle.

That these flames were shaped like tongues may point to the Spirit-empowered preaching about to take place. It may further suggest the effect that God's Word has on human hearts; it makes them burn (Luke 24:32; cf. Jeremiah 20:9).

AN UNQUENCHABLE FIRE

Those four "doughnuts" of black rubber on which our cars ride are infinitely better than the solid tires that were used on early automobiles. The smooth ride and precise handling that we enjoy in our cars are two of the numerous benefits of modern technology. However, there is a downside to these wonders: disposal. The state of California alone discards thirty million used tires every year, and that's a problem.

One summer day, near the town of Tracy, California, a pile of seven million used tires caught fire. The shape of tires makes such a fire very difficult to extinguish. Air is trapped and readily available to feed the fire even as water or other flame retardants are blocked from reaching it. Thus, months later, the "tire fire" was still burning out of control, sending a pall of black, pollutant-filled smoke over the countryside.

On the Day of Pentecost, a strange phenomenon occurred. The place where the apostles were gathered was filled with the roar of a "violent wind"—perhaps like the sound of a tornado. Then, what resembled a flame appeared on each of the apostles.

This was the beginning of a "fire" that has been impossible to extinguish. It was a fire that burned, not on the heads, but in the hearts of those who became fervent followers of Jesus Christ. Two millennia later, the message of the gospel is still a consuming fire that has spread around the world, burning the pollution of sin out of the hearts of those who yield to the cleansing power of Jesus.   —C. R. B.

4. All of them were filled with the Holy Spirit and began to speak in other tongues as the Spirit enabled them.

The last two events were another pair of miracles. First, the *Holy Spirit* of God *filled* twelve ordinary human beings. The second miracle gave the apostles the ability they needed to preach directly to the hearts of the crowd that was gathering. The *Spirit enabled* the Twelve to speak to each group in its native tongue or dialect.

II. THE CROWD RESPONDS (ACTS 2:37-41)

Peter and the apostles used this unique opportunity to proclaim publicly for the first time that Jesus of Nazareth is the Lord of glory and the Messiah whom Israel had awaited for so long. Central to his message was the fact that, though they had crucified Jesus, God had raised him from the dead (v. 32). Peter's declaration that God had made Jesus "both Lord and Christ" (v. 36) struck a blow at the people's messianic hopes. They had rejected the very Messiah they had awaited for centuries—what hope was left for them?

A. INSPIRED INSTRUCTIONS (vv. 37, 38)

37. When the people heard this, they were cut to the heart and said to Peter and the other apostles, "Brothers, what shall we do?"

The sting of guilt *cut to the heart* of many in the crowd like a sharp knife. When they realized what they had done in crucifying the Son of God, they pleaded to the *apostles, "Brothers, what shall we do?"* Should they offer an abundance of animals as a sacrifice for their sins? Should they pray for God to forgive them? Should they promise to be better and try harder? Should they punish themselves for the terrible thing they had done?

Similarly, many today realize that they have disobeyed God; and they too wonder what they should do about it. Listen to Peter's answer.

38. Peter replied, "Repent and be baptized, every one of you, in the name of Jesus Christ for the forgiveness of your sins. And you will receive the gift of the Holy Spirit.

WHAT DO YOU THINK?

The apostles' preaching in languages they had never studied or learned was a powerful demonstration that God was the author of their message. How can we convince people today that the gospel is true and of God?

[Encourage your students to tell how they have been able to make headway with convincing unbelievers to accept the truth of the Bible. If discussion is slow, consider factors that make this task so difficult. Then ask the class to suggest ways to deal with each factor cited.]

WHAT DO YOU THINK?

The people who heard Peter's accusation that they had crucified the One who was "both Lord and Christ" were "cut to the heart"— they felt guilty. How appropriate is it to use guilt as a motivating factor to lead people to Christ? Can you use guilt without manipulating a person? If so, how?

"Repent, and be baptized every one of you in the name of Jesus Christ for the remission of sins, and ye shall receive the gift of the Holy Ghost." *Acts 2:38*

Display today's visual as you prepare to discuss today's Key Verse, Acts 2:38.

Peter responded with two commands and two promises. The first command was that those who believe in Jesus as the Messiah must *repent.* To repent is to turn around, to turn from sin and self-centeredness to obedience to God. This change of attitude results in a change of life, as we begin to embrace new habits and new goals. Repentance does not mean that we suddenly become perfect, but rather that we start moving in a new direction, daily striving to become more like Christ.

The second command was that those who believed and repented should *be baptized . . . in the name of Jesus Christ.* Water baptism was designed by God to be a common experience uniting all Christians (Ephesians 4:4-6). Sadly, baptism has often divided Christians instead of uniting them. Perhaps it would help to note that certain conditions must exist before an act can be called Christian baptism.

First, the person who is baptized must believe in Jesus Christ (Mark 16:15, 16). Baptism without personal faith is not biblical baptism. Being baptized is an act of faith; it is not a work that we do to please God. In fact, we cannot baptize ourselves. Baptism is passive—it is something we allow another to do to us. Christian baptism is to be done *in the name of Jesus Christ*—that is, under his authority and by his terms. In baptism we reenact what Jesus did for us: we die (to sin, in repentance), we are buried (in the water), and we are resurrected, or brought forth from the water, so that we can "live a new life" (Romans 6:1-4).

Second, baptism is a decision that each person must make for himself. Just as *every one* of us must decide to repent, so each of us must decide to be baptized.

Third, God expects each person who believes in Christ to be baptized into him. The New Testament knows nothing of the idea of an unbaptized believer. As baptism assumes faith, faith also assumes baptism. Jesus expected that anyone who decided to be his disciple after his death, resurrection, and ascension should be baptized (Matthew 28:19, 20).

The two promises attached to faith in Jesus, expressed in repentance and baptism, are the *forgiveness* of sins and the reception of the *Holy Spirit.* We should not think that God forgives our sins as a "reward" for our faith, repentance, and baptism. We are saved by the grace of what Jesus did for us, not by any goodness of anything we do for him. The *gift of the Holy Spirit* comes to dwell within us and renew us so that we may grow daily to become more like Christ. As forgiveness removes the condemnation of our sin, so the Holy Spirit breaks our slavery to sin.

WHAT DO YOU THINK?

The gospel breaks down the barriers that divide and separate people. In what ways have you seen the gospel break down barriers? How can we be more effective in taking the gospel across barriers in our own community?

[Consider Romans 10:12, 13; Galatians 3:28; and Colossians 3:11 in your discussion.]

B. WARNING WORDS (vv. 39-41)

39. "The promise is for you and your children and for all who are far off—for all whom the Lord our God will call."

Peter told his audience that this *promise* was for three groups. The first was the crowd before him who had gathered to observe Pentecost. They represented all of that generation of Jews. The second group comprised the *children* of those gathered—in other words, the generation that was to come. This indicated that God's promise was not limited simply to the time of the apostles' ministry.

The third group included *all* others, no matter how *far off* they were, which indicated that the promise of the gospel was not to be limited by any national or geographical boundaries. Peter himself later saw the church incorporate both Jews and Gentiles into one body, worshiping the same Lord. God delights in shattering all man-made barriers with the gospel of Jesus Christ.

The phrase *all whom the Lord our God will call* brings to mind the concluding words of Joel's prophecy (Joel 2:32). It should be noted that this verse also includes the words, "Everyone who calls on the name of the Lord will be saved." Thus God's call does not diminish the need for human responsibility. We answer God's call by calling on his name (Acts 22:16).

40. With many other words he warned them; and he pleaded with them, "Save yourselves from this corrupt generation."

This indicates that, while many in the crowd were convicted, they were not yet saved. They were part of the *generation* whose lives were *corrupt*. The most obvious sign of their corruption was their rejection and crucifixion of Jesus Christ.

41. Those who accepted his message were baptized, and about three thousand were added to their number that day.

With this verse, Luke announces the spiritual harvest that the Lord reaped at the harvest festival of Pentecost. Those in the crowd who believed what Peter preached about Jesus, who in turn were ready to put their faith in Jesus, and who were prepared to repent of their sins *were baptized*—most likely in some of the many pools in Jerusalem. To baptize this many people on the same *day* should not be considered impossible. The apostles would not have had to do all the baptizing. If those who had been baptized in turn baptized others, the entire group of *three thousand* could have been baptized in a few hours.

YES OR NO?

For decades Jack Smith was a popular columnist for the *Los Angeles Times*. One of his most memorable columns was entitled, "The Everlasting Yea—or Nay." In it he compared the way computer circuits respond only to 1 or 0 (on or off, yes or no) with the way the human brain functions. His conclusion was that even life's most complicated quandaries can be resolved by asking the right simple questions.

For example, do we get up? Go to work? Stay at home in bed? These simple questions can have a profound influence on our lives, and the answers to them are simply *yes* or *no*. Everything from our choice of dinner menu to our choice of a life's mate can be boiled down to a *yes* or a *no*.

Smith noted that even great, history-making questions (Should the American colonies declare independence? Should Imperial Japan attack Pearl Harbor? Should America drop the atomic bomb?) all were decided with a simple *yes*.

When the gospel was presented to the crowd that had gathered on that Pentecost, the key issue came down to a simple *yes* or *no*. It still does: those who gladly receive the apostolic message of the crucified and risen Christ say *yes* to what he has done and respond to him in faith-filled obedience.   —C. R. B.

III. THE CHURCH GROWS (ACTS 2:42-47)

A. PRIMARY PRACTICES (v. 42)

42. They devoted themselves to the apostles' teaching and to the fellowship, to the breaking of bread and to prayer.

The early Christians were a devoted people; they lived their faith devotedly in regard to four essential elements of church life. First, all came under the instruction of the *apostles' teaching*, whether in large groups at the temple or in smaller groups in homes (v. 46). Second, the Jerusalem church devoted itself to *fellowship*—a commonly shared life. They created a new and close community within the city as they supported and encouraged each other.

The third and fourth items to which these believers committed themselves relate to their worship. While *breaking of bread* may simply mean sharing a meal, here Luke probably means the Lord's Supper, or Communion. Finally, *prayer* was a vital part of the early church—a theme emphasized throughout Acts (4:24-31; 6:4, 6; 11:4, 5; 12:5; 13:3; 14:23; 16:25; 22:17; 28:8).

B. STARTLING SIGNS (v. 43)

43. Everyone was filled with awe, and many wonders and miraculous signs were done by the apostles.

WHAT DO YOU THINK?

The early church won three thousand converts on its first day of operation. What can we learn from their strategy that can help us have that kind of success in our evangelistic efforts?

HOW TO SAY IT

Galileans. Gal-uh-LEE-unz.
Matthias. Muh-THIGH-us.
messianic. mess-ee-AN-ick.

Many wonders and miraculous signs supported the authority of the apostles' teaching, for such demonstrations of God's power indicated that they spoke on his behalf (Hebrews 2:3, 4). Luke gives several examples of such miracles in the rest of his account (Acts 3:1-10; 5:12-16; 8:13; 9:32-42; 14:8-10; 19:11, 12; 20:9-12; 28:7-9).

C. COMMON CONCERN (vv. 44-47)

44, 45. All the believers were together and had everything in common. Selling their possessions and goods, they gave to anyone as he had need.

What Luke describes here is not the establishment of an early Christian commune; it is simply a description of how wealthier Christians helped their poorer brothers and sisters. Some sold *their possessions and goods* and *gave* to those who *had need*. This was an example of voluntary generosity, not a continuing pattern that was meant to be compulsory for all Christians for all time. (That certain families kept their private homes is clear from the next verse.)

46. Every day they continued to meet together in the temple courts. They broke bread in their homes and ate together with glad and sincere hearts.

At this early stage in the development of the church, Christians and Jews could still worship in the same areas without animosity. The daily meetings *in the temple courts* probably took place during the regular prayer times and may have included teaching sessions conducted by the apostles. In addition, these Christians met together in private *homes* to share their meals and their joy.

47. . . . praising God and enjoying the favor of all the people. And the Lord added to their number daily those who were being saved.

Although the Christians would continue to be faithful in *praising God*, the *favor* of the public was something that the church could not expect to enjoy forever. This "honeymoon period" would soon be replaced by opposition and persecution. But *the Lord* was able to use both good times and bad to keep adding *to their number daily those who were being saved* (as he still is). The Lord blesses human efforts in his behalf and brings growth to the church (1 Corinthians 3:7-9).

New Christians become a part of the church at the same moment that they are saved. They must not be left alone, for they have been born into a spiritual family who should care for them, nourish them, and encourage them. Each of us must work to ensure that our church does not produce "spiritual orphans" who feel abandoned the moment they get out of the baptistery.

CONCLUSION

Luke's record indicates that every Christian has four joyful responsibilities that come with being a follower of Jesus Christ. First, we are responsible to worship and obey God. Second, we are responsible to learn the teaching of the apostles and submit to it. Third, we are responsible to encourage, share with, and worship with one another. And fourth, we are responsible to the people of the world, to share with them the good news of God's love found in Jesus Christ. God's Spirit will work through our words to convince them of the truth of the gospel. Then, when they accept Christ, we can continue the process by teaching them these four responsibilities so that they in turn may teach them to others.

As we pursue these tasks, let us remember that we are empowered by the same God who sent his Spirit to his church on the Day of Pentecost. We can preach the same gospel, call for the same kind of response, teach the same apostles' doctrine, share the same fellowship, and accept the same responsibilities as the early church. As we do, we will see that the Lord is faithful and that he can still add to our number daily those who are being saved.

WHAT DO YOU THINK?

The success of the early church was due in part to the willingness of all to share what they had with those who were in need. How can we live out that principle in the church today?

[Consider Romans 12:13; Galatians 6:10; and Hebrews 13:1.]

PRAYER

O God of Pentecost! You sent your Son to save us and your Word to guide us. You sent your Spirit to empower us and your people to encourage us. May we as your church be faithful to the example and design you have given us in the Holy Bible, and may all that we do give you praise forever. Through Jesus Christ, amen.

THOUGHT TO REMEMBER

God's church, which began on Pentecost, is the same church whose purpose and activities we seek to reproduce today around the world.

Discovery Learning

This page contains an alternate lesson plan emphasizing learning activities. Classes desiring such student involvement will find these suggestions helpful. The next page is a reproducible activity page to further enhance discovery learning.

LEARNING GOALS

After participating in this lesson, each student will be able to:

1. Describe the events of Pentecost and the earliest days of the church.

2. Explain the importance of each element of worship cited in Acts 2:42.

3. Consider one of the elements cited in Acts 2:42 and suggest some specific steps he or she can take to grow in maturity in that area.

INTO THE LESSON

Nothing parallels the excitement of starting a new congregation. The participants in planting a new church must grapple with the essential elements that make the church the unique institution that God has ordained. Tell your class members to pretend that they are the planning committee for planting a new church. Distribute copies of the reproducible activity "New Church Plant" from the next page. Allow a few minutes for the learners to complete the activity; then ask them to turn to the persons seated next to them and spend a minute or two describing the essential features of the church.

Make the transition to the Bible study by saying, "We have been wrestling with what constitutes the essential features of the church. Our text today spells out those qualities in the historical account of the establishment of the first church—the church formed on the Day of Pentecost in Acts 2."

INTO THE WORD

Use one or more of the following activities to involve your students in a study of today's lesson text.

NEWSPAPER REPORT

Ask your class members to pretend that they are newspaper reporters assigned by *The Jerusalem Herald* to cover the events on the Day of Pentecost described in Acts 2. Newspapers should present a balanced story that covers the five basic "W" questions—"Who?" "What?" "When?" "Where?" and "Why?"—as well as "How?"

Warm up for writing by having your class members read the text at least twice. Then establish an outline of the events to be covered. Decide which participants should be interviewed and quoted in the article. Conclude by brainstorming for an eye-catching headline.

(Use the reproducible masthead from page 244 to make a worksheet for writing these articles.)

DIARY OR JOURNAL ENTRY

The Day of Pentecost recorded in Acts 2 was a unique and memorable day in history. What impact did these events have on those who were present?

Ask your class members to write a diary or journal entry as if they were present for the events recorded in Acts 2. In preparation for writing, have your students read the text several times.

INTO LIFE

Use one or more of the following activities to help your students make application of today's lesson text.

Make a large copy of the following chart to compare the characteristics of the church in Acts 2 with your church. Characteristics from Acts 2 are identified on the left. Note similar practices in your church on the right. If your church does not have a corresponding practice or experience, suggest an appropriate activity that the class can plan to encourage growth in that area.

TEXT	ACTS 2 CHURCH	OUR CHURCH
2:37	people cut to the heart	
2:38	repentance, baptism	
2:39	promise is universal	
2:40	powerful preaching	
2:41	baptism	
2:42	apostles' teaching	
	fellowship	
	breaking of bread	
	prayer	
2:43	sense of awe	
2:44	togetherness	
2:45	shared with needy	
2:46	happily eating together	
2:47	praising God	

Distribute copies of the activity "We Can Do Better" from the reproducible page that follows. Ask your class to evaluate your church in each of the four areas cited in Acts 2:42: the apostles' teaching, fellowship, breaking of bread, and prayer. Discuss some ideas of how to imitate the Acts 2:42 model better. Then develop a plan to improve your church in one of those areas.

New Church Plant

Nothing parallels the excitement of starting a new congregation. The participants in planting a new church must grapple with the essential elements that make the church the unique institution that God has ordained. Pretend that you are on the planning committee for planting a new church. What features would you like to see in the new church? List as many features as you can think of. Then go back and evaluate each item by making a check (✔) in the appropriate column—essential (it just is not a church without these), desirable (these would be very good to have, but not essential), expected (these features are traditionally found in churches, but there is no Scriptural basis for them), or preferred (some churches may not have these, but I personally like to be involved in a church that does).

POSSIBLE FEATURES	ESSENTIAL	DESIRABLE	EXPECTED	PREFERRED

We Can Do Better

Choose one or more of the areas cited in Acts 2:42 in which you think our church could improve. Suggest some specific ways to do better in that area.

apostles' teaching

fellowship

breaking of bread

prayer

THE HOLY SPIRIT WORKS WITH POWER

LESSON 3

Mar
18

DEVOTIONAL READING:
1 CORINTHIANS 1:26-31

BACKGROUND SCRIPTURE:
ACTS 3:1—4:22

PRINTED TEXT:
ACTS 3:1-10; 4:1-4, 13

WHY TEACH THIS LESSON?

Expectations. We talked about them in practical ministries class in seminary. We talked about them in the counselor's office as we looked forward to getting married. We do well to consider them whenever we begin to work with other people—what do they expect of us? What can we expect of them? Are the expectations warranted and reasonable?

What do your learners expect when they enter your classroom? What do they expect from their faith? Today you will encounter a man at the temple in Jerusalem whose expectations—no, his wildest dreams—were surpassed by the power of Jesus Christ. Challenge your learners to expect the same kind of power to work in their own lives.

INTRODUCTION

A. MAJORING IN "MINOR PEOPLE"

All around us are people who might be called "minor" characters—people who pass in and out of our days so quickly and quietly that we tend to ignore them. (Of course, we can also be minor characters in other people's lives.)

What changes someone from a minor character into a "real" person? That usually takes place when we choose to focus on such a one and to care about him or her as someone made in the image of God. We begin looking directly at that individual, speaking with and really listening to the person. We make a connection that goes beneath mere surface concerns.

Some people seem doomed to the continual role of a "minor character"—just a part of the scenery in other peoples' lives. They wait for someone to notice (*really* notice) them in their loneliness and isolation. Today's lesson focuses on an incident when Peter transformed a lame man's life by really seeing him, speaking to him, and taking his hand in Jesus' name. This action and the events that followed resulted in many coming to faith in Christ and in an opportunity for Peter and John to demonstrate the character of Christ.

And it all began with majoring in what seemed to be a "minor" person.

B. LESSON BACKGROUND

Part of last week's lesson was taken from the closing verses of Acts 2, where Luke describes the life of the early church in Jerusalem. He notes that the Christians continued to worship in the temple, that the apostles were empowered to do miracles as a sign of God's blessing on their message, and that the church was growing daily. Moving from these general descriptions, Luke then focuses on one specific incident that illustrates how the Spirit empowered the apostles' ministry.

This particular incident is also pivotal in showing the beginning of opposition to the preaching of the gospel. As was the case with Jesus, the primary adversaries

LESSON AIMS

After this lesson students should be able to:

1. Tell how the Spirit's power was seen in the healing of the lame man and in Peter and John's response before the Sanhedrin.

2. Explain how our treatment of society's "outcasts" demonstrates whether we have "been with Jesus."

3. Form a plan for ministering to someone in their neighborhood or community whose situation and needs are often ignored.

KEY VERSE

When they saw the courage of Peter and John and realized that they were unschooled, ordinary men, they were astonished and they took note that these men had been with Jesus.   —Acts 4:13

of the apostles were the Jewish religious leaders. A miracle of healing impressed the crowds and led many to be open to the preaching of Peter. This openness was not shared by the temple leaders, however, and they moved quickly to attempt to silence the apostles. The way in which Peter and John responded to being jailed and interrogated had a telling impact on the Sanhedrin (the Jewish ruling council). These leaders seemed to consider the boldness and wisdom of Peter and John to be as miraculous as the healing of a lame man. And this is a "miracle" that God can reproduce in us.

I. APOSTOLIC MIRACLE (ACTS 3:1-10)

A. A BEGGAR'S REQUEST (vv. 1-5)

1. One day Peter and John were going up to the temple at the time of prayer—at three in the afternoon.

Peter and John are prominent both in the Gospels and in the early chapters of Acts. Here they went up together to the temple. (They literally went up, for the temple grounds were higher than the city, and the temple itself sat atop four ascending terraces.) The Jews paused for prayer three times each day: at the time of the morning sacrifice (9:00 A.M.), the time of the evening sacrifice (3:00 P.M.), and at sunset. Thus this incident occurred during the second time of prayer on this day—at three in the afternoon.

2, 3. Now a man crippled from birth was being carried to the temple gate called Beautiful, where he was put every day to beg from those going into the temple courts. When he saw Peter and John about to enter, he asked them for money.

As the two apostles entered the temple grounds, they passed a man crippled from birth begging from the worshipers who passed by. Throughout this passage, "Dr. Luke" seems to take a particularly medical interest in this man. First, he notes that the man's condition was a congenital problem, making it especially unlikely that he could ever be helped (John 9:32). Second, the man was over forty years old (Acts 4:22). This was not a case of temporary paralysis; the man's condition was well-known. He always had to be carried to the temple, since he was unable to walk on his own. His primary means of support was begging from passersby.

The lame man was laid every day at the temple gate called Beautiful. This was most likely the great Eastern gate (Nicanor Gate), the largest entrance to the temple area. When the man saw Peter and John approaching, he asked them for money.

4, 5. Peter looked straight at him, as did John. Then Peter said, "Look at us!" So the man gave them his attention, expecting to get something from them.

Both of the apostles stopped and focused their attention on the lame beggar. They did not have to stop; like most in the crowds around them, Peter and John could have walked right by the man. But they acted as Jesus would. They gave time and attention to one who meant little or nothing in most people's eyes. In fact, many thought that such a congenital deformity as this man's was a sign of God's judgment on the sin of either the man or his parents (John 9:2). But Jesus had taught the apostles that this was not so (John 9:3). Today Christians also need to be on the lookout for the physically challenged and for others who are often treated as though they were invisible.

B. PETER'S RESPONSE (vv. 6-8)

6. Then Peter said, "Silver or gold I do not have, but what I have I give you. In the name of Jesus Christ of Nazareth, walk."

Peter removed the beggar's false expectations so that he could replace them with far greater ones. The apostle informed the poor man that he would get no money from Peter because he had none. Instead, what the beggar was about to

WHAT DO YOU THINK?

Peter and John focused their full attention on the lame man and his obvious need. Why do we sometimes have a hard time seeing the needs of the people around us? How can we do a better job of being sensitive to other people's needs?

receive was of far greater value than any amount of money. What Peter did have was the power given by the Holy Spirit to perform signs and wonders. Thus he gave the man a second command: *In the name of Jesus Christ of Nazareth, walk.*
7. Taking him by the right hand, he helped him up, and instantly the man's feet and ankles became strong.

With a firm grasp, Peter took the beggar *by the right hand* and *helped him up*. As he did so, sudden changes took place in the lame man's body. The physician Luke carefully describes both the speed of the healing and its location. He uses very specific terms for the *feet and ankles*. When he says that these bones *became strong*, he uses a medical term that commonly described the mending of broken bones. Such healing usually involves a lengthy, tiring process, but in this instance it happened *instantly* by the power of God. The lame man felt this dramatic change in his long-standing condition and responded just as dramatically.
8. He jumped to his feet and began to walk. Then he went with them into the temple courts, walking and jumping, and praising God.

Now the beggar completed the action that Peter's initiative began. For the first time in his forty-some years, he *jumped to his feet*! He *began to walk*, getting used to the sensation of carrying his own weight instead of being carried by others.

Then the joy of this man's healing and his new freedom took hold of him. As he accompanied the apostles into the *temple* area, he began *jumping* up and down and shouting praise to the God who had set him free. Such worship might have seemed excessive and far too exuberant for those calmly strolling toward the temple to pray. But this man's life had been suddenly and radically changed. Now he could go anywhere and do anything; he could live a normal life. No wonder he could not stop *walking and jumping, and praising God*! The wonder is that many of us who have been set free by Christ have forgotten how to rejoice and praise God for the glorious things he has done for us.

A REMARKABLE CURE

In 1999 Lance Armstrong became only the second American ever to win the classic Tour de France bicycle race. But when he won the grueling, 2,288-mile, three-week-long ride over the mountains and plains of France, it wasn't his nationality that made his victory such a spectacular achievement.

Three years earlier, Armstrong had been told that he had an aggressive cancer in his abdomen, lungs, and brain. There was a fifty percent chance that he would die and only a ten percent chance that he would ever ride a bicycle in competition again. When he conquered these seemingly insurmountable odds to win the Tour de France, one sportswriter called his victory "the greatest comeback in the history of all sports." Some even called it a "miracle."

The lame man in our lesson text today had even less of a chance at a normal life than Lance Armstrong did. Forget any idea of athletic competition: this man had *never* walked in his entire life! No "miracle cures" of modern medical science and no "grit" and determination such as Armstrong displayed in his recovery could overcome the fact that this man simply *could not walk*. But God's power immediately turned this man into a leaping, praising "athlete"!

Thanks be to him who can accomplish what man's ability cannot.   —C. R. B.

C. THE CROWD'S REACTION (vv. 9, 10)
9, 10. When all the people saw him walking and praising God, they recognized him as the same man who used to sit begging at the temple gate called Beautiful, and they were filled with wonder and amazement at what had happened to him.

The actions and shouts of the healed man soon caught the attention of those in the temple. For a moment they were likely annoyed by someone interrupting the

WHAT DO YOU THINK?

Peter took the right hand of the lame man and helped him stand up. We, too, want to help people in need. Unfortunately, we often go to one of two extremes on this issue. One extreme is to say we can't help everyone, so we won't help anyone. The other temptation is to do too much for people in need. As a result, we stifle their own initiative and make them dependent on the help we and others provide. How can we chart a course between those extremes to give people in need a helping hand?

WHAT DO YOU THINK?

When the lame man was healed, he began jumping and shouting, praising God for the miracle. No doubt many of those who saw him were annoyed by his emotional outburst, thinking it inappropriate for a place of worship. Why are many of us reluctant to be emotional about the good things that God does in our lives?

HOW TO SAY IT

Galileans. Gal-uh-LEE-unz.
Khrushchev. KROOSH-shef.
Levites. LEE-vites.
Nazareth. NAZ-uh-reth.
Nicanor. Nye-CAY-nor.
Sadducees. SAD-you-seez.
Sanhedrin. San-HEED-run or
SAN-huh-drin.

solemn time of prayer. Then those who knew the man saw his face and realized that, incredibly, this was the lame man they had just passed and had passed so many times before *at the temple gate.* An excited murmur spread through the crowd. A miracle *had happened!* The worshipers were *filled with wonder and amazement.* As they gathered around the apostles and the formerly lame man, the stage was set for Peter and John to explain this remarkable turn of events.

II. APOSTOLIC MESSAGE (ACTS 4:1-4, 13)

In Acts 3:12-26 Luke records Peter's words to the throng gathered in the temple area. First, he made it clear that he and John did not heal the lame man by their own power. God had healed him in order to glorify Jesus Christ, the very one whom these crowds had disowned and killed, but whom God had raised to life. The lame man's healing demonstrated that the name of Jesus was as authoritative now as when he was on earth.

Peter then called for the people to repent of their sins, turn to God, and believe in Jesus Christ. He warned them that this same Jesus will one day return and restore the universe and will judge those who have not obeyed him. The crowds listened intently, and many did respond to Peter's preaching (Acts 4:4). However, this sudden interruption in the worship schedule had not gone unnoticed by those charged with keeping peace in the temple.

A. PRODUCING OPPOSITION (vv. 1-3)

1. The priests and the captain of the temple guard and the Sadducees came up to Peter and John while they were speaking to the people.

While *Peter and John* were still preaching, they were suddenly surrounded by a group of angry men. The leader was *the captain of the temple guard*, who was the priest in charge of the temple police. He was second only to the high priest in authority, and he was charged with keeping order in all the courts of the temple.

The *Sadducees* were the dominant party among the priests and controlled the office of the high priest. They rejected any belief in angels or in the resurrection of the dead (Acts 23:8). Many were wealthy landowners, and, to remain financially secure, were willing to cooperate with the hated Romans when necessary. They knew that the Roman army could be called in to crush any civil disorder (such as the uproar caused by the preaching of the apostles after the healing of the lame man). Something had to be done.

2. They were greatly disturbed because the apostles were teaching the people and proclaiming in Jesus the resurrection of the dead.

These Jewish leaders were deeply *disturbed* by the apostles' actions on two counts. First, they were upset that *the apostles were teaching the people* who gathered for worship in the temple. As the officials saw it, the apostles were agitators stirring up unrest among the crowds. They were interrupting the established order of worship for the day and keeping the people from fulfilling their religious duties. Furthermore, the apostles were threatening the authority of the religious leaders by publicly *teaching* new doctrines that had not been cleared by the officially sanctioned teachers of the law. The right to teach the people was a privilege that was jealously guarded by the Jewish authorities for themselves alone.

Second, the religious leaders were disturbed because of the content of the apostles' teaching. Peter and John were *proclaiming in Jesus the resurrection from the dead.* This would have especially enraged the Sadducees, who had publicly argued for years that a resurrection from the dead was a myth. The apostles had to be stopped. After all, when they preached that Jesus was raised from the dead, they not only implicitly taught that the Sadducees were wrong to deny the resurrection,

WHAT DO YOU THINK?

The temple authorities wanted to stop Peter and John from talking about Jesus Christ. Why is there opposition to the preaching of the gospel? Why do some people always get angry when the name "Jesus" comes up?

but they also charged the Jewish religious leaders with being responsible for the crucifixion of one whom God had glorified by bringing him up from the grave. To protect their reputation and authority, the temple elite had to act immediately.

3. They seized Peter and John, and because it was evening, they put them in jail until the next day.

The temple guards arrested the apostles under the authority of the captain of the temple and with the approval of the Sadducees. The arrest seems to have included the healed lame man, since later he is described as "standing there with" the apostles before the Jewish leaders (Acts 4:14). The prisoners were then taken to some place of custody to be jailed overnight. This was probably a guarded room near the temple.

The apostles were held *until the next day* because it was too late for the people who would judge them to convene and hold a hearing. Apparently Peter's sermon was considerably longer than the excerpt Luke has recorded, since the healing occurred at around 3:00 P.M. (see verse 1) and it was now *evening*.

The apostles' hearing was to be held before the Jewish high council, or Sanhedrin. It was composed of seventy priests, Levites, and elders, with the high priest serving as the leader. Most of these men lived in Jerusalem, but many of them also had country estates outside of the city. Thus, it would take time to notify all the council members and gather them together to deal with Peter and John.

B. BEARING FRUIT (v. 4)

4. But many who heard the message believed, and the number of men grew to about five thousand.

In spite of the fact that the two preachers had just been arrested, the response to their message was extremely positive: *many who heard the message believed*. Aside from Peter and John, there must have been many other Christians in the crowd going to the temple to pray that day. These unknown believers must have completed the work of the apostles by baptizing the new converts and helping them to get started in their new life with Christ. Here Luke notes that the total *number* of believing *men grew to about five thousand*; thus this figure does not include the women and children in the church at that time.

At this point, Luke goes on to describe what happened when the apostles and the lame man appeared before the Sanhedrin the next day. By the power of the Holy Spirit, Peter gave a simple yet courageous defense for the apostolic preaching in Jesus' name. His argument was based on the undeniable fact of two miracles: the healing of a man crippled from birth and the resurrection of Jesus Christ from the dead. His conclusion was that Jesus Christ is the one and only means of salvation (v. 12). Luke then notes the Sanhedrin's reaction to the apostles' words.

C. CAUSING WONDER (v. 13)

13. When they saw the courage of Peter and John and realized that they were unschooled, ordinary men, they were astonished and they took note that these men had been with Jesus.

This Jewish ruling council was composed of some of the most powerful and intelligent men in all Judea. These men were experts in interpreting the Old Testament law. Most of the common prisoners brought before such a court were too intimidated to present a powerful and coherent case in their defense. But the apostles were an exception. They were confident in Christ and empowered with *courage* by the Holy Spirit.

The members of the council realized that the apostles *were unschooled, ordinary men*; that is, they had had no formal rabbinical training in interpreting the

DAILY BIBLE READINGS

   Monday, Mar. 12—Peter Heals a Lame Beggar (Acts 3:1-10)

   Tuesday, Mar. 13—Peter's Sermon in Solomon's Porch (Acts 3:11-16)

   Wednesday, Mar. 14—Peter Calls for Repentance (Acts 3:17-21)

   Thursday, Mar. 15—Jesus Is the Promised Messiah (Acts 3:22-26)

   Friday, Mar. 16—The Rise of Persecution (Acts 4:1-4)

   Saturday, Mar. 17—Peter and John Before the Council (Acts 4:8-12)

   Sunday, Mar. 18—No Boasting in God's Presence (1 Corinthians 1:26-31)

Today's visual dramatizes the conflict between Jesus' disciples and the Sanhedrin. Display it as you discuss verse 13.

Since we have "been with Jesus," we will "obey God rather than men."
Acts 4:13 & 5:29

Old Testament Scriptures. They were common people, not priests or experts in the law. They held no public office or titles; they were ordinary men. How were they to explain the remarkable courage and clarity of these two untrained Galileans? And how could they explain the man who was healed who stood beside the apostles? The men of the Sanhedrin *were astonished* at the seeming contradiction between the commonness and the power of Peter and John. Then the truth began to dawn on them.

Not long before, someone else had stood before the council. He too was a commoner from Galilee with no formal training. But he had also spoken with extraordinary power and performed wondrous miracles. He was the very one whom these apostles proclaimed as the Savior risen from the dead. It became obvious that Peter and John had to have *been with Jesus*—walking with him, learning from him, and growing more like him. Jesus Christ was the only possible explanation for the transformed lives of these men. By the power of Jesus, lame men began to leap and cowards became courageous. Today it should also be obvious from our lives that we are living with Jesus and are being transformed into his likeness.

UNLIKELY SPOKESMEN

During what came to be called the famous "kitchen debate" in Moscow, Russia, on July 24, 1959, Nikita Khrushchev told then-Vice President Richard Nixon, "In another seven years we will be on the same level as America. . . . We will bury you." By this he meant that capitalism would die and that Marxist Communism would be victorious in the battle for political primacy in the world.

So it was that an unlikely candidate for United States citizenship took his oath of citizenship on another July day, exactly forty years later. This person was none other than Khrushchev's son, Sergei. The younger Khrushchev and his wife had been living and working in America since 1991. They had come to enjoy the fruits of the capitalism that was supposed to have been "buried" long ago. They have now become the unlikely spokespersons of the American way of life. In fact, they own two cars and have a suburban house with central air conditioning, a Jacuzzi, and an entertainment center!

The Jewish Sanhedrin had had enough trouble with the "unschooled" rabbi from Nazareth who had won the hearts of the Jewish people with his criticism of the Jewish aristocracy. Now they were forced to deal with the powerful witness of some unlikely spokesmen—Jesus' equally "unschooled" followers. They did not realize that truth cannot be silenced, even though it is spoken by unsophisticated, "common" people.

—C. R. B.

CONCLUSION

Peter and John risked becoming major people in a minor person's life. They cared enough to step out of the background and get involved. Because they were willing to serve one person in Jesus' name, they gained a greater opportunity to serve many people in Jesus' name. And when confronted by opposition, the apostles responded with Christlike courage and wisdom, so that even their enemies could see the character of Christ in their lives.

Every day each of us encounters people who could simply remain "minor characters" in our lives if we choose to ignore them and go our way. But what if we consciously notice them, speak to them, and actually get to know them? If we treat them as Jesus would, we might see how the Lord can heal their hearts through our words and our touch. And when they look into our eyes and see the compassion and respect there, they might tell us that now they know that we have been with Jesus because they see his love in us.

Discovery Learning

This page contains an alternate lesson plan emphasizing learning activities. Classes desiring such student involvement will find these suggestions helpful. The next page is a reproducible activity page to further enhance discovery learning.

LEARNING GOALS

After this lesson students should be able to:

1. Tell how the Spirit's power was seen in the healing of the lame man and in Peter and John's response before the Sanhedrin.

2. Explain how our treatment of society's "outcasts" demonstrates whether we have "been with Jesus."

3. Form a plan for ministering to someone in their neighborhood or community whose situation and needs are often ignored.

INTO THE LESSON

Have your class brainstorm for the qualities and characteristics that identify a true Christian. List your class members' responses on a white board or overhead projector—or tape a large piece of paper to the wall and use a broad-tipped marker. Explain to your class that in brainstorming you do not stop to evaluate answers—just keep writing them as fast as possible and let students "feed on" other students' responses.

Say, "The last verse of our text today says that the Jewish leaders took note that the disciples 'had been with Jesus.' As we study today's lesson, watch for the qualities and characteristics we have listed to see how many of them show up in the disciples' lives."

OPTION

Invite a children's class to visit your class with a rendition of the song, "Peter and John Went to Pray." Older adults especially enjoy the vitality of singing children. The song will provide a natural entrance into today's study.

INTO THE WORD

Divide your class into small groups—no more than four to a group. Have the members of each group select one or two of them to play characters mentioned in today's text. (Possible characters to portray include Peter and John, the former lame man, the leader of the Sanhedrin, the captain of the temple guard, a couple from the crowd, and one or two of the five thousand believers.) The other members of the group will interview these characters, asking them questions about the events recorded in Acts 3 and 4. Allow time for the group to prepare; then ask each group to record its interview on a cassette tape. If you have time, you can play some or all of these recordings like a radio broadcast.

While each group is recording its interview, help the remaining students make a second chart similar to the one created in the brainstorming activity above, this time listing characteristics and qualities demonstrated in the lives of the apostles in today's text. List the verse numbers and write the qualities that your class members identify from each verse. For example:

3:1—They were regular in prayer.
3:4—They noticed the poor and needy out of the crowds of people.
3:6—They explained what they were going to do.
3:7—They personally touched the poor and needy man.

OPTION

Distribute copies of the "Word Maze" from the next page. Allow a few minutes for the students to work and then review the puzzle, explaining the text as you note each word in the puzzle.

INTO LIFE

Have each learner compare the list of qualities from the brainstorming activity and the characteristics identified in the apostles and make a revised list of the qualities that identify a true Christian. Then ask the learners to evaluate where they are in their personal development. Say, "On a scale from 0 to 5, where 0 means 'I haven't even started yet!' and 5 means 'I am mature in this characteristic,' put your numbers in the right margin in the character study."

Today's text shows that followers of Jesus are sensitive to the poor and needy of society. Have your class plan a visit to a nursing home or resident home for adults with mental retardation. Preparing small favors for residents and sharing a favorite verse are two ways of helping visitors interact with residents.

Close your class with a time of prayer for the persecuted church. Have a leader pray for various missionaries and the problems they face. (Missionaries whom your church supports, or their forwarding agents, can provide you with information for specific prayer.) After the leader prays for each group, have the class respond in unison with a prayer based on Acts 4:13 like this one:

"Lord, give courage to these disciples, as you did to Peter and John. May their detractors be astonished, not by their education or abilities, but by the fact that they have been with Jesus."

Word Maze

Read Acts 3:1-10; 4:1-4, 13. Find as many words from our text in the word maze below as you can. All are in the vertical (top to bottom) or horizontal (left to right) position. (If you want a little help, use the word list below to help you know what to look for.)

APOSTLES   NAZARETH   SILVER   BEAUTIFUL   PRAISING
SPIRIT   BELIEVED   PROCLAIM   STRONG   DEAD
RESURRECTION   TEMPLE   GOD   SADDUCEES   UNSCHOOLED
LAME   SANHEDRIN

```
R E S U R R E C T I O N O D A S W E R T
B C A E R T Y H B F V B N M M O N A W A
G S D R R E D D F E R F B S T R O N G S
T E D A S D T F G H I J K I M C V E R T
Y U U R T B E A U T I F U L F D S A B E
H I C W A S M S C C D E E V H J K L E D
N J E E W E P T R E D P R E T G B N L C
M O E W E R L Y U I O P P R O C L A I M
J F S A N H E D R I N W E D T Y H U E O
U C F P E R F D F R A R U E T G B Y V N
I A K O N R E D D L Z K N L H O L T E D
K Q U S S D I O P R A I S I N G P R D T
L W E T A S C E F K R R C K E O G E D D
O S R L A M E B H U E G H U G D E A D K
P E F E N R E D D E T B O E F A D E S U
Z R O S P I R I T R H O O R L R E D D E
X T R E D P R E T G B I L N U N T K S R
C R I E N R T D N A Z C E R E D D U D E
V E A S B R E D P R E T D B L M J E D F
B F E T G B S M S C C D E E V H A R T S
```

Don't Overlook the Overlooked

People in the service trades are often overlooked. Do you notice the people who empty your garbage cans? Do you notice the person's name who takes your order at the fast-food restaurant? Develop a plan for recognizing these people, acknowledging their presence, and expressing appreciation for their service. Include a winsome witness for Jesus Christ, the ultimate Servant.

OBEDIENT TO THE SPIRIT

LESSON 4

WHY TEACH THIS LESSON?

I don't play golf. I don't even watch it on television. But I admire golfers. Golf seems to be one of the few sports that still prize "sportsmanship."

I don't remember the golfer's name, but I heard of one who disqualified himself from a prestigious tournament. It seems he had made a special golf club for his young son so he could teach the boy how to play. It was altogether too short for his own use, but somehow it got put into his bag before the tournament.

In the course of one game, the golfer discovered the extra club, which put him over the allowed maximum number of clubs in his bag. His caddie suggested he hide it and play on—no one would know. "I would know," he replied. Then he reported the error to a tournament official and was disqualified.

Such a commitment to doing what is right is rare today. We see it in the apostles. When told not to preach, they replied, "We must obey God rather than men!" We must do the right thing no matter what anyone else says or does. Challenging your students to that level of commitment is the goal of today's lesson.

INTRODUCTION

A. HOW CAN I BE BOLD?

Boldness is a willingness to take risks. It chooses to stand and state clearly what must be said, regardless of the cost. For a Christian, boldness involves using every available opportunity to act and speak in ways that honor God, even when others may disapprove and our hearts are pounding with fear. Boldness is courage in action. But boldness is difficult for many of us because we do not like to offend anyone or risk the pain of rejection or persecution.

Today we will see how the apostles boldly gave their witness before a hostile audience. Though confronted with persecution and the possibility of death, their faith in Christ enabled them to proclaim him without compromise and to experience joy through their suffering. Their example encourages us to be bold in Christ.

B. LESSON BACKGROUND

From last week's study of Acts 4, we learned how the Sanhedrin (the Jewish ruling council) tried to stop Peter and John from preaching about Jesus. The apostles were released with a warning to stop evangelizing. Instead, they returned to the group of believers and organized a prayer meeting to ask God for greater boldness in preaching Jesus. God responded by empowering those present so that they "spoke the word of God boldly" (Acts 4:31).

At the beginning of Acts 5, we read of a Christian couple who tried to cover their greed with a show of generosity. Ananias and Sapphira dropped dead because of their sin, and, as a result, a respectful fear spread through the church (v. 11). Still, the church grew as the apostles preached and healed many people. Their successful evangelism soon aroused the jealous wrath of the Sanhedrin, who had all the apostles arrested and held overnight for trial.

Near dawn an angel came and released the apostles, telling them to go back to the temple and resume their preaching. Thus, when the Sanhedrin sent for the

---

DEVOTIONAL READING:
PSALM 103:15-18
BACKGROUND SCRIPTURE:
ACTS 5
PRINTED TEXT:
ACTS 5:27-42

Mar
25

LESSON AIMS

After this lesson students should be able to:

1. Summarize the viewpoints expressed at the apostles' trial before the Sanhedrin and the outcome of the trial.

2. Tell how joyful obedience in the face of opposition can testify to the power of the gospel.

3. Ask God for boldness in confronting a specific situation where a Christian's testimony is needed.

KEY VERSE

Peter and the other apostles replied: "We must obey God rather than men!" —Acts 5:29

jailed prisoners, the officers sent found no one in the cells. While they were reporting to the council that the Twelve were missing, another messenger announced that the apostles were back in the temple grounds—preaching again! The captain of the guard took some men to re-arrest the apostles (quietly) and to return them for trial.

Amazingly, the council seemed uninterested in how the miraculous escape from jail had occurred. This group was far more concerned with the apostles' stubborn refusal to keep silent about Jesus.

I. APOSTLES' TESTIMONY (ACTS 5:27-32)

A. CHARGE OF DISOBEDIENCE (vv. 27, 28)

27. Having brought the apostles, they made them appear before the Sanhedrin to be questioned by the high priest.

Previously only Peter and John had faced this group of educated, powerful men. *The Sanhedrin* (consisting of seventy such men) regarded with suspicion these disciples of Jesus who could heal the sick and escape from locked and guarded rooms. The *high priest* (most likely Annas, as noted in Acts 4:6) was the president of the council and thus began the hearing. The same group that tried Jesus was about to put his disciples on trial.

28. "We gave you strict orders not to teach in this name," he said. "Yet you have filled Jerusalem with your teaching and are determined to make us guilty of this man's blood."

The high priest brought three charges against the apostles. First, they had ignored the previous warning given to Peter and John *not to teach in Jesus' name* (Acts 4:18). Notice that the high priest refused even to say the word, "Jesus"; he simply stated that the apostles were teaching *in this name*. He then stated the second charge against the apostles: they had not only refused to be silent concerning Jesus, but they had also *filled* the entire city with their *teaching*. They had made Jesus "the talk of the town." The high priest, however, tried to diminish this accomplishment by claiming that the doctrine the apostles taught was theirs, originating from them and not from God.

The third accusation against the apostles was that they had blamed the Sanhedrin for Jesus' death. The high priest's reference to bringing Jesus' *blood* upon the Sanhedrin may reflect what transpired during his trial before Pilate. After the Roman governor had declared Jesus to be innocent and had publicly washed his hands, he stated that he was innocent of the blood of Jesus. Then the crowd (spurred by the religious leaders) shouted back at Pilate that they would accept the responsibility for Jesus' blood (Matthew 27:24, 25). Perhaps these men feared that their words were coming back to haunt them.

B. DEFENSE OF OBEDIENCE (vv. 29-32)

29. Peter and the other apostles replied: "We must obey God rather than men!

Peter's defense is quite similar to the one he made to the Sanhedrin the last time that he and John appeared before them (Acts 4:19): what *God* says is more important than what *men* say.

30. "The God of our fathers raised Jesus from the dead—whom you had killed by hanging him on a tree.

Peter then called attention to another contrast between the will of God and the will of the council. God *raised Jesus from the dead* after the council *had killed* him *by hanging him on a tree* (the cross).

The law of Moses declared that the body of anyone who was executed for a crime should be hung on a tree for public display and that such a person had God's curse upon him (Deuteronomy 21:22, 23). The members of the council

WHAT DO YOU THINK?

It has always been easier to make a promise than to keep it. The Jewish leaders incited the crowd at Jesus' trial to cry out, "Let his blood be on us and on our children!" (Matthew 27:25). But in the apostles' trial, the leaders objected to having Jesus' blood brought on them. Why is it so hard to accept responsibility for our actions—even if we have promised to do so? What safeguards against making rash promises can you suggest?

WHAT DO YOU THINK?

The same Peter who said, "We must obey God rather than men" also wrote, "Submit yourselves . . . to every authority instituted among men" (1 Peter 2:13). How can we tell when we are in a situation where we need to choose to obey God's will rather than man's laws?

had treated Jesus in this manner, intending to humiliate him. They did not realize that in so doing, they were fulfilling the promises made by God to their fathers. The curse associated with Jesus' death was not for his own sins; he redeemed us by "becoming a curse for us" (Galatians 3:13) and taking the punishment that we rightfully deserved for our sins.

31. "God exalted him to his own right hand as Prince and Savior that he might give repentance and forgiveness of sins to Israel.

For someone to be *exalted . . . to the right hand* of a monarch meant that the ruler had given that individual both honor and authority. This is also clear from the titles of *Prince* and *Savior* that are used to describe Jesus.

Peter then elaborated on how Jesus provides salvation. First, Jesus is said to *give repentance.* This does not mean that Jesus forces anyone to repent, but he provides what is necessary for us to carry out this crucial step of returning to God. Jesus has sent the Holy Spirit to convict us of our sins (John 16:7-11). He has shown us the love of God by giving his life to pay for our sins (1 John 4:9, 10). Because of this, it is now possible for us to turn from our sins and turn back to God.

Second, when we repent we receive *forgiveness of sins* through Christ's sacrifice for us. As Peter preached on the Day of Pentecost, repentance and forgiveness are closely linked (Acts 2:38). Only Jesus could provide these blessings, not only for *Israel* but for the entire world.

32. "We are witnesses of these things, and so is the Holy Spirit, whom God has given to those who obey him."

Peter concluded his defense by stating the *witnesses* whose testimony supported his case. This was in keeping with the requirements of the law of Moses (Deuteronomy 17:6). Peter himself, along with the rest of the apostles, made up one group of witnesses to who Jesus is and what he has done. The second witness was the *Holy Spirit,* who supported the apostles' testimony by empowering them to do miraculous signs (Hebrews 2:3, 4).

Peter then reminded the Sanhedrin that God gives his Spirit only *to those who obey him* (Acts 2:38). The apostles were obeying God by continuing to preach Jesus, even when this meant disobeying the council. (Peter's words implied that the Sanhedrin was disobeying God by hampering the apostles' ministry.)

II. GAMALIEL'S ADVICE (ACTS 5:33-39)

A. LEARN FROM THE PAST (vv. 33-37)

33. When they heard this, they were furious and wanted to put them to death.

The members of the Sanhedrin realized that only *death* could stop the apostles' testimony, and, at that moment, the council was so outraged that they actually might have executed the Twelve (as they later did Stephen).

34. But a Pharisee named Gamaliel, a teacher of the law, who was honored by all the people, stood up in the Sanhedrin and ordered that the men be put outside for a little while.

At this pivotal moment, the Lord supplied a voice of calm and reason. *Gamaliel* was the greatest Jewish *teacher* of his day. The apostle Paul (when he was Saul) studied under Gamaliel before he became a Christian (Acts 22:3).

Gamaliel was the head of an important rabbinical school in Jerusalem, the school of Hillel (named for Gamaliel's grandfather). This school promoted a rather loose interpretation of the law of Moses while remaining true to the traditions of the Pharisees. (The other school in Jerusalem, named after a Rabbi Shammai, was much more strict.) Gamaliel demonstrated his broad-minded attitude in his suggestion on how to deal with the apostles. First, he had them removed so that he could speak freely about their case.

Use the same visual as you used last week to illustrate today's lesson. Refer to it as you discuss verse 29.

WHAT DO YOU THINK?

The council reacted to the apostles' witnessing with murderous rage. What are some more common reactions to the gospel? How can we improve the chances that our witnessing will receive a favorable reaction?

WHAT DO YOU THINK?

Sometimes help comes from unexpected places. Gamaliel—who certainly was no friend of the Christians—actually came to their defense. Why, do you suppose, did he do that? What, if anything, can we learn from this incident?

35, 36. Then he addressed them: "Men of Israel, consider carefully what you intend to do to these men. Some time ago Theudas appeared, claiming to be somebody, and about four hundred men rallied to him. He was killed, all his followers were dispersed, and it all came to nothing.

Gamaliel began by solemnly warning the Jewish leaders to be careful in their handling of these followers of Jesus. He separated himself from his companions' murderous intent by stating that it was they who needed to evaluate their thinking. In typical rabbinical style, Gamaliel appealed to recent well-known events to remind his hearers of the lessons of history.

Gamaliel's first illustration called attention to a man named *Theudas*. The only information we know about this person and his followers is what Gamaliel tells us. In 4 B.C. King Herod the Great died. In the power vacuum that followed, many insurrectionists rose up trying to seize control. The situation became so bad that the Roman army came in to put down all the uprisings. Theudas may well have been one of these insurgent leaders. His boast *to be somebody* was likely a claim to be a prophet of God or even the Messiah.

Theudas attracted a small following of *four hundred men* (many more than Jesus' twelve). However, as soon as Theudas was killed, his movement fell apart. Gamaliel was suggesting that perhaps Jesus' cause would also end up as a pointless attempt to gather a following.

37. "After him, Judas the Galilean appeared in the days of the census and led a band of people in revolt. He too was killed, and all his followers were scattered.

Thanks to the writings of a first-century historian named Josephus, we know more about *Judas the Galilean*. In A.D. 6 the Roman governor of Syria and Judea, Quirinius (mentioned in Luke 2:2), took a *census* of the territories he controlled in order to determine how much he could raise in taxes from them. Judas of Galilee publicly opposed the census and its taxation, claiming that this action was just the first step to enslaving the Jews and causing them to serve another god.

To protect the liberty of his people and to uphold the holy name of the Lord, Judas called on all Jews to oppose this taxation—by force if necessary. He attracted a large following to his endeavor. However, once more the might of Rome crushed the uprising through a series of violent campaigns, and Judas died. Afterward, all the people whom Judas had persuaded to join his cause *were scattered* and returned to their normal lives, except for those injured or killed.

Although Judas the Galilean had been very popular for a time, at this point the only group who followed his anti-Roman philosophy was the group known as the Zealots. Gamaliel seemed to be saying that the Sanhedrin tolerated the Zealot movement, so why not be equally tolerant of these followers of Jesus?

B. LEAVE THESE MEN ALONE (vv. 38, 39)

38. "Therefore, in the present case I advise you: Leave these men alone! Let them go! For if their purpose or activity is of human origin, it will fail.

Gamaliel now stated his position: *Leave these men alone! Let them go!* Whatever the apostles' plans and activities may be, if their movement is merely the remains left over from the followers of some dead fanatical leader, it will disappear on its own without help from the Sanhedrin. The council should just be patient, and perhaps this latest "fad" will die out on its own or be destroyed as the others were. There was, however, another possibility to consider.

39. "But if it is from God, you will not be able to stop these men; you will only find yourselves fighting against God."

Gamaliel went on to say something like this: "What if these followers of Jesus are telling the truth and doing God's bidding? Do you really think we can be

HOW TO SAY IT

Ananias. An-uh-NYE-us.

Annas. AN-nus.

Gamaliel. Guh-MAY-lih-ul.

Hillel. HILL-el.

Josephus. Jo-SEE-fus.

Pharisee. FAIR-ih-see.

Quirinius. Kwy-RIN-ee-us.

Sanhedrin. San-HEED-run or SAN-huh-drin.

Sapphira. Suh-FYE-ruh.

Shammai. SHAM-eye.

Theudas. THOO-dus.

Zealots. ZEL-uts.

successful in *fighting against God?* We are supposed to be the religious leaders of our people; do we want to appear to be God's enemies? No! So again I say, leave these men alone!"

Gamaliel's argument does make a certain amount of sense. And yet, while it is true that Christ's disciples will win in the end, that does not mean that, in the here and now, it will always appear that we are winning. Sometimes, for a certain period of time, it may seem as if the church is failing miserably or even dying. Such a momentary setback does not mean that we are not truly doing the will of God. Nor is it true that apparent success and growth of false teachers' ministries are evidence that these are being blessed by God.

Thus, despite what Gamaliel advised, momentary victories or defeats do not reveal what will ultimately be approved or disapproved before the Lord. God has shown us his will through Jesus and in the Bible; our job is to be faithful in following his will, whether we seem to be winning or losing at any particular time.

GOOD ADVICE

"Dear Abby" once advised a woman not to have the local newspaper correct the obituary of her recently deceased mother. The obituary had incorrectly added nine years to the mother's age. Abby's response was, "Let it alone."

Abby then quoted a series of small-town newspaper ads that continued to compound an error printed in the first ad. A man was selling a sewing machine. Buyers were instructed to call after 7 P.M. and "ask for Mrs. Kelly who lives with him cheap." The following day the editor published a correction: "ask for Mrs. Kelly who lives with him after 7 P.M." On the third day came another correction: "ask for Mrs. Kelly who loves with him."

Finally, the seller of the sewing machine placed an ad saying that he no longer had a sewing machine for sale. He had smashed it and disconnected his phone! He added, "I have not been carrying on with Mrs. Kelly. Until yesterday she was my housekeeper, but she quit."

The members of the Sanhedrin were somewhat like that poor editor. The more they tried to address their concerns about the apostles, the more their frustration grew. Gamaliel reminded them of some recent history and then gave some good advice: If God is not in this movement, don't worry about it; but be careful—lest you find yourselves fighting against God.   —C. R. B.

III. TRIAL'S OUTCOME (ACTS 5:40-42)
A. COUNCIL'S DECISION (v. 40)
40. His speech persuaded them. They called the apostles in and had them flogged. Then they ordered them not to speak in the name of Jesus, and let them go.

The members of the Sanhedrin were *persuaded* by Gamaliel that killing the apostles would not be wise. At the same time, these men had to be given some kind of punishment for disobeying the explicit instructions of the council. So each apostle was *flogged*, most likely with the standard thirty-nine lashes. The number was carefully counted so that the punishment did not exceed the forty lashes allowed by the law (Deuteronomy 25:3).

The Sanhedrin then solemnly repeated to the Twelve the commandment that they had already broken: do not ever preach *in the name of Jesus* again. Then the apostles were released. The members of the council no doubt hoped that the sting of the whip would silence these troublemakers. How wrong they were!

B. APOSTLES' RESPONSE (vv. 41, 42)
41. The apostles left the Sanhedrin, rejoicing because they had been counted worthy of suffering disgrace for the Name.

WHAT DO YOU THINK?

After being threatened and beaten by the Sanhedrin, the apostles thought it a privilege to be "counted worthy of suffering disgrace for the Name." How can we develop such an attitude? How important is it to do so?

PRAYER

Our Father, help us to be the ambassadors you have called us to be. Each day, give us opportunities. Each opportunity, give us boldness to respond. Each response, give us wisdom to listen and to speak wisely. And in all we do, may your love be seen in us. We pray to be like Jesus. In his name, amen.

THOUGHT TO REMEMBER

Godly boldness is the willingness to take risks in fulfilling our service to God.

DAILY BIBLE READINGS

Monday, Mar. 19—*Ananias and Sapphira Sin and Die (Acts 5:1-11)*

Tuesday, Mar. 20—*The Power of the Apostles (Acts 5: 12-16)*

Wednesday, Mar. 21—*Life and Faith of Believers (1 Thessalonians 1)*

Thursday, Mar. 22—*Persecution and Release (Acts 5: 17-23)*

Friday, Mar. 23—*Arrest and Accusation (Acts 5:24-28)*

Saturday, Mar. 24—*The Answer of the Apostles (Acts 5:29-32)*

Sunday, Mar. 25—*The Warning of Gamaliel (Acts 5: 34-42)*

The apostles' will to serve Jesus was not broken by the beating they received; on the contrary, *they left the Sanhedrin* determined more than ever to proclaim his message. In spite of their pain, these men were *rejoicing!* They were honored to be dishonored for Jesus, and dignified by their indignity on his behalf.

42. Day after day, in the temple courts and from house to house, they never stopped teaching and proclaiming the good news that Jesus is the Christ.

The apostles made it their daily practice to go right back to the *temple* grounds where they had been arrested to teach and proclaim *that Jesus is the Christ*—the very "crime" for which they had been arrested and beaten. In addition, they continued to instruct the believers in their homes. Thus, whether in public or in private settings, regardless of the cost, they *never stopped* telling others about Jesus. The example of their unconquerable faith and devotion continues to challenge us today.

THEY COULD NOT BE SILENCED

San Francisco, California, is said to be a city that takes nostalgia seriously. Many are familiar with the old popular song about the "little cable cars" that "climb halfway to the stars." The city spends millions of dollars to keep those quaint remnants of the romantic past in operation.

San Francisco is also famous for its fog—and its foghorns. At one time years ago, more than fifty foghorns located around San Francisco Bay warned ships of dangerous shoals and shores. In November of 1992, the last of the old foghorns was silenced and replaced by an electronic beeper. However, the citizens of San Francisco wouldn't stand for this. Historians denounced the beeper, civic leaders weighed in on the side of history, and radio station KFOG began a campaign to raise the money needed to revive the old foghorns. After three weeks, the U.S. Coast Guard gave in, and a compromise was reached. If the city would pay for their operation, a couple of the old foghorns would be reactivated.

The Sanhedrin believed that a stern warning followed by a severe beating would silence the apostles. These men had become noisy reminders of an embarrassing, recent past. The Sanhedrin thought that they could get rid of them by dealing with them as they had dealt with Jesus. But the Sanhedrin did not take into account the faith of the apostles. These followers of Jesus knew that he was alive, and they could not be silenced.

Can the same be said of us?   —C. R. B.

CONCLUSION

What was the secret of the incredible boldness of the apostles? Consider the following:

First, the apostles clearly were convinced of the truth of what they were saying and the importance of their message. Their faith in Jesus Christ was the "driving force" behind who they were and what they did. We need to recognize that we are also called to be Christ's ambassadors, just as the apostles were (2 Corinthians 5:20).

Second, the early church prayed for boldness to preach and teach Jesus and used the power given to accomplish that task. We, too, ought to pray for power to do the tasks that God has given us and do them to his glory (Ephesians 3:20, 21).

Third, the apostles were absolutely committed to obeying the Lord regardless of how others might react. They were not surprised by opposition; they expected and accepted it. In fact, they rejoiced in their suffering, considering it an honor to serve Jesus in this manner.

No one ever said that serving Jesus would be always easy or that it would be accepted by others. But we know that as we confess Jesus to others, he will confess us to God (Matthew 10:32, 33). As we honor his name, he will honor ours.

Discovery Learning

This page contains an alternate lesson plan emphasizing learning activities. Classes desiring such student involvement will find these suggestions helpful. The next page is a reproducible activity page to further enhance discovery learning.

LEARNING GOALS

After this lesson students should be able to:

1. Summarize the viewpoints expressed at the apostles' trial before the Sanhedrin and the outcome of the trial.

2. Tell how joyful obedience in the face of opposition can testify to the power of the gospel.

3. Ask God for boldness in confronting a specific situation where a Christian's testimony is needed.

INTO THE LESSON

Put the words "Boldness is . . ." on a large sheet of poster paper taped to the wall. As your class members enter the room, have each person complete the sentence in his or her own words.

If your classroom does not lend itself to posting something on the walls, or if your students prefer not to write on such a poster, then open the session by asking the class to complete the sentence verbally. Give each person an opportunity to respond with a one-sentence answer before anyone may respond twice.

Make the transition to the Bible study by saying, "Today's lesson looks at a graphic example of boldness. As we read the Scripture text, check to see if the answers we have given describe Peter and John's response during their appearance before the Sanhedrin."

INTO THE WORD

Have a volunteer read Acts 5:27-42 aloud. Distribute copies of the reproducible activity page that follows. Allow a few minutes for the learners to complete the puzzle; then review. Ask learners to identify the verse from which each answer is discerned. Use the commentary section to point out significant details concerning each verse as it is noted.

If there is time, or if your class does not like crossword puzzles, ask your students to suppose that Peter were able to visit or write to your class to help each person be bolder in witnessing for Jesus. Read the text again, one verse at a time, and after each verse ask, "What does this verse suggest that Peter might say to us today?" For example, Acts 5:27 might suggest, "Also be prepared because you never know when you will be called to testify for Jesus."

Or have your class members write a letter such as Peter might have written to encourage Christians to be obedient and bold in sharing their faith in Jesus. Ask half the class to write a letter that Peter might have written the night before his appearance before the Sanhedrin. Have the other half write a letter that Peter might have written the evening after his trial.

INTO LIFE

Have each class member write a song to a familiar melody using the ideas in today's text. Warm up for the writing by working together to list words and ideas the students might want to include. Such a brainstorming might generate this list: *bold, speak up, preach, proclaim, teach, obey, witness, courage, fearless, testify.* If a student were to select the melody of "Stand Up, Stand Up for Jesus," he might then write as follows:

"Speak up! Speak up for Jesus.
Proclaim his name each day.
With boldness tell of Jesus;
It's God we must obey!"

Then distribute copies of the following True/False quiz. Ask each student to complete the quiz as a self-evaluation. (No one will need to reveal his or her results to anyone else in the class. This activity is intended as a personal challenge.)

T F 1. I find it easy to talk to others about my faith in Christ.

T F 2. I often engage others in conversations about Christ.

T F 3. I have personally led a person to become a Christian.

T F 4. I am not ashamed to speak up for Jesus Christ with my family.

T F 5. Everyone at my job knows that I am a Christian.

T F 6. I am always ready to share my faith with others.

T F 7. I often invite people to come to church with me.

T F 8. I am a part of my church's evangelism ministry.

T F 9. I often give people Christian tracts and booklets.

T F 10. I am a bold and confident witness for Jesus Christ.

Close your class session with a prayer. Ask God to help the students evaluate themselves honestly and to yield to his Spirit in those areas where they discern weakness. Pray that each one will be bold in giving witness of Jesus.

Crossword Puzzle

Read Acts 5:17-42. Then complete the crossword puzzle below. Identify the verse from which each answer is learned.

ACROSS

1. Type of orders given to the apostles.
3. Party associated with the high priest.
5. The Twelve.
12. Along with the apostles, the Holy Spirit is a _____.
13. What God wanted to give to Israel.
14. Deity.
17. The apostles were counted _____.
18. What the apostles suffered.
20. City that was filled with the apostles' teaching.
21. What the officials did to the apostles.
22. Spokesman for the apostles.
23. The Jewish high court.

DOWN

2. This man had been "claiming to be somebody."
4. A Jewish leader.
6. Title for Jesus.
7. Jesus was hanged on one.
8. Another title for Jesus.
9. A rebel during the time of the census.
10. Do this for God rather than for men.
11. The apostles never stopped _____.
14. What the apostles never stopped teaching (2 words).
15. 9 Down was this.
16. The high _____ questioned the apostles.
19. The apostles suffered disgrace for the _____ of Jesus.

EMPOWERED TO SERVE

LESSON 5

WHY TEACH THIS LESSON?

In Revelation 2:10, Jesus promises that those who remain faithful to him until death, or "to the point of death," will receive a "crown of life." The word *crown* there is the Greek word *stephanos,* from which we get the name Stephen.

In today's lesson we meet Stephen, who was the first to receive the "crown of life" for being "faithful . . . to the point of death." Let his name and his faithfulness be ever a reminder to your students of the crown that awaits them as well.

INTRODUCTION

A. APRIL FOOL?

Grandma was an enthusiastic gardener. She eagerly waited each year for the time when she could get her tools and her hands into the rich soil of her vegetable bed and begin growing good things to eat once again. The first of April was usually about the right time for groundbreaking.

One year Grandma hoped to have some help from younger and stronger hands. Her grandson had taken to muscle building with an eagerness at least as great as Grandma's zest for gardening. His iron pumping was producing visible results that he was not reluctant to display before any willing audience. The backyard garden plot would be a great place for a demonstration.

Things didn't work out quite that way, though. Garden tools just didn't fit hands better suited to iron weights, and arms that were impressive at lifting barbells just couldn't manage a hoe. There was power in those young muscles, but to gardening with Grandma they responded with only an "April Fool!"

Today (April 1) might be a good time to ask what our God-given abilities were designed for and what we are doing with them. Are we playing the fool by putting these abilities on display for self-promotion? Or are we giving the kind of service that is due the Giver? Stephen served—to the ultimate degree!

B. LESSON BACKGROUND

The first five chapters of Acts expand on the promise given by Jesus to the eleven apostles just before he ascended into Heaven: "You will receive power when the Holy Spirit comes on you; and you will be my witnesses in Jerusalem, and in all Judea and Samaria, and to the ends of the earth" (Acts 1:8). Acts 1–5 is concerned primarily with the spread of the gospel throughout Jerusalem and Judea.

Acts 5:14 notes that, following the sudden and sobering deaths of Ananias and Sapphira and the continued working of miracles by the apostles, "more and more men and women believed in the Lord and were added to their number." Not even the threats of the Jewish ruling council could stifle this movement. The apostles, who were beaten on orders from the council, responded by "rejoicing because they had been counted worthy of suffering disgrace" for the name of their Lord (v. 41). The concluding verse of chapter 5 notes their continued zeal: "Day after day, in the temple courts and from house to house, they never stopped teaching and proclaiming the good news that Jesus is the Christ" (v. 42). With such growth, however, came new problems and challenges that the church had to address.

DEVOTIONAL READING:
MICAH 4:1-8
BACKGROUND SCRIPTURE:
ACTS 6:1—8:3
PRINTED TEXT:
ACTS 6:1-8; 7:55—8:1a

Apr
1

LESSON AIMS

After this lesson students should be able to:

1. Relate how Stephen faithfully served the Lord through helping the needy and through giving his life for Christ.

2. Tell why every act of service, whether great or small, is needed in Christ's kingdom.

3. Identify someone who has faithfully served the Lord for many years, and make specific plans to express appreciation to that person.

KEY VERSE

So the word of God spread. The number of disciples in Jerusalem increased rapidly, and a large number of priests became obedient to the faith. —Acts 6:7

LESSON 5 NOTES

I. SEVEN MEN CHOSEN (ACTS 6:1-8)

A. SENSITIVE MATTER (v. 1)

1. *In those days when the number of disciples was increasing, the Grecian Jews among them complained against the Hebraic Jews because their widows were being overlooked in the daily distribution of food.*

Those days describes a time of growth and opportunity for the church that continued in spite of the threats against the apostles recounted in the previous chapter. Before the Day of Pentecost, one hundred and twenty had prayed together (Acts 1:15); then on that day three thousand declared themselves obedient followers of Jesus as Lord and Christ (Acts 2:41). Daily additions soon brought the number of converts to five thousand men (Acts 2:47; 4:4), and to that were added the "multitudes" mentioned in Acts 5:14. Here *the number of disciples was increasing.*

At this point in the church's growth, all of these believers were Jewish. Most were Jews by birth; they lived in the land promised to Abraham and his descendants, spoke its language (Aramaic), and followed its customs. Others were proselytes (Gentile converts to Judaism). They were Jews, but they were *Grecian* in language and culture. Some of these may have been among the three thousand converted on the Day of Pentecost (note the various lands mentioned in Acts 2:8-11). They may have remained in Jerusalem to become a part of the fellowship of believers in Jesus (Acts 2:42-47). Not having homes or employment in Jerusalem, some of these—and especially the *widows*—would have been among those who were most dependent on the *daily distribution of food* provided from the pooled resources of the church.

It would be difficult for any organization to continue for very long in a collection and distribution of material resources without someone's being—or feeling—slighted. "We/they" feelings are hard to avoid where distinct groups of people are involved. Occasionally those who are "outsiders" may complain because they see the more "established" participants as the beneficiaries of special favors.

WHAT DO YOU THINK?

The Grecian widows felt there was some discrimination in the early church. What should we do to assure that this is not a problem today?

[Discuss how your church ministers to people of every racial, ethnic, social, gender, and age distinction. Do you deliberately aim for a homogeneous congregation? If so, what do you do for the sake of the people in other demographic categories?]

B. PROPOSED SOLUTION (vv. 2-4)

2. *So the Twelve gathered all the disciples together and said, "It would not be right for us to neglect the ministry of the word of God in order to wait on tables.*

The *Twelve* (the apostles) had been chosen, appointed, empowered, and instructed by Jesus to preach, teach, and work miracles in bearing witness to his death and resurrection. For them to begin giving so much time to benevolence management that they neglected their divinely assigned work would be definitely wrong. Caring for the needy was right and good, but it did not have to be administrated by the apostles.

A similar problem is faced when ministers of the gospel find themselves busy with matters involving facilities or finances. It is also faced by every Christian in choosing how he or she will spend available time. Choices must be made, not only between the good and the bad, but between the good and the better. One has to allow others to do what can be done by others and give priority to doing what God has uniquely called him or her to do.

3. *"Brothers, choose seven men from among you who are known to be full of the Spirit and wisdom. We will turn this responsibility over to them.*

The problem had arisen among the people, so it was only right that the solution be found *among* them. Apostolic authority would lead in shaping the program, but the people must *choose* the personnel from among themselves. *Seven men* would be adequate to lead in addressing the concern. In order to preserve the

WHAT DO YOU THINK?

The apostles said, in essence, "This is not our job. Find someone else to take care of it." When is it appropriate for a person to refuse to participate in a worthy ministry, and when would refusal be an act of arrogance? Why?

sacred purpose of the entire enterprise, they must be *full of the Spirit*. To steer the right course in personal relationships, they must possess godly *wisdom*.

These seven men are often referred to as "deacons," from the Greek *diakonos*. The basis for this seems to be the use of two other words from the same root as *diakonos* in this passage. The daily "distribution" in verse 1 is from *diakonia*, and the verb for "wait on tables" in verse 2 is from *diakoneo*. However, the Bible never explicitly refers to the seven as deacons. While modern deacons are often responsible for the more "material" matters of church life, the two best known of the seven (Stephen and Philip) were especially noted for their speaking and evangelism (Acts 6:9, 10; 8:5, 26-40; 21:8).

4. ". . . and will give our attention to prayer and the ministry of the word."

The apostles were not taking a "sabbatical." They would give full-time *ministry*, or service (again the word is *diakonia*), to their primary assignment of providing spiritual leadership through teaching and *prayer*.

NO SPIRITUAL ROBOTS

At one time or another, many busy persons have wished that they could duplicate themselves so they could do all the work that they just don't seem to have time to accomplish. A Georgia preacher, inspired by Disney World's robotic figure of President Lincoln, has tried to do something like this. Just as the Jerusalem church chose seven helpers, this preacher has built seven robots to help him preach the gospel! One of the figures cost a quarter of a million dollars: it is an "apostle Paul" that is able to shake hands, cross its leg, and deliver a thirteen-minute sermon about Jesus' appearance to Paul (Saul at the time) on the road to Damascus.

The apostles found themselves unable to administer the Jerusalem church's benevolence program to widows. The seven men chosen by the church to carry out this ministry were not just "clones" of the apostles; they were men "full of the Spirit and wisdom." They were genuine men of God whom the church knew could be entrusted with this important task.

The world may be amused by robotic figures that can imitate human behavior and even deliver a speech in mechanical fashion. However, if we wish to amaze the world with the power of the gospel as the first-century Christians did, it will require more of us than merely "going through the motions," mechanically giving lip service to Christ, or doing good deeds because it is what we have been "programmed" to do.   —C. R. B.

C. UNANIMOUS APPROVAL (vv. 5, 6)

5. This proposal pleased the whole group. They chose Stephen, a man full of faith and of the Holy Spirit; also Philip, Procorus, Nicanor, Timon, Parmenas, and Nicolas from Antioch, a convert to Judaism.

We are not told exactly how the choice of the seven men was made. It must have reflected a procedure that was familiar and generally accepted among the believers. All of the seven chosen had Greek names; thus it would appear that the Grecians' complaint was being respected. But we must not attach too much importance to the names, for two of the twelve apostles (Andrew and another Philip) also had Greek names.

Stephen is named first among the seven and is described most fully. That prepares the reader for the record of Stephen's activity that will follow. *Philip*, later referred to as "the evangelist" (Acts 21:8), is named second. The reference to *Nicolas* as a *a convert to Judaism* from *Antioch* foreshadows the prominence of Antioch as a city where the gospel was first preached to Jews and Gentiles alike, and where the disciples were first called Christians (Acts 11:19-26).

HOW TO SAY IT

Ananias. An-uh-NYE-us.
Antioch. AN-tee-ock.
Aramaic. Air-uh-MAY-ick.
diakoneo (Greek). dih-AH-ko-NEH-o.
diakonia (Greek). dih-AH-ko-NEE-uh.
diakonos (Greek). dih-AH-ko-nawss.
Grecians. GREE-shunz.
Jairus. JYE-rus or JAY-ih-rus.
Judaism. JOO-day-iz-um.
Lazarus. LAZ-uh-rus.
Nicanor. Nye-CAY-nor.
Nicolas. NICK-uh-lus.
Parmenas. PAR-meh-nas.
Procorus. PROCK-uh-rus.
proselyte. PRAHSS-uh-light.
Samaria. Suh-MARE-ee-uh.
Sanhedrin. San-HEED-run or SAN-huh-drin.
Sapphira. Suh-FYE-ruh.
stephanos (Greek). STEFF-ah-noss.
Timon. TY-mon.

WHAT DO YOU THINK?

How important do you think the successful handling of the matter of care for the widows was to the church growth reported in verse 7? Why?

Use today's visual to note the rapid growth of the early church. Discuss how the modern church can recapture the same vitality as the early church had.

6. They presented these men to the apostles, who prayed and laid their hands on them.

The "whole group" of believers (v. 5) made their choices and presented their candidates for apostolic commissioning (similar to the modern practice of "ordination" of certain leaders). The laying on of the apostles' hands provided the special endowment by which Stephen and Philip were able to work miracles (Acts 6:8; 8:5-8, 13-20). Perhaps others of the seven also performed miracles, but we are not told of this in the Scriptures.

D. ASTONISHING RESULTS (vv. 7, 8)
7. So the word of God spread. The number of disciples in Jerusalem increased rapidly, and a large number of priests became obedient to the faith.

Positive results came almost immediately from the wise and effective handling of the Grecians' complaint. *The word of God spread*: the gospel went forth bearing additional fruit among folk who observed and respected what was done. The words *increased rapidly* are used to describe the church's phenomenal growth. Most astonishingly, many converts came from the group that had most vigorously opposed the apostles' preaching—the *priests* (Acts 4:1-3; 5:17, 18).
8. Now Stephen, a man full of God's grace and power, did great wonders and miraculous signs among the people.

At this point our attention is directed to *Stephen*, where it remains through the account of his message and martyrdom.

Beyond the measure of the Spirit and of wisdom required of the seven (v. 3) and the degree of faith found in Stephen personally (v. 5), he is here described as *full of God's grace and power*. He moved swiftly beyond a serving of tables to the working of *wonders and miraculous signs*, thus presenting the message of Christ most effectively *among the people* who had chosen him and to whom he was committed.

Not everyone, however, was favorably impressed with Stephen. Some, apparently of mixed national backgrounds, disputed with him. Failing in that effort to discredit Stephen's ministry, they brought charges of blasphemy against him before the Sanhedrin; and he was brought to trial to answer the charges. In response, Stephen traced the course of Jewish history from its beginning to the current hour. He highlighted the continual rejection by God's people of both his message and his messengers. The crowning sin, said Stephen, lay in the Jewish leaders' rejection and killing of Jesus. That accusation brought an immediate and hostile reaction from the council (Acts 6:9—7:54).

II. ONE MAN MARTYRED (ACTS 7:55—8:1a)
A. STEPHEN SEES JESUS (vv. 55, 56)
55. But Stephen, full of the Holy Spirit, looked up to heaven and saw the glory of God, and Jesus standing at the right hand of God.

WHAT DO YOU THINK?

Stephen saw Jesus standing at the right hand of the Father. Elsewhere the Bible tells us he sat down *at the Father's side (Hebrews 1:3). What significance do you see in the fact that Jesus was standing in Stephen's vision?*

Stephen had already demonstrated a loyalty to Christ that was oblivious to the threats and attacks of his accusers. His attention was riveted on a vision infinitely higher than the hate-contorted faces of his accusers. That vision was reflected in his own face, which they had already seen "like the face of an angel" (Acts 6:15).

As Isaiah had seen God's glorious presence when he received his prophetic assignment (Isaiah 6:1-5), so Stephen now *saw* it in the closing hour of his earthly life. But he also saw something more. In the position of highest honor and authority, *at the right hand of God*, he saw Jesus. Jesus had said that he would be seen in *glory* seated at the right hand of power (Matthew 26:64; cf. Ephesians 1:20; Colossians 3:1; Hebrews 1:3). What everyone will see at last, Stephen saw at that moment. But Stephen saw yet more; he saw Jesus *standing*—perhaps even rising to his feet as though to welcome his faithful witness home in a magnificent gesture of divine approval.

56. "Look," he said, "I see heaven open and the Son of Man standing at the right hand of God."

As clearly as a man with perfect eyesight sees what is before him on an earthly plane, Stephen saw beyond the wide-flung door of *heaven*. He saw, not simply a man called Jesus, but the one who had offended the Jewish leaders by describing himself with the messianic term *Son of Man*. The Sanhedrin had charged Jesus with blasphemy because of his use of this title (Mark 14:61-64). Now Stephen was about to be charged with this same offense because he had dared to refer to Jesus in the same way. Furthermore, he had magnified his offense by saying that he saw in Heaven that very one *standing at the right hand of* Almighty *God!* It was enough to throw the council into a screaming rage!

B. STEPHEN IS STONED (vv. 57, 58)

57. At this they covered their ears and, yelling at the top of their voices, they all rushed at him.

The accusers had heard more than enough. This presumptuous miracle worker had to be silenced! To make sure they heard no more, they *covered their ears* (by either putting their fingers into their ears or their hands over them). Then, with all reasonable communication ended, *they all rushed at him* like a pack of wolves. They were united in one mindless purpose—to destroy their victim.

58. . . . dragged him out of the city and began to stone him. Meanwhile, the witnesses laid their clothes at the feet of a young man named Saul.

Leviticus 24:16 prescribed death by stoning as punishment for blaspheming the name of the Lord; Deuteronomy 17:2-7 directed taking the offender to the city gate for the execution. The *witnesses* whose testimony convicted the offender were to throw the first stones.

In order to give their arms more freedom of movement, those casting stones laid aside their heavy outer garments and put them *at the feet of . . . Saul* (later Paul), who may have been an observer for the Sanhedrin at this execution. What a remarkable introduction to the man who would later become the Lord's apostle to the Gentiles!

C. STEPHEN DIES (vv. 59—8:1a)

59. While they were stoning him, Stephen prayed, "Lord Jesus, receive my spirit."

While the hurtled stones were taking their toll, Stephen was praying loudly enough to be heard and understood over every other sound. His words echoed Jesus' prayer from the cross: "Father, into your hands I commit *my spirit*" (Luke 23:46).

60. Then he fell on his knees and cried out, "Lord, do not hold this sin against them." When he had said this, he fell asleep.

Did Stephen at this point sink to his *knees* in weakness or deliberately in prayer? That he *cried out* his final words, like those of his crucified Lord (Luke 23:46), indicates a continuing force of will and a clear mind. Stephen's words of forgiveness are once again similar to those of the Master: "Father, forgive them, for they do not know what they are doing" (Luke 23:34).

The reference to death as a falling *asleep*—as a rest from labor and suffering—was used by Jesus in reference to Jairus's young daughter (Luke 8:52, 53) and to Lazarus (John 11:11-14). The figure is nowhere more appropriate than

WHAT DO YOU THINK?

The natural reaction of one who is hurt by another is to seek vengeance—or at least justice. But Stephen prayed for mercy on behalf of his attackers, just as Jesus had done. How can disciples today develop a gracious spirit that seeks mercy even for those who hurt them?

THOUGHT TO REMEMBER

Whatever you are doing in the Lord's work, be faithful.

DAILY BIBLE READINGS

in reference to Stephen's well-earned rest at the end of a turbulent day and at the end of service rendered courageously in the name of Christ Jesus.

MARTYRS

As the Vietnam war spilled over into neighboring countries, Cambodia fell to the Khmer Rouge (Kuh-*mair* Rouge)—the Communists who would later immerse the country in a veritable blood-bath. Minh Tien Voan (Min *Tee*-en *Vo*-an) was a Cambodian staff member of World Vision, a Christian relief organization. As the attack began on Phnom Penh (Peh-*nahm* Pen), the capital of Cambodia, Minh had an opportunity to leave the country by chartered plane. World Vision personnel urged him to do so and thus save his life. He refused with these words: "The people will need us Christians when the country starts to suffer."

A few days later, U.S. government personnel began to evacuate the American embassy in Phnom Penh, in the face of an inevitable Communist takeover of the city. The Americans offered Minh a seat on a helicopter with them. He refused this offer as well. Eventually Minh was arrested and executed for giving Bibles to the peasants.

We who live in a free nation and enjoy safety from persecution for our Christianity may find it hard to relate to stories of people like Minh Tien Voan and Stephen. Seldom, if ever, are we called upon to risk much of anything for our faith. But the life-and-death stories of these and many other Christian martyrs, both ancient and modern, testify to what it means to be committed—*really* committed—to Christ.

—C. R. B.

8:1a. And Saul was there, giving approval to his death.

Saul's role here may have been more active than is apparent. The Sanhedrin risked being called to account for this illegal act—since only the Romans could authorize capital punishment. But it is difficult to identify specific persons in the midst of mob violence; only those who stand out in some way are easily fingered. Some have suggested that Saul's *giving approval* took the form of accepting personal responsibility for the stoning of Stephen by putting himself in a conspicuous position, guarding the cloaks of the actual assailants.

This scene remained etched in Paul's memory. Concerning his own apostleship he wrote, "I am the least of the apostles and do not even deserve to be called an apostle, because I persecuted the church of God" (1 Corinthians 15:9). After his conversion, when he had returned to Jerusalem he prayed, "When the blood of your martyr Stephen was shed, I stood there giving my approval and guarding the clothes of those who were killing him" (Acts 22:17-20). To Timothy, Paul described himself as one who "was once a blasphemer and a persecutor and a violent man" but "was shown mercy" (1 Timothy 1:13). Thus Stephen's willingness to die in the name of Jesus was transformed from an act that Saul supported to one that reminded him of God's wondrous grace.

CONCLUSION

Perhaps it is hard to think of Stephen as one chosen, appointed, and empowered to "wait on tables"—the time-consuming task for which the apostles could ill afford to neglect their God-given responsibilities. What a waste of this man's superior ability! But suppose Stephen had refused or neglected the less notable service? How would he have received the subsequent opportunities to serve the Lord through miracles, the brilliant defense of the gospel, and a heroic likeness to his Lord in death?

Jesus once said, "Whoever can be trusted with very little can also be trusted with much" (Luke 16:10). Remember that in the work of the Lord no one is "just" anything. There are no unworthy opportunities to serve to the glory of God!

Discovery Learning

This page contains an alternate lesson plan emphasizing learning activities. Classes desiring such student involvement will find these suggestions helpful. The next page is a reproducible activity page to further enhance discovery learning.

LEARNING GOALS

After this lesson students should be able to:

1. Relate how Stephen faithfully served the Lord by helping the needy and by giving his life for Christ.

2. Tell why every act of service, whether great or small, is needed in Christ's kingdom.

3. Identify someone who has faithfully served the Lord for many years, and make specific plans to express appreciation to that person.

INTO THE LESSON

To introduce the lesson, use one or more of the following activities.

HELP WANTED ADS

Have your class write help wanted ads for positions in Christian service. What qualities would be essential? What qualities would be helpful? What would the compensation package look like?

For example, a help wanted ad from Acts 6:1-4 might read, "Large metropolitan church seeks several men to administer benevolence program for church widows. Applicants must be full of the Holy Spirit and wisdom, responsible, and able to function without close supervision. Grecian heritage would be helpful. Apply in person to the twelve apostles."

CIRCLE RESPONSE

On a poster taped to the wall or on a white board write: "Nothing is more spiritual than the way a person handles money." Ask each person to tell why he or she agrees or disagrees with this statement with a one-sentence response. No one may respond twice until each person has had the chance to respond once. This activity will help less vocal members to venture out and participate. It will also help to quiet more vocal members who may unintentionally dominate the class.

INTO THE WORD

A dramatic reading of today's text will help bring the account to life for your class members. Warm up for the dramatic reading by identifying the emotions and attitudes of the voices in each verse. Decide whether each narrative verse should be read by a man or a woman. Then assign members to be narrators, an apostle, and Stephen; and have the cast read Acts 6:1-8; 7:55—8:1a.

To explore the passage, give a copy of the text—with wide margins—to each class member. Have your students read the text and make a mark in the margin beside each verse, using one of the marks defined below:

?   "I have a question about this verse."

*   "I have a comment I'd like to make about this verse."

+   "We need more of this in our church!"

↑   "I am inspired and challenged by what this verse says."

Complete the activity in class yourself; this will provide a good gauge of how long to allow for the activity. Then ask the following questions:

"Who has a verse marked with a question mark?" Field the questions, looking for answers in the text as much as possible.

"Who has a verse marked with an asterisk?" Take the comments and discuss the observations made for as long as you think is appropriate.

"Who has a verse marked with a plus sign?" What items or activities do the students think are needed? Why? Can your class help to make these things happen?

"Who has a verse marked with an *up* arrow?" Discuss what the students find challenging. What will they do about these challenges?

INTO LIFE

SERVICE PROJECT

Widows have always had a special place in the life of the church. And some widows have always been neglected by the church. Probably there are widows in your church and community who feel neglected. Lead your class in planning a project that will minister to the needs of widows in your church. Possibilities include help with transportation, friendly visits in person and by phone, completing chores requiring strength and agility, household repairs, etc.

RECOGNITION CERTIFICATE

Lead your class in writing certificates of recognition for people who have demonstrated a Stephen-like dedication to whatever needs to be done. (Use the reproducible page that follows.) People should exhibit the qualities of Stephen, must have served in more than one capacity, and must have moved on to positions of greater responsibilities.

Recognition

Today's lesson looks at those who are chosen to serve. Every congregation has a few shining examples of what it means to serve Christ faithfully in whatever capacity he directs. Use this certificate to honor such a person in your congregation.

In Grateful Recognition

for the Consistent Demonstration of a

Servant's Spirit

_____

(Name)

Is Honored on

_____

(Date)

by

_____

(Church)

Signed _____

_____

WITNESSING BEYOND JERUSALEM

LESSON 6

WHY TEACH THIS LESSON?

Sometimes a job needs to be done, but you have to let someone else do it. It's not that you can't do the job; you could do it well. But you have other responsibilities, and there are others who can and should get involved. So you refuse. We saw the apostles do that in last week's lesson. Caring for the widows was a noble task, but they could not add it to their duties. Seven other faithful men were recruited.

In today's lesson another job comes up. This time it is one of the Seven who is challenged to do something outside of his "job description." Rather than deferring it to another, however, Philip takes on the task. With the church scattering (Acts 8:3), his care for the widows apparently was no longer needed.

Thus, today's lesson will challenge your students to be flexible. Philip's example is opposite the apostles' except for one detail: he, like the apostles, was doing the Lord's will for the good of the church. If your learners will take that attitude, they will have learned a valuable lesson.

INTRODUCTION

A. STIRRING UP THE NEST

Residents of our retirement home sit for hours to watch a dozen tiny birds whose residence is a glass-enclosed aviary. Most fascinating is the emergence of recently hatched babies from their nests to make use of the flying space provided. One wee bird stayed too long in his crowded nest and became so crippled that he remained a "hopper" among those flying above and around him. That is a condition not to be desired, either among God's creatures or God's people.

Moses made this point in his song celebrating God's deliverance of Israel from Egypt: "He shielded him and cared for him; . . . like an eagle that stirs up its nest and hovers over its young, that spreads its wings to catch them and carries them on its pinions. The Lord alone led him; . . . . He made him ride on the heights of the land" (Deuteronomy 32:10-13).

Similarly, the persecution endured by the early church in Jerusalem may be seen as a stirring up of the nest in which it came into being. Thus was it persuaded to tumble out and to use and develop its wings in order to embark on the worldwide flight for which it was intended. Today's lesson recounts some of the first brief flights beyond the church's "hatching nest."

B. LESSON BACKGROUND

While the Jerusalem church began "enjoying the favor of all the people" (Acts 2:47), conditions did not remain favorable. The apostles, as the Lord's spokesmen and the leaders of the church, endured persecution (Acts 4:1-3; 5:17-42). Later, opposition was directed against Stephen (one of the Seven chosen to help administer the benevolence ministry for widows). Saul of Tarsus, who kept watch

DEVOTIONAL READING:
JOHN 4:19-24
BACKGROUND SCRIPTURE:
ACTS 8
PRINTED TEXT:
ACTS 8:4-8, 26-39

Apr
8

LESSON AIMS

After this lesson each student should be able to:

1. Summarize Philip's evangelistic efforts among the people of Samaria and with the Ethiopian eunuch.

2. Tell how Philip's encounter with the eunuch illustrates important principles of personal evangelism.

3. Plan a specific way to use these principles in his or her witness to someone this week.

KEY VERSE

Those who had been scattered preached the word wherever they went. —Acts 8:4

over the clothing of those who stoned Stephen to death, quickly rose to leadership in the persecution of the believers in Jerusalem. Acts 8:1-3 tells the story: "On that day a great persecution broke out against the church at Jerusalem, and all except the apostles were scattered throughout Judea and Samaria."

Thus the believers were dispersed in all directions: southward and westward in Judea and northward to Samaria. Meanwhile, the apostles continued to carry on their special work in Jerusalem.

I. TO SAMARITANS NEARBY (ACTS 8:4-8)

A. GOING AND TELLING (vv. 4, 5)

4. Those who had been scattered preached the word wherever they went.

The early disciples of Jesus took the gospel with them *wherever they went*. They probably did not announce formal gatherings where they addressed audiences with sermons and lectures. A more likely scenario is excitement generated in personal conversation, heralding the good news that had changed the believers' lives and driven them from their homes. As strangers in a community, they had every reason to say why they were there. The *word* of Christ was the dominant, motivating power in their lives. What else was there to talk about?

What, by the way, should a Christian today talk about when he introduces himself to a stranger?

5. Philip went down to a city in Samaria and proclaimed the Christ there.

The *Philip* mentioned here was not the apostle; the apostles had remained in Jerusalem. This man was one of the seven men selected to conduct the daily distribution of supplies to the needy (Acts 6:1-6). He was known some years later as "Philip the evangelist" (Acts 21:8). By then he was living in Caesarea and serving as host to Paul and his companions (including Luke, who is part of the "we" mentioned in the record) on their way to Jerusalem.

The *city in Samaria* to which Philip *went* may have been the ancient capital of the northern kingdom of Israel (known as Sebaste in the first century), or it may have been another city in Samaria, such as the one where Jesus talked with the woman at Jacob's well (John 4:4-7).

B. CONFIRMING THE WORD (vv. 6, 7)

6. When the crowds heard Philip and saw the miraculous signs he did, they all paid close attention to what he said.

If Philip's hearers included individuals who had witnessed Jesus' visits to their territory, then a foundation for faith existed already. Added was the evidence provided through Philip's ability to do *miraculous signs*. This power apparently came with the laying on of the apostles' hands when the Seven were set apart to their task (Acts 6:5-8; 8:14-19). The word and the works made a convincing combination.

7. With shrieks, evil spirits came out of many, and many paralytics and cripples were healed.

The scope of Philip's miracle-working ministry resembled that of Jesus. First noted are those with spiritual afflictions—corrected, though not without the departing demons' noisy objections. Then mentioned are those suffering from various kinds of physical afflictions—*paralytics and cripples*. The fact that *many . . . were healed* had a powerful impact.

C. ENJOYING THE RESULTS (v. 8)

8. So there was great joy in that city.

This outcome seems obvious, but most appropriate. Bodies and spirits had been made whole. Most significant, eternal life had been received by many; for "when they believed Philip as he preached the good news of the kingdom of God and the name of Jesus Christ, they were baptized, both men and women" (v. 12).

The remainder of our printed text tells how *joy* came to another person to whom Philip brought the word of life in Christ.

CHURCH ON FIRE

In June of 1990, fire ravaged a church building in Burlingame, California, doing a million dollars worth of damage. Eventually, the minister of the congregation admitted to pouring gasoline on the building and lighting it. He had wanted to collect the insurance money so that his church could update the fifty-five-year-old structure.

The minister claimed that he didn't mean to burn down the entire building; his plan simply got out of hand. In fact, one of his fellow ministers came to his defense, describing him as "a very dedicated man . . . a real man of God, with a genuine concern." Apparently, having a "genuine concern" for others is not all that is required to be a leader of God's people. A sense of integrity would also help!

Of course, many ministers would like to "set the church on fire"—in a spiritual sense. Those who are most successful at this follow the example of Philip: they proclaim Christ faithfully and watch the gospel bear fruit in the lives of individuals who commit themselves to Christ. In every time and place the transformation that occurs in those who accept Christ proves that God is still creating spectacular changes in human beings through those who are "on fire" for him.   —C. R. B.

Today's visual suggests a number of modern applications of Acts 8:4. Discuss additional ways you and your class can spread the good news.

II. TO ONE FROM FAR AWAY (ACTS 8:26-39)

Acts 8:9-25 includes the account of two men named Simon and their relationship to Philip's ministry among the Samaritans. One Simon, a skillful illusionist, or magician, became convinced of the gospel through seeing that Philip's miracles were real. This Simon was among those who were baptized. The other Simon (the apostle Peter) came with John from Jerusalem to see what was happening in Samaria and to convey special powers of the Spirit by laying hands on the believers. When Simon the magician tried to buy this ability to give the Spirit to others, Peter responded with a stern rebuke. After further ministry in this location, the two apostles returned to Jerusalem, preaching in other Samaritan villages along the way.

A. DIRECTIONS FROM HEAVEN (vv. 26-29)
26. Now an angel of the Lord said to Philip, "Go south to the road—the desert road—that goes down from Jerusalem to Gaza."

Why was Philip to make this journey? What was there to justify his leaving the evangelizing of Samaria and taking a long walk alone into the *desert* country of Judea? Such questions must have occurred to him, but he accepted the message of the *angel* as God's directive. He knew that his responsibility was to obey. *Gaza* was the southernmost of five ancient Philistine cities and was located near the Mediterranean coast.

27. So he started out, and on his way he met an Ethiopian eunuch, an important official in charge of all the treasury of Candace, queen of the Ethiopians. This man had gone to Jerusalem to worship,

Breathtakingly abrupt, the narrative leaps from Philip's departure—*he started out*—to his encounter with a man from Ethiopia (modern Sudan), located south of Egypt. This man served as an official responsible for *the treasury of Candace, queen of the Ethiopians.* (*Candace* was a title of queens in Ethiopia much as *Caesar* was a title of Roman emperors.)

In addition, this man was a *eunuch*, as were many attendants in royal courts. (Eunuchs were believed to be less likely to become involved in questionable

WHAT DO YOU THINK?

An angel told Philip where to go to find a receptive person with whom to share the gospel. How do we determine when and where to share the gospel today? How do we find people who are receptive to the message?

HOW TO SAY IT

Ashdod. ASH-*dod.*

Azotus. Uh-ZO-*tus.*

Caesar. SEE-*zer.*

Caesarea. Sess-uh-REE-*uh.*

Candace. CAN-*duh-see.*

Ethiopians. Ee-thee-O-pea-*unz.*

eunuch. YOU-*nick.*

Gaza. GAY-*zuh.*

Isaiah. Eye-ZAY-*uh.*

Mediterranean. MED-uh-tuh-RAY-*nee-un.*

Philistine. Fuh-LISS-*teen or* FILL-*us-teen.*

Samaria. Suh-MARE-ee-*uh.*

Samaritans. Suh-MARE-uh-*tunz.*

Sebaste. Seh-BAS-*tee.*

Septuagint. Sep-TOO-ih-*jent.*

Tarsus. TAR-*sus.*

behavior with any ladies of the court.) He had traveled *to Jerusalem to worship,* perhaps at one of the major national feasts. Whether he was born a Jew or had become a proselyte (a convert to the Jewish faith), we do not know. But being a eunuch, he would not have been permitted to go inside the courts of the temple at Jerusalem (Deuteronomy 23:1).

28. . . . *and on his way home was sitting in his chariot reading the book of Isaiah the prophet.*

No doubt this journey by *chariot* from Jerusalem to the eunuch's homeland (well over a thousand miles) must have been uncomfortable at times. But we know how he was spending some of the long hours: he was reading his Bible! Specifically he was reading from a scroll of *Isaiah,* perhaps in the Greek translation (the Septuagint), made approximately three centuries earlier in Egypt. Some suggest that the eunuch purchased the Isaiah scroll in Jerusalem during his visit there and was now taking the opportunity to examine it.

29. *The Spirit told Philip, "Go to that chariot and stay near it."*

If God had something in mind for this man in the *chariot,* why did he not convey that message directly by his angel or by his *Spirit* and leave Philip to continue his work in Samaria? For whatever reason, that is not the way God works. Each person receives the gospel of Christ from another person. "How can they believe in the one of whom they have not heard? And how can they hear without someone preaching to them?" (Romans 10:14). The preacher may be an apostle such as John, conveying the saving gospel through Scripture (John 20:30, 31). It may be a Christian friend saying through letters what is sometimes spoken. But a human messenger of the gospel has always been God's instrument for the salvation of mankind—even "hand-picked" prospects such as the Ethiopian eunuch and Saul of Tarsus (Acts 9:6).

THE DISTASTEFUL ONES

A long-cherished myth of evolutionary biology involves the viceroy butterfly. It was believed to mimic the coloration of monarch and queen butterflies, which have a taste that birds do not like. In 1862 Walter Bates developed a theory that one species can learn to mimic the sound, appearance, or smell of another species in order to deceive its predators.

One hundred and thirty years later, two Florida biologists decided to test Bates's hypothesis and found that (at least in the case of the three species mentioned above) it was not true! They removed the wings from specimens of the three varieties of butterflies and discovered that birds found them *all* to be distasteful. It wasn't the viceroy's protective coloration that caused birds to avoid them after all.

In New Testament times, most Jews found it "distasteful" to have contact with certain classes of people—Gentiles, Samaritans, tax collectors, and eunuchs, for examples. But then came Philip, preaching the gospel of Christ among the Samaritans and then responding to the call of God to tell an Ethiopian eunuch about Christ—and all of this apparently with no reluctance! His example says that no one is "distasteful" to God; no one is outside the circle of his love.

Have *we* drawn any circles that leave certain "distasteful" people on the outside?

—C. R. B.

WHAT DO YOU THINK?

Philip heard the Ethiopian reading a prophecy about Jesus, and this gave him a good idea about how to approach the man with the good news. How can we broach the subject of Jesus with people? What opportunities should we watch for?

B. QUESTIONS RAISED (vv. 30, 31)

30. *Then Philip ran up to the chariot and heard the man reading Isaiah the prophet. "Do you understand what you are reading?" Philip asked.*

The man in *the chariot* was *reading* aloud, perhaps to fix his own attention on the text, or possibly to include an otherwise unmentioned driver of the chariot. Philip *heard* enough to know what was being read and to ask a very wise question about it. No one could fully *understand* the passage being read by the eunuch without recognizing its links to the gospel of Christ. The question was a rather direct one to ask of a complete stranger, but this reader did not mind.

31. *"How can I," he said, "unless someone explains it to me?" So he invited Philip to come up and sit with him.*

Far from being offended by Philip's question, the eunuch welcomed it as a possible solution to his problem. There was room in the chariot for another passenger, and Philip was warmly invited to *sit with* the treasurer. Neither of these two men, so different in nationality and background, hesitated for a moment to examine God's Word with the other!

C. TEXT PROVIDED (vv. 32-35)

32, 33. *The eunuch was reading this passage of Scripture: "He was led like a sheep to the slaughter, and as a lamb before the shearer is silent, so he did not open his mouth. In his humiliation he was deprived of justice. Who can speak of his descendants? For his life was taken from the earth."*

The source of the eunuch's reading was the best known of Isaiah's songs about God's Suffering Servant. We find it in Isaiah 53:7, 8. It compares God's servant with a *sheep* or a *lamb* in the creature's quiet acceptance of the most violent treatment, whether in shearing or in *slaughter*. One is led to think of Jesus' steadfast refusal to answer or complain against the slander and *humiliation* to which he was subjected before and during his crucifixion (1 Peter 2:21-23).

In all of this, as Isaiah prophesied, Jesus *was deprived of justice*; he was denied every basic right to a fair trial, either by the Jewish council or by the Roman court. Justice gave way to the clamor for his crucifixion. The question, *Who can speak of his descendants?* continues the tone of sorrow in this portion of Isaiah's prophecy. It seems to be asking how Jesus can have any descendants if *his life* is *taken from the earth*.

One may wonder why this text in Acts differs in places from the passage as found in Isaiah 53. What we see in Acts is a translation that more closely resembles the Greek text that was commonly used in New Testament times.

34. *The eunuch asked Philip, "Tell me, please, who is the prophet talking about, himself or someone else?"*

Obviously Isaiah was describing someone. Was it *himself or someone else* who fulfilled the role of God's Suffering Servant? The same question remains troublesome to those who deny its obvious answer in Jesus of Nazareth! To them it produces an uneasiness that they often find difficult to cope with.

35. *Then Philip began with that very passage of Scripture and told him the good news about Jesus.*

What an opportunity was presented to the evangelist, and what a text was provided! It was both natural and necessary for Philip to show how the facts of the gospel fulfilled the word picture drawn by Isaiah. From the eunuch's question that followed (verse 36), it is apparent that Philip's preaching *the good news about Jesus* to him included showing how a believer participates in the death and resurrection of Jesus through being baptized—buried and raised according to his command (Matthew 28:18-20; Romans 6:1-4; Colossians 2:11, 12).

D. GOSPEL ACCEPTED (vv. 36-38)

36. *As they traveled along the road, they came to some water and the eunuch said, "Look, here is water. Why shouldn't I be baptized?"*

Even the desert country of Judah is not entirely without springs, streams, and pools. Such waters seem to have been rare enough to excite the eunuch when he saw one. Having been taught by Philip concerning baptism, the eunuch was eager to fulfill this command.

Note that while the teaching about salvation had to come from Philip, the idea of immediate action came from the eunuch. No pressure, prodding, or exhortation was needed here. This man believed and desired to do as he had been taught.

37. (footnote) Philip said, "If you believe with all your heart, you may." The eunuch answered, "I believe that Jesus Christ is the Son of God."

This verse does not appear in some early manuscripts of Acts, nor in most of the newer translations. It is, however, quoted in some very early Christian writings, and it appears to represent a procedure that was followed in the early church. Baptism was, and is, for believers—believers in *Jesus Christ as the Son of God*.

38. And he gave orders to stop the chariot. Then both Philip and the eunuch went down into the water and Philip baptized him.

The Scripture is explicit in recording the procedure that was followed. Did the inspired historian consider that future generations might question the need for the burial aspect of baptism? Otherwise why should he be so specific that both the baptizer and the candidate *went down into the water* to carry out the act (immersion) that is inherent in the word *baptized*? The eunuch deliberately made an all-out commitment. A limited expression was not, and is not, appropriate. His dripping garment would dry out; his spirit of obedience to the Lord would not!

E. MEN SEPARATED (v. 39)

39. When they came up out of the water, the Spirit of the Lord suddenly took Philip away, and the eunuch did not see him again, but went on his way rejoicing.

The Holy *Spirit*, who had brought Philip into contact with the homeward-bound Ethiopian (v. 29), had other work for the evangelist to do in towns along the Mediterranean coast, from Azotus (known as Philistine Ashdod in the Old Testament) and finally to Caesarea (v. 40). There Paul and Luke found him approximately a quarter of a century later (Acts 21:8)—the final time Philip is mentioned in the New Testament.

The newly baptized eunuch apparently continued *on his way* to Gaza, Egypt, and home to Ethiopia. While we know nothing certain of what became of him there, we would like to think that (in keeping with the spirit of the book of Acts) he told others of the Christ he had found through the prophecy of Isaiah and the testimony of the man who approached him as he traveled homeward. With him, as with the Samaritans to whom Philip had taken the gospel, there was *rejoicing*.

CONCLUSION

"I'll go on my way rejoicing."

A friend of mine said this habitually as he took his departure. The words were those used to describe the Ethiopian eunuch following his obedience to the gospel, but the spirit of joy was my friend's own and it was real. What was he rejoicing about? Almost everything, but mostly things related to Jesus and the life available in him. If you asked him to be specific, you didn't have time to hear him recite, one by one, all the reasons for his joy.

What, though, were the causes of the eunuch's rejoicing? They are not named, and we can't know them all. Surely these are some: he had been introduced to the Savior prophesied by Isaiah; that Savior had come to die for him and for people throughout the world; God could be worshiped in his homeland of Ethiopia as well as in Jerusalem; and life eternal was his in Jesus Christ. The list of blessings was endless. Why shouldn't he go on his way rejoicing?

Why shouldn't we?

Discovery Learning

This page contains an alternate lesson plan emphasizing learning activities. Classes desiring such student involvement will find these suggestions helpful. The next page is a reproducible activity page to further enhance discovery learning.

LEARNING GOALS

After this lesson each student will be able to:

1. Summarize Philip's evangelistic efforts among the people of Samaria and with the Ethiopian eunuch.

2. Tell how Philip's encounter with the eunuch illustrates important principles of personal evangelism.

3. Plan a specific way to use these principles in his or her witness to someone this week.

INTO THE LESSON

Say to your class, "In sixty seconds, tell the person sitting next to you about the person who shared the gospel with you the first time it made sense. After sixty seconds, it will be your partner's turn. Remember that you have only sixty seconds, so be brief. Ready, set, go."

Make the transition to the Bible study by saying, "Our Bible lesson today looks at two groups that were influenced by the evangelism of Philip. As we study our text today, maybe we can see some insights that will be helpful in our efforts to present the gospel in a way that 'makes sense' to those with whom we share it."

If this "neighbor nudge" activity doesn't seem right for your class, then guide the class in brainstorming for ethnic and cultural groups that are often neglected in local church evangelism. Tape a large poster to the wall and use a broad-tipped marker to list the groups the students mention.

Make the transition to the Bible study by saying, "Our Bible lesson today looks at two ethnic and cultural groups that were influenced by Philip. Let's look for some insights that will be helpful in our efforts to take the gospel to the ends of the earth."

INTO THE WORD

Have a volunteer read Acts 8:4-8, 26-39 aloud. Observe that almost every verse of this text suggests principles of evangelism that are true and valid for all times and for all cultures.

Provide paper and pens and challenge your class members to identify principles of evangelism for every verse that is appropriate. For example, Acts 8:4 shows that all Christians are to announce the Word wherever we go. Acts 8:5 gives us the central focus of our message—we proclaim Christ. Acts 8:8 assures us that joy will fill the place where Christ is preached and acknowledged. Acts 8:26 teaches us to be sensitive to God's leading. Acts 8:27 illustrates immediate obedience and the inclusion of high-profile, influential people in our efforts. Acts 8:28 suggests watching for people who have an interest in the Bible or in spiritual matters. Acts 8:29 shows that God will guide those who are open to his leading. Acts 8:30 illustrates urgency, listening to others, and asking pointed questions to discern understanding. Acts 8:31 cautions to wait for an invitation to move closer. Acts 8:32-35 shows that we should be able to begin at any point in Scripture and share the gospel of Jesus. Acts 8:36 indicates that baptism is important as a part of one's accepting Christ. Acts 8:38 makes it clear that baptism is by immersion. Acts 8:39 tells us to expect joy in the life of the new convert to Christ.

OPTION

We often use Bible drama with children, but it is also effective with adults. The characters can all read their lines from their Bibles; memorizing lines is not necessary. Understanding the character and projecting the emotions and concerns of the character are important.

Acts 8:4-8 lends itself to drama with a narrator. Prepare a group to dramatize this and note the serious nature of the demonic elements. For Acts 8:26-39, assign parts for a narrator, the angel, the Holy Spirit, Philip, and the Ethiopian.

INTO LIFE

Provide pens and paper for your class to write evangelistic letters to people with whom they would like to share the gospel. Explain that they could introduce the topic like this: "In our Bible class today, we studied the account of Philip talking to a man about Christ, and I thought about how I've been wanting to talk to you about Jesus. The man in the story was interested in religious discussion, just as you are. Our lesson said that Philip told him the good news about Jesus, and I would like to do the same with you."

Invite class members to read their letters aloud. It will encourage the listeners, and the reader will be encouraged by the response of the listeners. Ask for suggestions to improve each presentation.

Close the class period by dividing into prayer partners to pray for the letters and their impact on the recipients. Then encourage the students to mail the letters early this week.

Evangelistic Verses

Write out each of the verses listed below. As you are copying, ask God to show you how each verse applies to your efforts to share your faith in Jesus Christ.

John 3:16

Acts 1:8

Matthew 28:18-20

Mark 16:15, 16

Romans 10:11-13

Just Do It!

"Do not merely listen to the word, and so deceive yourselves. Do what it says" (James 1:22). What is your plan for putting into practice the things you are learning in this study? Don't have one? Write one out here.

PROCLAIMING THE RISEN LORD

LESSON 7

WHY TEACH THIS LESSON?

What do you think of when you hear the word *primary*? The word basically means "first," but it can be first *in time* or first *in importance or significance*.

Today we will look at the primary witnesses of Jesus' resurrection. The women were primary witnesses in that they were the first to tell the good news. Paul, it can be argued, became the primary witness of the resurrection in that he is the most significant. His prominence in the book of Acts and his contribution to the writing of the New Testament bear that out.

These primary witnesses will remind your learners that proclaiming the risen Lord is their "primary" task as believers!

INTRODUCTION

A. THE DARKEST HOUR

"The darkest hour is just before the dawn."

Most of us have heard this saying. Perhaps we have spoken the words in an effort to encourage someone during a difficult time. But if anyone has examined it literally in relation to nights and mornings, we have not seen his report.

There is an all-important area, however, in which this adage is true; and it is an area that touches every person's life in a very significant and powerful way. We refer to Jesus' death and resurrection and to the difference that those events make in how one deals with death whenever he has to confront its harsh reality. At that critical point, resurrection becomes more than just a doctrine; it is the unshakable basis of hope for one who believes and lives in Jesus.

Here is a summary of that message of hope: "That Christ died for our sins according to the Scriptures, that he was buried, that he was raised on the third day according to the Scriptures, and that he appeared"—to many who knew him best and grieved most deeply at his dying (1 Corinthians 15:3-8). In Jesus the deepest darkness does give way to brightest dawn—a truth that demands to be reported.

B. LESSON BACKGROUND

One man, Luke, served as God's recorder for both passages of Scripture before us today. The two passages have this feature in common: each follows an account of death and resurrection, and each leads to the spreading of the news that Jesus is risen.

Luke 23 tells how the Jewish council delivered Jesus to the Roman authorities, who were persuaded to crucify him. The final two verses of the chapter note that Galilean women who had followed Jesus and supported his ministry (Luke 8:1-3) witnessed his death, then watched as his body was entombed by Joseph of Arimathea (John 19:38-42). Not satisfied with the hundred pounds of myrrh and aloes already used to wrap Jesus' body, the women prepared spices and ointments

DEVOTIONAL READING:
JOHN 20:1, 11-18
BACKGROUND SCRIPTURE:
LUKE 24:1-12; ACTS 9:1-31
PRINTED TEXT:
LUKE 24:1-10; ACTS 9:19b-22, 26-28

LESSON AIMS

After this lesson a student should be able to:

Apr
15

1. Describe the appearance of angels to the women at Jesus' tomb and Saul's earliest testimony of the resurrection.

2. Tell how the evidence for Jesus' resurrection is convincing for believers today.

3. Praise God for Jesus' resurrection and for the gospel message it validates.

KEY VERSE

Why do you look for the living among the dead? He is not here; he has risen! —Luke 24:5, 6

LESSON 7 NOTES

to show their own respect for Jesus. Then, beginning at sundown on Friday, they rested through the Sabbath, as the law prescribed, before visiting the tomb and hearing the astonishing news that Jesus had risen.

Acts 9 carries us approximately seven years forward into the history of the church and to the life of Saul, a fervent Pharisee and opponent of the gospel. His eagerness to persecute Christians took him to Damascus, where he expected to arrest believers and bring them to Jerusalem for punishment. But Saul himself was "arrested" on the way by Jesus himself, speaking from Heaven. Saul "surrendered" and asked for orders. Those orders took him on to Damascus for further instructions, given by a disciple named Ananias: "Get up, be baptized and wash your sins away, calling on his name" (Acts 22:16).

Saul (the apostle Paul) later referred to his baptism as a death-and-resurrection experience with Christ: "Don't you know that all of us who were baptized into Christ Jesus were baptized into his death? We were therefore buried with him through baptism into death in order that, just as Christ was raised from the dead through the glory of the Father, we too may live a new life" (Romans 6:3, 4).

What happened in Jerusalem after Jesus' resurrection? We learn this from Luke 24. And what happened in Damascus after Saul's spiritual resurrection in Christ? We learn this from Acts 9.

I. THE WOMEN SEE AND TELL (LUKE 24:1-10)
A. AMAZING DISCOVERY (VV. 1-3)
1. On the first day of the week, very early in the morning, the women took the spices they had prepared and went to the tomb.

The first day of the week is usually called Sunday; but because of what happened on this day, Christians often refer to it as the Lord's Day. This is most likely the meaning of John's reference to "the Lord's Day" in Revelation 1:10.

We have noted Luke's reference to the women from Galilee who witnessed Jesus' death and burial (Luke 23:55, 56). Mentioned earlier as ones "who had been cured of evil spirits and diseases" (Luke 8:1-4) are Mary Magdalene, Joanna (the wife of the manager of Herod's household), Susanna, and "many others." Two of these, Mary Magdalene and Joanna, are mentioned with the group at the tomb, along with Mary the mother of James and "others with them" (Luke 24:10).

From the other Gospel accounts we learn that one of these women was Salome (Mark 16:1). We also learn that, while Mary Magdalene came to the tomb with the other women, at some point she became separated from them. John's account (John 20:1, 2) indicates that when Mary saw that the stone had been rolled away from the tomb, she immediately ran to tell Peter and John that someone had taken the body of Jesus (though she was mistaken). Peter and John then ran to the tomb to investigate (though Luke mentions only Peter's journey in v. 12). Mary Magdalene returned alone to the tomb, where Jesus appeared to her (John 20:11-18).

2. They found the stone rolled away from the tomb.

Joseph of Arimathea had completed his burial of Jesus by rolling a great *stone* before the opening of the *tomb*. Pilate had ordered the stone sealed and guarded to prevent the removal of Jesus' body (Matthew 27:62-66). This stone had been a subject of concern to the women as they approached the tomb (Mark 16:3), but they quickly discovered that their anxiety was unnecessary. An angel from Heaven had *rolled away* the stone. Thus were all hindrances removed that would keep anyone from entering and examining the empty burial place (Matthew 28:2-4). As some have noted, the stone was rolled away, not to let Jesus out, but to let witnesses in.

WHAT DO YOU THINK?

From the different Gospel accounts we get different details about the events of the resurrection. How would you reply to someone who challenged the accuracy of the Gospel reports on the basis of these differences?

3. . . . but when they entered, they did not find the body of the Lord Jesus.

The women *entered* and looked around. The *body* of Jesus was gone, but its wrappings lay in place, and to one side was the cloth that had been about Jesus' head. This was noted especially by Peter and John when they were summoned to the tomb a short while later (John 20:1-8).

B. WONDERFUL NEWS (vv. 4-8)

4. While they were wondering about this, suddenly two men in clothes that gleamed like lightning stood beside them.

It is only natural that the women were *wondering about* what they saw: the once-secure tomb was opened, and the body they had watched being placed inside was missing—without a trace of forcible removal.

Both the apparel and the message of the *two men* who *suddenly* appeared identified them as angels. One had removed the stone from the doorway of the tomb and proceeded to address the women (Matthew 28:2-7).

5. In their fright the women bowed down with their faces to the ground, but the men said to them, "Why do you look for the living among the dead?

Zechariah (the father of John the Baptist), Mary the mother of Jesus, and the shepherds near Bethlehem all had shown the same natural response to the sudden and glorious appearance of angels (Luke 1:12, 29, 30; 2:9, 10). The women *bowed . . . to the ground* to avoid facing the brilliance before them.

The angels' message was blunt: *Why do you look for the living among the dead?* It sounds like a rebuke, but how else could their news be expressed so briefly, plainly, and powerfully? A tomb is no place to look for a living person.

6. "He is not here; he has risen! Remember how he told you, while he was still with you in Galilee.

The angels' statement that Jesus *is not here,* but *has risen* confirmed the news implied in the angel's question. The announcement should not have come as a surprise, however, to anyone who had followed Jesus' ministry and heard his teaching in these women's home district of *Galilee.* Jesus' own predictions of his suffering, death, and resurrection had been directed mostly to his apostles (Matthew 16:21; 17:22, 23; Mark 8:31; 9:31; Luke 9:21, 22; 18:31-33), but they were a part of his public teaching available to men and women alike. Now the teaching was authenticated by a dramatic visual aid.

7. "'The Son of Man must be delivered into the hands of sinful men, be crucified and on the third day be raised again.'"

Jesus had been clear about the events of his final days. Judas betrayed Jesus *into the hands* of the Jewish leaders, who in turn delivered him to the Romans with a demand that he *be crucified.* Those events happened as predicted; therefore, why shouldn't his resurrection *on the third day* have been expected? There was really no place for uncertainty or confusion.

Should we be surprised, however, at the disciples' failure to hear and understand Jesus' words? Are we better than they at shaping our actions to what God's Word says, rather than to what we expect or wish it to say?

8. Then they remembered his words.

These women needed only to have the truth brought to their attention. Having *remembered* what Jesus said and having experienced the fulfillment of *his words,* they were ready to go and tell others.

C. EXCITED REPORT (vv. 9, 10)

9. When they came back from the tomb, they told all these things to the Eleven and to all the others.

Display today's visual as you discuss Luke 24:4. Discuss: "While we can't all see angels to assure us that Jesus has risen, how can we have confidence in the resurrection?"

"Why seek ye the living among the dead? He is not here, but is risen." Luke 24:5, 6

WHAT DO YOU THINK?

The women who came to the tomb of Jesus must have had a vivid memory of much that Jesus said and did during his ministry. Why do you think they did not remember what he said about his resurrection?

Apparently the women from Galilee were lodging together in Jerusalem and were in close contact with the apostles. So they returned to share with their fellow disciples the glorious news of Jesus' resurrection. Such news is still important enough to be told with breathless excitement wherever we can find a hearer.

The *Eleven* had been the Twelve until the defection and self-destruction of Judas. Peter and John were the first of the group to learn of the empty tomb, and they did not at first grasp the entire story (John 20:1-10). They ran to the scene to examine the empty tomb.

10. It was Mary Magdalene, Joanna, Mary the mother of James, and the others with them who told this to the apostles.

Mary Magdalene and *Joanna* are named among the Galileans whom Jesus had healed of evil spirits and various diseases (Luke 8:2, 3). *Mary the mother of James* seems to have had a son among the apostles—"James the younger" (Mark 15:40). He and his companions, however, did not accept the report. To them, talk of a resurrection seemed like "nonsense" (v. 11).

Luke's summary lists the women together, but we have already noted that Mary Magdalene had made her report to Peter and John separately—apparently without having seen the angels (John 20:2). Peter and John, then, must have been separated from the other apostles and were evidently closer to the tomb than they. Mary Magdalene had time to find them and to return to the tomb behind them before the other women made their report. Mark 16:9 tells us that Jesus "appeared first to Mary Magdalene" outside the tomb (as reported in John 20:11-17). His second appearance was to the other women as they were on the way to tell the apostles about seeing the angels at the tomb (Matthew 28:9). At some point the apostles all came together, except for Thomas, and Jesus appeared to them as well (Luke 24:33-49; John 20:19-24).

NOT A HOAX

Leroy Johnson is an authority on the history of Death Valley National Park. In 1998 a friend told him that he had found a wooden chest containing the possessions of one of the "forty-niners" (the miners who flocked westward during the California "gold rush"). A document in the chest was dated January 2, 1850. At first, Johnson believed it to be authentic.

However, as Johnson and other historians examined the chest and its contents more carefully, they found several discrepancies. A ceramic bowl bore a distinctive trademark that was not in use until 1914. Two tintype photos in the chest were of a kind not patented until several years after 1850. It became obvious that the chest was a hoax—though the man who said he found it continued to claim otherwise.

Throughout history skeptics have called the resurrection of Christ a hoax. But the Gospel accounts will not allow such a view to stand. They include the testimony of the women who were first to arrive at the tomb and discover it empty. (Women in that society were already held in disregard; imagine the added scorn that would result from concocting such an outlandish story.) Eventually the men to whom they told the news were able to examine the evidence and believe.

None of these individuals had anything to gain by fabricating a hoax that would have made them look foolish. Today, because of their testimony, we can declare with confidence, "Christ has indeed been raised from the dead" (1 Corinthians 15:20).　　　　　　　　　—C. R. B.

II. SAUL TESTIFIES OF JESUS (ACTS 9:19b-22, 26-28)

Here our focus shifts to a man whose name as well as his life was changed by his proclamation of the risen Christ. When first we meet him in the Scripture, he is known as Saul of Tarsus.

WHAT DO YOU THINK?

We often talk about "doubting Thomas," but the Gospel records are clear that none of the apostles believed in the resurrection until he actually saw Jesus. So how can we convince people today? What kind of evidences can we provide for people to whom the claims of the resurrection seem like "nonsense"?

HOW TO SAY IT

Ananias. An-uh-NYE-us.
Arabia. Uh-RAY-bee-uh.
Arimathea. AIR-uh-muh-THEE-uh.
Barnabas. BAR-nuh-bus.
Caesarea. Sess-uh-REE-uh.
Cornelius. Cor-NEEL-yus.
Damascus. Duh-MASS-cus.
Galileans. Gal-uh-LEE-unz.
Magdalene. MAG-duh-leen or Mag-duh-LEE-nee.
Pharisee. FAIR-ih-see.
synagogues. SIN-uh-gogs.
Tarsus. TAR-sus.
Zechariah. Zek-uh-RYE-uh.

A. IN DAMASCUS (vv. 19b-22)

19b. Saul spent several days with the disciples in Damascus.

This verse follows the account of Saul's baptism into Christ, after which he was given nourishment. For *several days* he remained *in Damascus* in the company of followers of Jesus, who were now his friends, not his foes.

20. At once he began to preach in the synagogues that Jesus is the Son of God.

Saul had come to Damascus with letters to the *synagogues* authorizing him to seek out and arrest any who believed *Jesus* was *the Son of God* (Acts 9:1, 2). Now he entered those synagogues to convince unbelievers to believe that very fact!

In Damascus Saul began the pattern that he followed throughout his evangelistic career. The gospel was the power of God for salvation to every believer, "first for the Jew, then for the Gentile" (Romans 1:16). So in every city the apostle first went to the synagogue, where he would find Jews who possessed a knowledge of the prophetic Scriptures and thus a background for understanding the gospel. He would preach in the synagogue as long as he had a receptive hearing and leave only when he was rejected and compelled to do so (Acts 13:45, 46; 17:1-9).

21. All those who heard him were astonished and asked, "Isn't he the man who raised havoc in Jerusalem among those who call on this name? And hasn't he come here to take them as prisoners to the chief priests?"

Saul's hearers *were astonished.* His reputation had preceded him to Damascus, especially among those who had the most to fear from his arrival there. Included in that number was Ananias, the disciple whom God persuaded to lead Saul to the new life in Christ (Acts 9:10-18).

22. Yet Saul grew more and more powerful and baffled the Jews living in Damascus by proving that Jesus is the Christ.

As time passed, Saul *grew more and more powerful* in his presentation of the gospel. He thwarted the objections of *the Jews in Damascus* by his ready answers to their arguments and assertions. By laying the Old Testament Scriptures alongside the facts of Jesus' life, death, and resurrection, Saul proved that *Jesus is* indeed the *Christ*, the promised Messiah.

Verses 23-25 (not included in the printed text) note that "after many days" the Jews made plans to kill Saul, forcing him to leave the city. The "many days" apparently includes the three years mentioned in Galatians 1:15-18, during which Saul went to Arabia and then returned to Damascus. The Scripture does not say what he did in Arabia. Perhaps the Lord instructed him during this time, preparing him for the special ministry he would have.

A GRAVE MATTER

The "Y2K bug" generated a lot of hoopla and consternation in the last few years leading up to January 1, 2000. Our tendency to rely on high-tech solutions to even the most mundane of life's problems created some rather interesting dilemmas.

One form of the "bug" that received little hype was very low-tech in nature. Many older people whose spouses had died had dual headstones placed on the grave plots where they would eventually be buried with their mates. On each stone, beneath the person's own name, had been engraved the numerals "19" followed by a blank space to be filled in at the time of the person's death. In the late 1990s, it was estimated that a quarter of a million gravestones were inscribed this way. The cost for changing the "19" to "20" ran as high as two thousand dollars.

Saul had a different "gravestone" problem. His encounter with the risen Christ was a "grave" matter, for it forced him to acknowledge that Jesus' gravestone had indeed been rolled away. When he finally admitted this, it revolutionized his life. He began proving that Jesus was the Messiah, confounding those who had known him formerly as a persecutor of the church.

DAILY BIBLE READINGS

Monday, Apr. 9—The Empty Tomb (Luke 24:1-10)

Tuesday, Apr. 10—Jesus Appears to Saul (Acts 9:1-9)

Wednesday, Apr. 11—Ananias, a Reluctant Witness (Acts 9:10-19a)

Thursday, Apr. 12—Saul Preaches and Leaves Damascus (Acts 9:19b-25)

Friday, Apr. 13—Saul in Jerusalem (Acts 9:26-31)

Saturday, Apr. 14—Peter Heals Aeneas and Raises Dorcas (Acts 9:32-43)

Sunday, Apr. 15—Have Faith! God Will Provide (Psalm 63)

Regardless of when we live—whether early in the first millennium as Saul did, or early in the third as we do now—once the risen Christ takes control of our lives, all things become new.

—C. R. B.

B. IN JERUSALEM (vv. 26-28)

26. When he came to Jerusalem, he tried to join the disciples, but they were all afraid of him, not believing that he really was a disciple.

Rescued from the wrath of the unbelieving Jews, Saul returned *to Jerusalem*, where once more his reputation preceded him. There he *tried to join the disciples*. But the Jerusalem faithful were skeptical. Was this an effort to spy on them in an attempt to arrest and punish even more of their number?

27. But Barnabas took him and brought him to the apostles. He told them how Saul on his journey had seen the Lord and that the Lord had spoken to him, and how in Damascus he had preached fearlessly in the name of Jesus.

Saul could not have found a better "sponsor" in his efforts to work with the church at Jerusalem than *Barnabas* provided in bringing him *to the apostles*. Specifically, Peter and James (the Lord's brother) are mentioned in Galatians 1:18, 19. (That James is called an apostle in this passage most likely reflects his position of leadership in the Jerusalem church.)

Barnabas's willingness to "go out on a limb" for someone whose conversion was being questioned was an appropriate gesture for one known as the "Son of Encouragement" (Acts 4:36). He also seems to have done his homework by investigating the reports of Saul's conversion. He was able to report confidently that Jesus had appeared and *spoken* to Saul on the way to *Damascus*, and that Saul had risked his life to speak *fearlessly* for Christ in that city.

We wonder why the details of Saul's conversion were not better known by the apostles. Perhaps it was simply that Saul talked about Jesus rather than himself.

28. So Saul stayed with them and moved about freely in Jerusalem, speaking boldly in the name of the Lord.

Barnabas's support on behalf of Saul accomplished its purpose. Saul *stayed with* the disciples *in Jerusalem*. He continued *speaking boldly in the name of the Lord*—a proclamation in which he seems never to have been as effective in Jerusalem as he was afterward in other places. Apparently the disciples could forgive his acts of persecution more readily than the Jews could forgive his conversion!

CONCLUSION

When Peter stood before those gathered in the house of Cornelius in Caesarea, he spoke plainly of the life and ministry and the death and resurrection of Jesus. He said that God showed the risen Savior openly; however, he was "not seen by all the people, but by witnesses whom God had already chosen—by us who ate and drank with him after he rose from the dead. He commanded us to preach to the people" (Acts 10:40-42).

Peter was right, but now that we have reviewed the events of the resurrection morning, we know the rest of the story: Peter didn't know that Jesus was alive again until some women told him, and at first he didn't believe what he heard! Consider also the case of Saul of Tarsus, who saw and heard Jesus on the Damascus road. An otherwise unknown disciple named Ananias was responsible for giving Saul further instructions once he entered Damascus.

Frontline proclaimers of the gospel still have a constant need for supportive, encouraging, and sometimes direct "nudges" from common folk in the congregation. Whether one's task is done in public or behind the scenes, we are *all* essential to the effective proclamation of the gospel.

Discovery Learning

This page contains an alternate lesson plan emphasizing learning activities. Classes desiring such student involvement will find these suggestions helpful. The next page is a reproducible activity page to further enhance discovery learning.

LEARNING GOALS

After this lesson each student should be able to:

1. Describe the appearance of angels to the women at Jesus' tomb and Saul's earliest testimony of the resurrection.

2. Tell how the evidence for Jesus' resurrection is convincing for believers today.

3. Praise God for Jesus' resurrection and for the gospel message it validates.

INTO THE LESSON

Have your class members sit in groups of four to discuss these two statements: "The resurrection of Jesus Christ is the best-attested event in history," and "The resurrection of Jesus Christ is the most controversial event in history."

Make the transition to the Bible study by saying, "The resurrection of Jesus Christ is the foundational doctrine of Christianity. Today's lesson includes a look at the effect of the resurrection of Jesus Christ on the apostle Paul. Be watching in today's study for how the resurrection of Jesus should affect us today."

INTO THE WORD

Have one or two volunteers read aloud Luke 24:1-10; Acts 9:19b-22, 26-28. Then choose one or more of the following activities to lead a study of the text.

DRAMATIC MONOLOGUE

A dramatic monologue tells a story from the perspective of the author but with the dimensions of emotion and excitement added by the reader. Ask the learners to work in groups of two or three to identify the emotion behind the account. Have them give reading instructions for each verse. For example, Luke 24:1 should be read in a subdued and sad voice, with verse two swelling with question and wonder. Acts 9:19 should be read with excitement and awe; verse 20, with boldness.

VIDEO VIEWING

An excellent video of the book of Acts based on the *New International Version* is produced by The Visual Bible and is available at most Christian bookstores or through Visual International, 5201 Maryland Way, Brentwood, TN 37027. Show the portions that cover today's text.

OUTLINE THE TEXT

Provide a pen and a copy of the reproducible page that follows for each class member. Have the learners work in groups of four or five to outline today's text. If there is time, ask the group members to develop a paraphrase of the text as well. Encourage originality and creativity.

INTO LIFE

Choose one or more of the following activities to conclude your session.

HYMN STUDY

Distribute hymnals to the learners and have each one identify his or her favorite resurrection hymn. Then have them find as many allusions, references, or quotations of today's text as they can find in the hymns they chose.

Close the session by singing one stanza and a chorus of each of several favorite hymns.

PERSONAL TESTIMONY

Ask each learner to prepare a two-minute testimony on the topic, "What the resurrection of Jesus means to me." Prepare by asking these questions: How do you know for sure that Jesus rose from the dead? What was your life like before you accepted Christ? What specific changes has the resurrection of Jesus made in your life?

POETRY WRITING

Several people in your class probably enjoy poetry, and even people who do not necessarily like poetry will write a simple kind of poetry called a cinquain (*sing-cane*) if you walk them through the steps. Write a cinquain with your whole class by writing the answers to these questions on successive lines on a poster.

• What is a one-word title for this episode?
• What are two words that describe the title?
• What three words describe your feelings about the title?
• What four words express action about the title?
• What is a one-word synonym for the title?

Here is an example based on Luke 24:1-10.

RISEN
ALIVE AGAIN
FILLED WITH JOY
TELLING OTHERS THE NEWS
RESURRECTION

Outline

Outlining is an important Bible study method because it requires identifying the main ideas of a particular text. Outline today's text with one main point for each section identified below. Provide one or two subpoints if you would like to.

I.   Luke 24:1-10

II.   Acts 9:19b-22

III.   Acts 9:26-28

Paraphrase

A paraphrase restates the author's ideas in one's own words, including explanations. Luke 24:1 might be paraphrased, "Early Sunday morning, just as it was beginning to dawn, the women arrived at the tomb that Joseph of Arimathea had made available for the burial of the body of Jesus. They had prepared spices to use in the formal burial of Jesus' body." Try your hand at writing a paraphrase of today's text.

GENTILES
RECEIVE THE SPIRIT

LESSON 8

WHY TEACH THIS LESSON?

Unless you teach a class of Jewish learners, this lesson ought to be one of the most exciting ever! Peter and the other Jewish believers, even the leaders of the newly established church, had blinders on regarding the salvation of non-Jewish people. Had those blinders not come off, we would never have known the gospel was for us! That is exciting.

It is also humbling. Peter, who traveled with Jesus for over three years, could not understand the scope of the gospel plan of salvation without a dramatic divine sign. If Peter could be so mistaken, we ought to be very cautious when we disagree with other believers. There is no room for dogmatism, but rather an open and honest appeal to God's revealed plan. That is what this lesson is all about.

INTRODUCTION

A. BARRIERS

All too familiar in our time are the walls, both visible and invisible, that separate ethnic groups, nations, and other categories of humanity. No division is more deeply rooted than the biblically recognized cleavage of humanity between Jew and Gentile—between those who have "citizenship in Israel" and those considered "foreigners to the covenants of the promise" (Ephesians 2:12). That division was most forcefully presented in the stern warning carved in the wall separating the outer court of the temple in Jerusalem from the inner courts: "No foreigner may enter within the barricade which surrounds the temple and enclosure. Anyone who is caught doing so will have himself to blame for his ensuing death."

B. LESSON BACKGROUND

The church came into being in Jerusalem during a Jewish feast (Pentecost) through the preaching of the apostles (all Jewish) to Jews from many places. While Jesus had commanded his followers to teach all nations (Matthew 28:18-20) and to go into all the world with the gospel (Mark 16:15, 16), the church was slow to grasp the all-inclusive scope of that commission. It took some dramatic nudging on God's part to convince even the most outspoken apostle that Gentiles, too, were legitimate recipients of divine grace through the gospel.

Cornelius, the first Gentile to hear the gospel, was a centurion in the Roman army. He was stationed in the city of Caesarea, located on the Mediterranean coast about sixty-five miles northwest of Jerusalem. This man worshiped the one true God, practicing the virtues expected of devout Jews, such as prayer, fasting, and generosity to the poor (Acts 10:1, 2, 22, 30). Such was the strength of his example that "all his family" followed the same pattern of living (v. 2).

An angel appeared to Cornelius one day as he was praying during the middle of the afternoon. He directed Cornelius to send for the apostle Peter, who was at

DEVOTIONAL READING:
GALATIANS 3:11-14
BACKGROUND SCRIPTURE:
ACTS 10:1—11:18
PRINTED TEXT:
ACTS 10:30-40, 43-48

LESSON AIMS

After this lesson students should be able to:

1. Recall significant details of the conversion of Cornelius and his household.

2. Tell how this event demonstrates the universal nature of the gospel.

Apr
22

3. Identify a group in their own community that has little or no presence in the church, and make plans to reach people within that group with the gospel.

KEY VERSE

God does not show favoritism but accepts men from every nation who fear him and do what is right.   —Acts 10:34, 35

WHAT DO YOU THINK?

For Peter and others, observance of the law was a mark of identity and evidence of faithfulness. Even though Peter was a Christian, he was still a Jew. Up until this time, submission to the New Covenant had never challenged his continued faithfulness to the Old. That is the reason his experience was so disturbing to him. He was asked to do something that violated his conscience and threatened his identity. As a Christian, how do you decide how far outside your comfort zone you are willing to go to reach out to someone who is not yet a Christian?

WHAT DO YOU THINK?

The lesson writer says, "God honored Cornelius's devotion by making special arrangements for him to hear about Jesus." Do you think God always honors devotion in this way? Why or why not?

[Be careful to distinguish between what we may want to be true, what might be true, and what the Bible assures us really is true.]

Joppa, about thirty miles down the coast. The angel told precisely where the apostle would be found and what his message would be. Immediately Cornelius dispatched three of his trusted servants to Joppa (Acts 10:1-8).

When the travelers reached their destination the next day, Peter was on the rooftop of the house where he was staying, awaiting his noon meal. While there he "fell into a trance" and saw a vision of various creatures being let down before him in what appeared to be a sheet. He then heard a voice command him to slay and eat these animals. Peter refused, claiming that they were "impure." The voice told Peter that he should not label as impure what God had cleansed. This vision occurred three times, and Peter was left wondering what it meant (vv. 9-17).

At that very moment, the delegation from Caesarea arrived and asked for Peter. He received the men and arranged for them to be lodged overnight. The next day he left with them, accompanied by six fellow Christians from Joppa (Acts 11:12). When the men arrived at Caesarea, they found Cornelius awaiting them, along with many friends and relatives whom he had invited to his home. Cornelius had to be dissuaded from bowing before the apostle, who went on to explain that God had persuaded him to break the Jewish/Gentile barrier by accepting Cornelius's invitation.

Peter then inquired, "May I ask why you sent for me?" (vv. 17-29). Today's printed text begins with Cornelius's answer.

I. AN AUDIENCE IS PREPARED (ACTS 10:30-33)

A. ANGEL'S MESSAGE (vv. 30-32)

30. Cornelius answered: "Four days ago I was in my house praying at this hour, at three in the afternoon. Suddenly a man in shining clothes stood before me.

Cornelius began by recounting what had happened *four days* earlier. The *man in shining clothes* was later identified by Cornelius's messengers to Peter as "a holy angel" (Acts 10:22). He had appeared to Cornelius *at three in the afternoon.*

31. ". . . and said, 'Cornelius, God has heard your prayer and remembered your gifts to the poor.

Certainly Cornelius was living in a manner that fulfilled God's desire for his people under the Old Covenant: "to act justly and to love mercy and to walk humbly with your God" (Micah 6:8). God honored Cornelius's devotion by making special arrangements for him to hear about Jesus.

32. "'Send to Joppa for Simon who is called Peter. He is a guest in the home of Simon the tanner, who lives by the sea.'

The angel's directions were clear. They included names, a location, and an occupation. It is worth noting that Peter was staying with a *tanner,* whose work would have required handling the skins of dead animals. Since these were unclean according to Jewish law (see Leviticus 11), some see this as an indication that Peter was already starting to rid himself of certain Jewish prejudices even before his vision of the unclean animals.

Here, as in the case of the Ethiopian eunuch (Acts 8:26-39) and Saul of Tarsus (Acts 22:6-16), divine intervention brought the hearer and the messenger together; the human messenger brought the gospel. That was the reason Peter was going to Cornelius's house: to "bring . . . a message through which you and all your household will be saved" (Acts 11:14).

B. CORNELIUS'S RESPONSE (v. 33)

33. "So I sent for you immediately, and it was good of you to come. Now we are all here in the presence of God to listen to everything the Lord has commanded you to tell us."

Could any evangelist find a better prepared audience than the one that welcomed Peter that day? The people had come together on their own initiative with a desire to *listen*. They recognized a responsibility *in the presence of God* to hear his instructions. They were not interested in small talk and human opinion; they wanted their preacher to tell them what God had to say.

II. AN APOSTLE SPEAKS (ACTS 10:34-40, 43)

A. GOD HAS NO FAVORITES (vv. 34, 35)

34. Then Peter began to speak: "I now realize how true it is that God does not show favoritism.

God had just given Peter a "crash course" on the truth that he *does not show favoritism*. Peter now understood how that lesson applied to the present situation.

35. ". . . but accepts men from every nation who fear him and do what is right.

The Old Testament provides examples of God's interest in people of *every nation*, not just those of Israel. One is Ruth the Moabitess, who believed in and served God and is named among the human ancestors of the Lord Jesus (Matthew 1:5).

We are not to assume from this verse that people can become acceptable to God through their works. For one to possess true righteousness before God means doing so on his terms, not one's own. That means having the "righteousness . . . which is through faith in Christ—the righteousness that comes from God and is by faith" (Philippians 3:9). This is what Cornelius lacked.

A FUNDAMENTAL TRUTH

In February of 1942, President Franklin D. Roosevelt signed Executive Order 9066—the decree that caused approximately 120,000 Japanese-Americans to be interned until World War II was over. The order came just two months after the Japanese attack on Pearl Harbor, amidst a widespread hysteria about foreigners, particularly those who looked different from the "average" American. Rumors about "treasonous" Japanese circulated widely. For example, some were claiming that Japanese farmers were planting their tomato crops in arrow-shaped patches that would direct Japanese bombers toward California armament factories!

After the war, it became obvious that certain U.S. officials had knowingly lied to the American people. There was no evidence that any of the Japanese-Americans were siding with Japan. Attorney General Francis Biddle would later say that the internment of the Japanese was "ill-advised, unnecessary, and unnecessarily cruel."

This statement also describes what happens when Christians allow racial and cultural pride and/or paranoia to affect the way they treat others in the church or withhold the gospel from others in society. In our text, Peter stated a fundamental principle of the gospel and then acted on it by telling Cornelius and those gathered with him about Christ.

The gospel is *the* solution to the racial and cultural divisions in the world and in the church. Has this truth found its place in *our* hearts?   —C. R. B.

B. JESUS IS SAVIOR OF ALL (vv. 36-38)

36. "You know the message God sent to the people of Israel, telling the good news of peace through Jesus Christ, who is Lord of all.

Jesus was born and grew up as one of *the people of Israel*, and his ministry was to them first (Matthew 10:5, 6; Mark 7:27). However, Peter also noted that *Jesus . . . is Lord of all*, including those Gentiles whom he was addressing.

37. "You know what has happened throughout Judea, beginning in Galilee after the baptism that John preached.

Peter's hearers were not totally "in the dark" concerning Jesus. They did *know* something about him. As a Roman army officer, Cornelius must have been aware

---

WHAT DO YOU THINK?

It was not easy for Peter to say, "I now realize that I have been wrong about what I believed regarding God's plan for the Gentiles." Nor is it easy for us to say, "I now realize that I didn't have all the facts," or, "I now realize that I was misinformed," or, "I now realize that I was too quick to pass judgment," or, "I now realize that my understanding of that passage of Scripture was inadequate." Does the phrase, "I now realize" have a familiar ring to you? In what circumstances have you had to admit a realization of past ignorance or mistakes? What kind of results have you seen from such humble honesty?

Today's visual is a vivid reminder of the truth that Peter perceived at the home of Cornelius: God does not play favorites!

God is no respecter of persons: but in every nation he that feareth him, and worketh righteousness, is accepted with him.

Acts 10:34, 35

of events that had some impact on the peace and safety of the area under his jurisdiction (even if he were not stationed in Caesarea during Jesus' ministry). Such information would have included the news of multitudes who flocked to the Jordan valley to hear *John* the Baptist and to obey his command of *baptism*. Even greater multitudes were attracted by the teaching and miracles of Jesus in *Galilee*. In Capernaum Jesus had healed the servant of another Roman centurion who humbly requested it (Matthew 8:5-13). Reports of this probably would have been of special interest to Cornelius.

38. ". . . how God anointed Jesus of Nazareth with the Holy Spirit and power, and how he went around doing good and healing all who were under the power of the devil, because God was with him.

Peter called attention to two aspects of Jesus' public ministry: that it was a ministry of *power* provided by the *Holy Spirit* (Luke 4:17-19) and that this power was used for *doing good* to others. Jesus never used his power to his own advantage, but always for the *healing* of others—to make them spiritually and physically whole. This placed Jesus in continual conflict with *the devil*, whom he had come to destroy (Hebrews 2:14, 15; 1 John 3:8).

C. OTHERS BEAR WITNESS (vv. 39, 40, 43)

39. "We are witnesses of everything he did in the country of the Jews and in Jerusalem. They killed him by hanging him on a tree.

In contrast to the widely published reports of Jesus' ministry was the more precise and intimate testimony of the apostles, whom the Lord chose to be in his company throughout his ministry from its beginning at John's baptism until his ascension into Heaven (Acts 1:21, 22). This group was the *we* for whom Peter spoke.

The phrase *the country of the Jews* describes Palestine in general and also points to the Jewish leaders as the ones who opposed Jesus and brought about his crucifixion. Their hostility stands in stark contrast to the loving work of God in empowering, approving, and glorifying his one and only Son. The reference to *hanging him on a tree* identifies the crucifixion with the curse pronounced in Deuteronomy 21:22, 23 and referred to in Galatians 3:13, where we are told that Jesus became "a curse for us." There was no limit to the shame and suffering that Jesus bore for us!

40. ". . . but God raised him from the dead on the third day and caused him to be seen.

God's definitive answer to man's hostility toward Jesus was given in Jesus' resurrection *on the third day* following his death. The appearances of Jesus after his resurrection were done openly, leaving no doubt in the witnesses' minds that Jesus was indeed alive.

43. "All the prophets testify about him that everyone who believes in him receives forgiveness of sins through his name."

Cornelius was likely familiar with some of the teachings of the Old Testament *prophets*. Now he was able to see their words in a new light, as he understood that they testified *about* the Christ of whom Peter spoke. *Forgiveness of sins* in the *name* of Jesus was the theme of Jesus' commission to his apostles (Luke 24:47) and of their preaching (Acts 2:38).

III. THE SPIRIT SHOWS APPROVAL (ACTS 10:44-48)

A. AMAZING INTERRUPTION (vv. 44-46a)

44. While Peter was still speaking these words, the Holy Spirit came on all who heard the message.

Peter had fulfilled his assignment; now God took over, showing his approval of what was taking place. The sudden coming of *the Holy Spirit* indicated that these who were hearing the gospel were allowed to do so without regard to their nationality. Acts 11:15 tells how Peter reported the matter later to the church in Jerusalem: "As I began to speak, the Holy Spirit *came on* them as he had come on us at the beginning."

Peter's reference to the "beginning" clearly refers to what the apostles experienced on the Day of Pentecost (Acts 2:1-4). However, what happened in Jerusalem and what was happening in Caesarea were not exactly the same. On the former occasion, the Spirit fell on the apostles before they spoke, enabling them to be heard in languages familiar to their widely mixed audience. Here the Spirit came on the listeners and ended the sermon. At Pentecost the Spirit put the stamp of God's power on the speakers and the message; here he put the stamp of God's approval on the hearers and their reception of the *message*.

45, 46a. The circumcised believers who had come with Peter were astonished that the gift of the Holy Spirit had been poured out even on the Gentiles. For they heard them speaking in tongues and praising God.

Peter had been wise in taking with him six fellow Christians—all Jewish, of course—when he accompanied Cornelius's messengers to Caesarea. (They could later serve as witnesses to what had happened.) This was an extraordinary experience for these men. They are described as being *circumcised*, which highlights their distinction from *the Gentiles* gathered with them (cf. Ephesians 2:11). And now they saw and heard evidence that these Gentiles were receiving an outpouring *of the Holy Spirit* similar to what the apostles received on the Day of Pentecost. These Gentiles were *speaking in tongues*, or languages, that they had not learned (just as the apostles had done on Pentecost), and they were obviously expressing praise to God.

B. APOSTLE'S QUESTION (vv. 46b, 47)

46b, 47. Then Peter said, "Can anyone keep these people from being baptized with water? They have received the Holy Spirit just as we have."

Whereas Peter had "doubted" the meaning of the vision that he had seen earlier in Joppa (Acts 10:17), here he grasped immediately the significance of what had happened. A seemingly impregnable barrier was coming down. These Gentiles who had just heard the gospel should be *baptized* as readily as any of the Jews who had expressed a desire to follow Christ.

Some may question whether the sequence of events described here indicates that Cornelius and those Gentiles gathered with him *received the Holy Spirit* prior to their baptism in *water* (mentioned in the next verse). But this "receiving" experienced by the Gentiles was Peter's way of referring to the baptism of the Spirit that the apostles (*we*) had received at Pentecost. (Note his words in Acts 11:15, 16.) *Just as* the baptism of the Spirit at Pentecost had preceded the instructions about baptism to Jews, here it preceded the instructions about baptism to Gentiles. It indicated to Peter that the "keys of the kingdom" (Matthew 16:19) were to be used to allow Gentiles—who had been previously excluded—to enter. Thus Peter proceeded to offer to the Gentiles in Caesarea the opportunity to obey the gospel and to be baptized. They would then receive the indwelling of the Spirit promised to every baptized believer, according to Acts 2:38.

ARTISTIC LICENSE

Think for a moment about the works of some famous artists: Salvador Dali's surreal "landscapes," for example; or Pablo Picasso's distorted human faces; or Henry

WHAT DO YOU THINK?

Peter was wise to take six fellow Christians with him to Caesarea. They could later serve as witnesses to what had happened. In what situations should Christian leaders today demonstrate the same kind of wisdom?

DAILY BIBLE READINGS

Monday, Apr. 16—Cornelius Sends for Peter (Acts 10:1-8)

Tuesday, Apr. 17—Peter's Vision (Acts 10:9-16)

Wednesday, Apr. 18—The Men at the Gate (Acts 10:17-23a)

Thursday, Apr. 19—Peter Goes to Caesarea (Acts 10:23b-33)

Friday, Apr. 20—Gentiles Hear the Good News (Acts 10:34-43)

Saturday, Apr. 21—Gentiles Receive the Holy Spirit (Acts 10:44-48)

Sunday, Apr. 22—Peter's Report in Jerusalem (Acts 11:1-18)

Moore's heavy, rounded interpretations of human or animal figures. "Artistic license" is how we describe the process that is involved in creating all of these designs.

A strange example of this phenomenon can be found on the wall of the Pacific Bell building in Los Angeles. It is a sculptured map of the world, with the continents represented fairly accurately—but that's where reality stops. The position of the continents has been changed so that the eastern tip of Brazil lies just west of Alaska, the tip of South Africa rests above the northern reaches of Norway, and Australia pretty well fills the gap between Panama and Spain. The world as we know it has been strikingly rearranged.

When God poured out his Spirit on the Gentiles in Cornelius's house, he was rearranging the spiritual world as Peter had known it. Peter saw the implications of this and asked, "Can anyone keep these people from being baptized with water?" The answer then, as now, is that the gates to God's kingdom are open to all peoples in all places.

God's "artistic license" has given us a completely new way of looking at the world. Isn't it a beautiful piece of work?   —C. R. B.

C. GENTILES' BAPTISM (v. 48)

48. So he ordered that they be baptized in the name of Jesus Christ. Then they asked Peter to stay with them for a few days.

This matter was important and was not to be delayed. Peter had begun the teaching of these individuals; now he conveyed the command for them to *be baptized*. His work, however, did not end there. *A few days*—we know not how many—of fellowship and teaching were necessary in order for these new converts to learn the Lord's commands and to embark on an exciting walk with him.

CONCLUSION

A. WHO WAS ADDRESSED?

God had sent his angel, not to present the gospel to Cornelius, but to provide a human preacher of the saving word. But this occasion also provided a vital learning experience for many besides Cornelius. These others needed to learn the lessons that it taught.

Peter needed to learn that Jesus is the Savior of Jew and Gentile alike. Peter received his lesson on a rooftop in Joppa; he saw it illustrated in Caesarea.

Other Jewish Christians stood in great need of the same lesson. A beginning was made with the six believing Jews who had gone with Peter to Caesarea. Later they were present with him in Jerusalem when he explained to the church there exactly what had happened in the house of Cornelius (Acts 11:12-18).

The family and friends whom Cornelius had gathered to hear the gospel learned a priceless lesson—that God is no respecter of persons and that Jesus is a Savior for *every* person. That, however, was a lesson that the church needed to learn as well—and it took time for the lesson to sink in.

B. WHO IS ADDRESSED?

A vastly larger audience is affected by the "double-barreled" message of the Scripture before us today. First, the gospel message is for everyone of every ethnic, national, political, economic, social, and religious background and persuasion. Second, the message of salvation is the same for all: "that Christ died for our sins according to the Scriptures, that he was buried, that he was raised on the third day according to the Scriptures" (1 Corinthians 15:3, 4).

If Christ is the Savior of all, it follows, then, that there is no other Savior for any! And if we who are followers of that Savior do not let others know of him, who will?

Discovery Learning

This page contains an alternate lesson plan emphasizing learning activities. Classes desiring such student involvement will find these suggestions helpful. The next page is a reproducible activity page to further enhance discovery learning.

LEARNING GOALS

After this lesson students should be able to:

1. Recall significant details of the conversion of Cornelius and his household.

2. Tell how this event demonstrates the universal nature of the gospel.

3. Identify a group in their own community that has little or no presence in the church, and make plans to reach people within that group with the gospel.

INTO THE LESSON

Begin your class by giving a copy of the following agree-disagree survey to each class member. Have each learner mark his or her level of agreement or disagreement, on a scale of 9 to 1, before each statement (9=strongest agreement; 5=completely neutral, no opinion; 1=strongest disagreement).

___ 1. Our church needs to be more diverse in its ethnic and cultural makeup.

___ 2. Our congregation needs to reach out to people with different national origins.

___ 3. People of different ethnic and cultural backgrounds would be comfortable in our church.

___ 4. If converts from our missionaries visited our congregation, they would be warmly received.

___ 5. Appealing to one ethnic (homogeneous) group is a valid church growth principle.

INTO THE WORD

Ask a volunteer to read aloud Acts 10:30-48. Then choose one or both of the following activities to explore the meaning of the text.

JOURNAL OR DIARY ENTRY

Provide pens and paper for your class to write journal or diary entries that Peter, Cornelius, a member of Cornelius's household, or one of Peter's Jewish Christian companions might have written during the three days covered in our text. Try to make sure that at least one learner is writing an entry for each character in the text.

Ask the participants to prepare by reading the text with the perspective of the selected person in mind. For example, when Peter saw his vision, he probably did not yet understand its full meaning or implication. After his presentation of the gospel to Cornelius, his understanding was broadened, and he had to change lifelong habits and attitudes.

Allow about ten minutes for writing. Then ask volunteers to read their journal entries aloud.

DRAMATIC READING

Assign people in your class to prepare a dramatic reading of today's text. Assign the parts to Cornelius, the angel, Peter, and a narrator.

Read through the text a verse at a time, and discuss the voice, tone, and attitude of the speaker in each verse. For example, consider Cornelius's tone in Acts 10:30 and 31. Was he proud of his piety that prompted the visit of an angel? Probably not, but how does he relate the information in verses 30 and 31 without sounding arrogant or filled with pious pride? Verse 33 would be spoken with rising excitement and anticipation. How will you portray the outbreak of tongues in verses 44-46? This will doubtless prompt a discussion of the nature of tongues. Make sure you have read the commentary section thoroughly or have obtained help from another reliable source.

Once those questions are answered, have the "cast" read through the text in dramatic fashion.

INTO LIFE

Provide a sheet of poster board, some markers, and some mounting tape for every four students. Ask these groups to make posters with verses that describe the universal nature of the gospel. Encourage your learners to examine the following verses: Matthew 28:18-20; Mark 16:15, 16; John 3:16; Acts 1:8; or Romans 10:11-13. Ask the group to write the selected verse in large letters and decorate the poster for display.

In addition, or instead of, the poster project, challenge your class to list the ethnic, cultural, or national groups living within the circle of influence of your congregation who are not being effectively evangelized by your church. Are there any changes in attitude, style, or action that your congregation would have to make in order to reach these groups more effectively? What efforts have been made to reach them in the past? What leaders would need to be contacted to implement an outreach project to these groups?

A third option for applying this lesson is to use the reproducible activity on the page that follows.

Scripture Search

The hour from 11:00 A.M. to noon on Sunday has been called "the most segregated hour of the week." This reflects a sad truth in our society. The church in Acts struggled diligently to break out of its cultural heritage and include believers of all ethnic, cultural, and national backgrounds. We need the same kind of diligent struggle for unity in the midst of diversity. Study these passages and write out some implications from each of them.

Psalm 133:1

John 17:20-23

Romans 15:5, 6

Ephesians 4:3

Colossians 2:2

1 Corinthians 1:10

Colossians 2:12-20

THE CHURCH IN ANTIOCH

LESSON 9

WHY TEACH THIS LESSON?

Lynn Anderson has written an excellent book on leadership in the church, entitled *They Smell Like Sheep*. In it he notes that shepherds do more than care for sheep—they live with them. They handle them, looking for injuries that need mending. They carry the weak or the young. They spend so much time so close to the sheep that "they smell like sheep"!

One way for a leader to "smell like sheep," the author says, is to divide his time between "problem people" and "possibility people." Anderson says leaders too often focus all their ministry efforts on "problem people," those people who need for the leaders to minister to them, to help them. Anderson says that the wise leader will not invest all of his or her efforts on people who are "objects" of ministry, but instead will recruit "allies" in ministry.

Barnabas knew that. When he saw the potential in Antioch, he recruited an ally in the person of a relatively new Christian who showed a lot of promise. He recruited Saul of Tarsus!

This lesson will encourage your learners to be possibility people and to recruit possibility people.

INTRODUCTION

Experts in gardening offer this advice: "If you want to get rid of that undesirable growth in your flower bed, don't try to dig it out. All of the little roots will just reach out in every direction. Let the ground lie fallow for about two years. Each time a sprout comes up, give it a shot of weed killer. After a while it will all die, and you can plant your flowers."

Undesirable objects, when aggressively attacked, often seem to thrive. The desires and intentions of the attacker backfire. Those who initially found the church "undesirable" found it equally resistant to their efforts to stamp it out. Persecution only made it stronger!

A. THEY CRUCIFIED JESUS

"This will bring an end to it," the authorities thought as they watched Jesus die the agonizing death of crucifixion. But their actions were subject to an authority higher than theirs. The crucifixion was part of God's grand plan "before the creation of the world" (1 Peter 1:20). It demonstrated his love and his grace, and it was the prelude to the resurrection of Jesus, which destroyed the power of death once for all.

B. THEY STONED STEPHEN

"No one can talk to the powers that be like that. We'll show these followers of Jesus who's really in control." But the ones who hurled the stones that brought about Stephen's death heard only forgiveness and hope from the dying martyr's lips. The results were definitely not what they anticipated: "Those who had been scattered preached the word wherever they went" (Acts 8:4). The church at Antioch, as we shall see, began as a result of that scattering.

DEVOTIONAL READING:
EPHESIANS 3:7-12
BACKGROUND SCRIPTURE:
ACTS 11:19-30; 13:1-3
PRINTED TEXT:
ACTS 11:19-30; 13:1-3

LESSON AIMS

After this lesson a student should be able to:

1. Recount how the church at Antioch was strengthened in its growth and how it then sent forth workers to expand the church's outreach.

2. Explain the importance of developing godly leadership in the church.

3. Identify an individual who needs encouragement in the Lord's work, and plan a specific way to become a "Barnabas" to that person.

Apr
29

KEY VERSE

While they were worshiping the Lord and fasting, the Holy Spirit said, "Set apart for me Barnabas and Saul for the work to which I have called them."
—Acts 13:2

C. THEY KILLED JAMES

Not long after the church at Antioch began, "King Herod arrested some who belonged to the church, intending to persecute them. He had James, the brother of John, put to death with the sword" (Acts 12:1, 2). Perhaps Herod figured that an assault on the key leadership of the church would silence its voice. That strategy failed just as badly as the others had. The church was briefly vexed, but quickly vitalized. One apostle's death did not stop its witness; it stirred and strengthened it.

D. LESSON BACKGROUND

In last week's lesson, we watched God certify the Gentiles as candidates for his kingdom by using Peter to extend his invitation to them. The Holy Spirit's stamp of approval (demonstrated in the same manner as Peter had seen it manifested on the Day of Pentecost with the apostles) made it all "official": God wants Gentiles in his family!

In today's lesson we shall see how a church full of Gentiles not only received approval and encouragement (from God and from Barnabas), but also seized the initiative in serving others and in carrying out Jesus' Great Commission.

I. PRODUCING A CHURCH (ACTS 11:19-21)

A. TALKING TO BRETHREN (v. 19)

19. Now those who had been scattered by the persecution in connection with Stephen traveled as far as Phoenicia, Cyprus and Antioch, telling the message only to Jews.

Earlier we cited Acts 8:4, which notes how *the persecution in connection with Stephen* (following his martyrdom) resulted in the followers of Jesus being *scattered* abroad. Here we see additional "fallout" from that futile effort to silence believers. In trying to quench the fire surrounding Jesus, the religious authorities succeeded only in fanning the flames. Fearing for their lives, the followers of Jesus left their homes and possessions—but they didn't leave their faith.

Three areas of ministry are mentioned in this verse. The first is *Phoenicia*. This area was located northward, beyond Samaria and Galilee, and included the long fertile plain between the Lebanon mountains and the Mediterranean Sea. It also included the cities of Tyre and Sidon. That churches were established in these important cities is evident from Acts 21:3, 4 and 27:3. *Cyprus* was the foremost island of the eastern Mediterranean. It was the home of Barnabas (Acts 4:36).

Most important in today's study is the city of *Antioch*. (This was Antioch of Syria, not the Pisidian Antioch mentioned in Acts 13:14.) Antioch provided fertile soil for the gospel, for many Jews resided here. At this time in history, Antioch was the third largest city in the world (following Rome and Alexandria, Egypt). It was also a corrupt city, badly in need of spiritual and moral revival. But that was about to change.

B. CROSSING BARRIERS (v. 20)

20. Some of them, however, men from Cyprus and Cyrene, went to Antioch and began to speak to Greeks also, telling them the good news about the Lord Jesus.

Some of these believers had come to Jerusalem *from Cyprus* and from *Cyrene* (located in northern Africa), and there they had embraced the good news. They were anxious to share it with their fellow Jews in *Antioch*, but they had a passion to do more. So they started to tell their neighbors who were *Greeks* about the *Lord Jesus*.

WHAT DO YOU THINK?

The believers described in Acts 11:19-21 were obviously enthusiastic about sharing their faith in Jesus Christ. How can we stir up more enthusiasm in our congregation for witnessing and evangelism?

C. RECEIVING GOD'S BLESSING (v. 21)

21. The Lord's hand was with them, and a great number of people believed and turned to the Lord.

The enthusiasm of these followers of Jesus caught people's attention, the truth reached hungry hearts, and a great number of people believed.

II. RESPONDING TO A NEED (ACTS 11:22-24)

A. PROPER CONCERN (v. 22)

22. News of this reached the ears of the church at Jerusalem, and they sent Barnabas to Antioch.

Many of the leaders in the church at Jerusalem may have been quite puzzled by the news of events in Antioch. Could God really be blessing this surge among the Gentiles?

We must, however, give these men credit for being open to the possibility that what was happening in Antioch was of God. They searched among themselves for someone to send and decided on the man who had come to be called the "Son of Encouragement" (Acts 4:36). He was someone known for his fair play; the apostles knew he would make an honest assessment.

When a need for an encourager arises in the church, are people likely to think of you?

B. PROPER REPRESENTATIVE (vv. 23, 24)

23, 24. When he arrived and saw the evidence of the grace of God, he was glad and encouraged them all to remain true to the Lord with all their hearts. He was a good man, full of the Holy Spirit and faith, and a great number of people were brought to the Lord.

Barnabas is this writer's favorite Christian. What a man! Wouldn't it be great if your friends and loved ones would feel constrained to print verse 24 on your headstone?

It seemed to take no time at all for Barnabas to discern the Holy Spirit's blessing on the Antioch church. True to his reputation, Barnabas encouraged them all to remain true to the Lord.

Barnabas also realized that he did not want to return to Jerusalem. Exciting things were happening in Antioch, and he was not content with merely observing them. He wanted to share a piece of the action! He also thought of someone else whose passion and abilities made him well suited for ministering in the thriving church at Antioch.

III. MATURING (ACTS 11:25-30)

A. TEAM TEACHING (vv. 25, 26)

25, 26. Then Barnabas went to Tarsus to look for Saul, and when he found him, he brought him to Antioch. So for a whole year Barnabas and Saul met with the church and taught great numbers of people. The disciples were called Christians first at Antioch.

Acts 9:30 notes that Saul had been sent away to Tarsus (his hometown) when some in Jerusalem had plotted to kill him. That was where Barnabas found him. He brought Saul to Antioch, recognizing that the church there needed his kind of personality, commitment, and gifts, and that Saul needed a place to serve. The two men worked well together in Antioch; whereas "a great number of people" had been led to the Lord (v. 24), now great numbers of people were taught.

Some believe that the disciples were being ridiculed when the locals began to call them Christians. Others suggest that it was a grudging kind of admiration:

DAILY BIBLE READINGS

Monday, Apr. 23—The Church in Syrian Antioch (Acts 11:19-24)

Tuesday, Apr. 24—Barnabas and Saul in Antioch (Acts 11:25-30)

Wednesday, Apr. 25—James Killed and Peter Imprisoned (Acts 12:1-5)

Thursday, Apr. 26—Peter Delivered From Prison (Acts 12:6-19)

Friday, Apr. 27—Barnabas and Saul Commissioned (Acts 12:24—13:3)

Saturday, Apr. 28—Paul, a Prisoner for Christ Jesus (Ephesians 3:1-6)

Sunday, Apr. 29—Paul's Ministry to the Gentiles (Ephesians 3:7-13)

WHAT DO YOU THINK?

Barnabas went and found Saul and brought him back to Antioch to help with the work there. How important do you think it is today to find a partner with whom we can share in the Lord's work? Why?

[Does Mark 6:7 or Luke 10:1 help in this discussion?]

"All those people can talk about is Jesus Christ. Christ this! Christ that! They're *Christ*-ians!"

Still others believe that the name *Christians* was a name given by God to the followers of Jesus. They note that the Greek word translated *called* in this verse is used elsewhere in the New Testament of God's calling, warning, or speaking to someone. Many who hold this view see this name as the fulfillment of a prophecy in Isaiah 62:2: "The nations will see your righteousness, and all kings your glory; you will be called by a new name that the mouth of the Lord will bestow." The "new name" of *Christians* would have been particularly appropriate for the believers in Antioch, where the gospel had begun to make significant inroads among Gentiles.

B. PROPHETIC WARNING (vv. 27, 28)

27, 28. During this time some prophets came down from Jerusalem to Antioch. One of them, named Agabus, stood up and through the Spirit predicted that a severe famine would spread over the entire Roman world. (This happened during the reign of Claudius.)

Communication between the church at Jerusalem and the church at Antioch continued through *prophets* who traveled *from Jerusalem to Antioch*. Here God used a man named *Agabus* to foretell a period of *severe famine* that *would spread over the entire Roman world*. According to records of that time, famines occurred in various parts of the empire during the reign of *Claudius*, A.D. 41-54. (This incident also introduces Luke's readers to Agabus, who predicted Paul's arrest in Jerusalem in Acts 21:10-14.)

C. GENUINE CARING (vv. 29, 30)

29, 30. The disciples, each according to his ability, decided to provide help for the brothers living in Judea. This they did, sending their gift to the elders by Barnabas and Saul.

This is another demonstration that the assessment Barnabas made concerning the church at Antioch was on target. The grace of God was evident in those people (v. 23), and it manifested itself in their eager response when confronted with the need of fellow believers *in Judea*. They gave *each according to his ability*—a plan similar to that which Paul recommended to the Corinthians (1 Corinthians 16:1, 2).

The *brothers* in Judea would have suffered particular hardships from any famine. Many had been impoverished because of the persecution of Christians that followed the martyrdom of Stephen (Acts 8:1). Since the gospel had come to Antioch as a consequence of that persecution (Acts 11:19, 20), the believers in that city felt a special responsibility to assist fellow Christians in Jerusalem and the surrounding area.

The church in Antioch sent their *gift* with *Barnabas and Saul* (perhaps these two led a delegation from the church). No one man's integrity was compromised by having him carry that money alone. Sending the most notable leaders in the church with the offering gave the gesture a special measure of dignity. In addition, the fact that the men who brought the offering had some ties to the Jerusalem church (especially Barnabas) would serve to strengthen the bond between that church and the church in Antioch.

WHAT DO YOU THINK?

We could say that the church at Antioch was successful in "growing through giving." What role does stewardship play in the growth of the church today? How can we encourage believers to grow in this area of their faith?

GROWING UP

For several years we have been hearing a lot about aging "baby boomers." If we were to believe some of the reports in the media, we would think that this is the first generation ever to be faced with wrinkles, graying hair (or balding scalp), and the onset of that chubbiness around the waist known as "middle-age spread."

One "boomer" has described his generation as "the most populous, schooled, indulged, narcissistic and persistently adolescent generation in American history." Nevertheless, "Father Time" has a way of making his presence known. The last of the boomers are now approaching forty years of age, the clock is ticking, and some are not handling it well!

However, at some point members of every generation have to acknowledge that they are no longer young and must learn to "grow up." This usually means starting to look outward and considering what legacy they will leave behind.

We have no evidence that the church in Antioch was particularly preoccupied with its own welfare. What we *do* find is that this congregation was "growing up." The Christians there took upon themselves the responsibility of sending famine relief to Christians in Judea. No adolescent self-centeredness was present; the church exhibited a sincere concern for others. It is a model that every maturing congregation should follow. —C. R. B.

IV. REACHING OUT (ACTS 13:1-3)

A. EXPANDING LEADERSHIP (v. 1)

1. In the church at Antioch there were prophets and teachers: Barnabas, Simeon called Niger, Lucius of Cyrene, Manaen (who had been brought up with Herod the tetrarch) and Saul.

Apparently *Barnabas* and *Saul* had been able to do some mentoring with the Antioch church, resulting in the assembling of a leadership team. Like most good teams, this one brought several different personalities and backgrounds together.

The nickname of *Simeon* suggests that he may have been a dark-complexioned man. Some think that he was the man known as Simon of Cyrene (a man from Africa and probably black), who carried the cross for Jesus (Matthew 27:32).

Lucius, who is identified as being from *Cyrene*, could very well have been one of the "men from Cyprus and Cyrene" who first began sharing the gospel with the Gentiles in Antioch (Acts 11:20). The Greek text says that *Manaen* was literally a "foster brother" of *Herod the tetrarch* (that is, Herod Antipas), who was the son of Herod the Great; thus, Manaen was *brought up with* Herod. Herod Antipas had John the Baptist killed, and he participated in the trials of Jesus (Matthew 14:1-11; Luke 23:6-12). Obviously Manaen's life took a very different turn!

B. EXTENDED CONCERN (vv. 2, 3)

2, 3. While they were worshiping the Lord and fasting, the Holy Spirit said, "Set apart for me Barnabas and Saul for the work to which I have called them." So after they had fasted and prayed, they placed their hands on them and sent them off.

Observe that God had brought these men together as leaders; now it was time for two of them to be *set apart* from the others and begin an important new venture in the Lord's *work*. It is evident that all of these men had been seeking the Lord's leading for their ministry, not only in Antioch but to the world. Their desire for his leading was clear from their actions: they *fasted and prayed*.

Fasting is still an important spiritual discipline for the church and for individual Christians. Fasting can take place when an individual has a reason to repent and to seek God's forgiveness and renewal. It can be done when one is seeking some specific direction from God. And it can be done when a church is setting men and women aside to a special purpose in the business of Christ's kingdom.

WHAT DO YOU THINK?

How desirable would you say it is to draw in people of different personalities and backgrounds to form a leadership team? Why?

WHAT DO YOU THINK?

What are some ways in which the church at Antioch provides a model for the church that aspires to be a great missionary church today?

PRAYER

Dear God, empower us with the courage that will make us more like these first Christians, who could not keep the good news to themselves and who let it have an impact on every facet of their lives and their church. Thank you for sending your Holy Spirit to work in your church. We pray that you will be pleased at seeing that power at work in us, and that our neighbors will know our passion so well that they will call us **Christians***. In Jesus' name, amen.*

Use the visual for today's lesson to challenge your students to make your church like the church at Antioch.

THOUGHT TO REMEMBER

Encouragement is a most important key to a growing church.

That is what was taking place in Antioch: "God, we want your will to be done here on earth (and all over the earth) as it is in Heaven."

THINKING "YOUNG"

A "senior moment" is what happens occasionally to many people in their fifties and older—a friend's name, a familiar word, or even an entire thought just slips from one's mind. It happens to everyone: studies show that most people lose thirty percent of their memory between the ages of twenty and seventy-five.

A memory training specialist at Stanford University has apparently found a way to reverse this trend. She teaches a two-week-long course for senior adults that encourages them to "think young." This involves trying to look at certain objects the way younger people would—for example, analyzing details in paintings and thus, in the words of a psychiatrist at Stanford, "increasing their visual imaging ability." The psychiatrist notes that eighty-five percent of the students increased their memory skills from thirty to fifty percent over a five-year period.

Churches grow older, too, and often forget their reason for existence. Leaders settle into comfortable positions and sometimes stay there by insisting on maintaining the status quo and by never entertaining any new ideas.

How different was the church in Antioch! Its leaders were visionary, energetic, and responsive to the leading of the Spirit of God. They could imagine the whole world wanting to know about Jesus. So they sent out some of their best and brightest on a journey that eventually filled the pagan Roman Empire with the gospel!

—C. R. B.

CONCLUSION

A. A GREAT CHURCH'S WITNESS

The church at Antioch was a great church because it began through the efforts of Christians who refused to have their faith snuffed out by persecution. They left the things that were less important and carried with them the one thing that was (and is) forever important. And they didn't keep this to themselves. They seemed to be indifferent to financial loss, to the pressure of persecution, and to the anxiety caused by having to "pull up stakes" and relocate their families.

B. A GREAT CHURCH'S LEADERS

Antioch was also a great church because its leaders responded to opportunities for service. Barnabas recognized that Saul possessed abilities that the church needed and made a determined effort to find him and add him to the leadership team. Then they multiplied themselves by working with and training "reliable men" who were ready to step up and serve (2 Timothy 2:2). And these men were totally unselfish. While they could have remained together and watched great things unfold in Antioch, they sensed the world's need and heard the world's call—which was really the call of Christ to carry his message to the world. So they commissioned two members of their team and sent them out.

C. A GREAT CHURCH'S ENCOURAGEMENTS

In addition, Antioch was a great church because it watched and imitated the style of an encourager (Barnabas). Notice, church leader, the privilege and the sobering reality in this! A congregation, to a significant degree, will take on the personality of its leaders. No church can grow past the spiritual strength, the personal faith, and the passion for Christ that dwells in the hearts of its leaders. When the "mother church" in Jerusalem had a need, the "daughter church" in Antioch rushed to her aid and offered its encouragement. And the disciples sent their best—both in a financial and a personal sense—to fulfill that need.

Discovery Learning

This page contains an alternate lesson plan emphasizing learning activities. Classes desiring such student involvement will find these suggestions helpful. The next page is a reproducible activity page to further enhance discovery learning.

LEARNING GOALS

After this lesson each student will be able to:

1. Recount how the church at Antioch was strengthened in its growth and how it then sent forth workers to expand the church's outreach.

2. Explain the importance of developing godly leadership in the church.

3. Identify an individual who needs encouragement in the Lord's work, and plan a specific way to become a "Barnabas" to that person.

INTO THE LESSON

Say, "Turn to the person next to you and tell him or her all you can about the most encouraging person that you know. After thirty seconds your partner will have a chance to describe his or her most encouraging person."

OPTION

Ask two of your learners to prepare a skit showing a typical couple looking for a new church home. Each person is adamant that his or her interests and concerns be heard. Issues might include the preacher, the worship style, the time factor, the youth program, the people, etc.

Make the transition to the Bible study by saying, "What is it that people *need* to be looking for in a church? Today we are going to study a great church in the Bible—the church at Antioch. Let's see if we can find what made it a great church."

INTO THE WORD

Ask a volunteer to read aloud Acts 11:19-30; 13:1-3. Then choose one or more of the following activities.

CHARACTER STUDY

Give each person a copy of the reproducible page that follows. Ask them to work individually or in small groups to develop a character sketch of Barnabas, using the Scripture references provided. Perhaps they could pretend that they have to introduce Barnabas as the speaker at a special church event. They could use the information they gather to write some introduction notes.

GROUP STUDY

Assign your learners to groups of three or four. Ask them to study today's text and put together a description of a great church. They may want to design a church brochure for the church at Antioch. What qualities of this congregation should be included? What design features would be important to it? Each group should be ready to share the brochure with the rest of the class.

ACROSTIC

"The disciples were called Christians first at Antioch" (Acts 11:26). Use the word *Christian* as an acrostic to list the qualities that make a person or church "Christian." Write the word *Christian* in large letters vertically down a piece of poster board. Then use each letter to identify a characteristic or quality that defines a person or a church as "Christian." For example, the letter "S" in *Christian* could stand for "Speaking About Christ" (Acts 11:19, 20).

INTO LIFE

Use one or both of these activities to close the class session with application.

ENCOURAGEMENT PROJECT

Observe that Joseph was renamed Barnabas ("Son of Encouragement," Acts 4:36) by the apostles. He was an encourager! Every congregation has people who are in desperate need of encouragement. Design a Barnabas project in which you encourage someone who needs it—and we all do!

How do you encourage someone? A word fitly spoken, a note or small gift at just the right time, a hand on the shoulder or pat on the back, a helping hand in a difficult project, or recognition for what the person has done or is doing. What fits your situation? Make your plan and put it into practice.

PRAYER PYRAMID

Have your class divide into pairs. Ask each pair to take two minutes to offer prayers of thanks for the *history* of your church. After two minutes, ask each pair to join another pair and pray for two minutes for the *purpose* of your church. After two minutes, ask each group of four to join another group of four and pray for your *church leaders* for two minutes. After two minutes, ask each group of eight to join another group of eight and pray for your church's *missionaries*. Continue the process until everyone is in one big circle praying together for the church.

Character Study

Barnabas is a fascinating character. He peeks out of the text at the end of Acts 4. Then he appears briefly to encourage Saul's acceptance. Our text is really just the beginning of his place in the New Testament. Use these references to develop a bigger picture of this godly man. Write your insights beside each reference.

Acts 4:36, 37

Acts 9:26, 27

Acts 11:22-30

Acts 12:25—15:39

1 Corinthians 9:6

Galatians 2:1, 9, 11-13

Colossians 4:10

Introducing . . .

Imagine that Barnabas is going to be the speaker at an event in your church. You have been asked to introduce him. From the information you pulled together in the previous activity, write an introduction for Barnabas below.

Continuing Jesus' Work
Unit 3: Spreading the Gospel Into All the World
(Lessons 9-13)

MISSION TO GENTILES

LESSON 10

WHY TEACH THIS LESSON?

I love roller coasters. I don't know why, but there is just something about climbing those high hills and then hurtling down—seemingly out of control—at breakneck speeds around twists and turns until the ride comes to a stop.

Emotional roller coasters are another matter, entirely. The highs are great, but the dips are no fun. But we all find ourselves on those "rides" from time to time, so we have to deal with them.

Paul did not know what a roller coaster was, but he must surely have been on an emotional one. In our text we find him having success—and having to leave town! We find him winning converts—and losing a co-worker. But in it all, God's work was done, and the church grew.

Use this lesson to reassure your learners that, no matter what kind of "ride" they might be on, God is in control. He will bring the car to a safe stop.

INTRODUCTION

A. A TEAM EFFORT

A few years ago, a Christian leader, speaking at a workshop, reported a conversation that he had with a new convert. This leader had cared about the other man for quite some time. Patiently he had worked at building a relationship, studying the Bible, speaking to him about Jesus, and answering his questions. Then the man was ready to declare his faith. The leader had the privilege of baptizing him into Christ. A few days later, while they were talking about his new life, the teacher seemed to take great pride in how he had led the man to faith in Christ. The new believer told his friend, "You know, you're not the only one who led me to Christ. Several other people helped me come to this decision. It was just that you were in the right place at the right time to finish the job."

Paul put it in these terms: "I planted the seed, Apollos watered it, but God made it grow" (1 Corinthians 3:6). That's one of the beautiful things about the church; it's a *body*. Every Christian is called to use his gifts and his personality for the good of the body's growth. One of us can talk easily. Another can understand the deeper doctrinal issues and thus add insights to our classes. Still another does a wonderful job of demonstrating the mercy of God and the love of Christ through personal kindnesses and eager service. Others are very good at demonstrating and promoting Christian fellowship.

Shortly after the verse cited above, Paul added, "We are God's fellow workers" (1 Corinthians 3:9). We are to work *together* in order to present the gospel to those who desperately need good news. Some of us plant, others water, and, in time, the harvest comes. Sometimes it comes in ways that we will never see this side of Heaven.

B. LESSON BACKGROUND

Last week we watched the church in Antioch begin, mature through sound teaching, share its blessings, develop leaders, and commission Barnabas and Saul to go (on Christ's behalf and as their representatives) to places as yet untouched

DEVOTIONAL READING:
PSALM 96

BACKGROUND SCRIPTURE:
ACTS 13, 14

PRINTED TEXT:
ACTS 13:4, 13-15, 42-52

LESSON AIMS

After this lesson a student should be able to:

1. Summarize Paul's message in Pisidian Antioch and the people's responses.

2. Compare Paul and Barnabas's methods of evangelism with modern evangelistic practices.

3. Write a letter to a missionary or missionary family, encouraging them in their important work for the Lord.

WHAT DO YOU THINK?

Paul described evangelism in terms of one person's planting and another's watering (1 Corinthians 3:6-8). What are some evangelistic tasks members can perform in today's church?

May
6

KEY VERSE

"I have made you a light for the Gentiles, that you may bring salvation to the ends of the earth." —Acts 13:47

by the gospel. Today's lesson begins where last week's ended. The two men are on their way.

I. THE MISSION BEGINS (ACTS 13:4, 13-15)

A. FIRST STOP—CYPRUS (v. 4)

4. The two of them, sent on their way by the Holy Spirit, went down to Seleucia and sailed from there to Cyprus.

Acts 13:3 (the final verse of last week's printed text) notes that "they" (the prophets and teachers in the Antioch church) sent Barnabas and Saul on their mission. Verse 4 emphasizes that the *two* men were *sent on their way by the Holy Spirit.* Recall from last week's study that, following the leading of the Spirit, the other prophets and teachers in the Antioch church had "placed their hands" on Barnabas and Saul and commissioned them to this special venture. Fasting and prayer also accompanied this pivotal response to the need of the world for the gospel.

Both in his Gospel and in the book of Acts, Luke demonstrates a close attention to details. This becomes clear as one reads his account of Paul's missionary endeavors. Here he notes that Barnabas and Saul *went down to Seleucia.* Seleucia was the seaport city of Antioch, located about sixteen miles westward. The town has no other significance than being the place from which the missionary team left.

The team's first stop was the island of *Cyprus.* Why Cyprus? That was the home of Barnabas (Acts 4:36). Since he was known there, it would be a somewhat easier place to get a hearing. In addition, believers from Cyprus had come to Antioch to help start the church there (Acts 11:19, 20). Thus Barnabas and Saul may have been hoping to begin their task in rather friendly surroundings.

WHAT DO YOU THINK?

Paul was so put out with John Mark for not completing the first missionary trip that he refused to take him on the next one. The issue even caused Paul and Barnabas to separate (Acts 15:36-41). In time, however, the rift was healed. What do you think is the key to resolving conflicts between Christian brothers?

B. ADJUSTMENT MADE AT PERGA (v. 13)

13. From Paphos, Paul and his companions sailed to Perga in Pamphylia, where John left them to return to Jerusalem.

Our printed text does not include the record of what took place on Cyprus. The team began preaching at Salamis, on the eastern coast of Cyprus. They then moved westward approximately one hundred miles to *Paphos,* on the other side of the island. There Sergius Paulus, a local official, wanted to hear the word of God from Barnabas and Saul. But Bar-Jesus (Elymas), a sorcerer who was an attendant of the official, "opposed them" and "tried to turn the proconsul from the faith" (v. 8). Saul (who in verse 9 is called Paul for the first time) told the sorcerer that the Lord would strike him with blindness, which immediately happened. Sergius Paulus, who must have witnessed all of this with astonishment, "believed, for he was amazed at the teaching about the Lord" (v. 12).

The team then traveled northward (over the Mediterranean Sea) to what is now western Turkey. Specifically, they *sailed to* the province of *Pamphylia,* located along the southern coast, and arrived at *Perga,* the capital of the province. At this point, *John* Mark, who had been serving Barnabas and Saul as a "helper" (v. 5), *left them to return* to his home in *Jerusalem.*

Exactly why John Mark left the group has been the subject of much speculation. Some believe that he became homesick or missed his mother—apparently a committed Christian woman who provided accommodations for the church (Acts 12:12). He may have resented how Paul had begun to take on more leadership responsibilities than Barnabas, who was, after all, a relative of John Mark (Colossians 4:10). Others suggest that John Mark feared the more rugged, threatening terrain and inhabitants that awaited the group in the territory of Pamphylia.

Whatever Mark's reason, Paul seems to have considered it unjustified. He refused to include John Mark on a second trip (Acts 15:36-39). In time, however, John Mark's service was valued by Paul and he became a "comfort" to the apostle (Colossians 4:10, 11).

C. PATTERN SET IN ANTIOCH (vv. 14, 15)

14. From Perga they went on to Pisidian Antioch. On the Sabbath they entered the synagogue and sat down.

From *Perga*, Paul and Barnabas proceeded to *Pisidian Antioch* (a province to the north), about one hundred ten miles away. This city had a large Jewish population. It was here that Paul and Barnabas established a pattern that they and their co-workers would follow whenever they began to evangelize a city. They *entered the synagogue* first and took part in the *Sabbath* day worship. The synagogue was a natural place to present Jesus as the Christ to Jews, whose knowledge of the Scriptures provided a foundation on which Paul and his companions could build.

TARGETING THE AUDIENCE

The *National Enquirer,* the *Weekly World News*, and the *Star* are tabloids found at the checkout lanes in supermarkets just about everywhere. The purchase of one or more is part of the weekly shopping ritual for many people. Even those of us who don't buy the tabloids must admit to occasionally scanning the eye-catching headlines.

A headline that few of us could keep from noticing was seen in one issue of the *Weekly World News*. It read, "Satan Escapes From Hell." Beside the headline was pictured a cloud of oily smoke escaping from an exploding oil well. With a bit of imagination, one could see a grotesque face in the cloud.

There is a ready audience for salacious gossip and incredible stories—a subculture easily tapped by the tabloid editors, who know that placing their publications by the supermarket checkout lanes will entice the buyers. That's an important principle of marketing.

Paul and Barnabas knew that certain people could be counted on to be present at a specific place and time: they could be found in the synagogue on the Sabbath day. Here was an audience—a subculture—already prepared to hear the gospel because it was familiar with the Old Testament Scriptures, which Jesus had come to fulfill. It was an open door that Paul and Barnabas used, with encouraging results.

The sensationalism of the tabloids is not a good model for us in sharing the gospel, but the wisdom of the apostles is.   —C. R. B.

15. After the reading from the Law and the Prophets, the synagogue rulers sent word to them, saying, "Brothers, if you have a message of encouragement for the people, please speak."

In a synagogue service, portions *from the Law and the Prophets* were read, then someone in the assembly addressed those who had gathered. One of the responsibilities of *the synagogue rulers* was to designate someone for this duty. Often visitors, such as Paul and Barnabas, were asked to *speak*. Paul would have been an especially appropriate choice, given his background of training in the Jewish faith (Acts 22:3).

II. THE MISSION EXPANDS (ACTS 13:42, 43)

A. GENTILE SEEKERS (v. 42)

42. As Paul and Barnabas were leaving the synagogue, the people invited them to speak further about these things on the next Sabbath.

HOW TO SAY IT

Antioch. AN-tee-ock.
Apollos. Uh-PAHL-us.
Bar-Jesus. Bar-JEE-zus.
Barnabas. BAR-nuh-bus.
Cyprus. SIGH-prus.
Elymas. EL-ih-mass.
Iconium. Eye-CO-nee-um.
Pamphylia. Pam-FILL-ee-uh.
Paphos. PAY-fahss.
Perga. PER-guh.
Pisidian. Pih-SID-ee-un.
Seleucia. Sih-LEW-shuh.
Sergius Paulus. SER-jih-us
   PAUL-us.

WHAT DO YOU THINK?

"The people invited [Paul and Barnabas] to speak further about these things . . ." (Acts 13:42). That indicates a wonderful openness to the gospel. Who in our culture—in our community—is open to the gospel? How can we tell? What if we assumed that people were open to the gospel? How would that affect the way we approach them?

Our printed text moves to the outcome of Paul's address in the *synagogue*, which began with God's deliverance of Israel from bondage in Egypt and concluded with a proclamation of Jesus as the one through whom "everyone who believes is justified from everything you could not be justified from by the law of Moses" (Acts 13:39). Most likely those present that day had never heard anything like this before. Yet the message was received favorably, particularly by Gentiles who wanted to hear more about it *on the next Sabbath*.

B. JEWISH SEEKERS (v. 43)

43. When the congregation was dismissed, many of the Jews and devout converts to Judaism followed Paul and Barnabas, who talked with them and urged them to continue in the grace of God.

Some in *the congregation* did not want to wait a week. They were so eager to learn more of what *Paul and Barnabas* were saying about Jesus that they *followed* these two, clinging to their every word. These results were, thus far, just what the missionaries had wanted. They were preaching Jesus as the promised Messiah to their brethren, *the Jews*; and they were also able to introduce him to the Gentiles by way of the *devout converts to Judaism*.

Obviously these individuals were not far from the kingdom. The good news was drawing them. And Paul and Barnabas were excited to encourage them to keep moving forward, growing in their understanding of *the grace of God*.

III. THE MISSION MATURES (ACTS 13:44-52)

A. DEALING WITH JEALOUSY (vv. 44, 45)

44, 45. On the next Sabbath almost the whole city gathered to hear the word of the Lord. When the Jews saw the crowds, they were filled with jealousy and talked abusively against what Paul was saying.

New ideas are fine, unless they begin to supplant established ones. And they are fine as long as they do not engage the interest of significant numbers of people. When, *on the next Sabbath almost the whole city gathered* to *hear* what Paul and Barnabas had to say, the Jewish leaders could feel their control slipping away. Perhaps it appeared to them that their synagogue was being taken over by these "outsiders."

The issue at hand was not a matter of right and wrong, nor was it a doctrinal disagreement, at least initially. True, these men had said some shocking things— things that seemed radical to some. But it seems that the authorities became concerned only when those teachings began to draw a popular following and to threaten the status quo. So *filled with jealousy* were they that they mounted a mud-slinging campaign in an attempt to discredit Paul and Barnabas. Unfortunately, the scenario described in these verses proved to be "par for the course" for the missionary team as they moved from city to city.

B. ENCOURAGING THE GENTILES (vv. 46-48)

46. Then Paul and Barnabas answered them boldly: "We had to speak the word of God to you first. Since you reject it and do not consider yourselves worthy of eternal life, we now turn to the Gentiles.

Paul and Barnabas refused to ignore those who had for so long been God's chosen people. As Paul would later write to the Roman Christians, "I am not ashamed of the gospel, because it is the power of God for the salvation of everyone who believes: first for the Jew, then for the Gentile" (Romans 1:16; cf. 2:10). The Jews would get the *first* opportunity to embrace the New Covenant relationship and the *eternal life* that God was offering through Jesus. But when they rejected it, Paul

WHAT DO YOU THINK?

Paul and Barnabas broke off their evangelistic efforts toward the Jews to concentrate on teaching the Gentiles. What are some factors that might lead us to curtail our evangelistic efforts toward a particular individual or family?

and Barnabas were prepared to *turn* immediately to the *Gentiles*, who were eager to hear.

47. For this is what the Lord has commanded us: "'I have made you a light for the Gentiles, that you may bring salvation to the ends of the earth.'"

That the gospel invitation should go to *the Gentiles* was in keeping with God's plan as revealed in the Old Testament. Here Isaiah 49:6 is quoted, in which God's servant is *commanded* to be *a light for the Gentiles*. Simeon had alluded to this passage when Joseph and Mary brought Jesus to the temple (Luke 2:32). And while Jesus is the light of the world (John 8:12), he has also appointed his followers to be the light of the world (Matthew 5:14) and to go *to the ends of the earth*. (Read again Jesus' Great Commission as recorded in Acts 1:8.)

48. When the Gentiles heard this, they were glad and honored the word of the Lord; and all who were appointed for eternal life believed.

These Jews in Antioch scorned the idea that they were not worthy (v. 46) of God's favor. But the *Gentiles* (needless to say) were thrilled. Those who *honored the word of the Lord* and were ready to accept God's grace were ready to receive the gift of *eternal life* (Romans 6:23).

The phrase *all who were appointed for eternal life believed* does not mean that certain individuals were chosen to believe. The verb translated "appointed" can also mean "placed, positioned, or determined" and appears in the Greek text in a form that can signify an action done by one's self to one's self. It means that those who wanted to place themselves in a position to receive eternal life believed. (Others, such as the Jews described in verse 46, did not want to place themselves in that position.)

THE "NIMBY" SYNDROME

Some time ago, when the world seemed like a kinder and gentler place, the prospect of a new church building going up in a neighborhood was seen as a positive thing. A new church was an indication that "good people" were in the neighborhood and that the social order would be preserved and strengthened.

But times have changed. Today, communities are more likely to resist the construction of a new church building in their midst. People don't want to put up with the noise and traffic it will bring. And if it is the "wrong kind" of church—either architecturally or theologically—people are fearful of the effect it will have on the community. (And we must admit that what is called a "church" today *is* sometimes rather weird—in either architecture or doctrine!) It's another example of what has been labeled the "NIMBY" syndrome—*Not In My Back Yard*: "Don't bother me. Go somewhere else if you want to change things."

While that was the attitude of the Jewish leaders in Antioch, it certainly wasn't what the Gentile community was thinking. They *liked* what they heard about the Christian faith. They *wanted* the church in their "back yard" because the gospel offered them forgiveness and hope.

Does *our* church offer the community a similar message?   —C. R. B.

C. SUCCESS AND DISTRESS (vv. 49-52)

49. The word of the Lord spread through the whole region.

Not only to those in Antioch but *through the whole region* the message proclaimed by Paul and Barnabas spread. Most likely this resulted from the efforts of new believers, not the missionary team. The gospel moves so much more quickly that way—and that's as true today as it was on that first missionary journey.

50. But the Jews incited the God-fearing women of high standing and the leading men of the city. They stirred up persecution against Paul and Barnabas, and expelled them from their region.

I have set thee to be a light of the Gentiles, that thou shouldest be for salvation unto the ends of the earth.
Acts 13:47

Use today's visual to illustrate verse 47 of the text. Discuss how Christians today can be a "light" to those who do not know Jesus.

WHAT DO YOU THINK?

The lesson writer notes how quickly the gospel can be spread by new believers. How can we make the best possible use of the evangelistic enthusiasm of new believers?

PRAYER

Our Father, we acknowledge that we are those who are responsible to carry the message of eternal life to others. If we do not, who will? You do not want us to ignore anyone. Give us the energy, insight, compassion, and clarity to share the good news of Jesus and to carry out that task regardless of how our hearers respond. In Jesus' name, amen.

THOUGHT TO REMEMBER

"The Lord is not slow in keeping his promise, as some understand slowness. He is patient with you, not wanting anyone to perish, but everyone to come to repentance" (2 Peter 3:9). God wants us all!

In Paul's day, as is true in our day, trouble in the church is spread much more successfully through indirect means than by direct. If the Jewish leaders had stood up and lectured against Paul and Barnabas, it might have had little effect. But they *stirred up* trouble behind the scenes. "Did you know that these men are not dependable people?" Then the one who heard that told another person, "I heard from a reliable source that you can't count on what this Paul says. He's a troublemaker." And a third person, if his emotions have been deeply stirred, will say (with more anger than the first two), "We have to get these people out of here. They're trying to force their beliefs on everyone!" If you ask that third person to explain what he means and where he got his information, he probably can't tell you. But he's sure that it's true.

This verse notes that the Jews in Antioch aimed their disruptive efforts at some of the *God-fearing women* and the *leading men of the city*. (Some believe that these women were the wives of the leading men.) It was easier for the "city fathers" simply to get rid of the source of the nuisance than to take time to investigate what was happening and see that justice was done. So Paul and Barnabas were told to leave the *region* surrounding the city.

51. So they shook the dust from their feet in protest against them and went to Iconium.

When Paul and Barnabas *shook the dust from their feet*, they were signaling the end of their responsibility toward the unreceptive Jewish authorities. Certainly they must have been frustrated at having to leave the new believers behind so soon. But we can see from the next verse that the seed of the gospel had taken root.

52. And the disciples were filled with joy and with the Holy Spirit.

These young Christians in Antioch demonstrated exemplary dedication. We might have expected them to become frightened or angry when their teachers were forced out of town. But they were *filled with joy* because of their salvation. And *the Holy Spirit* was working in their lives and in their church. Later, when Paul and Barnabas came back through Antioch, they could set aside leaders (Acts 14:21-23) and encourage the believers to remain faithful.

CONCLUSION

A. THE PROTECTIVE

Many times we have heard how difficult it is to move some people from their familiar neighborhoods. Their surroundings may be dangerous or even life-threatening. The living conditions may be primitive. An opportunity for a healthier, more peaceful environment is offered. But "we want to stay home." As someone once put it, "Come weal or come woe, our status is quo."

Was the message that Paul and Barnabas were preaching true? To the Jewish leaders in Antioch, that didn't matter. It was different—that was the real problem.

It is not the Jews who shrank back to protect the comfort of their synagogue who should be our models. They judged themselves unworthy of eternal life.

B. THE RECEPTIVE

Our heroes in Antioch should be those who *did* judge themselves worthy of eternal life. They were filled with joy to hear about the forgiveness of sins and about the one whom God had raised from the dead to provide that forgiveness. They were receptive to an offer from God that would provide the life that they were unable to provide for themselves. This was good news. This was *great* news!

Yes, it would change things. But these people were ready to be changed. What a joy to find and to teach such receptive hearts!

Discovery Learning

This page contains an alternate lesson plan emphasizing learning activities. Classes desiring such student involvement will find these suggestions helpful. The next page is a reproducible activity page to further enhance discovery learning.

LEARNING GOALS

After participating in this lesson, each student should be able to:

1. Summarize Paul's message in Pisidian Antioch and the people's responses.

2. Compare Paul and Barnabas's methods of evangelism with modern evangelistic practices.

3. Write a letter to a missionary or to a missionary family, encouraging them in their important work for the Lord.

INTO THE LESSON

Many new churches have been planted with well-developed strategies. As a result, these churches have had impressive beginnings and immediate growth. Check with your preacher—he probably knows of such a church. If there is one nearby, you may be able to get someone to come and tell their story. Or you can contact an evangelistic or church-planting ministry in your area and invite someone from the organization to come and address the class.

After this report, divide the class into groups of four or five. Ask each group to develop a strategy for planting a new church. The location has no nucleus of believers to begin the work, so the church is starting from scratch. Give each group a chance to report on its suggested strategy to the rest of the class.

Make the transition to the Bible study by saying, "The beginning of a new church can lay the foundation for years of growth, or it can sow the seeds of self-destruction. We've heard some modern-day plans for a new church planting. Now let's look at one of the first church-planting teams and study its strategy."

INTO THE WORD

Have a volunteer read Acts 13:4, 13-15, 42-52. Then divide your class into four groups to explore this text. Give each group one of the assignments below.

GROUP 1: SUMMARY

Today's lesson focuses on the portion of Acts 13 that records the ministry of Paul and Barnabas in Antioch of Pisidia. First, summarize the message that Paul and Barnabas preached there, and second, summarize the response of the people. Be ready to report the results of your study with the rest of the class.

GROUP 2: CONCORDANCE STUDY

Assign this group to find what the rest of the New Testament says about John Mark. Look at each of the passages, and don't forget the Gospel of Mark: Acts 12:12, 25; 13:5; 15:37-39; Colossians 4:10; 2 Timothy 4:11; Philemon 24; and 1 Peter 5:13. Be ready to share the results of your study with the entire class.

GROUP 3: MAP STUDY

Provide copies of the reproducible page that follows for this group to study. Ask the group to trace the travels of Paul and Barnabas through Acts 13. Be sure to distinguish between and locate the two cities with the name of Antioch. Be ready to share the results of your study with the entire class.

GROUP 4: PRINCIPLES OF EVANGELISM

The fourth group has the assignment of identifying some principles of evangelism from Acts 13. For example, verse 1 could suggest that well-developed churches should be receptive to the opportunity to share leaders to plant new congregations. Verse 2 implies that fasting and prayer are essential to the planting of new churches. Verse 4 records that Barnabas began his trip by returning to the island of his birth. Jesus said to the former demoniac, "Go home to your family and tell them how much the Lord has done for you, and how he has had mercy on you" (Mark 5:19). Be ready to share the results of your study with the rest of the class.

INTO LIFE

Provide all of the materials for each of your class members to write a letter of encouragement to a missionary. Your missions committee will be glad to provide you with names and addresses of missionaries supported by your congregation.

Today many missionaries have access to e-mail. This medium has enabled missionaries to publish newsletters and distribute them worldwide immediately. Prayer requests and answers can be communicated instantaneously. You might even arrange for your class to visit an Internet chat room with a missionary for an on-line chat. Be aware of time zone differences.

Conclude the session with a time of prayer for specific missionaries your church supports, new churches in your area, and your own church's evangelistic efforts.

Map Study

Highlight or underline each geographical location when you read it in today's text. Keep this map and use it for the rest of these lessons from Acts.

THE JERUSALEM CONFERENCE

LESSON 11

WHY TEACH THIS LESSON?

I couldn't believe my ears. The Washington monument in Washington, D.C. was getting some much needed renovation. The work required that scaffolding be put up all around the monument, from the ground to the top. The monument was completely surrounded. That's when someone suggested that the scaffolding looked so good that maybe it should be left in place even after the work was done.

That sounds crazy! Scaffolding is a tool; it's put in place in order to do a job. Once the job is done, it is removed to allow the true work of art to be seen.

The early Jewish Christians had the same problem: they had fallen in love with the scaffolding, the law that prepared the world for the Messiah. It's understandable. That scaffolding had been in place for a millennium and a half! But it was still the scaffolding. The real plan, the New Covenant, was finally in place.

Use this lesson to challenge your students to remove whatever scaffolding may be blocking their view of the Savior. It might be hard, but they will be better for it!

INTRODUCTION

A. JUMPING THROUGH HOOPS

About a dozen young adults in medical school at the local university attend church together. It has been a great encouragement to see their steadfast faith and to hear them talk of their experiences. It's exciting to think about the many years of ministry they can have as professional healers who know the real Healer.

One day, during a conversation with a third-year student, the preacher asked, "Why are your supervisors so hard on you? Why the long hours, the 'all-nighters'? Is there some lesson that they're trying to teach you? Do they want to toughen you up, or teach you how to handle sleep deprivation so that you will be better able to handle those early-morning emergencies? There's got to be a reason for it."

"Actually there's not," she said. "The supervisors put us through it only because *their* supervisors and teachers put *them* through it. There's no real reason for it at all. There's nothing about it that is designed to make us better doctors."

The "rules of the game" often dictate that to be legitimate, you must jump through the same hoops everyone else had to jump through. It wouldn't be right for you to have the same credentials as I if you took an easier route to get them!

Does that happen in the church? Today's lesson focuses on a time when it did.

B. LESSON BACKGROUND

In last week's lesson, we considered both the successes and the frustrations that were experienced by Paul and Barnabas and their co-workers during the first missionary journey. Acts 14 (the chapter between last week's lesson and today's printed text) tells what else took place on that journey. In some respects conditions became worse: in Lystra, for example, Paul was stoned and left for dead

DEVOTIONAL READING:
ROMANS 3:21-26

BACKGROUND SCRIPTURE:
ACTS 15:1-35

PRINTED TEXT:
ACTS 15:1, 2, 6-15a, 19, 20

LESSON AIMS

After this lesson students should be able to:

1. Explain the issue that occasioned the Jerusalem Conference, and summarize how the Conference addressed it.

2. Tell how traditions sometimes obscure the simplicity of the gospel of grace.

3. Confess any burdensome "yokes" that they have placed on others, and praise God for the grace freely given in Jesus Christ.

May
13

KEY VERSE

We believe it is through the grace of our Lord Jesus that we are saved, just as they are.
—Acts 15:11

LESSON 11 NOTES

(Acts 14:19, 20). But there were blessings, too: people kept turning to Christ, and they came in numbers large enough for the team to go back through all of the towns where they had preached and ordain elders in the churches that had been established there (Acts 14:21-23).

The conclusion of chapter 14 records the team's return to its sending congregation in Antioch of Syria. There they reported to that remarkably vibrant young church all that had happened during their endeavor. They also determined to stay in Antioch and work with the church there for a "long time" (vv. 24-28). They were set to enjoy the kind of furlough that the most fortunate missionaries today enjoy—exchanging blessings with the sponsoring congregation and its leaders, and being refreshed and encouraged for the next trip. Then trouble came to town.

I. CONTROVERSY (ACTS 15:1, 2)

A. THE ISSUE (v. 1)

1. Some men came down from Judea to Antioch and were teaching the brothers: "Unless you are circumcised, according to the custom taught by Moses, you cannot be saved."

These *men who came down from Judea to Antioch and were teaching the brothers* had no authority to do so. In the letter that was composed as a result of the meeting in Jerusalem, the leadership in Jerusalem noted that "some went out from us without our authorization" (Acts 15:24). They may well be the same ones whom Paul described as "false brothers [who] had infiltrated our ranks to spy on the freedom we have in Christ Jesus and to make us slaves" (Galatians 2:4).

These unauthorized visitors said, *Unless you are circumcised, according to the custom taught by Moses, you cannot be saved.* Of course, there was more involved in this matter than circumcision. As Paul explained, "Every man who lets himself be circumcised . . . is obligated to obey the whole law" (Galatians 5:3). In effect, the Gentile Christians in Antioch were being told that, without following the system of Jewish ritual observance, they could not be considered Christians.

A BEAUTIFUL WORLD

We don't often see globes anymore, but it used to be that every public library (as well as many private homes) had one. The various land areas and seas were shown, as were the political boundaries separating the nations.

Now, for those who have an interest in globes (and in works of art), there is a particular one advertised as "the world's finest." It features lapis lazuli oceans and countries represented by amethyst, jade, jasper, and other semi-precious stones. An effort has been made to use the stones in the areas of the globe appropriate to their origins. The price, almost eight hundred dollars, guarantees that most of your neighbors won't have one—your view of "the world" will be unique among your circle of friends.

The Jewish Christians who came to Antioch and made certain demands of the Gentile Christians had their own unique view of the world, and they did not appreciate the variety that others were trying to bring to it. For them, the church could be only Jewish; the law of Moses was the only "mosaic" they could imagine.

These people did not realize that what God has in mind for his church is a far more beautiful "globe"—one made up of precious stones from every people of the world, not just a few. It's an idea that some Christians still find difficult to accept.

—C. R. B.

WHAT DO YOU THINK?

Most churches have their share of "dispute and debate." When is that a legitimate part of the church's business, and when is it merely disruptive?

B. THE DISAGREEMENT (v. 2)

2. This brought Paul and Barnabas into sharp dispute and debate with them. So Paul and Barnabas were appointed, along with some other believers, to go up to Jerusalem to see the apostles and elders about this question.

One can easily see how a *sharp dispute and debate* arose as a result of this turn of events, especially in light of Paul and Barnabas's recent missionary travels among the Gentiles. They had been preaching and teaching "that through Jesus the forgiveness of sins is proclaimed to you. Through him everyone who believes is justified from everything you could not be justified from by the law of Moses" (Acts 13:38, 39). To sanction what the other teachers were proposing would have had the effect of negating all that they had just accomplished.

Since the two groups disagreed so strongly on such a crucial matter (that is, what was necessary for salvation), they agreed to take the *question* to the *apostles and elders* in the well-established church in *Jerusalem*.

II. CONFIRMATION (ACTS 15:6-15a)

A. PETER'S TESTIMONY (vv. 6-11)

6, 7. The apostles and elders met to consider this question. After much discussion, Peter got up and addressed them: "Brothers, you know that some time ago God made a choice among you that the Gentiles might hear from my lips the message of the gospel and believe.

This gathering (often referred to as the Jerusalem Conference) seems to have been preceded by a private meeting in which Paul and Barnabas related details of their ministry among the *Gentiles* to the elders and apostles (Acts 15:4; Galatians 2:2). The public discussion began with the proposition expressed by some believers who also were (or had been) Pharisees, insisting that the Gentiles comply with the law of Moses (v. 5). Perhaps these were the same teachers who had taught this doctrine in Antioch, calling forth the need for this conference.

As in Antioch, there was *much discussion* over the issue. Then *Peter got up* to speak. He was the one whom God had used to expand the church's outreach to include the Gentiles. Peter reminded those present that the issue they were discussing was something God had already decided *some time ago*. God had sent Peter a vision (the same one three times) in order to teach him that God "does not show favoritism" (Acts 10:34). Peter went straight from the vision and its explanation to meet some men who had been sent from Cornelius. He correctly put the two events together and went with them to Cornelius's house in Caesarea.

8. "God, who knows the heart, showed that he accepted them by giving the Holy Spirit to them, just as he did to us.

While the apostle was talking about Jesus to those gathered in Cornelius's home, *the Holy Spirit* fell on those Gentiles in a Pentecost-like manifestation (note Peter's words *just as he did to us*), thus certifying that God did indeed want these people to receive his salvation (Acts 10:44-47).

9. "He made no distinction between us and them, for he purified their hearts by faith.

Peter did not suggest that these Gentiles be circumcised, but baptized, as the expression of their *faith* in Jesus as Lord and Christ (Acts 10:47). This was similar to what had occurred on Pentecost, when, following the coming of the Holy Spirit on the apostles, Peter had preached to the Jews in Jerusalem and held them responsible for the crucifixion of Jesus, whom "God has made . . . both Lord and Christ" (Acts 2:36). He then called for his listeners to repent and to be baptized (v. 38).

Thus both Jews and Gentiles had been given the same opportunity to be justified *by faith*. Without circumcision! Without a commitment to keeping the law! There was *no distinction* in how Jews and Gentiles could be saved.

10. "Now then, why do you try to test God by putting on the necks of the disciples a yoke that neither we nor our fathers have been able to bear?

The issue was not what Peter had said or done, but what *God* had decided. He has established a new way—a better way—for individuals to become his children.

WHAT DO YOU THINK?

God "knows the heart" of those with whom we share the gospel. How important do you think it is to keep that in mind? Why?

WHAT DO YOU THINK?

What kinds of unscriptural "yokes" have you seen some Christians try to put on the necks of others? How can we be sure we are not guilty of the same?

"We believe that through the grace of the Lord Jesus Christ we shall be saved, even as they." Acts 15:11

The visual that corresponds with lesson 11 illustrates Acts 15:11. It is also an important reminder for any believer in Jesus.

"Who has ever kept all the law?" Peter's question implied. It is a *yoke* too heavy for anyone *to bear*. Now that it has been replaced, it is wrong to force it on anyone.

11. "No! We believe it is through the grace of our Lord Jesus that we are saved, just as they are."

Jesus is the way, the truth, and the life (John 14:6). He is the one through whom Jews, who have failed to keep the law of Moses, are *saved*. He is the one through whom Gentiles, who have failed to live up to the law "written on their hearts" (Romans 2:15), are *saved*. The way of law has been rendered obsolete by *the grace of our Lord Jesus*.

B. JAMES'S COUNSEL (vv. 12-15a)

12. The whole assembly became silent as they listened to Barnabas and Paul telling about the miraculous signs and wonders God had done among the Gentiles through them.

Barnabas and Paul followed Peter's testimony with their report of what God had done through them during their missionary travels. They testified of the *miraculous signs and wonders God had done among the Gentiles*. It was clear that God had been in this entire undertaking, as he "confirmed his word" and "testified to it" through these signs (Mark 16:20; Hebrews 2:3, 4).

13. When they finished, James spoke up: "Brothers, listen to me.

The next speaker was *James*, who summarized what had been said thus far and offered a plan to address the issue at hand. While there were two apostles known as James, this James was most likely the half-brother of Jesus (Matthew 13:55) and author of the epistle of James. James the brother of John had already been put to death (Acts 12:1, 2), and James the son of Alpheus is never mentioned except in lists of the apostles. John notes that during Jesus' earthly ministry his brothers "did not believe in him" (John 7:5) as the Son of God. But the risen Christ appeared to James (1 Corinthians 15:7), and he became a prominent leader, one of those "reputed to be pillars" (Galatians 2:9), in the Jerusalem church.

14. "Simon has described to us how God at first showed his concern by taking from the Gentiles a people for himself.

James used Peter's Hebrew name of *Simon*, perhaps because he was appealing primarily to Jewish Christians. Peter had summarized his experience in the house of Cornelius and its significance. Those *Gentiles* who were willing to accept the gospel were to be welcomed into God's New Covenant *people*. James emphasized this and then cited the authority that his hearers would respect the most.

15a. "The words of the prophets are in agreement with this.

Prophets such as Isaiah (Isaiah 11:10; 54:3), Jeremiah (Jeremiah 16:19), and Malachi (Malachi 1:11) looked ahead to a time when Gentiles would be included among those who acknowledged God's name. In his remarks, James proceeded to quote from the prophet Amos (Amos 9:11, 12), emphasizing the Lord's promise to "rebuild David's fallen tent" so that Gentiles might seek the Lord (Acts 15:16-18). Thus, what was happening with the Gentiles was not Peter's idea or Barnabas and Paul's doing; it was the fulfillment of God's plan.

III. CAUTIONS (ACTS 15:19, 20)

A. FOR THE JEWISH BELIEVERS (v. 19)

19. "It is my judgment, therefore, that we should not make it difficult for the Gentiles who are turning to God.

James declared his *judgment* regarding this sensitive matter. The Gentile believers had been troubled by the teaching being spread by those who had come from Judea to Antioch. They would have been especially concerned about attempts to make them keep the complicated code of regulations that had been developed by the Pharisees and teachers of the law. None of the Jewish people (not even the leaders) had been able to keep every regulation.

"God is not imposing such rigid standards on these new believers," James asserted. Jews and Gentiles enter the kingdom of God in the same way, and keeping the law is not the way. Trusting Jesus is the way. However, there were some areas of concern that the Gentile believers needed to be aware of, and James proceeded to mention those.

"DON'T MAKE IT DIFFICULT"

What do you think is *essential* to the Christian faith? What might be placed in the category of *opinion*? Church history includes many attempts to move items up the list from opinion to essential, creating new "churches" or denominations as a result.

Even the movements that have claimed to be "non-denominational" have had to struggle with this problem. The "Restoration Movement," which began around the turn of the nineteenth century "to unite Christians in all the sects" (as the founders put it), has divided over many issues. One of the familiar slogans of this movement is, "In matters of faith, unity; in matters of opinion, liberty; in all things, love." However, like many summations of truth, this one is easy to remember but difficult to apply!

First-century Jewish Christians were telling Gentiles that they couldn't keep their Gentile culture and still be Christians. In essence, they had to become Jews. But the apostles answered, "Don't make it difficult" for these believers with matters that are not essential. That's good advice for us as well. It doesn't quite answer all of our questions, but it does indicate the spirit with which we should approach sensitive issues.

God sent the Savior to smooth the pathway to Heaven, not to place obstacles on it.
                —C. R. B.

B. FOR THE GENTILE BELIEVERS (v. 20)

20. *"Instead we should write to them, telling them to abstain from food polluted by idols, from sexual immorality, from the meat of strangled animals and from blood."*

In some respects, this list of requirements is what we might expect; in others, it may seem rather surprising. The command to *abstain from . . . sexual immorality* is certainly understandable. God had commanded his people Israel not to commit adultery (Exodus 20:14). Throughout the Scriptures there are strong warnings against any form of sexual immorality.

The command to *abstain from food polluted by idols* was especially appropriate for Gentile Christians. The pagan worship in cities where the gospel was making inroads often included a mixture of idol worship and illicit sexual activity. Offerings of food were believed to provide the pagan gods with their meals. Christians must distance themselves from such actions and the worship of false gods associated with those actions.

These last two items, abstaining *from the meat of strangled animals and from blood,* appear to cover concerns that were important in the Jewish law (Genesis 9:4; Leviticus 17:13, 14; Deuteronomy 12:16, 23, 27). They are never emphasized in any proclamation of the gospel. Why impose them on Gentiles?

Some students believe that these commands, along with the command to abstain from food polluted by idols, were added as an aid to Christian fellowship—not as a requirement for salvation. An important part of fellowship, especially in the early church where people with Jewish and non-Jewish backgrounds were coming together, was the readiness to understand and appreciate the sensitivities of others in the church. (It still is important.) The idea of eating food that had been offered to idols, eating the meat of strangled animals, or eating blood would have been highly offensive to Jewish believers. For the Gentile believers to respect

---

HOW TO SAY IT

Alpheus. Al-FEE-us.
Antioch. AN-tee-ock.
Barnabas. BAR-nuh-bus.
Caesarea. Sess-uh-REE-uh.
Cornelius. Cor-NEEL-yus.
Isaiah. Eye-ZAY-uh.
Jeremiah. Jair-uh-MY-uh.
Lystra. LISS-truh.
Malachi. MAL-uh-kye.
Syria. SEAR-ee-uh.

WHAT DO YOU THINK?

Suppose a new believer said to you, "I thought we lived under grace! Why, then, did the apostles and elders send this letter with *rules to follow?*" How would you respond?

PRAYER

Lord, in a difficult world please strengthen your church that she might be what you wish her to be. Use us all, both leaders and followers, to spread the good news that Jesus Christ has come to save and that he is Lord. Through him we pray, amen.

THOUGHT TO REMEMBER

"How good and pleasant it is when brothers live together in unity!" (Psalm 133:1).

these sensitive areas would make fellowship between Jews and Gentiles (particularly sharing meals together) much more harmonious.

Some may question whether there is a contradiction between the command to abstain from food polluted by idols and other Scriptures where Paul seems to be more tolerant of such activity (Romans 14:13-23; 1 Corinthians 8). In these Scriptures, Paul may have been addressing situations involving primarily Gentile Christians. There the issue was not so much having fellowship with Jews as it was causing fellow believers to fall away from Christ through a poor example (Romans 14:19-21; 1 Corinthians 8:9-13). Even so, the common ground in both situations is the need to abstain from such foods for the good of another.

CONCLUSION

A. IT'S EASY TO BULLY

The Jewish Christians in Jerusalem had history on their side. They were from God's chosen people. The apostles (the leaders of the church) were Jews. The Gentile Christians were fewer and newer. They had much to learn about their new faith. If the leaders in Jerusalem had chosen to exercise their full authority, most likely whatever they decreed would have been done by those new (Gentile) Christians.

It's easy for the more prominent, more "official" individuals involved in a disagreement to exert their authority, state their demands, and get their way. But it isn't Christlike.

B. IT'S EASY TO SPLIT

The tension between Jewish Christians and Gentile Christians could have increased to the point where the church suffered a major setback. The Gentile believers in Antioch could have reacted in anger to the teachings of the ones who came from Judea. They could have started "their own church," one more sensitive to the Gentile heritage. That's what many Christians do today when there is conflict. One group becomes two—and the credibility of the church in the eyes of the community is strained.

C. IT'S HARDER TO HEAL, BUT RIGHT

Better than bullying and better than splitting is healing. That is what the churches of Antioch and Jerusalem did. Contributing to this peaceful resolution, no doubt, was the fact that some effort had already been made to build bridges between the two churches. Upon hearing of the spread of the gospel into Antioch, Jerusalem had sent Barnabas to encourage the new believers (Acts 11:22, 23). Upon hearing of a coming famine, the Antioch church had sent a relief offering to the Christians in Judea. Barnabas was instrumental in this as well (Acts 11:27-30). It is easier for churches (or individual Christians) to find healing in strained relationships when those relationships are built around the love of Jesus.

Healed relationships mean that everyone has to do some giving. When it is the right thing to do, some apologies have to be made—and accepted. Compromises must be worked out in matters that are not of primary importance. Probably no one will get his way entirely; no group will get all it wants.

How do we respond if we are involved in such a situation? Do we "hang in there" and make the sacrifices necessary to maintaining peace? Or do we "throw a fit" and go home angry?

These are the times when it helps to think about what God wants. How does he respond to division within his family? How does he respond to the demonstration of love and encouragement? It should not be hard for us to know when he is smiling and when he is sad.

Discovery Learning

This page contains an alternate lesson plan emphasizing learning activities. Classes desiring such student involvement will find these suggestions helpful. The next page is a reproducible activity page to further enhance discovery learning.

LEARNING GOALS

After this lesson students should be able to:

1. Explain the issue that occasioned the Jerusalem Conference, and summarize how the Conference addressed it.

2. Tell how traditions sometimes obscure the simplicity of the gospel of grace.

3. Confess any burdensome "yokes" that they have placed on others, and praise God for the grace freely given in Jesus Christ.

INTO THE LESSON

Copy the story from the Introduction to the lesson, "Jumping Through Hoops." Ask a class member to read the illustration to introduce the lesson. Then ask your class to cite other examples of rigidly holding to the past long after the reason for doing so has expired. Here is a classic that you can have another person read:

Two sisters were discussing the preparation of ham for a family gathering. One asked the other why they always cut the end off the ham before putting it in the roaster pan. Her sister responded, "I don't know. That's just the way Mom always did it." Not satisfied with that explanation, they decided to call their mother to find the reason. "Mom, why did you always cut the end off the ham before putting it in the roaster pan?"

"Because, it was too long for the roaster pan," their mother replied.

INTO THE WORD

Have your class read today's text—Acts 15:1, 2, 6-15a, 19, 20—as a choral reading. Assign a person or group of people to read the parts of a narrator, the Jewish believers, Peter, and James.

The narrator will read verse 1 until the Jewish believers speak. The narrator will read verses 2, 6, and 7 until Peter speaks. The narrator will read verses 12 and 13 until James speaks. (You could have one or two persons compose the report that Barnabas and Paul gave, as summarized in verse 12, and give that report before going on to verse 13.) James finishes the printed text.

Ask the class to form small groups (four to six members in each) and study each verse for insights to use in resolving church problems. For example, verse 1 might suggest that disputes should be expected. We should not be so naive as to assume that there will be no con-flicts in church life. Verse 2 infers that if there is a sharp dispute and debate, those involved can appeal to church leaders, even from another congregation, to sort out disagreements. Verse 6 says that the apostles and elders met to consider this question, which implies that the discussion was the primary purpose of the meeting. Have a class member write each group's insights on a poster or on the chalkboard.

OPTION

Distribute copies of the reproducible page that follows. Have the class work in small groups, with half the groups completing the first activity and half doing the second. Call for reports after ten minutes.

INTO LIFE

In Acts 15:11, Peter turns the phrase on the Jews by saying, "We believe it is through the grace of our Lord Jesus that we are saved, just as they are." In other words, "We get to Heaven the same way they do!"

This verse echoes down the corridors of time and still resounds as truth. Encourage your class to memorize this verse together. Read the verse aloud in unison. Each time you read it, emphasize a different word. Take time to discuss the importance of the word emphasized. For example, the word *we* shows that Peter's belief is in stark contrast to the belief of the Jewish brethren who wanted the Gentiles to follow the Jewish law, including the practice of circumcision. The term *grace* stands in contrast to human effort or legalistic requirements of the law.

Point out that while the issue in Acts 15 is whether a person must be circumcised to be saved, today's churches wrestle with other issues relating to salvation. Give your class copies of the following "Yes-No" quiz. Learners are to tell whether the Bible mentions each action as necessary for a person to be saved. Have your Bible and a concordance ready for the lively discussion that will follow!

1. Observe the Lord's Supper
2. Confess their sins
3. Repent
4. Go forward in a church service
5. Tithe
6. Pray the sinner's prayer
7. Confess that Jesus is Lord
8. Be baptized
9. Join your local church

Close your class time with a period of directed prayer. Include confession for relying too rigidly on tradition as well as praise for God's grace freely given in Christ Jesus.

Gentiles Included in God's Plan

The following references show that God always intended that the Gentiles were to be included in his plan. Write a short summary of the teaching of each passage.

Genesis 12:3 (and 22:18; 28:14)

Isaiah 9:1

Isaiah 42:6

Isaiah 49:6

Isaiah 49:22

Matthew 4:15

Matthew 10:5

Matthew 10:18

Luke 2:32

Acts 9:15

Commentary Study

Acts 15:20 says, "Instead we should write to them, telling them to abstain from food polluted by idols, from sexual immorality, from the meat of strangled animals and from blood." Four restrictions were given to the Gentiles. Get a commentary from your church library (or see your preacher). Study these four instructions and summarize the purpose and meaning of each:

"abstain from food polluted by idols"

"abstain from sexual immorality"

"abstain from the meat of strangled animals"

"abstain from blood"

RESPONDING TO NEED

LESSON 12

WHY TEACH THIS LESSON?

"Now if you need anything, you be sure and call me." How often we say that to someone, perhaps a grieving widow at the funeral home, or a new mother who has just brought her infant home from the hospital. Unfortunately, they seldom call! Maybe we know they won't, but at least we offered, right?

How much better to suggest some real help and not wait for an invitation. "I'll bring you something for supper on Tuesday night, okay?" Paul did not wait for an invitation. Oh, it's true, he was in Macedonia because of an invitation in a vision (Acts 16:9, 10). But he did not wait to be invited to the riverside Bible study, where Lydia met the Lord and was baptized. He did not wait for the servant girl to request his help. He did not ask permission from the jailer to hold the midnight praise service. He just did it!

This lesson should challenge your learners to do what they can for the Lord, with or without an "invitation."

INTRODUCTION

A. DECISIONS

One of the most impressive qualities distinguishing the apostle Paul is his decisiveness. Certainly there were times when he was tentative and even afraid (cf. 1 Corinthians 2:3). But generally speaking, he seems to have been a man who was able to make a decision and move forward aggressively without turning back or regretting what he had done.

Someone may respond, "Well, if God gave me a vision of what he wanted me to do [such as what we see in today's lesson], I'd move forward aggressively too!" And at times we may wish for such guidance. But we must never underestimate the importance of the guidance provided for us in the Scriptures. There God has provided general directions for us (and even some specific directions that can be learned from the teachings and experiences that are recorded).

Most likely all of us have wrestled with how God indicates his will for us in daily situations. Perhaps we have sensed times when God was blocking our plans, as he did when Paul's missionary team intended to go to Asia and Bithynia, but was forbidden by the Spirit (Acts 16:6, 7). At other times, even though we have not seen a vision offering us guidance, we have sensed that a certain course of action is God's will.

Many who claim that they want to know God's will have not spent sufficient time in the Book where it is found! If we determine to be decisive in obeying God's clear will as recorded in Scripture, we will be better prepared for trusting him on those occasions when his will is not as clear.

B. LESSON BACKGROUND

Armed with the confirmation of their ministry that had come from the decision of the Jerusalem Conference, Paul and Barnabas prepared to proceed with their task of taking the gospel to the Gentiles. First, they returned to Antioch and conveyed the decisions of the Conference, which brought great encouragement

---

DEVOTIONAL READING:
PHILIPPIANS 1:3-11

BACKGROUND SCRIPTURE:
ACTS 16:6-40

PRINTED TEXT:
ACTS 16:9-15, 25-33

LESSON AIMS

After this lesson each student should be able to:

1. Give the significant details of the conversions of Lydia and the jailer in Philippi.

2. Tell how these incidents demonstrate the importance of presenting the gospel in a manner that is sensitive to people's needs.

3. Pray for courage and sensitivity in presenting Christ to someone this week.

May
20

KEY VERSE

"Come over to Macedonia and help us." —Acts 16:9

to the church there. Jesus Christ *alone* is the way to salvation; Gentiles are *not* required to bear the additional weight of keeping the regulations and rituals of Judaism. One of the representatives from the Jerusalem church (Silas) enjoyed the fellowship in Antioch so much that he decided to stay for a while. (He probably did not anticipate that he would become Paul's next traveling companion.)

At one point during their stay in Antioch, Paul suggested to Barnabas, "Let's go back and visit the churches that were established on our last trip. We should see how they are doing."

"Great idea!" said Barnabas. "And why don't we take John Mark with us?"

"Oh, no!" said Paul. "Don't you remember how he deserted us? We don't need someone that unreliable."

Acts 15:39 notes that "they had such a sharp disagreement" that Paul and Barnabas decided to separate. Barnabas took Mark and headed for Cyprus. Paul chose Silas as his new partner and went to visit the churches that had been started during the first missionary journey.

Luke's account focuses on the travels of Paul and Silas. In Lystra, they were joined by Timothy, a young man who showed great promise and eventually became an exemplary leader. (That's what happens when experienced Christians invest time, prayer, example, and instruction in faithful and capable young people.)

While Paul desired to visit churches that were already established, he was also eager to break new ground with the gospel. He wanted to go westward into the province of Asia. In some manner, however, the Holy Spirit prohibited him from doing so. He then tried to turn northward. Again the Spirit said no.

Then Paul and his team came to Troas, where he received his "marching orders." Without delay, he responded!

I. SEEING A VISION (ACTS 16:9, 10)

A. A PLEADING MAN (v. 9)

9. During the night Paul had a vision of a man of Macedonia standing and begging him, "Come over to Macedonia and help us."

Across the Aegean Sea from Troas was the territory of *Macedonia*. (It is northern Greece today.) As God had earlier guided Peter by means of a *vision* (Acts 10:9-16), here he revealed to Paul what the next step of his journey should be.

B. A PREPARED MAN (v. 10)

10. After Paul had seen the vision, we got ready at once to leave for Macedonia, concluding that God had called us to preach the gospel to them.

Here is the decisiveness in Paul that was mentioned earlier. Plans were made *at once to leave for Macedonia*. Notice also that the travel team is described as *we*. This is the first of the *we* sections in the book of Acts (they are found in 16:10-17; 20:5—21:18; and 27:1—28:16). Here it means that Luke, the author of the book of Acts, joined Paul and his companions in Troas. (Verse 8 says that *they* "passed by Mysia and went down to Troas.") Now it is *we* until the imprisonment of Paul and Silas in Philippi.

RESPONDING TO A CALL OF DISTRESS

A distress call from off the Florida coast was received by the United States Coast Guard. When the rescue team arrived, it found a sixteen-foot boat being dragged in circles by something that had attached itself to the boat's anchor rope. Even the boat's ninety-horsepower engine was useless; it was being pulled steadily out to sea.

The Coast Guard rescue boat attached its winch to the motorboat's anchor rope. Eventually, the rescue team pulled to the surface a giant manta ray that measured

WHAT DO YOU THINK?

We do not expect a vision to direct us to a particular individual, family, or other group with the gospel. What are some ways in which we receive our "Macedonian call"?

WHAT DO YOU THINK?

The pronoun *we* in verse 10 indicates that Luke, the author of Acts, joined Paul's team. How important is building a team to the success of Christian ministries? How do you know when to enlist help and when to do the job yourself?

eighteen feet in width and was estimated to weigh more than a ton. It could have pulled the boat to the bottom of the ocean had it been able to reach deep water.

The man from Macedonia whom Paul saw in his vision was also issuing a distress call. His cry for help was a plea for someone to bring the gospel message to him and his people. They were feeling the devastating effects of a sinful pagan culture that was pulling them down to certain spiritual and moral destruction.

This crisis call was heard by those who had what was needed to accomplish a rescue: the right message and the right spirit. The gospel had the power to save, and Paul and his team were willing to take it to others. The church has the same message today and the world's need is the same. The question is whether the church has the right spirit—a willingness to go where the message is needed.   —C. R. B.

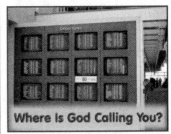

Where Is God Calling You?

Today's visual reminds us that not everyone is called to "Macedonia," but God does call each of us to service.

II. ANSWERING THE CALL (ACTS 16:11-15)

A. TRAVELING TO PHILIPPI (vv. 11, 12)

11. From Troas we put out to sea and sailed straight for Samothrace, and the next day on to Neapolis.

Notice, once again, Luke's careful attention to detail as he charts the course of the missionary team's travels. Apparently nothing significant happened on *Samothrace* (an island in the northeastern Aegean Sea) or in *Neapolis* (the seaport city for Philippi). These were simply stops made in the process of answering the "Macedonian call."

12. From there we traveled to Philippi, a Roman colony and the leading city of that district of Macedonia. And we stayed there several days.

Philippi was the first European city where Paul preached. Luke describes it as *the leading city*. This does not mean that Philippi was the capital city; Thessalonica was the capital. But *Macedonia* was divided into four districts, and Philippi was a leading city in the specific *district* of Macedonia where it was located. Philippi was also considered *a Roman colony*, meaning that it was self-governing and that the citizens were exempt from many of the taxes that were imposed on other portions of the empire.

B. FINDING A PLACE OF PRAYER (v. 13)

13. On the Sabbath we went outside the city gate to the river, where we expected to find a place of prayer. We sat down and began to speak to the women who had gathered there.

Earlier we noted that Paul's usual practice upon arrival in a city was to locate the synagogue and begin his evangelistic efforts there. Since Paul did not follow this same procedure in Philippi, most students conclude that there was no synagogue to be found there. Ten Jewish men were required to establish a synagogue, so the absence of a synagogue suggests that there were not many Jews in the city. Thus, *on the sabbath* Paul and his companions searched in the area *where they expected to find a place of prayer*. Here they found a group of *women*—perhaps Jewish, perhaps Gentile proselytes. No men are mentioned as leading or even participating; perhaps the women were quite eager to have some men present who would join them and teach them.

C. TEACHING LYDIA (vv. 14, 15)

14. One of those listening was a woman named Lydia, a dealer in purple cloth from the city of Thyatira, who was a worshiper of God. The Lord opened her heart to respond to Paul's message.

Out of all the women in the group (we do not know how many were present), one is mentioned by name—*Lydia*, a businesswoman from *Thyatira*. Our

HOW TO SAY IT

Aegean. Ay-JEE-un.
Antioch. AN-tee-ock.
Barnabas. BAR-nuh-bus.
Bithynia. Bih-THIN-ee-uh.
Chrysostom. KRIH-suss-tum or Krih-SAHSS-tum.
Corinth. COR-inth.
Lydia. LID-ee-uh.
Lystra. LISS-truh.
Macedonia. Mass-eh-DOE-nee-uh.
Mysia. MISH-ee-uh.
Neapolis. Nee-AP-o-lis.
Philippi. Fih-LIP-pie or FILL-ih-pie.
Philippian. Fih-LIP-ee-un.
Samothrace. SAM-o-thrace.
Thessalonica. THESS-uh-low-NYE-kuh.
Thyatira. THY-uh-TIE-ruh.
Troas. TRO-az.

text describes her as *a dealer in purple cloth*. Actually, the Greek term used here simply calls her a dealer in *purple*. That could mean that she sold cloth that had been dyed purple (as this translation suggests) or that she sold the dye that was used in the process. Perhaps she dealt in both. Since this was a rather expensive procedure and since purple garments were usually in demand, Lydia was probably quite well-to-do.

Lydia's hometown was a *city* in the Roman province of Asia and home of one of the seven churches addressed by Jesus in the book of Revelation (Revelation 2:18-29). Perhaps Lydia and her co-workers returned there with the gospel message and were instrumental in starting that church.

Luke's record also tells us that *the Lord opened* Lydia's *heart to respond to Paul's message*. This should be understood to mean that the Lord used the efforts of Paul and his companions (the message that they spoke and the sincerity of their lives) to prepare Lydia to believe the gospel and thus to open up a new field of service. Whatever is accomplished by the efforts of faithful Christian workers is considered the Lord's work (Acts 14:27; 15:12) and is done for his glory.

Lydia was one of those remarkably attentive, perceptive, and responsive individuals who are willing to hear and examine the gospel message and to accept it without hesitation as the truth. Remember that there have always been faithful women such as she who have played a significant role in the Lord's work.

15. When she and the members of her household were baptized, she invited us to her home. "If you consider me a believer in the Lord," she said, "come and stay at my house." And she persuaded us.

Lydia's *household* may have included other women who worked with her in the purple cloth/dye business, family members, or both. They had also come to the riverside to pray and had listened to Paul's message. They, too, accepted it as the truth, and, along with Lydia, they *were baptized*. Thus it is evident that when Paul talked about Jesus as the Son of God and urged those who listened to accept him as Savior and Lord, he must have talked about Christian baptism as the necessary and appropriate response.

Although a new convert, Lydia seems to have grasped immediately the importance of Christian hospitality. Apparently she either owned or rented (so that she could use it during business trips) a *house* in Philippi (another indication of her wealth). Evidently this was a fairly roomy house, for she and her household had room for living and sleeping; and there was enough additional room for providing temporary quarters for the traveling evangelists.

III. HELPING A JAILER (ACTS 16:25-33)
A. PRISONERS' PRAISE (v. 25)
25. About midnight Paul and Silas were praying and singing hymns to God, and the other prisoners were listening to them.

Not everything in Philippi went as smoothly as did the encounter with Lydia and the other women. Verses 16-24 of Acts 16 tell how the missionary team encountered a young woman who "had a spirit by which she predicted the future" and engaged in "fortune-telling." She identified Paul and his companions as servants of God who were proclaiming the way of salvation. After many days of this, Paul became "troubled" at the woman's behavior. She was speaking the truth; however, the gospel was not being helped by testimony from that kind of source! So Paul cast the spirit out of the woman. Her "handlers," who had been making plenty of money from her ability, became angry. They seized Paul and Silas, brought exaggerated charges against them to the authorities, and had them thrown into prison.

But Paul and Silas were not ordinary prisoners! Instead of cursing their fate, they *were praying* to God. And instead of complaining, they were *singing hymns*. Nor was this a private time of worship, for *the other prisoners were listening to them*.

PRAYING DURING A CRISIS

One foggy day, Amber Scott was sitting in her car at a railroad crossing, waiting for a train to pass. Suddenly, a truck rear-ended her car, shoving it under a freight car in the middle of the train. Unaware of what had happened, the engineer did not stop.

Scott's car was caught by the train and dragged down the tracks. During the terrifying seven-minute ride that followed, she called 911 on her cell phone. Her call was broken off, however, because the roar of the train made it impossible for the dispatcher to hear her voice. So she called her mother, but that call was also broken off.

Scott realized that she had one other resource at her disposal: she prayed. She later said, "I prayed to the Lord all the way down the track." At the end of the ordeal, her car was "totaled"; but she escaped with only minor injuries.

When Paul and Silas were arrested and imprisoned in Philippi, their response was the same as Amber Scott's: they prayed—and they sang hymns as well! As it turned out, they did not escape with "minor injuries," since they had been "severely flogged." Nevertheless, they knew where to turn for strength and help. The result was that God rescued them and that others were influenced by their faith.

The world is watching how we Christians deal with adversity. May our actions be a testimony to our faith.   —C. R. B.

B. SUDDEN EARTHQUAKE (v. 26)

26. Suddenly there was such a violent earthquake that the foundations of the prison were shaken. At once all the prison doors flew open, and everybody's chains came loose.

The other prisoners may have thought their new "guests" a bit strange, but the things that soon began to happen were even stranger! *Suddenly there was . . . a violent earthquake*. When the *prison doors flew open* and the restraining *chains came loose*, the prisoners could have escaped easily.

C. TROUBLED JAILER (vv. 27-30)

27. The jailer woke up, and when he saw the prison doors open, he drew his sword and was about to kill himself because he thought the prisoners had escaped.

The *jailer* had one main job—to keep his *prisoners* in custody. If they were to escape, his life was forfeit. Assuming that the prisoners had used the earthquake as their opportunity to flee, this jailer was certain that suicide would be less painful than the sentence that his superiors would carry out on him.

28. But Paul shouted, "Don't harm yourself! We are all here!"

If the jailer could not see the prisoners, how did *Paul* know what the jailer was about to do? Was it darker in the cell so that the prisoners could see the jailer but he could not see them? Did he give a cry of despair, announcing his lethal intentions? Did God reveal to Paul what the jailer was about to do? We do not know the answers, but we do know that Paul *shouted* from the darkness and assured the jailer that no one had fled.

29, 30. The jailer called for lights, rushed in and fell trembling before Paul and Silas. He then brought them out and asked, "Sirs, what must I do to be saved?"

Perhaps the jailer had heard about Paul and Silas or had even heard them speak prior to their arrest. Apparently he knew Paul and Silas were preaching a message of salvation. Now deeply distressed over the crisis confronting him, he turned to Paul and Silas for help: "I have heard you talking about salvation—*what must I do to be saved?*"

DAILY BIBLE READINGS

Monday, May 14—Paul's Vision About Macedonia (Acts 16:6-10)

Tuesday, May 15—In Philippi: The Conversion of Lydia (Acts 16:11-15)

Wednesday, May 16—Paul and Silas in Prison (Acts 16:16-24)

Thursday, May 17—Songs at Midnight (Acts 16:25-29)

Friday, May 18—The Message of Salvation (Acts 16:30-34)

Saturday, May 19—An Invitation to Abundant Life (Isaiah 55:1-11)

Sunday, May 20—Public Exoneration (Acts 16:35-40)

D. JOYFUL HOUSEHOLD (vv. 31-33)

31. They replied, "Believe in the Lord Jesus, and you will be saved—you and your household."

Paul and Silas gave a short answer that required a longer explanation. The next verse tells us about that.

32. Then they spoke the word of the Lord to him and to all the others in his house.

Paul and Silas continued to teach *the word of the Lord* to both the jailer and *his house* (servants who lived with him or members of his family or both). They explained who the Lord Jesus Christ is and what believing in him involves.

33. At that hour of the night the jailer took them and washed their wounds; then immediately he and all his family were baptized.

The jailer demonstrated his gratitude for how Paul and Silas had saved his life, both in a physical and in a spiritual sense. He *washed their wounds*, cleaning the lacerations that had been caused by the earlier beating. Then *immediately* the believing household was taken to a place where they could be buried and raised with Christ in baptism. John Chrysostom, one of the outstanding preachers of early church history, wrote of the Philippian jailer: "He washed and was washed. He washed them from their stripes, and he himself was washed from his sins."

CONCLUSION

A. A CHANGED FAMILY

The jailer did not neglect his duty when he took Paul and Silas to his house, where he could care for their wounds. They were still in his custody—just not in the prison. It was the city officials who had neglected their duty (Acts 16:35-40).

We are told that the jailer "was filled with joy because he had come to believe in God—he and his whole family" (v. 34). Undoubtedly Heaven rejoiced as well (Luke 15:7). Everything in a household changes when those within it are "in Christ"—when he is recognized as the true Head of that home. Those in Philippi who saw the jailer the next day noticed a different man.

B. AN ENLARGED FAMILY

Lydia was already a God-fearer before she became a Christian. She was also a successful businesswoman. She provided a living for those employees within her "household." She likely had a rather large sphere of influence.

When Lydia became a Christian, she expressed her newfound faith by granting the missionaries the hospitality of her home. She had become part of a new and different kind of household—the "family of believers" (Galatians 6:10).

When we become "in Christ," we join a worldwide fellowship of brothers and sisters. Our family becomes larger.

C. A FAMILY OF NEW INDIVIDUALS

Whatever happened to the fortune-telling girl in Philippi after the spirit of divination was cast out of her? It requires an assumption for us to say that she became part of the church in Philippi, but some believe that she did. She knew something about Jesus, even when she was telling fortunes. Perhaps she continued to learn of him after being set free from the control of the evil spirit.

Paul later wrote to the church that would soon be established south of Philippi (in Corinth), "Therefore, if anyone is in Christ, he is a new creation; the old has gone, the new has come!" (2 Corinthians 5:17). When we are in Christ, we are part of a family of forgiven individuals who, by God's Spirit, begin living the lives of new people.

WHAT DO YOU THINK?

Both Lydia and the jailer expressed some form of Christian grace immediately upon their conversions. Lydia provided the missionaries a place to stay, and the jailer brought them to his home and fed them. How important are such behaviors in the life of a new Christian? Why?

[Consider these Scriptures in your discussion: Matthew 3:8; Romans 6:4; 2 Corinthians 5:17.]

PRAYER

Having considered, Father, how Paul and his companions responded to your call, we ask that you would reinforce our determination to respond—quickly and decisively—to the needs in our sin-scarred world. In Jesus' name. Amen.

THOUGHT TO REMEMBER

"After Paul had seen the vision, we got ready at once to leave for Macedonia" (Acts 16:10).

Discovery Learning

*This page contains an alternate lesson plan emphasizing learning activities. Classes
desiring such student involvement will find these suggestions helpful. The next page
is a reproducible activity page to further enhance discovery learning.*

LEARNING GOALS

After this lesson each student will be able to:

1. Give the significant details of the conversions of
Lydia and the jailer in Philippi.

2. Tell how these incidents demonstrate the importance of presenting the gospel in a manner that is sensitive to people's needs.

3. Pray for courage and sensitivity in presenting
Christ to someone this week.

INTO THE LESSON

To open today's class period, sing a hymn that describes the desire of Paul's heart evidenced in today's
lesson. A good choice is "I'll Go Where You Want Me to
Go." Provide copies for all members or project the
words on a screen or wall where everyone can see them.
(This hymn is in the public domain. If you choose another, be sure it is also in the public domain or that you
have permission from the copyright holder to copy it.)
Sing through all stanzas of the hymn. Then discuss the
words with your class.

Make the transition to the Bible study by saying,
"This hymn describes a commitment to share God's
message wherever he wants us to go. Our lesson today
finds Paul searching for his next ministry location and
following God's leading."

INTO THE WORD

If your class has both men and women, you may
want to divide them into two groups. Ask the women to
study Acts 16:9-15 and the men to study Acts 16:16-33.
As they study, have them look for information that could
be used if they were assigned to introduce Lydia (or the
Philippian jailer) as the speaker for a women's (men's)
retreat. They should include family, occupation/busi-
ness, how she (he) became a Christian, and the impact
the gospel has made in her (his) life.

OPTIONS

Word Search. Use the word search puzzle on the next
page to introduce key words from today's text. After allowing time for the learners to locate each of the terms,
discuss the significance of each one.

Map Study. Ask the learners to trace the travels of
Paul in Acts 16 on a map of the Mediterranean world.
(Use the map on page 316.) Listed below are the cities

and regions mentioned in Acts 16. Use your Bible to
note which sites Paul visited and what is said about the
locations on the list that he did not visit.

Cities: Derbe, Lystra, Iconium, Troas, Neapolis,
Philippi, and Thyatira.

Larger Regions: Phrygia, Galatia, Asia, Mysia, Bithynia,
Macedonia, and Samothrace.

Third Option. Have half the class work on the word
search puzzle and the other half on the map. Review the
key terms from both to cover the text.

INTO LIFE

Paul and his companions went looking for people like
Lydia. Lydia was a religious woman who was open,
ready, and receptive to the gospel message they had to
offer. Have each of the learners select a partner to go
with him or her (as Paul did). Brainstorm for a list of
people who might be open to listening to the gospel.
Then say, "Choose one person whom you and your
partner will go to see this week. Develop a plan for how
you and your partner will share the gospel with this person. Choose a method from this list that you will use:
invite the person to a church event (worship service,
Bible study, or other), share your personal testimony,
give the person a Christian tract, write a witnessing letter, share a meal with the person, or your better idea!"

In contrast to Lydia, whom Paul went seeking, the
jailer in Acts 16 was a person whom God brought into
Paul's life. Often we are unprepared to strike up a conversation with such people. Have your class consider each
of these statements and check any that might be good to
use:

1. "I'll bet it's been a long time since someone invited
you to a Bible study. How long has it been?"

2. "I find that our preacher's messages are easy to listen to and have practical application to my life. Would
you like to go with me to church next Sunday?"

3. "I'm supposed to talk to someone about the good
news of Jesus for a class I'm in at church. Could I talk to
you for a few minutes?"

4. "I am really enjoying our Bible study at church.
Would you like to go with me next week?"

5. "Did you know that you can know for sure that
you are going to Heaven?"

6. "If someone were to ask you, 'What must I do to
be saved?' what would you tell them?"

Word Search

Find these words from our text in the word search below. (All are in the vertical or horizontal position.)

BAPTIZED
JESUS
SAMOTHRACE
PAUL
DOORS
MACEDONIA
EARTHQUAKE
PHILIPPI
SILAS
MIDNIGHT
PRAYER
THYATIRA
JAILER
NEAPOLIS
SABBATH
TROAS

```
M A C E D O N I A N R E D D Z P A U L O
R F E E L W E A S D H S A E E F H E E X
B G U E B L A N E V E A N L E I D U E R
G T Y U C S P T T E U B I T U L C Y U B
T Y W Y T R O A S U Y B E N Y O I W Y G
Y U P W H E L N E Y W A L O W P D P W T
H I E C Y U I T S W P T S P H P B N E Y
N D U G A Y S A M O T H R A C E A A U H
M O Y H T W O L N N T H S A Y A T O Y N
J O W L I P A S D H E A L Y E S T P W M
U R E N R L P O I U M T G E F A S D P J
I S I L A S D F J A I L E R B V B C S U
K N R A D U E T E F D A E F P R A Y E R
L M F G Q W H S S D N G U I E R P G H K
O N D H S D L D U R I P P M N C T E L E
P H G T I O I V S N G U W E A S I T E O
Z E T K O L G S S E H A P P I N Z E W P
X F H A S D A E A R T H Q U A K E T A Z
E D R T O P O N R E D D E T B I D Y S X
N P H I L I P P I D E N R E D D E T W E
```

"Come over to Macedonia and help us."

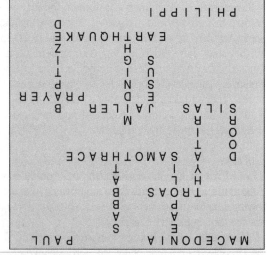

SERVING WITH HUMILITY

LESSON 13

WHY TEACH THIS LESSON?

One of the most clever print ads I ever saw was for an electronic commerce consulting firm. Next to a pack of wolves stood a lamb, partially obscured by the hide of a wolf. The message was clear: electronic commerce is highly competitive, dominated by fierce "wolves." The timid competitor, the lamb who pretends to be a wolf, is in big trouble!

Of course, it was the "lamb in wolf's clothing" that caught the eye. That's not normal! What is normal, though tragic, is the "wolf in sheep's clothing." It's not new. It's been around for a long time. But the ploy still works, so shepherds have to be on their guard.

Do you have shepherds in your class—elders, parents, youth sponsors? All of them, and others that might be present, must be ever vigilant for wolves. This lesson will remind them of that need.

INTRODUCTION

A. "KEEP WATCH OVER YOURSELVES"

Leadership in the Lord's church is not (and never has been) easy. No one ever said that it would be. Good leaders will not complain when the going gets tough, for they are aware that such times are unavoidable. They keep modeling faith. They keep growing. They keep caring. They determine to lead by loving, not lording; by modeling, not mandating; and by being servants, not sovereigns.

Good leaders do not take a defensive posture that assumes "those people in the pews don't know what they're talking about." Instead, they ask, "How can we serve more effectively and communicate our decisions and dreams more clearly?" They may go on a devotional retreat and pray. They may search the Scriptures together, reminding themselves of the divinely mandated dimensions of their task. They may divide into groups that study issues such as shepherding, peacemaking, and overseeing; then return to the larger group with suggested plans of action.

Such efforts as these can be part of the efforts that leaders make to "keep watch" over themselves. Their primary concern should be this: what can we do to be God's men and God's leaders over the flock that he has entrusted to our care?

B. "AND ALL THE FLOCK"

Most every congregation has people who are hurting. Some are hurting because of the self-inflicted pain of their sin. Some are hurting through no fault of their own; the sin of others has wrought havoc in their lives. Some hurt and don't know why. Some react to their hurt by trying to inflict pain on someone else.

Both those who are hurt and those who are hurting others need help—divine help and the help of mature Christians. The church's leaders are to be at the forefront of those who want to make a difference in such individuals' lives. Elders are to "keep watch" over the flock—the bleating, confused, vulnerable, sometimes stubborn flock—whom God loves and wants to keep in his fold. Their model is the Good Shepherd, who laid down his life for his sheep (John 10:15).

DEVOTIONAL READING:
1 CORINTHIANS 15:1-11
BACKGROUND SCRIPTURE:
ACTS 20:13-38
PRINTED TEXT:
ACTS 20:17-32

LESSON AIMS

After this lesson a student should be able to:

1. Summarize Paul's farewell speech and exhortation to the Ephesian elders.

2. Tell what this passage says about the responsibilities of leaders in the local church.

3. Plan a way to express encouragement to a leader in the church and purpose to do so more frequently.

KEY VERSE

However, I consider my life worth nothing to me, if only I may finish the race and complete the task the Lord Jesus has given me—the task of testifying to the gospel of God's grace.

—Acts 20:24

May
27

LESSON 13 NOTES

C. LESSON BACKGROUND

At one point Paul had desired to go into the province of Asia, where Ephesus was located, and preach the gospel. However, the Holy Spirit had forbidden him to do so (Acts 16:6). Shortly afterward, Paul saw a vision of a man from Macedonia pleading with him to come there. Paul's response to that vision was the beginning of his second missionary journey (described in Acts 16:11—18:22). Last week's lesson was taken from Paul's ministry in Philippi, which was his first preaching stop in Macedonia.

Paul did not forget about the needs in Asia. At the conclusion of his second missionary journey he finally arrived there, at Ephesus (Acts 18:18-21). There he left Priscilla and Aquila until he himself could return, which he did during his third missionary journey (Acts 19:1). He spent three years there (Acts 20:31), preaching and teaching, establishing a church, and developing capable leadership. Eventually Paul had to leave Ephesus when his evangelistic success threatened the local idol makers and caused a near riot (Acts 19:23-40).

However, Paul had done his work well; a healthy church was firmly in place, and a group of leaders had been set apart to guide it. But Paul's hasty departure meant that some of his work had gone undone. Returning from his third journey, Paul determined to sail past Ephesus in order to reach Jerusalem by the celebration of Pentecost (Acts 20:16). (Perhaps the situation was still too tense in Ephesus, and Paul thought it better not to go back in person.)

Still, Paul was quite concerned about the church in Ephesus. When the ship on which he was traveling stopped at Miletus (about thirty miles south of Ephesus), Paul determined that he would have enough time to send for the elders of the church and meet with them. He reminded these men of what they had been taught before, called their attention to the kind of loving leadership that he had modeled, warned them of threats to their flock, and encouraged them to remain faithful. His words continue to speak powerfully to leaders in Christ's church today.

I. PAUL'S EXAMPLE (ACTS 20:17-27)

A. CONSISTENT IN LIFESTYLE (vv. 17, 18)

17. From Miletus, Paul sent to Ephesus for the elders of the church.

As noted above, Paul had chosen to bypass *Ephesus* on his way to Jerusalem. But once the ship reached the harbor at *Miletus*, he realized that he would have time to contact the *elders of the church* in Ephesus and arrange a meeting. (Perhaps the ship had to remain at Miletus a while for repairs or loading.)

18. When they arrived, he said to them: "You know how I lived the whole time I was with you, from the first day I came into the province of Asia.

Paul began his remarks to the elders by reminding them of the foundation on which he had built his ministry with them. He had led by an example that began *from the first day* that he arrived in *the province of Asia*. The fact that Paul could say *you know* indicates that he had nothing to hide from these men. His conduct gave him no reason to be ashamed. Paul's example had remained intact *the whole time*: during both good times and times of pressure and persecution, his commitment to Christ never wavered. This was the kind of leadership that he had modeled for these elders and that he wanted them to demonstrate. Particularly during the difficult days that lay ahead (vv. 29, 30), they would need to be men of faith, wisdom, and service.

B. DETERMINED IN SERVICE (v. 19)

19. I served the Lord with great humility and with tears, although I was severely tested by the plots of the Jews.

WHAT DO YOU THINK?

While Ephesus was not far from Miletus, it must have required a significant amount of time for the elders to make the round trip and to meet with Paul. If any of these men were day laborers, the economic impact of such a trip would have been significant. What, if anything, can we learn from their example of sacrificing time and money for their "flock"?

Paul had a strong emotional attachment to the church of Ephesus, as noted by his reference to his *tears* (see also v. 31). No doubt that attachment helped to strengthen his resolve to minister to the Ephesians in spite of the obstacles he faced. We have already noted the opposition that arose from the silversmiths, recorded in Acts 19:23-41. Here we see that there was in Ephesus, as in many other cities, opposition from *the Jews* as well.

C. FAITHFUL IN TEACHING (vv. 20, 21)

20. You know that I have not hesitated to preach anything that would be helpful to you but have taught you publicly and from house to house.

Once again, Paul emphasized the open and aboveboard nature of his ministry: he kept back nothing. He shared with the Ephesians everything he knew about Christ and anything that would be *helpful* to their walk with him and their witness for him.

Publicly and from house to house is a good teaching pattern for church leaders in any era. If we are being faithful to Jesus' Great Commission to teach, baptize, and teach (Matthew 28:19, 20), then teaching opportunities—both in public settings and in the privacy of people's homes—will present themselves regularly. An elder should be able to teach in both settings.

21. I have declared to both Jews and Greeks that they must turn to God in repentance and have faith in our Lord Jesus.

The pattern of Paul's evangelistic outreach was "first for the Jew, then for the Gentile" (Romans 1:16). Whenever possible, Paul and his companions preached to *Jews* first when they entered a city, then shared with *Greeks* (Gentiles) as other doors opened.

The phrase *turn to God in repentance* expresses what repentance really means. In repentance there should be sorrow for sin and the confession of one's guilt before God. But what makes it true *repentance* is the turning around *to God*—the change of direction—in one's life. Before I am a Christian, I take my own advice and go my own way. I am my own boss. When I become a Christian, Jesus is my boss. Whereas I formerly answered to myself and no one else, I now answer to God.

In the same way, *faith* is described as being *in our Lord Jesus*. Our faith has meaning and substance. As John stated it in the purpose for writing his Gospel: "that you may believe that Jesus is the Christ, the Son of God, and that by believing you may have life in his name" (John 20:31).

D. UNDAUNTED BY SUFFERING (vv. 22-24)

22. And now, compelled by the Spirit, I am going to Jerusalem, not knowing what will happen to me there.

Paul was headed for *Jerusalem, not knowing what* he would face. True, there were those present in Jerusalem who were fiercely hostile to the gospel. But Paul wanted to bring the financial assistance that various churches had collected to help the poverty-stricken believers in that city (1 Corinthians 16:1-4; 2 Corinthians 9:1-5, 12-14).

The phrase *compelled by the Spirit* may refer to the fact that the Holy Spirit had warned Paul of the trials that awaited him (as he states in the next verse). The Greek wording may also mean "compelled in the spirit," which would signify Paul's personal compulsion (in his own spirit) to proceed to Jerusalem. Either way, we can see the urgency Paul felt about *going* there.

23. I only know that in every city the Holy Spirit warns me that prison and hardships are facing me.

WHAT DO YOU THINK?

Paul reminded the Ephesian elders of how he lived while he was among them—his example. How important is one's example? Why?

HOW TO SAY IT

Agabus. AG-uh-bus.
Aquila. ACK-wih-luh.
Ephesians. Ee-FIH-zhuns.
Ephesus. EF-uh-sus.
Macedonia. Mass-eh-DOE-nee-uh.
Miletus. My-LEE-tus.
Philippi. Fih-LIP-pie or FILL-ih-pie.
Priscilla. Prih-SIL-uh.

WHAT DO YOU THINK?

Paul was determined to complete his ministry. What would it mean for you to "complete your ministry"? What prioritizing needs to be in place for you to do that?

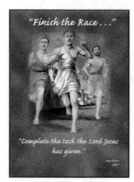

"Finish the Race..."

"Complete the task the Lord Jesus has given."

Today's visual illustrates verse 24 of the text and challenges the viewer to take the same attitude as Paul had toward ministry.

Paul was certain that he would experience opposition and even *prison* in Jerusalem. Later this was confirmed through a prophetic message from Agabus (Acts 21:10, 11).

24. However, I consider my life worth nothing to me, if only I may finish the race and complete the task the Lord Jesus has given me—the task of testifying to the gospel of God's grace.

Most important to Paul—more important to him than his personal welfare or safety—was his ministry. He had been assigned the introduction of *the gospel of God's grace* to the Gentiles. Like a marathon runner, Paul wanted to *finish the race* in triumph.

Did Paul finish the course as he planned? The answer is clear from the final chapter of 2 Timothy: "I have fought the good fight, I have finished the race, I have kept the faith" (2 Timothy 4:7).

E. WITHOUT REGRETS (vv. 25-27)

25. Now I know that none of you among whom I have gone about preaching the kingdom will ever see me again.

Paul's statement that *none of* the Ephesian elders would *ever see* him *again* raises a question, in light of the fact that it appears Paul did return to Ephesus at a later time (see 1 Timothy 1:3). Perhaps Paul was simply stating what he believed to be true at this point; in other instances, he made plans that he then had to change for some reason (2 Corinthians 1:15, 16, 23).

26, 27. Therefore, I declare to you today that I am innocent of the blood of all men. For I have not hesitated to proclaim to you the whole will of God.

Those in Ephesus and "all the Jews and Greeks who lived in the province of Asia" had "heard the word of the Lord" (Acts 19:10). Anyone who rejected the gospel had only himself to blame; his *blood* would be upon his own head. Paul had done his job.

LEADING BY DOING

James Russell Wiggins thinks retirement is a waste of labor and talent. Of people in their sixties who are still sound in mind and body, but who are relaxing in retirement communities, he asks, "How can a society support such idleness?"

Note that Wiggins is not some young fellow worrying about "old folks" getting so many Social Security benefits that the system may bankrupt itself long before *he* gets to retirement age. On the contrary, when Wiggins made those comments, he was ninety-five years old and still editing the *Ellsworth American,* a weekly newspaper in the town of Ellsworth, Maine. It's a job he's been doing since 1922! This gentleman is living up to the advice he gives to others.

The apostle Paul is someone else who lived up to the advice he gave. When the elders of the church at Ephesus came to meet him at Miletus, Paul gave them some advice about how they should conduct themselves as leaders of God's people. But this was not a case of "Do as I say, not as I do." He reminded these men of the character of his own life and leadership. He had given himself in service and faithfully declared "the whole will of God" to all who would listen.

It was a good example for that time, and it is for ours.   —C. R. B.

II. PAUL'S EXHORTATION (ACTS 20:28-32)

A. A CHARGE (v. 28)

28. Keep watch over yourselves and all the flock of which the Holy Spirit has made you overseers. Be shepherds of the church of God, which he bought with his own blood.

WHAT DO YOU THINK?

Paul urged the elders at Ephesus to "be shepherds of the church of God." How is that done today?

Here Paul's words provide a description of the purpose of leadership in the Lord's church. Leaders must first *keep watch over* themselves. Paul gave similar counsel to Timothy: "Watch your life and doctrine closely. Persevere in them, because if you do, you will save both yourself and your hearers" (1 Timothy 4:16). The leader's commitment to his own spiritual development determines how far and how well he will be able to lead others.

Paul also describes the elders of the church as *overseers*. Their task of oversight involves the duty to *be shepherds of the church of God*. Biblical oversight is not expressed primarily through decision-making or exerting authority in a dictatorial manner. Peter tells elders to "be shepherds of God's flock . . . serving as overseers—not because you must, but because you are willing, . . . not lording it over those entrusted to you, but being examples to the flock" (1 Peter 5:2, 3). Elders hold each other accountable; they meet the needs of their flock; they give responsible oversight to the direction of the church's ministries; they provide spiritual food by seeing that the Word of God is taught. After all, the church is not the elders'; it is *the church of God*.

Paul then gives an additional reason for taking such special care of God's church: it has been *bought with his own blood*. The Greek phrase can be translated, "the blood of his own," thus referring to the priceless sacrifice that Jesus made to obtain mankind's redemption from sin.

B. A WARNING (vv. 29-31)

29. I know that after I leave, savage wolves will come in among you and will not spare the flock.

The church is not exempt from attack by the devil and any whom he can use. In fact, he is constantly engaged in such activity! It is his intention to disrupt the church, to raise doubts in the minds of her members, and to put Christians at odds with each other. He will attack from outside the church, but often from the inside.

Paul's reference to *savage wolves* calls to mind Jesus' warning about wolves "in sheep's clothing" (Matthew 7:15). It may seem hard to imagine that a church could fall prey to the influence of such forces after three years of constant, faithful teaching from an apostle (Acts 20:31). And yet, later portions of the New Testament indicate that this was so. Paul sent 1 Timothy (and probably 2 Timothy) to Ephesus, where Timothy was having to confront those whose doctrine was suspect (1 Timothy 1:3, 4). Some have suggested that the epistle of 1 John was sent to the churches of Asia, which would have included Ephesus. There we read of the influence of false teachers who were questioning whether Jesus came in the flesh (1 John 4:1-3). Finally, Jesus' words to the church in Ephesus (Revelation 2:1-7) indicate that it was being influenced by corrupting and disruptive elements. It is no surprise that Paul counseled these elders to "be on your guard" (v. 31).

30. Even from your own number men will arise and distort the truth in order to draw away disciples after them.

Paul warned that the influences described in verse 29 would not come from outside the church; they would originate from their *own number*. Sadly, it is sometimes true that the church is severely harmed by its *own*—by *men* who are interested in building a following rather than following Jesus.

31. So be on your guard! Remember that for three years I never stopped warning each of you night and day with tears.

The depth of Paul's commitment to the believers in Ephesus is clear from these words. He poured both time (*night and day* for *three years*) and emotional involvement (*tears*) into their spiritual maturity. The "wolves" (v. 29) would have only their own selfish interests at heart.

WHAT DO YOU THINK?

The devil still seeks to undermine the church from within. What precautions can be taken to keep this from happening?

DAILY BIBLE READINGS

Monday, May 21—Paul in Athens (Acts 17:16-34)

Tuesday, May 22—Paul in Corinth (Acts 18:1-11)

Wednesday, May 23—Paul in Ephesus (Acts 19:1-10)

Thursday, May 24—Paul in Macedonia and Greece (Acts 20:1-6)

Friday, May 25—Paul in Troas and Miletus (Acts 20:7-16)

Saturday, May 26—Paul Speaks to the Ephesian Elders (Acts 20:17-24)

Sunday, May 27—Paul's Summary and Farewell (Acts 20:25-38)

PRAYER

Father in Heaven, more than to be leaders we want to be followers—followers of your Word, of your Son, and of the path of service to which you point us. If we are presently serving as leaders in our church, help us to do that with the courage, compassion, and humility that Paul displayed. We ask in the name of the head of the church, amen.

THOUGHT TO REMEMBER

Are you an elder, called to shepherd and oversee the flock of God (as the men from Ephesus in today's lesson)? Are you part of the flock? Each of us has the same responsibility: serve the Lord—faithfully, readily, and humbly!

C. A TRUST (v. 32)

32. Now I commit you to God and to the word of his grace, which can build you up and give you an inheritance among all those who are sanctified."

Although Paul (the Ephesians' teacher, encourager, and model for leadership) was leaving these elders, he was not leaving them alone. He could still *commit* these men *to God and to the word of his grace.* The apostolic instruction they had received would serve them well as a reliable guide in the face of future threats. Today we have these recorded in the New Testament Scriptures. By following them, we too can lay hold of the *inheritance* promised to all who faithfully serve Jesus.

"WIN ONE FOR THE GIPPER"

Perhaps the most famous plea in all of sports history is, "Win one for the Gipper." George Gipp played football for the University of Notre Dame. He was a "natural"—an outstanding athlete who became famous for leading his team to spectacular comeback victories over superior foes, sometimes playing exceptional football even with serious injuries.

Gipp played his last game during the 1920 season. Injured and sick with a fever, he came into a game against Northwestern for only one play and threw a fifty-five-yard touchdown pass. He died a few weeks later of pneumonia.

Eight years later, Notre Dame was playing a much stronger, undefeated Army team. At halftime neither team had scored. In the Notre Dame locker room, coach Knute Rockne said to his team, "Boys, I want to tell you a story." Then he related Gipp's deathbed conversation with him: "Sometime, Rock, when . . . things are going wrong and the breaks are beating the boys—tell them to go in there with all they've got and win just one for the Gipper." With the team sobbing, Rockne said, "All right, boys. This is the game. Let's get one for the Gipper." Notre Dame won the game that day, 12-6.

Paul's final words to the elders of the church at Ephesus were words of encouragement. He had set the example. He knew that final victory would be theirs. It can be ours, too, if we are faithful to follow that example and serve Jesus.—C. R. B.

CONCLUSION

A. BORN TO LEAD

We've all probably heard the term "born leader." There is certainly some measure of truth in that phrase. Some individuals possess a leadership personality that can be seen while they are still children. Their peers just naturally seem to follow them. Such individuals may lead well, or they may lead poorly. But they have an ability to convince and draw followers.

On the other hand, some very fine people never become leaders. They appear to lack that hard-to-define something that gains a following.

B. BUILT TO LEAD

It is incorrect, however, that only those born with certain instincts or a certain style of personality can lead. We can study the godly leaders of the Old and New Testaments and learn from the way they led. (We can also study bad examples and learn from them as well!) As we do so, we can seek to use the talents and abilities with which we are blessed to serve the Lord's church and to encourage others. In this way, many Christians "grow" into leadership positions. They are "built," not "born."

Any leader needs to keep in mind these words of Jesus: "From everyone who has been given much, much will be demanded" (Luke 12:48). If you are a leader in the Lord's church, determine above all else to be a follower of Jesus.

Discovery Learning

This page contains an alternate lesson plan emphasizing learning activities. Classes desiring such student involvement will find these suggestions helpful. The next page is a reproducible activity page to further enhance discovery learning.

LEARNING GOALS

After this lesson each student should be able to:

1. Summarize Paul's farewell speech and exhortation to the Ephesian elders.

2. Tell what this passage says about the responsibilities of leaders in the local church.

3. Plan a way to express encouragement to a leader in the church and purpose to do so more frequently.

INTO THE LESSON

Here is another chance to train and develop a new teacher! Probably there is someone in your class who has the potential of being a teacher. Ask that person to help you by preparing a brief lecture on the background material for today's lesson, a summary of Paul's travels recorded in Acts 16–20. Provide a copy of the commentary for this week. Help your prospective teacher have a successful experience. Offer help with content, especially with visuals. An outline in print or an overhead projection transparency would help any new teacher. Allow from three to five minutes for this part of the lesson. Be sure to follow up with a debriefing session, an evaluation of the lecture, and a thank-you note.

In addition to the activity above, or in place of it if time is short, have the following sentence written on a chalkboard in your room or on a poster prominently displayed: "What does it take to be a good leader?" If possible, arrange the chairs in small clusters of four to six. When the learners arrive, ask them to work in small groups to discuss this question. Have each group select someone to record and summarize the group's discussion and report to the whole class. Allow five to seven minutes for discussion; then ask for reports.

Option. Use the crossword puzzle on the reproducible page that follows to introduce today's theme and text.

INTO THE WORD

Ask a volunteer to read aloud Acts 20:17-32. Observe that this text and 1 Peter 5:1-4 are two of the most comprehensive descriptions of the office of elder, overseer, and shepherd (the three terms, or verb forms of the terms, are all used to describe the same group of men) in all of the New Testament. Assign a task force to compare these two passages by listing in two columns the teaching of each passage. The chart might begin something like this:

ACTS 20:17-32	1 PETER 5:1-4
All 3 terms used to describe the group	All 3 terms used to describe the group
The terms are all plural	The terms are all plural
Not because of greed	Not because of greed

Allow the task force to work while other groups of learners participate in the following activities. After ten or twelve minutes, call for reports from all groups.

LEADERSHIP STUDY POSTERS

Make three posters to use in studying Paul's teaching about leadership in Acts 20:17-32. Title the first poster, "COMMITMENT," the second, "CHARACTER," and the third, "CONDUCT." Assign a group and a recorder for each poster and provide a broad-tipped marker. As the group studies each verse, have the learners suggest words or phrases to be listed on each poster. A recorder can be selected to do the writing.

For instance, Paul's example is foundational in Acts 20:18, so the word *example* should go on the CONDUCT poster. *Serving with humility* goes on the CHARACTER poster, from verse 19. *Ready for persecution* is implied from verse 19 and should appear on the COMMITMENT poster. *Teaching publicly and in homes,* from verse 20, belongs on the CONDUCT poster.

BIBLE DICTIONARY

Adult Bible teachers have the responsibility not just to teach the Bible but also to teach their class members how to study the Bible for themselves. Borrow Bible dictionaries from your church library or your minister's study. Divide the class into small groups, and have each group research each of the following terms: elders (v. 17), church (v. 17), humility (v. 19), repentance (v. 21), faith (v. 21), grace (v. 24), gospel (v. 24), kingdom (v. 25), overseers (v. 28), and sanctified (v. 32).

INTO LIFE

Our churches are filled with leaders who have served for years with too little appreciation or encouragement. Probably someone in your class has a great testimony of how an elder in the church has influenced his or her life. Ask such a person to give a short testimony of such a man's service. Encourage all your learners to write notes with similar messages to other leaders in the church.

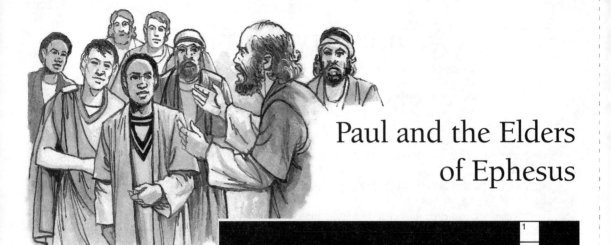

Paul and the Elders of Ephesus

From Acts 20 and the clues below, complete the following crossword puzzle.

ACROSS

2. Ephesian church leaders (v. 17).
3. What the elders were to shepherd (v. 28).
6. Paul testified to God's _____ (3 words) (v. 24).
10. Quality needed in addition to repentance (v. 21).
12. What accompanied Paul's warning (v. 31).
13. What Paul went about preaching (v. 25).
14. Gift given to all who are sanctified (v. 32).

DOWN

1. What the Holy Spirit made the Ephesian leaders (v. 28).
4. Gave Paul warning about prison and hardships (two words) (v. 23).
5. Those who are _____ receive an inheritance (v. 32).
7. Elders or overseers (v. 28).
8. Elders are to watch over themselves and the _____ (v. 28).
9. Paul declared the necessity of this (v. 21).
11. Characteristic of Paul's service (v. 19).

Copyright © 2000. STANDARD PUBLISHING, Cincinnati, Ohio. Permission is granted to reproduce this page for ministry purposes only. Not for resale.

Summer Quarter, 2001

Division and Decline

Special Features

Lessons

Unit 1: A Kingdom Divided

Unit 2: Prophecies of Judgment

Unit 3: Decline and Fall

About These Lessons

"United we stand; divided we fall." We've all heard those words, and the truth of them seems apparent. Yet we still find ourselves choosing up sides and dividing ourselves one from another. This series of lessons warns against such division. When the nation of Israel became two nations, both were weaker, and both eventually collapsed. Let the church heed the warning.

Jun 3

Jun 10

Jun 17

Jun 24

Jul 1

Jul 8

Jul 15

Jul 22

Jul 29

Aug 5

Aug 12

Aug 19

Aug 26

Lessons That Must Be Learned

by John W. Wade

Many agencies, public and private, are trying to address the problems of our civilization. Their efforts alone, however, offer no real solutions. The source of most of our problems lies deeply imbedded in our hearts. Like Isaiah, we are a people of "unclean lips," dwelling "among a people of unclean lips" (Isaiah 6:5).

That is the reason that the study of Old Testament history can be of great benefit in every age. In fact, that is the reason these ancient records have been preserved: "as examples and . . . warnings for us" (1 Corinthians 10:11).

UNIT 1: A KINGDOM DIVIDED

JUNE

Lesson 1 deals with the controversy that led to the tragic division of God's people into two nations. The differences that led to this division had been simmering beneath the surface for some time, but the arrogant, self-centered Rehoboam proved to be the catalyst that brought them to an explosive climax.

Lesson 2 introduces us to the prophet Elijah, who in many respects epitomizes the prophetic ministry of the Old Testament. He was a courageous man who spoke out against evil without concern for his personal safety.

Lesson 3 focuses on Elijah's dramatic confrontation with the prophets of Baal on Mount Carmel, where God's power triumphed decisively.

Micaiah is the hero of **lesson 4**. Although his brief encounter with Ahab is the only incident in Micaiah's life that the Bible relates, this episode shows us that Micaiah was a man of courage and character.

UNIT 2: PROPHECIES OF JUDGMENT

JULY

In **lesson 5** we learn about Amos, who spoke out with firmness and clarity against the people's greed, sexual immorality, and idolatry.

Lesson 6 provides further insight into the ministry of Amos. He denounced in no uncertain terms the people's empty, insincere worship.

Lesson 7 introduces us to Hosea, whose marriage became intertwined with his ministry. His wife's infidelity served as a symbol of Israel's unfaithfulness to God.

Lesson 8 tells how Hosea continued to plead with God's wayward people. God's refusal to give up on his people will encourage those who have been tempted to give up on unbelieving friends or family members.

Lesson 9 introduces us to Micah, who denounced false prophets, dishonest judges, and mercenary religious leaders.

UNIT 3: DECLINE AND FALL

AUGUST

Lesson 10 allows us to witness God's dramatic call to Isaiah. Isaiah was overwhelmed by a vision of God "high and exalted" (Isaiah 6:1).

Lesson 11 includes the prophecy that a virgin would bear a Son and call him Immanuel. This timely message of hope remains helpful even today.

Lesson 12 notes how Isaiah used a parable of a vineyard to show how God expected the "fruit" of justice and righteousness from his people, but instead they brought forth greed and oppression.

The last lesson of the quarter lowers the curtain on the nation of Israel. God permitted the Assyrians to overpower Israel and take her citizens into captivity.

Learning these lessons from history can help us avoid repeating some of the failures of God's people—but only if we have the courage to apply these lessons.

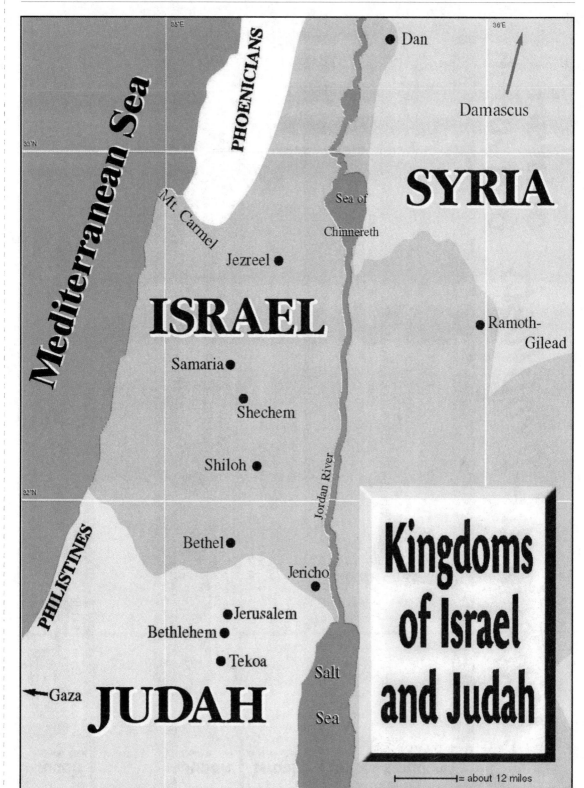

Kings and Prophets of Israel and Judah

United Kingdom

Kings: David, Solomon

Prophets / Kings — Israel
Kings / Prophets — Judah

B.C. 970 960 950 940 930 920 910 900 890 880 870 860 850 840 830 820

Israel Kings: Jeroboam I, Nadab, Baasha, Elah, Zimri, Omri, Ahab, Ahaziah, Joram, Jehu, Jehoahaz

Israel Prophets: Elijah, Elisha

Judah Kings: Rehoboam, Abijah, Asa, Jehoshaphat, Jehoram, Ahaziah, Athaliah, Joash

Judah Prophets: Obadiah, Joel

Israel / Judah

Prophets / Kings — Israel
Kings / Prophets — Judah

810 800 790 780 770 760 750 740 730 720 710 700 690 680 670 660

Israel Kings: Jehoahaz, Jehoash, Jeroboam II, Zechariah, Shallum, Menahem, Pekahiah, Pekah, Hoshea

Israel Prophets: Elisha, Jonah, Amos, Hosea

(Kingdom Ends)

Judah Kings: Joash, Amaziah, Uzziah, Jotham, Ahaz, Hezekiah, Manasseh

Judah Prophets: Isaiah, Micah

Judah

Prophets / Kings — Judah

650 640 630 620 610 600 590 580 570 560 550 540 530 520 510 500

Judah Kings: Manasseh, Amon, Josiah, Jehoahaz, Jehoiakim, Jehoiachin, Zedekiah

(Babylonian Captivity)

(Ruled by Governors)

Judah Prophets: Nahum, Zephaniah, Habakkuk, Jeremiah, Ezekiel, Daniel, Haggai, Zechariah, Malachi (430 B.C.)

REHOBOAM: AN UNWISE DECISION

LESSON 1

WHY TEACH THIS LESSON?

Today's lesson could have a very different application depending on the age of your learners. If you teach a class of older adults, especially older men, the temptation for them will be to become smug. "If only Rehoboam had listened to his elders, men like *us*, things would have turned out so much better!" For them you will need to deal with potential pride. It was not merely the age of the older counselors, but their wisdom, that Rehoboam should have respected. Age and wisdom do not always go together. Encourage your older learners to pursue wisdom.

If you teach younger adults, they will have a tendency to ignore the wisdom of the older generation—just as Rehoboam did. Encourage these learners not to dismiss the older generation just because they drive slower and are not necessarily computer literate. (Some of the older crowd may just surprise them on both scores, however!)

For each of your learners, the challenge is to understand and respect those of other generations. That is the lesson that you will seek to impart today.

INTRODUCTION

A. ADVICE NOT "FIT FOR A KING"

Kings George I, George II, and George III ruled England during the eighteenth century. The first two were weak, ineffective rulers. As a result, the English Parliament became more and more aggressive in governing the country. During this period of parliamentary rule, Britain's empire grew and her trade expanded. Then, in 1760, George III came to the throne. At his coronation his mother advised him, "Be king, George. Be king!"

One of the first steps George III took in his efforts to "be king" was to discharge his able prime minister, William Pitt. Then he began a series of measures that antagonized many leaders both in England and in her colonies. The eventual result was the American Revolution and the colonies' independence—all because George made the foolish mistake of listening to bad advice.

Rehoboam's efforts to "be king" led to similar tragic results—the division of his kingdom. He chose to listen to the brash words of his young advisers rather than heed the advice of his father, King Solomon: "Pride goes before destruction, a haughty spirit before a fall" (Proverbs 16:18).

B. LESSON BACKGROUND

King Solomon began his reign as king of Israel about 971 B.C. Because he realized that he was relatively young and inexperienced when he came to the throne, he humbly asked God for wisdom to rule his people well. God granted Solomon his request, and for some time his kingdom prospered. Solomon embarked on extensive building programs (including the temple in

DEVOTIONAL READING:
MATTHEW 11:27-30

BACKGROUND SCRIPTURE:
1 KINGS 12; 2 CHRONICLES 10:1—11:12

PRINTED TEXT:
1 KINGS 12:3-13a, 16

LESSON AIMS

After participating in this lesson, students should be able to:

1. Describe the circumstances that led to the division of Israel into two kingdoms.

2. Give illustrations (from current events or from their personal experiences) of how following bad advice produced problems.

3. Take steps to deal with a difficult decision or situation they are currently facing by seeking wise and godly counsel.

KEY VERSE

"If today you will be a servant to these people and serve them and give them a favorable answer, they will always be your servants." —1 Kings 12:7

The visuals packet contains a map of the divided kingdom that will be useful today and throughout the quarter. See page 349 for ordering information.

HOW TO SAY IT

Absalom. AB-suh-lum.

Ahijah. Uh-HIGH-juh.

Ebal. EE-bull.

Gerizim. Guh-RYE-zim or
    GAIR-ih-zeem.

Ish-Bosheth. Ish-BO-sheth.

Jeroboam. Jair-uh-BO-um.

Rehoboam. Ree-huh-BO-um.

Sheba. SHE-buh.

Shechem. SHEK-em or
    SHEE-kem.

Jerusalem and his own palace) that greatly enhanced the kingdom materially. But as the years passed, Solomon compromised his faith by entering foreign alliances that were "sealed" by his marriages to pagan wives. Many of these women brought their false religions to Israel, corrupting the people with their beliefs and practices.

This sad turn of events brought God's judgment upon Solomon: "The Lord became angry with Solomon because his heart had turned away from the Lord, the God of Israel, who had appeared to him twice" (1 Kings 11:9). God then sent the prophet Ahijah to seek out Jeroboam, whom Solomon had made a leader of one of the groups of laborers that Solomon commissioned from the tribes of Israel (1 Kings 5:13, 14; 11:28). Ahijah dramatized his message by taking his outer garment and tearing it into twelve pieces. These twelve pieces symbolized the twelve tribes of Israel. Ten of these pieces the prophet gave to Jeroboam, signifying that he would become the leader of ten of the tribes (1 Kings 11:29-31).

First Kings 11:26 notes that this incident amounted to an act of rebellion by Jeroboam against Solomon. Through some means the king apparently learned of it and sought to kill Jeroboam. Jeroboam fled to Egypt, where he remained until Solomon's death (1 Kings 11:40). When Solomon's son Rehoboam ascended the throne, he journeyed to Shechem for the coronation service, which is the point at which today's printed text begins.

I. THE PEOPLE'S REQUEST (1 KINGS 12:3-5)

A. PLEA FOR MERCY (vv. 3, 4)

3. So they sent for Jeroboam, and he and the whole assembly of Israel went to Rehoboam and said to him:

The city of Shechem was located about thirty miles north of Jerusalem in a valley between Mount Gerizim and Mount Ebal. It was a city with great historical significance for the nation of Israel. Abraham had built an altar there (Genesis 12:6, 7). Later Jacob purchased a "plot of ground" in that vicinity, where he pitched his tent and erected an altar (Genesis 33:18-20). "Jacob's well," which guides in the Holy Land still show to modern tourists, was also located in this territory (John 4:5, 6). Joshua's farewell address, during which he urged the Israelites to be faithful to God's covenant with them, was delivered at Shechem (Joshua 24:1ff.).

With so much history associated with it, one can see why Shechem was selected as the place for the coronation of *Rehoboam* as Israel's king. Of far greater significance, however, is that *he* went to Shechem rather than having the people come to Jerusalem "to make him king" (1 Kings 12:1). This suggests to many students that there was already a certain measure of dissension among the people.

Furthermore, the fact that the Israelites had *sent for Jeroboam* to return from Egypt (vv. 2, 3) provides additional evidence that trouble was brewing. Although Jeroboam had been in exile, he was apparently so well respected that the people wanted him to serve as their spokesman when they met with King Rehoboam. If Rehoboam was aware of his father's suspicions toward Jeroboam (1 Kings 11:40), the latter's return at this particular time surely must have been unsettling to Rehoboam.

4. "Your father put a heavy yoke on us, but now lighten the harsh labor and the heavy yoke he put on us, and we will serve you."

Years earlier, when the nation of Israel first wanted a king, Samuel had warned the people that having a king would carry certain negative consequences (1 Samuel

8:10-18). His dire predictions that a king would levy a heavy tax burden upon them and conscript their sons and daughters for his service had come to pass during the reign of Solomon (1 Kings 5:13, 14; 9:15, 22). Now the people wanted relief. They were not asking for the complete abolition of all taxes or other burdens laid upon them by Solomon. All they were asking was that Rehoboam would *lighten* their *heavy yoke,* and then they would *serve* him.

Certainly this was not an unreasonable request of a new king. Nor did the people complicate the issue by giving an ultimatum. Their statement left open the question of what they would do if Rehoboam denied their request.

B. REHOBOAM'S RESPONSE (v. 5)
5. Rehoboam answered, "Go away for three days and then come back to me." So the people went away.

Living in Solomon's palace, Rehoboam may well have been isolated from the people and their hardships. Thus it was reasonable for him to take some time to examine the facts and evaluate the situation before he made a decision. On the other hand, Rehoboam may simply have been stalling for time—like many politicians do today when they are confronted with hard decisions. Regardless of his motives, the people were willing to give him time to consider the matter.

II. REHOBOAM'S ADVISERS (1 KINGS 12:6-11)
A. OLDER MEN (vv. 6, 7)
6. Then King Rehoboam consulted the elders who had served his father Solomon during his lifetime. "How would you advise me to answer these people?" he asked.

The first step Rehoboam took in determining how to *answer these people* was a wise one. He *consulted the elders* who had counseled *his father Solomon*. They had observed the mistakes that had ruined Solomon's once-promising reign. They saw how his growing extravagance had placed an increasingly heavy burden on the people by demanding that they furnish both the manpower and the taxes necessary to complete and maintain his many projects and enterprises. No doubt, these men had heard some of the complaints that the people had made.

7. They replied, "If today you will be a servant to these people and serve them and give them a favorable answer, they will always be your servants."

These senior counselors advised Rehoboam to become *a servant to these people*. This was quite different from the usual demeanor of ancient monarchs, who were notorious for their arrogant and haughty behavior. The last thing in the world they would think of becoming was a servant. They desired instead to be served.

These wise elders, however, were declaring a great truth: a ruler who is willing to *serve* the people will soon have subjects who are willing to serve him. Jesus was a perfect model of this kind of servant leadership (Matthew 20:25-28). And while many pay lip service to it, few leaders in politics, business, or even the church have truly understood this principle.

LEADERSHIP = SERVANTSHIP
Nearly a millennium after Rehoboam's older and wiser advisers counseled the new king to "be a servant," Jesus of Nazareth taught, "If anyone wants to be first, he must be the very last, and the servant of all" (Mark 9:35). Those who are greatest in God's kingdom are those who lead by serving. Jesus is living proof of that truth. He came to serve and to save us, and he never wavered from that purpose. He illustrated servanthood dramatically when he stooped to wash his disciples' feet.

WHAT DO YOU THINK?

Rehoboam consulted some advisers when facing a decision. What are some ways to get good counsel when we are trying to make a crucial decision?

WHAT DO YOU THINK?

The elders whom Rehoboam consulted suggested that he "be a servant to these people." By hindsight we know their advice was better than the counsel of the young men. How good do you think it is for leaders today? What kind of leaders—political leaders, church leaders, any leaders?

Rehoboam rejected the wisdom of leading by serving. Instead, he looked for advice that would allow him to gratify his pride and exploit his power. His iron-handed tactics irreversibly divided the nation of Israel.

Someone has wisely observed, "You cannot teach what you do not know; you cannot lead where you will not go." All leaders (whether presidents, preachers, or parents) should hang this motto on their walls. Truly effective leadership results from humble servantship. Rather than grasping a scepter and wielding a sword, reach for a basin and a towel. That is what Jesus would do.   —R. W. B.

B. YOUNGER MEN (vv. 8-11)

8. But Rehoboam rejected the advice the elders gave him and consulted the young men who had grown up with him and were serving him.

We can only guess at Rehoboam's motives for rejecting *the advice the elders gave him.* Perhaps he had turned to them first simply out of courtesy, knowing ahead of time that he would not take their advice. Or he may have resented the fact that their words, in effect, criticized the actions of his father. Perhaps Rehoboam also realized that if he followed their counsel, he would have to do without some of the privileges that Solomon had enjoyed. Rehoboam was like many of us: when someone gives us advice we don't like, we turn to someone else who we think will give advice more to our liking.

In Rehoboam's case, this meant consulting some *young men.* This was a group of his peers—men whom he knew better, for they had *grown up with him.* We usually feel more comfortable among people we have grown up with or have known for a long time. Apparently these younger men had been Rehoboam's companions or servants in the palace, since they *were serving him.* They knew how he thought and knew the answers that he wanted to hear.

9. He asked them, "What is your advice? How should we answer these people who say to me, 'Lighten the yoke your father put on us'?"

In speaking to these younger men, Rehoboam posed his question differently from the way he consulted the older counselors. In speaking to the older men he asked, "How would **you** advise **me** to answer these people?" (v. 6). But to the young men he asked, *How should we answer these people?* Quite obviously Rehoboam identified with, and felt at ease with, the younger men more than the older men.

10. The young men who had grown up with him replied, "Tell these people who have said to you, 'Your father put a heavy yoke on us, but make our yoke lighter'—tell them, 'My little finger is thicker than my father's waist.

In sharp contrast to the response of the older counselors, the answer of these *young men* showed utter contempt for the *people.* As companions of Rehoboam, these men had probably lived lives of ease and comfort. Such a lifestyle had left them with little understanding of the plight of the general populace, who were burdened by a heavy tax load. Thus, these men had little or no sympathy for the people's suffering. No doubt, this was one reason Jeroboam was considered a fitting representative for the people (vv. 2, 3): he had worked among them (1 Kings 11:28) and was aware of their grievances.

The arrogance of these young advisers to Rehoboam is almost beyond belief. They acknowledged that Solomon had placed a *heavy yoke,* or burden, upon the people, but they urged Rehoboam to increase that burden rather than grant relief. They even told Rehoboam the words he should use: *My little finger is thicker than my father's waist.* The meaning of this proverbial expression was quite clear: Rehoboam's weakest actions would be more severe than his father's strongest actions.

WHAT DO YOU THINK?

The lesson writer notes that the younger counselors may have grown up in ease and comfort, and that this may have contributed to their lack of sensitivity to the people's plight. How can leaders identify with the people whom they lead, especially if they come from different backgrounds from their own?

WHAT DO YOU THINK?

The counsel of the younger men was opposite that of the elders, so Rehoboam had to evaluate the advice and make his own decision. He chose to take the advice that most nearly conformed to his own instincts and preferences, and the result was disastrous! How should we evaluate the counsel that we receive?

11. *My father laid on you a heavy yoke; I will make it even heavier. My father scourged you with whips; I will scourge you with scorpions.'"*

While the reference to *whips* and *scorpions* could have been figurative, on occasion Solomon's overseers may have used actual whips on their workers. Some commentators have suggested that *scorpions* describes an especially painful whip in which pieces of metal or bone were embedded to cause lacerations in the flesh of the victim.

III. REHOBOAM'S CHOICE (1 KINGS 12:12, 13a, 16)

A. HARSH REPLY (vv. 12, 13a)

12, 13a. Three days later Jeroboam and all the people returned to Rehoboam, as the king had said, "Come back to me in three days." The king answered the people harshly.

When the *three days* that *Rehoboam* had requested had passed, *all the people*, led by *Jeroboam*, again assembled to hear the king's response to their petition. No doubt they had used this time to discuss possible replies he might make. Had he responded favorably to their petition, they probably would have been willing to return home, supportive of Rehoboam. But they also must have considered the possibility that Rehoboam would reject their request.

Sadly, *the king answered the people harshly*, ignoring the wisdom of his father: "A gentle answer turns away wrath, but a harsh word stirs up anger" (Proverbs 15:1). Even a gentle answer might not have placated the people, but a harsh answer was certain to fan the flames of their dissatisfaction.

B. TRAGIC RESULTS (v. 16)

16. When all Israel saw that the king refused to listen to them, they answered the king: "What share do we have in David, what part in Jesse's son? To your tents, O Israel! Look after your own house, O David!" So the Israelites went home.

Rehoboam's brash rejection of the people's request broke open wounds that actually had been festering for many years. During the time of the judges, tensions manifested themselves on at least three occasions (Judges 8:1-3; 12:1-6; 20:1-48). Later, after King Saul's death, only Judah crowned David as king, while the northern tribes remained loyal to Saul's house, crowning his son Ish-Bosheth king (2 Samuel 2:8-10). In addition, following Absalom's revolt and David's return to power, the northern tribes briefly supported a rebel named Sheba (2 Samuel 19:41—20:22). In fact, the words spoken here to Rehoboam are strikingly reminiscent of those that initiated Sheba's revolt against David (2 Samuel 20:1).

To your tents, O Israel. Some students interpret this as a call to arms. It is a reasonable assumption, but not required. It may have been simply a call for the people to leave the meeting with the king and to depart to their homes. Regardless of the immediate intent, however, the eventual result of this response is clear. Negotiations between Rehoboam and the northern tribes were angrily terminated. The northern tribes voiced their allegiance to Jeroboam as king, and Ahijah's prophecy of the kingdom's division came to pass.

GENERATION GAPS

"Senior Saints" are sometimes heard to say, "I must have been born several years too late." They mean, of course, that they are not comfortable living in eras dominated by the tastes and preferences of a younger generation. On the other hand, the young are restless and rebellious because they too are uncomfortable with what they consider the rigid expectations and "old-fashioned" ways of their elders.

WHAT DO YOU THINK?

When Rehoboam acted unreasonably, the northern tribes rejected his leadership. On the other hand, David remained loyal even when King Saul tried to kill him. How should we respond when leaders act unreasonably?

VISUALS FOR THESE LESSONS

The visual pictured in each lesson (e.g., page 346) is a small reproduction of a large, full-color poster included in the Adult Visuals packet for the Summer Quarter. The packet is available from your supplier. Order No. 492.

PRAYER

Dear Lord, protect us from stubborn pride. Teach us to learn how to compromise gracefully over issues that are not vital to the Christian faith. Show us how to forgive when we have dealt harshly with others. In the name of the humble Lamb of God we pray. Amen.

THOUGHT TO REMEMBER

Be discerning about whose advice you follow. Seek counsel from godly people whom you know and trust.

Rehoboam is a prime example of this youthful rebelliousness, except that his issues and agendas held implications much more far-reaching than those normally faced by the younger generation. His choices and decisions affected thousands of people; indeed, the history of a nation was significantly altered by the generation gap between this "upstart" ruler and the "old men" who had served his father, but whose advice he curtly brushed aside.

The conflict that arose when Rehoboam took the throne was never resolved. The kingdom was divided and tribes of God's family became virtual enemies. Fortunately, families usually survive the generation gaps between teens and parents. But will the church overcome whatever generational conflicts threaten the "unity of the Spirit"? God help us if mere opinions and preferences are allowed to divide us!

—R. W. B.

CONCLUSION

A. CONFLICT OR COMPROMISE?

Throughout the centuries, the church has found itself in conflict with the forces of the secular world. In these situations the church has had to stand and fight, for to compromise with evil would lead the church to abandon its very reason for being. Jesus warned us to anticipate these struggles, and he has promised to be with us when we face them.

However, not all church fights have pitted the church against the world. All too often those who wore the name of Christ have fought against one another. In some situations the faithful have had little choice but to stand and fight. When those within the church seek to subvert the basic doctrines of the church—such as the authority of the Scriptures, the virgin birth of Christ, and the bodily resurrection of Christ—the faithful dare not compromise. We must "contend for the faith that was once for all entrusted to the saints" (Jude 3).

Yet candor forces us to acknowledge that not all the controversies within the church deal with crucial matters of faith. We may try to make it appear that we are contending for the faith when in reality we are contending only for our personal opinions. In situations such as this, reasonable compromise is certainly most appropriate. The "bigger picture"—the accomplishment of the mission of the church—must receive top priority.

One of Rehoboam's problems was that he could not distinguish between those policies that were essential to the strength of his kingdom and those that reflected his own personal preferences. He was more concerned about maintaining personal power than seeking the good of the entire kingdom. As a result, what power he did have was irreversibly weakened.

B. SPEAK SOFTLY

When Solomon came to the throne as a young man, he did so with appropriate humility. He confessed to God that he was "only a little child" not knowing "how to carry out my duties." With such an attitude, it is not surprising that he asked for wisdom to rule his people well (1 Kings 3:7-11). Unfortunately, the blessings that God granted Solomon gradually caused him to forget his initial humility and fall victim to pride.

As Rehoboam grew up in the royal household, pampered and surrounded by luxury, he saw few signs of Solomon's humility. Instead, he saw a degree of wealth and power that kept him from developing a compassion for the people whom he was called upon to lead. As we have noted, he seemed oblivious to his father's warnings about pride (Proverbs 16:18) and about the importance of a "gentle answer" (Proverbs 15:1). What a terrible price the nation paid for Rehoboam's negligence!

Discovery Learning

This page contains an alternate lesson plan emphasizing learning activities. Classes desiring such student involvement will find these suggestions helpful. The next page is a reproducible activity page to further enhance discovery learning.

LEARNING GOALS

After participating in this lesson students will be able to:

1. Describe the circumstances that led to the division of Israel into two kingdoms.

2. Cite illustrations (from current events or from their personal experiences) of how following bad advice produced problems.

3. Take steps to deal with a difficult decision or situation they are currently facing by seeking wise and godly counsel.

INTO THE LESSON

Distribute copies of the reproducible activity "Seeking Good Advice From Godly People" from the next page. Allow just a few minutes for the learners to complete the activity. Then discuss the value of seeking, not only *good* advice, but *godly* advice, when making a major decision. Make the transition to Bible study by pointing out that in today's lesson we have what might be called a "good bad example" in the matter of seeking godly advice!

INTO THE WORD

Give each person a letter-sized sheet of paper. At the top of the paper should be a major heading, "Making Decisions (1 Kings 12:3-13a, 16)." Over the first column write "Good Moves!" and over the second column write "Bad Moves!" Down the left-hand side of the page, list the following labels: verses 3 and 4, verse 5, verses 6 and 7, verse 8, verses 12 and 13a.

Before beginning the Bible study, give a brief lecture on the lesson background from your lesson commentary. Emphasize the circumstances that led to the division of Israel into two kingdoms. You may write the list of principal characters as you lecture about them (Solomon, Ahijah, Jeroboam, Rehoboam). You may also show a map of the divided kingdom of Israel. (Use visual 1 from the *Adult Visuals* pack. See page 346.)

After the mini-lecture, you may choose to have groups of five complete the worksheets together or have the learners work on them individually. Read the Scripture lesson. Ask the groups or individuals to go back and write the good moves or bad moves Rehoboam made in making his decision. The answers for the "Good Moves" column are as follows: *verses 3 and 4: Identify the problem; verse 5: Take time in making important decisions; verses 6*

and 7: Consult persons with experience. Verse 8 can be listed under both columns: *Consult friends.* Verses 12 and 13a will be listed under the "Bad Moves" column: *Followed bad advice.*

After completing this exercise, ask the following discussion questions: "Why do you think Rehoboam chose to favor the advice of the young men rather than that of the elders?" and "What was the impact of Rehoboam's decision on Israel?"

Make the transition to application by reminding the class that good counsel is extremely important in making good decisions.

INTO LIFE

The application will take place through three brief activities. The first activity is to brainstorm principles in seeking advice. Ask the class to share what they believe are important principles in seeking advice. While they suggest these principles, have a class member write them on a marker board or a chalkboard.

The second activity is to review the text for additional principles, or to reinforce those already stated. Distribute copies of the reproducible activity "Godly Advisers for Good People" from the next page. Allow three or four minutes for the learners to search the text for principles in seeking advice. Add to your list on the chalkboard any additional principles discovered.

The final step is to apply these principles to some hypothetical situations. List the following situations on poster board or a transparency, and have small groups answer these two questions about one of the situations: "Whom would you seek as advisers in this situation?" and "Why are these advisers appropriate?"

SITUATION 1: A church worship committee is considering making the worship service more contemporary by blending choruses with hymns and adding more instrumentation to the service.

SITUATION 2: A young mother and father have different views on disciplining their child.

SITUATION 3: A single Christian woman has been asked to marry a non-Christian young man who has been coming to church with her.

After completing the above exercise, remind the class that the same principles are appropriate when giving advice as when seeking it. Conclude by having the class read together the closing prayer printed on page 350.

Seeking Good Advice From Godly People

Today's lesson encourages us to seek good advice from godly people as we make important decisions. David echoes this principle in Psalm 1. Fill in the blanks from Psalm 1:1, 2. The highlighted letters will spell the result of seeking good advice from godly people.

is the man who does not

in the counsel of the

or

in the way of sinners or sit in the

of mockers.

But his

is in the law of the Lord, and on his law he

day and night. (Psalm 1:1, 2)

The one who seeks good advice from godly people will be

Godly Advisers for Good People

We can learn some lessons from today's text about how to counsel people. While the list below is not exhaustive, the principles are very significant. What principles do you find in this text that will help you to be a godly adviser?

Verse 5:

Verse 6:

Verses 8-10:

Verse 16:

"First Seek the Counsel of the Lord"

—King Jehoshaphat of Judah to Ahab, King of Israel (2 Chronicles 18:4)

ELIJAH:
A PROPHET APPEARS

LESSON 2

Jun
10

WHY TEACH THIS LESSON?

The opening verses of Romans 5 contain a wonderful promise. To know that our suffering can produce good results in our lives, particularly perseverance, character, and hope, is a comfort. Sometimes, it's not so easy to rejoice, however. I know one Christian sister whose family was under great stress. She said, "I told God if he would let up on my 'character development' for a while, I'd really work hard on it later [after her current stress was relieved]!"

I can sympathize with her, as can many of your learners who have experienced extended periods of trial. Such students should take comfort from today's lesson. During an extended period of famine—three and a half long years—it might have seemed that God had abandoned his people. Today's text gives clear examples that he was still making provision for his own. He still does!

INTRODUCTION

A. A TERMITE AND A PROPHET

According to an old legend, there once lived a wicked giant. The animals of the forest lived in fear of him because he often tortured and killed many of them just for sport. The giant lived in a castle perched high on a cliff overlooking the sea. From this vantage point he could observe anyone who dared approach him.

One day the animals met and began to plot how they might rid themselves of this evil tyrant. The elephant, the largest animal in the forest, volunteered to climb the steep path and attack the giant. But the giant saw him coming, rushed out to meet him, seized him, and threw him into the sea. After watching this, the animals were even more fearful. Finally, however, the lion—the bravest animal in the forest—agreed to try and fight the giant. But he met the same fate that had befallen the elephant.

As the animals cowered in fear, they heard a tiny voice say, "I have a plan to defeat the giant." Looking around, they discovered a tiny termite emerging from an old log. The other animals scoffed, "If the elephant and the lion could not defeat the giant, what chance do you have?"

"Be patient and wait," replied the little insect as he started toward the castle. Arriving there undetected by the giant, the termite crept inside the castle and began to eat away at one of the massive timbers that held the castle in place. Many months after the termite began his work, the castle suddenly collapsed into the sea, carrying the giant to his doom and securing a victory that the most powerful animals of the forest could not achieve.

This is similar to the situation that faced the northern kingdom of Israel. A wicked king, Ahab, and his wicked wife, Jezebel, were in power. God could have used the mighty armies of Israel's enemies to challenge Ahab. Instead, he chose

DEVOTIONAL READING:
JOB 36:5-11
BACKGROUND SCRIPTURE:
1 KINGS 17
PRINTED TEXT:
1 KINGS 17:1-16

LESSON AIMS

After this lesson students should be able to:

1. Tell how God provided for Elijah during the three-year famine described in the text.

2. Tell some ways in which God provides for his people today.

3. Suggest a specific way they can demonstrate dependence on the Lord.

KEY VERSE

The jar of flour was not used up and the jug of oil did not run dry, in keeping with the word of the LORD spoken by Elijah.
—1 Kings 17:16

DAILY BIBLE READINGS

Monday, June 4—*Omri Reigns Over Israel (1 Kings 16:21-28)*

Tuesday, June 5—*Ahab Reigns Over Israel (1 Kings 16:29-34)*

Wednesday, June 6—*Elijah Predicts a Drought in Israel (1 Kings 17:1-7)*

Thursday, June 7—*The Prayer of Faith (James 5:13-18)*

Friday, June 8—*The Widow of Zarephath (1 Kings 17:8-16)*

Saturday, June 9—*Elijah Raises the Widow's Son From Death (1 Kings 17:17-24)*

Sunday, June 10—*God's Goodness (Job 36:5-11)*

This listing of the kings and prophets of Israel and Judah is in the Adult Visuals packet. It will be useful throughout this quarter.

an obscure prophet, Elijah, who suddenly appeared on the scene to demonstrate to Ahab and to God's people who was really "in power."

B. LESSON BACKGROUND

Our previous lesson focused on Rehoboam, who became king when his father Solomon died. Rehoboam's arrogant rejection of the people's request for relief from the burdens of an extravagant reign led to a revolt that divided the kingdom.

For approximately the next three hundred and fifty years, the history of God's people comprised the history of two separate kingdoms—the northern kingdom (Israel) and the southern kingdom (Judah). During that time, relations between the two ranged from cooperation in the face of a common enemy to bitter conflict. The Bible notes that, following the division of the kingdom, "there was continual warfare between Rehoboam and Jeroboam" (1 Kings 14:30). Tensions continued during the reigns of later kings (1 Kings 15:16).

The northern kingdom never experienced any degree of stability until the reign of Omri, who came to power in approximately 885 B.C. (almost fifty years after the division). Although Omri brought prosperity to the northern kingdom, he "did evil in the eyes of the Lord and sinned more than all those [kings] before him" (1 Kings 16:25). Perhaps his most grievous evil was allowing the influence of his pagan neighbors to the north, who worshiped many false gods, to infiltrate his kingdom. This is indicated by the fact that Omri's son Ahab, who ascended the throne in 874 B.C., married Jezebel, described as "daughter of Ethbaal king of the Sidonians" (1 Kings 16:31). Most likely this was a marriage designed to seal an alliance between Israel and the Phoenicians to the north. Jezebel, however, was a strong-willed woman, who was also a fervent worshiper of Baal and never missed an opportunity to promote his worship. Thus this marriage, though arranged for political reasons, wrought spiritual disaster in Israel; for it allowed Baal worship to gain a foothold.

It was at this crucial time in the northern kingdom's history, when pagan worship was making serious inroads among God's people, that God called Elijah (in approximately 860 B.C.) to confront a powerful but corrupt couple and to counter their influence on behalf of the true God.

I. ELIJAH'S MINISTRY BEGINS (1 KINGS 17:1-7)

A. ELIJAH'S COURAGE (v. 1)

1. Now Elijah the Tishbite, from Tishbe in Gilead, said to Ahab, "As the LORD, the God of Israel, lives, whom I serve, there will be neither dew nor rain in the next few years except at my word."

The name *Elijah* means "The Lord is God." The Scriptures tell us nothing about Elijah's family; he appears rather suddenly, without any introduction. Even what we learn from this verse is not entirely clear. *Gilead* was the territory east of the Jordan River, extending from the northern end of the Dead Sea northward to the Yarmuk River, south of the Sea of Galilee. The location of *Tishbe* is not certain. Some place it north of the Jabbok River in Gilead. Others associate it with a site in the tribal land of Naphtali. If the latter is correct, then Elijah would have been a *Tishbite* by ancestry even though he was living in the land of Gilead at this time.

Ahab reigned over Israel twenty-two years. During that time he "did more evil in the eyes of the Lord than any of those before him." He worshiped Baal and even "set up an altar for Baal" in Samaria (the capital of Israel). He "did more to provoke the Lord, the God of Israel, to anger than did all the kings of Israel before him" (1 Kings 16:29-33). Elijah was called of God to confront Ahab with his sins and to remind him of Israel's real King, to whom Ahab was accountable.

The ministry of Elijah began with a sobering announcement of God's judgment. The prophet's first words authenticated his message: *As the Lord, the God of Israel, lives, whom I serve.* The Lord, not Baal, was still in charge of Israel, in spite of Jezebel's aggressive efforts on behalf of Baal. The judgment was that there would *be neither dew nor rain in the next few years.* (There are two references to this incident in the New Testament, Luke 4:25 and James 5:17, both indicating that *the next few years* amounted to three and a half years.) Elijah's words constituted a direct challenge to Baal on behalf of Israel's true God, for Baal was believed by his followers to be the god of fertility—both in human beings and in all of nature. Thus, it was believed, Baal controlled the rain and other factors that were necessary for crops to grow. Such a challenge as Elijah's would leave no doubt as to who was really in charge of the elements.

B. GOD'S CARE (vv. 2-7)

2, 3. Then the word of the LORD came to Elijah: "Leave here, turn eastward and hide in the Kerith Ravine, east of the Jordan.

Once Elijah had delivered his message, God ordered him to *hide.* During the time of famine, God's messenger and word would be withdrawn from his people. Most likely Elijah's personal safety was also a factor. Since Palestine has a dry season that generally lasts from May to October, some time may have elapsed before it became obvious that Elijah's prophecy was being fulfilled. When that became apparent, Ahab would probably try to kill him.

God instructed Elijah to go *eastward* and take refuge *in the Kerith Ravine.* While there is some disagreement about its location, this was probably a small stream *east of the Jordan* River, emptying into the Jordan or one of its tributaries.

4. You will drink from the brook, and I have ordered the ravens to feed you there."

God not only supplied a hiding place for Elijah, but he also provided water and food. The *brook,* which was probably fed by springs, would supply water for a time, and the food would be brought by *ravens.* Obviously such behavior would have been most unusual for ravens, but the God who created them would have no difficulty in commanding them to act in this manner.

UNUSUAL PROVIDENCE

My wife and I never had to miss or postpone any meals while raising three children on a preacher's salary (which can be a real challenge sometimes). But occasionally our provisions came from unlikely sources. No one in our family will ever forget the several meals whose source was a neighbor's pumpkin patch. Cooked pumpkin would have been an ordinary treat; we found batter-dipped, fried pumpkin *blossoms* to be an extraordinary treat! (They taste almost as good as morel mushrooms.)

I never would have guessed that God would supplement our grocery budget with such an unusual entrée. Elijah must have wondered, too, at God's rather bizarre providence. How could ravens possibly supply his food? Later, he must have been at least a little surprised that a penniless widow would be chosen to give him his "room and board."

Truly the Lord provides in unexpected and even miraculous ways. Elijah believed God's promise, despite the unlikely nature of the resources available. Dare we doubt his providence simply because we can't see the possibilities? God nurtures our trust by demonstrating his great, and often mysterious, faithfulness.   —R. W. B.

5. So he did what the LORD had told him. He went to the Kerith Ravine, east of the Jordan, and stayed there.

We wonder why Ahab did not seize Elijah immediately and either imprison him or kill him. Perhaps he did not believe that the prophet, or his God, could

---

WHAT DO YOU THINK?

If he had chosen to, God could have arranged to demonstrate his power over nature (and thus over the pagan gods) in a much shorter time period than three and a half years. What benefit do you see in his using such a slow process to teach his people this lesson?

WHAT DO YOU THINK?

God told Elijah to hide from Ahab. In other places God tells his followers to stand up and not be afraid of their enemies. How do you know when to stand up and confront the evil in society and when to retreat and "hide" for a time?

WHAT DO YOU THINK?

How long Elijah waited by the brook Kerith no one knows, but it seems to have been a period of some weeks, if not several months. What do you suppose he did during this time? What do you do with extended periods of "down time"?

WHAT DO YOU THINK?

The lesson writer notes that Elijah went to "the very center of Baal worship." How can we take the message of the gospel to the very centers of modern idolatry today—the centers of materialism, secularism, false spiritualism, and others?

harm him. Most likely Elijah did not tarry long in Ahab's presence to give the king time to act. He seems to have set out at once for the hiding place God had provided for him.

6. The ravens brought him bread and meat in the morning and bread and meat in the evening, and he drank from the brook.

The *brook* Kerith was isolated enough to provide both security and solitude for Elijah.

7. Some time later the brook dried up because there had been no rain in the land.

Although this *brook* was probably fed by springs, a prolonged drought would have dried up even these springs. God was signaling to Elijah that it was time for him to begin a new phase in his ministry.

II. GOD DIRECTS ELIJAH (1 KINGS 17:8-16)

A. WIDOW IN ZAREPHATH (vv. 8, 9)

8, 9. Then the word of the LORD came to him: "Go at once to Zarephath of Sidon and stay there. I have commanded a widow in that place to supply you with food."

This new phase in Elijah's ministry took him to *Zarephath*. This town was located on the Mediterranean Sea about halfway between the two Phoenician cities of Tyre and *Sidon*. At this point in history the town was under the control of Sidon.

Sending Elijah to Phoenicia, the very center of Baal worship, and telling him that he would find sustenance from a *widow* (often the poorest of the poor in the ancient world) may seem like another unusual way to provide for him. For now, however, God's hand of judgment (expressed through the famine) remained on the nation of Israel. His blessing was about to be experienced by a non-Israelite. Jesus later used this incident to rebuke those in the Nazareth synagogue for their scornful attitudes and to emphasize God's concern for others outside the scope of the "chosen people" (Luke 4:23-26).

B. ELIJAH'S REQUEST (vv. 10, 11)

10. So he went to Zarephath. When he came to the town gate, a widow was there gathering sticks. He called to her and asked, "Would you bring me a little water in a jar so I may have a drink?"

In making his way from his hiding place by the brook Kerith, it is likely that Elijah traveled along the east side of the Jordan River as far north as its headwaters at Dan. From there he would have traveled westward to *Zarephath*. By taking such a route, he would have been able to avoid Ahab, who had begun a search all over the kingdom for him (1 Kings 18:8-10).

When Elijah approached *the town gate,* he saw a *widow* who was *gathering sticks* to build a fire for cooking. At that point he apparently did not know that this was the woman who would feed him. Thirsty from his long travels, he asked for *a little water in a jar.* To provide a drink of water to strangers was considered a common courtesy in this part of the ancient world. Even though the drought had reached into Phoenicia, the springs there were fed from the peaks of the Lebanon Mountains and thus would still contain water when most other sources had dried up.

Judging from the widow's words to Elijah in verse 12, it is difficult to know whether she was a follower of the true God or was simply acknowledging the Lord as Elijah's God (note her reference to "*your* God"). Perhaps the woman was a refugee from Israel or had in some other way learned of the true God. We are reminded of Jesus' ministry in this same area, during which a Greek woman came desiring that Jesus cast a devil out of her daughter (Mark 7:25, 26).

11. As she was going to get it, he called, "And bring me, please, a piece of bread."

The widow's response to Elijah's request for a drink may have been the clue indicating to him that this was the woman whom God had mentioned earlier. So he added the request that she *bring* him *a piece of bread*—which would have been more available than any other food.

C. DESPERATE CONDITION (v. 12)

12. *"As surely as the LORD your God lives," she replied, "I don't have any bread—only a handful of flour in a jar and a little oil in a jug. I am gathering a few sticks to take home and make a meal for myself and my son, that we may eat it—and die."*

The widow was not immediately able to comply with the prophet's request. She did not have *any bread*. While this area of Phoenicia did have water available for drinking, it had not been able to escape other consequences of the drought. The widow had just enough *flour* and *oil* to provide something for her and her son to *eat*. After that they faced starvation. While some students interpret her reply as an excuse for denying food to Elijah, it is possible that the widow was offering an apology for not being able to provide for him more adequately.

D. ELIJAH'S ASSURANCE (vv. 13, 14)

13. *Elijah said to her, "Don't be afraid. Go home and do as you have said. But first make a small cake of bread for me from what you have and bring it to me, and then make something for yourself and your son.*

The words *don't be afraid* are found on several occasions in the Scriptures when a person was confronted with an overwhelming or frightening situation. This woman certainly needed such reassurance because she knew that she had barely enough flour and oil to prepare food for herself and her son. Yet this stranger was asking to be fed *first*!

14. *For this is what the LORD, the God of Israel, says: 'The jar of flour will not be used up and the jug of oil will not run dry until the day the LORD gives rain on the land.'"*

This is what the Lord, the God of Israel, says. By this expression Elijah stated the authority for his reassuring words to the woman. As is so often the case, when God gives he gives bountifully. He would provide the woman with *flour* and *oil* until the drought was over.

E. GOD'S PROVISION (vv. 15, 16)

15, 16. *She went away and did as Elijah had told her. So there was food every day for Elijah and for the woman and her family. For the jar of flour was not used up and the jug of oil did not run dry, in keeping with the word of the LORD spoken by Elijah.*

Encouraged by the prophet's words, the woman proceeded to do as *Elijah* had asked. And God did indeed miraculously provide for her, her son, and Elijah. *There was food every day* for all three of them—during not only the time that Elijah stayed with the woman, but during the time that passed until the rains returned.

THE GRACE OF GIVING

I can remember when my father's income was less than one-tenth of my present salary. Yet I know that Dad was a faithful tither to the church and gave other offerings besides. My parents believed God's promise to supply all of our needs (Philippians 4:19) when we make his kingdom our priority (Matthew 6:33). And God rewarded their faith by providing for our family.

Sacrificial giving is illustrated and commended repeatedly in Scripture. Jesus praised the widow who gave "everything—all she had to live on" (Mark 12:41-44)

HOW TO SAY IT

Ahab. AY-hab.
Baal. BAY-ul.
Elijah. Ee-LYE-juh.
Ethbaal. Eth-BAY-ul.
Gilead. GIL-ee-ud.
Jabbok. JAB-ok.
Jeroboam. Jair-uh-BO-um.
Jezebel. JEZ-uh-bel.
Kerith. KEY-rith.
Macedonians. Mass-eh-DOE-nee-uns.
Naphtali. NAF-tuh-lye.
Nazareth. NAZ-uh-reth.
Omri. AHM-rye.
Phoenicians. Fuh-NISH-uns.
Rehoboam. Ree-huh-BO-um.
Samaria. Suh-MARE-ee-uh.
Sidon. SIGH-dun.
Sidonians. Sigh-DOE-nee-uns.
Tishbe. TISH-be.
Tishbite. TISH-bite.
Tyre. Tire.
Yarmuk. YAR-mook.
Zarephath. ZAR-ih-fath.

to the temple treasury. She was perhaps unwittingly following the example of the widow in our lesson today, who also gave her very last resources to provide for the needs of God's prophet.

Writing to the Corinthian Christians, the apostle Paul illustrated the "grace of giving" by telling of the Macedonian Christians, who gave abundantly despite undergoing "the most severe trial" (2 Corinthians 8:1-4). They considered it a privilege to share their meager possessions with needy brothers and sisters. Paul exhorted the Corinthians to "excel in this grace of giving" (v. 7).

How many of today's Christians understand the "grace of giving"? The Macedonians did because they "gave themselves *first* to the Lord" (v. 5). So must we.

—R. W. B.

CONCLUSION
A. "What Goes Around Comes Around"

Most of us have probably heard this saying. And probably we would admit that, while what goes around may not *always* come around, quite often that statement proves true—as the widow in today's lesson learned. She was willing to give the last morsel of food she had to feed a hungry prophet. She had not asked for nor expected any reward for her sacrifice; nevertheless, she was rewarded by receiving enough food to last her and her son through a severe famine.

This principle still holds true today. A church in Georgia earned a reputation for helping other churches in time of need, including a Florida church whose building was struck by a hurricane. Then a disastrous flood seriously damaged the building of the congregation in Georgia. In the weeks that followed there was an outpouring of aid from those whom they had helped and from others who learned of their need. Indeed, in this case what went around came around.

Of course, the most vivid illustration of this principle is yet to come. In Matthew 25:31-46 we read of Jesus' description of the final judgment. It tells of what he will say to those who have involved themselves in such acts as giving food to the hungry, drink to the thirsty, and clothing to the naked. Although those who have provided such help have not done so for a reward, Jesus will grant them the greatest reward of all—a glorious welcome into Heaven.

B. Courage and Patience

Elijah was a man of great faith and courage. He needed both qualities to confront a wicked king like Ahab. But once he had pronounced God's judgment through the famine, God wisely took him "out of the picture" for some time. From what the Scriptures indicate, Elijah was a man of action, and he must have chafed while waiting until God was ready to use him again. Left to his own counsel, he might have preferred to remain near the king and his cohorts, caring little that it could mean death. However, raw courage must always be tempered with cautious wisdom. Although Elijah may have accepted God's restraint reluctantly, accept it he did—and survived to carry on a far more important ministry than dying a martyr's death.

In many places in the world today, Christians have to worship and carry out their ministries in secret. For example, in China there are perhaps thousands of "house churches" where Christians meet quietly and without any public announcement. Raw courage might lead some to want to proclaim their faith boldly in the streets, but to do so would certainly mean persecution or even death. Most of these believers have carried on their ministries with appropriate discretion, patiently praying and waiting for that day when they can proclaim their Lord from the housetops.

What Do You Think?

Read James 5:17. How would you explain to a new believer the point of this verse?

Prayer

Almighty God, we thank you for men like the prophet Elijah—men of faith, prayer, and courage, who were able to confront evildoers in places of power with your words of judgment. May we pray seeking similar faith and courage—not just for dramatic confrontations but for the little challenges that we face every day. In Jesus' name we pray. Amen.

Thought to Remember

Let us learn from the example of Elijah—"a man just like us" but whose prayer was "powerful and effective" (James 5:16-18).

Discovery Learning

This page contains an alternate lesson plan emphasizing learning activities. Classes desiring such student involvement will find these suggestions helpful. The next page is a reproducible activity page to further enhance discovery learning.

LEARNING GOALS

After this lesson students should be able to:

1. Tell how God provided for Elijah during the three-year famine described in the text.

2. Tell some ways in which God provides for his people today.

3. Suggest a specific way they can demonstrate dependence on the Lord.

INTO THE LESSON

Ask the class members to work in groups of three. Each learner is to tell the others in his or her group about someone whose life demonstrates *trusting God to provide for one's needs*. The learners should know personally the people whom they describe, but they are not to reveal names.

After the groups have finished sharing, summarize the story of Abraham's willingness to sacrifice his son Isaac in obedience to God's command (found in Genesis 22:1-14). Tell of how God provided a ram as a substitute for Isaac. As a result, Abraham called the place where this happened "The Lord Will Provide" (Genesis 22:14). Tell the class that God's care and provision for his people are also dramatically illustrated in today's text.

INTO THE WORD

During the week before class, ask a class member to prepare a brief lecture on, or a synopsis of, the lesson background and verse 1 of the text. Provide commentary and atlas support as needed.

To open the Bible study, tell the fable of the termite and the giant found on page 353. Be sure to include the concluding thoughts comparing this story with Ahab and Elijah. Then ask the person you have recruited to give a synopsis of the lesson background.

Ask a volunteer to read 1 Kings 17:1-16 aloud. Distribute copies of the puzzle on the next page, and allow time for learners to complete the exercise. Discuss the significance of each term as you review the word list.

In addition to, or instead of, the puzzle activity, discuss the following questions:

1. Why do you think Elijah used the phrase, "As the Lord, the God of Israel, lives"?

2. The text does not tell how Ahab responded to Elijah's message. How do you think he responded?

3. Why do you think God told Elijah to hide?

Read verses 8 and 9, and give a brief lecture on the background of Zarephath. Then ask the class to work in small groups to discuss and write one-sentence answers to these two questions:

1. Why do you think Elijah asked the widow to feed him first?

2. Why do you think she complied with his request?

After the groups have completed their study, tell the class that the story of the widow doesn't end here. As the remaining verses of 1 Kings 17 record, her son suddenly became ill and died. But Elijah, through God's power, restored the boy's life.

INTO LIFE

Prepare a visual with three columns under the major heading "The Lord Will Provide." Over column 1 write "Elijah." Over column 2 write "Widow." Over column 3 write "Believers Today." Appoint someone to act as "scribe" to write the class's answers on the visual.

Ask, "What did God provide for Elijah?" Answers may include food, water, safety, and assurance. Then ask what he provided for the widow. Answers may include food, security, her son's life, and a demonstration of his power.

Tell the class, "Now comes the tough question. What does this lesson teach us about God? What do we learn through Elijah about trust in and dependence on God? Will God always provide for our needs? Let's start with the easier question: 'What does God provide for every disciple of his?'" List their answers in column 3. Answers may include salvation, an inheritance, Heaven, hope, peace, a family, etc. The list could be long.

Observe that, even though God is our provider, he does not promise believers that they will *never* experience hardship or even extreme deprivation of basic needs. Ask the class to suggest illustrations of this truth. Summarize by pointing out that trusting God to provide is not always easy, but we know he will. Read Matthew 6:25-34.

To make the lesson personal, ask each class member to identify at least one area of his or her life that needs to demonstrate more patience and trust that God will provide. Ask them to write that at the top of a three-by-five card that you distribute. Then ask each learner to compose a one- or two-sentence prayer committing himself to trusting God in that situation. Each one is to carry the card through this coming week, praying each day the prayer written on it.

Word Search

Elijah, God's messenger to Ahab, had quite an adventure in our text. Search the grid below for words from Elijah's adventure in I Kings 17:1-16. Then check the box below to see how many of the thirty hidden words you found.

```
T N T I S H B E B A H A J I L E H C
D H W U U K H B J J L P G H R M F M
R M S R P V O T K E Y N T E C S Q W
L B O L P F W C A S F W B H Y N I O
E X M Q L L K R Z H I U K R T D T M
D L I O Y Y S B M V P R I S O P F A
R W U N M I A R G D Z E B W A O Z N
I R Z T C T B N T L N N R I S W K H
C E X K S S H S S I D O N A I D B U
H M K R S C R A V E N S R Y Z L V F
O V P A K N F A M I L Y O C C C U Q
S S G R C P R M W X O J R V I P Y L
T F K P I H K E E D R U L H W Q J U
M Z N H T J M H D A D A E L I G F R
Y J I I S Q N F I J T A C R X P S B
F X R W M B O N A D R O J Y D A V M
S E D L X O T R C V F Q U O Z K F Y
K B N G D A E R B S D F G A T E G D
```

ISRAEL: CALLED TO DECIDE

LESSON 3

WHY TEACH THIS LESSON?

Our church did one of those personality profiles once. It used animals to represent different personality types. The lion, for example, typified the aggressive, leadership type of personality. I don't remember what animal typified my personality, but it was not the lion. Decisiveness and quick action are not my forte!

Today's key verse sounds like it was written for people like me: "How long will you waver between two opinions?" the prophet Elijah asks. But I suspect the question loses something in the translation! *Opinions* hardly seems to describe the two ways set before the Israelites that day.

If you have students who sometimes waver between bacon or sausage, blue socks or gray, you will want to reassure them that such wavering is not the problem in our text. But if you have students who wrestle with doubt about the validity of their faith or about the ability of God to help them find victory over temptation, use this lesson to reaffirm their commitment to the Lord—the one true and living God.

INTRODUCTION

A. LOOKING FOR LOOPHOLES

Pericles, a respected statesman in ancient Athens, was once approached by a group of citizens who wanted a popular decree changed. "Don't you realize," said Pericles, "that we have a long-standing law that forbids the taking down of any tablet upon which a decree is written?"

"Yes, we understand the law," said one of the group, a lawyer noted for his cleverness. "But there is no need to take the tablet down. We need only to turn it around so that it can no longer be read. There is no law against that."

Times haven't changed much since then. In fact, this lawyer's viewpoint is quite prevalent in our society today. Those who hold this viewpoint do not come out openly and attack the moral standards that have served our society so well. Instead, they use legal technicalities (sometimes called "loopholes") to circumvent the obvious intent of laws, thereby violating their real spirit. Compounding this tragedy is the fact that this practice is becoming more prevalent among some of the most influential of leaders and seems to be widely approved by many citizens.

Christians need to stand as fearless Elijah did and ask, "How long will you waver between two opinions? If the Lord is God, follow him." We dare not be content with "loopholes."

B. LESSON BACKGROUND

The verses between last week's lesson and today's tell how Elijah left Phoenicia and returned to Israel. On his way to see King Ahab he met Obadiah, an official in Ahab's administration, who had been sent to hunt for water and grass for the king's animals. Through Obadiah, Elijah sent word that he wanted to speak with the king.

When the two met, Ahab's immediate response was to blame the prophet for the trouble that had befallen his kingdom: "Is that you, you troubler of Israel?"

DEVOTIONAL READING:
JOSHUA 24:14-18

BACKGROUND SCRIPTURE:
1 KINGS 18

PRINTED TEXT:
1 KINGS 18:20, 21, 30-39

Jun
17

LESSON AIMS

After this lesson students should be able to:

1. Give the important details of the confrontation on Mount Carmel between Elijah and the prophets of Baal.

2. Describe how people today "waver" between serving God and following "idols."

3. Express an uncompromising faith in the Lord God.

KEY VERSE

Elijah went before the people and said, "How long will you waver between two opinions? If the LORD is God, follow him; but if Baal is God, follow him."

—1 Kings 18:21

WHAT DO YOU THINK?

Ahab blamed Elijah for the drought in Israel. How should we respond to people who blame God for the difficulties they face in life?

The visual for today's lesson is a dramatic illustration of verse 21. Display it as you begin to discuss that verse.

WHAT DO YOU THINK?

Suppose a friend says he thinks it is unfair for God to demand people to live with uncompromising devotion to him. How would you answer your friend?

(1 Kings 18:17). Elijah quickly informed the king that *he*, Ahab, was the real troubler of Israel.

Elijah challenged the king to assemble all Israel on Mount Carmel, along with four hundred fifty prophets of Baal and four hundred "prophets of Asherah." The Canaanite goddess Asherah was considered the "lover" of the god Baal. Implied in Elijah's challenge—or perhaps explicitly stated but not recorded for brevity—was that some kind of test would be conducted that would demonstrate which god was superior and which of them (Elijah or Ahab) was really the "troubler of Israel."

Nothing more is said about the four hundred prophets of Asherah who were invited to Mount Carmel. Since they are described as those who ate at Jezebel's table (v. 19), perhaps she encouraged them not to participate in what she considered a foolish exercise.

I. THE SETTING (1 KINGS 18:20, 21)
A. AHAB'S SUMMONS (v. 20)
20. So Ahab sent word throughout all Israel and assembled the prophets on Mount Carmel.

Mount Carmel is a high ridge that projects out into the Mediterranean Sea, dividing the plain of Esdraelon to the northeast from the coastal plain to the southwest. It was approximately seventeen miles away from Jezreel, where Ahab kept a palace (1 Kings 21:1). Thus Mount Carmel was located where Baal worship was strongest.

We can only guess why Ahab would accept Elijah's challenge. The effects of the drought may have driven him to the point that he was willing to try anything to bring it to an end. Or perhaps he was arrogant enough to believe that the *prophets* of Baal would somehow overwhelm or embarrass Elijah and thus rid his kingdom of the man whom Ahab considered Israel's "troublemaker."

B. ELIJAH'S CHALLENGE (v. 21)
21. Elijah went before the people and said, "How long will you waver between two opinions? If the LORD is God, follow him; but if Baal is God, follow him."
    But the people said nothing.

When Elijah addressed those who had gathered on Mount Carmel, he wasted no time on diplomatic pleasantries but got right to the point: *How long will you waver between two opinions?* Some issues in life are best resolved by reasonable compromise. But on this issue there was no middle ground, no shade of gray. Elijah's plea is reminiscent of Joshua's: "Choose for yourselves this day whom you will serve" (Joshua 24:15).

Elijah's description of the people's behavior, translated here as *waver*, was a fitting one. The Hebrew word describes one who hops or walks with a limp. From that, it sometimes was used to refer figuratively to one who hesitated or wavered, as the people had been doing. The word also meant to leap or dance; in fact, it is used in verse 26 to describe the way the prophets of Baal "*danced* around the altar" as they cried out to him. Perhaps the biblical writer intended a little play on words by using it both of the Israelites' hesitation and of the prophets who led them to believe that they could serve both the Lord and Baal at the same time.

But Elijah would have none of this. The people must choose between either *the Lord* or *Baal*. Perhaps Elijah reminded his audience that the Lord was the God of their fathers—Abraham, Isaac, Jacob, and Moses. He is a God of mercy, but he is also a jealous and holy God who will tolerate no competition.

However, in the minds of the people there appeared to be some advantages to following Baal. He was the god of fertility, and his worshipers often engaged in illicit sexual activity as a religious rite. Furthermore, Baal worship was the religion of Ahab and Jezebel—and it is usually a good idea to be on the side of those in power.

Torn between these two alternatives, *the people said nothing*. They knew that if they acknowledged that they had violated the First Commandment ("You shall have no other gods before me"), they would have to repent and change their ways. And they also knew that they could not plead ignorance or mitigating circumstances, which might get them off the hook. On the other hand, they may have hoped that if they remained quiet perhaps Elijah would simply go away, or the false prophets would kill him. And so they said nothing! It was a very different response from the one that followed Joshua's similar appeal (Joshua 24:16-18). Their silence set the stage for the confrontation that followed.

SILENCE IS GOLDEN?

Whoever coined the phrase, "Silence is golden," just may have been the grandfather of twins and triplets, all born within a three-month period! I'm guessing that because I myself am such a grandfather. Having spent considerable time helping to care for my five new grandchildren, I have my own definition of peace: when no babies are crying!

As the phrase is normally used, "Silence is golden" means that saying nothing at all is often the best kind of communication. Certain circumstances call for few words—the kind of quiet that actually speaks volumes.

Elijah's challenge to the Israelites to state their religious loyalty was not such a time! Still, they "said nothing." They offered no refutation, no defense, no reply. Perhaps they felt the sting of God's reproach. Perhaps they had become so used to the pattern of compromise that they did not know how to respond when asked to take a stand.

Whatever the reason, Israel's weak and sorry condition teaches us an important lesson: sometimes silence is *not* golden; sometimes it's simply "yellow." —R. W. B.

II. THE PREPARATION (1 KINGS 18:30-35)

A. THE ALTAR (vv. 30-32)

30. Then Elijah said to all the people, "Come here to me." They came to him, and he repaired the altar of the LORD, which was in ruins.

Verses 22-29 provide the details of how the test was to be carried out. The prophets of Baal were to prepare a bull for sacrifice, laying it on firewood as a burnt offering without lighting it. Then they were to pray that Baal would send fire to consume the sacrifice. From morning until noon they called upon their god, but nothing happened. Elijah began to chide them, claiming that their god must be busy, or on a journey, or asleep. At this, the prophets of Baal cried louder and even cut themselves in their frenzy, yet when evening came "there was no response, no one answered, no one paid attention" (v. 29).

When it was more than obvious that nothing was going to happen, Elijah called the people to gather around him. He wanted to make sure that they were in a position to observe his actions carefully so that they could later serve as credible witnesses. First, he *repaired the altar of the Lord, which was in ruins*. This may have been one of the altars that were destroyed as a result of the promotion of Baal worship during Ahab's reign (1 Kings 16:32; 19:10). It was probably not an elaborate altar, but one made of rough, uncut stones that had been gathered in the area.

31, 32. Elijah took twelve stones, one for each of the tribes descended from Jacob, to whom the word of the LORD had come, saying, "Your name shall be Israel."

WHAT DO YOU THINK?

The people hesitated and said nothing after Elijah asked them to declare their loyalty to God or Baal. How does such indecision hurt the body of Christ today?

WHAT DO YOU THINK?

Elijah used twelve stones to build the altar, one for each of the tribes of Israel. How important are symbols to us today? What symbols are especially important to you?

With the stones he built an altar in the name of the LORD, and he dug a trench around it large enough to hold two seahs of seed.

Elijah selected *twelve stones* for the *altar*, representing the twelve *tribes* of Israel. Although the tribes were by now divided into two nations, Judah and Israel, the prophet's action conveyed the message that in the eyes of God they were still one nation.

Next, Elijah *dug a trench* around the altar. (No doubt this seemed quite odd to the onlookers.) A seah was a unit of measure equal to about a third of a bushel. If this refers to volume, the trench was not very large. Some, however, believe that the term is describing depth, which would make the trench much larger.

B. THE SACRIFICE (vv. 33-35)

33. He arranged the wood, cut the bull into pieces and laid it on the wood. Then he said to them, "Fill four large jars with water and pour it on the offering and on the wood."

That Elijah *arranged the wood* apparently means he prepared the sacrifice as prescribed in Leviticus 1:3-9. This would be another demonstration that the people were still living under God's laws and were expected to observe them.

Then Elijah did something especially unusual. He ordered that *four large jars* of *water* be poured over the sacrifice and *on the wood* used to start the fire. These jars are similar to those that women balanced on their heads when they carried water. One may wonder how this much water could have been available during a time of severe drought. Most likely a spring continued to flow somewhere down Mount Carmel—perhaps sustained by an underground source.

34, 35. "Do it again," he said, and they did it again.

"Do it a third time," he ordered, and they did it the third time. The water ran down around the altar and even filled the trench.

Elijah had water poured on the sacrifice a second then a *third time*. By now the purpose of the trench was obvious. So much water had been poured on *the altar* that it ran down and *filled the trench*. Such actions assured that there would be no basis whatsoever for any charges of fraud or trickery on Elijah's part.

III. THE CLIMAX (1 KINGS 18:36-39)

A. ELIJAH'S PRAYER (vv. 36, 37)

36. At the time of sacrifice, the prophet Elijah stepped forward and prayed: "O LORD, God of Abraham, Isaac and Israel, let it be known today that you are God in Israel and that I am your servant and have done all these things at your command.

The Hebrew text literally reads, "And it came to pass at the offering of *the sacrifice*." However, since the law required that two sacrifices be offered daily (Exodus 29:38-42), this was probably the time of the evening sacrifice (about 3:00 P.M.). Once again, Elijah's purpose may have been to remind the people of God's approved practice concerning sacrifice, even though the people of the north no longer worshiped in Jerusalem.

37. Answer me, O LORD, answer me, so these people will know that you, O LORD, are God, and that you are turning their hearts back again."

Elijah addressed his prayer to the *Lord*—that is, Jehovah—using God's unique name that he had revealed to Moses (Exodus 3:13, 14). Elijah was calling the people's attention to the God of the covenant—the covenant that had been made many centuries before with Abraham, Isaac, and Jacob. He was also calling the people to reaffirm their responsibilities under that covenant. *You are turning their hearts back again.* Elijah was so confident of the people's response that he prayed as if it had already happened.

B. GOD'S ANSWER (v. 38)

38. Then the fire of the LORD fell and burned up the sacrifice, the wood, the stones and the soil, and also licked up the water in the trench.

As soon as Elijah concluded his prayer, God acted—and with authority! *The fire of the Lord fell*, and in an awe-inspiring demonstration of his mighty power, everything used to arrange *the sacrifice* was instantly *burned up*.

Some, wishing to minimize the miraculous element in this event, propose that a bolt of lightning struck the altar and the sacrifice. If so, this would have been a most unusual lightning bolt, for there was no sign of rain at the time. The clouds and rain and any accompanying lightning came later (1 Kings 18:41-45). Even so, a bolt of lightning from a cloudless sky that hit at just the right time and in just the right place would have been just as much a miracle!

FIRE FROM HEAVEN

Fire possesses great potential for both productive energy and destructive power. The Chicago fire of 1871 is a classic illustration of the latter. So are the forest fires that annually scorch thousands of acres of land and result in the tragic loss of life and property.

On the productive side, fire heats our homes, generates energy for industry, cooks our food, and powers all sorts of engines. It can be either helpful or harmful, but it is nearly always evidence of power. In the Scriptures, fire is often a symbol of the power of God's Spirit. Perhaps the clearest illustration of this is when "what seemed to be tongues of fire" appeared over each of the apostles on the Day of Pentecost (Acts 2:1-4).

The fire that fell in response to Elijah's prayer was unmistakably a demonstration of the power of Israel's true God, and it fulfilled two important purposes. The sacrifice and altar that Elijah had prepared were consumed (along with everything surrounding them), but the faith of Israel was renewed and empowered.

God's Spirit provides "heat" to warm our hearts with love and conviction and "light" (through the words of the Scriptures) to guide our paths. The world needs to see such fire as evidence that "the Lord, he is God." Pray for fires of revival to be poured out on our nation and to the ends of the earth!   —R. W. B.

C. THE PEOPLE'S RESPONSE (v. 39)

39. When all the people saw this, they fell prostrate and cried, "The LORD—he is God! The LORD—he is God!"

The people's response was immediate. They knew very well that they had seen the powerful hand of God dramatically displayed. This was no time for theological discussions about the relative power of Jehovah and Baal. They knew what they had seen, and they acted accordingly: *they fell prostrate* (on their faces)! Western culture may not prescribe this posture, but in that time and culture it was an appropriate posture that showed fear, awe, and reverence.

Elijah had boldly challenged the people to choose between Jehovah and Baal. They now made their choice quite obvious: *The Lord—he is God! The Lord—he is God!* This manifestation of God's power could not be denied.

The remaining verses of 1 Kings 18 tell of some of the events that followed the incident at Mount Carmel. First, the prophets of Baal were taken down to the Kishon Valley (just north of Mount Carmel) and there executed. Then, after informing Ahab that rain was on the way, Elijah went to the top of Mount Carmel and began to pray. After praying, he sent his servant to look toward "the sea" (i.e., the Mediterranean Sea) for signs of rain. When he returned and reported that he saw nothing, Elijah sent him back again. This was repeated until the seventh time, when the servant returned with the message that he saw a cloud "as small as a

WHAT DO YOU THINK?

Wouldn't it be great to call fire from Heaven to vindicate us before the secularists and materialists today who scoff at the idea of serving God! What evidence can we cite for our faith?

DAILY BIBLE READINGS

Monday, June 11—Elijah Is Sent to Ahab (1 Kings 18:1-6)

Tuesday, June 12—Elijah Meets and Challenges Ahab (1 Kings 18:7-19)

Wednesday, June 13—Elijah and the Prophets of Baal (1 Kings 18:20-29)

Thursday, June 14—Choose Whom You Will Serve (Joshua 24:14-18)

Friday, June 15—Elijah's Triumph for God (1 Kings 18:30-40)

Saturday, June 16—The Drought Ends (1 Kings 18:41-46)

Sunday, June 17—Elijah Flees, Then Meets God (1 Kings 19:1-18)

man's hand." Soon the sky grew dark, then there was "a heavy rain." Ahab, following the prophet's earlier instructions to return to Jezreel, had already started back in his chariot; but Elijah ran ahead of the chariot and arrived at the city first. Clearly it was a day of triumph for the Lord's prophet.

CONCLUSION

A. LIKE KING, LIKE PEOPLE

Rulers, whether they are hereditary monarchs, military dictators, or elected officials, have an obligation before God to provide good government for their people. But just as important, though often overlooked, is their responsibility to provide good models for their people. The reigns of Omri and his son Ahab show the tragic results that follow when rulers do not live up to this second responsibility. These two rulers imported the worship of Baal into the northern kingdom and in the process infected their people with it. Ahab compounded the problem by marrying Jezebel, daughter of Ethbaal of the Sidonians (1 Kings 16:31). She became a vigorous missionary for the cause of Baal, assembling four hundred fifty prophets of Baal and four hundred prophets of Asherah. With such aggressive support for the worship of Baal, it should be no surprise that many of the people became followers of this false religion.

In recent years, we have seen the flouting of God's moral laws by various national leaders. As shocking as some of these activities have been, even more serious is the impact that this type of behavior has had on society in general. That our society is experiencing a serious decline in moral standards, both public and private, is obvious to anyone who takes a serious look at the situation. And, as in Elijah's time, those who take a stand for biblical teachings on morality are often labeled as "old-fashioned" or "bigoted" by those outside the church and sometimes as "legalists" by fellow believers.

B. WAVERING BETWEEN TWO OPINIONS

Jehovah God is a jealous God: "You shall have no other gods before me" (Exodus 20:3). He is an uncompromising God who is unwilling to accept divided allegiance from his followers. Jesus said, "You cannot serve both God and Money" (Matthew 6:24).

Satan, on the other hand, is quite willing to make whatever concessions are necessary to gain an entrance into people's hearts. He has no objection to people's attending church and even becoming "Christians" so long as he can maintain a foothold in their lives. His soothing message of compromise falls on receptive ears. If we listen to him long enough, we are likely to find ourselves ensnared in his trap.

This was the situation in Israel in Elijah's day. Many of the people probably considered themselves faithful followers of God. They had no real interest in becoming fully committed, dedicated followers of Baal. They wanted to serve Jehovah and at the same time enjoy some of the pleasures that the priests of Baal promised to his followers. Elijah confronted this attitude by hurling at the people a challenge that left no room for compromise: "How long will you waver between two opinions?"

When we fall for Satan's clever call to compromise, we find that the keen edge of moral discernment becomes blunted, and we no longer have the insights or the courage to stand firmly for the right. This is perhaps best illustrated by the people's response to Elijah's challenge: they "said nothing." They were drifting aimlessly in a sea of compromise, with no courage and no convictions.

May the words and example of Elijah encourage us to stand firmly on the truth of the Bible—without compromise.

PRAYER

Dear Lord, we thank you for servants such as Elijah, who stood faithfully in the face of overwhelming odds. Grant us, we pray, the same kind of courage to serve you where you have called us, even when the odds we are up against seem overwhelming. In our Master's name we pray. Amen.

THOUGHT TO REMEMBER

"Choose for yourselves this day whom you will serve" (Joshua 24:15).

Discovery Learning

This page contains an alternate lesson plan emphasizing learning activities. Classes desiring such student involvement will find these suggestions helpful. The next page is a reproducible activity page to further enhance discovery learning.

LEARNING GOALS

After participating in this lesson, students should be able to:

1. Give the important details of the confrontation on Mount Carmel between Elijah and the prophets of Baal.

2. Describe how people today "waver" between serving God and following "idols."

3. Express an uncompromising faith in the Lord God.

INTO THE LESSON

Use a large marker to write each of the letters of the word *faithful* on a different sheet of construction paper in large print. Begin the session by giving one sheet to each of eight class members. Ask them to arrange themselves so they spell a word. When they have formed the word *faithful*, thank them and ask them to mount their letters on a wall or bulletin board.

Then ask each class member to find a partner and to tell him or her the name of an Old Testament character who modeled faithfulness to God and how the character did so. After a few moments, make the transition to Bible study by telling the class that God has continually reminded his people of his expectation of faithfulness to him. Today's text provides one example, and it will serve as a reminder for us today.

INTO THE WORD

Read 1 Kings 18:20, 21, 30-39. Then divide the class into groups of four or five. Give each group a piece of poster board, a marker, and a piece of paper with one of the following three tasks. If you have more than three groups, give duplicate tasks to some. If you do not have enough learners to form three groups, then omit some of the tasks or do them as whole-class activities.

Task 1: Pretend you are a reporter covering this miraculous call to faithfulness. List approximately five significant facts about this event that need to be developed in the news article. Write a "quotable quote" from the event that can be used in the article. Write the opening line and a headline for the article.

Task 2: Decide what are crucial characteristics of a faithful follower of God. List those characteristics by building an acrostic around the word *faithful*. Example: using the letter "t" you might cite "truthful" as a characteristic. Other crucial characteristics may also be written on the poster.

Task 3: Select from the text a "key verse" that serves as a motto for this lesson. Print that verse on the poster board. Then identify and list "idols" that tempt people to be unfaithful to God.

After each group has completed the tasks, ask the group or groups with task 1 to report their findings. After the report, give a brief lecture about the temptations Baal brought to the Israelites. See the lesson commentary notes on the Lesson Background, verse 21, and the Conclusion. Then ask the group or groups with task 2 to report their findings. After this report ask the class to name additional characteristics of the faithful life. Write these new suggestions on the poster. After the group or groups with task 3 report, affirm the key verse. Then ask the class to suggest additional "idols" that cause today's believers to waver between faithfulness and unfaithfulness. Add these to the poster as they are given.

INTO LIFE

Make the transition to application by observing that most of us struggle with faithfulness in several areas of our lives. Most of us would like to honor God with greater faithfulness to him.

Give each person a letter-size sheet of paper with the heading "My Commitment to Faithfulness." Below the heading print these words: "As I read Elijah's call to faithfulness to God, I am thankful that I generally honor him with these characteristics of faithfulness. . . ." Almost midway down the page print, "As I read today's text I confess I feel guilty about not being faithful to God in this area of my life. . . ." Near the bottom of the page print, "My plan to honor God by being more faithful to him includes. . . ."

Ask the class members to look at the poster created earlier for task 2. Using this list of characteristics of a faithful life, learners should complete the first part of the worksheet. After they complete this task, ask them to identify areas of their lives where they need to demonstrate more faithfulness to God. Write those areas on the second part of the worksheet. Then give the learners time to complete the strategy exercise near the bottom of the worksheet.

Conclude by having the class sing "I Surrender All" or "I Give All." (Provide songbooks.) Close the lesson with a prayer for faithfulness, using the choral reading based on Psalm 119:1-16, 33, from the next page.

Choral Reading

Use the following in a group to perform a choral reading of the prayer for faithfulness from Psalm 119:1-16, 33.

LEADER
1. Blessed are they whose ways are blameless, who walk according to the law of the Lord.

MEN
2. Blessed are they who keep his statutes and seek him with all their heart.
3. They do nothing wrong; they walk in his ways.

LEADER
4. You have laid down precepts that are to be fully obeyed.

WOMEN
5. Oh, that my ways were steadfast in obeying your decrees!
6. Then I would not be put to shame when I consider all your commands.

ALL
7. I will praise you with an upright heart as I learn your righteous laws.
8. I will obey your decrees; do not utterly forsake me.

LEADER
9a. How can a young man keep his way pure?

MEN
9b. By living according to your word.

LEADER
10. I seek you with all my heart; do not let me stray from your commands.
11. I have hidden your word in my heart that I might not sin against you.

WOMEN
12. Praise be to you, O Lord; teach me your decrees.

MEN
13. With my lips I recount all the laws that come from your mouth.

WOMEN
14. I rejoice in following your statutes as one rejoices in great riches.

MEN
15. I meditate on your precepts and consider your ways.

WOMEN
16. I delight in your decrees; I will not neglect your word.

ALL
33. Teach me, O Lord, to follow your decrees; then I will keep them to the end.

MICAIAH:
COURAGEOUS PROPHET

LESSON 4

WHY TEACH THIS LESSON?

It's the stuff of action drama on television or in movies. The hero knows something important—the location of P.O.W.'s in Asia, the use of defective parts in a nuclear reactor, or details of some other injustice—but no one believes him. So he sets out singlehandedly to expose the truth and/or bring the bad guys to justice. Of course, the hero is always a strong and impressive sort, usually well-trained in the martial arts.

The "hero" in our text is not so impressive physically. Actually, we know nothing of his appearance, but he does not strike out against his opponents. He does not prove the rightness of his convictions by might. He simply speaks for the Lord and then trusts in God to vindicate him at the right time.

You won't see him in the movies, but he makes a much better role model for your students!

INTRODUCTION

A. AN EXCELLENT SPINE

Charles Spurgeon, the renowned nineteenth-century preacher, was once conducting a Bible study with a group of boys. One boy was asked to read from Daniel 6:3: "Then this Daniel was preferred above the presidents and princes, because an excellent spirit was in him" (*King James Version*). But the boy misread part of the verse and said, "An excellent spine was in him." We may smile at the boy's mistake; but even if his reading was wrong, he hit upon an important truth. Daniel *was* great because of his "excellent spine"—his great courage in the face of difficult circumstances.

Some two and a half centuries earlier, Micaiah demonstrated "an excellent spine" under similar conditions. Surrounded by false prophets who spoke words favorable to King Ahab, Micaiah refused to go along with the majority. As a result, he endured the scorn of the king, who had him imprisoned. But Ahab learned, at the cost of his life, that he could not imprison the Lord's truth.

B. LESSON BACKGROUND

The previous lesson focused on Elijah's confrontation with Ahab and the false prophets of Baal on Mount Carmel. The display of God's mighty power there should have brought Ahab to his knees in contrite repentance; however, his wife Jezebel determined to seek revenge against Elijah. The prophet fled to the wilderness of Judah, where God spoke to him and encouraged him to remain faithful to his prophetic task (1 Kings 19:1-18).

First Kings 20 then records Israel's involvement in two battles with Ben-Hadad, king of Syria (called Aram in our text), during a two-year span. On both occasions Ahab defeated the Syrian forces in fulfillment of a promise given by a prophet of

DEVOTIONAL READING:
PROVERBS 12:13-22

BACKGROUND SCRIPTURE:
1 KINGS 22:1-40

PRINTED TEXT:
1 KINGS 22:15-28

Jun 24

LESSON AIMS

After this lesson each student should be able to:

1. Recount the circumstances under which Micaiah courageously refused to compromise God's message.

2. Tell why standing for God's truth is such a challenge in today's world.

3. Express appreciation to someone who, like Micaiah, has paid a price for being true to God's message.

KEY VERSE

Micaiah said, "As surely as the LORD lives, I can tell him only what the LORD tells me."
—1 Kings 22:14

the Lord. After the second battle, Ahab made a treaty with Ben-Hadad (against the will of the Lord, as indicated in 1 Kings 20:34-43). Apparently this treaty involved the return of certain cities to Israel that the Syrians had captured. One of these was Ramoth in Gilead (called Ramoth Gilead in today's text). (For the location of Gilead, see the comments on 1 Kings 17:1 in lesson 2, page 354. Ramoth was located in the eastern part of this territory.)

The Syrians, however, had not honored Ahab's treaty. (Syria's possession of Ramoth gave the Syrians easier access to Israelite territory.) After three years had passed (1 Kings 22:1), Ahab decided to attack the Syrians. By this time he was on good terms with Jehoshaphat, the king of Judah. So when Jehoshaphat came to visit Ahab in Samaria, Ahab asked for his assistance in recapturing the city of Ramoth Gilead. Jehoshaphat was willing to ally himself with Ahab in such a venture, but he wanted to be sure that the campaign carried the blessings of the Lord. To reassure him, Ahab brought in four hundred men, apparently a group of court prophets, and asked them whether he should go into battle at Ramoth Gilead. To a man they agreed (1 Kings 22:6). But Jehoshaphat was suspicious of such a unanimous response. "Is there not a prophet of the Lord here whom we can inquire of?" he asked (v. 7).

Ahab admitted that there was such a prophet, Micaiah, but apparently he was in prison. "I hate him," said Ahab, "because he never prophesies anything good about me, but always bad" (v. 8). But Jehoshaphat insisted that he wanted to hear Micaiah, so Ahab reluctantly sent for him. The officer sent to bring Micaiah informed the prophet about the situation and urged him to bring the same message that the other prophets had brought. Micaiah, unwilling to compromise himself or his God, responded, "I can tell him only what the Lord tells me" (v. 14).

I. DISASTROUS PREDICTION (1 KINGS 22:15-18)

A. MICAIAH'S SARCASM (v. 15)

15. When he arrived, the king asked him, "Micaiah, shall we go to war against Ramoth Gilead, or shall I refrain?"

"Attack and be victorious," he answered, "for the LORD will give it into the king's hand."

Micaiah delivered the same message as that of the other prophets. But his words were so dripping with sarcasm that Ahab could not miss their real intent.

B. AHAB'S RESPONSE (v. 16)

16. The king said to him, "How many times must I make you swear to tell me nothing but the truth in the name of the LORD?"

Angered by Micaiah's reply, Ahab demanded that the prophet *tell . . . nothing but the truth*. But Ahab did not really want to hear the truth. This entire procedure was nothing more than a show for the benefit of Jehoshaphat. What Ahab really wanted Micaiah to say were words that would encourage Judah's king to accompany him in the campaign to take Ramoth Gilead from the Syrians.

It took great courage for Micaiah to tell King Ahab a truth he did not want to hear. And it takes courage today to speak truth that one knows will not be well received. Jesus is the truth (John 14:6), yet millions reject him and his teachings. Many do not want to hear our personal testimony of the Savior and Lord we know, but we remain "under oath" to speak all the truth—warnings as well as promises—in love.

Pray that God will make you a bold witness for him.   —R. W. B.

C. MICAIAH'S MESSAGE (v. 17)

17. *Then Micaiah answered, "I saw all Israel scattered on the hills like sheep without a shepherd, and the* LORD *said, 'These people have no master. Let each one go home in peace.'"*

Micaiah related two visions that revealed the true word of the Lord to Ahab. First, he described the nation of *Israel* as *sheep* who were *scattered* because there was no longer a *shepherd* to lead them.

D. AHAB'S DISGUST (v. 18)

18. *The king of Israel said to Jehoshaphat, "Didn't I tell you that he never prophesies anything good about me, but only bad?"*

Ahab did not need an interpreter to help him understand the meaning of Micaiah's vision. He quickly realized that the prophet was predicting Ahab's removal from office. The reason the people were pictured as having no "master," or leader, was because Ahab would no longer be present to lead them.

But instead of heeding Micaiah's warning, Ahab used it to prove his earlier charge (v. 8) that the prophet carried a grudge against him and was out to get him. This is a time-honored method of avoiding having to face painful truth: blame the messenger and ignore him, discredit him, or even dispose of him.

II. DISTRESSING VISION (1 KINGS 22:19-23)

A. THE LORD ON HIS THRONE (v. 19)

19. *Micaiah continued, "Therefore hear the word of the* LORD: *I saw the* LORD *sitting on his throne with all the host of heaven standing around him on his right and on his left.*

Micaiah was not easily intimidated. Though he realized that he could be endangering his life if he said any more, he refused to remain silent. He told of another vision in which he *saw the Lord* in a position similar to that of an ancient ruler: *sitting on his throne*. And, just as a ruler was often surrounded by his advisers, the Lord was surrounded by *all the host of heaven*. The word *host* often refers to armies; heavenly host or *host of heaven* refers both to celestial bodies and to spiritual beings such as angels who worship God (Nehemiah 9:6; Psalm 148:2). From the succeeding verses we know that the host in Micaiah's vision also included evil spirits—perhaps in the same way that Satan presented himself before the Lord in Job 1:6; 2:1.

B. A LYING SPIRIT (vv. 20-23)

20. *And the* LORD *said, 'Who will entice Ahab into attacking Ramoth Gilead and going to his death there?'*

"One suggested this, and another that.

Micaiah's vision continued with a description of how the Lord asked the members of the host of Heaven *who* would *entice Ahab* to go to his downfall *at Ramoth Gilead*. Again, this was similar to the way in which an earthly ruler would ask his advisers for help in solving a specific problem.

21-23. *"Finally, a spirit came forward, stood before the* LORD *and said, 'I will entice him.'*

HOW TO SAY IT

Ahab. AY-hab.
Ahaziah. Ay-huh-ZYE-uh.
Amon. AY-mun.
Aram. AIR-um.
Baal. BAY-ul.
Ben-Hadad. Ben-HAY-dad.
Carmel. CAR-mel.
Elijah. Ee-LYE-juh.
Jehoram. Jeh-HO-rum.
Jehoshaphat. Jeh-HOSH-uh-fat.
Jezebel. JEZ-uh-bel.
Joash. JO-ash.
Kenaanah. Kih-NAY-uh-nah.
Micaiah. My-KAY-uh.
Ramoth Gilead. RAY-muth
    GIL-ee-ud
Samaria. Suh-MARE-ee-uh.
Syria. SEAR-ee-uh.
Zedekiah. Zed-uh-KYE-uh.

WHAT DO YOU THINK?

Micaiah was a true prophet. When he said, "Hear the word of the Lord," he spoke with divine authority. How should we respond when a person claims to have a message from God?

"'By what means?' the LORD asked.

"'I will go out and be a lying spirit in the mouths of all his prophets,' he said.

"'You will succeed in enticing him,' said the LORD. 'Go and do it.'

"So now the LORD has put a lying spirit in the mouths of all these prophets of yours. The LORD has decreed disaster for you."

These verses (and the entire scene described in Micaiah's vision) have created no little controversy among Bible students. We are told clearly in Scripture that God cannot lie (Titus 1:2). Yet in this passage he appears to be encouraging, if not causing, lying. Two ways to understand Micaiah's vision have been suggested.

Some believe that the vision is not to be taken literally, as a description of actual events occurring in Heaven. They point out that God does not need the "advice" of the host of Heaven; he possesses all wisdom and knowledge. They also claim that the false prophets surrounding Ahab did not need an evil spirit to make them say what they did. They were guided primarily by their own selfish interests. In this view the *lying spirit* was a personification of the attitude that governed the false *prophets*, and the vision was a symbolic way of saying that God allowed the prophets to speak falsely and lure Ahab to his death. A second view takes the vision more literally. It holds that the lying spirit was a demon, or perhaps the devil himself. (Some suggest that one of God's spirits, or angels, could have assumed the role of a lying spirit in order to carry out God's judgment against Ahab.)

Whether we take this scene literally or figuratively, we must keep in mind that God's actions did not violate Ahab's freedom of choice in this matter. God allowed the lying spirit to work among him and the false prophets; but these men, by their own defiance of God and his truth, had opened their lives to such an influence. Ahab, because of his unparalleled wickedness (1 Kings 21:25, 26), had placed himself under God's judgment. He had rejected the path of life and chosen the path of death (Deuteronomy 30:19).

III. DISTURBING ANNOUNCEMENT (1 KINGS 22:24-28)

A. ZEDEKIAH'S ANGER (v. 24)

24. Then Zedekiah son of Kenaanah went up and slapped Micaiah in the face. "Which way did the spirit from the LORD go when he went from me to speak to you?" he asked.

Zedekiah was mentioned earlier in 1 Kings 22 as one of the prophets who predicted victory for Ahab and even used a visual aid to reinforce his "prophecy" (v. 11). He seems to have been the spokesman for the court prophets. He was so incensed by Micaiah's words that he *slapped* him *in the face*.

Zedekiah asked Micaiah, *"Which way did the spirit from the Lord go when he went from me to speak to you?"* The meaning of *spirit* here is different from that in verses 21-23. Zedekiah was asserting that he, not Micaiah, had the spirit of prophecy sent by God. (Quite possibly the word *spirit* should be capitalized to indicate the Holy Spirit; the *New International Version* suggests this in a footnote.) Zedekiah's sarcastic question asked, "How did God's Spirit leave me and go to you?"

B. MICAIAH'S REPLY (v. 25)

25. Micaiah replied, "You will find out on the day you go to hide in an inner room."

Micaiah's reply stated an important truth: the real test of any prophecy is whether or not it is fulfilled in the way it was stated (Deuteronomy 18:21, 22). Micaiah was quite willing to have his and the court prophets' conflicting prophecies tested in this manner. Would Ahab go into battle and meet disaster as Micaiah had predicted? Or would he go into battle and triumph as the court prophets had predicted? The answer would come, declared Micaiah, when Zedekiah would have to go into hiding from those who were angry that his advice had led to Ahab's death. At that point he would no longer be able to maintain the pretense that he really spoke for God. The fact that he had lied would be undeniable.

C. AHAB'S ANGER (vv. 26, 27)

26. The king of Israel then ordered, "Take Micaiah and send him back to Amon the ruler of the city and to Joash the king's son

Ahab was furious with Micaiah and his message. The king's immediate concern was that it might upset Jehoshaphat so much that he would return to Judah and not accompany him on his campaign against Syria. Thus he ordered *Amon the ruler* [perhaps we would use the term "mayor"] *of the city* of Samaria to put Micaiah *back* in prison (implying that he had been there previously). *Joash* may have been Amon's assistant or involved in some other way in administering the prison. He is called *the king's son*, which some commentators think may be a title for an important official rather than a description of Joash's relationship to Ahab.

27. ". . . and say, 'This is what the king says: Put this fellow in prison and give him nothing but bread and water until I return safely.'"

Ahab not only sent Micaiah to *prison* but placed him on a very restricted diet—*bread and water*—as further punishment. The king's words *until I return safely* had an ominous ring to them. Ahab meant that when he returned from battle, he would administer a more severe punishment to Micaiah, perhaps even death. But these words were ominous only for Ahab. He was being presumptuous to assume that he would return in peace, as the next verse indicates.

D. MICAIAH'S PROMISE (v. 28)

28. Micaiah declared, "If you ever return safely, the LORD has not spoken through me." Then he added, "Mark my words, all you people!"

Micaiah refused to be intimidated by Ahab or the court prophets. Instead of going back quietly to his cell, he made one further pronouncement. If Ahab *ever* did *return safely*, it would be clear evidence that Micaiah had *not spoken* the truth. Micaiah was willing to submit his prophecy to the test suggested in Deuteronomy 18:21, 22. By these words he signed his own death warrant, in effect, for if Ahab did return, he almost certainly would execute the prophet.

Mark my words, all you people! Micaiah's final words before being taken to prison were not limited to those around him. He wanted as many as possible to be aware of what had just transpired, so that all of them could later recognize who really spoke for God.

STRETCHING THE TRUTH

A wife chided her husband: "I don't mind your little half-truths, but you keep telling me the wrong half!" Some individuals justify themselves when they tell less than the whole truth by rationalizing: "It was just a little white lie." Sometimes truth is stretched so far that it snaps back with destructive force.

Micaiah resisted any temptation to tell a lie that would have favored King Ahab and secured his own freedom from imprisonment. Micaiah recognized that he was accountable to a far greater King than Ahab. That King had issued a command against giving "false testimony." That King hates a "lying tongue" (Proverbs 6:17), and he warns that unrepentant liars shall join other unforgiven sinners one day in the "fiery lake of burning sulfur" (Revelation 21:8). The concept of "little" or "white" lies reflects man's thinking, not God's.

Don't try to stretch the truth; "stretch" your life so that it conforms to the truth.

—R. W. B.

Hearken, O people, every one of you.

1 Kings 22:28b

Today's visual draws from Micaiah's warning in verse 28 to challenge believers today to hearken to the Word of God.

WHAT DO YOU THINK?

When someone challenges the truthfulness or accuracy of what we have said, the natural response is to make a defense. Micaiah was willing to say, "Wait and see." When should we take a "wait and see" attitude, and when should we defend our position?

WHAT DO YOU THINK?

"Mark my words, all you people!" Thus Micaiah warned those who heard him to pay attention to what God had said. The language sounds somewhat outdated, but the message is needed just as much today. How can we urge contemporary people to pay attention to what God says?

CONCLUSION

A. THE REST OF THE STORY

Our lesson text ends with Micaiah's prediction of disaster for Ahab if he went into battle against the Syrians. In the concluding verses of 1 Kings 22 we see that Ahab chose to disregard Micaiah's warning and was able to persuade Jehoshaphat to accompany him on the campaign to retake Ramoth Gilead. However, to provide some additional "insurance" that Micaiah's prediction would not come true, Ahab persuaded Jehoshaphat to wear his clothing into battle.

Predictably, the results were nearly disastrous for the king of Judah. The king of Syria had ordered his troops to concentrate on capturing or killing Ahab. Seeing someone dressed in the garb of Ahab, they attacked Jehoshaphat's chariot and might have seized him had he not cried out.

Elsewhere on the battlefield Ahab apparently was feeling quite secure in his disguise. Suddenly an arrow shot at random found a chink in the king's armor, and Ahab bled to death in his chariot. Without a leader the soldiers of Israel left the battlefield and scattered to their homes, fulfilling Micaiah's prophecy (v. 17). Ahab's body was carried back to Samaria and buried. Later his chariot was washed out, and the dogs licked up his blood, fulfilling a prophecy of Elijah (1 Kings 21:19).

The Scriptures are silent about what happened to Micaiah. With Ahab dead, he may have been released from prison. On the other hand, Jezebel remained the real power behind Ahab's two sons and successors, Ahaziah and Jehoram. She may have had the prophet executed.

B. A RARE COMMODITY

Some months ago I was speaking to a friend who is a businessman in a different part of the state where I live. When I inquired about how his business was doing, he informed me that he had sold it. When I asked him what kind of a sales contract he had entered into to complete the transaction, he replied, "We didn't sign a contract. We just shook hands on the deal."

"But," I protested, "you can't do business on a handshake."

"You can still do it that way down where I live," came his reply.

This conversation caused me to stop and think a bit about the business climate where I and most people live. In our society integrity has become an increasingly rare commodity. We feel its absence in every area of our lives. As a result, we have become cynical about our relationships in all kinds of circumstances.

Modern advertising usually tells some truth about the product it attempts to sell, but it doesn't tell us all the truth. When we see a good deal advertised, we have learned to ask, "What about the fine print?" Experience has taught us that the fine print often nullifies what the headlines advertise.

Politicians have built their careers on promising what they cannot (or do not intend to) deliver. Lawyers can cleverly twist words in such a way that their clients can avoid the legal consequences of their deeds. Students habitually cheat, claiming that "everybody does it." Even religious leaders sometimes betray their sacred calling, leading astray many in their flocks through either a theology or a lifestyle that rejects biblical standards.

Must we as Christians be reduced to a cynicism that accepts this decline of values that is so prevalent in what many call a "post-Christian" culture? Or can we resist? The examples of Elijah and Micaiah show us that we do not have to surrender to the values of our culture. Their lives demonstrated a commitment to God that left no room for compromise. And they demonstrated that commitment by their integrity—a rare commodity in our times, but one that the world must see if our witness is to communicate clearly on Christ's behalf.

PRAYER

O God, you have called us out of this world to become your holy servants. Now send us back into the world to serve the needs of those all about us who have lost their way and need the light that only you can offer. In Jesus' name we pray. Amen.

THOUGHT TO REMEMBER

One person and God make a majority.

Discovery Learning

This page contains an alternate lesson plan emphasizing learning activities. Classes desiring such student involvement will find these suggestions helpful. The next page is a reproducible activity page to further enhance discovery learning.

LEARNING GOALS

After participating in this lesson, each student should be able to:

1. Recount the circumstances under which Micaiah courageously refused to compromise God's message.

2. Tell why standing for God's truth is such a challenge in today's world.

3. Express appreciation to someone who, like Micaiah, has paid a price for being true to God's message.

INTO THE LESSON

Tell the class that there are times when it is tough to speak God's truth. For example, the listener might be hostile or antagonistic to Christianity or be too close of a friend. Ask the class members to share what they think would be a tough situation for them to speak a truth from God. They may do this in small groups or share with the whole class. As they report these situations, list them on a marker board or chalkboard.

Make the transition to Bible study by telling the class that we are going to be encouraged by someone who successfully shared God's truth in a threatening situation. This little-known character probably had a degree of fear because he was facing a powerful authority. His courageous truthfulness did get him in trouble, but he faithfully delivered God's message. His adventure teaches us a lesson about courage, truthfulness, integrity, and priorities. The man's name is Micaiah. (Write *Micaiah* on the board.) Like Elijah, he was a prophet during the reign of King Ahab.

INTO THE WORD

Read 1 Kings 22:15-28 and deliver a brief lecture on the lesson background. Then ask the learners to form groups of five or six people. Each group will work together to write the dialogue of the main characters in contemporary English and then act out the incident, using their paraphrased dialogues for scripts.

To prepare for this activity, make large name tags for each main character: King Ahab, Micaiah, Jehoshaphat (even though he doesn't speak), and Zedekiah. (Write each name on a letter size piece of paper and use a string to hang it from the appropriate actor's neck.) Preparations for the activity should also include a piece of paper for each class member, listing the verses and speaker down the left side. The group will write their paraphrase down the right side. The left-side column should list v. 15, King Ahab to Micaiah, Micaiah to King Ahab; v. 16, King Ahab to Micaiah; v. 17, Micaiah's vision/prophecy; v. 18, King Ahab to Jehoshaphat; vv. 19-23, Micaiah's vision/prophecy; vv. 24, 25, Zedekiah to Micaiah, Micaiah to Zedekiah; vv. 26, 27, King Ahab (to court prophets?); v. 28, Micaiah to King Ahab (and to the people).

Give each group a photocopy of the lesson commentary notes on verses 21-24 with the words *lying spirit* and *Zedekiah* highlighted. This material will help groups interpret and paraphrase the dialogue. Be ready also to visit each group and clarify sections of the story as needed.

After the groups have finished, ask them to assign readers and read the paraphrase to their own groups. Then ask one of the groups to perform its dialogue for the entire class. Give the readers the name tags to help class members remember the characters.

After the reading (and applause!), give a brief lecture. Use this time to fill in details and to clarify the story as needed.

INTO LIFE

Use the following discussion questions to guide the class in applying this Scripture to life.

1. Focus on the prophet Micaiah for a moment. What do you learn about godly living from this event in his life? (List the answers given on the chalkboard.)

2. Micaiah took a courageous stand for truth in a hostile environment. Today's Western world is also becoming increasingly hostile to Christianity. What lessons do you learn for today's Christian living in today's world?

3. Who are some persons you have known who have taken a courageous stand for Christ's truth? They may have even paid a price for that stand!

If there is time, or instead of the discussion described above, distribute copies of the reproducible page that follows, and allow time for the learners to complete the chart. Allow volunteers to report some of their responses.

Remind the class that, to have this kind of courageous testimony, we must do two things: we must know God's Word, and we must make a determination to be faithful to the truth *before* a confrontation challenges us. Give the learners three-by-five cards and ask each to write a personal vow to God that addresses both issues above. Some may wish to tape these commitments to the inside covers of their Bibles.

Truthfully Speaking

    Micaiah was confronted with a situation where he could speak God's truth, or he could simply say what the king wanted to hear. Today's Christians are also often faced with similar frightening opportunities. Consider the following persons and situations. What might these persons like or WANT to hear, and what truth from God do you think they SHOULD hear?

PERSON / SITUATION	WANT TO HEAR	SHOULD HEAR
President of U.S. (If you live outside the U.S., substitute the executive head of your country.)		
Educators		
Abortionists		
Entertainers		
Parents		
A Couple Considering Divorce		
Today's Church		
My Church		
Me		

JUDGMENT ON JUDAH AND ISRAEL

LESSON 5

WHY TEACH THIS LESSON?

"They should do something about this!" How many times have you heard something like that? And did you ever wonder who "they" were? It is easy, and even common, to assume that some "powers that be" ought to take responsibility for correcting the problems around us. Rare is the one who takes on the much harder task of assuming responsibility for making improvements.

Amos was such a character. Without credentials or position, he obeyed the Lord's call to declare the truth. Not everyone appreciated it. But he was faithful to the task, and his name has been honored for nearly three millennia since.

If your students would be among the rare few who do something instead of just talk about what ought to be done, then they will appreciate today's lesson.

INTRODUCTION

A. WITHOUT OFFICIAL APPROVAL

"I was neither a prophet nor a prophet's son," confessed Amos (Amos 7:14), frankly admitting that he was not a card-carrying member of the "prophets' union" and thus lacked any official status in recognized clerical circles.

But Amos was neither the first nor the last to proclaim God's message outside "official" channels. Consider Micaiah, who proclaimed God's message without hesitation in spite of how it contradicted Ahab's court prophets. Consider John the Baptist, whose rustic lifestyle seemed eccentric to some but whose powerful preaching prepared the way for the Messiah. Consider Jesus, of whom the religious leaders of his day asked, "How did this man get such learning without having studied?" (John 7:15). Finally, consider Jesus' apostles. Although recognized as "unschooled, ordinary men," their boldness on behalf of Jesus caused the Jewish leaders to marvel (Acts 4:13).

God can use anyone to declare his good news. In some cases his most effective witnesses are those who have "non-professional" status.

B. LESSON BACKGROUND

During the approximate century that passed since the events covered in last week's lesson, a number of significant changes occurred in Israel (the northern kingdom). The dynasty of Omri (which included Omri, Ahab, and his two sons, Ahaziah and Jehoram) had been replaced by the dynasty of Jehu. Under this dynasty Israel enjoyed substantial prosperity, which reached its peak during the long reign of Jeroboam II, who ruled from 785 to 745 B.C. The prophetic ministry of Amos occurred near the middle of Jeroboam's reign, at about 760 B.C.

Perhaps the main reason for Israel's prosperity during this time was the weakness of its neighbors, particularly the Syrians to the north and the Assyrians to the east. Both of these peoples had caused problems for Israel during the previous

DEVOTIONAL READING:
HEBREWS 10:26-31

BACKGROUND SCRIPTURE:
AMOS 1, 2

PRINTED TEXT:
AMOS 1:1, 2; 2:4-10

Jul
1

LESSON AIMS

After this lesson each of your students should be able to:

1. Summarize Amos's message of judgment against Judah and Israel in today's text.

2. Illustrate how the sins that Amos cited are prevalent in our society.

3. Develop a message of warning of God's judgment on contemporary sin.

KEY VERSE

This is what the LORD says: "For three sins of Judah, even for four, I will not turn back my wrath. . . . they have rejected the law of the LORD and have not kept his decrees." —Amos 2:4

LESSON 5 NOTES

century. During this power vacuum, Jeroboam II expanded his territory, regaining some of the land that had been lost by his predecessors. The result was a growing prosperity that reminded some of the "glory days" under David and Solomon. Despite the nation's impressive outward appearance, however, its spiritual condition was deteriorating rapidly. This was the problem that Amos had come to address.

I. AMOS THE PROPHET (AMOS 1:1, 2)

A. THE MAN (v. 1)

1. *The words of Amos, one of the shepherds of Tekoa—what he saw concerning Israel two years before the earthquake, when Uzziah was king of Judah and Jeroboam son of Jehoash was king of Israel.*

Amos was the earliest of four eighth-century prophets who brought God's message to all of God's people: Amos and Hosea preached in *Israel*; Micah and Isaiah brought God's message to *Judah*.

All that we know about Amos is what we learn from his writing. Here we are told that he was *one of the shepherds of Tekoa*. He later describes himself as one who had been "tending the flock" (Amos 7:15). He also mentions that he "took care of sycamore-fig trees" (7:14). His hometown of *Tekoa* was located on a ridge about six or seven miles south of Bethlehem.

As noted earlier, Amos had no official credentials to serve as a prophet. When he was challenged by Amaziah, the priest at Bethel, he frankly acknowledged that he was not a prophet in the generally accepted sense, nor was he "a prophet's son" (Amos 7:14). This probably means that Amos was not one of the "company of the prophets" (2 Kings 4:38; 6:1), who apparently comprised a kind of "training school." His authority came directly from God: "The Lord took me from tending the flock and said to me, 'Go, prophesy to my people Israel'" (Amos 7:15).

Amos carried out his ministry during the reigns of *Uzziah* in *Judah* and of *Jeroboam* II in *Israel*. The prophet adds a specific chronological reference to date his ministry—*two years before the earthquake*. This earthquake is also referred to in Zechariah 14:5. Archaeological excavations at Hazor, a city in Israel eight or ten miles north of the Sea of Galilee, have provided evidence of an earthquake that occurred sometime around 760 B.C.

B. THE MESSAGE (v. 2)

2. *He said:*

> "The LORD roars from Zion
>   and thunders from Jerusalem;
> the pastures of the shepherds dry up,
>   and the top of Carmel withers."

Amos journeyed from Tekoa to Bethel, a distance of about twenty-five miles. Bethel was one of two places (Dan was the other) where Jeroboam I had set up golden calves to keep his subjects in the northern kingdom from going to worship at the temple in Jerusalem (1 Kings 12:25-29). Bethel became the more prominent of the two locations and was known as "the king's sanctuary" (Amos 7:13).

The Lord is depicted as a roaring lion, terrifying in his judgment. Such language reflects the world of the shepherd, with which Amos was familiar. While the Lord wanted to be the protecting Shepherd of Israel (Psalm 23), here he is portrayed as a lion coming to harm Israel as he exercises judgment on her for her sins.

Zion was a common designation for *Jerusalem*. Here was located the temple, the earthly symbol of God's presence with his people. Amos reminded his audience that it was from here that God would pronounce judgment, not from Dan or Bethel, where the rulers of Israel had set up rival sanctuaries.

WHAT DO YOU THINK?

Amos acknowledged that he was not an official "prophet" (7:14). God often chooses people from unlikely backgrounds for special tasks. What are some of the characteristics that mark spokespersons for God?

WHAT DO YOU THINK?

Amos pictured the Lord as a lion about to plunder the flock of Israel. That image was contrary to the popular image of the Lord as a shepherd and must have been startling to Amos's hearers. What images do people today have of God? How might we appropriately challenge those images to call people to repentance?

The pastures of the shepherds dry up. God's judgment would include a drought that would make it difficult for shepherds to find places to feed their sheep. So severe would be the effects of this drought that even *the top of Carmel withers.* Recall the extended drought that God sent during the time of Elijah and Ahab. Even when this drought was at its worst, Elijah was able to get water on Mount Carmel to pour on top of his sacrifice (1 Kings 18:33-35). Thus, for this location to wither signified a severe drought indeed.

"HERE COMES THE JUDGE"

The late Sammy Davis, Jr., is remembered both for his musical talent and for his work as a comedian. One of his most memorable routines was called "Here Comes the Judge." Davis wore a judge's robe and sat behind a huge bench as if in a courtroom. Many found the unorthodox "judgments" that his character handed down to be entertaining. Harry Anderson, star of the television series *Night Court,* got laughs as well with his caricature of a judge who dressed and behaved in a non-conformist style. There is often genuine humor in characterizations that are non-stereotypical.

Amos was no "stereotypical" or "cookie cutter" clone of the prophets of his time and place. He really did not have the credentials considered necessary to qualify him for such a job. He *was* authorized, however, by the Supreme Judge of all the earth. It was God's indictment that he boldly brought against Israel and Judah. He needed no other validation, degree, or license.

God often appoints unlikely candidates to deliver his messages and render his judgments. Consider the "motley crew" of twelve whom he used to begin the church. Consider *us,* whom he has commissioned to preach "repentance and forgiveness of sins" to the nations (Luke 24:47). His commandment alone qualifies us to be "prophets" and "judges" to our time and to our world.   —R. W. B.

II. JUDGMENT AGAINST JUDAH (AMOS 2:4, 5)

A. THE REASON (v. 4)

4. This is what the LORD says:
   "For three sins of Judah,
      even for four, I will not turn back my wrath.
   Because they have rejected the law of the LORD
      and have not kept his decrees,
   because they have been led astray by false gods,
      the gods their ancestors followed.

In the intervening verses of chapters 1 and 2, Amos had pronounced God's judgment on many of Israel's neighbors—Syria, called Aram in our text (1:3-5), Philistia (1:6-8), Phoenicia (1:9, 10), Edom (1:11, 12), Ammon (1:13-15), and Moab (2:1-3). He then turned his attention to *Judah.* By including Judah in his condemnations, Amos indicated to his audience that he was not just a preacher from Judah who was expressing a personal prejudice against Israel.

As Amos preached against Israel's enemies, his audience may have voiced hearty approval. These peoples had often been a "thorn in the side" of God's people. Many would have been just as enthusiastic when Amos condemned Judah, for the enmity between Israel and Judah was long-standing. A few, however, might have realized where Amos's line of reasoning was leading—straight toward Israel.

With the phrase *for three sins of Judah, even for four,* Amos was not specifically enumerating only three or four sins. This appears to be a rhetorical device that the prophet used to introduce each of the Lord's condemnations. It was a way of saying that the sins of a nation had accumulated to the point where God could no longer withhold his judgment. In condemning the other nations, Amos mentioned specific sins of which they were guilty. He followed the same pattern in

The Lord will roar from Zion, and utter his voice from Jerusalem ... and the top of Carmel shall wither. *Amos 1:2*

The visual for today's lesson dramatically illustrates God's warning in verse 2. Display this poster as you begin your Bible study.

WHAT DO YOU THINK?

Amos cited specific sins of which his people were guilty: rejecting God's law, breaking his commandments, worshiping false gods, and continuing in their ancestors' sins. If God sent a prophet to denounce the sins of our nation, what specific sins would he condemn? What can we do to turn people away from such sins?

[Be sure to stay specific on sins, and not on sinners! There is a danger that things could get personal, but the discussion need not go that direction.]

HOW TO SAY IT

Ahab. AY-hab.

Ahaziah. Ay-huh-ZYE-uh.

Amaziah. Am-uh-ZYE-uh.

Ammon. AM-mun.

Amorites. AM-uh-rites.

Aram. AIR-um.

Assyrians. Uh-SEAR-ee-unz.

Babylon. BAB-uh-lun.

Carmel. CAR-mel.

Edom. EE-dum.

Elijah. Ee-LYE-juh.

Hazor. HAY-zor.

Hosea. Ho-ZAY-uh.

Jehoash. Jeh-HO-ash.

Jehoram. Jeh-HO-rum.

Jehu. JAY-hew.

Jeroboam. Jair-uh-BO-um.

Micaiah. My-KAY-uh.

Moab. MO-ab.

Nebuchadnezzar. NEB-yuh-kud-NEZ-er.

Omri. AHM-rye.

Philistia. Fuh-LISS-tee-uh.

Phoenicia. Fuh-NISH-uh.

Tekoa. Tih-KO-uh.

Uzziah. Uh-ZYE-uh.

denouncing Judah's sins. The people had *rejected the law of the Lord*, thus violating his covenant with them. Duplicating the sins that *their ancestors* had committed, they had been *led astray by false gods*, worshiping them instead of the true God.

B. THE RESULT (v. 5)

5. "... *I will send fire upon Judah*
     that will consume the fortresses of Jerusalem."

In Amos's indictment of *Judah, Jerusalem* was specifically singled out for punishment. This was the center of Judah, both religiously and politically, and its leaders bore a great deal of the responsibility for the sins of the people. For that reason, Jerusalem would be subjected to a *fire*, probably as a result of invading armies. The fulfillment of Amos's words occurred when the army of Nebuchadnezzar, king of Babylon, destroyed the city, including the temple, in 586 B.C.

INTOLERABLE TOLERANCE

Twenty-first century society is bending over backward to grant the moral freedom of choice to every soul, no matter how a person's choices may offend God, endanger lives, and/or contaminate the culture. It is called "tolerance." Calling sin "sin" is viewed as judgmental and unsophisticated. Standing for God's absolutes is ridiculed as "primitive" or at least "ultra-conservative." All manner of perversion, obscenity, exploitation, and godlessness is tolerated in the name of "freedom" and "choice."

The moral uncertainty of our time is not so very different from that of Amos's day. His neighbors, too, tolerated all kinds of sinful and ungodly behavior. They needed to be told of impending punishment for their sins. God was about to deliver them into the hands of their enemies because they were disobedient and unrepentant.

So-called "tolerance" eventually becomes intolerable to God. True, he is patient with us, for he wants no one to perish (2 Peter 3:9). But justice ultimately will prevail. Sin will earn its wages (Romans 6:23). Unforgiven unbelievers will suffer "the second death" (Revelation 21:8).

Who, like Amos, will warn them? Who will call them to repentance? —R. W. B.

III. JUDGMENT AGAINST ISRAEL (AMOS 2:6-8)

A. GREED (vv. 6, 7a)

6. *This is what the* LORD *says:*
     "*For three sins of Israel,*
         even for four, I will not turn back my wrath.
     They sell the righteous for silver,
         and the needy for a pair of sandals.

Some students believe that the first sin for which Israel was indicted was that of bribing judges so that they would return false verdicts against the *righteous*. However, the rest of the sentence, which seems to be a repetition of the first part, appears to be directed at the sin of selling *needy* people into slavery. A man who fell into debt and could not pay his way out would be sold as a slave. Even his wife and children might be enslaved in this manner. The people had so trivialized human life that they would sell a person *for a pair of sandals*.

7a. "*They trample on the heads of the poor*
     as upon the dust of the ground
     and deny justice to the oppressed.

Amos employed a striking image in his indictment of the people's callous attitude: *they trample on the heads of the poor as upon the dust of the ground*. They cared as little for the poor as they did for the dust on which they walked.

The Hebrew word rendered *trample* can also mean "pant." The *New American Standard Bible* translates the verse as follows: "These who pant after the very dust of the earth on the head of the helpless." This may be a way of saying that the greed of the rich for land had become so intense that they wanted even this meager amount of dust. Perhaps it refers to how the poor sprinkled dust in their hair as a sign of mourning over their impoverished state. The rich wanted to deny them even this small token of their despair. Regardless of how the passage is translated, the emphasis on the heartless greed of the people is clear.

B. IMMORALITY (v. 7b)

7b. "Father and son use the same girl
    and so profane my holy name.

This may refer to a *father and son* who both used a female slave for their sexual pleasures or to both men consorting with the *same* prostitute. Some students take the view that such a woman was a sacred prostitute, and in visiting her these two men were engaging in pagan worship as well as in breaking the law that forbade sexual promiscuity. God's law demanded sexual purity, and those who violated that law were guilty of profaning his *holy name*. How tragic that a father would set such a disgusting example for his son!

C. BLASPHEMY (v. 8)

8. "They lie down beside every altar
    on garments taken in pledge.
In the house of their god
    they drink wine taken as fines.

The phrase *garments taken in pledge* describes the heavy outer garments that the poor wore during the day and used as a cover at night. When such a garment was held as security for a debt, it was to be returned by nightfall so that the debtor would not have to sleep without protection from the cold (Exodus 22:26; Deuteronomy 24:12, 13). But instead of observing the law, the creditors were keeping the garments and using them as their own in the temple. Given what Amos said in verse 7b, it may be that their lying down *beside every altar* involved the kind of sacred prostitution encouraged by pagan worship.

They drink wine taken as fines. Apparently people were consuming wine paid as a fine during drunken gatherings that took place *in the house of their god*. The worship of some of the pagan gods included such occasions of drunken revelry.

IV. LESSONS FROM THE PAST (AMOS 2:9, 10)

A. JUDGMENT AGAINST THE AMORITES (v. 9)

9. "I destroyed the Amorite before them,
    though he was tall as the cedars
    and strong as the oaks.
I destroyed his fruit above
    and his roots below.

The personal pronoun *I* here emphasizes God's faithfulness to his people as contrasted with the people's unfaithfulness to him. *The Amorite* is a general term for the people who inhabited Canaan when the Israelites entered the promised land (Genesis 15:16). Amos's descriptive words (*tall as the cedars* and *strong as the oaks*) recall the Israelites' description of the Canaanites' size (Numbers 13:33). But God had given the Israelites victory over these foes—a victory so complete that it is described as including both the *fruit* and the *roots* of these mighty *oaks*.

The message here is a two-edged sword. On the one hand it is a fearsome reminder of what can happen when God judges a people. Just as he removed the Amorite (Canaanites) from the land, he can remove Israel from the land when

---

WHAT DO YOU THINK?

Amos chastised the Israelites for their greed and sexual promiscuity. The same sins had plagued the nation before and would continue to grieve God at later dates in history. These two sins are devastating to God's people. How do they gain access and even acceptance among God's elect?

WHAT DO YOU THINK?

With the example of the Amorites, God was calling his people to look back at history to discover what would happen to the disobedient. What lessons from history could we cite to show that God's judgment will eventually be rendered on his unfaithful people?

PRAYER

We thank you, Father, for men like Amos who boldly proclaimed the truth in a society that did not want to hear the truth. Grant us the same courage to speak forthrightly to our own society. In Jesus' name we pray. Amen.

THOUGHT TO REMEMBER

The same God who gave a ministry to Amos, a humble shepherd, has a ministry for each of us—regardless of our occupation.

their sin becomes similar to that of their predecessors. The other side is a message of comfort. God can take care of his people, as surely as he cared for them in giving them the land in the first place.

B. DELIVERANCE IN THE EXODUS (v. 10)

10. "I brought you up out of Egypt,
    and I led you forty years in the desert
    to give you the land of the Amorites."

During the exodus from Egypt, God demonstrated his power in various ways. The *forty years* of wandering were the result of the Israelites' disobedience. Still, God had guided them and provided them food and water as they traveled. Their clothes did not wear out during their wandering (Deuteronomy 8:4).

Although Amos preached a message that strongly condemned the sins of God's people, he also offered them the opportunity to repent and return to God. By referring to significant events in Israel's history, the prophet reminded the people of how much God had loved and cared for them. How could they be so callous toward a God who had done so much for them?

CONCLUSION

Anyone who takes a stand for truth is likely to be accused of being judgmental or a hypocrite. In our tolerant, anything-goes society, to be so branded marks one as a pariah and even an outcast in some groups. Of course, it never seems to occur to the person making the charges that in so doing he is being judgmental.

Those who accuse others of being judgmental often quote Jesus' words: "Do not judge, or you too will be judged" (Matthew 7:1). What such people fail to understand is that Jesus was condemning biased, misguided judgments. Only a few sentences later he urges his listeners to make all kinds of judgments: to choose the narrow gate rather than the wide way, to beware of false prophets, and to judge a tree by its fruit (vv. 13-20).

There is certainly nothing wrong with making judgments. In fact, it is impossible to exist without making judgments. And many of the judgments we make are about trivial matters—which tie goes best with this suit or which restaurant we shall patronize today. Other judgments are far more important, although they may not involve moral decisions—such as which college I will attend or which job offer I shall accept.

Still other judgments are profoundly moral and have life-changing implications. The most important judgment we will ever make in this life is the answer we give to the question, "What do you think about the Christ?" (Matthew 22:42).

By contemporary standards Amos would have been branded "judgmental." In fact, he went out of his way to be judgmental, leaving his home in Judah and traveling to the neighboring kingdom of Israel to make his judgmental pronouncements. It is quite obvious that Amos did not receive a very friendly welcome in Bethel, especially from those whom he was criticizing. The priest at Bethel, Amaziah, accused him of conspiring against the king, Jeroboam II.

The next time you are called judgmental for standing for the truth, avoiding sinful actions, or criticizing someone who is engaging in immoral activities, count it a compliment. You are in good company—Amos, John the Baptist, the apostle Paul, and Jesus Christ, among others. Just be sure of one thing, however: make certain that you are standing firm for the right, not just for your opinion of what is right. Amos received a special revelation from God for his ministry. We cannot expect that kind of revelation, but we do have God's revelation in the Bible. On it we can and must stand firm.

Discovery Learning

This page contains an alternate lesson plan emphasizing learning activities. Classes desiring such student involvement will find these suggestions helpful. The next page is a reproducible activity page to further enhance discovery learning.

LEARNING GOALS

After this lesson each student should be able to:

1. Summarize Amos's message of judgment against Judah and Israel in today's text.

2. Illustrate how the sins that Amos cited are prevalent in our society.

3. Develop a message of warning of God's judgment on contemporary sin.

INTO THE LESSON

Prepare a handout with a large "Behavior Meter" on it. (See below.) Give the handout to groups of five or six people and ask each group to indicate a place on the meter that the members believe best characterizes our nation's society. Then ask where they would put the meter mark for the society of the 1950s. Where do they think the mark will go twenty years from now?

BEHAVIOR METER

Say, "We are going to study a prophet who became a 'behavior meter' for Israel. He listed their sins and pronounced God's judgment to come."

INTO THE WORD

Prepare a brief lecture to introduce the setting for today's study. Prepare a poster or an overhead projector transparency with the following outline: Prosperity and Poverty, The Prophetic Quartet, Amos's Occupation, Amos's Credentials, The Timing and Target of the Prophecy. The notes in the lesson commentary on the Lesson Background and verses 1 and 2 (pages 377, 378) will give the information needed for this presentation.

Next, give each learner a highlighting marker and a photocopy of Amos 2:4-10. Explain the words "for three sins . . . even for four" in verses 4 and 6 (see page 379). Then ask each person to highlight words or phrases in the text that give word pictures or images of sin or of God's punishment.

When they have finished, display a visual on which you have already listed the word pictures or images of sin. (They "rejected the law of the Lord," had "not kept his decrees," had "been led astray by false gods," v. 4; they sold

"the righteous for silver, and the needy for a pair of sandals," v. 6; they would "trample on the heads of the poor as upon the dust of the ground and deny justice to the oppressed," "father and son use the same girl," v. 7; they would "lie down beside every altar on garments taken in pledge," and "drink wine taken as fines," v. 8.) Use your lesson commentary to explain the more confusing images.

Second, review the list of sins and ask the class members to write a contemporary name for, or an illustration of, each sin. (*For example, selling the righteous for silver might be the equivalent of taking advantage of one's employees to make a bigger profit at their expense.*) Write these names or illustrations beside (or under) the sins listed, using a different color marker.

Third, ask the class to identify which of these sins the prophet would also charge against our nation. Place an asterisk (*) beside these.

INTO LIFE

Tell the students that "we have identified the sins and punishments of the Israelites in Amos's list, and we have also identified some of the sins of our culture. Let's imagine that you are the prophet to carry God's message of warning to our nation. What would you say?" Give the original groups of five or six people another handout, as described below, on which they can write a judgment and warning to our nation. They will use Amos's prophecy as a pattern. Use terminology similar to verses 4-8 ("for three sins . . . even for four," etc.), but with modern locations and modern sins taken from your earlier list).

After the groups complete this exercise, ask them to read their pronouncements to the rest of the class. If you have a large class with many groups, two groups can simply exchange papers and read each other's pronouncements.

Then ask the class to share ideas about what we can do about these sins present in our society. Ask a volunteer to write abbreviations of answers on a chalkboard. After the list is completed, share in a prayer time for our nation. Choose five class members, and ask each to word a prayer for one of the following: forgiveness for our nation's sinfulness, guidance for our national, state, and local political leaders, guidance for the education of our children, strength for our churches, and a faithful testimony for each class member.

Judah and Israel's Web Page

Can you imagine what Judah and Israel would list on their web page if they only could cite items mentioned by the prophet Amos? Read Amos 2:4-10. Then write a few "bullets" about the following issues that could be included on the page according to Amos.

Our Gods:

Our View and Treatment of the Poor of Our Nation:

Our Sexual Standards:

Our Religious Life:

My Personal Virus Check

It is difficult to live in a country and not have its values and behavior infiltrate your own life. As you read Amos's prophecy and as you see the sins of our culture, identify one of these values or behaviors you find tempting and infecting your life and write it here:

Now, note how you can delete this from your life so you may be pleasing and acceptable in God's sight.

EMPTY OFFERINGS

WHY TEACH THIS LESSON?

An editor has two concerns when working with a piece of writing. One is what it says: factual content, proper vocabulary, grammar, and punctuation are the issue here. The other is how it looks: this concerns position of the type on the page, size of type, consistency in format, and the like. Sometimes, to make a page "look right," the editor has to change the wording slightly.

I sometimes feel guilty about that. Am I sacrificing the content for the form? The goal is to make form and content come together as a unit, but achieving that goal is never easy.

The same balance is critical to worship. So much time and effort is given to a discussion of the proper form for worship, one wonders if content has not been forgotten—or, at least, been given second place. It happened to the Israelites. It can happen to us. Today's lesson warns us about that very issue.

INTRODUCTION

A. A HEART FULL OF WHALES

A whaling vessel was in port being prepared for a long voyage in search of whales. On Sunday the captain of the ship attended worship services in the little village chapel. He seemed quite attentive throughout the sermon, but later, when the minister spoke to him, it was obvious that the sermon had made no impression on him. "How is it," asked the minister, "that you could seem so attentive during a sermon and yet apparently never hear a word I said?"

"The fact is," replied the captain, "all the time you were preaching I was thinking about where I would be most likely to find whales. There was no room in my heart for anything but whales."

Probably not many today attend worship services with their hearts full of whales. But, as in Amos's day, some fill their hearts with thoughts of making profits and pursuing pleasures.

B. LESSON BACKGROUND

Many blame poverty for the many social ills we face, and it is true that poverty provides a variety of temptations. But prosperity carries with it its own temptations. While people sometimes blame God for their difficulties and fail to thank him for the blessings they have, those who are doing well are tempted to credit their prosperity to their own intelligence and hard work, neglecting to thank God for their blessings. Sometimes they are inclined to look scornfully at the poor, blaming their plight on their own laziness or ignorance.

Greed also impairs one's worship. When material comforts control a person's life, that one is not likely to engage in meaningful worship. During the period of today's lesson, Israel was enjoying general prosperity. The affluent Israelites may have attended worship services regularly and given generously, but they did so with wrong motives. Jesus called his disciples' attention to the same problem when he commended a widow and her two copper coins in contrast to the much larger donations given by the rich (Mark 12:41-44; Luke 21:1-4). Empty ritual

DEVOTIONAL READING:
MALACHI 1:6-14
BACKGROUND SCRIPTURE:
AMOS 3–5
PRINTED TEXT:
AMOS 4:2-5; 5:18-24

LESSON AIMS

After participating in this lesson, each student should be able to:

Jul
8

1. Recite key points of Amos's condemnation of Israel's misuse of wealth and its empty rituals of worship.

2. Explain the connection between true worship and a godly life, and tell why that link must never be broken.

3. Take steps to make times of corporate worship more realistic and less ritualistic.

KEY VERSE

Let justice roll on like a river, righteousness like a never-failing stream! —Amos 5:24

can never substitute for the kind of relationship with God that gives worshipers a genuine concern for others.

As we study this lesson today, we should be able to see many parallels between conditions in ancient Israel and conditions in our own country today. In doing so, we should also keep in mind that less than forty years after Amos prophesied, God's punishment came upon Israel in the form of Assyrian armies who crushed the nation and carried thousands away into captivity.

In the first verse of Amos 4, the prophet directed his words to the "cows of Bashan." Bashan was the fertile plateau east of the Jordan River, stretching to the north from the Yarmuk River south of the Sea of Galilee to Mount Hermon. In the ancient world it was famous for the exceptional cattle that were nourished on its lush pastures. Here "cows of Bashan" is used as a metaphor to describe the rich women of Samaria who oppressed the poor to maintain their luxuriant lifestyle.

I. GOD'S CONDEMNATION OF ISRAEL (AMOS 4:2-5)

A. ARROGANCE IN PROSPERITY (vv. 2, 3)

2, 3. *The Sovereign LORD has sworn by his holiness:*
"The time will surely come
when you will be taken away with hooks,
the last of you with fishhooks.
You will each go straight out
through breaks in the wall,
and you will be cast out toward Harmon,"
declares the LORD.

WHAT DO YOU THINK?

During Amos's day, Israel was enjoying a period of prosperity. For them, wealth was like a poison. But it is not just Israelites who succumb to the deceit of becoming self-sufficient. How can having too much affect our relationship with God?

The plight of the poor and oppressed in Israel had not gone unnoticed. God had withheld his judgment for a time, but *his holiness* now arose to demand punishment. Amos described the impending disaster in store for Samaria: the people would be led away like fish on *hooks*. Some of the reliefs (pictures engraved on stone) and inscriptions left behind by the Assyrians portray this treatment of captive peoples. Usually they were led away with a rope fastened to a hook that pierced the nose or lower lip. (Note the description, in 2 Kings 19:28, of how God promised to treat the Assyrians.) Amos states that none of the arrogant women would escape this punishment: even *the last* of them would be *taken away. You will each go straight out through breaks in the wall.* The destruction of the walls of Samaria would leave gaping holes through which the captives could be led out.

The phrase translated *you will be cast out toward Harmon* is vague, so it is hard to know how to translate it. Perhaps it is a reference to Mount Hermon or to some other area where the people's captors would take them.

OBLIGATIONS OF AFFLUENCE

Being a Christian in the Western world today poses both special privileges and special responsibilities. We enjoy freedom of worship, and we usually don't have to fear imprisonment or torture for expressing our faith. But there is a certain peril in privilege, particularly where material wealth is concerned. Our stewardship responsibilities are greater because we are stewards over more possessions. Jesus said, "From everyone who has been given much, much will be demanded; and from the one who has been entrusted with much, much more will be asked" (Luke 12:48).

There is always the temptation to credit ourselves instead of God's blessing for our abundance. If we yield to this temptation, we will be less likely to make appropriate preparations for Jesus' return. We will also have far less influence for Christ in this world than we could have.

Israel, too, was prosperous; its people had come to trust in their wealth and what it brought them rather than in God. But the inescapable judgment of God, declared Amos, was sentencing them to defeat and exile. Can we learn from Israel's experience? Will we avoid the same sins?

Sadly, history can and does repeat itself. Pray that our nation will forsake its wicked ways and turn to God, who will hear from Heaven and heal our land (2 Chronicles 7:14).   —R. W. B.

B. EMPTINESS IN WORSHIP (vv. 4, 5)

4. "Go to Bethel and sin;
    go to Gilgal and sin yet more.
  Bring your sacrifices every morning,
    your tithes every three years.

Jeroboam I had established a center of worship at *Bethel* to keep the people of the northern kingdom from going to the temple in Jerusalem to worship (1 Kings 12:25-30). Amos boldly stepped forward and challenged this unauthorized practice. He condemned the false worship at Bethel by sarcastically urging the people to continue in it: *Go to Bethel and sin.* They were sinning, both through their worship at an unapproved site and by their attempts to worship God while living in defiance of his authority in their daily conduct.

Gilgal was the site where the Israelites camped after crossing the Jordan River, just prior to beginning their conquest of Canaan (Joshua 4:19). Apparently it, like Bethel, had become a center of worship (Hosea 4:15; 12:11; Amos 5:5).

The fact that the people brought *sacrifices every morning* indicates that they had erected altars at Bethel and Gilgal. Thus they were careful to observe certain commands set forth in the law (morning and evening sacrifices are commanded in Exodus 29:38-42). Yet in Bethel these sacrifices were being offered to the golden calf set up there by Jeroboam, not to the true God.

The phrase *your tithes every three years* calls to mind the teaching of the law of Moses about tithing. The law commanded that every three years the Israelites were to bring the tithes of that year's produce and store it away in order to provide for the needs of Levites, strangers, orphans, and widows (Deuteronomy 14:28, 29; 26:12). Students disagree as to whether this "third-year tithe" was the same as, or in addition to, the annual tithe (Deuteronomy 14:22). The Hebrew term may also be rendered "every three days." If this translation is accepted, then Amos would have been using sarcasm once again to highlight the people's spiritual condition. Even if they offered tithes every three days, it would be meaningless in view of their failure to obey God's law in their daily living.

5. Burn leavened bread as a thank offering
  and brag about your freewill offerings—
  boast about them, you Israelites,
    for this is what you love to do,"
        declares the Sovereign LORD.

Continuing his sarcastic tone, Amos urged the people to *burn leavened bread as a thank offering.* Including leaven in any offering involving fire was forbidden (Leviticus 2:11). By doing so the people were once more substituting their will for the expressed will of God in his law.

Amos also told his audience to *brag about your freewill offerings . . . for this is what you love to do.* The people liked to receive public acclaim for their offerings. Instead of coming humbly with their gifts, they were coming boastfully because this brought them the praise of others. Consider how Jesus described the phony worshipers of his day: "And when you pray, do not be like the hypocrites, for they love to pray standing in the synagogues and on the street corners to be seen by men" (Matthew 6:5).

WHAT DO YOU THINK?

Amos 4:4, 5 describes Israel's empty and ritualistic worship. Some would accuse today's church of practicing empty worship as well. How do we distinguish real worship from empty worship?

[Consider Matthew 15:8; John 4:23, 24; and Psalm 95:6 in your discussion.]

HOW TO SAY IT

Assyrians. Uh-SEAR-ee-unz.
Bashan. BAY-shan.
Gilgal. GIL-gal.
Harmon. HAR-mun.
Hermon. HER-mun.
Jeroboam. Jair-uh-BO-um.
Samaria. Suh-MARE-ee-uh.
Yarmuk. YAR-mook.

II. THE DAY OF THE LORD (AMOS 5:18-20)
A. NO LIGHT (v. 18)
18. Woe to you who long
> for the day of the LORD!
> Why do you long for the day of the LORD?
>> That day will be darkness, not light.

The day of judgment on God's enemies is often referred to in Scripture as *the day of the Lord.* (See also Isaiah 13:6, 9; Joel 1:15; 2:1, 2, 11, 31; 1 Thessalonians 5:2; 2 Peter 3:10.) Those to whom Amos preached believed that such a day was coming—they even longed for it. The problem was that they did not see this as a day of judgment against them. Amos made it clear that a time of judgment was coming on the people of Israel. Clearly God was not pleased with them. But their prosperity had blinded them to spiritual realities. With times so good (so they thought), how could the day of the Lord possibly be a day of *darkness, not light?*

Are we in any way like these ancient Israelites? Is our measure of contentment based on how well we are doing materially? Every day that passes brings us one day closer to the time that we will be called to stand before the judgment seat of Christ (Romans 14:10). What are we doing to prepare ourselves for that day?

B. NO ESCAPE (v. 19)
19. It will be as though a man fled from a lion
> only to meet a bear,
> as though he entered his house
>> and rested his hand on the wall
>> only to have a snake bite him.

To explain what the day of the Lord would be like for unprepared people, Amos used illustrations that were familiar to his audience. The *lion* has been extinct in Palestine for centuries, but in ancient times it frequented the thickets along rivers. Both Samson (Judges 14:5, 6) and David (1 Samuel 17:34, 35) had successful encounters with lions. The *bear* refers to the Syrian brown bear, now also extinct in Palestine.

Imagine the humor in the word picture painted by Amos. A man is running for his life to escape from a lion. He reaches a point where he figures he can finally relax, only to see a bear coming! He flees from the bear and eventually comes to his *house,* thinking that surely he will be safe there. Feeling at ease, he leans his *hand on the wall*—and a *snake* bites him! (This probably refers to an opening in a wall, perhaps a window, where a snake could hide.) The point of Amos's illustration is obvious: when the day of the Lord arrives, there will be no way to escape the wrath of God.

C. ONLY DARKNESS (v. 20)
20. Will not the day of the LORD be darkness, not light—
> pitch-dark, without a ray of brightness?

Darkness is often associated with God's judgment or with that which is evil or undesirable. Jesus speaks of those who in the day of judgment will be cast "outside, into the darkness" (Matthew 8:12; 25:30). Whether that day will be one of light or of darkness is up to us and is determined by our relationship with Jesus.

III. INDICTMENT OF FALSE WORSHIP (AMOS 5:21-24)
A. FEAST DAYS AND ASSEMBLIES (v. 21)
21. "I hate, I despise your religious feasts;
> I cannot stand your assemblies.

WHAT DO YOU THINK?

First John 5:13 assures us that we can "know" that we have eternal life. While it is important that we have that confidence, is it possible to become overconfident regarding judgment—even as the people in Israel did? What should be our attitude regarding "the day of the Lord"?

WHAT DO YOU THINK?

The language of Amos 5:21 is strikingly harsh. What do you think would cause God to "hate" or "despise" our worship assemblies or practices today? What should be our response?

Although the people were keeping the prescribed *feasts*, God rejected their worship because there was such a glaring contradiction between their profession of faith and their daily living. The statement *I cannot stand your assemblies* reads, according to the Hebrew text, "I cannot smell in your assemblies." When God gave instructions in the law of Moses concerning sacrifices, he had described "an aroma pleasing to the Lord" that would rise from them (Leviticus 1:9, 13, 17). But God had also warned that if his people rebelled against him, dire consequences would follow: "I will turn your cities into ruins and lay waste your sanctuaries, and I will take no delight in the pleasing aroma of your offerings" (Leviticus 26:31). Amos was announcing that Israel had deteriorated to such a sorry state.

B. OFFERINGS (v. 22)

22. "Even though you bring me burnt offerings and grain offerings,
    I will not accept them.
Though you bring choice fellowship offerings,
    I will have no regard for them.

In the previous verse Amos had condemned the people's "assemblies," which had become nothing more than empty rituals and a perversion of true worship. Now he turned his attention to the various offerings that the people brought.

The *burnt offerings* are the most commonly mentioned offerings in the Old Testament. Only male animals (without blemish) were used for this offering, and the entire animal was burned on the altar. Leviticus 1 includes the regulations concerning the burnt offering. The *grain offerings* were made of "fine flour." These were the only bloodless offerings required by the law of Moses. Regulations for them are found in Leviticus 2. *Fellowship offerings* could be made with either male or female animals. A portion of the animal was eaten by the priests and the rest by the worshiper. These are further described in Leviticus 3.

C. MUSIC (v. 23)

23. "Away with the noise of your songs!
    I will not listen to the music of your harps.

David and other psalmists wrote many *songs* that had become incorporated into Israel's worship. The building of Solomon's temple had stimulated the development of *music*, both vocal and instrumental, as a part of public worship. Apparently this emphasis on music had been continued in the places of worship established in the northern kingdom. God's objections were not to the music itself, but to the attitudes of the worshipers. Perhaps their emotions were soothed by the pleasant sounds. But unless they came before God with humble hearts, what they did was merely for personal pleasure. It was not true worship.

D. GOD'S DESIRE (v. 24)

24. "But let justice roll on like a river,
    righteousness like a never-failing stream!"

Amos wanted both *justice* and *righteousness* to govern the people's relationship with their fellow Israelites. Of course, both of these qualities can never become a reality without a proper relationship with God. The Ten Commandments are instructive here: the first four deal with man's relationship with God while the other six cover man's relationship with others. Neither part of the Commandments is complete without the other.

Using a vivid word picture once again, Amos pleaded with the people to allow justice and righteousness to flood the land like a *never-failing stream*. He pictured the change as something that would be ongoing—not like a desert wadi (where

Let judgment run down as waters, and righteousness as a mighty stream.

Today's visual features a dramatic photograph of Yellowstone Falls to illustrate the message of Amos 5:24. Post it as you begin to discuss that verse.

WHAT DO YOU THINK?

What can we do, as individuals or as a church, to "let justice roll on like a river, righteousness like a never-failing stream"?

[Talk about specific needs in your own community that need to be addressed. Is there a homeless shelter that you could help to equip or staff? Is there a family who lost its home to a fire or other disaster? Are there single mothers who could use some help with their children? Are there issues coming up on the ballot this fall that demand a united front from believers to secure justice for some segment of the community? Of course, in all these matters, do not overlook the power of prayer!]

PRAYER

Father, we are often disturbed by the suffering and injustice that we see all about us. Sometimes it seems overwhelming. Keep us from comfortably accepting our world as it is. Give us the strength and wisdom to do whatever we can wherever we are to bring about the justice and righteousness that Amos spoke about. Through the Prince of peace we pray. Amen.

THOUGHT TO REMEMBER

Empty, hollow worship will neither please God nor have an impact on the world for him.

water ran after a sudden rain only to dry up later), but like a perennial stream that issued life-giving water throughout the year.

SEVEN-DAY RELIGION

Times really don't change much. Hundreds of years after Amos delivered God's warnings to the Israelites concerning their neglect of justice and righteousness, Jesus had to teach the worshipers of his day the same lessons. "Woe to you, teachers of the law and Pharisees, you hypocrites! You give a tenth of your spices—mint, dill and cummin. But you have neglected the more important matters of the law—justice, mercy and faithfulness. You should have practiced the latter, without neglecting the former" (Matthew 23:23). Same sin—same condemnation!

True religion is walked as well as talked. Sabbath-keepers in ancient Israel were failing to live by their professed faith. Today Sunday superficiality is the practice of many Christians who give just one day a week to God. They categorize their time as either "spiritual" or "secular." Worship is fine in its place, but "business is business."

Many churches have recognized the importance of using the church facilities seven days a week. Even more essential is the living out of Christian principles and gospel truth seven days a week. God will be pleased, and the world will be given a clearer view of what Christianity really is.　　　　　　　—R. W. B.

CONCLUSION

For much of the previous century, conservative, Bible-believing Christians (often referred to as evangelicals) were not leaders in working for social justice. There were historical reasons for this. Early in the century, theological liberals, having abandoned many of the beliefs essential to the Christian faith, turned their energies to working for social justice in the world. The focus on these efforts led to the term "social gospel," which became associated with liberal theology. Evangelicals, wanting nothing to do with liberalism in any form, abandoned these concerns for social justice, giving their energies instead to evangelism and missions.

It would be unfair, however, to accuse evangelicals of abandoning all concern for the needy and helpless. They have built orphanages and homes for the elderly. They have supported missions in the inner cities, ministering to drug addicts, alcoholics, prostitutes, and the homeless. They have given generously to international parachurch organizations that minister to human needs around the world.

If Amos were to return in the twenty-first century, how would he view our society? Evangelicals generally hold that the best route to social reform is to convert people to Jesus Christ. If people are genuinely committed to Jesus and his teachings, they will be concerned for individuals such as the sick, the homeless, the orphans, the widows, and the hungry. Certainly Amos would approve of this.

At the same time, many of the evils of our society are deeply imbedded in our social structures and our laws. Those of us who live in democratic societies, where as citizens we have an opportunity to shape our laws, must recognize the special responsibility that is ours to work for justice in our society. As Christian citizens, we need to keep ourselves well informed about public issues and express our beliefs through the ballot box and through whatever involvement in public life that we believe is God's desire for us. This will be no easy task, for in a chaotic society like ours there are often no simple answers to complicated problems. In some instances we may have to accept compromises, settling for something that may be an improvement but falls short of achieving the best.

Amos was an advocate of both justice and righteousness. Let us work for both of these important goals—for righteousness, in bringing people into a right relationship with God through Jesus Christ, and for justice, in bringing a Christian perspective to the issues of our day that are crying for solid answers.

Discovery Learning

This page contains an alternate lesson plan emphasizing learning activities. Classes desiring such student involvement will find these suggestions helpful. The next page is a reproducible activity page to further enhance discovery learning.

LEARNING GOALS

After this lesson each student will be able to:

1. Recite key points of Amos's condemnation of Israel's misuse of wealth and its empty rituals of worship.

2. Explain the connection between true worship and a godly life, and tell why that link must never be broken.

3. Take steps to make times of corporate worship more realistic and less ritualistic.

INTO THE LESSON

Observe that children will sometimes call other children names when they are angry. Sometimes they use the names of animals. Ask the class what a child might imply when calling someone a chicken. A pig. A dog. A cow.

Tell the class that you know of an *adult* who called a number of prominent women "cows." And he was a preacher! Ask, "Why do you think a preacher would call women 'cows'? What do you think he was implying?"

Let the class suggest answers, but do not comment on the answers one way or the other. After some discussion, say, "Actually, this preacher was making a point about the worship these women and others in Israel practiced. We will see what he meant in today's adventure with Amos."

INTO THE WORD

Prepare a visual to help your learners understand the lesson background. The visual should have the heading "Empty Offerings." Under this should be listed four major points for your brief presentation: Israel's Prosperity, Diluted Worship, Cows of Bashan, Coming Captivity. Use the Lesson Background and commentary notes (see pages 385, 386) to prepare and deliver a brief lecture on these four points. Then tell the class that the focus of Amos's address is the approach of God's judgment against the people's empty, ritualistic worship.

Read Amos 4:2-5 and ask, "Why does Amos tell his listeners to go to Bethel and Gilgal to sin? What is he implying?" Then explain these phrases: "Bring your sacrifices every morning," "your tithes every three years," "thank offering," and "freewill offerings." Use the commentary section for help.

Ask a volunteer to read Amos 5:18-24. Then form small groups to discuss the following sets of questions based on this text. (You should have these questions printed on a handout or a large visual to which the groups can refer.)

1. The Israelites longed for the "day of the Lord." What do you think they expected to happen on the day of the Lord? Why would Amos pronounce "woe" to these expectant Israelites?

2. Why would God hate their religious feasts and not accept their offerings and music?

3. Why the pronouncement in verse 24? What did God expect of the Israelites?

After a few minutes, ask for group reports and discuss these issues as a class.

INTO LIFE

Ask each group to stay together and to complete one of the following tasks. (If you have more than three groups, have some of the groups do the same task.)

Task 1: Innocent children sometimes suffer the consequences of their parents' sins (Amos 4:2, 3). Cite contemporary illustrations of this principle and write recommendations for parents.

Task 2: Amos emphasizes social responsibility. Read Matthew 25:31-46; then list some of the characteristics of a person who fulfills God's will in this area. List implications this passage suggests for today's church.

Task 3: Worship is influenced by our values and behavior. Considering what happened to the worship of the Israelites, offer suggestions of how to keep Christian worship expressions genuine and not merely ritualistic.

After the groups finish, introduce Group 1 by telling the class there are often helpful subtopics packed into the big picture of Scripture. One of those is in today's text, and it concerns the effects of sin on our children.

Introduce Group 2 by telling the class that this group addressed one of the major issues of Amos's message—social justice and responsibility.

Introduce Group 3 by reminding the class that the worship of the Israelites was not acceptable because of their hearts and behavior. Allow a representative from Group 3 to offer suggestions on how to keep worship fresh, personal, and genuine. After the report, remind the class that God seeks worshipers whose lives reflect worship of him, not simply people who go to worship.

Distribute copies of the reproducible page that follows. Ask the students to complete the right column first (about the nation); then discuss the results. Then have them complete the left side. Discuss how your church can improve in the areas cited by the class.

Contemporary Judgments

If Amos were to speak for God to your church or to your nation, what judgments do you think he would bring? What activities and values would he compliment? What would he condemn?

I believe the Lord appreciates these activities and values of my church:	**I believe the Lord appreciates these activities and values of my nation:**
I am concerned Amos might denounce these activities and values of my church:	**I am concerned Amos might denounce these activities and values of my nation:**

GOD'S LOVE FOR ISRAEL

LESSON 7

WHY TEACH THIS LESSON?

Today's lesson is one of good news—really great news! Now, it doesn't exactly sound like good news at first. "You are not my people! I am not your God!" This doesn't sound at all like good news. Israel, who had been God's people, was judged unworthy. God was separating himself from her.

But then comes the good news: this separation did not need to be permanent. Israel could and would be restored. They would be God's people again. That's the good news.

The really great news is that all those who were not God's people—the Gentiles, you and I—can also be God's people. That's a piece of news that you just can't ignore.

INTRODUCTION

A. BLASTED INTO USEFULNESS

Several years ago my family and I stood on the bank of the Saint Lawrence River and watched great ocean freighters lock through the Saint Lawrence Seaway. Across the river we could see Canada and the city of Montreal, but we did not see a single ship on the river. At this point the river, while it was quite wide, was too swift and shallow for navigation.

"Why," asked one of our children, "can the big ships go through here but not on the river?"

"Blasting," was my reply. "Blasting a channel through solid rock by using tons of dynamite. It was a long, hard job, but it was the only way the river could be made navigable. It had to be blasted into usefulness."

Hosea may have been a thoughtful, sensitive person even before God called him to be a prophet. Yet for him to be effective in carrying out his ministry, it was necessary for God to deepen his sensitivity. Thus God used Hosea's personal tragedy of a broken marriage, painful though it was, as a means of making him a more compassionate and insightful prophet. In effect, Hosea was blasted into usefulness.

B. LESSON BACKGROUND

Like Amos, Hosea's ministry was to Israel (the northern kingdom); but unlike Amos, who was from Judah (the southern kingdom), Hosea was most likely from Israel. Like Amos, Hosea prophesied during the reign of Jeroboam II, who ruled Israel from 793 to 753 B.C. (Hosea 1:1; Amos 1:1). Unlike Amos, Hosea is described as prophesying during the reigns of four kings of Judah—Uzziah, Jotham, Ahaz, and Hezekiah (Hosea 1:1). This means that Hosea's ministry probably lasted into the final quarter of the eighth century B.C. If so, he may well have witnessed the fall of the northern kingdom to Assyria in 722 B.C. (which Amos may not have). Since the only king of Judah that Amos mentions is Uzziah (Amos 1:1), Hosea was probably a younger contemporary of Amos. He was also a contemporary of the prophets Isaiah and Micah.

DEVOTIONAL READING:
PSALM 100

BACKGROUND SCRIPTURE:
HOSEA 1, 2

PRINTED TEXT:
HOSEA 1:2—2:4

LESSON AIMS

After this lesson each student will be able to:

1. Tell how Hosea's marriage to an unfaithful wife illustrates God's love for his people, even when they are unfaithful.

2. Suggest how Christians may be tempted toward spiritual infidelity even as Israel was.

3. Offer a prayer of repentance for past infidelities to the Lord.

Jul
15

KEY VERSE

Yet I will show love to the house of Judah; and I will save them . . . by the LORD their God.
—Hosea 1:7

LESSON 7 NOTES

I. AN UNUSUAL MARRIAGE (HOSEA 1:2-9)

A. CHOICE OF A WIFE (vv. 2, 3a)

2. When the LORD began to speak through Hosea, the LORD said to him, "Go, take to yourself an adulterous wife and children of unfaithfulness, because the land is guilty of the vilest adultery in departing from the LORD."

It was noted during the studies from Amos (lesson 5, page 377) that Israel experienced great prosperity during the reign of Jeroboam II. Spiritually and morally, however, the nation was undergoing a serious decline. *To speak* the word of *the Lord* during such times required someone specially prepared for the heartbreak of scorn and rejection. God was about to guide Hosea through such a period of preparation.

The command to *take . . . an adulterous wife* seems shocking, even inconceivable, to us. As a result, some students take this incident as a vision or an allegory rather than the record of actual events. However, no mention is made of a dream or vision; and the fact that the woman's name (Gomer) has no allegorical significance seems to rule out this approach.

Although Gomer was described as *an adulterous wife,* this does not necessarily mean that she was an immoral woman when Hosea married her. It may be a description of what she became through the influence of the sexually promiscuous society in which she lived. While faithful to Hosea at the beginning of their marriage, eventually Gomer yielded to the temptations surrounding her and turned to a life of immorality. The phrase *an adulterous wife* thus warned Hosea of the heartache that lay ahead for him.

The reason given for Hosea's marriage—*because the land is guilty of the vilest adultery in departing from the Lord*—fits well with the understanding of Hosea and Gomer's relationship described in the previous paragraph. Just as Israel began as God's faithful people, then departed from his way, so did Gomer begin as a faithful wife to her husband Hosea, only to "depart" from him to pursue other lovers.

The reference to *children of unfaithfulness* seems to indicate that the children born following Hosea and Gomer's marriage would follow the sordid lifestyle of their mother, not the righteous lifestyle of their father. This would have been as painful for Hosea to see as was the adulterous activity of his wife.

3a. So he married Gomer daughter of Diblaim.

Even though Hosea may have had serious reservations about God's command, he obeyed without voicing these—an indication that God had selected the right man for this very unusual and demanding task.

B. BIRTH OF A SON (vv. 3b-5)

3b. . . . and she conceived and bore him a son.

The text makes it clear (by saying *bore him a son*) that this first child was the child of Hosea and not the child of an illicit relationship.

4. Then the LORD said to Hosea, "Call him Jezreel, because I will soon punish the house of Jehu for the massacre at Jezreel, and I will put an end to the kingdom of Israel.

God chose the name for the son, *Jezreel,* which means "God sows" or "scatters." This was also the name of a city located south and west of the Sea of Galilee, overlooking the valley of Jezreel. Approximately a hundred years earlier Jezreel had been the scene of Jehu's *massacre* of Jezebel and the house of Ahab (2 Kings 9:30-37; 10:1-7, 11). Following these actions, *Jehu* had attempted to bring about a religious reform by carrying out a bloody purge of the followers of Baal (2 Kings 10:18-28). God rewarded Jehu's efforts by declaring that four generations

---

WHAT DO YOU THINK?

Gomer was certainly a spiritual mismatch for one of God's prophets. More importantly, she represented the spiritual misfits of the day. What social practices of today are "out of step" with God's call and damaging to spiritual health? How can we take a positive stand for the biblical view of morality in a way that is winsome and credible, a way that will have some influence with others?

WHAT DO YOU THINK?

The lesson writer observes that Hosea obeyed the Lord in spite of any reservations he may have had about God's command. What have you done in spite of personal reservations simply because you believed it was the right thing to do? How has God blessed you for that?

of his descendants would reign on the throne of Israel, though God was not pleased with the excessive amount of blood shed nor with Jehu's failure to keep his law faithfully (10:30, 31). As a result, a punishment similar to the one that had befallen Ahab's house awaited *the house of Jehu.*

In 753 B.C. Jeroboam died. He was succeeded by his son Zechariah, who was assassinated within six months, thus ending the rule of the fourth generation (2 Kings 15:8-12). Only some thirty years remained until the destruction of *the kingdom of Israel* in 722 B.C.

5. *"In that day I will break Israel's bow in the Valley of Jezreel."*

Israel's bow represented Israel's might. Following the death of Jeroboam II, Israel never again regained her military strength. Certain portions of the land such as the *Valley of Jezreel* (to the north of the city of Jezreel) fell prey to the Assyrians in 733 B.C., several years before Israel itself fell.

C. BIRTH OF A DAUGHTER (vv. 6, 7)

6. *Gomer conceived again and gave birth to a daughter. Then the LORD said to Hosea, "Call her Lo-Ruhamah, for I will no longer show love to the house of Israel, that I should at all forgive them.*

Hosea's second child was *a daughter,* who also was given an unusual name— *Lo-Ruhamah,* which means "not pitied" or "no mercy." Commentators have noted that this child is not said to have been born to Hosea, unlike Jezreel (v. 3, she "bore *him* a son"). This may indicate that this second child was born through an illicit relationship, thus marking the beginning of Gomer's adultery.

The message behind the name Lo-Ruhamah was closely tied to that of Jezreel, for both signified God's judgment upon *the house of Israel.* Israel's repeated rejection of God and his covenant had exhausted his patience. *No longer* would they be shown *love.*

GOD'S "LAST NERVE"

Sometimes a parent who is running out of patience with his or her young children is heard to say, "You kids are getting on my last nerve!" Unless the children's behavior improves, some form of punishment usually will follow—especially after Dad's or Mom's last nerve has "snapped." Even the most kind and loving parents occasionally exhaust every last shred of patience; then justice is administered swiftly, and often painfully, upon strong-willed children who disregard clear instructions and ample warnings.

Israel had become a childish nation. She had been privileged to experience God's love and care in many unique ways. His covenant commandments were unmistakably clear. Yet the "chosen nation" repeatedly rebelled and disobeyed, in spite of God's warnings about such behavior. Finally the people got on "God's last nerve." The message came through Hosea: "I will no longer show love to the house of Israel, that I should at all forgive them."

The parallels to our contemporary moral and spiritual bankruptcy are sobering, to say the least. Will our nation be wise enough to learn from the lessons of history? Such wisdom begins with fearing the Lord. Our Father's patience does have limits. —R. W. B.

7. *"Yet I will show love to the house of Judah; and I will save them—not by bow, sword or battle, or by horses and horsemen, but by the LORD their God."*

Although Judah had followed Israel into idolatry and apostasy, she had not fallen so far that her situation was beyond God's *love.* Nearly twenty years after the destruction of the northern kingdom, Judah, like Israel, felt the wrath of Assyria at its very doorstep. But then *the Lord their God,* without using any of the

The Poster Children for Israel

Display visual 7 at the beginning of your class time today. It pictures the three children of Hosea's wife and their very significant names.

WHAT DO YOU THINK?

God said that he would judge Israel, but Judah would be spared. Their deliverance would come, not by their own strength, "but by the Lord their God." What lessons, if any, do you think that has for us today?

usual weapons of war, destroyed the entire Assyrian army and spared his people and his city (2 Kings 19:32-37).

D. Birth of a Second Son (vv. 8, 9)

8, 9. *After she had weaned Lo-Ruhamah, Gomer had another son. Then the Lord said, "Call him Lo-Ammi, for you are not my people, and I am not your God.*

Since mothers in the ancient Near East nursed their children up to three years, this amount of time probably had lapsed between the birth of the daughter and the birth of the second *son*. Again, note that this child is not described as born to Hosea.

This son's name, *Lo-Ammi*, meant *not my people*. God's explanation for this name amounted to a reversal of his earlier promise that Israel would be his people and that he would be their God (Leviticus 26:12). However, as the following verses indicate, this was not God's final word on the matter. Just as his promise could be reversed, so could his judgment.

II. PROMISE OF BETTER TIMES (HOSEA 1:10—2:1)

A. God's People Multiplied (v. 10)

10. "*Yet the Israelites will be like the sand on the seashore, which cannot be measured or counted. In the place where it was said to them, 'You are not my people,' they will be called 'sons of the living God.'*

Verses 10 and 11 mark a sharp break with the previous verses, which had been filled with gloom and impending judgment. Hosea's inspired vision saw beyond the destruction of his people to a day when they would *be like the sand on the seashore, which cannot be measured or counted*. Though once rejected and shown no love (v. 6), they would again be called *sons of the living God*. This may refer to the time when some of the descendants of those taken captive in 722 B.C., along with some of the refugees from Judah, were able to return from their captivity in 538 B.C. and make the promised land their home.

Note, however, Paul's quotation of this passage in Romans 9:26. Here the apostle sees Hosea's promise as embracing not just the physical descendants of Abraham, but his spiritual seed as well—Christians, who by faith are considered children of Abraham (Galatians 3:6-9). This makes the reference to the sand of the seashore significant, for it is reminiscent of the promise God made to Abraham concerning his descendants (Genesis 22:15-18).

B. God's People United (1:11; 2:1)

11. "*The people of Judah and the people of Israel will be reunited, and they will appoint one leader and will come up out of the land, for great will be the day of Jezreel.*

Hosea also described the day when *Judah* and *Israel*, divided for some two hundred years at the time of his ministry, would once more be *reunited* under *one leader* and would *come up out of the land*. Some suggest that his words were fulfilled when Cyrus the Great conquered the Babylonian Empire and issued a decree allowing the Jewish captives who chose to do so to leave the land of their captivity and return to their homeland (Ezra 1:1-4).

But the return from captivity in Babylon is but a shadow of the full implications of this passage. Like the previous verse, it should be viewed as a messianic prophecy looking forward to the coming of Christ. Only then will the unity described in this verse come to pass, as individuals from both Judah and Israel (along with Gentile believers) are brought together in the church under *one leader*, Jesus Christ, to make up the "Israel of God" (Galatians 6:16).

What Do You Think?

God cited several blessings that would come when those who were formerly not his people could be called the "sons of the living God." Paul cites this passage in Romans 9:26, and Peter alludes to it in 1 Peter 2:10. What blessings have you experienced since becoming a part of the people of God? What blessings do you imagine we would see if a large majority of our nation turned to the Lord?

The verse concludes with the promise that *great will be the day of Jezreel.* Earlier Jezreel was described as a place associated with Israel's punishment (Hosea 1:4, 5). Now, however, the situation is reversed, and Jezreel becomes a place of blessing. The name Jezreel ("God scatters" or "sows") takes on a positive meaning in this verse, as God "scatters" the people, not in judgment as before, but in a sowing that will result in abundant growth.

IRON HANDS/VELVET GLOVES

Parenting may be the most difficult job in the world. One of its biggest challenges involves administering discipline. Even permissive parents realize sooner or later that children need to be punished in some manner. The hard part is balancing justice with mercy.

Our Father in Heaven is a master of loving discipline. In fact, "the Lord disciplines those he loves" (Hebrews 12:6); and it really does "hurt him more" when he punishes his children. Israel had to be chastened severely, yet even with Hosea's prophecy of imminent punishment came the additional promise of God's merciful plan to bring his people together—a plan that came to pass under the saving lordship of Jesus Christ.

Our God is indeed an awesome God—perfectly just, yet full of compassion. His love is often tough, but his "iron hands" are clothed with "velvet gloves." His mercy is everlasting.   —R. W. B.

2:1. "Say of your brothers, 'My people,' and of your sisters, 'My loved one.'

Having just promised better times for God's people, Hosea was told to remove the *Lo* that had prefixed the names of his children. *Lo* is the Hebrew word for "not"; thus the names reflected the brighter future ahead. (*Ammi* means "my people"; *Ruhamah* means "receiving mercy.") Those who are part of God's people under the New Covenant will recognize each other as *brothers* and as *sisters* on the basis of the mercy of God that all have experienced.

Later in this chapter Hosea reiterates these promises by using the names of the three children (vv. 22, 23). Peter used similar language when he described what God has done for all those who were formerly excluded from the people of God but who, through Jesus, are now included (1 Peter 2:10).

III. HEARTBREAK OF SIN (HOSEA 2:2-4)

A. MARRIAGE VOWS BROKEN (v. 2)

2. "Rebuke your mother, rebuke her,
    for she is not my wife,
    and I am not her husband.
Let her remove the adulterous look from her face
    and the unfaithfulness from between her breasts.

In spite of Hosea's words concerning the glorious future that lay ahead for God's people, the prophet had to confront the painful reality of the present situation involving his wayward wife. Hosea's children were asked to *rebuke* their *mother* (Gomer), for by this time she had left Hosea to live a life of immorality. Perhaps Hosea himself had tried and failed to win her back. Failing in this effort, he had declared the marriage covenant broken: *she is not my wife, and I am not her husband.*

Hosea's children were to beg their mother to *remove the adulterous look from her face and the unfaithfulness from between her breasts.* This seems to describe the seductive adornment by which Gomer attracted her partners. It was not enough for her simply to leave a life of adultery; she had to leave behind anything that was associated with that lifestyle and that might tempt her to return to it.

HOW TO SAY IT

Ahab. AY-hab.
Ahaz. AY-haz.
Ammi. AM-my.
Assyrian. Uh-SEAR-ee-un.
Baal. BAY-ul.
Babylonian. Bab-uh-LOW-nee-un.
Cyrus. SIGH-russ.
Diblaim. Dib-LAY-im.
Gomer. GO-mer.
Hezekiah. Hez-ih-KYE-uh.
Hosea. Ho-ZAY-uh.
Isaiah. Eye-ZAY-uh.
Jehu. JAY-hew.
Jeroboam. Jair-uh-BO-um.
Jezebel. JEZ-uh-bel.
Jezreel. JEZ-ree-el or JEZ-reel.
Jotham. JO-thum.
Lo-Ammi. Lo-AM-my.
Lo-Ruhamah. LO-roo-HAH-muh.
Micah. MY-kuh.
Ruhamah. Roo-HAH-muh.
Uzziah. Uh-ZYE-uh.
Zechariah. Zek-uh-RYE-uh.

PRAYER

O holy God, we pray that you will give us the strength and the understanding to speak to our times. Hold back your judgment upon us—a judgment that we clearly deserve—and grant your mercy that we may yet repent and turn to you. In your Son's name we pray. Amen.

THOUGHT TO REMEMBER

Both an unfaithful person and an unfaithful nation will eventually experience the wrath of God.

B. INFIDELITY PUNISHED (vv. 3, 4)

3. "Otherwise I will strip her naked
      and make her as bare as on the day she was born;
    I will make her like a desert,
      turn her into a parched land,
      and slay her with thirst.

A husband was responsible to provide clothes and other needs for his wife (Exodus 21:10). Hosea, the betrayed husband, was prepared to take away all the gifts of clothing and other adornments that he had showered on his wife. In the same way, God (the betrayed "husband" of Israel) would *strip* Israel of all the blessings he had provided for her in such abundance.

The phrase *as the day she was born* probably refers to the time when Israel was enslaved in Egypt and was called to be God's "holy nation" (Exodus 19:6). At that time she was as *naked* and helpless as a newborn baby.

Hosea then used another word picture to depict Israel's desolate condition resulting from her punishment—a *desert* and a *parched land*. This comparison reminded the Israelites of the nation's forty years of wandering in the wilderness after the exodus. Unless Israel repented of her wicked ways and returned to the Lord, she would revert to a condition similar to the desperation of those days. At that time God had provided water in the desert, but this time he would *slay her with thirst.*

4. "I will not show my love to her children,
      because they are the children of adultery."

One of the great tragedies of sin is its impact upon the children of those who become caught in its deadly snare. The *children* of Gomer would become known as *children of adultery*—participants in the same shameful acts as their mother. They would experience the judgment of God upon the northern kingdom, which was just a few years away.

CONCLUSION

Hosea had to cope with a double tragedy—the infidelity of his wife and the moral collapse of his nation. When did Hosea first realize that Gomer was unfaithful to him? Did some of her actions arouse suspicions that he ignored at first, refusing to believe that his beloved had betrayed him? Or did the realization come suddenly, on the day she left home to pursue openly her adulterous activities? Although we are spared the sordid details of Hosea's broken marriage, we are aware of enough broken homes and marriages to understand the situation.

When did Hosea first realize that Israel was guilty of spiritual infidelity in her relations with the Lord? Perhaps he realized, long before his prophetic ministry began, the moral decadence into which Israel had fallen. He may have spoken out occasionally against many of the actions that he knew were wrong. Yet he was not ready to speak with authority until God called him to his unique ministry.

Suppose Hosea were to return today. He would not need the eyes of a divinely inspired prophet to see that our nation is trapped in the quicksand of depravity. If we continue on this course, our judgment will be as certain as that of ancient Israel.

Hosea certainly did not enjoy being a prophet of gloom and doom, yet that was the message he had to deliver to Israel. In the same way, most of us do not enjoy being the bearers of bad tidings. Yet if we are to fulfill our responsibilities as Christian parents and leaders, we must speak out and do so in no uncertain terms. We must call out for integrity and justice in high places, marketplaces, and remote places.

WHAT DO YOU THINK?

In Hosea 2:3, 4 the prophet metaphorically described the results of Gomer's unfaithfulness. What are some of the results that can be expected when God's people turn their backs on him?

DAILY BIBLE READINGS

Monday, July 9—The Prophet Hosea's Marriage (Hosea 1:1-5)

Tuesday, July 10—The Births of Lo-Ruhamah and Lo-Ammi (Hosea 1:6-9)

Wednesday, July 11—Blessing Followed by Chastisement (Hosea 1:10—2:7)

Thursday, July 12—Israel's Humiliation and Punishment (Hosea 2:8-13)

Friday, July 13—The Lord's Hope for His People (Hosea 2:14-18)

Saturday, July 14—Unfaithful Israel to Be Restored (Hosea 2:19-23)

Sunday, July 15—Invitation to Praise (Psalm 100)

Discovery Learning

*This page contains an alternate lesson plan emphasizing learning activities. Classes
desiring such student involvement will find these suggestions helpful. The next page
is a reproducible activity page to further enhance discovery learning.*

LEARNING GOALS

After this lesson each student will be able to:

1. Tell how Hosea's marriage to an unfaithful wife illustrates God's love for his people, even when they are unfaithful.

2. Suggest how Christians may be tempted toward spiritual infidelity even as Israel was.

3. Offer a prayer of repentance for past infidelities to the Lord.

INTO THE LESSON

If a class member is currently dealing with infidelity in his or her marriage, make adjustments to the lesson plan as needed to be sensitive.

Select two women and three men from among the early arrivals to the classroom to prepare a drama giving a synopsis of Hosea's marriage (Hosea 1:2-8; 3:1-3). They should not use a narrator but dramatize the story in first person. Give them signs to wear. These signs should have the names of Hosea, Gomer, Jezreel, Lo-Ruhamah, and Lo-Ammi on them. Send the group to a hallway, a corner, or another room to make preparations.

While the drama group makes preparations, give the rest of the class copies of the reproducible activity "Infidelity Hurts" from the next page. Allow three or four minutes for the learners to work; then discuss the results. Note that marital infidelity is often used as a metaphor for unfaithfulness to God. Our lesson text is one example.

INTO THE WORD

Begin your Bible study with an explanation of Hosea's background and God's command to him about marriage. Note that Hosea's wife bore three children; then distribute copies of the reproducible activity "God's Judgment on Unfaithful Israel" from the next page. Divide the class into three teams, and ask each team to discover the significance of the name of one of Hosea's children. Provide each team a photocopy of a portion of the lesson commentary as follows: Jezreel team: 1:3b-5; Lo-Ruhamah team: 1:6, 7; Lo-Ammi team: 1:8, 9. After they have finished their work but before they report, ask the drama team to make its presentation. Then ask representatives from the study teams to report on the significance of the children's names.

After these presentations, have a volunteer read aloud Hosea 1:2—2:4. Then deliver a short lecture emphasizing the following points: Israel's unfaithfulness or adultery; the imagery in Hosea's marriage; Israel's fall (see the commentary on 1:5, 6, 8, 9); Judah's hope (see the commentary on 1:7); Israel's hope (see the commentary on 1:10, 11); God's plea (see the commentary on 2:1-4). Help the class members follow the lecture by putting these points on strips of poster board. As you mention each point, tape or fasten the appropriate piece of poster board to the wall.

INTO LIFE

Remind the class that spiritual infidelity is the real theme of this drama in Hosea's life. Draw the class's attention back to the questions discussed in the lesson Introduction. Ask the same questions but with an emphasis on unfaithfulness to God.

1. What are some of the causes or reasons for unfaithfulness to God?

2. What is the fallout or damage caused from unfaithfulness to him?

3. Why is reconciliation often difficult? For whom is it most difficult—us or God? Why?

Then tell the groups, "Your task is to warn today's believers about how Christians are tempted to be spiritually unfaithful. How can you do that?" Ask each group to choose one of the following means to communicate the warning and to write or prepare the prophetic message. A group may write a radio announcement, write an e-mail notice to churches, write a description of a video game, or prepare a poster. If time does not permit this activity, simply ask these discussion questions: "What are some of the ways Satan tempts contemporary Christians to be spiritually unfaithful? What do you think are some of his favorite and most effective tools?"

Ask, "What can our Sunday school class do to encourage Christians to remain faithful?" List the answers on poster board.

Then ask the class to let this lesson become very personal. All of us have been unfaithful to our Heavenly Father at times. Otherwise we wouldn't need a Savior. Give each class member a three-by-five card. As they reflect on their sins, they are to write a prayer of repentance. The prayer should start with these words: "I am sorry, Lord, because. . . ." They should also write their gratitude for God's grace. Begin this part of the prayer with "I thank you, Lord, for. . . ."

God's Judgment on Unfaithful Israel

God sent a message to Israel by choosing names that had special significance. Write in the speech bubbles below what message you think God was sending Israel through these names. The meaning of the names is in parentheses.

Infidelity Hurts

Unfaithfulness seriously damages a marriage, and it damages our relationship with God. What are the causes of marital infidelity?

What preventive measures can a person take to protect his or her marriage from infidelity?

What are some of the consequences of infidelity . . .

To one's spouse?

To God?

What makes reconciliation so difficult after infidelity? What can be done to make it easier?

GOD'S COMPASSION FOR ISRAEL

LESSON 8

WHY TEACH THIS LESSON?

This lesson contains one of the most moving pictures of God in all of Scripture. God the Holy One must punish sin, but God the Heavenly Father hates to see his children suffer. The emotional turmoil in God's own heart is something we often fail to consider. If we will consider it, however, we will better appreciate the depth of God's love for us.

It is said that some people fail to appreciate the concept of God as our Father because their own fathers were abusive or absent from their lives. For that reason, some have argued against using the Father image. Much better is it to redefine the Father image for such ones. This lesson will go a long way toward defining it properly.

INTRODUCTION

A. WHOSE HAND IS ON THE WHEEL?

Years ago, when I was about six or seven, I went for a ride with my father in the family car. After a while Dad said to me, "Would you like to drive, Son?" Of course, like any boy my age, I wanted to drive; so I climbed onto Dad's lap and grabbed the steering wheel. Under my guidance the car veered first to the right and then to the left, but somehow it managed to stay on the street and even to stop at a corner.

During my drive I saw a friend standing on the sidewalk beside the street. I shouted, "Look at me—I'm driving!" Later, he questioned whether I was really driving. "Sure I was," I answered. "Didn't you see me holding the steering wheel?"

In reality, of course, it was my father's strong arms that handled the steering wheel. It was his steady feet that controlled the brake, the clutch, and the accelerator. I was like the Israelites in Hosea's day, who thought that all the blessings they had received had come through their own efforts. They had forgotten, to their shame, that God was the one who had provided all those blessings.

B. LESSON BACKGROUND

In last week's study we noted that Hosea was called to his prophetic ministry at a time when Israel was experiencing great prosperity. We also saw how God used the tragedy of Hosea's broken marriage to illustrate his love for Israel. In spite of Gomer's infidelity, Hosea later attempted to rescue her from the slavery that her prostitution had brought upon her (Hosea 3:1-3). This painful series of events helped Hosea gain a deeper understanding of God's love for Israel—a nation that had committed spiritual prostitution by spurning God's love and pursuing the gods of her pagan neighbors.

DEVOTIONAL READING:
PSALM 103:8-14

BACKGROUND SCRIPTURE:
HOSEA 11

PRINTED TEXT:
HOSEA 11:1-9

LESSON AIMS

After participating in this lesson, each student should be able to:

1. Summarize Hosea's message of God's compassion for his people.

Jul
22

2. Tell how God's words and actions toward Israel modeled those of a loving parent.

3. Give thanks for the stubborn, steadfast love of our heavenly Father.

KEY VERSE

I led them with cords of human kindness, with ties of love; I lifted the yoke from their neck and bent down to feed them.
—Hosea 11:4

LESSON 8 NOTES

While Hosea reminded God's people of his love for them, he also had to warn them of coming judgment, which would be executed through the conquering armies of Assyria. Yet those warnings were also indicators of God's love, for he was encouraging the people to repent and return to him so that they could be spared that judgment.

I. HISTORY OF GOD'S LOVE (HOSEA 11:1-4)

A. LOVE EXTENDED (v. 1)

1. *"When Israel was a child, I loved him,*
and out of Egypt I called my son.

WHAT DO YOU THINK?

Hosea called on the people to remember their roots and their relationship to God as children. What would remind us of how God has changed us and how we need to depend on him?

Old Testament history includes frequent references to Israel's bondage in Egypt and to the glorious deliverance that God accomplished through the exodus. These references were a way of reminding the people of God's mercy toward them and of their responsibility to obey him (1 Samuel 12:6-8; Nehemiah 9:6-9; Psalm 78:12-55; Jeremiah 7:21-26; Daniel 9:15). Often they describe the exodus in terms of the mighty power that God demonstrated. Here Hosea uses it as an illustration of how much God *loved* his people.

The reference to *Israel* as a *child* seems to call attention to the fact that the Egyptian bondage occurred at a time when Israel was just beginning to develop as a nation. Hosea may also have desired to picture God's people being as helpless as children, totally unable to free themselves from their slavery. Like little children, they could not defend themselves. But when they "cried . . . because of their slavery," God "heard their groaning" (Exodus 2:23, 24) and came to their rescue. Just as a newborn child needs extra care, so did the nation of Israel in her infancy.

Out of Egypt I called my son. God instructed Moses to say to Pharaoh, "Israel is my firstborn son, and I told you, 'Let my son go, so he may worship me'" (Exodus 4:22, 23). Matthew says this prophecy was fulfilled again when Joseph and Mary took the child Jesus to Egypt and remained there until after the death of Herod (Matthew 2:13-15).

B. LOVE REJECTED (v. 2)

2. *"But the more I called Israel,*
the further they went from me.
They sacrificed to the Baals
and they burned incense to images.

Whereas Israel's departure from God was illustrated earlier by a wayward wife, here it is illustrated by a wayward son. *The more I called Israel, the further they went from me.* Many times God had appealed to his people through the prophets. Yet they rejected those messengers just as callously as they had forgotten their deliverance from Egypt. "For many years you were patient with them. By your Spirit you admonished them through your prophets. Yet they paid no attention" (Nehemiah 9:30).

"I drew them with cords of a man, with bands of love."
Hosea 11:4

The visual for today's lesson pictures a tender scene of a father walking with his child. Display it at the beginning of your session.

While the Israelites were in Egypt, they may have been tempted to serve some of the Egyptian gods; but once they entered Canaan, they were enticed by the Canaanite deities—here described as the *Baals*. Baal was considered the head of the Canaanite gods and was worshiped as the source of fertility and productivity. Because Palestine received minimal rainfall, its pagan inhabitants considered it important to appease a fertility god like Baal to insure good crops and families with many children. The fertility rites in which worshipers of Baal participated often involved immoral activity with sacred prostitutes. Some of this also involved burning *incense to images.* This was a clear violation of the Second Commandment (Exodus 20:4).

C. LOVE LIKE A PARENT'S (vv. 3, 4)

3a. "It was I who taught Ephraim to walk,
    taking them by the arms.

Ephraim and Manasseh were sons of Joseph. Ephraim had received a special blessing from his grandfather, Jacob (Genesis 48:5-22), and the tribe of Ephraim came to occupy a position of prominence when the Israelites reached the promised land. When the kingdom became divided, Jeroboam, who was from the tribe of Ephraim (1 Kings 11:26), became king of the northern kingdom (Israel). Perhaps for that reason Ephraim appears to have been acknowledged as the leading tribe of the north. The designation *Ephraim* is often applied to the entire northern kingdom, as in this verse and throughout Hosea.

Hosea depicts a parent teaching a child *to walk*. Parents tend to be very protective during the early stages of their children's development. They watch their young ones carefully as they pull themselves up and take a few hesitating steps while hanging on to the crib railing or a chair. From time to time the parents offer them a hand and help them take a few awkward steps. Finally, when they take those steps without any help or support, the parents express their approval and support with enthusiasm. What a wonderful picture of the care and patience of our loving God!

3b. "but they did not realize
    it was I who healed them.

Even today, with all of our miracle drugs, little children sometimes become desperately ill. During those anxious times the parents keep a constant watch over their little ones, trying to soothe their pain and provide whatever comfort they can. Every other concern becomes secondary to that of nursing the children back to health. This is a beautiful description of God's love for Israel, as well as his compassion for us.

Note, however, how God's people responded to his concern. Usually when children fall and cut or bruise themselves, they know they can turn to their parents for help, for experience has taught them to do so. But the Israelites seemed completely oblivious to all that God had done for them and treated his kindness toward them with contempt.

4. "I led them with cords of human kindness,
    with ties of love;
    I lifted the yoke from their neck
    and bent down to feed them.

Here Hosea uses yet another word picture to illustrate God's love for his people. He compares God's dealings with Israel with those of a farmer with one of his animals. The portrayal of those who *lifted the yoke from their neck* may describe how a farmer removed the heavy wooden yoke from around the face of an animal (such as an ox) so that the animal could eat more easily. It may also picture what took place at the end of a day when the animal's work was done. Thus had God dealt gently with his people. He had not forced affection from them, but *led them with cords of human kindness*.

And bent down to feed them. Mealtime (or the end of a day) brought, not only relief from the burden of the yoke, but also food.

II. HEARTBREAK OF GOD'S LOVE (HOSEA 11:5-9)

A. ISRAEL'S PUNISHMENT (vv. 5, 6)

5. "Will they not return to Egypt
    and will not Assyria rule over them
    because they refuse to repent?

WHAT DO YOU THINK?

In Hosea 11:3 is a beautiful illustration of God's guiding Ephraim as a parent teaches a child how to walk. What help do we need from God as we learn to walk in his ways?

WHAT DO YOU THINK?

The picture of God dealing with Israel as a kind farmer cares for his animals is very similar to the familiar shepherd metaphor (Psalm 23; John 10). What other word pictures can you think of to describe God's care for his people? What makes these images significant to you?

Hosea turned rather abruptly from speaking of God's love to declaring God's judgment. *Will they not return to Egypt?* Hosea had stated previously that the people would return to Egypt (Hosea 8:13; 9:3). Apparently he was speaking figuratively, using the Israelites' experience in Egypt to represent the nation's future bondage to Assyria. Some students believe that the mention of Egypt is a reference to Israel's attempts to ally itself with Egypt in order to gain assistance in its struggle against Assyria. These attempts were part of the reason that the Assyrians eventually invaded Israel and destroyed Samaria (2 Kings 17:3-6). If that understanding is correct, then Hosea was predicting that those attempts would fail.

At that point *Assyria* would *rule over* Israel. Approximately a century earlier the Assyrian ruler Shalmaneser III had traveled westward and forced Jehu, king of Israel, to pay him tribute. But then Assyrian power waned. By the time Jeroboam II was king, Israel found itself free of the threat of Assyrian interference and enjoyed a period of significant prosperity. That prosperity would come to a bitter end when the revitalized Assyrians returned westward with a renewed military might that was virtually impossible to withstand.

The reason for this tragic turn of events was really quite simple: the people had refused *to repent.* Their continual rejection of God and his covenant, in spite of frequent warnings, could result only in their receiving his punishment.

NOT SLOW, BUT PATIENT

Parents who threaten misbehaving children with repeated ultimatums, yet never follow through with punishment, are training their offspring to ignore all disciplinary warnings. They are creating individuals who will learn how to disregard authority and flaunt disobedience, and whose actions will come to have far more serious consequences for society. Such methods are unhealthy and destructive, and they certainly do the children no favors.

God's warnings to Israel were not empty threats. He always means what he says and says what he means. And though God takes no delight in the punishment of his beloved children (Ezekiel 33:11), he does chasten all whom he loves (Hebrews 12:6).

That God's punishment is not always immediate has sometimes been misunderstood as indifference on his part. Backsliders in Hosea's day allowed themselves to be lulled into complacency. They were lured into sinful unfaithfulness by what seemed to them an absence of retribution for their transgressions. Like the scoffers described by Peter (2 Peter 3:3, 4), they thought, "Nothing has changed; we see no reason to worry or to repent." Skeptics of our day also doubt that they will ever have to pay the "wages of sin."

But make no mistake—"payday" will come! The unrepentant and the unforgiven "will be punished with everlasting destruction and shut out from the presence of the Lord" (2 Thessalonians 1:9). Remember, however, that this is not how God wants to treat us. He "is patient . . . not wanting anyone to perish, but everyone to come to repentance" (2 Peter 3:9).   —R. W. B.

6. *"Swords will flash in their cities,*
      will destroy the bars of their gates
      and put an end to their plans.

The Israelites may have believed that they would be safe inside Samaria and their other fortified *cities;* but no walls would be able to protect them from the devastation of the coming Assyrian onslaught. *The bars of* the *gates* (an important part of any city's defenses) would be broken, and the *swords* would *flash* inside the cities as enemy soldiers broke through. Eventually Samaria itself fell, following a three-year siege (2 Kings 17:5). Assyrian records from this time note that approximately thirty thousand Israelites were carried into captivity. Whatever *plans* the people had devised to counter the Assyrian menace proved worthless.

B. ISRAEL'S BACKSLIDING (v. 7)

7. "My people are determined to turn from me.
    Even if they call to the Most High,
    he will by no means exalt them.

The phrase *determined to turn from me* pictures *people* who are stubbornly moving away from God. The Israelites' rebellion against God was not an uncommon or infrequent action; it was an established pattern of behavior. Tragically, they had reached a point where their cries to God would no longer be heard: *even if they call to the Most High, he will by no means exalt them.* The nation was ripe for judgment.

C. GOD'S STUBBORN LOVE (vv. 8, 9)

8. "How can I give you up, Ephraim?
    How can I hand you over, Israel?
    How can I treat you like Admah?
    How can I make you like Zeboiim?
    My heart is changed within me;
    all my compassion is aroused.

Yet again God expressed his never-dying love for his people, in spite of their ongoing rebellion against him. If God administered the judgment they deserved, they would be utterly destroyed, as were *Admah* and *Zeboiim*. These two cities were located in the Valley of Siddim at the southern end of the Dead Sea (Genesis 10:19; 14:2, 3). Because of their sinfulness, they were destroyed along with Sodom and Gomorrah in the time of Lot (Deuteronomy 29:23). If the Israelites remembered their history, they realized that these cities had been destroyed without leaving a trace. It should have served as a grim reminder of the punishment that lay in store for them, unless they repented of their rebellion.

That God's *heart is changed* (literally, "turned") *within* him suggested the inward turmoil he was experiencing because his righteousness required him to punish his people, yet his *compassion* made him reluctant to do so. It is not unlike the feeling a loving parent experiences when he realizes that a child must be punished for a particular action and that there is no alternative.

9. "I will not carry out my fierce anger,
    nor will I turn and devastate Ephraim.
    For I am God, and not man—
    the Holy One among you.
    I will not come in wrath.

Because of his compassion, God would not utterly *devastate Ephraim*. God's mercy would prevail over his justice. God is *not man*, who, in a similar situation of being betrayed, might completely unleash his anger upon his offender. Though betrayed by his people, God would not give up on them. He declared, *I will not come in wrath*—for the purpose of bringing complete destruction.

In the verses that follow, Hosea allows a gleam of hope to penetrate the desolation in Israel's immediate future. The people would indeed suffer under the heavy hand of Assyrian oppression and be carried into captivity; yet the time would come when the Lord would "settle them in their homes" (Hosea 11:10, 11).

WHAT DO YOU THINK?

To be both tender and tough as we handle our children causes us inner turmoil. See how it affected God (verses 8 and 9). What happens to church leaders when they are called upon to discipline a disobedient child of God? (It may be possible to think of specific examples.)

PRAYER

O God, we pray that we will humbly receive from this ancient prophet the message you have for us. Like Hosea, may we surrender our lives to you so that we can share that message with others. Thank you for your steadfast love. In our Lord's name we pray. Amen.

THOUGHT TO REMEMBER

"The Lord disciplines those he loves" (Hebrews 12:6).

CONCLUSION

A. A BACKSLIDING NATION

God used his miracle-working power to free the Hebrew people from bondage in Egypt. He guided them through the wilderness—an experience that should have lasted only a few months but, because of their unbelief (Hebrews 3:16-19), was extended to forty years. He further blessed his people by leading them into the promised land, where they were able to live in houses that they had not built and to enjoy fruit from vines they had not planted. Yet, even as they were enjoying these blessings, they were enticed by pagan gods and repeatedly turned away from the Lord Jehovah.

God did not allow this backsliding to go unpunished. He allowed neighboring peoples to oppress his people. However, before each occurrence of discipline, God sent first the judges and then the prophets to call his people back to him. Hosea was one of the last of these messengers to warn the northern kingdom. The failure of the north to heed his warning led to its destruction within a few years after Hosea conveyed the word of the Lord.

And yet, through all of these failures, there was always a remnant—a handful of the faithful—who gave heed to God's message and did repent. God used this faithful remnant to keep alive the hope of a Messiah who would offer salvation, not only to Israel but to the entire world.

Our nation, like ancient Israel, has become a backsliding nation, forgetting all the blessings God has poured out upon us. By almost every standard that can be applied, our nation has abandoned the values that made us great. Crime, drugs, broken homes, illegitimate births, and abortions give evidence of our decline.

Our nation has no shortage of messengers to call us from our backsliding. From church pulpits and over radio and television come constant appeals to hear and obey the message that can save us. But many have closed their ears, preferring instead to worship at the shrines of our modern Baals—success, affluence, and pleasure.

Is there any hope for our nation, or have we already gone beyond the point of no return? We could very well allow ourselves to become paralyzed by pessimism. It is vital, as we study ancient messengers of God such as Hosea, that we take hope in the fact that God is exceedingly patient in dealing with wayward people. Hosea also shows how God can use a faithful remnant to accomplish his purposes. May we commit ourselves to being a part of that remnant.

B. "THIS IS GOING TO HURT ME"

When we were youngsters and got into trouble that warranted serious punishment, our parents sometimes prefaced their actions with the words: "This is going to hurt me more than it will you." We didn't believe it at the time, and only later, when we had become parents, did we begin to understand what our parents were talking about.

In today's lesson Hosea describes God's "parenting" of his child Israel. He also tells us that, although God had to administer punishment to Israel, he took no pleasure in it. It was going to hurt him more than it did the Israelites.

We often think of God as being high and exalted and quite different from us—and, of course, he is! But he is also a loving Father who feels pain when we turn away from him and who never ceases to love us and long for our return. If our nation is to return to God, it will happen only when a faithful remnant begins to demonstrate through their lives an eagerness to love others and a fervent desire to serve sacrificially so that the Lord's kingdom may grow.

Discovery Learning

This page contains an alternate lesson plan emphasizing learning activities. Classes desiring such student involvement will find these suggestions helpful. The next page is a reproducible activity page to further enhance discovery learning.

LEARNING GOALS

After this lesson each student will be able to:

1. Summarize Hosea's message of God's compassion for his people.

2. Tell how God's words and actions toward Israel modeled those of a loving parent.

3. Give thanks for the stubborn, steadfast love of our heavenly Father.

INTO THE LESSON

Before class, prepare enough slips of paper to tape one to the bottom of every chair in the classroom. Use three colors of paper, one color for each of the following questions. On one-third of the papers write, "When I think of a good parent, _____'s name comes to mind because. . . ." On another third write, "One thing I want from or for my child is _____ because. . . ." On the remaining third write, "I think the most difficult aspect of parenting young children is _____ because. . . ."

Ask each person to reach under his or her seat, remove the slip of paper taped there, and write a response to the statement. Give the students two or three minutes to do this. Then have the learners form groups of three to six people, making sure that at least one person with each of the three questions is included in each group. Allow the group members to share their answers and viewpoints with each other. Then ask a few volunteers to share their responses with the whole class.

Make the transition to Bible study by noting that God uses several different images to describe his relationship with his people. And one of those images, the one that fills our text, is that of a parent.

INTO THE WORD

From last week's lesson, review the story of Hosea's broken marriage and Gomer's infidelity. Explain that this marriage illustrates Israel's infidelity and God's love, which will be important in this lesson as well. Also explain the name "Ephraim" in verse 3. Tell the class that today's text gives the heart of God's message to Israel and packs warnings and encouragements to our nation and churches today.

Put the following outline on a large visual.

1. Two Imageries (rebellious children and farmer caring for one of his animals) (vv. 1-4)

2. Judgment and Punishment (vv. 5, 6)

3. "Determined" Israel (v. 7)

4. God's Stubborn Love (vv. 8, 9)

Ask each group (from the earlier grouping) to paraphrase a portion of the text, using imagery and words easily understood in our culture. Each group should be assigned one of the sections of the outline. A recorder is to write the group's paraphrase on poster board.

After the group reports on verses 1-4, explain "Baals" and emphasize the unfaithful history and continual rebellion of Israel. (See page 402.) After the group shares its paraphrase of verses 5 and 6, use your lesson commentary to tell of Assyria's impact on Israel. After the group reports on verse 7, comment on how the people's disobedience had reached the point where they had become "determined" to turn from the Lord. After the last group offers its paraphrase of verses 8 and 9, emphasize God's compassionate love, in spite of the people's defiant attitude.

INTO LIFE

Ask the class to continue to work in their groups as we apply the lesson to life. Ask the groups to jot down notes about what they think God would say to our nation through the prophet about the following:

1. The prophet's word about our roots and formative years.

2. The prophet's evidences of our unfaithfulness.

3. The prophet's word about God's heartache concerning our nation's unfaithfulness.

4. The prophet's encouraging word to the faithful followers in our nation.

After they complete this task, ask representatives of the groups to share their findings about the issues above.

Distribute copies of the reproducible activity page that follows. Allow time for the students to work; then ask for volunteers to share some of their ideas. Ask, "What issues from our study are matters that you think we should pray about?" Have the learners suggest specific prayer requests for the church, the nation, and for individual believers. Write these on the chalkboard.

When you have three good lists, ask the groups to pray together. Assign one of the lists to each group, and ask each group member to pray concerning one or two of the issues on the group's list. At the end of the class session, encourage the learners to take their lists home and to pray about these matters on a daily basis.

Prophetic Preaching

If God were speaking through Hosea to your country, your church, and to you, what do you think he would say? What specific issues would the prophet challenge?

TO YOUR COUNTRY

What would Hosea say to your nation? What warnings or condemnations would he give? What hope or encouragement?

TO YOUR CHURCH

What would Hosea say to your church? What warnings or condemnations would he give? What hope or encouragement?

TO YOU!

What would Hosea say to you? What warnings or condemnations would he give? What hope or encouragement?

WHAT GOD REQUIRES

LESSON 9

WHY TEACH THIS LESSON?

"What do you *want* from me?" Have you ever said that—or wanted to? Perhaps you had a boss who was never satisfied with the amount of work you did. Perhaps a former friend just will not let go of a wrong you did him, no matter how much you try to do to make it right.

Some of your students may be in situations where they feel they just can't please certain people in their lives. Maybe they even feel that way about God. Today's lesson text provides reassurance. Our key verse sounds much like Jesus' words in Matthew 22:37-40. The entire "Law and the Prophets," Jesus said, can be summed up in two commandments: love God, and love your neighbor. Point out to your students that "Act justly . . . love mercy and . . . walk humbly with your God" really says the same thing!

INTRODUCTION

A. CANINE THEOLOGY

A story is told about a medieval monastery located in a high Alpine pass. This monastery served as a refuge and rescue station for travelers caught in snowstorms in the mountains. The monks had worked many years training their renowned Saint Bernard dogs to aid them in their rescue work.

On one occasion an important church official was visiting the monastery. During his visit a terrible blizzard swept across the mountains, and, as usual, the monks sent out their rescue dogs to search for travelers. Soon the dogs returned with two half-frozen men. When they were revived, it was discovered that they were considered heretics and that they had been caught in the storm as they fled the wrath of the church authorities.

The visiting church official was furious that these men had been rescued. "Why didn't the dogs leave them out there to suffer the fate they deserved?" he stormed.

Finally one of the monks spoke up. "It takes many months to train a dog to do rescue work. We find it impossible to teach them the finer points of theology. All they seem able to learn is mercy."

In a world where religious strife has left many people confused about Christianity, we might be better off if differences could be settled by a "canine theology" that taught mercy before it addressed the finer points of theology.

B. LESSON BACKGROUND

The Scriptures tell us little about the prophet Micah. What we do know about him is found in the first verse of the book of Micah. He was from Moresheth, a small town located about twenty-five or thirty miles southwest of Jerusalem. He prophesied during the reigns of three kings of Judah: Jotham, Ahaz, and Hezekiah, dating him from around 740 B.C. to as late as 690 B.C. This would have made Micah a contemporary of Hosea and Isaiah.

Like Isaiah, Micah's ministry was primarily to Judah, the southern kingdom. As Micah began his ministry, both Judah and Israel were still enjoying the prosperity that they had experienced through much of the first half of the eighth century B.C.

DEVOTIONAL READING:
PROVERBS 21:2, 3
BACKGROUND SCRIPTURE:
MICAH 3; 6:1-8
PRINTED TEXT:
MICAH 3:5-12; 6:3-8

LESSON AIMS

After this lesson your students will be able to:

1. Tell how Micah contrasted the message of false prophets with the true requirements of following the Lord.

2. Explain how people today try to please God in ways other than those prescribed by him.

3. Memorize Micah 6:8, and make it the governing principle of their conduct each day this week.

Jul
29

KEY VERSE

He has showed you, O man, what is good. And what does the LORD require of you? To act justly and to love mercy and to walk humbly with your God.

—Micah 6:8

LESSON 9 NOTES

But these good times would not last. In 745 B.C. Tiglath-Pileser III came to power in Assyria. Under his aggressive leadership, Assyria experienced a resurgence of power, while, at the same time, Israel was becoming increasingly unstable. In 725 B.C. the Assyrians began a siege of Samaria that lasted three years and ended in 722 with the fall of the city and the captivity of thousands of Israel's citizens.

By the end of the eighth century, Jerusalem was also feeling the threat of the Assyrians. But God intervened miraculously, and the city was spared (2 Kings 19:35).

While Micah grew up in a rural area, he was quite aware of the problems that plagued the land—self-serving leaders, greedy priests, counterfeit prophets, and a populace unconcerned about the injustices that were occurring regularly. He was given the thankless task of warning the people of God's wrath if they did not repent and return to God. But Micah was also given a glimpse beyond the dismal state of affairs around him to a time when God would one day bless his people in a marvelous way: "You will again have compassion on us; you will tread our sins underfoot and hurl all our iniquities into the depths of the sea" (Micah 7:19).

I. FALSE PROPHETS (MICAH 3:5-7)

A. THEIR DECEPTIVE MESSAGE (v. 5)

5. *This is what the LORD says:*
> *"As for the prophets*
>   *who lead my people astray,*
> *if one feeds them,*
>   *they proclaim 'peace';*
> *if he does not,*
>   *they prepare to wage war against him.*

WHAT DO YOU THINK?

*The so-called prophets in Micah's day told the people what they **wanted** to hear rather than what they **needed**. Why would they neglect their office so flagrantly? To what degree is this a danger among church leaders today?*

Micah had already brought sharp words of rebuke against the political leaders of God's people—the "leaders of Jacob" and the "rulers of the house of Israel" (Micah 3:1). He would return to them later; now he turned his attention to the religious leaders—in particular, *the prophets who lead my people astray*. The prophets were responsible for monitoring the moral condition of the nation and for holding the political leaders accountable when their actions violated God's standards.

Micah accused the false prophets of prophesying merely for the sake of financial gain. As long as the false prophets were well taken care of, *if one feeds them*, they eagerly spoke words of *peace*, saying exactly what their supporters wanted them to say. If an individual refused to provide anything for them and would not support them, these phony prophets determined *to wage war against him*.

B. THEIR EVENTUAL DESTINY (vv. 6, 7)

6. *"Therefore night will come over you, without visions,*
>   *and darkness, without divination.*
> *The sun will set for the prophets,*
>   *and the day will go dark for them.*

These self-proclaimed *prophets* were really frauds, but they were clever enough to fool many of the people. Micah refused to be intimidated by them: he predicted that the end of their clever schemes was at hand. When the Assyrians eventually entered the northern kingdom and ravaged the land, the false prophets' declaration of peace would be proven empty. No longer would they claim to have a vision, and no more would they practice *divination*. This word refers to the methods of some false prophets, who obtained their messages from the observation of events in nature, such as the flight of birds or the appearance of the entrails of an animal killed in order to discern the will of the gods. Such practices were strictly forbidden by God (Deuteronomy 18:9-14).

7. *"The seers will be ashamed*
    and the diviners disgraced.
 They will all cover their faces
    because there is no answer from God."

    Seers received their messages through dreams or visions from God. In some such manner, Micah "saw" the word of the Lord (Micah 1:1). Those who claimed to have seen such visions but had not (cf. Jeremiah 23:16) would *be ashamed.*

    Diviners, as noted under the previous verse, received their messages by means that God had declared to be unacceptable. Such deceivers would eventually be *disgraced.* They would *all cover their faces,* most likely as an expression of their shame. It would be clear to everyone that God had not spoken through them.

II. MICAH, A TRUE PROPHET (MICAH 3:8-12)

A. DECLARING HIS AUTHORITY (v. 8)

8. *But as for me, I am filled with power,*
    with the Spirit of the LORD,
    and with justice and might,
 to declare to Jacob his transgression,
    to Israel his sin.

    Having swept aside the claims of the false prophets, Micah presented his own credentials. His prophecies did not originate in his imagination, nor were they spoken to make money. Instead, he was *filled with power, with the Spirit of the Lord.*

    No doubt the false prophets made similar claims concerning their authority. Recall lesson 4, in which Zedekiah, a false prophet, asserted that he had just as much of the Spirit of the Lord as God's true prophet Micaiah (1 Kings 22:24). Micaiah said the proof of which prophet spoke the truth would come when the predicted events either came to pass or not (1 Kings 22:25-28). And so it would be in Micah's case. Part of what he predicted (the destruction of Samaria, for example) would come to pass within the lifetime of some of his listeners.

B. CONDEMNING LEADERS (vv. 9-11)

9. *Hear this, you leaders of the house of Jacob,*
    you rulers of the house of Israel,
 who despise justice
    and distort all that is right.

    Having established his credibility, Micah directed attention once more to the *leaders of the house of Jacob* and the *rulers of the house of Israel.* As indicated by verses 10-12, his focus seems to be especially on Jerusalem, also known as Zion.

    The corruption of high officials in government has been occurring as long as there have been governments. Whatever the tactics and whatever the era of history, the results are the same: the principles of *justice* and fairness are perverted.

10. *who build Zion with bloodshed,*
    and Jerusalem with wickedness.

    Micah's indictment of building *Zion with bloodshed* may have been literally true. The resources to build palaces and other imposing buildings in *Jerusalem* may, in some cases, have been gained through violence. It is more likely, however, that Micah was using forceful figurative language. The rich and powerful had used shady business deals and clever legal strategies to exploit the poor and powerless and achieve their desired ends. They did not care who was hurt in the process.

11. *Her leaders judge for a bribe,*
    her priests teach for a price,
    and her prophets tell fortunes for money.

What does the Lord require of me?

To do justly;

to love mercy;

to walk humbly

with Him.

—*from Micah 6:8*

    Today's visual, an attractive representation of Micah 6:8, is one you may want to frame and display at any time in your church building, not just to illustrate this lesson.

How to Say It
Ahaz. AY-haz.
Assyria. Uh-SEAR-ee-uh.
Balaam. BAY-lum.
Balak. BAY-lack.
Beor. BE-or.
Gilgal. GIL-gal.
Hezekiah. Hez-ih-KYE-uh.
Hosea. Ho-ZAY-uh.
Isaiah. Eye-ZAY-uh.
Jeremiah. Jair-uh-MY-uh.
Jericho. JAIR-ih-ko.
Jotham. JO-thum.
Micah. MY-kuh.
Micaiah. My-KAY-uh.
Miriam. MEER-ee-um.
Moab. MO-ab.
Moresheth. MO-resh-eth.
Samaria. Suh-MARE-ee-uh.
Shittim. Shih-TEEM.
Tiglath-Pileser. TIG-lath-Pih-LEE-zer.
Zedekiah. Zed-uh-KYE-uh.

Yet they lean upon the LORD and say,
"Is not the LORD among us?
No disaster will come upon us."

Here Micah targeted his indictment to include those *leaders* who *judge for a bribe*, the *priests* who *teach for a price*, and the *prophets* who *tell fortunes for money*. Corrupt judges were bad enough, but when priests and prophets—God's representatives and spokesmen—participated in the same selfish practices, the impact on the nation was especially devastating. Worse yet, these leaders insisted that *the Lord* was *among* them, giving his blessing to their actions. They believed themselves to be immune from any *disaster* that would indicate the judgment of God.

"No New Sin Under the Sun"

The ancient Persians devised an effective deterrent to judicial corruption. A judge convicted of being influenced by bribes was executed, and his hide was flayed from his body, tanned, and used to upholster the next judge's chair. Sitting on such a seat of judgment reminded successors of the stiff punishment for courtroom dishonesty!

Bribery of public officials seems to be a practice common to every society regardless of time and place. Micah noted that in Judah the "leaders judge for a bribe" (Micah 3:11). Today we often read or hear of similar actions by which elected officials betray the trust that people have placed in them. Such incidents remind us that sin remains essentially the same because the human heart remains the same—"deceitful above all things and beyond cure" (Jeremiah 17:9).

All too often our world wants to address the ills of society by lowering the standards of what is right and wrong. But God's standards don't need any "tinkering." We need to adjust our lives to his standards! —R. W. B.

C. Predicting Judgment (v. 12)

12. Therefore because of you,
Zion will be plowed like a field,
Jerusalem will become a heap of rubble,
the temple hill a mound overgrown with thickets.

This verse gives us a clue about the timing of Micah's prophecy because it is cited in Jeremiah 26:18, 19. There we learn that Hezekiah was king of Judah when Micah spoke these words. That means that Samaria probably had fallen to the Assyrians by this time.

How could the people of Judah ignore the implications of this tragedy for them? Did they think that they could escape a similar punishment without making some drastic changes? The passage in Jeremiah also gives us the good news that they did not ignore Micah's prophecy, but turned to God in repentance. Hezekiah himself led in that repentance, but it apparently did not last. The remainder of our printed text comes from a later portion of Micah, and the prophet once again is pleading with the people to repent.

III. GOD'S CHALLENGE (MICAH 6:3-5)

A. His Question (v. 3)

3. "My people, what have I done to you?
How have I burdened you? Answer me.

Micah 6 begins with God's statement that he was "lodging a charge" against his people (v. 2). The setting is similar to a courtroom scene in which witnesses are called to testify. God calls the mountains and the "everlasting foundations of the earth" to speak. Having been in existence since long before Israel became a nation, they have observed Israel's behavior throughout history. They can testify as to whether God's "charge" was justified.

However, the tone of the words in verse 3 is not that of a condemning Judge. This is a loving Father agonizing over his children gone astray. Judah had received blessing after blessing from God, and yet the people had turned from him. In light of this, how could they *answer* God's question? Parents who have attempted to reason with wayward children understand the anguish in God's heart here.

B. HIS REMINDERS (vv. 4, 5)
4. *"I brought you up out of Egypt*
*   and redeemed you from the land of slavery.*
* I sent Moses to lead you,*
*   also Aaron and Miriam.*

God had not given his people any reason to be "burdened" (v. 3). Their history was filled with evidence of his love. The clearest piece of evidence was their deliverance from bondage in the land *of Egypt*. There was no way that Israel could have escaped from that misery without God's miraculous intervention or apart from *Moses . . . Aaron and Miriam*, whom God had sent to provide leadership. Each contributed significantly to Israel's beginnings as a nation: Moses was the lawgiver, Aaron was the first high priest, and Miriam was a prophetess (Exodus 15:20, 21).

5. *"My people, remember*
*   what Balak king of Moab counseled*
*   and what Balaam son of Beor answered.*
Remember your journey from Shittim to Gilgal,
*   that you may know the righteous acts of the LORD."*

The incident involving *Balak king of Moab* and *Balaam* is found in Numbers 22–24. *Shittim* was located in Moab, north of the Dead Sea and east of Jericho. It was one of the last campsites of the Israelites as they prepared to enter the promised land (Joshua 3:1). *Gilgal* was situated between the Jordan River and Jericho and was the people's first place of encampment after they crossed the Jordan River (Joshua 4:19).

As the Israelites proceeded toward the promised land, they conquered the peoples in some of the territories who had stood in their way and refused to let them pass through (Numbers 21:21-35). Balak, realizing the danger that the Israelites posed to his people, hired the prophet Balaam to pronounce a curse upon Israel. But God permitted Balaam to speak only words of blessing on Israel. This was another example of how God had protected and cared for his people.

All of these acts had been done to teach Israel to *know the righteous acts of the Lord*. God could not be blamed for the people's sorry condition; he had demonstrated his love for them on numerous occasions.

IV. GOD'S REQUIREMENTS (MICAH 6:6-8)
A. SUGGESTED ANSWERS (vv. 6, 7)
6, 7. *With what shall I come before the LORD*
*   and bow down before the exalted God?*
Shall I come before him with burnt offerings,
*   with calves a year old?*
Will the LORD be pleased with thousands of rams,
*   with ten thousand rivers of oil?*
Shall I offer my firstborn for my transgression,
*   the fruit of my body for the sin of my soul?*

Here Micah puts himself in the position of the people as they respond to the charges that God has brought against them. What must they do to please the Lord? What does he want?

DAILY BIBLE READINGS
    Monday, July 23—*Wicked Rulers and Prophets (Micah 3)*
    Tuesday, July 24—*Peace and Security Through Obedience (Micah 4:1-5)*
    Wednesday, July 25—*Restoration Promised After Exile (Micah 4:6—5:1)*
    Thursday, July 26—*The Ruler From Bethlehem (Micah 5:2-6)*
    Friday, July 27—*Future Role of the Remnant (Micah 5:7-15)*
    Saturday, July 28—*God Challenges Israel (Micah 6:1-5)*
    Sunday, July 29—*What God Requires (Micah 6:6-16)*

WHAT DO YOU THINK?

Micah called on the people to consider what they should do to come back to the Lord. While some of the measures seem rather extreme, they were nonetheless futile! How "extreme" should we become to make sure that we are maintaining a close relationship to God? What will make our efforts more successful than those of the Israelites?

WHAT DO YOU THINK?

Micah makes a distinction between knowing what we are to do and actually doing it. In our personal walk with God, what are those areas where it is tougher to walk the walk rather than just to talk the talk?

PRAYER

God of mercy and justice, teach us how to be humble before you and obedient to you. May our lives so resonate with these virtues that the world will see and become followers of Jesus as we are. In his name we pray. Amen.

THOUGHT TO REMEMBER

God's priorities must become our priorities.

A series of possible answers follows. *Burnt offerings* were commanded in the law of Moses (Leviticus 1). Animals of *a year old* (including *calves*) were often required for sacrifices (Leviticus 9:2, 3; 12:6; 14:10, 11). On the other hand, perhaps God was interested more in quantity of sacrifices than quality: *will the Lord be pleased with thousands of rams, with ten thousand rivers of oil?* (Oil frequently accompanied certain offerings, such as those described in Leviticus 2.)

Finally the prophet proposed a radical act: *shall I offer my firstborn for my transgression?* Certainly God never commanded his people to do anything like this! But would he be pleased with someone's desire to give him something as precious as the firstborn of his children?

B. THE RIGHT ANSWER (v. 8)

8. He has showed you, O man, what is good.
    And what does the LORD require of you?
  To act justly and to love mercy
    and to walk humbly with your God.

Micah did not mean to imply that the people of Judah should not offer the sacrifices that God had commanded in the law. His point was that all of these sacrifices were meaningless unless they led to a lifestyle that pleased God and followed after what he considered important: seeking justice, loving *mercy*, and walking *humbly* before God. None of this had been kept secret from the people; as Micah said, *he has showed you . . . what is good.* But the people chose to ignore these concerns. It has always been easier to follow prescribed rituals than to live out one's faith in everyday settings.

KEEPING THE MAIN THING THE MAIN THING

Most of us can recall various neighborhood clubs that we belonged to as children. Usually these clubs got started on rainy or otherwise boring days when we found ourselves sitting in someone's basement or tree house with nothing to do. Someone would say, "I know! Let's start a club!" Immediate interest was aroused and, before long, officers were elected, secret passwords were decided on, and initiation rites were created. Sometimes dues and dress codes were stipulated. The longer it rained, the more organized we became. And the more organized, regulated, and regimented we became, the less likely was the club to exist longer than a week or so. We became so bogged down with details that we forgot our purpose—to have fun!

The people of Judah in Micah's day had become obsessed with rites, rituals, and ceremonies. They were substituting formal sacrifices and programmed "pomp and circumstance" for a humble walk with God and a heartfelt compassion for others. The main things of their religion had ceased to be the main things.

God "has showed [us] what is good." Are we paying attention?   —R. W. B.

CONCLUSION

None of what Micah states as important before God requires involvement in elaborate rituals or colorful ceremonies. Even the most simple worship service can produce the changes in us that God requires. All too often (perhaps even unconsciously) we substitute activity and "busyness" for the kind of worship that God really wants.

As the twenty-first century unfolds, we hope for a better century than the twentieth, which was so filled with injustice and so lacking in mercy and humility before God. But in the process of looking forward, we must also look backward to the eighth century B.C. and heed the words of Micah. If we put his challenge into practice, we can help to eliminate some of the violence and bitterness that have plagued our society in recent years.

Discovery Learning

This page contains an alternate lesson plan emphasizing learning activities. Classes desiring such student involvement will find these suggestions helpful. The next page is a reproducible activity page to further enhance discovery learning.

LEARNING GOALS

After this lesson your students will be able to:

1. Tell how Micah contrasted the message of false prophets with the true requirements of following the Lord.

2. Explain how people today try to please God in ways other than those prescribed by him.

3. Memorize Micah 6:8, and make it the governing principle of their conduct each day this week.

INTO THE LESSON

Ask the class to suggest some qualities of a good teacher or preacher. Write their ideas on the chalkboard. Remind the class that no teacher or preacher will fit all of these ideals. However, some qualities must be present in any leader. Ask the class to select from your list one or two qualities that must be present in *every* teacher. Place a check mark (✔) beside the answers given. Then put a circle around the qualities that emphasize faithfulness to God's Word. Tell the class, "Teachers and preachers must speak for God; they must be faithful to God's Word and his will. However, there have always been religious leaders who were not. The contrast between the two kinds is seen in today's lesson."

INTO THE WORD

Early in the week, ask a class member to read the incident of Balak and Balaam in Numbers 22–24. Ask this person to prepare a brief summary to relate to the class.

Begin the Bible study with a brief lecture about Micah and his prophecies. Use the Lesson Background in the lesson commentary. Conclude this lecture by telling the class that, earlier in the book, Micah had condemned the political leaders of Judah. Now he turns his attention to the religious leaders—the prophets and priests.

Ask the class to work in teams of two or three. The teams' first task is to read Micah 3:5-12 and paraphrase each verse by reducing it to one word, one phrase, or one brief sentence. Give this example from verse 9: "Listen up, you religious extortionists!" After the groups have finished, ask a couple of teams to read their paraphrases.

Note that these self-acclaimed prophets were frauds! Use the commentary on verses 6 and 7 to describe these leaders. Point out that Micah, by contrast, came to speak God's truth (v. 8). He indicts these false leaders, saying that they are going to fail and be exposed.

Before studying Micah 6:3-8, tell the class this passage reads like a trial scene. Ask the learners to look at verses 1 and 2. Distribute copies of the reproducible activity "Religious Requirements Reiterated" from the next page. Make an overhead transparency of the activity as well, or copy the information on a large poster. As you mention these positions and persons, fill in your visual with the following: "Accused: Israel; Plaintiff: The Lord; Jury: The mountains, hills, and earth."

Divide the class into small groups; ask the groups to read Micah 6:3-8 and discuss the questions on the handout. After the groups have finished their discussion, ask for volunteers to give answers to questions 1 and 2. (*The charge against Israel: refusing to follow the Lord; why the Israelites' slavery in Egypt is cited: God's deliverance proves his love for Israel.*)

Then ask the person you recruited earlier in the week to relate his summary of Balak and Balaam's incident. Ask the class, "Why would God include this incident in his argument?" (*The incident is a reminder to be faithful to God's Word and will.*) Continue by asking volunteers to give their answers to questions 3 and 4. (*Why God asked the questions in verses 6 and 7: the people thought ceremonial acts could excuse sinful acts; the bottom line: verse 8.*)

INTO LIFE

Discuss the following questions.

1. What does this text imply about contemporary religious leaders—our ministers, teachers, Bible study leaders, youth coaches, and others?

2. The people hearing Micah's message may have been enthusiastic about offerings and sacrifices, but they missed the point of godly living. What are some of the actions believers today may do as a substitute for godly living? What illustrations would Micah use if he were citing religious practices that we substitute for godly living?

3. Look at Micah 6:8. What does it mean "to act justly" in 2001? What does it mean for Christians today to "love mercy"? How can we "walk humbly with [our] God"?

Distribute three-by-five cards, and ask each learner to draw a scroll on his or her card and to write the words of Micah 6:8 in the scroll. Ask the students to carry these scrolls this week, memorize the words, and make this verse a governing principle for godly conduct in their daily lives.

In Plain and Pointed Language

Read Micah 3:5-12. Reduce each verse to one word, one phrase, or one sentence that makes Micah's message to religious leaders easy to understand.

Verse 5: "Listen up, you religious extortionists!"

Verse 6:

Verse 7:

Verse 8:

Verses 9 and 10:

Verse 11:

Verse 12:

Religious Requirements Reiterated

Read Micah 6:1-8. In this passage, the Lord reminds the people of his expectations for godly living. In this trial scene, who or what is:

The Accused? _____

The Plaintiff? _____

The Jury? _____

Now develop the case further by answering the following questions.

1. What is the charge implied against Israel?

2. Why does the Lord cite slavery in Egypt in his argument?

3. Why did God ask the questions in verses 6 and 7? What is he implying?

4. What is the bottom line God expects of his followers?

ISAIAH'S CALL

LESSON 10

WHY TEACH THIS LESSON?

The scene described in today's text is one of the most awe-inspiring in all the Bible. A teacher would like to think that, after this lesson, each learner in the classroom would leave in a reverent spirit of worship, but it probably won't happen. The average Sunday school class deals with far too many distractions to be caught up into such a rapturous state.

This lesson can have a dramatic effect on your students, however. While the emotional impact may have to be postponed to a time of quiet meditation, your students will have the opportunity to focus on the greatness of God's majesty. And the challenge of Isaiah's response will be clear. In view of the glory of the one who calls us, how can we answer anything else but, "Here am I. Send me"?

INTRODUCTION

A. WHEN THE KING CALLS

When World War I broke out, railroad stations in London were overwhelmed by individuals trying to reach their destinations before travel restrictions were imposed. Amid the confusion, one man, whose clothes, face, and hands were covered with soot and oil, pushed his way to the head of the line, purchased a ticket, and boarded the train. As soon as he sat down, he fell asleep.

When other passengers got on the train and saw the man, they woke him up and complained about his behavior and appearance. He replied, "I am a reservist, and my unit has been called up for duty. I am a stoker on a coal-burning ship—a very dirty job. I had put in twenty hours at my job with no break when I received my call. I didn't take time to clean up, because when the king calls, a loyal subject doesn't say, 'Wait until I'm ready!' He responds immediately!"

Isaiah could have made excuses when the Lord asked, "Whom shall I send? And who will go for us?" When the King of kings called, Isaiah responded without delay: "Here am I. Send me!"

B. LESSON BACKGROUND

Isaiah was a contemporary of Micah, whose message we studied in last week's lesson. His lengthy ministry was carried out in Judah during the reigns of Uzziah, Jotham, Ahaz, and Hezekiah (Isaiah 1:1), meaning that it probably covered well over fifty years (approximately 745 B.C. to 690 B.C.). When Isaiah was first called to the prophetic ministry, Judah, along with Israel, was continuing to experience prosperous times, mainly because Assyria remained in a period of decline. However, as noted in the Lesson Background of last week's lesson, this changed drastically during the second half of the eighth century B.C. Before Isaiah's ministry was concluded, the prophet would see his homeland ravaged by the Assyrians.

According to Isaiah 1:1, Isaiah's father was named Amoz (not to be confused with the prophet Amos). Isaiah was married and had two sons (Isaiah 7:3; 8:1-4). Unlike most other prophets, Isaiah seems to have had easy access to the royal court and was able to speak with kings such as Ahaz and Hezekiah (Isaiah 7:3; 38:1). A later Jewish tradition says that Isaiah was sawn in two during the reign

DEVOTIONAL READING:
ACTS 26:12-20
BACKGROUND SCRIPTURE:
ISAIAH 6
PRINTED TEXT:
ISAIAH 6

LESSON AIMS

After this lesson a student should be able to:

1. Retell the story of Isaiah's vision and call, including his unreserved response.

2. Describe both the privilege and the frustrations of serving the Lord.

3. State the ministry to which he or she believes God is calling, and answer, "Here am I. Send me!"

Aug
5

KEY VERSE

Then I heard the voice of the Lord saying, "Whom shall I send? And who will go for us?"

And I said, "Here am I. Send me!" —Isaiah 6:8

of the wicked king Manasseh. (This may be the incident to which the writer of Hebrews refers in Hebrews 11:37.)

Isaiah's elevated literary style has earned him the title of the greatest of the writing prophets. He shows a keen sense of God's activity in history, anticipating a day when many nations and peoples would come to the Lord. Because of Isaiah's numerous messianic prophecies, his book has been called the "fifth Gospel."

I. ISAIAH'S TEMPLE VISION (ISAIAH 6:1-4)

A. THE LORD SEATED (v. 1)

1. In the year that King Uzziah died, I saw the Lord seated on a throne, high and exalted, and the train of his robe filled the temple.

Uzziah, who is also called Azariah in the Scriptures (2 Kings 15:1), had a lengthy reign as *king* of Judah, from 792 B.C. until *the year* he *died*, which was 740 B.C. During the early part of his reign, he apparently served as a co-regent (or co-ruler) with his father, Amaziah. On the whole Uzziah was a good king, and Judah enjoyed prosperity under his rule. Near the end of his reign, however, he arrogantly tried to usurp the authority of the priests. As a result, he was stricken with leprosy and had to live in a separate house while his son Jotham served as a co-regent until Uzziah's death (2 Chronicles 26:16-23).

Some commentators believe that Isaiah 6 records Isaiah's initial call to the prophetic ministry, and it certainly reads as if it could be just that. However, the fact that this call is not recorded until the sixth chapter rather than in the first suggests to many that Isaiah was already active as a prophet before this event. If so, then his ministry must have taken on a new and more specific direction at this time. Perhaps this experience came after King Uzziah's death to remind Isaiah that *the Lord* was Judah's real King and was still in control.

I saw the Lord. How can this be, when John 1:18 tells us that "no one has ever seen God"? We should understand Isaiah's experience as a vision rather than a direct encounter with God. It is likely that Isaiah regularly attended the temple; perhaps this vision occurred during one of these occasions.

In his vision Isaiah saw the Lord *seated on a throne*, signifying his power and authority. Like an earthly king he wore a *robe* with a long *train*, which was so vast that it *filled the temple*, giving further evidence of his majesty.

B. SERAPHIM STANDING (v. 2)

2. Above him were seraphs, each with six wings: With two wings they covered their faces, with two they covered their feet, and with two they were flying.

This is the only place in the Bible where *seraphs* are mentioned. (While there are similarities between the seraphs and the "beasts" described in Revelation 4:6-8, the latter are never called *seraphs*.) Apparently they had human form except that *each* one had *six wings*. *Two* of these *wings* were used to cover *their faces* (perhaps to protect the seraphs from beholding the glory of God) and *two* to cover *their feet*. The third pair of wings was used so that the seraphs could fly.

The primary function of the seraphs appears to have been to praise God and to serve as his messengers. The term *seraphs* comes from a Hebrew word meaning "to burn"; thus the seraphs were the "burning ones." Some see that as suggestive of their role as purifying agents, as in verses 6 and 7.

C. PRAISE SPOKEN (vv. 3, 4)

3. And they were calling to one another:
  Holy, holy, holy is the LORD Almighty;
    the whole earth is full of his glory."

Some people think that Isaiah's grief over King Uzziah's death played a significant part in the timing of this vision. What kind of events cause us to search for God? Do "crisis" oriented encounters with God have a longer lasting impact on us than encounters we have planned, such as regular worship services, revival meetings, retreats, or camps? Why or why not?

Holy, holy, holy: the repetition was likely for emphasis. Some think that speaking these words *to one another* represents an antiphonal choir, singing in response to one another.

While we usually associate the word *holy* with words like *righteous, pure,* and *good,* the basic meaning of the term is "set apart." God's nature sets him so far apart from sinful humans, or even from the angels, that these divine qualities have become the basis for our understanding of what it is to be holy.

4. At the sound of their voices the doorposts and thresholds shook and the temple was filled with smoke.

The energy generated by the praise of the seraphs caused the temple (a solidly built structure) to shake. The filling of *the temple* with *smoke* is an indication of the glory of God's presence (Exodus 19:18; 20:18).

II. ISAIAH'S CALL TO SERVICE (ISAIAH 6:5-8)

A. HIS UNWORTHINESS (v. 5)

5. "Woe to me!" I cried. "I am ruined! For I am a man of unclean lips, and I live among a people of unclean lips, and my eyes have seen the King, the LORD Almighty."

Isaiah's distress, reflected in his cry *Woe to me*, reflects a sense of reverence and overwhelming awe in the presence of *Almighty* God (something that many today, even among Christians, have lost). Isaiah knew that he was in no way worthy to be experiencing what he was experiencing.

I am ruined, confessed Isaiah. His *unclean lips* had uttered words that were offensive to God. Furthermore, Isaiah realized that he was not alone in his predicament; he lived *among a people of unclean lips.* Isaiah did not say this to excuse his condition; he was simply aware that he could not escape the impact of his corrupt surroundings. We need to be aware of how we are affected by our culture and how we often have substituted the world's values for God's standards in our thoughts, words, actions, and priorities. Isaiah had come to the alarming realization of who he was before a holy God—a sinner, condemned and unclean.

B. HIS CLEANSING (vv. 6, 7)

6, 7. Then one of the seraphs flew to me with a live coal in his hand, which he had taken with tongs from the altar. With it he touched my mouth and said, "See, this has touched your lips; your guilt is taken away and your sin atoned for."

Isaiah's situation was not hopeless. God knew his need and responded to it by allowing one of the *seraphs* to take a *live coal . . . from the altar*—most likely the golden altar in the Holy Place, from which coals of fire were taken into the Most Holy Place on the Day of Atonement (Leviticus 16:12). The seraph then touched Isaiah's lips with the coal. The contact with fire symbolized a cleansing that purged Isaiah from his *sin.* (Thus the significance of obtaining one of the coals normally used on the Day of Atonement is clear.) The presence of fire also indicates that Isaiah's cleansing was thorough, but it further suggests that it was painful. Few experiences are more soul-wrenching than having to confess our sins and accept the responsibility for them and for the punishment that often follows.

C. HIS RESPONSE (v. 8)

8. Then I heard the voice of the Lord saying, "Whom shall I send? And who will go for us?"

And I said, "Here am I. Send me!"

I heard the voice of the Lord. Up to this point, God had not spoken. There had been no need; his very presence had communicated everything Isaiah needed to

WHAT DO YOU THINK?

Out of the millions of people who lived during Old and New Testament times, only several dozen people received a special "call" from God. All others received a general call. In what ways today does God "call" people to serve him? What response does God want from each person?

HOW TO SAY IT

Ahaz. AY-haz.
Amaziah. Am-uh-ZYE-uh.
Amoz. AY-mahz.
Assyria. Uh-SEAR-ee-uh.
Azariah. Az-uh-RYE-uh.
Babylon. BAB-uh-lun.
Damascus. Duh-MASS-kus.
Hezekiah. Hez-ih-KYE-uh.
Jotham. JO-thum.
Manasseh. Muh-NASS-uh.
messianic. mess-ee-AN-ick.
Micah. MY-kuh.
seraph. SAIR-uff.
terebinth. TER-uh-binth.
Uzziah. Uh-ZYE-uh.

know. When God did speak, he asked a question: *Whom shall I send? And who will go for us?* His words do not seem to have been directed specifically to Isaiah. It was almost as if Isaiah were overhearing a conversation in the courts of Heaven. But in Isaiah's mind there was no doubt that the questions were aimed at him.

Note the change in pronouns from singular (*I*) to plural (*us*). While this may indicate that God was including the seraphs in his question, some believe that this reflects the presence of the three Persons of the Godhead, much as Genesis 1:26 does ("Let *us* make man in *our* image").

Apparently Isaiah's response was immediate: *Here am I. Send me!* He did not ask for time to think the matter over or to count the cost. He volunteered without a moment's hesitation, not even knowing what a *yes* answer might entail.

In Isaiah's case the call to God's service was not specific. It rarely is. When one becomes a member of his nation's armed forces, he usually has no idea where he will eventually serve. In the same way, the moment one becomes a Christian he enlists in the struggle with Satan and becomes a soldier in God's army. But he may have little or no idea where he will eventually be used in that struggle or the price he will have to pay.

HEED THE CALL

Moses received his assignment to lead the Israelites out of bondage in Egypt during a unique encounter with a burning bush. The apostle Paul received his "wake-up call" in the form of a blinding light on the road to Damascus. Most of us do not experience such a dramatic summons into the Lord's service. I remember how my father was called into the ministry by the quiet discipling efforts of faithful church elders. It was not a spectacular "call," but it certainly made an impact on his life.

No universal pattern of circumstances characterizes God's call to Christian service. It comes in a variety of ways. However, Isaiah's call teaches us certain particulars that prepare us to receive God's call, no matter the circumstances in which that call may come. Isaiah was *humble* before the Lord; he was *remorseful* and *penitent* in acknowledging his sin; and he responded as a *willing* servant to God's plea for workers.

In one way or another, God calls each of his children to work in his kingdom. To what task is he calling you? Are you listening for his still small voice with humility, penitence, and willingness? You, too, can hear and heed his call.   —R. W. B.

III. ISAIAH'S MISSION (ISAIAH 6:9-13)

A. DIFFICULT TASK (v. 9)

9. He said, "Go and tell this people:

"'Be ever hearing, but never understanding;
be ever seeing, but never perceiving.'

Isaiah's task consisted of a pair of actions—he was to go and tell. The message he was to deliver was also stated in pairs: *Be ever hearing, but never understanding; be ever seeing, but never perceiving.* The Hebrew text suggests the meaning, "Keep on hearing, yet never understanding; and keep on seeing, yet never perceiving."

While Isaiah had readily volunteered to do God's bidding, God said his efforts were, for the most part, destined to fail. In spite of all his pleading, *this people* would refuse to pay attention. This does not mean that every individual in the nation would close his ears and eyes to Isaiah's call to repentance. But the nation as a whole was determined to go its own way. Its rejection of God's prophet would confirm the judgment that God had already reserved for his people.

GO AND TELL

It was "Show and Tell" day at my elementary school—a fact that I had failed to remind my mother of until it was time to leave the house! At the last minute, Mom shoved our family bread plate into my hand and sent me off to school. The plate did possess unusual color and texture, but neither my mother nor I had any idea how unique and valuable it was. My teacher, however, recognized it as a fine specimen of centuries-old *Majolica* (Muh-*jah*-lick-uh) ware "worth who-knows-what." Needless to say, I returned home that day with not just a bread plate, but a priceless antique—wrapped, padded, and tied securely. I still own and cherish that plate.

Isaiah's call to "go and tell" was a typical charge to prophets. He was to be God's messenger; his message of divine truth was priceless. But it was, for the most part, negative news—not nearly as well received as my plate story and certainly not as happily heard as the good news shared by gospel ambassadors of reconciliation.

The going and telling of Christians in response to Christ's commission is definitely a more joyful job than Isaiah's. Though we must warn sinners of God's wrath and justice, the primary thrust of our message is God's love and mercy. Both warnings and promises are designed to bring people to repentance and salvation. So let us "go, show, and tell," never forgetting the priceless worth of the gospel. —R. W. B.

B. DISCOURAGING RESPONSE (v. 10)

10. *"Make the heart of this people calloused;*
 make their ears dull
 and close their eyes.
Otherwise they might see with their eyes,
 hear with their ears,
 understand with their hearts,
and turn and be healed."

Prosperity tends to make people oblivious to warnings. So when Isaiah challenged the prosperous people of Judah to return to God, they would instead take the easy way, continuing on the same path. Their hearts would be *calloused*, their *eyes* would not *see*, and their *ears* would not *hear*. Thus there was no repentance, no conversion, and no healing. Both Jesus and Paul used this text to describe the adverse reaction of some to their messages (Matthew 13:14, 15; Acts 28:25-27).

C. DURATION OF THE MISSION (vv. 11, 12)

11, 12. *Then I said, "For how long, O Lord?"*
And he answered:
"Until the cities lie ruined
 and without inhabitant,
until the houses are left deserted
 and the fields ruined and ravaged,
until the LORD has sent everyone far away
 and the land is utterly forsaken.

To be called to a difficult task is challenging enough; to be called to a task that holds no hope of success can overwhelm an individual with discouragement. Isaiah cried out in anguish, *For how long, O Lord?* "Is there no end to this message of judgment?" he seemed to be asking.

God's answer was hardly reassuring. Yes, there would be a conclusion to his seemingly hopeless task, but not before disaster had ravaged the land. The *cities* of Judah would be *ruined and without inhabitant*, and the *houses* would be *deserted*.

Why would such desolation occur? Because *the Lord* would send *everyone far away*, leaving the *land . . . utterly forsaken*. Even as Isaiah's call was taking place, international changes were occurring that, within twenty years, would bring the Assyrian hordes upon Israel to the north and carry her people away. About twenty years later, this dreaded foe was camped outside Jerusalem threatening to do there what it had done to Samaria. Jerusalem was spared then (Isaiah 37:36, 37), but

DAILY BIBLE READINGS

Monday, July 30—*The Wickedness of Judah (Isaiah 1:1-9)*

Tuesday, July 31—*Isaiah's Transforming Vision (Isaiah 6: 1-8)*

Wednesday, Aug. 1—*Daniel's Vision of God's Glory (Daniel 10:1-11)*

Thursday, Aug. 2—*John's Vision of Christ (Revelation 1: 9-18)*

Friday, Aug. 3—*Isaiah's Commission (Isaiah 6:9-13)*

Saturday, Aug. 4—*A Prayer of Trust (Psalm 25:1-10)*

Sunday, Aug. 5—*Paul's Vision on the Road to Damascus (Acts 26:12-20)*

WHAT DO YOU THINK?

Isaiah was told that, in spite of his preaching, Judah's spiritual condition would not improve. What do you think kept Isaiah motivated? What helps you to remain motivated to persevere in God's work when it seems not to be appreciated or fruitful?

ANSWERS TO PUZZLE ON P. 424

ACROSS	DOWN
1. throne	1. train
3. calloused	2. oak
5. understanding	3. coal
9. inhabitant	4. terebinth
10. tongs	5. Uzziah
11. earth	6. king
13. seated	7. smoke
14. tenth	8. thresholds
16. ruined	12. ravaged
18. atoned	13. stumps
19. seraphs	15. forsaken
21. holy	17. dull
22. lips	20. ruined
23. seeing	21. holy
24. flying	22. long
25. deserted	23. six
	24. far

that was not the end of her troubles. Within a hundred years, another foreign power, Babylon, would descend on Judah and carry still more captives far away.

D. DECLARATION OF HOPE (v. 13)

13. *"And though a tenth remains in the land,*
   it will again be laid waste.
But as the terebinth and oak
   leave stumps when they are cut down,
    so the holy seed will be the stump in the land."

Even the *tenth*—the portion of those who remained *in the land*—would *again be laid waste*, meaning that they would suffer additional ravaging attacks from their enemies. However, like a strong, resilient tree, this remnant would survive in spite of being subjected to such treatment.

The *terebinth* tree was common in the lower elevations of Israel and Judah. Its great size and long life resembled those of the *oak*. These trees (each symbolic of Judah) would be *cut down* by Judah's enemies, but their *stumps* would provide the *holy seed* that would keep alive a remnant of God's people so that his covenant with Abraham would still be fulfilled through the coming of the Messiah. A similar promise is found in Isaiah 11:1.

CONCLUSION

A. CLEANSED AND CALLED

Isaiah's stirring account of his vision of the Lord reminds us that, in one way or another, God calls every Christian to a ministry. But it also points out that, if we are to be effective in that ministry, we must first of all be cleansed, laying aside "everything that hinders and the sin that so easily entangles" (Hebrews 12:1). Just as the cleansing was an agonizing experience for Isaiah, so it is likely to be for us. Yet, the "finished product" will be, in Paul's words, "an instrument . . . made holy, useful to the Master and prepared to do any good work" (2 Timothy 2:21).

B. MISSION IMPOSSIBLE

Several years ago "Mission Impossible" was a popular television program. Each week a team of agents—the "Impossible Missions Force"—was assigned an extremely dangerous task considered to be "impossible." By clever strategies, incredible devices, and great courage they were always able to accomplish their "impossible" mission.

The title of this television program could well summarize the challenge that confronted Isaiah. He was sent to the people of Judah, who had turned away from God, with a message of repentance. But his mission appeared impossible; the people had closed their minds and their ears to that message. As discouraging as this task may have been for Isaiah, he did not fail; he was faithful to his duty. Let us remember that God counts faithfulness as more important than success.

A few of us may be called to some distant and difficult mission field; however, most of us will be called to closer and less dramatic mission fields. Some might consider teaching a junior boys' class an "impossible" mission, yet certain individuals have succeeded in spite of the difficulties. Others would consider ministering to those suffering from drug and alcohol addiction as another task to be filed in the "impossible" category. Yet some have carried out this ministry faithfully in spite of numerous disappointments and setbacks. Others have found their "impossible" mission in bringing hope and comfort to the terminally ill through hospice care.

Is God calling you to a seemingly impossible mission? If so, accept it as Isaiah did. And never forget that God specializes in the impossible.

Discovery Learning

This page contains an alternate lesson plan emphasizing learning activities. Classes desiring such student involvement will find these suggestions helpful. The next page is a reproducible activity page to further enhance discovery learning.

LEARNING GOALS

After this lesson a student should be able to:

1. Retell the story of Isaiah's vision and call, including his unreserved response.

2. Describe both the privilege and the frustrations of serving the Lord.

3. State the ministry to which he or she believes God is calling, and answer, "Here am I. Send me!"

INTO THE LESSON

Remind the class of the old TV series *Mission Impossible*, which was about government agents assigned to tasks or missions that had been deemed "impossible" for other agencies to complete. Ask, "If God were to call you to an 'impossible mission,' which of these assignments might that be?" Then read the following list:

• Teach a junior high boys' class.

• Make teaching calls to prospective Christians.

• Supervise a church building remodeling project.

• Lead music in a worship service.

• Lead a midweek Bible study group.

Ask the class members to call out the mission that would be the most difficult for them to fulfill. Ask a few persons why they think the jobs they mentioned would be "impossible missions."

Then ask, "How would you feel if the Lord asked you to do something that was bound to fail? That's exactly what God asked one of his prophets to do. But Isaiah's willing response becomes a model of humble and unquestioning service for believers today."

INTO THE WORD

Give a short lecture on the setting for today's lesson, using the lesson commentary notes on the Lesson Background and verse 1. Divide the class into three groups. Give each group one of the following assignments.

Group 1: Heavenly Worship. Read Isaiah 6:1-4 and Revelation 4:6b-8. List the similarities in these two glimpses of Heavenly worship. Tell what lessons you find implied for today's worship services in these visions.

Group 2: Moment in God's Presence. Read Isaiah 6:1-8. Tell what the phrases "a man of unclean lips" and "a people of unclean lips" imply about our attitudes and relationship with God. Explain the significance of the live coal being laid on Isaiah's mouth. What might the pain of this experience imply about confession of sin?

Group 3: Call to Service. (Give this group a photocopy of the lesson commentary for verses 8-13.) Read Isaiah 6:8-13 and the lesson commentary notes on this passage. Be ready to explain Isaiah's "impossible mission": What was his task? How would Judah respond? Why did God bother to send Isaiah? What would be in Judah's future? Review this text by allowing the group members to report their findings.

INTO LIFE

Distribute a "Personal Assessment Sheet," as follows. As a heading for the left column, write, "My Experience With the Lord." Below that list the following:

__ 1. The "angel" who placed the "live coal" on the lips of my life was

    A. a stranger

    B. a parent

    C. a church leader

    D. a friend

    E. I'm still waiting for my "angel."

__ 2. If I've had one worship experience where I've had a taste of Heavenly worship, it was

    A. at a church camp.

    B. in a personal devotional time.

    C. at my home church.

    D. in a nature setting.

    E. Other _____

Column two should have the heading "My Experience in Service." Under it write:

1. List the areas of service in which you are presently involved through your church.

2. Suppose God called you to one of the following ministries. Check (✔) the ones that would surprise you.

__ Leading public worship

__ Teaching children/youth

__ Teaching adults

__ Being a foreign missionary

__ Sharing Christ at work

__ Leading a Bible study

__ Preparing to be a minister

__ Providing meals for the homeless

__ Showing hospitality

Ask each learner to circle the task or ministry he or she feels "called" to do, even though it may be frightening. Close with prayer, asking people to tell the Lord they will be open to his leading.

Commission Puzzle

There is no need to be puzzled about Isaiah's commission in Isaiah 6. Read the following clues to solve the crossword puzzle. Isaiah 6 will provide the answers. (Or see page 421 of *The NIV Standard Lesson Commentary*.)

ACROSS

1. Where the Lord was seated during Isaiah's vision.
3. The heart of the people would be made _____.
5. Isaiah's hearers would be ever hearing, but never _____.
9. Isaiah was to preach until the cities were without _____.
10. What tool did Isaiah see in this vision?
11. What is full of the Lord's glory?
13. The posture of the Lord on the throne.
14. How many people would remain in the land after the destruction and deportation?
16. Isaiah cried, "I am ____!"
18. What did the live coal do for Isaiah's sin?
19. The creatures who worshiped the Lord in Isaiah's vision.
21. The word used three times to describe "the Lord Almighty."
22. Isaiah said he was a man of unclean _____.
23. Isaiah's hearers would be ever _____, but never perceiving.
24. Two wings of the creatures covered their faces, two covered their feet, and with two the creatures were _____.
25. The houses would be _____.

DOWN

1. What part of the Lord's robe filled the temple?
2. A tree of that region.
3. What did the creature have in his hand?
4. Another tree of that region.
5. The name of the king who died in the year of Isaiah's vision.
6. What was Uzziah's title and position?
7. What, besides the train of the robe, filled the temple?
8. What, besides the doorposts, shook?
12. The fields would be ruined and _____.
13. What would the terebinth and the oak leave?
15. The land would be utterly _____.
17. The people's ears would be _____.
20. Isaiah was to preach until what was the condition of the cities?
21. What type of seed would be the stump of the Lord?
22. Isaiah asked God, "For how _____?"
23. The number of wings that each of the creatures in this vision had.
24. The Lord would send everyone _____ away.

ISAIAH'S CHALLENGE TO RELY ON GOD

LESSON 11

WHY TEACH THIS LESSON?

If ever there were a time to "rely on God," as our lesson title mentions, it is now! One look at the front page of the morning paper is enough to convince us of that. Yet all was not well in Isaiah's day either. Enemy armies were advancing on his homeland. Corrupt officials denied justice to the weak. If ever there were a time for divine intervention, it was then.

But the king was looking elsewhere for help! And the source of help he chose would eventually turn out to be more foe than friend. Again, Isaiah's world parallels our own. Looking for help from the government, the education system, or even the free market, so many people today have failed to see that the only source of real help is from the Lord, Immanuel, God with us—to help us and to deliver us. The only source of help is in Jesus Christ!

Let this lesson issue your students *that* challenge to rely on God.

INTRODUCTION

A. GOD IS THE PILOT

The story is told of a mother and her three children who were taking a long flight together aboard a commercial airliner. About an hour into the flight, the plane unexpectedly ran into some turbulence, which caused it to drop suddenly and shake violently. The passengers became alarmed and some began to scream and cry out. But one of the three children, a six-year-old boy, remained calm throughout the whole episode.

Later one of the attendants stopped and complimented the lad for his remarkable courage when everyone else seemed to panic. "Oh, I didn't have any reason to be afraid," responded the boy. "My daddy is the pilot!"

King Ahaz and the people of Judah, learning that Israel and Syria were conspiring against them, became so frightened that their hearts were shaking like the "trees of the forest are shaken by the wind" (Isaiah 7:2). The Lord sent Isaiah to Ahaz to give the troubled king the assurance that Judah had nothing to fear from this threat. After all, God—the "pilot" of the universe—was still handling the controls.

B. LESSON BACKGROUND

In last week's lesson we studied Isaiah's special call to the prophetic ministry in the year that King Uzziah died (Isaiah 6:1). Jotham, who had served as a co-regent with his father, then became king. Although he did not carry out certain needed religious reforms, the Bible includes these words of approval: "he did what was right in the eyes of the Lord" (2 Kings 15:34).

Jotham was succeeded by his son, Ahaz, who did not follow the good examples set by his father and grandfather. Ahaz "did *not* do what was right in the eyes

DEVOTIONAL READING:
PSALM 33:1-12

BACKGROUND SCRIPTURE:
ISAIAH 7; 2 KINGS 16; 2 CHRONICLES 28

PRINTED TEXT:
ISAIAH 7:1-6, 10-17

LESSON AIMS

After participating in this lesson, each student will be able to:

1. Summarize the message that Isaiah gave Ahaz and how the message demonstrated God's control to King Ahaz and the people of Judah.

2. Cite reasons that people today need reassurance of God's control.

3. Share the message of "Immanuel" with someone facing particularly difficult circumstances.

Aug
12

KEY VERSE

Therefore the Lord himself will give you a sign: The virgin will be with child and will give birth to a son, and will call him Immanuel.　　—Isaiah 7:14

LESSON 11 NOTES

of the Lord" (2 Kings 16:2). This created a particularly difficult situation for Judah, in light of the changing international scene at that time. Assyria, under the aggressive leadership of Tiglath-Pileser III, had begun making inroads into Israel (the northern kingdom) and Syria. These two nations, which had been at war with each other during the days of the prophet Elijah (see the Lesson Background of lesson 4) had formed a coalition to thwart the Assyrian menace. They were trying to pressure Judah into joining their coalition—a situation that produced the crisis described in the opening verses of our printed text.

I. ISAIAH REASSURES AHAZ (ISAIAH 7:1-6)

A. A NATION TROUBLED (vv. 1, 2)

1. When Ahaz son of Jotham, the son of Uzziah, was king of Judah, King Rezin of Aram and Pekah son of Remaliah king of Israel marched up to fight against Jerusalem, but they could not overpower it.

King Rezin of Aram (that is, Syria) and *Pekah . . . king of Israel* were the leaders who had formed a coalition to resist the threat of Assyria. They wanted Judah to join this alliance. When *Ahaz* refused, both Israel and Syria sent forces to Judah in an attempt to coerce Ahaz's compliance with their demand. The biblical record in 2 Chronicles 28:1-8 notes that Judah was soundly defeated during these invasions. "In one day Pekah [the king of Israel] . . . killed a hundred and twenty thousand soldiers in Judah" (v. 6). The record in Chronicles is clear that all of this took place because Ahaz and Judah "had forsaken the Lord, the God of their fathers" (v. 6). Among other detestable sins, Ahaz had offered his children to be sacrificed in the fire to pagan gods (v. 3).

It may have been after these attacks that the incident recorded in Isaiah 7 occurred, when Israel and Syria *marched up to fight against Jerusalem*. In spite of the significant casualties Israel and Syria had inflicted earlier upon Judah, they *could not overpower* Jerusalem's formidable defenses. However, Judah had been so weakened by its losses that Ahaz and his people had good reason to fear still another assault. Verse 6 of our text indicates that the purpose of such an attack would be to remove Ahaz from the throne, most likely in order to replace him with a king who would be more cooperative with the proposed alliance against Assyria.

2. Now the house of David was told, "Aram has allied itself with Ephraim"; so the hearts of Ahaz and his people were shaken, as the trees of the forest are shaken by the wind.

The phrase *house of David* could refer to either the royal court of Ahaz or to the entire nation of Judah. It seems that the nation was gripped with a sense of panic upon receiving word of the approaching armies: *the hearts of Ahaz and his people were shaken, as the trees of the forest are shaken by the wind.* Apparently they had lost all hope.

B. A PROPHET SENT (v. 3)

3. Then the LORD said to Isaiah, "Go out, you and your son Shear-Jashub, to meet Ahaz at the end of the aqueduct of the Upper Pool, on the road to the Washerman's Field.

At this point, Ahaz desperately needed reassurance, and *the Lord*, knowing that need, spoke to *Isaiah* and sent him to *meet* with the troubled king. God also ordered Isaiah to take his *son, Shear-Jashub,* with him. The son's unusual name served as an object lesson, for it meant "a remnant will return"—a message similar to that which Isaiah had received during his call from the Lord (Isaiah 6:13).

The meeting between Ahaz and Isaiah occurred *at the end of the aqueduct of the Upper Pool, on the road to the Washerman's Field.* The exact location of this site is

---

WHAT DO YOU THINK?

Isaiah took his son with him as an object lesson. What benefits do you think came to Shear-Jashub by being present? In what ways would the church be stronger if more Christians took their children or grandchildren along to observe or share in spiritual endeavors?

unknown. Perhaps the king was conducting a tour of the city's water sources in anticipation of another siege.

C. A KING ENCOURAGED (vv. 4-6)

4. "Say to him, 'Be careful, keep calm and don't be afraid. Do not lose heart because of these two smoldering stubs of firewood—because of the fierce anger of Rezin and Aram and of the son of Remaliah.

Don't be afraid—how often we read these words in Scripture at the beginning of a message of hope and encouragement! The phrase *these two smoldering stubs of firewood* describes *Rezin*, king of Syria, and *the son of Remaliah*, who was Pekah, king of Israel. (Pekah was a usurper, an army officer who had murdered the previous king in order to seize the throne. Many scholars believe it is contempt for his behavior that causes him to be referred to, not by his name, but merely as *the son of Remaliah*.) Like torches, these kings' *fierce anger* against Ahaz (for not joining their coalition) would blaze for a short time and then burn out.

5, 6. "'Aram, Ephraim and Remaliah's son have plotted your ruin, saying, "Let us invade Judah; let us tear it apart and divide it among ourselves, and make the son of Tabeel king over it."'"

Aram was the nation we now call Syria. *Ephraim* was the most prominent tribe of the northern kingdom; sometimes its name was used to refer to the entire kingdom. The two kings who were allied against Ahaz had failed in their earlier attempts to capture Jerusalem, but they were determined to try yet again. If they were successful, they intended to place someone described as the *son of Tabeel* on the throne. We know nothing about this person, though he was probably someone who was sympathetic to the proposed alliance against Assyria.

WHOM DO YOU TRUST?

During World War I, the United States and Russia were enemies. During World War II, the same two countries were allies, for at that point they were facing a common enemy in Germany. Sometimes conflict creates alliances between unlikely powers. Siblings who constantly quarrel and bicker will usually join forces against "outsiders" who threaten either or both of them.

A common enemy (Assyria) made "strange bedfellows" out of Israel and her former enemy, Syria. Those two allied themselves against Judah, which in turn established an alliance with Assyria (2 Kings 16:7), of which the prophet Isaiah strongly disapproved. Far better would have been the outcome if all of God's chosen people in both the northern and southern kingdoms had presented a united front that trusted not in chariots, swords, and spears, but in Jehovah God.

Although the opposition to Christians today seems intimidating at times, we need to trust in and depend on God's strength as we fight our battle "against the spiritual forces of evil" (Ephesians 6:12). All the resources that we need to achieve victory have been provided, but we must determine to use them.   —R. W. B.

II. GOD SPEAKS TO AHAZ (ISAIAH 7:10-13)

A. GOD'S REQUEST (vv. 10, 11)

10, 11. Again the LORD spoke to Ahaz, "Ask the LORD your God for a sign, whether in the deepest depths or in the highest heights."

In verses 7-9 Isaiah gave Ahaz further encouragement that the campaign directed against him would not stand. There was also, however, a warning issued to Ahaz, whose faith had been less than exemplary to this point: "If you do not stand firm in your faith, you will not stand at all" (v. 9).

Again the Lord spoke to Ahaz. Perhaps some time passed until this next occasion when God spoke to the king through Isaiah. It appears that Ahaz had been

HOW TO SAY IT

Aram. AIR-um.
Ahaz. AY-haz.
Assyria. Uh-SEAR-ee-uh.
Damascus. Duh-MASS-kus.
Elijah. Ee-LYE-juh.
Ephraim. EE-fray-im.
Gideon. GID-ee-un.
Hezekiah. Hez-ih-KYE-uh.
Immanuel. Ih-MAN-you-el.
Isaiah. Eye-ZAY-uh.
Jeroboam. Jair-uh-BO-um.
Jotham. JO-thum.
Massah. MASS-uh.
messianic. mess-ee-AN-ick.
Pekah. PEEK-uh.
Pharisees. FAIR-ih-sees.
Rehoboam. Ree-huh-BO-um.
Remaliah. Rem-uh-LYE-uh.
Rezin. REE-zin.
Septuagint. Sep-TOO-ih-jent.
Shear-Jashub. SHE-are-JAH-shub.
Syria. SEAR-ee-uh.
Tabeel. TAY-be-el.
Tiglath-Pileser. TIG-lath-Pih-LEE-zer.
Uzziah. Uh-ZYE-uh.
Zechariah. Zek-uh-RYE-uh.

WHAT DO YOU THINK?

Many people have longed for a "sign" from God. What do you think they are wishing for as a result of a sign? What signs has God already provided for us? How would another sign make a difference?

unwilling to accept Isaiah's previous message of hope; so the prophet was sent to him again. This time Isaiah encouraged the spiritually unsteady king to *ask* for some kind of *sign* that would convince him of the truth of the prophet's message.

Certainly there are times when asking for a sign is wrong. During Jesus' ministry the Pharisees asked for signs, not to confirm their faith but to find a way to curtail Jesus' popularity (Matthew 12:38-40). Zechariah was made mute for asking, "How can I be sure of this?" regarding God's promise (Luke 1:18-20). However, when Gideon asked for a sign, God complied (Judges 6:36-40). God knows the heart of the person. He knows whether the request for a sign comes from a true desire to know his will or is an act of doubt and disbelief.

The case before us is different from the above examples because the initiative for the sign came from God. God told Ahaz to ask for a sign, and he gave him a wide range of items for which he could ask: *whether in the deepest depths or in the highest heights* (probably meaning "anything on earth or in the sky"). While this language suggests a miraculous sign, a sign could involve some natural event that occurred in such a way as to convey a message. In effect, God presented Ahaz with a blank check.

B. AHAZ'S REFUSAL (v. 12)
12. But Ahaz said, "I will not ask; I will not put the LORD to the test."

In rejecting God's offer to *ask* for a sign, Ahaz seems to appear very pious and reverent toward God: "*I will not put the Lord to the test.*" Deuteronomy 6:16 states, "Do not test the Lord your God as you did at Massah" (referring to the incident found in Exodus 17:1-7). But since God was giving this opportunity to Ahaz, the king's response was actually a blatant defiance of God's authority and a declaration that he himself (without God's help) would determine what he and his nation would do.

WHAT DO YOU THINK?

Ahaz had put his faith in a political solution, an alliance with Assyria, rather than in God. What can the church do to help Christians increase their trust in God rather than in political solutions? What can we do as Christians to encourage national leaders to seek a godly course first?

It appears that Ahaz had already made up his mind to ask Assyria for help against his enemies, which he proceeded to do (or, perhaps, had already done), according to 2 Kings 16:7-9. Ahaz refused to acknowledge Judah's real King. He trusted the Assyrians (that is, man's power) more than he trusted God. It was a decision he would live to regret (v. 17).

TO SIGN OR NOT TO SIGN?

In recent years great interest has arisen among the general public in angels, miracles, and the "spirit world." The print, film, and video media have responded to and heightened that interest through articles, books, movies, and television shows on these themes. People are reporting miracles of healing and even of "resurrection" (when a person who has been pronounced clinically dead returns to life). Alleged angel and spirit "sightings" seem to be frequent. Human nature strongly desires to believe in the supernatural. That desire can be satisfied by fantasy, superstition, coincidence—or by real evidence.

Ahaz was given the opportunity to name the sign by which the divine nature of Isaiah's message would be validated. However, receiving such a sign would have required the king's personal repentance and obedience. Thus, when offered this unique opportunity, the king declined the invitation. He preferred to continue in sin for another season and to trust in the military might of a godless neighbor (Assyria).

Demanding signs from God can reflect an attitude of doubt rather than faith. But ignoring the evidence that *God himself* freely offers reflects intentional and stubborn disbelief. Sinful cynics must take a "leap of doubt" when they refuse to consider the compelling amount of evidence that brings true seekers to the certainty that God "exists and . . . rewards those who earnestly seek him" (Hebrews 11:6).

God has given us numerous signs of his great faithfulness that we dare not reject or ignore. As the hymn says, "Morning by morning new mercies I see; All I have needed Thy hand hath provided."   —R. W. B.

C. GOD'S REBUKE (v. 13)

13. Then Isaiah said, "Hear now, you house of David! Is it not enough to try the patience of men? Will you try the patience of my God also?

The message concerning the Israelite/Syrian coalition had been sent to the *house of David* (v. 2), so the Lord's response given through Isaiah was addressed to it as well. Isaiah had grown tired of Ahaz's arrogance and obstinacy, but even more significant, *God* had grown weary of it as well. His *patience* was running thin.

While Isaiah had spoken to Ahaz of "your God" in verse 11, in this verse he referred to *my God*. The prophet subtly indicated that Ahaz, through his stubborn disbelief, had severed ties with God and his purposes.

III. AHAZ RECEIVES A SIGN (ISAIAH 7:14-17)

A. A VIRGIN'S SPECIAL SON (v. 14)

14. "Therefore the Lord himself will give you a sign: The virgin will be with child and will give birth to a son, and will call him Immanuel.

Even though Ahaz had refused to ask for a *sign, the Lord* offered to *give* one anyway. The sign is directed to *you,* which is plural in the Hebrew. Thus this sign was not only for Ahaz but for the whole "house of David" (v. 13), or the nation of Judah.

The sign was this: *The virgin will be with child and will give birth to a son, and will call him Immanuel.* Christians understand this to be one of the most significant of the messianic prophecies (cited in Matthew 1:22, 23). While there has been frequent discussion over the years about the Hebrew word that is translated *virgin,* it is clear from a study of the Hebrew word used by Isaiah in this verse that *virgin* is the best translation of the term. The word is used nine times in the Old Testament, five times in the plural and four times in the singular. In every case the word clearly describes an unmarried woman, though in one instance (Proverbs 30:19) it describes an immoral one. However, for Isaiah's sign to have the significance attached to it, an immoral woman having a child would hardly be appropriate. Also worth noting is the fact that this word has the definite article before it: "*the* virgin." This calls attention to the fact that a special virgin is being described. The Septuagint (the Greek translation of the Old Testament) used a word that clearly means *virgin.*

Some believe that the virgin mentioned by Isaiah was a woman who was a virgin at the time of the prophecy, but who was married (perhaps to Isaiah) at the time the promised child was conceived. Many of these students suggest that the child mentioned in Isaiah 8:1-4 is the same one as prophesied here. As attractive as that kind of consistency may be, the structure of the Hebrew in this verse clearly indicates that the virgin would be a virgin at the time of the conception. Moreover, the birth of a child to a woman who was unmarried at the time of the prophecy and who later married would hardly provide the kind of exceptional "sign" that the Lord had challenged Ahaz to request in verse 11.

Isaiah then proceeded to call attention to the special *son* whom the virgin would bear. The child's uniqueness is clear from his name: *Immanuel,* meaning "God with us." Our finite minds find it difficult to comprehend how an infinite God could, through his Son, take on a human form and live among us as a human being. Yet that is exactly what the incarnation means: "the Word was God" and "the Word became flesh and made his dwelling among us" (John 1:1, 14).

PRAYER

Almighty God, help us to learn to trust you for help and guidance instead of relying on our own fallible judgments. May we look to Immanuel—God with us—as our source of strength and wisdom. In his name we pray. Amen.

THOUGHT TO REMEMBER

Immanuel—God with us. What a wonderful thought!

B. A NATION'S DISMAL FUTURE (vv. 15-17)

15, 16. *"He will eat curds and honey when he knows enough to reject the wrong and choose the right. But before the boy knows enough to reject the wrong and choose the right, the land of the two kings you dread will be laid waste.*

Isaiah then used the infancy of the promised child to indicate the time that Judah would be in danger from the current threat of Israel and Syria. He stated that the child's diet would consist of *curds and honey.* These foods reflect a humble diet, consistent with that of a family of limited financial resources, as Jesus' earthly family was. It is also consistent with the difficult times to come upon Judah because of Ahaz's reliance on Assyria (vv. 20-22). This is what the child would *eat when*—or it may be translated "up until the time that"—*he knows enough to reject the wrong and choose the right. But before* he reaches that stage of maturity, the threat of Israel and Syria would pass.

How long does it take a child to learn right from wrong? At a very early age (within just a few years) this process is taking place. This meant that the coalition formed by *the two kings* against Judah would be short-lived. In fact, within three years after the invasion by Israel and Syria, the Assyrians captured Damascus (capital of Syria) and forced Pekah, king of Israel, from his throne. Thus both Israel and Syria, which had caused Ahaz and Judah so much anxiety, were *laid waste.*

17. *"The LORD will bring on you and on your people and on the house of your father a time unlike any since Ephraim broke away from Judah—he will bring the king of Assyria."*

Isaiah then informed Ahaz that his land would suffer as it had not suffered in nearly two hundred years—*since Ephraim broke away from Judah.* This phrase refers to the *time* (in 931 B.C.) when the nation of God's people was divided into Ephraim (that is, Israel—the northern kingdom) and Judah (the southern kingdom). During the reigns of Jeroboam I (the first king of the north) and Rehoboam (the first king of the south) there was continual war (1 Kings 14:30). Isaiah foretold a similar period of chaos that *the king of Assyria* would bring about in Judah.

As noted earlier, Ahaz placed more trust in the king of Assyria (Tiglath-Pileser III) than he did in the God of Judah. He appealed to Tiglath-Pileser for help against Israel and Syria (2 Kings 16:7-9). While Ahaz may have considered this a solution to his present crisis, in the long run he caused Judah far more problems than he solved. Many of these problems would be left to his son Hezekiah to address (2 Kings 18:13—19:37).

CONCLUSION

Although God used Isaiah as his spokesman and as a special channel to convey his message, the prophet could not have understood fully all the implications of his predictions of God's future acts. He knew, of course, that *Immanuel* meant "God with us." Did he also recognize that he was describing the most significant event in history? Could he have dared to expect the coming of God's own Son into the world?

Of course, we today know how Isaiah's words were fulfilled. We have read Matthew, and he explains it (1:22, 23). May we never allow our familiarity with this passage to diminish our sense of wonder at the glorious thought of Immanuel! It is unfortunate that we usually limit our teaching about the incarnation to the few weeks during the Christmas season. Every day we need to remind ourselves that God's Son did come into the world and that we can receive forgiveness of our sins because he was willing to die for us.

Discovery Learning

This page contains an alternate lesson plan emphasizing learning activities. Classes desiring such student involvement will find these suggestions helpful. The next page is a reproducible activity page to further enhance discovery learning.

LEARNING GOALS

After this lesson each student will be able to:

1. Summarize the message that Isaiah gave Ahaz and how the message demonstrated God's control to King Ahaz and the people of Judah.

2. Cite reasons that people today need reassurance of God's control.

3. Share the message of "Immanuel" with someone facing particularly difficult circumstances.

INTO THE LESSON

Have the chairs arranged in circles of four or five, preferably at tables, as students arrive. At each table have a sheet of poster board, a marker, and several hymn and chorus books. Ask students to find lines in songs that indicate God is in control or that we should trust him as the pilot of our lives. They are to write the name of the song and the specific line(s) reflecting this concept. Examples you might give are "Jesus, Savior, Pilot Me," "This Is My Father's World," or "I Will Call Upon the Lord." Post these lists on a wall as groups report.

Make the transition to Bible study by telling the class that trusting God brings peace to life. Many of our hymns and choruses reflect his care. However, trusting him is easier said than done. Our study in Isaiah reminds us that God sees the big picture and is faithful to his people, even when they are in difficult circumstances.

INTO THE WORD

Use the information in the Lesson Background and the notes on verses 1 and 2 to set the stage for the events of today's lesson. Use a map of Israel and Judah to show how Jerusalem was under attack. Tell the class that God sent Isaiah to bring hope and good advice to the troubled King Ahaz and the people of Judah.

Since this passage has the potential to be quite confusing, keep the class members together for this study. Read the printed text. Then discuss the following questions as you work in information from the commentary.

1. God told Isaiah to take his son to meet Ahaz (v. 3). The son's unusual name, Shear-Jashub, means "a remnant will return." Why do you think God asked for him to be present?

2. God called the enemies "smoldering stubs of firewood" (vv. 4-6). What do you think he meant by this description of the kings of Syria and Israel?

3. Isaiah, in previous chapters, had already told of Judah's doom (vv. 4-6). Why would God now send a message of assurance? (Note: this is a good place to identify Ephraim and Tabeel. Also, use the brief summary of verses 7-9, on page 427, to stress God's encouragement and offer of hope.)

4. Why do you suppose Isaiah told Ahaz to ask for a sign from the Lord, and why did Ahaz refuse (vv. 10-12)? (Explain God's response in verse 13.)

5. Why would a prophecy about Jesus' birth be an appropriate and adequate sign (vv. 14-16)?

6. What was to be the result of Ahaz's faithless choice to call for the Assyrians to deliver Judah (v. 17)? Use the commentary notes to point out that the prophecies about suffering and captivity would come true. They are colorfully emphasized in verses 18-25. However, the prophecies about the remnant also teach us that God was with Judah, guiding the nation in difficult times.

INTO LIFE

God used his prophecy about Immanuel to demonstrate to Ahaz his never-ending care for his people and that he remained in control. Even though they were to face severe hardship and judgment, God demonstrated his mercy. People still need that assurance.

Use the following "case study" to help your students talk about why people need to know that God is in control in life's difficult circumstances and that the coming of Immanuel gives hope.

Albert is a thirty-six-year-old family man. He has two children: Kara is thirteen years old and Chad is ten. Albert's wife, Abby, has just been told she has developed a disease that will cause severe physical disabilities within the next few years. (1) What do Albert and Abby need to remember about God's character and how he works in the lives of his people? (2) What can they tell their children about the Lord through this experience? (3) Why are Christians able to respond differently to trying circumstances from the way unbelievers respond?

Distribute copies of the reproducible page that follows. Have the learners work in the same small groups as earlier to complete the first activity. Take a few minutes to review the groups' findings.

Then discuss the questions in the lower activity together. Encourage broad participation, as this will be encouraging to all who are present.

God Is in Control—735 B.C.

Isaiah's prophecy is dated about 735 B.C. or slightly later. His prophecy in Isaiah 7:1-6, 10-17 was meant to let Ahaz know that God is still in control. God even offered a sign that was meant to reassure Ahaz and his people.

What are the encouraging words Isaiah was to deliver to Ahaz?

Be _____

Keep _____

Don't be _____

Do not _____ _____

What was the sign Isaiah prophesied for Ahaz?

How was this sign meant to encourage?

God Is Still in Control—A.D. 2001

Even the faithful believers may sometimes doubt if God is active and in control of our universe and of our individual lives. What are some things that may cause believers to experience this doubt?

What are reasons to believe that God is still in control?

What are some reasons that you know God is active and working in *your* life?

The mind controlled by the Spirit is life and peace.
—Romans 8:6

PRONOUNCEMENT OF DOOM

LESSON 12

WHY TEACH THIS LESSON?

The title of today's lesson does not inspire eagerness to present it: "Pronouncement of *Doom*"! Those of us who grew up on animated "specials" featuring the characters created by the late Charles Schultz can just hear the voice of Linus as he intones, "We're *doomed*, Charlie Brown!"

While the session need not take on a "gloom and doom" atmosphere, it does sound a needed warning. In this age of grace, we sometimes take for granted that our sins are forgiven in Christ. But sin is still a serious matter, as this lesson shows.

It has been said that grace is free, but it's not cheap. Let today's reminder of the seriousness of sin be also a reminder of the blessing of grace.

INTRODUCTION
A. "WHAT HAVE YOU DONE LATELY?"

Alben Barkley, vice-president of the United States under President Harry Truman, once told of an incident that occurred when he was a senator from Kentucky. He learned that one of his staunch supporters had backed an opponent in a recent election. Later the senator confronted the man and began to remind him of all the favors he had done for him in the past.

"When you were out of work, didn't I get you a government job?" asked Senator Barkley.

"Yes, you did," the man replied.

"And when your uncle was in jail, didn't I persuade the judge to release him without bail?"

"That's right."

"And didn't I recommend your son for an appointment to the Naval Academy?"

"You sure did."

"Well then," asked the senator, "why did you work on behalf of my opponent after all I had done for you?"

"But, Senator," complained the man, "what have you done for me lately?"

This man's lack of gratitude is regrettable, but it is not as shocking as the ingratitude of the people of Judah in Isaiah's day. God had blessed them in countless ways, yet repeatedly they had turned away from him to worship pagan gods and engage in immoral living. It was part of Isaiah's responsibility as God's prophet to deliver the message that God's patience with Israel had reached an end. His judgment was close at hand.

B. LESSON BACKGROUND

"It was the best of times, it was the worst of times." This well-known opening statement from Charles Dickens's *A Tale of Two Cities* appropriately describes the situation in Judah when Isaiah began his ministry. Economically, these were "the

DEVOTIONAL READING:
MARK 12:1-9

BACKGROUND SCRIPTURE:
ISAIAH 5

PRINTED TEXT:
ISAIAH 5:1-8, 11, 18-23

LESSON AIMS

After this lesson each of the students should be able to:

1. Retell Isaiah's parable of the vineyard, and list the sins prevalent in Judah that prompted it.

2. Compare the list of sins with conditions in his or her own community.

3. Suggest a specific action that he or she can take to resist one of the sins cited by Isaiah.

KEY VERSE

Aug
19

Woe to those who call evil good and good evil, who put darkness for light and light for darkness, who put bitter for sweet and sweet for bitter. —Isaiah 5:20

HOW TO SAY IT

Ahaz. AY-haz.
Bathsheba. Bath-SHE-buh.
Corinth. COR-inth.
Hezekiah. Hez-ih-KYE-uh.
Isaiah. Eye-ZAY-uh.
Micah. MY-kuh.
Sophists. SAH-fists.

WHAT DO YOU THINK?

The lesson writer compares Isaiah's approach with that of Nathan in 2 Samuel 12. Of course, we are familiar with Jesus' use of parables, too. How might we use parables today to make a spiritual point?

best of times." But these were also "the worst of times" because the nation was experiencing serious spiritual and moral decline. Isaiah faced a difficult ministry, to say the least! (See Isaiah 6:9-13.) The challenges he faced were not greatly different from those that Christian leaders today confront, as economic prosperity causes many to feel apathetic about spiritual matters.

All told, Isaiah's labors covered a period of more than fifty years. It has already been noted that Isaiah seems to have had frequent access to the royal court, for he was able to speak with kings such as Ahaz and Hezekiah (Isaiah 7:3; 38:1). Some students believe he probably served as a kind of counselor to the kings of Judah.

Today's lesson text is taken from Isaiah 5. This chapter does not seem to be directly connected with either the chapters that immediately precede it or those that follow. As a result, there is no consensus among Bible students about where to place this chapter chronologically in Isaiah's ministry, although there is general agreement that it came early in his career.

I. PARABLE OF THE VINEYARD (ISAIAH 5:1-7)

A. LOCATION (v. 1)

1. I will sing for the one I love
　　a song about his vineyard:
　My loved one had a vineyard
　　on a fertile hillside.

Isaiah began with the words, *I will sing*. Perhaps Isaiah actually sang his message as a kind of ballad. Some have suggested that he did so at the Feast of Tabernacles, which was held in the fall in Jerusalem (v. 3) and which celebrated the harvest gathered from the vineyards (Deuteronomy 16:13). Many people would have been in the city for such a joyous occasion, and by singing his message, Isaiah might have attracted a larger audience than he would have otherwise.

The song is actually a parable, a story that makes a strong point. Isaiah's use of a parable here reminds us of how the prophet Nathan used a parable to expose David's sin with Bathsheba (2 Samuel 12:1-7).

B. PREPARATION (v. 2a)

2a. He dug it up and cleared it of stones
　　and planted it with the choicest vines.
　He built a watchtower in it
　　and cut out a winepress as well.

Having chosen a site for his vineyard, the owner *dug* in the soil and *cleared* the field of *stones* so that he could plant the *vines*. This was a common practice in Palestine, where there was little topsoil and many stones. The plot thus prepared was *planted* with *the choicest vines*, and a *watchtower* was built in the middle of it. This watchtower would allow the owner to guard the vineyard against thieves and marauding animals. Finally, a *winepress* was built. This was usually a basin, cut out of the limestone, where the grapes were squeezed by trampling. Below this basin was a second basin into which the juice flowed.

C. DISAPPOINTMENT (v. 2b)

2b. Then he looked for a crop of good grapes,
　　but it yielded only bad fruit.

Everything had been done to insure a bountiful harvest of *good grapes*, and the owner of the vineyard had good reason to expect such a crop. But to his disappointment, the vines *yielded only bad fruit*. These grapes were small, sour, and seedy—completely useless.

D. QUESTIONS (vv. 3, 4)

3, 4. *"Now you dwellers in Jerusalem and men of Judah,*
judge between me and my vineyard.
What more could have been done for my vineyard
than I have done for it?
When I looked for good grapes,
why did it yield only bad?

To apply this parable to his audience, Isaiah assumed the role of the "loved one." He asked two pointed questions: *What more could have been done for my vineyard? Why,* after all the time and effort I had invested, *did it yield only bad* grapes?

E. JUDGMENT (vv. 5, 6)

5. *"Now I will tell you*
what I am going to do to my vineyard:
I will take away its hedge,
and it will be destroyed;
I will break down its wall,
and it will be trampled.

Normally a *vineyard* was protected by a *hedge* of thick, thorny shrubs or cactuses. (Even today one may see garden plots or houses in Palestine protected in this manner.) The vineyard had become such a disappointment that the owner decided to remove its protection: *I will take away its hedge, and . . . will break down its wall.* Wild animals could then enter the vineyard and trample it.

6. *"I will make it a wasteland,*
neither pruned nor cultivated,
and briers and thorns will grow there.
I will command the clouds
not to rain on it."

Neglect would *make* the vineyard a *wasteland* in a very short time. Any plot of ground where the plants are not pruned or cultivated soon becomes an eyesore.

Thus far, Isaiah's reaction to the disappointing vineyard was no different from what anyone else's would have been. But when he said, *I will command the clouds not to rain on it*, the prophet seems to have been leading to the application of this parable to God's dealings with his people. Only he has authority over the clouds.

F. EXPLANATION (v. 7)

7. *The vineyard of the LORD Almighty*
is the house of Israel,
and the men of Judah
are the garden of his delight.
And he looked for justice, but saw bloodshed;
for righteousness, but heard cries of distress.

The indictment was directed at all of God's people— *the house of Israel* in the north and *Judah* in the south. The Lord had "planted" his people in a "fertile" (v. 1) land. He had done all he could to provide for and protect his vineyard. For centuries he had blessed his people with deliverance and protection from the nations around them. God did this for his people so that they would be his "holy nation" (Exodus 19:6) and would produce "fruit" appropriate for such a people.

But God was sadly disappointed. He *looked for justice*; instead he found *bloodshed*. The rulers and the rich were using all kinds of clever schemes to exploit people and keep them under their control. Instead of *righteousness*, there were *cries*, most likely the anguished outcries of the oppressed.

DAILY BIBLE READINGS

Monday, Aug. 13—*The Song of the Vineyard (Isaiah 5:1-7)*

Tuesday, Aug. 14—*Woe Unto Extortioners and Carousers (Isaiah 5:8-17)*

Wednesday, Aug. 15—*Woe Unto Scoffers (Isaiah 5:18-23)*

Thursday, Aug. 16—*Foreign Invasion Predicted (Isaiah 5:24-30)*

Friday, Aug. 17—*The Anger of the Almighty (Isaiah 9:11—10:4)*

Saturday, Aug. 18—*Assyria Also Judged (Isaiah 10:5-12)*

Sunday, Aug. 19—*Wicked Tenants of the Vineyard (Mark 12:1-9)*

WHAT DO YOU THINK?

Suggest different analogies (besides a vineyard) that might be used in a parable to describe our nation's present moral condition and the danger of God's judgment.

Because of such a poor "harvest," God determined to do to his vineyard what the owner in the parable did to his. He would remove the "hedge" of protection from his people, abandoning them to their enemies.

SOUR GRAPES

In contemporary vernacular, "sour grapes" is a term used to describe disparaging remarks from someone who is jealous of someone else's success. Examples of sour grapes include a contest loser's criticism that the prize was not worth winning anyhow or a small church's put-down of a larger church's methods.

Such jealousy is not among the sins condemned by Isaiah in his poetic parable. The prophet decried the ingratitude of the Israelites and their tragic betrayal of God's trust. God was the owner of the vineyard (the people of Israel and Judah). He prepared and provided everything necessary for the productivity and security of his people. He had every reason to expect a bountiful harvest of delicious grapes (obedient, faithful lives). Instead, all God reaped was wild, sour, seedy fruit—a sorry crop worth nothing. No wonder God allowed the "vineyard" to be destroyed.

What more could God have done for Israel? What more can he do for us? He supplies every need, both physical and spiritual. He wants us to "bear much fruit" (John 15:8). Are we producing fruit—or only sour grapes? —R. W. B.

II. APPLICATION (ISAIAH 5:8, 11, 18-23)

After pronouncing God's sentence upon Judah, Isaiah then introduced six specific charges against the people. Each of them begins with the ominous word *Woe.*

A. WOE TO THE COVETOUS (v. 8)

8. Woe to you who add house to house
and join field to field
till no space is left
and you live alone in the land.

WHAT DO YOU THINK?

What are some "woes" God might pronounce on our nation or on an average congregation? How can these woes be effectively communicated to people today?

[Use Isaiah's style in today's text to develop this list. The focus can be either on issues that pervade all of society or specific issues of local importance.]

Woe is a strong word, signifying much more than a gentle slap on the wrist. It carries the weight of God's righteous indignation.

Like Amos before him (Amos 8:4) and Micah, his contemporary (Micah 2:2), Isaiah condemned the people's greed. The rich added *house to house* by buying up all the property they could until their houses touched one another. Apparently they did this at the expense of the poor, creating a kind of monopoly for themselves. Perhaps those who did this rented out houses as a source of income.

The rich would *join field to field,* acquiring land adjoining their own. Small farmers who fell into debt often sold their land to pay off their debts. The law required that in the Year of Jubilee such land was to be returned to the original owners or their heirs (Leviticus 25:8-17), but the rich often had clever schemes to circumvent this law. As a result they were able to *live alone* amid their vast holdings.

B. WOE TO THE CAROUSERS (v. 11)

11. Woe to those who rise early in the morning
to run after their drinks,
who stay up late at night
till they are inflamed with wine.

Those who *rise early in the morning* are usually hard-working persons who are to be commended for their diligence. Isaiah's second *woe* is reserved for those who show the same kind of enthusiasm for strong drink. They are so addicted to alcohol that they start early and *stay up late at night* to continue drinking. Obviously, only the rich could do this. A common laborer would soon become impoverished and unable to provide himself with basic necessities—or with more *wine!*

C. WOE TO THE SCOFFERS (vv. 18, 19)

18. Woe to those who draw sin along with cords of deceit,
and wickedness as with cart ropes.

The third *woe* was directed toward the arrogant scoffers. The figure of men rather than oxen straining to pull a heavy *cart* is striking. Commentators express different views as to its meaning. Perhaps the best explanation is that these men were having to bear the weight of their sin (and its consequences). "The evil deeds of a wicked man ensnare him; the cords of his sin hold him fast" (Proverbs 5:22).

19. to those who say, "Let God hurry,
let him hasten his work
so we may see it.
Let it approach,
let the plan of the Holy One of Israel come,
so we may know it."

These scoffers were telling Isaiah, "You claim that God is working in history. But we don't see it. Show us—give us a sign—and then we will believe." They sound like some of Jesus' enemies who demanded a sign (Matthew 12:38). These men were not seeking after truth; they were interested only in making Jesus look bad. They had closed their minds. Even when Jesus was on the cross, they challenged him, "He's the King of Israel! Let him come down now from the cross, and we will believe in him" (Matthew 27:42). But even such a dramatic miracle as that would not have changed their stubborn minds. Peter notes that "scoffers" continue to question whether Jesus will return (2 Peter 3:3, 4).

D. WOE TO THE PERVERTED (v. 20)

20. Woe to those who call evil good
and good evil,
who put darkness for light
and light for darkness,
who put bitter for sweet
and sweet for bitter.

The Sophists, a school of philosophers in ancient Greece, earned a reputation for being able to "make the worse appear the better part." It is obvious that some in Isaiah's day had preceded the Greeks in mastering this skill. Even now there seems to be no shortage of those proficient in this art! Certain lawyers have brought disrepute on their profession by cleverly defining terms in such a way that their clients can avoid the consequences of their evil deeds. Advocates of abortion define the issue as one of "choice." They call an unborn baby a "fetus," not a human being. Those who want to justify homosexuality speak of an "alternate lifestyle," as if that would make such behavior more acceptable to God.

Many church members fall into the same trap. They don't want to believe that a "loving" God could consign anyone to Hell. They lose their evangelistic zeal by embracing the belief that "one religion is as good as another." Isaiah did not hesitate to pronounce a woe upon those who practice such verbal and moral sleight of hand.

E. WOE TO THE ARROGANT (v. 21)

21. Woe to those who are wise in their own eyes
and clever in their own sight.

The apostle Paul said there were some in the church at Corinth who would "measure themselves by themselves and compare themselves with themselves." As a result, he said, these people were not *wise* (2 Corinthians 10:12). Many today reject God's standards of right and wrong and substitute their own. Since these are

The humorous illustration of a person misreading the chart during an eye exam reminds us we all need to examine how we "spell" good and evil.

"Woe unto them that call evil good, and good evil." Isaiah 5:20

WHAT DO YOU THINK?

List the ways that people today give sin other names so that they "call evil good." How do such labels become accepted, and what harm does that acceptance do? How can we ensure that we are not "brainwashed" by the ungodly changes around us?

PRAYER

O God, from whom all blessings flow, may we never forget that you are the source of all our blessings. Grant us the wisdom and the courage to accept the responsibilities that accompany these blessings. Help us to be fruitful in your service. In Jesus' name, amen.

THOUGHT TO REMEMBER

Responsibilities should not be seen as burdens to be borne, but as opportunities to help others and to bring glory to God.

WHAT DO YOU THINK?

Christians have proposed many ways to combat the moral drift of our culture. What are some pros and cons of relying on any of the following: (a) focusing only on evangelistic outreach, (b) developing programs that help Christians grow in holiness, (c) starting organizations like MADD (Mothers Against Drunk Driving) to attack moral evils, or (d) developing government programs like DARE (a drug use prevention program) to attack moral evils?

almost always easier to meet than God's standards, such individuals begin to feel proud and self-righteous when they are able to live up to their revised standards.

F. WOE TO THE DRUNKARDS (vv. 22, 23)

22, 23. *Woe to those who are heroes at drinking wine*
    and champions at mixing drinks,
who acquit the guilty for a bribe,
    but deny justice to the innocent.

The sixth of Isaiah's "woes" might seem like a repetition of his second (v. 11), but there is a difference. In the second "woe" Isaiah condemns those who have succumbed to the power of strong drink. They begin drinking early in the morning, they drink all day, and they are still drinking at night. Here the *woe* seems directed at some kind of public officials who engage in what we might call "binge drinking." They like to demonstrate what *heroes* they are and what *champions* they are *at mixing drinks*. But their drinking smooths the path toward corruption. Their senses and their moral values are dulled so that they *acquit the guilty for a bribe* and *deny justice to the innocent*. When we note the heartaches caused by the abuse of alcohol today, we are reminded once more of just how contemporary the words of Isaiah are, even though they were uttered some twenty-seven centuries ago.

SIX DEADLY SINS

The "seven deadly sins" named during the Middle Ages were pride, avarice, gluttony, lust, sloth, envy, and anger. Isaiah spoke of only six "woes" in our text, but anyone can see that these were "deadly" to the perpetrators: covetousness, carousing, scoffing, perversion of the truth, arrogance, and injustice (sparked by drunkenness).

The end of Isaiah 5 tells of the punishment that would come to these unrepentant sinners. Their destruction and defeat are described in terms of fire, decay, beatings, earthquakes, noise, and darkness. God's judgment will be no Sunday school picnic!

Regardless of the number or the seriousness of your sins, they are punishable by the same "wages"—death (Romans 6:23). Jesus has paid that penalty for you, but you must appropriate his gift of redemption by trusting and obedient faith (John 1:12; Acts 2:38).

"How shall we escape if we ignore such a great salvation?" (Hebrews 2:3). *Woe to us!* —R. W. B.

CONCLUSION

When Isaiah began his ministry in ancient Judah, his nation was enjoying a prosperity similar to that experienced when David was king. These blessings had come from the hand of God, who had been watching over his people from the time of Abraham. But the nation had forgotten that God was the source of their blessings, and because of that, they were using his blessings in the wrong way. Many had become greedy, and this greed had lured them into bribery and other corrupt practices. In a land where there was plenty for everyone to be well fed and properly clothed and housed, the rich were becoming richer at the expense of the poor. Isaiah eloquently pointed out that with all blessings come responsibilities, and the greater the blessings, the greater the responsibilities.

If we cannot see the obvious parallels between our society and the one to which Isaiah preached, then we are either morally blind or willfully ignorant. It should be clear that we who live under the New Covenant instituted by Jesus Christ have received greater blessings than the people of Isaiah's time, and as a result we have far greater responsibilities. Are we living up to them?

Remember Jesus' words: "From everyone who has been given much, much will be demanded" (Luke 12:48).

Discovery Learning

This page contains an alternate lesson plan emphasizing learning activities. Classes desiring such student involvement will find these suggestions helpful. The next page is a reproducible activity page to further enhance discovery learning.

LEARNING GOALS

After this lesson each student will be able to:

1. Retell Isaiah's parable of the vineyard, and list the sins prevalent in Judah that prompted it.

2. Compare the list of sins with conditions in his or her own community.

3. Suggest a specific action that he or she can take to resist one of the sins cited by Isaiah.

INTO THE LESSON

Write the words *Love Songs* on the chalkboard or on a large poster. As students arrive, have romantic music playing on a CD or cassette player. Ask students to name their favorite love songs and to tell the songs' themes. Examples of themes are declarations of love, disappointment or heartache, separation, and the like. If your class is small, you may hear each person's favorite. Larger classes could have trios or small groups identify their favorites with each other.

Tell the students that today we will read a sad love song. The song is packed with emotion—deep love, tender care, a disappointed lover, anger, and desertion. It is a parable about God's relationship with unfaithful Israel and Judah. It is a powerful parable that teaches us about God's expectations for believers today.

INTO THE WORD

Use the Lesson Background in the commentary pages to set the scene for this study. Be sure to note that this chapter is in poetic form.

During the week before this lesson, ask a person who reads or memorizes Scripture well to be prepared to recite or read Isaiah 5:1-8, 11, 18-23 for the class. This early request will give the person time to become familiar with the flow of the words in this passage of Scripture. Before the reading or recitation, ask the class to close their eyes and enjoy hearing this unusual love song. They will study it closely in a few moments.

After the reading, tell the class that the poetry is written in two verses or thoughts. The first is the song of the vineyard, and the second is the condemnation of sins. First, review the imagery of Israel and Judah hidden in the song of the vineyard (vv. 1-7). Distribute copies of the reproducible activity page that follows. Have the learners work individually or in small groups to complete the activity; then discuss their results.

To study the second part of the poetry, tell the class that Isaiah applies the parable by specifically mentioning six charges or sins. Each charge is introduced with the strong word *woe*. Ask the class to define *woe*. (*Strong word of rebuke, signifying God's righteous indignation.*) Then ask them to locate the six "woes" in the text and to identify the sin condemned in each.

Have a class member write these six sins on the chalkboard as they are identified. They may include greed (v. 8), alcohol addiction (v. 11), arrogant scoffing of God (vv. 18, 19), false advice or rationalization of their sins (v. 20), spiritual arrogance (v. 21), and drunkenness that leads to a perversion of justice (vv. 22, 23).

INTO LIFE

Tell the class that Isaiah's words are very contemporary. Ask students to work in teams of two or three persons each to write notes about how each of the six sins are evidenced in today's society. Give each group a piece of poster board with the heading "Applying Isaiah to Life Today." Over the left column write, "Woe to. . . ." Over the right column write, "Contemporary Acts or Evidences of Sin." The teams are to identify and list the sins against which Isaiah invoked the divine "woe" down the left column. In the right column, they are to cite ways these sins are evidenced in life today. Since the discussion could become lengthy, encourage groups to work quickly. They should also spend more time on the sins more prevalent in our culture. Ask volunteers to tell a few of their answers to the whole class.

Remind the class that even though God was speaking to a nation, his heart was breaking because individuals had been unfaithful to his love. He responds similarly when individuals sin today. To make the lesson personal, ask each learner to think of some sins or areas of temptation that trouble him or her personally. Give each person a three-by-five card and say, "I'd like each of you to write a prayer on this card. Thank God for his love and patience, confess to God the problem area you have identified, and ask God's guidance in overcoming this temptation." Assure the learners that no one will be required to reveal the information on the card to anyone but God. Encourage them to use these in the coming week to seek God's provision for their spiritual needs. Then close with prayer.

Poetic Imagery

Isaiah uses poetic form and imagery to communicate God's love, disappointment, and judgment upon Israel and Judah. Use the following chart to interpret and apply the parable in Isaiah 5:1-7 to God's people. See verse 7 for clues in interpreting this love song.

THE IMAGERY	INTERPRETATION OR APPLICATION
The vineyard	
The fertile hillside	
Clearing the stones	
The watchtower	
The winepress	
Bad fruit	
Removing the hedge and the wall	
No pruning nor care	
No rain	

ISRAEL TAKEN INTO CAPTIVITY

LESSON 13

WHY TEACH THIS LESSON?

"That's the last straw!" How often we have reached the point of exasperation with a strong-willed child, an uncooperative co-worker, or an unreasonable employer. Perhaps it has even been with a brother or sister in Christ with whom we have trouble getting along.

Today's lesson tells how God reached such a point with Israel. The easy application might be to justify our severing relations with some disagreeable acquaintance. But challenge your students to look deeper. Look at the long list of abuses God tolerated from Israel before finally allowing the nation to be taken into captivity. And note further—even the deportation was for the sake of purging a remnant. The separation was not permanent.

The lesson is really one of patience, not of punishment alone.

INTRODUCTION

A. WHEN FOUNDATIONS ERODE

Several months ago as my family and I were traveling on an interstate highway, the traffic slowed and almost stopped. Up ahead we could see that construction work was in progress. As we approached the construction area, our two lanes were narrowed down to one lane. Soon we came to a bridge, and there the problem became obvious. The fill on the bridge approach had eroded away and the pavement had collapsed. When I later asked about what happened, I was told that at the base of the fill was a spring that had not been properly capped and drained away. As a result, the spring continued to flow, slowly washing away the fill and allowing the pavement to collapse.

The fall of Israel (the northern kingdom) occurred in a similar manner. Its spiritual and moral weaknesses gradually eroded away its strength. Although the collapse of the nation took place in 722 B.C., the seeds of judgment had been sown over many generations. Only the final destruction came suddenly. Is there a lesson in this for us? And are we willing to heed it?

B. LESSON BACKGROUND

Today's lesson concludes this quarter's studies, entitled "Division and Decline." We saw *division* in the first lesson, where we studied Rehoboam. It was his decision to listen to foolish counsel that resulted in the division of the kingdom of Israel. Other lessons during the quarter highlighted the *decline* that occurred in both Israel and Judah as the people and their leaders yielded more and more to sin. In today's lesson we see the tragic, but inevitable, result of this pattern: the judgment of Almighty God.

A visitor to Israel and Judah in 750 B.C. would have found both nations prospering and enjoying peace with their neighbors. At the time, both nations were

DEVOTIONAL READING:
EXODUS 20:1-6

BACKGROUND SCRIPTURE:
2 KINGS 17:1-23

PRINTED TEXT:
2 KINGS 17:6-18

LESSON AIMS

After participating in this lesson, students should be able to:

1. Tell what today's text says about why the northern kingdom fell to the Assyrians.

2. Tell why God's judgment must be a crucial part of the church's message today.

3. Suggest some credible ways to express God's judgment against sin.

KEY VERSE

So the LORD was very angry with Israel and removed them from his presence. Only the tribe of Judah was left.
—2 Kings 17:18

LESSON 13 NOTES

being ruled by strong kings—Jeroboam II in Israel and Uzziah in Judah. In part, the good times had come because Assyria, the primary power to the northeast, was in a period of decline. But the apparent good times were not to last much longer. The external prosperity of Israel in particular masked serious spiritual and moral problems. These problems, however, could not be masked from God, nor from his prophets, who warned of imminent judgment.

In 745 B.C. Tiglath-Pileser III came to power in Assyria. He gave immediate attention to reviving its prominence on the world stage. He soon turned his attention westward to Syria and Israel. These two nations had been bitter enemies at one time, but, fearing Assyria's might, they formed a coalition against Tiglath-Pileser and tried to force Judah to join them. But none of Israel's efforts, no matter how valiant, could save her from the might of Assyria—for Assyria was God's instrument of judgment against his people.

I. ISRAEL'S FALL (2 KINGS 17:6)
A. Samaria Destroyed (v. 6a)
6a. In the ninth year of Hoshea, the king of Assyria captured Samaria.

The death of Jeroboam II brought a period of turmoil to Israel. Five men occupied her throne in less than twenty years. Sometime around 738 B.C. the Assyrians, under Tiglath-Pileser III, seized portions of the land and took captives to Assyria (2 Kings 15:29). The king, Pekah, was later assassinated as the result of a conspiracy led by Hoshea, who then replaced him on the throne. (In Assyrian records Tiglath-Pileser III claims responsibility for placing Hoshea on the throne. He may have backed Hoshea in order to gain a more cooperative king to be his vassal.)

However, after about six years, Hoshea rebelled against Assyria (2 Kings 17:4). As a result Shalmaneser V, who had replaced Tiglath-Pileser III as king of Assyria, marched against Israel. In 725 B.C. the Assyrians laid siege to Samaria, the capital of Israel. Samaria had been strongly fortified and was able to withstand the siege for three years, finally falling in 722 B.C.

B. Captives Taken (v. 6b)
6b. . . . and deported the Israelites to Assyria. He settled them in Halah, in Gozan on the Habor River and in the towns of the Medes.

According to the records of Sargon II (who succeeded Shalmaneser V), the Assyrians *deported* 27,290 people from Samaria. Deportation served two purposes: it provided slaves for the Assyrians, and, by deporting the nation's leaders, it decreased the likelihood of another revolt. As an additional defense against further insurrection, the Assyrians settled in Israel conquered people from other parts of their empire.

The exact location of *Halah* is unknown, but some scholars place it north and east of Nineveh, Assyria's capital. The *Habor River* emptied into the Euphrates River, and *Gozan* was a city situated on the Habor. The *Medes* occupied an area east of the Tigris River in what is modern Iran.

II. A HISTORY OF SIN (2 KINGS 17:7-12)
A. Fearing Other Gods (v. 7)
7. All this took place because the Israelites had sinned against the LORD their God, who had brought them up out of Egypt from under the power of Pharaoh king of Egypt. They worshiped other gods.

The first six verses of this chapter give an explanation of some of the international maneuvering for power that took place during the nine years of Hoshea's reign. These verses seem to place the blame for Israel's fall on Hoshea's flawed

Use the same map as you used for lesson 1 to set the scene for today's lesson.

political schemes. The verse before us, however, makes it clear that Hoshea was not the only one responsible for the punishment that God administered to the nation. *The Israelites had sinned*; the people, along with the king, were guilty. They had *worshiped other gods* in spite of the many centuries during which the true God had blessed them and watched over them. They had forgotten all that he had done for them, including the event that had made them a nation: when he *brought them up out of Egypt*.

This verse should not be taken to imply that everyone in Israel had turned away from the Lord. Just as in Elijah's day, there were certainly many who had remained faithful to God (1 Kings 19:18). One of the great tragedies of sin is that in a time of national disaster, the faithful and innocent often have to suffer along with the wicked.

B. LIVING AS THE PAGANS (v. 8)
8. . . . and followed the practices of the nations the LORD had driven out before them, as well as the practices that the kings of Israel had introduced.

Every person, whether he acknowledges it or not, orders his life according to some kind of a moral code. Even though that code may not be chiseled in stone or printed in law books, it is still the guide that orders that person's life. It may be rigid and unbending, or it may be very flexible, changing with every new situation. Through Moses, God had given his people the Ten Commandments, written in stone, and along with them other laws covering many aspects of their daily living and their worship of God.

Many people try to combine religious codes with their own personal codes of conduct, resulting in interesting, and often contradictory, systems of right and wrong. This was the situation in ancient Israel. Most of the citizens of Israel probably would have insisted that they were faithful to the laws of Moses. At the same time, they *followed the practices of the* pagan *nations* around them.

When the Israelites entered the land of Canaan, the pagan inhabitants there practiced such sinful acts as cult prostitution and child sacrifice. God ordered the Israelites to drive out these sinful people (Deuteronomy 7:1-5), but this command was never completely carried out. Later, godless *kings of Israel* such as Jeroboam I and Ahab (spurred on by his wife Jezebel) invented pagan gods or imported them from foreign lands and encouraged the people to follow statutes made by men, not ordained by God (1 Kings 12:25-33; 16:30-33; 21:25, 26).

ETCHED IN STONE
"It's not etched in stone," we sometimes hear a person say. Such a statement usually means, "Hey, I'm flexible! I'm willing to consider another idea. I'm not locked into this suggestion or rule or date or whatever." If something isn't "etched in stone," it is subject to change.

Israel had treated God's law as if its statutes could be altered, modified, or even erased. But they had intentionally forgotten that the divine Commandments that formed the basis of the law *were* etched in stone—literally! The tablets that Moses brought down from Sinai were inscribed indelibly, and they are part of God's words that "will never pass away" (Matthew 24:35).

Many people today live by a "revised version" of the Bible. Moral relativity, situation ethics, and the very popular "How could it be wrong when it feels so right?" all play fast and loose with God's truth. But when a command or prohibition is "in the Book," no alterations are allowed. "If anyone takes words away from this book of prophecy, God will take away from him his share in the tree of life and in the holy city, which are described in this book" (Revelation 22:19).

It's etched in stone!

—R. W. B.

WHAT DO YOU THINK?

Who is responsible for the moral decline in a nation: the leaders or the citizens? Why? What ought the church to do to fulfill its responsibility regarding moral decline? How?

HOW TO SAY IT
Ahab. AY-hab.
Asherah. Uh-SHE-ruh.
Assyria. Uh-SEAR-ee-uh.
Baal. BAY-ul.
Canaanite. KAY-nuh-nite.
Elijah. Ee-LYE-juh.
Euphrates. You-FRAY-teez.
Gozan. GO-zan.
Habor. HAY-bor.
Halah. HAY-luh.
Hoshea. Ho-SHAY-uh.
Jeroboam. Jair-uh-BO-um.
Jezebel. JEZ-uh-bel.
Medes. Meeds.
Molech. MO-lek.
Nineveh. NIN-uh-vuh.
Pekah. PEEK-uh.
Pharaoh. FAIR-o *or* FAY-ro.
Rehoboam. Ree-huh-BO-um.
Samaria. Suh-MARE-ee-uh.
Sargon. SAR-gon.
Shalmaneser. Shal-mun-EE-zer.
Sinai. SIGH-nigh *or* SIGH-nay-eye.
Syria. SEAR-ee-uh.
Tiglath-Pileser. TIG-lath-Pih-LEE-zer.
Tigris. TIE-griss.
Uzziah. Uh-ZYE-uh.

C. BUILDING IDOLS (vv. 9-12)

9. The Israelites secretly did things against the LORD their God that were not right. From watchtower to fortified city they built themselves high places in all their towns.

This verse and those that follow mention specific ways in which the people did *things against the Lord their God*—things *that were not right*.

The sins of the people included practices done *secretly* and others that were carried out publicly, at the various *high places*. Earlier in Israel's history, some of these places were used in worshiping the Lord (1 Samuel 9:11-14; 1 Kings 3:2). But by the time described in our text, the high places were devoted mainly to pagan worship.

The phrase *from watchtower to fortified city* means "throughout the whole land," from the most isolated vineyard (where a tower was built in order to watch for thieves or animals) to the most well-defended city. The corruption of the people was a national disgrace.

10. They set up sacred stones and Asherah poles on every high hill and under every spreading tree.

These *sacred stones* or obelisks were monuments that were set up as objects of worship. The making of such images was strictly forbidden by the Second Commandment (Exodus 20:4).

The term *Asherah poles* refers to trunks of trees or posts set up as places of worship for the Canaanite goddess Asherah. Asherah was a pagan fertility goddess, whose "worship" often included illicit sex acts performed in order to induce her to grant fertility to humans, livestock, and crops.

11, 12. At every high place they burned incense, as the nations whom the LORD had driven out before them had done. They did wicked things that provoked the LORD to anger. They worshiped idols, though the LORD had said, "You shall not do this."

Incense was recognized as a symbol of prayer (Psalm 141:2). In this case, the incense was a symbol of prayers offered to pagan gods, not to the Lord. The phrase *whom the Lord had driven out before them* hinted at the punishment the Israelites were to suffer. God had given his people clear warning of this when he first issued his law. If the Israelites failed to obey the Lord, they would be treated as those whom the Lord had driven out of the land (Leviticus 18:26-28).

III. A HISTORY OF WARNINGS (2 KINGS 17:13-18)

A. PROPHETS SENT (v. 13)

13. The LORD warned Israel and Judah through all his prophets and seers: "Turn from your evil ways. Observe my commands and decrees, in accordance with the entire Law that I commanded your fathers to obey and that I delivered to you through my servants the prophets."

God gave the Israelites his *Law* in order to show them how to live as his people. But that was not all he did. He raised up judges to deliver them from their oppressors in the promised land. He permitted them to have kings, though he recognized that such a request was really not in the people's best interests. In addition the Lord sent *prophets and seers* who *warned* the people to *turn from* their *evil ways*. While the term *prophets* describes the office these messengers held, *seers* calls attention to the means by which they often received their messages from God—through dreams and visions.

B. WARNINGS REJECTED (vv. 14-17)

14. But they would not listen and were as stiff-necked as their fathers, who did not trust in the LORD their God.

WHAT DO YOU THINK?

Who or what are the idols in our nation? What sacrifices are being offered to these idols? Which has the most negative influence on the average person: the practices of Christian neighbors or non-Christian neighbors? Why?

DAILY BIBLE READINGS

Monday, Aug. 20—Assyria Defeats King Hoshea (2 Kings 17:1-6)

Tuesday, Aug. 21—Israel Sinned and Disobeyed God (2 Kings 17:7-13)

Wednesday, Aug. 22—Reasons for Israel's Captivity (2 Kings 17:14-18)

Thursday, Aug. 23—Summary of Israel's Iniquity (2 Kings 17:19-23)

Friday, Aug. 24—Assyria Resettles Samaria (2 Kings 17:24-28)

Saturday, Aug. 25—Pagan Worship Prevails in Samaria (2 Kings 17:29-41)

Sunday, Aug. 26—The One True God (Exodus 20:1-6)

In spite of God's efforts to turn his wayward people back from their sinful ways, the words of his messengers fell on deaf ears. They stiffened their necks like stubborn animals that refuse to obey the person who holds the reins.

15. They rejected his decrees and the covenant he had made with their fathers and the warnings he had given them. They followed worthless idols and themselves became worthless. They imitated the nations around them although the LORD had ordered them, "Do not do as they do," and they did the things the LORD had forbidden them to do.

They rejected his decrees and the covenant that God *had made with their fathers* at Mount Sinai. Instead of God's law becoming a testimony to the people's faithfulness toward him, it testified against them. Instead of building their faith on the many clear evidences of God's guidance, they preferred following the emptiness of the false gods that were really no gods at all. Thus they *became worthless* to God—that is, they failed to fulfill the purpose for which he had called them out of Egypt to be a nation.

16. They forsook all the commands of the LORD their God and made for themselves two idols cast in the shape of calves, and an Asherah pole. They bowed down to all the starry hosts, and they worshiped Baal.

The *idols* mentioned here were made by melting precious metal and pouring it into a *cast* or mold. Specifically noted were the *two* golden *calves* that Jeroboam I had set up at Dan and at Bethel after the kingdom had divided in 931 B.C. (1 Kings 12:25-29). As noted under verse 10, the word *Asherah pole* describes a trunk or pole set up for the worship of the pagan goddess Asherah. Asherah was a consort of *Baal*, whose worship was encouraged by Ahab and Jezebel (1 Kings 16:31, 32).

17. They sacrificed their sons and daughters in the fire. They practiced divination and sorcery and sold themselves to do evil in the eyes of the LORD, provoking him to anger.

Child sacrifice was common to the worship of the pagan god Molech. The Israelites had substituted the God of love with the god of brutality. Is it any wonder that God was provoked to *anger*? Will God be any less angry with our society, which has sacrificed countless numbers of unborn babies a year through abortion?

Divination is the practice of attempting to learn the future through means forbidden by God. Sometimes this was accomplished through trances or dreams. In other cases the entrails of sacrificed animals were "interpreted," or lots were cast, to provide such information. God condemned such practices (Deuteronomy 18:9-14).

The word *sorcery* describes the efforts of magicians to invoke the aid of evil spirits to influence human affairs. These activities were also condemned by God. When people turn away from serving God, they often turn to strange and bizarre practices. We see many in our time who have departed from God and his revealed truth to embrace the so-called "New Age" philosophy or some other deceptive cult—or even the occult.

C. JUDGMENT CARRIED OUT (v. 18)

18. So the LORD was very angry with Israel and removed them from his presence. Only the tribe of Judah was left.

Secular historians might attribute Israel's decline and fall solely to political or military factors. But the divinely inspired historian saw something else. He saw the hand of God's judgment using pagan powers to execute his judgment. *The Lord was very angry with Israel*—and with good reason. For centuries he had watched over Israel, guiding her, protecting her, and sending prophets to

WHAT DO YOU THINK?

Though Israel followed in the sins of "their fathers," younger generations often tend to act differently from the previous ones. What would it take for the current younger generation to "rebel" by drawing closer to God rather than going farther away from God? What can the church do today to influence the younger generation in this "radical" direction?

WHAT DO YOU THINK?

How harmless or destructive are the culturally accepted "divination" practices like horoscopes and psychic hotlines? Why do you hold this view?

warn her when she departed from God's ways. Time and again she had rejected these warnings. And so God *removed them from his presence*, and *only the tribe of Judah* survived. But Judah did not learn from Israel's experience, and it also felt God's anger about a hundred twenty years later. The enemy was different (Babylon), but the reason Judah fell was the same reason Israel did—disobedience.

BARRICADES ON THE ROAD TO HELL

Some partying teens were speeding down a rural road one night, oblivious to warnings that a bridge was out not far ahead. They flew past a huge yellow and black sign that announced: ROAD CLOSED, 1/2 MILE. Without noticing, they sped past another sign with blinking lights attached: BRIDGE OUT, ROAD CLOSED, 1/4 MILE. In seconds they saw the barricade blocking the edge of a gaping chasm where the bridge used to stand. Startled out of his drunken stupor, the driver slammed on his brakes; but the car crashed through the barrier and plunged into the dark abyss. There were no survivors.

Israel had been warned—repeatedly—of the consequences of its rebellious behavior. God spoke his message of certain judgment through his many prophets. But Israel ignored each barricade that God erected on the slippery slope to destruction. The nation did not survive.

Millions around us are speeding down the road to spiritual death and eternal condemnation. God has provided the barricades of conscience, conviction, and Christ to halt their race toward Hell. Most ignore the warnings, oblivious to the truth. They continue to rebel and resist and reject God's salvation. Among such there will be no survivors.

　　　　　　　　　　　　　　　　　　　　　　　　　　　　　—R. W. B.

CONCLUSION

Many are acquainted with the saying, "Though the mills of God grind slowly, yet they grind exceeding small." This one brief statement is a fitting summary of the history of Israel.

From the time that God led his people out of Egypt and into the promised land, he blessed them in many ways. Yet on numerous occasions the people turned from him and followed other gods. At times they may have fallen into sin unwittingly, simply aping the activities of their neighbors without thinking about the consequences. At other times their sins were a flagrant defiance of God's laws. But whether the people acted unwittingly or arrogantly, God's mills continued to grind toward a day of reckoning.

There were instances in which God gave his people glimpses of what lay ahead for them if they did not repent. During the time of the judges, he allowed them to be threatened and harassed by many of their neighbors. Such treatment usually brought them to their senses (if only briefly), and then the sorry cycle began again. This scenario was repeated, particularly during the time of the divided kingdom, and in spite of the fact that God repeatedly sent prophets to warn his people of the inevitable outcome if they continued in sin. Finally, as recorded in today's lesson, the divine Miller carried out his judgment on the northern kingdom. The promised "grinding" had come to pass.

There ought to be a sobering lesson in this for us today. Our nation has been greatly blessed, materially and spiritually, yet how have we used these blessings? All too often we have squandered them on selfish and sinful pursuits. Do we think that we are any better than ancient Israel or that we can devise a way to avoid judgment?

Listen carefully! Can you hear, above the din of our busy and noisy lives, the steady and ominous grinding of God's righteous mills?

Discovery Learning

This page contains an alternate lesson plan emphasizing learning activities. Classes desiring such student involvement will find these suggestions helpful. The next page is a reproducible activity page to further enhance discovery learning.

LEARNING GOALS

After this lesson each student will be able to:

1. Tell what today's text says about why the northern kingdom fell to the Assyrians.

2. Tell why God's judgment must be a crucial part of the church's message today.

3. Suggest some credible ways to express God's judgment against sin.

INTO THE LESSON

Write *Warning!* in large letters at the top of your chalkboard or marker board. Ask, "What warning from your parents did you ignore that got you into some trouble?" Allow each learner to relate an experience to two or three other persons. You may also wish to ask a couple of people to tell the entire class about their experiences.

Tell the class that a foolish disregard of a parent's warning often brings trouble. Even so, when we disobeyed, our parents did not remove us from the family or disown us. There are times when parents, however, do go through the heart-wrenching experience of separating themselves from their children. Ask, "What kind of extreme circumstances might cause a parent to disown his child?" After the class suggests a few answers, emphasize how difficult this action would be for the parent. Observe that, in today's Bible study, we will see what happened when God finally reached a similar point with his people Israel. Along the way we will discover key lessons about living faithfully for the Lord.

INTO THE WORD

Use the notes in the Lesson Background and under verse 6 to establish the setting for today's lesson.

Prepare handouts as follows. Reproduce today's printed text at the top of the page and list these discussion questions below. (Do not include the italicized answers; they are for your convenience.)

1. What was the strategy behind resettling people from captive lands? (*Resettled people were less likely to revolt because they would not be defending their homeland.*)

2. What does verse 7 imply about how widespread idolatry had become? (*Surely not everyone turned away from God, but the vast majority had. Idolatry was very common in the land.*)

3. Why do you think the Israelites were so tempted to follow the practices of the pagans? (*The presence of pagan peoples and their practices were a source of temptation. Their behavior, while sinful, appealed to the base lusts of the Israelites.*)

4. Explain the expression "stiff-necked" in verse 14. (*Stubborn resistance to efforts to turn the people away from their wrong behavior.*)

Distribute the handouts and highlighter pens to the learners in groups of two to four people. (These activities could also be done by the whole class together.) First, ask the groups to read the text and highlight each sin mentioned. Ask them to write in the margins of their handouts a definition, interpretation, or modern application of each sin. Then ask the groups to discuss the questions that are printed on their sheets.

After a few minutes, allow a few volunteers to summarize their answers. You may need to use your lesson commentary to answer questions they may raise about the text. Explain the "sacred stones" and "Asherah poles" that are mentioned in verse 10 and the sinful practices mentioned in verse 17.

INTO LIFE

Discuss what this lesson implies about teaching God's will and judgment to today's world. Ask the learners to suggest some ways to accomplish that task. Then say, "Every person, whether he acknowledges it or not, orders his life according to some moral code. We are going to allow you to begin defining your moral code and developing a life mission statement."

Distribute copies of the reproducible activity entitled "Living by a Moral Code" from the next page. Allow a few minutes for each student to answer the questions under "Defining My Personal Code" privately. Then allow a brief time for volunteers to share some of their answers.

Then discuss the questions under the heading, "Summing It Up." More important than the actual answers each student might write are ideas on how to determine these answers. After a brief discussion, give learners time to write down their personal responses.

Then ask the learners to consider the final question, "What corrections do I need to make in my moral code, my practices, and my goals if I am going to bring honor to the Lord God?" After some time for reflection, have a period of prayer, seeking courage for each one to make the changes they believe God wants them to make.

Living by a Moral Code

Every person, whether he acknowledges it or not, orders his life according to some moral code. That code guides one's daily behavior, his preparations for the future, and his spiritual life. The children of Israel had developed a code of living that displeased God. It is good for us to periodically examine and adjust the codes that govern our lives to continually stay in tune with God's will for our lives. To help you define your personal code for living, answer the following questions honestly and frankly.

DEFINING MY PERSONAL CODE

What do I value most in life?

What am I passionate about?

What are three things that make me angry?

What are three things that bring me joy?

Where do I spend most of my money?

If I had lots of money, where would I spend more of it?

Where or for what tasks do I volunteer?

What are my most significant life accomplishments thus far?

What areas of my life get the most attention in "personal development"?

What is the ultimate goal for my life?

For what would I like to be remembered after I die?

SUMMING IT UP

Why do I believe that I exist?

What do I believe is God's purpose for my life?

SO NOW WHAT?

What corrections do I need to make in my moral code, my practices, and my goals if I am going to bring honor to the Lord God?